The Political Economy of Japan

Volume 2

The Political Economy of Japan
is a three-volume work under the
general editorship of Yasusuke
Murakami and Hugh T. Patrick.

Volume 1 is *The Domestic
Transformation*, edited by Kozo
Yamamura and Yasukichi Yasuba.
Volume 3, currently in preparation,
is *Cultural and Social Dynamics*,
edited by Shumpei Kumon and
Henry Rosovsky.

Edited by Takashi Inoguchi and Daniel I. Okimoto

The Political Economy of Japan

Volume 2

The Changing International Context

 Stanford University Press, Stanford, California 1988

Stanford University Press
Stanford, California
© 1988 by the Board of Trustees of the
Leland Stanford Junior University
Printed in the United States of America

Japanese language rights assigned to
the National Institute for Research Advancement
37F Shinjuku Mitsui Building, 2-1-1 Nishi-Shinjuku,
Shinjuku-ku, Tokyo, Japan

CIP data appear at the end of the book

Published with the
assistance of the Japan Foundation

To our mothers,

    Mitsuko Inoguchi

    Kirie and Taeko Okimoto

The Japan Political Economy Research Committee acknowledges with deep appreciation the support provided by the two core funding institutions for the project, the National Institute for Research Advancement, Tokyo, and the East-West Center, Honolulu.

Contents

Tables

Figures

Contributors

Robert G. Gilpin, Professor, Woodrow Wilson School of Public and International Affairs, Princeton University.

Koichi Hamada, Professor, Department of Economics, Yale University.

Donald C. Hellmann, Professor, Department of Political Science, University of Washington.

Takashi Inoguchi, Associate Professor, Institute of Oriental Culture, University of Tokyo.

Motoshige Itoh, Associate Professor, Department of Economics, University of Tokyo.

Peter J. Katzenstein, Professor, Department of Government, Cornell University.

Ryutaro Komiya, Professor, Department of Economics, University of Tokyo.

Stephen D. Krasner, Professor, Department of Political Science, Stanford University.

Shumpei Kumon, Professor, International Relations, College of Arts and Sciences, University of Tokyo.

Charles E. Morrison, Research Fellow, East-West Center, University of Hawaii and the Japan Center for International Exchange.

Yasusuke Murakami, Professor, College of Arts and Sciences, University of Tokyo.

Daniel I. Okimoto, Associate Professor, Department of Political Science, Stanford University.

Hugh T. Patrick, Professor, Graduate School of Business, Columbia University.

Kenneth B. Pyle, Director, Henry M. Jackson School of International Studies, University of Washington.

Bruce Russett, Professor, Department of Political Science, Yale University.

Gary R. Saxonhouse, Professor, Department of Economics, University of Michigan.

Yoichi Shinkai, Professor, Department of Economics, Osaka University.

Akihiko Tanaka, Associate Professor, International Relations, College of Arts and Sciences, University of Tokyo.

Preface by the General Editors

The genesis of the three volumes that make up *The Political Economy of Japan* lies in the profound transformation of both Japan and the global political-economic system since World War II. Japan's sustained surge of rapid economic growth has brought it to the forefront of nations. The implications continue to be far-reaching and deep—within Japan in terms of societal and cultural as well as economic and political change, and internationally in terms of the mutual accommodation between the global system and Japan at a time of Japanese resurgence on the one hand and a decline in the capacity of the United States to serve as world leader on the other.

A new era is emerging—for Japan and the world as a whole. Since the early 1970s, Japan's political economy, and the international system as well, have undergone a sea change. In historical perspective—by economic criteria at least, such as living standards, levels of technology, and growth rates—the changes were so great that by 1980 the postwar era could be said to have come to an end. Japan is now in a transition to a new era, the major features of which can only be sensed imperfectly. Yet even with its economic transformation Japan is a remarkably stable democracy and society, seemingly without major political, economic, or social problems. Nor are there ideological or social schisms so pervasive or profound as to threaten that stability. Embedded in Japanese culture are great historical continuities that endure and yet are unusually susceptible to pragmatic adaptation as conditions change. These characteristics are well reflected in the ongoing evolution of economic, political, and social institutions.

The major purpose of these volumes is to evaluate the political economy of Japan as it approaches the 1990s. Explaining where Japan is today requires some explanation of how it arrived at that point; our intention, however, is not a history of the evolution of Japan's postwar political economy. The papers in these volumes are in principle future-oriented —they raise questions about where Japan is going as it approaches the twenty-first century and offer insights, albeit speculative, about future tendencies, prospects, and problems. The analysis of Japan's political economy is important in its own right. In addition, it will help us better understand the present and future of all industrial democracies; they face similar problems, and their futures will be inextricably linked.

Japan's economic performance and behavior over the long run, and particularly in transition periods, cannot be explained by standard economic variables alone. Nor can Japanese political performance and behavior be explained solely by political variables. The rules of the game, matters of policy, and the institutional environment are determined by the state—bureaucrats and politicians. Hence the political economy approach of these volumes. Yet even that is too narrow. A broader interdisciplinary, analytical approach is needed to take into account social and cultural variables, some of them changing significantly, others important for their very stability. In the short run it may be possible to isolate and analyze certain phenomena on the assumption that nothing else changes, but in the longer run one must take into account an intricate web of complex interactions between economic, political, social, and cultural forces and structures. However, social science has yet to develop generally accepted, comprehensive analytical frameworks that are operational. Each of the participants in this project found that even a political economy approach required substantial stretching beyond standard disciplinary boundaries.

What major changes marked the end of the postwar era? From a Japanese perspective, Japan in the 1970s had finally "caught up with the West." From a Western perspective, Japan had become a major affluent, industrial, high-technology power, the world's second largest market economy, and indeed the major challenger to U.S. industrial and technological supremacy. By 1970 Japan's domestic economic policies and performance had such an impact on the United States and Western Europe by way of trade that it could no longer be dismissed as a "small-country economy." Rather, U.S. and European government and business decision makers felt increasingly compelled to respond to Japanese competitive pressure; and Japan in turn could no longer take the world political-economic environment as a given. By the late 1970s, some Japanese large firms were at the technological frontiers in virtually every civilian goods industry and in the commercial application of basic scientific research, though not in basic science itself. By the mid-1980s, Japan had become the world's largest net exporter of capital in the now highly developed system of international financial markets.

Japan's economic prowess stands in sharp contrast to its modest military strength. Since World War II, Japan has persisted in a very low military posture of only limited self-defense capabilities. It has become an economic superpower, commensurate with the United States and Western Europe, while abjuring military power. Japan has depended for military security on its alliance with the United States, also by far its most important economic partner. This comprehensive alliance has been crucial for Japan; it has also become increasingly important for the United States.

The international political and economic environment has changed dramatically in the past fifteen years or so. Détente came to an end; the Soviet Union rose to nuclear parity with the United States. The hegemonic power—military and economic—of the United States declined but by no means disappeared. The Bretton Woods system of fixed exchange rates collapsed, to be replaced by a system of flexible exchange rates that has developed problems of its own. The two oil shocks of the 1970s contributed greatly to world inflation, a slowing of world growth, high interest rates, subsequent disinflation, an intractable Third World debt problem, and emergent protectionism in the United States and Western Europe. The international trading and monetary systems have come under immense strain. The sharp decline in world oil prices, interest rates, and the overvalued dollar in the mid-1980s continue the uncertain process of international adjustment and transition.

Japan has been as much affected by these international shocks and systemic changes as any other major nation. For these as well as internal reasons, Japan's formerly super-fast economic growth rate slowed sharply after 1973. Japan has nonetheless achieved more rapid economic growth than other industrial nations and has performed better in such areas as employment, price stability, productivity improvement, and structural adjustment. It has also fared better in terms of political and social stability. Even so, the sharp appreciation of the yen in the mid-1980s must have a substantial impact on domestic economic structure and performance, with implications for the rest of the world as well.

The question of where the present period of transition is leading pervades the papers in these volumes. Within Japan, we can anticipate an aging population; still further urbanization; and increased homogenization as mass media reduce regional and other variations, coupled, however, with the increased individuality of an affluent new middle class that forms Japan's great majority. Yet Japan's economy and institutions may well manifest greater decentralization, reflecting new opportunities as well as heterogeneity within a homogeneous society. Japan may well become the new, information-based society par excellence as a new technological era comes to dominate the turn of the new century.

Undoubtedly economic, political, and social institutions will continue to evolve in response to changing needs and pressures. Basic values and behavioral patterns, however, change more slowly. Indeed, they are a major source of domestic stability; yet they are also a source of international misunderstanding, confusion, and even conflict. Nonetheless, values, and the behavior they shape, are not static. Will the transition be predominantly technological and economic? To what extent will the new era embody even more profound societal and cultural changes? Or will basic values and preferred behavior patterns provide the stability to make the transition easier to deal with?

The international system—economic, political, military—also appears to be in transition, with its future characteristics unclear. The U.S.-USSR confrontation continues to dominate the global military arena. The rise of Japan to major international economic prominence has generated pressures from the United States and Western Europe for Japan to play a far greater role in maintaining and strengthening the open international economic system, to prevent a systemic retreat into protectionism. The foreign desire for Japanese leadership has been matched so far by Japanese caution. Will a new era of reduced U.S.-USSR military tension emerge? Will Japan's economic role be stabilizing or destabilizing? Will protectionism become more significant, and if so, will it be sectoral rather than geographic? We do not pretend to answer these or a host of other questions comprehensively, but at least they are addressed.

The editors of each volume of *The Political Economy of Japan* expand upon the general themes raised here in their introductions to the volumes, setting the themes in their particular context. Volume 1, subtitled *The Domestic Transformation*, takes essentially a domestic approach, while recognizing the impact of the rest of the world on Japan and Japan's interaction with it. Volume 2, *The Changing International Context*, correspondingly takes an international approach, while examining the global effects on Japan's domestic political economy. Volume 3, *Cultural and Social Dynamics*, presents a quite different but equally essential perspective. Culture is the medium in which economic and political behavior rests; it embodies underlying norms, values, and tastes. Society and its institutions are essential features of any political economy. The linkages between Japan's political economy, society, and culture are clearly important. They are also extraordinarily difficult to analyze. In Volume 3, a wider range of social scientists analyze certain of these linkages. Whereas Volumes 1 and 2 aim to be definitive, Volume 3 is overtly exploratory. Its aim is to open new avenues of research for our understanding of Japan.

The basic themes and issues addressed in the volumes are broad and comprehensive. Every nation, like every individual, has its unique features. But far more important are the similarities, and the subtle degree and specific nature of the differences. In principle, these studies are explicitly comparative, interdisciplinary, and future-oriented. These are difficult goals to achieve, as anyone conversant with the current state of social science theory and methodology knows full well. In practice, most of the comparisons are between Japan and the major, market-oriented industrial democracies of the West, particularly the United States. In many respects they are the most appropriate comparison group. Financial and human resource constraints precluded an even more ambitious approach. The Japanese economy, polity, society, culture, and people are not nearly so monolithic, centralized, homogeneous, or vertically structured as they have on occasion been stereotypically portrayed in the West. Nor are they as unique as some Japanese would maintain. On the other hand, the United States stands at the opposite pole among the industrial nations in terms of heterogeneity and decentralization. A comparison between Japan and the United States, the world's largest market economies, is therefore of crucial importance in our search for insights into Japan's political economy.

The contributors to these volumes confronted a complex mixture of evolutionary change, discontinuous change, and enduring continuities in their analyses of Japan's current state and future possibilities. They bravely responded by delving beyond their normal, comfortable disciplinary limits. We believe that, thanks to their efforts, these volumes will contribute substantially to establishing both the substance and the approach of future social science research on Japan. Although these studies push forward the frontiers of our knowledge, we still have much to do.

In recognition that no one scholar could adequately address the array of topics and issues incorporated in these volumes, in 1982 the binational Japan Political Economy Research Committee was formed, with Yasusuke Murakami and Hugh Patrick as co-chairmen, in order to plan and carry out this comprehensive project. The committee, together with other scholars, held numerous planning workshops to prepare six substantive conferences between 1984 and 1987, two for each volume.

The committee members were: Takashi Inoguchi (Political Science, University of Tokyo), Kazuo Koike (Economics, University of Kyoto), Ryutaro Komiya (Economics, University of Tokyo), Shumpei Kumon (Social Systems Analysis, University of Tokyo), Yasusuke Murakami (Economics, University of Tokyo), Yukio Noguchi (Economics, Hitotsubashi University), Daniel I. Okimoto (Political Science, Stanford University), Hugh T. Patrick (Economics, Columbia University), Kenneth B. Pyle (History, University of Washington), Thomas P. Rohlen (Anthropology, Stanford University), Henry Rosovsky (Economics, Harvard University),

Seizaburo Sato (Political Science, University of Tokyo), Gary Saxonhouse (Economics, University of Michigan), Akio Watanabe (International Relations, University of Tokyo), Kozo Yamamura (Economics, University of Washington), and Yasukichi Yasuba (Economics, Osaka University). The committee benefited greatly from the participation of many other scholars in the planning, particularly Marius Jansen (History, Princeton University), Barbara Ruch (Japanese Literature and Culture, Columbia University), and Robert Smith (Anthropology, Cornell University).

The project and its scope were made possible by the visionary funding commitments made early in the planning stage by the National Institute for Research Advancement (NIRA) in Tokyo and the East-West Center in Honolulu. Their early enthusiasm and financial underwriting were crucial. Additional funding for various key components of the intellectual package was received from the Mellon Foundation, the Japan–United States Educational Commission, the United States–Japan Friendship Commission, and the Japan Foundation.

Our great debt, as co-chairmen of the committee, is to the scholars who have written, rewritten, and rewritten again the papers appearing in these volumes. This was no ordinary project and certainly no ordinary series of conferences. Each author made a deep intellectual commitment, reflected in immense amounts of time and energy devoted to planning and meeting as well as research and writing. We thank especially the editors of each of the three volumes for their dedication, leadership, and sheer hard work. By far the greatest financial source of support for this project, as with much social scientific research, was the cost of the scholars' time, borne by their universities; all too often we take for granted the universities' central role in making such research efforts possible.

The project had a rather loose, semiautonomous administrative structure, which worked—from beginning to final publication—because of the behind-the-scenes efforts of many persons, all of whom we deeply thank. We mention only three stalwarts by name: Mikio Kato, Executive Director of the International House in Tokyo, who administered the NIRA grant and the three conferences and many planning sessions held in Tokyo; Charles Morrison, Research Fellow at the East-West Center, who oversaw the East-West Center's role as conference host and funder; and Grant Barnes, Director of Stanford University Press, who personally shepherded these manuscripts through the publication process.

Yasusuke Murakami
Hugh T. Patrick

The Political Economy of Japan

Volume 2

Daniel I. Okimoto and Takashi Inoguchi

Introduction

Even though losers in modern wars suffer devastating damages, they often rebound with astounding speed and vigor, and within fifteen to twenty years, as A. F. K. Organski and Jacek Kugler point out, they often succeed in bringing their industrial economies back to prewar levels. Sometimes, vanquished nations grow so rapidly that they even overtake the economic position of their wartime conquerors.[1]

The resilience of defeated nations can lead, over a few short decades, to a restructuring of the international system and the redistribution of power among nation-states. Even though a victor may have stepped forward to assume the mantle of hegemonic leadership, the rapid resurgence of one or more of the vanquished nations is capable of transforming the international status quo and eroding the hegemon's base of power. Whether the redistribution of power is stabilizing or destabilizing depends largely on two factors: the capacity of the hegemon to adjust to the far-reaching consequences of the loser's re-emergence[2] and the willingness of the resurgent countries to accept more responsibility for maintaining the stability of the international system.

Japan's Postwar Metamorphosis

The story of Japan following its crushing defeat in 1945 illustrates the historic pattern of phoenix-like recovery from war, leading to the restructuring of the international system. Japan's metamorphosis from military power to peaceful commercial state must be counted as a seminal development in twentieth-century history. In 35 years—only a generation's time—Japan has advanced from being another late-developing, Third World economy, only 5 per cent of the United States's size in 1952, to the status of an economic colossus by 1988. It is today the second-largest economy in the world—larger even than the Soviet Union, one of the world's two military superpowers, and more than half the size of the United States.

It is ironic, but hardly surprising, that as a peaceful merchant state, Japan has come to feel far more secure than it ever did as a military state. Japan owes its economic security and prosperity, in no small measure, to the openness and vigor of the international system created in the wake of World War II. In particular, the liberal system of trade based on the General Agreement on Tariffs and Trade (GATT) and the international monetary regime based on a fixed and then floating system of exchange rates, provided a stable framework for Japan and other countries to pursue policies of rapid economic expansion. The United States, Japan's conqueror, was the prime mover behind the construction of the postwar international system and has served as its primary pillar of support.

From the very beginning, Japan's *volte face* and resurgence have been closely aligned with, and dependent upon, America's willingness to serve as postwar hegemon and in that role to sustain such indispensable public goods as liberal trade and financial regimes and global politico-military stability. For both countries—to say nothing of the Pacific region and world at large, the U.S.–Japan alliance has turned out to be a development of monumental significance. At one stroke, this historic alliance replaced the biggest rivalry in prewar Asia with a much more stable structure of regional alignments.

The Impact of Japan's Economic Re-emergence

The impact of Japan's rise to economic prominence on the structure of the international system has been far-reaching. Whether it be in merchandise trade, capital movements, national security, or the structure of international regimes, the United States and other countries have had trouble adjusting to the consequences of Japan's economic advance. In an astoundingly short period of time, for example, Japanese industries have overtaken Western front-runners in the production of steel, automobiles, and consumer electronics, giving rise to serious structural dislocation in the United States and Western Europe, whose shares of world markets have shrunk as Japan's has expanded. Late-developing countries have not had to cope with such problems of domestic dislocation; for Third World states, open access to the Japanese market, also regarded as a problem for the advanced industrial states, is the over-riding issue.

In the United States and Western Europe, old-line manufacturing sectors like steel and automobiles—among the hardest hit by Japanese competition—have had a hard time altering what had been (until Japan's industrial resurgence) relatively successful patterns of behavior. Although the need has been obvious for some kind of adaptation to meet the more demanding parameters of competition set by the Japanese, the old-line manufacturing producers in the West have yet to show themselves capable of rising to the Japanese challenge.

In such industries, Japan's export "deluges" have generated strong political reactions. Traditionally in advanced industrial states, the steel and automobile industries have employed large numbers of workers, organized into politically active labor unions. What has added to their political clout has been their concentration in certain regions, where they have accounted for disproportionate shares of economic output. Inevitably, this has led to political pressures for import protection, designed to shield domestic producers from the full force of Japanese and other major foreign competition.

From the standpoint of the United States and other importing countries, the influx of Japanese manufactured products has been particularly disruptive because of their concentration in a few product categories: automobiles, steel, and electrical machinery and equipment. Taken together, these three categories account for well over half of what Japan has sold abroad. Such density means that Japanese imports have tended to crowd out or directly displace domestic products.

Few other big industrial states have such high levels of export concentration. Trade between the United States and Western Europe, for example, is characterized by a much higher level of intra-industry transactions (that is, the exchange of differentiated products within the same industry). Because intra-industry trade does not appear to require painful domestic adjustments, it generates lower levels of trade tension.[3] Owing to the sheer quantity and direct displacement effects of trade with Japan, especially in such "strategic" sectors as heavy manufacturing and high technology, the level of bilateral conflict is often extremely high and politically difficult to contain.

In addition to the political pressures caused by the heavy concentration of Japanese imports, the United States, Japan's biggest trade partner and military protector, has begun to worry about the national security implications of its decline in such key sectors as semiconductors, machine tools, robotics, and other areas of high technology. This concern with national security goes well beyond traditional fears of excessive dependence on foreign procurements or the potential costs of supply disruption. In the case of semiconductors, national security appears to be tied to the commercial viability of the semiconductor industry, its relationship to defense contractors, and their collective capacity to innovate at the cutting edges of technology.[4]

The national security line of reasoning is straightforward: Should the U.S. semiconductor industry be crippled by Japanese competition, U.S.

government officials and industrial leaders fear, it might undermine the country's capacity to stay a technological step or two ahead of the Soviet Union. Because America's whole defense posture rests on the premise of technological superiority to offset Soviet advantages in sheer firepower, any impairment of the U.S. capacity to innovate could jeopardize the country's national security (to say nothing of the security of the Western alliance). Japanese trade has thus become entangled with complex issues of national security, and depending on what happens in the commercial competition in high technology, the military balance of power could be tipped in one direction or the other.

National security concerns have also surfaced in connection with the massive outflow of Japanese capital. In 1986, the net outflow of Japanese capital exceeded $86 billion, with nearly $60 billion going toward the purchase of foreign securities and bonds. Over $60 billion entered the United States, helping to underwrite the large American fiscal deficits. For the United States, the high level of dependence on Japanese capital raises disquieting questions of potential vulnerability. If the influx of Japanese money were to be cut off or even curtailed, the United States might be hard pressed to meet its need for capital. Without a concomitant cut in national spending, interest rates would soar and the U.S. economy would plunge into a severe recession or depression.

Whether the Japanese could find alternative markets in which to invest their surplus savings is another obvious question. Few markets outside the United States are capable of absorbing such huge amounts of capital. Moreover, exactly how long the Japanese will remain the world's biggest supplier of capital is not entirely clear; the country's savings rate may fall as the population ages or as domestic consumption expands.

Nevertheless, even if its reign as the world's biggest money lender is brief—less than three decades, as in the cases of Great Britain and the United States before it—Japan is still going to accumulate vast overseas assets over time, especially in the United States. Any withdrawal of even relatively small fractions of Japan's cumulative assets could have far-reaching consequences for the U.S. economy. Once the world's leading creditor nation, the United States has swung to the opposite extreme, becoming the world's largest debtor nation. The swing, as big and abrupt as it has been, is in keeping with historical patterns of hegemonic dominance and decay, to which Robert Gilpin calls attention.[5]

A noteworthy aspect of Japan's huge export of capital is its growing portfolio of direct overseas investments; in 1985, Japan invested around $12 billion in physical assets abroad. The yearly figure has increased significantly over the past decade, as the yen has strengthened and threats of protectionism overseas have risen. With Japanese companies establishing overseas subsidiaries and seeking to acquire foreign corporations, questions of national security have arisen once again. Wary of possible Japanese domination in sophisticated semiconductor components, for example, U.S. government officials in 1987 opposed Fujitsu's bid to acquire Fairchild, one of the first companies in Silicon Valley. U.S. government officials have had serious misgivings about allowing Japanese companies to have direct, immediate access to critical, state-of-the-art technology in the United States. As in the case of capital dependence, the issue of direct Japanese investments has thus brought into public focus complicated questions of national security, underscoring at the same time the decline of Pax Americana.

Japan has also had an unsettling impact on the system of world trade because of the aggregate approach of its companies and foreign perceptions of the government's role in "tilting" the playing field in Japan's favor. Foreign competitors have complained vociferously about a variety of "unfair" practices that they believe have given rise to current account imbalances, including the emphasis on aggregate savings over consumption, export-led growth and recovery from recession, the undervaluation of the yen relative to the dollar, industrial policy "targeting," and government subsidies for the cultivation of strategic industries. Such policies are said to emerge from, and reflect, narrow self-interest and a general lack of concern for the international consequences of Japan's commercial behavior.

From the perspective of the international system, the problem encountered in trying to "level off" the playing field is that such actions as industrial "targeting" fall outside the scope of trade-related rules and regulations. The GATT system was set up to deal only with formal barriers to trade at the national borders. It was not designed to treat domestic differences in macroeconomic or industrial policies within nation-states—even though such policies often have a far greater impact on worldwide patterns of trade than tariffs, quotas, or other formal barriers within GATT's balliwick.

Outside Japan, the perception that Japanese macroeconomic and industrial policies violate the unwritten norms of fair competition is widespread, even though the violations may not be illegal under strict interpretations of specific GATT provisions. What Japan's export success has brought to light, therefore, is the limited capacity of the GATT-based regime to cope with many of the underlying factors that determine trade flows and give rise to trade conflicts. Countries running large deficits with Japan, including the United States and most European states, have responded to the flood of Japanese imports by negotiating—outside the framework of GATT—voluntary export restraints (VERs) on an ad hoc, bilateral basis. Whether, and to what extent, the GATT regime can long endure, as it is currently constituted, in the face of lopsided bilateral trade imbalances, mounting conflicts and tensions, and the proliferation of bilateral restrictions remains to be seen.

But the expanding scope and escalating intensity of trade frictions should be placed in proper structural perspective. What such conflicts reflect is a very significant historical development: namely, the unprecedented expansion of international interdependence. International linkages have grown far beyond anything that could have been anticipated, given the long-run secular trends toward economic involution stretching from the late 1920s to the end of World War II. Ties of interdependence have proliferated in all areas of economic activity—merchandise trade, capital movements, direct foreign investments, technology transfers, and strategic corporate alliances. The surge of goods and services, money, and technology across national borders has had the effect of increasing the demands made on international regimes, including those for finances and exchange rates. Here again, Japan's emergence as a major economic power has served as a catalyst for, as well as a barometer of, fundamental changes taking place in the structure of the international system.

Clearly, Japan's postwar development and the evolution of the postwar international system cannot be understood apart from each other. The two have been, and are, inextricably intertwined. Japan could not have reached its present status without the supportive structure of the liberal international system that was put into place in the wake of World War II. Similarly, the structure of the international system has been permanently transformed by Japan's rapid emergence as an economic, but not military, power.

In the future, the evolution of the two will continue to be intertwined. Japan's well-being will hinge on the viability of the international system in the face of severe strains occasioned by the unprecedented and still expanding scope of interdependence. To a significant extent, the world's capacity to endure as a liberal and open system will rest, in turn, on Japan's willingness to accept greater global responsibilities commensurate with its growing power and status as a major actor in the international economic order.

Questions and Themes

This book, the second of three volumes on Japan's political economy, explores the complex relationship between Japan and the international system. It analyzes the impact of international forces on the emerging shape of Japan's domestic political economy; and, conversely, it examines the ramifications of Japan's development for the changing structure of the international system. In exploring the interplay between Japan and the international system, a number of key questions and recurrent themes are dealt with; they fall into three different levels of analysis: the world system, the external-internal interplay, and Japan's domestic structure and policymaking processes:

I. World System

—Has the world entered an unstable era of power transition? If so, what are the implications?

—In what ways is the international system changing?

—Can national differences in institutional structure and public policies be accommodated within the international system without giving certain countries (like Japan) "unfair" advantages? Or must national differences be "harmonized" somehow?

—How should Japan's role in the international system be characterized: as a free rider, supporter, or challenger?

II. The External-Internal Interplay

—In what ways is Japan influencing the emerging shape of the international system, and in what ways, in turn, is Japan's political economy being shaped by the international environment?

—How has the U.S.–Japan alliance been affected by the erosion of American power and the rapid expansion of Japanese economic capabilities?

—Are American pressures and demands pushing Japan in the direction of supporting or undermining the structure of the liberal economic order?

—Will Japan continue to generate conflicts with other countries as a by-product of its distinctive institutions, vigorous economic behavior, and aggressive export orientation?

III. Domestic Structure and Policymaking Processes

—How different is Japan from the political economies of the United States, Western Europe, and other advanced industrial states?

—Do the differences pose special problems for Japan's integration into the international community?

—Are the differences diminishing over time as Japanese institutions and attitudes undergo the processes of "internationalization"?

—Is Japan capable of assuming some of the responsibilities of hegemonic leadership, or at least a significantly expanded role as system supporter?

The papers in this book, written by distinguished Japanese and American scholars, address the key issues enumerated above. In wrestling with these and other questions, the papers help fill a void in the burgeoning literature on Japan's political economy: namely, the complex interplay between Japan, other important national actors (especially the United States), and the international system. The Japan we see today is a product of the on-going interplay between international and domestic factors. To understand how Japan is changing, and where it appears to be headed, requires an analysis not only of its domestic institutions and processes but also, equally important, of the changing international environment within which Japan's political economy functions. Perhaps the strongest impetus for change in Japan comes not from within, but from the impingement of international developments and foreign pressures.

Japan's World Role

This book opens with Takashi Inoguchi's overview of Japanese foreign policy. A searching analysis moving at three distinct levels—domestic structure, internal-external interactions, and international system—this paper provides a broad introduction to the central questions and themes subsequently dealt with in this book. All readers, but especially those without much prior background on Japanese foreign policy, are urged to read and ponder this paper before moving on to the others.

As a means of imposing order on a mass of empirical information, Inoguchi makes use of three analytical categories, which can be seen as summary interpretations of the different roles Japan is thought to have played in the international system: namely, that of free rider, supporter, and challenger. Which of the three comes closest to capturing the essence of Japan's role in the world?

Some would argue that in the pursuit of narrow self-interest, Japan has adroitly sidestepped the burdens of providing for the world's collective good; the country's low level of defense spending is often cited as the most visible (but not sole) indicator of its self-centered approach (free rider).[6] Others would insist that Japan has contributed more than its fair share to the common defense and to the maintenance of a stable international system (supporter).[7] Still others would say that Japan's reemergence constitutes the most serious threat to the stability of the international status quo, a formidable economic threat to U.S. hegemony (challenger).[8]

As these conflicting images suggest, there is no consensus on the correct interpretation. Evidence can be marshaled in support of each of them. Indeed, Inoguchi argues that Japan's international behavior is far too complex and varied, over time and across issue areas, to permit the selection of a single interpretive category in which to pigeonhole Japan's international behavior.

Elements of all three coexist and are mingled together. In the defense domain, Japan has found security under the umbrella of the United States; yet, this has not deterred Japan from mounting an all-out challenge to American pre-eminence in high technology (which may have the effect of undermining America's technology edge in military hardware). At the same time, Japan has made constructive contributions to the stabilization of exchange rates and problems of Third World debt. Thus, Japan's role in the world has been too multifaceted and complex to capture by choosing a single interpretive label like free rider, supporter, or challenger.

After reviewing postwar policies, Inoguchi peers into the future and predicts, like most of the other authors in this volume, that Japan is unlikely to veer very sharply from its past course. Instead, it will probably continue to adhere to the same basic principles that have served the country's national interests so well. Japan may make incremental adjustments at the margins, depending on the nature of external and domestic circumstances (such as incremental increases in defense expenditures), but the central thrust of its foreign policy will remain the same: close ties with the United States and the separation of economic from politico-military power.

The International System

To understand Japan's role in the world requires, first, that we analyze the evolving structure of the international system within which Japan and other nation-states function. The paper by Shumpei Kumon and Akihiko Tanaka provides a very broad-gauged, macro-historical framework within which the present international system can be understood. In their view of modern history, the dominant mode of interaction between nation-states has shifted over the centuries from the struggle for military supremacy and territorial security (the "power game," to use their term) to that of commercial competition and economic advantage (the "wealth game"). From a preoccupation with the production of material wealth, the world may be headed toward what Kumon and Tanaka call the "wisdom game," a new pattern of competition featuring the production and application of knowledge as the primary repository of power.

Owing to the strengths of its institutional structure, Japan may be in an advantageous position to compete in the emerging "wisdom game." However, because the basic parameters of the game are as yet unclear, Kumon and Tanaka point out that it is difficult to tell whether institutions like the state or the corporation will function as the decisive units of action as they have in the past. Based on simple extrapolations from recent history, one can assume that they will and that Japan will continue to compete effectively in the international arena. But by placing the rise of postwar Japan against the background of system transformation, Kumon and Tanaka cast Japan's future in a more complex light than that suggested by the stereotyped image of an invincible economic juggernaut.

How has Japan's re-emergence affected the structure of the postwar international system? Has it been stabilizing or destabilizing? As is pointed out by several papers in this volume, the impact has been mixed: to the extent that Japan's postwar growth has led to the erosion of hegemonic stability or to the unraveling of specific international regimes, the impact might be considered negative; on the other hand, to the extent that Japan's growth has helped spur worldwide output and economic efficiency, it has invigorated the international system.

To date (though the picture may change over time), the positive consequences appear heavily to outweigh the negatives, especially in comparison with the turmoil caused by Germany's re-emergence during the interwar period.[9] No doubt, the decoupling of economic and military power has made Japan's reintegration much less threatening to the international status quo than would otherwise have been the case. Japan's overnight conversion from military power to commercial state has not only neutralized the danger of Japan's own military recrudescence; it has also contributed to the stabilization of East Asia, a region of chronic instability from the nineteenth to the mid-twentieth century.

There is no denying, however, that certain dislocations, conflicts, and uncertainties have also been caused by Japan's spectacular successes as a commercial state. From a systemic perspective, one could argue that Japan's rise has contributed inadvertently but directly to America's relative decline as world hegemon. If this is so, and if orthodox theories of hegemonic stability are correct, Japan's continued economic ascent could alter the international distribution of power in ways that destabilize the international system. Not only might the hegemon's preponderance of power be diminished, but the structure of international regimes governing capital flows, exchange rates, monetary policies, and merchandise trade might also collapse under the weight of new demands.

Has Japan's meteoric rise led to the eclipse of U.S. power? Has the postwar world witnessed a serious erosion of American hegemonic influence? The standard answer—indeed, the orthodox presumption—on the part of specialists of international relations theory is, yes, the United States's power base has been weakening perceptibly over time.[10] Whether America's decline is due to Japan's ascendance is not clear; but there seems to be little doubt about the erosion of U.S. power.

Yet in his chapter for this volume, Bruce Russett questions the empirical accuracy of this notion. Drawing a distinction between the hegemon's power base (structure) and its capacity to influence outcomes around the world (the application of power), Russett argues that while the structure of its power base may have atrophied to some extent, the United States's capacity to influence outcomes has not declined nearly as much. If Russett's assessment is correct, then Japan's rapid rise probably has not been achieved at the cost of a proportional decline in the United States's hegemonic power, at least not yet.

If Russett's definition of power is adopted, and a country's power base is differentiated from its capacity to determine outcomes in specific issue areas, then Japan's power can be seen to be more modest and constrained than the image implied by an "emerging Japanese superstate." Indeed, compared with the United States, which continues to influence the course of world events despite the steady contraction of its objective power base, Japan is still a long way from superpower status. Even middle-ranking states, like China, that lack a modern economic infrastructure appear more capable of bringing their weight to bear on international issues of crucial importance.

If cultural influence is factored into the question, as Russett feels it should be, Japan's actual power in the world would have to be considered weaker still. Japanese culture, the product of many centuries of endogenous evolution, is neither easily understood nor universally appealing to most people of the world; nor, because of its distinctive nature, is Japanese culture as likely as British and American culture to serve as a standard for the rest of the world. Even if, in the twenty-first century, Japan achieved economic and military parity with the United States, it would probably still be unable to exercise a comparable degree of influence, if only because of the particularistic nature of its culture, as Russett and Stephen Krasner point out.

Indeed, cultural particularism has come to be perceived as an impediment for foreign companies engaged in trade with Japan. The distinctive characteristics of Japanese society and culture have had the effect of raising unintended but formidable barriers to entry for foreign producers seeking to penetrate Japanese markets. The barriers are not just the obvious ones associated with any non-Western country—a difficult language, unfamiliar business customs, geographic distance, and different legal traditions. The sociocultural barriers are widespread in scope, diverse in nature, and deeply ingrained in the basic fabric of Japanese industrial organization and politico-economic organization.

This suggests that Japan is strikingly different from the advanced industrial countries of the West and uncommonly difficult for non-Japanese (as well as non-mainstream Japanese) to break into.[11] Structural impediments, reflecting cultural differences, include extensive intercorporate stockholding, close banking-business ties, parent company–subcontractor networks, interindustry groupings, close government-business interactions, and so on. As trade surpluses have ballooned, foreign competitors have become increasingly vocal about the de facto barriers raised by the peculiarities of Japan's structural-cultural characteristics.

The trade problem—not just for Japan but for the world—is greatly aggravated by the uncertainties surrounding present international financial and monetary institutions, especially the unpredictability of fluctuating foreign exchange rates. Imbalances in merchandise trade can be seen as outcroppings of underlying monetary and financial forces at work. This means that trade imbalances cannot be corrected on a sector-specific basis. The causes run far below the surface of sector-specific factors, involving such deep-seated problems as imperfect exchange-rate mechanisms and conflict-generating variations in the macroeconomic policies of major nation-states.

International Regimes

As we pointed out earlier, because the GATT system was designed to deal only with barriers to trade at national borders, it has not been able to neutralize the alleged advantages gained from national variations in culture, industrial organization, and macroeconomic policy. Under the Bretton Woods system, the mechanism of fixed exchange rates could be used to adjust the value of national currencies in response to variations in national tax, fiscal, and industrial policies. In theory, the system of floating exchange rates is supposed to make automatic adjustments to perturbations in merchandise trade flows. However, as Koichi Hamada and Hugh Patrick point out in their paper, the "black box" has failed to function in practice as it was designed to; in consequence, the post–Bretton Woods international system has seen countries like Japan (in 1984–85) run huge merchandise trade surpluses while at the same time their currencies have been undervalued.

Why has the floating exchange rate not functioned according to theory? What alternatives, if any, are there? Would it be possible and desirable to return to some form of fixed exchange rate system, or is the present system functioning satisfactorily? These questions have a central bearing on Japan's economic future, including its trade relationship with other countries. In their paper, Hamada and Patrick provide an overview of the evolution of the postwar financial system, with special reference to Japan, and offer some scenarios about the system's future direction.

The failure of the floating exchange-rate system to respond automatically to trade flow signals—at a time when ties of international economic interdependence have proliferated to historically unprecedented levels—has brought into focus the vexing question of how to deal at the international regime level with national differences in institutions and public policies. Since perfectly uniform standards cannot be imposed, what, if anything, can be done? Should there be a coordinated effort to "harmonize" national variations so that the playing field is at least level enough to eliminate "unfair" advantages?

This question, pointedly raised by Robert Gilpin and alluded to by several other authors in this volume, is a critical one from the standpoint of maintaining a relatively open, liberal trade regime. Serious doubts are being expressed that the liberal GATT regime can survive intact when one of its most dynamic member countries differs so much from the others in history, institutions, and sociocultural context. With Japan, the first non-Western country to break into the select circle of affluent industrial states, at the center of this political controversy, its interests are bound to be affected by the way in which the question is resolved or left unresolved.

For most advanced industrial countries, including the United States, trade issues have become highly charged and politicized. As Gilpin points out, the world has entered an era of "new protectionism," wherein international trade involving a growing number of key commodities like steel and automobiles has become subject to quantitative restrictions based on bilateral negotiations. The "new protectionism" differs from that of the 1930s in that the restrictions are informal, "voluntary," and temporary, not formally legislated tariffs and quotas.

Although the proliferation of voluntary export restraints (VERs) has curtailed trade in certain commodities, it has not constricted the aggregate flow of trade. To the contrary, as Gary Saxonhouse points out in his paper, the aggregate flow of trade has expanded far beyond that of any time in history. The two have not been mutually exclusive. In fact, some scholars believe that the proliferation of voluntary restraints is both a manifestation and an inevitable by-product of the unprecedented growth of international trade.[12] Thus, by limiting the need for the importing countries to make politically painful adjustments at home, the imposition of VERs in specific product commodities may have actually permitted the global expansion of trade, albeit at some cost to efficiency in the worldwide allocation of resources.

Even if one views VERs as a necessary evil, however, Gilpin warns that the dangers of relying on informal, bilateral cartels for market share allocation are substantial, especially if one accepts the notion that it can lead the world down a slippery slope toward more formal modes of beggar-thy-neighbor protectionism. Notwithstanding such troubling scenarios, Gilpin expects that the period of "negotiated" or "managed" trade will continue. If so, Japan—as one of the world's most active exporting countries—may be forced to swallow more voluntary export restraints. Whether a liberal trade regime can stand up to the cumulative weight of protective pressures is unclear.

This bleak picture of international trade is not universally shared. Ryutaro Komiya and Motoshige Itoh offer a more optimistic view. Although the GATT system has weakened, as countries have deviated from the letter and spirit of GATT principles, Komiya and Itoh feel that the liberal trade regime is far from dead. Because current circumstances differ from those of the Great Depression, they see little chance of the world reverting to the destructive, beggar-thy-neighbor policies of the 1930s. Nor do they believe, contrary to Gilpin, that managed or negotiated trade will become the dominant mode of world commerce. The Gilpin and Komiya-Itoh papers thus pose contrasting views of the future of the international system and by extension, the prospects for Japan's future.

Internationalization: Japan's Adaptation

As Japan has grown and expanded its ties of economic interdependence, how has the structure of its domestic economy changed? According to Gary Saxonhouse, Japan has undergone the most extensive structural transformation over the postwar period of all the major advanced industrial nations. This is observable in the profound changes that have taken place in the structure of industrial production, labor force allocation, and export composition.

In terms of imports, on the other hand, the scope of change has been very limited. There is thus a glaring and puzzling discrepancy in the speed and scope of change between export and import sectors in Japan. Does the discrepancy confirm suspicions of unfair import protection? Has Japan kept foreign products at bay, especially manufactured imports? To answer the question, Saxonhouse constructs a formal model of trade built on the assumption of no import barriers, compares this with Japan's actual pattern of trade, and then looks at the results in terms of import patterns of other countries.

Saxonhouse finds that Japan's import structure is not at all abnormal; when placed within the context of comparative factor endowments, its structure falls well within the range of what economists would consider normal. What accounts, then, for Japan's low level of manufactured imports? According to Saxonhouse, the low percentage of manufactured imports stems from Japan's small size, conspicuous lack of natural resources, and geographic distance from other advanced industrial economies. If Japan were larger, located closer to its trading partners (as the

European countries are to one another, or the United States and Canada are), and blessed with richer resources, its import structure would be virtually identical to those of other countries.

To drive this point home, Saxonhouse calls attention to a highly improbable but illuminating scenario: namely, the idea of United States giving Alaska, a vast storehouse of raw materials, to Japan. What effect would such a transfer have? The answer is that the composition of Japan's imports would become virtually indistinguishable from that of the United States and most European countries. By implication, therefore, Japan's export and import structures cannot be considered to be outrageously out of line with those of other advanced industrial countries, given its factor endowments.

As Japan changes in response to the external environment, is it coming to resemble other advanced industrial countries? Are the powerful forces of internationalization relentlessly transforming the structure of domestic institutions like Japan's financial system? Given that the Japanese capital market is one of the world's two or three biggest, and that the country's insulated and heavily regulated financial system has been an essential part of the government's capacity to steer the economy, the question of where Japan's financial system is headed is of global and national importance.

Japan's financial system, as Yoichi Shinkai discusses in his paper, is changing rapidly under the dual impact of deregulation and internationalization. Until the 1980s, Japan's financial system had been sealed off from international capital markets. The isolation permitted the Ministry of Finance to exercise considerable regulatory control. Under the old system, large amounts of household savings were cycled through banking institutions to the business sector, enabling companies to sustain very high rates of capital investment. By supplying huge amounts of capital at below-market-clearing interest rates (set by the state), Japan's financial system is thought to have given Japanese corporations a major competitive advantage over foreign producers.

Whether the costs of capital were indeed lower for Japanese companies is a controversial issue; but even if the old system gave Japanese producers a substantial edge in capital costs, that edge is being eroded as regulatory controls are removed and the financial system is progressively exposed to the force of internationalization. Japan's full integration into international financial markets should have the effect of leveling off any differentials in capital costs. Where companies choose to raise capital—whether in New York, London, or Tokyo—should make little or no difference in terms of the costs incurred.

The changes currently under way could have far-reaching implications for Japan's domestic political economy. Not only might they erode the government's capacity to administer macroeconomic and industrial policies; they might also alter the relative balance of power between the government and private sector in Japan, tipping the balance further in the direction of the private sector. As companies gain greater access to money abroad, and as banks find more outlets for their capital overseas, the unusually high debt-to-equity ratio for Japanese corporations could fall significantly, leading to a loosening of traditional ties between banks and businesses. Would such a change lead to the loss of the long-term time horizon for which Japanese companies have become famous? Would market-share maximization be supplanted by the same preoccupation with quarterly profits that plagues American companies? Shinkai expresses doubts that Japanese *kaisha* (large, blue-chip corporations) will suffer the same affliction, at least not to the same extent that foreign companies do.

To return, then, to the question posed earlier: Is there an irresistable trend toward convergence? Will Japan's political economy begin to lose its distinctive characteristics as it is integrated more fully into the international system? Shinkai's paper, as well as those of Okimoto, Katzenstein, Krasner, Pyle, and Hellmann, cast doubt on theories of eventual convergence. Although Japan is adapting constantly to changes in the external environment, its domestic system is not apt to lose all the features that have set it apart from advanced industrial countries in the West.

As changes take place in the international environment, where is the U.S.–Japan alliance headed? The future of this alliance, which has served as the central axis for Japanese foreign policy, is bound to be of seminal importance for the regional and global environment, as Stephen Krasner points out. Will the alliance hold together in the face of changing relative power capabilities, the erosion of international regimes, mounting trade frictions, and fundamental differences in culture and social organization? Can the present pattern of interaction be sustained, based on fierce competition in the economic sphere and American protection in the politico-military sphere? Krasner surveys the range of possibilities, drawing upon relevant international theory and the available empirical evidence. His assessment of the U.S.–Japan relationship is thought-provoking because it explicitly takes into account, and interweaves, all levels of analysis, including systemic as well as national factors.

Political Institutions and Policymaking in Comparative Perspective

From the broadest and most abstract level of analysis—the international system, international regimes, and Japan's adaptation to the external environment—the discussion narrows to more concrete subjects, focusing on national and subnational institutions in Japan. Three pa-

pers—by Peter Katzenstein, Daniel Okimoto, and Donald Hellmann—
focus on Japanese political institutions and the policymaking processes.
In contrast to the papers by Saxonhouse and Shinkai, which examine
the impact of external forces on developments within Japan, most of the
remaining papers look at the external-internal interplay the other way
round: namely, the impact of Japanese institutions on the external environment and on nations that regularly interact with Japan.

Peter Katzenstein begins this section with an unusual and intriguing
comparison between Japan and Switzerland, a small, affluent, and open
European country. In spite of many obvious dissimilarities—such as
their very different historical experiences, their different societies and
cultures, and the size of their economies—Katzenstein uncovers some
fascinating similarities, such as their capacity to take collective action in
the face of adverse shifts in the external environment. However, he does
note that behind the common capacity to adapt, there are significant differences in domestic political structure. Switzerland is characterized as
corporatist, Japan as statist.

How is it that two countries so dissimilar in background and structure
both demonstrate a talent for adaptability? Katzenstein finds the reason
in the existence of a common denominator: namely, the extraordinarily
high perception of vulnerability in both countries vis-à-vis the international environment. When faced with external shocks and national
crises, this sense of vulnerability has galvanized actors in the public and
private sectors to pull together for the achievement of collective goals.

The Japanese and the Swiss have adapted comparatively well to an increasingly adverse economic environment, one in which access to overseas markets has become increasingly restricted. Japan and Switzerland
have managed to respond to short-term pressures with effective policies
that have averted costly crises and no-win confrontations. Among the
palliative measures taken by the Japanese have been positive cooperation in yen revaluation, financial deregulation and internationalization,
stimulation of domestic demand, and sector-specific market-opening
programs.

In looking at Japan's pattern of response to foreign demands for greater
market access, however, an inconsistency of behavior across sectors and
product markets is as striking as it is puzzling. Japan may bend over
backward to accommodate foreign demands for greater shares of the
Japanese market in, say, semiconductors; but it may turn around and
stonewall in response to similar demands in, say, processed lumber
products. Why do the Japanese respond flexibly in one area but not in
another? How can we make sense of these inconsistencies?

In his paper, Daniel Okimoto provides a political explanation, based
on the relationship between the bureaucracies, the Liberal Democratic

Party (LDP), and the LDP's grand coalition of support groups. He argues that the degree of freedom from interest group pressures and political interference varies over time and by issue area for the various bureaucracies (not to mention bureaus and divisions within each ministry). The structure of Japanese government (notwithstanding images of "Japan, Inc.") is far from monolithic; there are wide variations across institutions and policymaking coalitions with respect to levels of politicization, interest group pressures, bureaucratic autonomy, and the intervention of party politicians.

Okimoto's model for policymaking in sector-specific, trade-related issues poses a contrast to the model of policymaking outlined by Donald Hellmann for national security issues. Whereas the policymaking apparatus seems to function fairly effectively in resolving trade frictions in most manufacturing sectors, Hellmann's paper points out that it functions much less effectively in matters of politico-military security. This asymmetry may strike American readers as surprising, because the situation with which they are familiar is just the reverse. In the United States, trade issues are open to free-for-all lobbying, as special interest groups descend on elected representatives and Congressional committees (which are susceptible to constituency pressures); but most national security issues tend to be handled in a more coherent fashion, largely under the guidance of the President and Department of Defense.

Several reasons can be cited for the curious disparity in Japanese policymaking capabilities across issue areas, the most relevant of which may be the existence of noteworthy differences in administrative power and policymaking between the Ministry of International Trade and Industry (MITI) (for trade in manufactured goods) and the Ministry of Foreign Affairs and Defense Agency (for national defense). Hellmann calls attention to several other factors. Policymaking authority is not adequately centralized in Japan; consensus is generally hard to reach; and the consensual process is enormously time-consuming and susceptible to long delays, if not prone to chronic immobilism. For these reasons, Hellmann argues, Japan lacks the policymaking infrastructure necessary to implement a coherent foreign policy. The structural flaws will become more painfully apparent as Japan continues to grow and as the "greenhouse" protection provided by the U.S. military umbrella weakens.

Hellmann's pessimistic projection poses a major counterpoint to the generally optimistic picture of Japan's future depicted by other papers in this volume. The implications of his assessment are deeply disquieting for those who hope that Japan will play an increasingly constructive and stabilizing role in the world. If Hellmann is correct, Japan is apt to stumble from one crisis to another, causing serious problems for itself and other countries (especially the United States).

If Hellmann's prognosis is correct, it also suggests a host of disquieting questions. What will happen as the United States's power declines and the international system enters an unstable period of power transition? Is Japan incapable of sharing more of the burdens of hegemonic leadership? Would heavier Japanese rearmament be dangerous, given present inadequacies in Japan's policymaking infrastructure, or would it force the country to undergo a thorough restructuring of its policymaking apparatus?

Whither Japan?

If Japan cannot be expected to serve as a surrogate power, or even to assist in maintaining the system of hegemonic stability, where might Japan be able to play a constructive role? The region where Japan is most likely to play a positive role is Southeast Asia, a region not exactly in Japan's backyard but not as far removed as other areas. Southeast Asia is a region of great strategic importance and enormous potential for economic growth; at the same time, it is racked with unresolved conflicts, domestic unrest, and the constant threat of violent political upheaval. It also happens to be a region where, for a variety of reasons, the United States has had trouble projecting its power. Over the years, the United States has had to reduce its force deployments and cut back its foreign aid to Southeast Asia, even though private American companies have stepped up the pace of foreign direct investments there.

Japan's involvement in Southeast Asia, dating as far back as the early twentieth century, is an indication of the region's importance to Japan, particularly as a source of natural resources. Today, Southeast Asia is arguably of greater importance than ever before, because of its central place in the Pacific Basin (the world's new center of economic dynamism) and because of Japan's growing ties of economic interdependence (including exports and imports, joint ventures, foreign direct investments, and technology transfers).

For Japan, Southeast Asia can be considered a kind of test case for the question posed above: Is there a constructive role Japan can play somewhere? As is true in Northeast Asia, Japan's ability to affect outcomes is constrained not only by its own set of internal inhibitions, but also by the lingering memories of Japanese aggression. The countries of Southeast Asia are wary of Japan's playing a greater politico-military role in the region and are worried about the dangers of economic domination.

In spite of the inhibitions and constraints, Japan has adopted a higher posture in Southeast Asia than anywhere else in the world. As Charles Morrison points out, Japan has taken an increasingly active role, for example, in providing economic aid. Even without prodding from the

United States, Japan has acted to help compensate for the decline in U.S. influence in the region. Morrison describes Japan's efforts to bolster America's waning power in Southeast Asia as the actions of a loyal ally. Here, in short, is an area where Japan can be considered a system "supporter," to recall Inoguchi's three broad categories.

What role do Japanese leaders and opinion-makers see for their own country, free rider, supporter, or challenger? Kenneth Pyle summarizes the lively public debate now taking place among Japanese opinion leaders about the role their country ought to play in the world. How leading Japanese intellectuals see their own country and its future in a constantly evolving international system reveals a great deal about their hopes and fears, aspirations and goals, national character and values— the very elements, in short, that will help to chart whatever course the country takes in the next century.

Given its particularistic culture and past history of military aggression, is it likely that Japan will attempt to reawaken its prewar visions of military grandeur? Although Pyle notes the recent growth of a "formless and free-floating national pride," he discounts the likelihood that the prewar brand of militant, jingoistic nationalism will rear its head again.

In the future, as in the past, Japan's international behavior will emerge from the ongoing interplay between the international environment and domestic institutions and concrete policy choices. Even more than in the past, Japanese attitudes and actions will register, in turn, an increasingly powerful impact on the shape of the emerging international system.

Acknowledgment

As editors of this volume, we would like to thank a number of people who had a hand in its publication. Kris England, Stacey Green, and Nancy Okimoto, at the Northeast Asia–United States Forum on International Policy at Stanford University, provided a great deal of behind-the-scenes help. John R. Ziemer did a superlative job of editing. We would like to single out for special thanks Muriel Bell at Stanford University Press for the superb work she did in getting the manuscript over the final hurdles. Her efforts went far beyond the call of duty.

Part I

The World System

Takashi Inoguchi

The Ideas and Structures of Foreign Policy: Looking Ahead with Caution

On August 2, 1985, a leading economic daily, *Nihon keizai shimbun*, carried articles on the following topics.

1. The U.S. Congress discusses anti-Japanese trade legislation in response to Japan's Action Program for trade access.

2. U.S. government guidelines for the new round of GATT focus on market access for investment in high-tech areas.

3. A Bank of Japan study suggests a stronger yen to solve the current-account deficit problem.

4. The Resource and Energy Agency of the Ministry of International Trade and Industry (MITI) publishes a report on cooperative utilization of coal in the Pacific area.

5. U.S. biotechnological advances may undercut Japanese rice production.

6. The Soviet vice-minister of foreign trade proposes joint Soviet-Japanese production of machinery and technological cooperation in high-tech areas.

7. CANON decides to produce 100 per cent of its photocopying machines in the EEC to avoid trade frictions.

8. Fujitsu establishes Fujitsu Canada, Inc., to expand computer sales in Canada.

9. "Japan bashing" heats up in Washington, D.C.; relations with U.S. states remain relatively cordial.

10. Prime Minister Nakasone comments in a television interview on the U.S. use of atomic bombs in Hiroshima and Nagasaki and pleads for more understanding of the Action Program that the Japanese government will implement in the following three years.

With Japan's economic growth, the almost daily newspaper coverage of topics such as these have contributed to the complexity of views of Japan as a phenomenon. Several contending images of Japan have dominated recent debates throughout the world. Perhaps at no time in history have images of Japan been so complex.[1] At one extreme, some critics of Japan tenaciously perceive it as a free-rider. This perception seems vindicated if one looks at Japan's small defense spending compared with that of the United States. These critics note that even compared with the military outlays of the United States' Atlantic allies, Japan's defense budget has been exceedingly small.[2]

The argument seems convincing given, for example, the lack of a direct Japanese contribution to the defense of the Persian Gulf, whose security assures 65 per cent of Japanese oil consumption but merely 3 per cent of U.S. oil consumption.[3] Why should the United States spend so much money to defend remote areas where its Japanese and West European allies have much more at stake? Why can't Japan send aircraft carriers to the Indian Ocean and the Persian Gulf to secure its oil?

More generally, it is argued that U.S. responsibilities for defending Japan should be steadily lessened to allow Japan to shoulder a larger load. Burden sharing commensurate with Japan's economic capability is the basic formula implicit in this argument.[4] To restore and reshape a sounder U.S. hegemony, it is vital that the United States "discipline" its allies to follow U.S. policy lines by playing up the Soviet threat to the nonsocialist world as a whole.[5] Since Japan has long benefited from U.S. security assurances and economic benevolence, it is high time, the argument goes, that a rich Japan do more for the rest of the world community.

A similar perception persists in the area of foreign aid. Although the absolute amount of Japan's official development assistance (ODA) amounted to half that of the United States in 1984, as a percentage of GNP or of total grants, it was not very high.[6] The argument is thus that Japan is stingy and irresponsible and does not understand the responsibilities of noblesse oblige. Furthermore, citing the Japanese emphasis on industrial infrastructure building, critics argue that Japan donates aid only to serve its own politico-economic interests, especially its own manufacturing and financial interests, which are allowed to grab the bulk of the business associated with Japanese foreign aid.[7] It is further argued that Japan's aid should extend to areas not immediately adjacent to Japan. As a global economic power, Japan should shoulder more responsibilities in regions beyond East and Southeast Asia—the Middle East and North Africa, sub-Saharan Africa, the Caribbean, and Central and South America.[8] The underlying assumption is that Japan has benefited enormously without shouldering many international responsibilities. In short, Japan is the world's ultimate egoist.[9]

At the other extreme, Japan's potential as a challenger is mentioned with increasing frequency and intensity.[10] (This image is often compatible with the free-rider image.) The first sign is found in manufacturing and trade. The Japanese advances in exports of televisions, automobiles, steel, video tape recorders, and electronic goods tend to foster this image. Skillful translation of technological breakthroughs into commodity production and worldwide marketing is seen as a Japanese characteristic. Japanese mass production allows for both variety and quality, and market targeting enables Japan to capture large portions of the market quickly. Japan's export-led economic recovery after the first oil crisis further reinforced the challenger impression.

Japanese advances in robotics, enabling production of manufactured goods with efficiency and precision, has also strengthened its image as a challenger. This makes some uneasy about the future prospects for their own economies, where unemployment rates are already high. With the largest percentage of robot-aided manufacturing facilities in the world, is Japan producing commodities more efficiently and causing unemployment abroad and thereby weakening the economic abilities of importing countries? The image that friends are in fact foes has been gaining a secure position in some quarters.[11] The nightmare is that the increasing Japanese share of the world automobile and electronics markets might extend to other areas as well. What if Japan achieves a superior competitive position vis-à-vis the United States in all manufacturing sectors, as Chalmers Johnson sees for the year 2000, between the two extremes of "hamburgers and ICBMs"?[12]

If the U.S. Defense Department's procurement of Japanese electronics components for high-precision weapons goes beyond a certain threshold, will Japan not acquire enormous leverage over the United States? Indeed, former CIA Director William J. Casey denounced Japan's large holdings in U.S. computer companies as "Trojan horses."[13] With the steady increase in direct Japanese investment (from $32 billion in 1980 to an estimated $150 billion in 1990), the national security argument is gaining strength.[14]

Japan is also portrayed as a challenger in international finance. One finance economist has calculated that Japan will seize a commanding share of the global financial market by 1990. Japan's overseas lending, which amounted to $42.6 billion in 1982, is likely to grow to $211 billion in 1990, with

Japanese trade surpluses and influx of foreign portfolio investment abroad providing the Japanese banks with plenty of new dollar deposits, which can then be onlent through the Euromarket. . . . The Yen dominated-bond market will exceed the Eurobond market in new issues. . . . Oil will be priced in yen, speeding the development of the yen currency bloc in the Far East. . . . Interest rate movements in Japan will be completely liberalized. . . . A relentless series of mergers through the 1980s will make the world's five largest banks all Japanese. . . . In 1990 one yen will equal one cent, the Japanese GNP will be the largest in the world.[15]

This image is further reinforced by the recent Japanese military buildup and the average 7.1 per cent annual budgetary increase between 1980 and 1985.[16] Japan could become a formidable military power in two or three decades if it so chooses, given its advanced technological level and vast economic and demographic size. According to this image, the gradual Japanese economic advance is nothing but a step toward overall Japanese supremacy. If Japan assumes a military burden commensurate with its economic capability, as opposed to the current $10 billion or 1 per cent of GNP,[17] this will strengthen the notion of Japan as a challenger. The uneasy asymmetry between Japan's economic and military power will be broken sooner or later, the argument goes, since historically no major economic power has remained such without transforming itself into a major military power.[18]

A third image portrays Japan as a supporter of international economic and political arrangements. Recently, however, the other two images have tended to overshadow the supporter image. According to this argument, Japan's increasingly positive role in military burden sharing, political cooperation, foreign aid, debt rescheduling, and foreign direct investment are best characterized as those of a supporter.

Japan is now the second largest aid donor next to the United States and the largest aid donor in many countries east of Pakistan. It is argued that Japan's emphasis on foreign aid to build industrial infrastructure compensates for the two major U.S. priorities: basic needs and weapons. In terms of geographical coverage, Japan has significantly expanded its aid donations from East and Southeast Asia to other parts of the world. The major recipients of Japanese foreign aid are not only the resource-rich countries on which Japan is fundamentally dependent but also the countries whose security is a major concern for the United States and therefore, at least indirectly, for Japan as well. Not only such neighboring countries as South Korea, China, and Indonesia but also countries like Pakistan, Turkey, Egypt, Saudi Arabia, and pro-U.S. Central American countries are now major recipients of Japanese foreign aid.[19] Furthermore, Japanese foreign aid increasingly emphasizes humanitarian aid and basic needs as it comes to focus on sub-Saharan Africa and South Asia.[20]

Japan has recently become the second largest contributor to the World Bank after the United States. Japan's contribution to the Asian Development Bank has been the largest since the bank began. Despite its large contributions to such organizations, Japan is said to maintain a low profile and to be interested more in the economic health and growth of recipient countries than with outright promotion of narrowly conceived Japanese national interests.[21]

Moreover, by 1983 Japan had become the second largest country after the United States in terms of outstanding net external assets. In proportion to the increase in these assets, Japan's syndicated loans and foreign direct investment have grown by leaps and bounds in the 1980s. Japan's syndicated loans, which amounted to $32.1 billion in 1982, have three major characteristics that, when combined, corroborate Japan's supporter role very well. The first is lower spreads and higher maturity on average than OPEC or most of U.S. lending. The second is that Japanese agents have been taking risks as leading managers or co-managers of consortiums, often in cooperation with U.S. banks. In 1983, the Bank of Tokyo was the number-two leading manager next to the Bank of America. In 1986 Nomura Securities was the number-two leading manager of Eurobonds, after Crédit Suisse First Boston, and in fixed-rate Eurobonds it was the leading manager. The third is that Japanese banks have shown themselves adept in conducting debt rescheduling to some developing countries, again in cooperation with U.S. banks.[22]

Japan's foreign direct investment has grown radically in the 1980s. In 1983 it registered $32.2 billion, fourth in the world.[23] In 1986, it rose to $105.9 billion. Japan's foreign direct investment in the United States increased fivefold between 1977 and 1982. Japan's overall willingness to accept minority ownership also befits its supporter role.[24]

In terms of security, the increasing burden sharing with the United States is prominent, ranging from budget sharing for U.S. bases in Japan to the Japan-U.S. division of labor in naval intelligence and blockade activities in joint military exercises in the Western Pacific.[25] It is argued that the Japanese government's strong support for the deployment of cruise and Pershing II missiles in Western Europe in 1983 is an indication that Japan quite cautiously plays a supporter's role.[26] Similar instances of political cooperation often cited are (1) resolving the loan issues with South Korea before Prime Minister Yasuhiro Nakasone's visit to the United States in 1981; (2) keeping diplomatic channels open with Iran and Iraq and trying to mediate between them since shortly after the Gulf war started in 1978; (3) supporting the United States in calling for a new round of GATT negotiations sometime after 1986 and prodding other countries to join it in the economic summit of May 1985; and (4) helping the United States in September 1985 by jointly persuading initially reluctant West Germany, France, and Great Britain to make concerted interventions in the market to lower the value of the dollar.

These three contending images of Japan—free-rider, supporter, and challenger—coexist with amazing ease if only because Japan is an enigma to the rest of the world. The confusing coexistence of the three images in the minds of many reflects the complex position Japan occupies in various areas of the international system, Japan's wide-ranging options vis-à-vis the international system, and the various ways Japan's policy mix determines its role in the international system.

In the following, I first summarize three characteristics of the third quarter of this century with longer-term implications for Japan. Then in greater detail, I focus on the post-1973 world, delineating major environmental changes and corresponding modifications in Japanese assumptions about economic and security policies. Third, I describe the domestic context that allowed Japan's ascension as a world power and that determine and constrain the way it adapts to international changes and modify its role, focusing on domestic preferences and policy priorities. Fourth, I speculate on the prospects for Japan and the rest of the world, discussing Japan's aspirations and capabilities and the sustainability and stability of alternate systemic possibilities.

Japan, 1950-2000

Japan's basic preoccupations before the early 1970s concentrated on internal economics and politics. Following the difficult immediate postwar years, its economy, effectively insulated from external disturbances, performed well for most of the 1960s. The real economic growth rate averaged about 10 per cent until the first oil crisis in 1973, and political stability, with a major emphasis on economic growth, reigned. From July 1960 until July 1972, there was only one change of prime minister.

Despite occasional disturbances both inside and outside Japan, most years of the third quarter of the century provided a favorable international environment, compared with the first decade of the fourth quarter, 1975–85. Aside from the immediate postwar years, Japan had a "sort of vacation" from most of the painful international and political complications that it experienced between the mid-nineteenth century and the mid-twentieth century.[27] During those one hundred years, Japan was plagued and shaped largely by national insecurity.[28] The third quarter of the century was an exceptional period compared with the more tumultuous fourth quarter.

Many favorable conditions enabled Japan to achieve high economic growth and continuous political stability. Among them, the most important are (1) the upward trend of the world economy in the third quarter of the century; (2) latecomer effects in industrialization; and (3) the resilient U.S. hegemonic umbrella in both the military and the economic areas.

Even the most cursory comparison of the 1950s and 1960s with the 1930s and 1940s or with the 1970s and 1980s makes the overall differences between them clear. The four criteria Kondratieff utilized to identify long-term conjunctional change—wars, technological innovation, gold production (or, in more contemporary terms, money supply), and agricultural production (resource constraints)—are useful measures in this regard.[29]

The third quarter of the century was an era of global economic upturn by most criteria. World War II, the cold war, the Korean war, and the Vietnam war played important roles in initiating or accelerating an upward trend or in effect precipitating the end of such an upturn. The waves of technological innovations and their rapid diffusion over the globe, in fields from steel to automobiles to petrochemicals to nuclear energy, were largely unprecedented in terms of their variety and enormous impact on production. The money supply expanded greatly in many countries, accommodating flourishing business activities and accelerating inflation. Resource constraints were hardly felt during most of the period. For the most part, commodity prices remained low during the 1950s and 1960s.

It was quite fortunate for Japan that it underwent its recovery and expanded growth during a period of world economic prosperity. Without this coincidence, Japan's economic growth would have taken a much longer and more hazardous path. Japan's previous spurt in industrialization took place in the increasingly unfriendly environment of the 1930s and 1940s.[30] Difficulties on a worldwide scale in trade and monetary transactions, in technology transfers, and in resource utilization and the eventual involvement in hostilities on all fronts forced Japan to mobilize economic resources for war. At least temporarily, this prematurely terminated Japan's industrial growth. Furthermore, national insecurity heavily influenced the forms of economic and political institutions throughout the period. The strong duality in industrial structure (with more secure, larger industries, on the one hand, and less secure, smaller industries, often the former's subcontractors, on the other hand) and political authoritarianism were two examples.[31] In the 1950s and 1960s, such unfavorable conditions did not exist.

Latecomer effects give a certain advantage to being industrially backward.[32] A latecomer can achieve more rapid economic growth because of lower costs and technological improvements by learning from the forerunners. Most crucially, a latecomer can dispense with a large amount of R&D because the pioneers have already explored the technological frontiers and the subsequent technological diffusion usually enables cheaper acquisition of new technologies.[33] Japan's contributions to technological innovation were concentrated more in manufacturing than in scientific discovery. With the markets for certain products already created by the early starters, those Japanese products with quality, cost, and other comparative advantages slowly and steadily penetrated the market. It is sometimes difficult to recall that Japan was the lonely forerunner of the newly industrializing countries outside Western Europe and North America in the 1950s and early 1960s and that Japan was a recipient of IMF loans until the mid-1960s. The latecomer effect accounts for much of the Japanese economic expansion.

The U.S. hegemonic umbrella ensured Japan access to the world market and allowed Japan to dispense more or less with military expenditures. The U.S. hegemonic position in the international system came about during World War II. First, the United States was the most effective contributor to the military and economic weakening of Germany and Japan.[34] Second, the United States steadily rooted out British colonial positions around the world in the process of working out the postwar international economic, political, and military framework of the U.S.-dominated neo-liberal imperium.[35] Although the Soviet Union also emerged as a victor, the contrast between the two countries was stark: the United States lost 290,000 men in the war whereas the USSR lost about 20 million; the United States had an enormous supply arsenal, the USSR found it difficult to acquire production facilities and fuel; the United States produced more than 60 per cent of the world's manufactured products, the USSR a much smaller amount. In short, the U.S. preponderance in the economic and military fields far outweighed the rest of the world.[36] Owing to these dominant economic, military, and even cultural positions, the United States shaped and remolded the postwar international system. The IMF and World Bank as economic institutions, NATO and other alliances as military institutions, and the United Nations and other organizations as political institutions were imprinted with U.S. hegemony in loosely institutionalized forms.[37]

For Japan, the U.S. hegemonic umbrella meant primarily three things.[38] With Japan's security tied to U.S. global strategies and U.S. military bases in Japan, Japan could dispense with most military expenditures. The ratio of military expenditures to overall government spending has been about 5 per cent and its ratio to GNP has been less than 1 per cent for the past two decades. This is a minuscule amount compared with that spent by the other major OECD powers (approximately 10–30 per cent of total government spending).

Economically, Japan enjoyed liberal access to the world market, both for exports of manufactured goods and imports of natural resources. Without this unprecedented liberal economic order, Japan would have found it difficult to develop its present-day trading pattern with the rest of the world. The yen-dollar exchange rate was favorable to Japanese exports, and Japan benefited much from this for most of the third quarter of this century. The fixed exchange-rate system provided much needed stability and predictability for Japanese manufacturers and traders.

Politically, U.S. support of the conservatives during the Occupation allowed them to recuperate from the disgrace of defeat and the damages of the early Occupational reforms. Without active U.S. support, it would have been more difficult for the Japanese conservatives to occupy what is called in political theory the Downsian center of the electoral spectrum, as they gradually did during the early 1950s after labor unions were fully legitimized, tenants liberated, business conglomerates disbanded, and many political and economic leaders purged from office by the early Occupation reforms. If the predominant party system was, as is often said, a major source of political stability and economic success in the 1950s and 1960s, then some credit goes to the United States, at least from the Japanese conservatives' point of view.

A major turnabout became increasingly clear in the 1970s and 1980s, when the three major conditions supporting Japan's political economy in the third quarter of the century eroded to a considerable extent. First, the world economy is experiencing a reversal in the fourth quarter of the century. The average growth rate in real income in the OECD countries registered an unmistakable decline in the beginning of the fourth quarter.[39] The Vietnam war, a major conflict in terms of its consequences on the belligerent countries and the world as a whole, ended with an unequivocal outcome in 1975. With the beginning of détente in the early 1970s, military activities slackened, at least in the United States. Although technological innovation continued to be as vigorous as before, its ability to stimulate economic activities became less powerful, despite its variety. The expansion of the money supply, however, did not increase as rapidly as the economic growth rate because of prolonged stagflation; resource constraints were felt less strongly because some resources, like oil, had already reached their upper limits shortly before. In the early 1980s, the worldwide supply of oil and the U.S. supply of wheat and corn, for example, were plentiful; manufactured products were also in oversupply, but demand was sluggish and unemployment soared.

Second, much of the latecomer effect became less pronounced because of Japan's admirable success. Such phenomena as the high population growth rate, the high percentage of the population working, the high investment in production equipment and socioeconomic infrastructure, the high growth rate of real gross fixed-capital formation, and the preponderance of the manufacturing sector in the economy either ceased to exist or weakened substantially. During the past decade, some of the latecomer attributes characterizing the Japanese model disappeared, although they continue to be much commented on both inside and outside Japan.[40]

Yet Japan's economic performance is still one of the best in the world, causing nightmares for both North America and Western Europe. Many articles published in the United States portray Japan as engaging in an economic Pearl Harbor.[41] As one of the few beneficiaries of the Reagan boom of the mid-1980s, Japan has caused envy and enmity throughout the world, including in the United States itself. But Japan is facing an unenviable situation in which the weakening of its latecomer attributes and its increasing international burden sharing will steadily slow its growth potential. Economic liberalization and higher integration with the U.S. economy increase Japan's vulnerabilities to a U.S. recession, as well as to U.S. whims.[42] In Europe, many Japanese visitors have been told that European life would be much easier without a militarily threatening USSR and an economically formidable Japan.[43]

Third, U.S. hegemony has been eroding slowly. The abandonment of the gold standard in 1971 was taken as a painful U.S. announcement of its abjuration of its position as the preponderant and sole responsible molder of the international monetary system. The U.S. withdrawal from Vietnam in 1973 was viewed as a grudging U.S. admission of its inability to assume the role of the sole arbiter of international conflict. Militarily, the USSR has been catching up steadily with the U.S., especially during the 1970s, when the United States slowed or stopped much of its military expansion efforts. Neither the United States nor the USSR, however, seems clearly superior to the other. A series of large-scale U.S. and Soviet military and naval maneuvers at various key spots in the past decade seems to document both their difficult-to-hide insecurity and their drive for power.

The Reaganite response to the U.S. decline was manifested first in the form of a prosperity based on a large-scale tax cut and second in the form of ever-increasing defense spending financed by unprecedented government deficits.[44] Although U.S. military hegemony and monetary sovereignty have not changed fundamentally, during the first decade of the fourth quarter of the century, they have become major disturbing, disquieting, and disorganizing forces in the international system.

Altered Environments and Modified Assumptions

Global Economic Metamorphoses

The two basic changes in the international economic environment since 1973 are the floating exchange-rate system and creeping protectionism combined with trade liberalization. The United States, which created and sustained after World War II what Ronald McKinnon calls the world dollar standard system, abandoned it abruptly in 1971 because it could no longer maintain it.[45] Keeping the U.S. dollar as virtually the sole international currency created three difficulties.[46] First, the overvalued dollar according to the fixed exchange-rate system with dollar-gold convertibility is considered to have contributed to the enormous U.S. trade deficits. Second, the large amount of dollars flowing easily in and out of the United States is thought to have lessened the effectiveness of domestic economic management. Third, the enormous capital outflows following multinational companies abroad are believed to have caused a gradual shortage of capital investment for domestic industries, resulting in a steady loss of competitiveness.

Since 1973, a more efficient floating exchange-rate system than that of 1971 has been installed. Its most important feature is credit expansion. Throughout the post–oil crisis period, the major factors contributing to credit expansion have been the separation of the dollar and gold, the institutional innovation of credit lending through consortia, the financial liberalization spearheaded by the United States, and the great fluctuations in the U.S. money supply expansion rate. Other than credit expansion, this capital regime was not a perfect solution. Two important problems are that exchange rates have been subject to somewhat wild vibrations and domestic macroeconomic management is no more effective than before.

Instability and disorder in the international system in the 1970s and 1980s have further accelerated speculative flows of capital. The long business slump since 1974 has led many banks and firms throughout the world, especially in surplus countries (first the OPEC countries and then Japan) and U.S.-based banks and multinational companies, to earn profits by investing in stocks and bonds. The decade-long global economic slowdown has meant surplus capacity for business firms, which have become large conglomerations of banks, security houses, mutual security societies, general trading companies, and think tanks, in addition to their primary function as manufacturing factories. Many big business firms are now speculators. Money moves across borders on the order of $150–200 billion a day.

Most troublesome for the first half of the 1980s was the overvalued dollar, caused primarily since the late 1970s by high U.S. interest rates. The dollar's high value has contributed to the U.S. trade deficits. It encouraged the alarming amount of capital inflows into the United States that made it a world debtor country by the end of 1984, seventy years after its status changed from debtor to creditor. The possibility of vast amounts of foreign capital leaving the United States, thus causing a sudden large-scale depreciation of the dollar once interest rates are lowered drastically to encourage the economy, has been a real possibility, especially for the past few years.[47]

Furthermore, the United States has asked and pressured Japan to liberalize its domestic financial institutions toward fully accommodating foreign financial institutions' activities in Japan and to internationalize its domestic financial markets to enable Japanese financial firms to conduct business abroad freely.[48] The floating exchange-rate system has so encouraged short-run capital flows that Japan cannot remain an exception in international finance. Second, the saturation and suppression of domestic demand in Japan and the large amount of surplus funds have forced Japanese firms, banks, and security houses to pursue more opportunities abroad in terms of syndicated loans, Eurobond underwriting, and foreign direct investment.

The transition to the floating exchange-rate system was thus the first important change in the international economic environment that effected an economic metamorphosis in Japan. Since the shift to the floating exchange-rate system was beyond the control of the Japanese authorities, we can call it environmental. The sheer size, the extraordinary resource dependence, and the ever-growing economic interdependence that characterize the Japanese economy fostered a strong sense of vulnerability throughout the 1970s and into the 1980s.[49]

The second environmental change is creeping protectionism combined with trade liberalization.[50] The onset of the global recession in 1973 accelerated the significant advances of economies that had not been major forces in world production and trade.[51] They are, along with Japan, a dozen or so newly industrializing countries (NICs). Taking advantage of the relative decline in competitiveness in certain manufacturing sectors of the major industrialized countries in Western Europe and North America, they have captured increasingly large export-market shares in the industrialized countries in, among other sectors, textiles, shipbuilding, steel, automobiles, electric appliances, and electronic components and equipment. Industrial adjustment in such industries has been slow and faced dogged resistance, revealing their inability to phase out, in large part because of self-complacency and sociopolitical rigidities.[52]

The result has been creeping protectionism in Western Europe and North America. Often, overt nontariff barriers are used. Manufacturing sectors benefiting from overt nontariff barriers in the 1970s and early 1980s accounted for 34 per cent of the market for U.S. manufacturing, 10 per cent for Canada, 20 per cent for Germany, 32 per cent for France, 34 per cent for Italy, 22 per cent for Great Britain, and 7 per cent for Japan.[53] An economist has estimated, however, the overall loss to Japanese exports incurred because of the toughest measures threatened by protectionist hard-liners at 10 per cent.[54] Sometimes outright restrictions are imposed, as in France with Japanese videotape recorders. Sometimes bilateral agreements curtail the expansion of imports, as with NIC textiles and Japanese automobiles. New entrants have posed a serious problem to old GATT members, who are accustomed to dealing with problems emanating from economies "similarly structured." They use protectionist threats to induce the up-and-coming countries to "behave well," that is, according to their norms and rules.[55]

The Tokyo Round Free Trade Agreement, concluded in 1979 and to be implemented by 1987, will lower tariff barriers to an unprecedented degree. Since 1979, there has been a combination of free trade rhetoric on the one hand and a delayed implementation of the agreement and creeping protectionism using nontariff barriers on the other hand. The high export dependence and the lack of "similarly structured" economies in Asia have made Japan all the more concerned about the creeping tide of protectionism.

Yet a larger trend is the increasing volume of trade across and against national barriers. For the dozen years since the global recession began in 1973, only once—in 1982—did world trade register an absolute decline. Creeping trade protectionism seems, therefore, a politico-economic manifestation of the relative maladjustment of a sector or an industry in the face of increasingly strong global forces penetrating national economies.

Two Japanese Assumptions Altered

Along with these two fundamental changes in the international economic environment have come two fundamental changes in Japanese assumptions on economic management in the 1980s. The first assumption is that a small economy does not influence other economies, whereas a large economy does. The second is that an economy can be isolated and regulate external forces at its borders.

The small economy assumption was discarded with the rapid expansion of the Japanese economy, an economy that has come to affect the world economy significantly. Starting with geographically adjacent economies, a number of countries bordering the Western Pacific are strongly affected by Japan. Business conditions in the latter often crucially affect economic directions in the former. Most noteworthy are the Far Eastern NICs, whose manufacturing and trade crucially depend on the imports of capital goods from Japan and enormous borrowing of Japanese capital.[56] Japan is the number-one trade partner and/or the number-one aid donor for more than half the countries in the Western Pacific.[57] Many of them have trade deficits with Japan.

More important from a global point of view is the increasing trade interdependence of the United States. The ratio of exports to GNP in the United States almost doubled during the 1970s. The United States could no longer realistically aspire to become an independent Fortress America, as was the case with the Energy Independence project of the early 1970s. A large part of U.S. trade is its Pacific trade, which by 1977 had surpassed its Atlantic trade.

Not only in trade but also in finance, Japan has ceased to be a small country.[58] Japan's foreign direct investment tripled between 1981 and 1983. Japan's direct investment in the United States accounted for 87 of the 325 cases of foreign direct investment in the United States in 1984.[59]

Capital inflows into the United States from Japan as well as from elsewhere have become so immense that the United States could not risk
alienating foreign capital by suddenly lowering interest rates, which
could result only in a sharp decline in the dollar's value. Japan's financial
ties with the rest of the world have become very tight and dense over the
past few years.

The closed economy assumption has also become unsustainable. Before 1973, the Japanese economy was characterized by a constellation
of localized competitive systems.[60] Since business firms desperately
needed financial resources for high-level investment in a high-growth
economy and since the Japanese economy was basically closed, financial
authorities were effectively able to regulate financial flows to firms, sector by sector, through commercial banks with official guidance and
financial intermediation. The large amounts of savings captured by quasi-
governmental financial institutions like the Postal Savings system enabled
the financial authorities to adopt this system of regulation. The consequences were that the financial market was highly regulated whereas
the product market was not and that intrasectoral competition was fierce
(localized competition) whereas the national market as a whole was
compartmentalized. Thus, the somewhat enigmatic picture emerged of
strict state regulation in finance coexisting with fierce market competition in manufacturing.

After the first oil crisis, however, the direction of financial flows was
reversed.[61] Instead of money flowing from the public sector to the private sector in large amounts, as was the case before 1973, money has
come to flow more from the private sector to the public sector, primarily
in the form of government bond purchases. Overloaded by swollen expenditures created especially by the large-scale introduction of social security programs at the end of the high growth period, the government
was forced to issue an enormous amount of government bonds and requested that the private sector "digest" them.[62]

One of the structural components that enabled the government to
regulate the private sector has been eroded by the change in the tide of
monetary flows. Since the net savings rate remained as high as before,
government bonds were digested without causing inflation in Japan, unlike the case in the United States.[63] The consequence was, however, to
strengthen the influence of private financial institutions vis-à-vis the government.[64] This trend was furthered by the strong global tide of financial liberalization and internationalization ushered in by the transition
from the world dollar-standard system to the floating exchange-rate system.[65] Under the floating exchange-rate system, short-term capital movements have become a major feature of international transactions. Hand
in hand with this trend, the overall demand for financial liberalization

and internationalization has been intensified, starting with the United States and then proliferating steadily among other OECD countries and the NICs.

This tide partly resulted from the expansion and performance of the Japanese economy. First, the rapid expansion of the Japanese economy in terms of GNP, gross fixed-capital formation, exports and imports, and foreign reserves has made it difficult for the Japanese economy to remain isolated from foreign economic influence. The enormous success of the Japanese economic expansion has made Japan more visible and more susceptible to criticism that it does not guarantee reciprocity in the openness of markets, both product and financial. Japan's soaring trade balances and growing foreign market shares for certain products have made it difficult to argue against this contention. Second, the good performance of the Japanese economy has been evidenced twice since the first oil crisis in the overall appreciation of the yen. Over the long term, demand for the yen as an international currency will increase. As of 1983, yen-dominated foreign reserves account for a mere 3.9 per cent of total world reserves.[66]

For these reasons, the days of the neatly insulated and effectively managed economy are gone, and the economy has become far more susceptible to international market forces. As domestic demand for manufactured goods is saturated, foreign direct investment increases. As allegations that Japanese exports generate unemployment in importing countries grow harsh, foreign direct investment again increases. As accusations of Japanese resource exploitation increase, foreign direct investment and official development assistance rise. As domestic bond markets become saturated, business firms increasingly draft foreign bonds or Eurobonds abroad, denominated either in dollars or in yen. Conversely, foreign business firms will increasingly draft yen-denominated bonds in Japan. As Japan's surplus capital increases, given its high saving rate, the volume of syndicated Eurocurrency credits increases. The consequences of these changes for international manufacturing and financial patterns are not yet clear. But there is one positive consequence that can be surmised but not yet empirically proved.

The horizon of activities in financing and marketing has been broadened and globalized. Financing and sales abroad are now much easier, and business firms are likely to depend far more strongly on foreign markets. Unless a thorough domestic financial liberalization is achieved simultaneously and unless Japan moves upward in technological and industrial innovation by not comforting itself with manufacturing abroad and foreign sales in markets it now dominates, the possibility exists that the international competitiveness of Japanese products will decline.

The U.S. experience in the 1950s, 1960s, and 1970s is instructive in this regard. Production abroad by U.S. multinational firms mushroomed when opportunities abounded under U.S. hegemony.[67] By the mid-1960s, however, capital outflows from U.S. banks financing these multinationals became unbearable because of balance-of-payments problems. Moreover, the Euromoney market developed beyond U.S. regulation, and capital outflows continued in the form of offshore markets. The fixed exchange-rate system with dollar-gold convertibility was finally abandoned by 1971. Since then, enormous amounts of capital have flowed out of the United States. These capital outflows seemed to have contributed considerably to the "deindustrialization" of the U.S. economy.[68]

As a result, domestic manufacturing sectors have not received sufficient investment. When the economy finally started to recover, enormous capital inflows from abroad attracted by high interest rates helped make the United States a debtor country.[69]

To sum up, Japan has ceased to be a small and closed economy in the past decade. It made the transition to the floating exchange-rate system in 1973, agreed to trade liberalization at the Tokyo Round of GATT in 1979, signed the Japan-U.S. agreement on Japanese financial liberalization and internationalization in 1984, and announced the three-year Action Program of economic liberalization and market access in 1985. In other words, Japan is now a large and rapidly liberalizing economy.

Global Security Metamorphoses

Japan's security environment has not changed as dramatically as its economic environment; continuity has been stronger than discontinuity in this area. Nevertheless, two significant changes in the security environment have occurred: renewed competition between the United States and the USSR, and U.S. hegemonic pressure on its allies.

The first change, from détente to renewed hostility between the United States and the USSR,[70] is the most important change in the Japanese security environment since the heyday of détente in the early and mid-1970s. Since Japan has been under the U.S. security umbrella, any alteration in basic U.S. foreign policy needs careful attention from Japan.

During the 1970s, the Americans and the Soviets interpreted détente very differently. The United States viewed détente as mutual restraint in excessive military buildup. (Recall Harold Brown's testimony: "When we build, they build; when we cut, they build."[71]) The USSR took détente as U.S. restraint in furthering U.S. nuclear superiority vis-à-vis the USSR, given the U.S. difficulties in Vietnam and the post–oil crisis recession. The United States thought of détente as moderation of Soviet expansionary efforts; the USSR took détente as U.S. restraint in blocking the forces of liberation and revolution in the Third World, especially since the Soviets perceived the "correlation of forces" as favoring the progressive forces of the world.

Besides these interpretive differences, the domestic contexts of the two countries, especially the conservative resurgence in the United States and secondarily the post-revolutionary stagnant conservatism in the late Brezhnev and post-Brezhnev eras, have been conducive to renewed animosity.[72] The resumption of a large-scale nuclear arms race in the late 1970s coincided with increasing strains and conflicts within each of the two blocs loosely headed by the two countries. Some Soviet clients and ex-clients were openly defiant (the turmoil in Poland, the anti-government war in Afghanistan, and China's invasion of Vietnam).[73] In the view of the U.S. government, some of its Western allies were moving toward "finlandization," and Japan was becoming an economic menace and hindering the U.S. restoration and reindustrialization program.[74]

The second change, the U.S. attempt to align its allies under its schemes far more strongly than before, is related to the first change. With a somewhat exaggerated perception of the Soviet military threat, the United States has been attempting to make its allies more cohesive and more supportive of its scheme to restore a reinvigorated hegemony. Efforts to reassert U.S. hegemony have focused on three areas of U.S. superiority: sophisticated weapons, high-tech communications, and international finance. In particular, the reinforced U.S. nuclear superiority over its allies has no parallel since 1945.[75] The principal U.S. concerns have been not to let the Europeans be lured into finlandization or Euroneutralism and not to allow either the Europeans or the Japanese to conduct business as usual with the Soviet bloc.

Two Japanese Assumptions Shaken

With these environmental changes as systematic constraints, Japan's security policy has undergone a metamorphosis. Like the small-country assumption in the economic area, the Japan-as-a-free-rider assumption rested on its small size and light weight. The sheer economic size of Japan, however, had rendered the first assumption ridiculous to many observers by the late 1970s. Similarly, the fast advances of Japanese high technology—in communications equipment, new materials, robotics, and electronic components—had made Japan very visible and rendered the free-rider assumption obsolete by the late 1970s.[76]

Nonetheless, the Japanese economy has not expanded to such a degree as to enable Japan to pursue a "go it alone" posture. The policy line of Mao's China in 1957 (both economic and nuclear) has not been a viable option for China, let alone for Japan. De Gaulle's 1964 decision to depart NATO has not been considered an attractive option either. Most thoughtful Japanese apparently think that working with the United States as a second-rate power—or a junior partner—is the prudent choice for Japan in the foreseeable future.[77] Japan's course is thus to contribute as much as possible to U.S. policy out of its abundant economic resources since few in Japan have fundamentally questioned the U.S.-Japan security alliance.

One way that Japan plays this positive supportive role is to emphasize the multidimensional nature of national security, using the notion of "comprehensive security" proposed by a study group established during Prime Minister Ohira's tenure (1978–80).[78] The hope hidden in this notion is that Japan's contributions to global economic welfare (foreign aid, debt rescheduling, and contributions to international organizations) will be conceived as security-related, supportive contributions. The notion of comprehensive security succeeded an emphasis on economic security in the mid-1970s.[79] The first oil crisis brought home to the Japanese that Japan's survival depended virtually on every corner of the world and forced Japan to plan for emergencies with such economic security programs as energy and resource diversification, energy conservation, and self-sufficiency in food. When the notion of economic security was discussed after the first oil crisis, many people still assumed that Japan could avoid involvement in conflicts in other parts of the world. What Japan has to do is to secure energy, food, other natural resources, and, of course, product markets, all despite wars. With the advent of the second cold war, this assumption has also been rejected.[80]

The other aspect of the Japanese security metamorphosis is the gradual erosion of the island of peace assumption, the mindset of most Japanese that grew out of the lesson they drew from the events of the 1930s and 1940s.[81] Most Japanese assume that as long as Japan is not armed and does not harbor any intent of military aggrandizement, foreign countries will respect Japanese sovereignty. Therefore, Japan ought to refrain from any activities that might involve Japan in an armed conflict. The postwar appeal of pacifism to most Japanese has not yet subsided.

The Ohira government considered policy alignment with the United States vital, and it came to describe Japan as "a member of the Western alliance."[82] The drastic change in tone of the 1979 White Paper on Defense reflects the government's fine-tuning in line with the change in U.S. policy during the late Carter administration. The Suzuki government (1980–82) took "two steps forward, one step backward" on the question of policy alignment, using the word "alliance" in the Japan-U.S. joint communiqué of 1981, but later giving the word an interpretation tailored to the domestic audience. The Nakasone government (1982–   ) has unequivocally supported the Reagan administration against the USSR. Its vehement opposition to the Soviet introduction of intermediate-range nuclear forces targeted at Western Europe and its explicit linkage of Japanese security with European and thus global security were a clear departure from past policy. On the whole, however, the Nakasone government's policy toward Japan's military buildup, security-related technological cooperation, and joint naval and military exercises is largely a continuation of the Ohira and Suzuki governments' policies.

Countering this trend of policy alignment with the United States is pacifism, which has undertones of isolationism, unilateralism, and free-ridership. Isolationism is manifested in the belief that if Japan avoids weapons and conflicts, peace is bound to prevail. The unilateral pledge to the cause of peace in Article 9 of the Japanese constitution is thought to have had good effects for Japan. The importance of free-ridership is clear. The island of peace has been kept intact under the U.S. security umbrella and sphere of influence since 1945. The Japanese have been ambivalent about acknowledging the U.S. umbrella since they fear that the U.S. forces in Japan (with or without nuclear weapons) might induce or invite an attack by a third party against Japan.

The reinvigorated military and naval forces of the Soviet Union over and adjacent to Japanese territories and general Soviet provocations since the mid-1970s have, however, aroused dissonant feelings within the Japanese government. This has been especially true since the Soviet provocations followed the adoption in 1976 of the Self-Defense Policy program based on the assumptions of the détente period of the early and mid-1970s.

On top of this, U.S. pressure for burden sharing led the Japanese government to be more conscious of the security ties with the United States. The overriding motive of the Japanese government in accommodating the U.S. government's requests and pressures in this respect and others is a strong sense of Japan's vulnerabilities and the incalculable cost associated with security independence.[83] Japanese compliance over the past few years with U.S. demands in such areas as defense cooperation, trade liberalization, and liberalization of finance and capital markets cannot be explained without fathoming Japan's deep sense of vulnerability.

The government has moved cautiously toward accommodation while being attentive not to arouse public pacifism. The basic cost-benefit calculation of the Japanese government seems to be that the economic costs of accommodation are basically manageable and that the psychological costs have to be lowered by "educating" the Japanese public.[84] Gradual intensification of the key word used to characterize the security ties with the United States are part of this process: "a member of the Western bloc" (Ohira), "a U.S. ally" (Suzuki), and "an unsinkable fortress" (Nakasone). The inevitable retreats associated with the revelation of these characterizations are designed to appease the intensely pacifist domestic audience and evidence some of the difficulties that lie ahead for the government. Although the Japanese government has been scared by the seriousness with which the U.S. government has been thinking about the possibilities of Japanese fighting together with Americans, it has so far cooperated.

How far the Japanese government can go is a moot question, however. The Japanese military capability is still extremely limited, especially in light of the contingencies that the U.S. government expects the Japanese Self-Defense Forces to meet. Since the Japanese government does not believe that the Soviet intermediate-range nuclear forces are primarily and massively targeted at Japan, it can avoid the hard decision over which defense posture Japan should develop in relation to the Japan-U.S. alliance.[85]

In sum, Japan has cautiously been modifying the two assumptions that governed its security policy until recently—the free-rider assumption and the island of peace assumption—and has started to assume more of a supporter's role in direct response to changes in the security environment as well as in U.S. policy.

Internal Logic

If changes in the global, economic, and security environments include systemic requirements that demand Japanese adaptation, then domestic values and structures work as a basis and a filter for adaptation and thus render change more compatible with internal logic and more amenable to it.[86] Internal logic is robust and resilient to change when values and structures have been shaped and restructured incrementally over forty years of successes in achieving the two basic priorities of maintaining peace and achieving prosperity.

A Resilient Pattern of Priorities

Most revealing of the Japanese preference pattern is the record, shared by few countries, of having waged no wars since World War II.[87] This contrasts with the fifty years preceding 1945, when Japan was one of the most intensely war-waging nations in the world.[88] The postwar Japanese commitment to self-restraint in this respect cannot be overexaggerated.

Having been barred from heavily rearming itself because of its defeat in World War II and the subsequent U.S. occupation, Japan's policy with respect to economic well-being and military spending has been weighted overwhelmingly in favor of the former. Japan relegates most of its critical military roles to the U.S. forces inside and outside Japan. It was President Truman who overruled Prime Minister Churchill's advice to allow Japan to retain a small army after the war and provided the Japanese with a constitution in which Japan relinquished any military role.[89] In other words, the United States imposed security free-ridership on Japan.

During the Occupation, the United States maintained its policy on Japanese national security, but did drastically alter its policy in order to transform Japan into an industrially strong ally from which U.S. forces could operate effectively to contain communist forces nearby, whether they were Soviet, Chinese, or North Korean. This response emerged from the intensified cold war in the late 1940s, particularly after the outbreak in 1950 of the Korean war, but U.S. policy on Japanese national security as such was consistent.[90]

The U.S. and the Japanese governments' positions on Japan's national security formula roughly converged. The Japan-U.S. Mutual Security Treaty signed and ratified in 1951 and put into effect in 1952 in tandem with Japan's regaining its independence makes it crystal clear that the U.S. forces bear most of the responsibility for assuring Japan's national security.[91] The Japanese government and most Japanese wanted the Self-Defense Forces to play a minor role. The primary and secondary roles of the Self-Defense Forces in the early years were to help maintain law and order at a time of political and economic turmoil and Left-Right confrontation and to serve as a disaster-relief force. Only gradually has their role in national defense come to be perceived as primary.[92]

The primary concern of the Japanese government during the first two postwar decades was economic recovery and reconstruction. Few would have welcomed a defense burden during this period. As GNP expanded in the 1960s and 1970s, defense expenditure declined in proportion to the total budget. When the growth rate of government revenues far exceeded the estimated growth rate of the economy in the early 1970s, the Tanaka government (1972–74) decided to expand social welfare to an overwhelming proportion.[93] Cries for improvements in social welfare and the environment in reaction to some of the negative social consequences of growth-first economic management, together with criticisms from abroad, encouraged the government to do so.[94] Shortly after the government reaffirmed its butter-first policy in the 1970s, the Miki government (1974–76), leaning to the left within the Liberal Democratic Party (LDP), put a cap on the expansion of the defense budget in relation to GNP.[95] Aided by the sheer growth of GNP, this semibinding threshold was maintained for the succeeding ten years, even when both superpowers began the second cold war in the late 1970s. All this amply illustrates the stability and robustness of the Japanese government's guns-and-butter policy mix.

The data in Table 1 further support this evaluation. It is clear that the expansion rate of defense expenditures was held lower than other categories of expenditures such as social security, public works, and education until the onset of the second cold war and the subsequent change in

TABLE 1

Major Categories of Japanese Expenditure, General Account Budget, 1955–1987

(¥100 million)

Expenditure	Fiscal year			
	1955	1965	1975	1980
National debt	434	220	10,394	53,104
	(4.4)	(0.6)	(4.9)	(12.5)
Local government	1,374	7,162	44,086	65,452
	(13.9)	(19.6)	(20.7)	(15.4)
General account				
Social security	1,043	5,183	39,282	82,124
	(10.5)	(14.2)	(18.5)	(19.3)
Veterans pensions	895	1,693	7,558	16,399
	(9.0)	(4.6)	(3.5)	(3.9)
Education/science	1,308	4,751	25,921	45,191
	(13.2)	(13.0)	(12.2)	(10.6)
Local finance	—	—	215	8,425
	—	—	(0.1)	(2.0)
Defense	1,349	3,014	13,273	22,302
	(13.6)	(8.2)	(6.2)	(5.2)
Public works	1,635	7,333	29,120	66,554
	(16.5)	(20.0)	(13.7)	(15.6)
Economic assistance	101	271	1,926	3,826
	(1.0)	(0.7)	(0.9)	(0.9)
Small business	26	217	1,273	2,439
	(0.3)	(0.6)	(0.6)	(0.6)
Energy	—	—	884	4,241
	—	—	(0.4)	(1.0)
Food management	—	1,055	9,086	9,556
	—	(2.9)	(4.3)	(2.2)
Others	1,670	5,182	26,870	42,775
	(16.8)	(14.2)	(12.6)	(10.0)
Emergency items	80	500	3,000	3,500
	(0.8)	(1.4)	(1.4)	(0.8)
Gen'l acc't subtotal	8,107	29,199	158,408	307,332
	(81.7)	(79.8)	(74.4)	(72.1)
TOTAL	9,915	36,581	212,888	425,888
	(100.0)	(100.0)	(100.0)	(100.0)

the international economic and security environments. The small size of Japan's defense expenditures in comparison with those of other major countries is shown in Table 2.

It is immediately clear from Table 1 that Japanese "butter" is produced mostly on a small scale. The level of Japanese wealth is not reflected in a proportionate level of investment in nonindustrial socioeconomic infrastructure. Most salient in this regard are houses, roads, sewers, and

TABLE 1 (cont'd)

Expenditure	Fiscal year			
	1984	1985	1986	1987
National debt	91,551	102,241	113,195	113,335
	(18.1)	(19.5)	(10.7)	(0.1)
Local government	88,864	96,601	101,850	101,841
	(17.5)	(18.5)	(5.1)	(−0.0)
General account				
Social security	93,211	95,737	98,346	100,896
	(18.4)	(18.2)	(2.7)	(2.6)
Veterans pensions	18,859	18,637	18,501	18,956
	(3.7)	(3.6)	(−0.7)	(2.5)
Education/science	48,323	48,409	48,409	48,497
	(9.5)	(9.2)	(0.1)	(0.1)
Local finance	1,829	—	—	—
	(0.4)	—	—	—
Defense	29,346	31,371	33,435	35,174
	(5.7)	(6.0)	(6.6)	(5.2)
Public works	65,200	63,689	62,233	60,824
	(12.9)	(12.1)	(−2.3)	(−2.3)
Economic assistance	5,439	5,863	6,232	6,492
	(1.1)	(1.1)	(0.3)	(4.2)
Small business	2,292	2,162	2,052	1,973
	(0.5)	(0.4)	(−5.1)	(−21.4)
Energy	6,032	6,288	6,297	4,952
	(1.2)	(1.2)	(0.1)	(−21.4)
Food management	8,132	6,954	5,962	5,406
	(1.6)	(1.3)	(−14.3)	(−9.3)
Others	43,694	43,244	40,837	39,163
	(8.6)	(8.2)	(−5.6)	(−4.1)
Emergency items	3,500	3,500	3,500	3,500
	(0.7)	(0.7)	(0.0)	(0.0)
Gen'l acc't subtotal	325,857	325,854	325,842	325,834
	(64.4)	(62.1)	(−0.0)	(−0.0)
TOTAL	506,272	524,696	540,886	541,101
	(100.0)	(100.0)	(100.0)	(100.0)

SOURCE: Zaisei Seisaku Kenyūkai, ed., *Korekara no zaisei to kokusai hakko* (Finance and bond issues in the future) (Ōkura zaimu kyōkai), 1985, p. 60; 1987, p. 30.
NOTE: Figures in parentheses are percentages of total.

TABLE 2
Defense Expenditure Patterns of Selected OECD Countries, 1978–1986

Year	Japan	U.S.	U.K.	FRG	France
1978	5.5%	23.5%	14.4%	19.4%	17.5%
1979	5.4	23.5	14.8	19.0	17.3
1980	5.2	23.6	14.7	19.0	17.4
1981	5.3	24.2	14.6	19.0	17.5
1982	5.5	26.2	15.8	18.8	18.3
1983	5.5	26.6	13.1	19.6	17.1
1984	5.8	26.8	13.5	19.7	18.2
1985	6.0	27.2	11.6	19.8	18.2
1986	6.2	27.6	—	19.9	—

SOURCE: Nihon ginkō chōsa tōkei kyoku, *Nihon keizai o chūshin tosuru Kokusai hikaku tōkei* (Comparative Economic and Financial Statistics, Japan and Other Major Countries) (Tokyo: Nihon ginkō), 1986, p. 88; 1987, p. 88.

TABLE 3
Japanese Expenditure Patterns Before and After the First Oil Crisis, 1973 and 1985
(¥ billion)

	1973	1985	Growth rate
Tax revenue	13,370	38,550	2.9%
Size of General Account Budget	14,780	52,500	3.6
Social security	2,220	9,570	4.3
Education and science	1,640	4,840	2.9
Public works	2,560	6,370	2.5
Defense	950	3,140	3.3
CPI (1980 = 100)	55.4	112.1[a]	2.02
Annual GNP	116,600	314,600	2.7

SOURCE: Same as Table 1; p. 61.
[a]1984

parks.[96] One could argue that the financial and administrative austerity policy of the past few years has led the government to rely more on the private sector than before, even in the area of infrastructure consolidation, and that the austerity policy accords well with the public's mild distrust of government spending habits. Even if this argument is accepted, one cannot deny that government expenditures on public works have been the primary target of the austerity policy. In fact, among government expenditures on social security, education, public works, and defense, public works recorded the lowest expansion rate between 1973 and 1985 (see Table 3).

Judging from the far from admirable achievements in this area, it seems that the Japanese miracle was a Pyrrhic victory based largely on the ephemeral advantage of economic backwardness and the adroitness in adaptation the Japanese were forced to acquire by perceived structural weaknesses, such as relative geographical isolation and the relative lack of natural and financial resources and of military might. One could even argue that both the wise allocation of resources to industrial manufacturing and infrastructure in the 1950s and 1960s and the respectable management of the economy in the 1970s and 1980s were made possible, however reluctantly, by sacrifices in the area of nonindustrial infrastructure.[97] The primacy of economic growth over social well-being in the former period and the primacy of anti-inflation policies over public spending in the latter period aptly sum up the priorities of the Japanese government and people. Since this policy priority pattern seems so robust, we need to look more closely at the most recent decade when policy priorities have shifted incrementally but without fundamentally altering the basic pattern of expenditures.

Self-restructuring Under Recession

The most salient feature of domestic management from 1973 to 1985 was the preoccupation with internal equilibrium. Domestic management of the economy and polity continued to absorb much of the government's energy and effort throughout the 1970s. This strong internal orientation contributed to the diffusion of externalities to the rest of the world, to the exacerbation of external issues, and thus to the difficulty of restructuring Japanese foreign policy in the 1980s.

In economic management, the first oil crisis was the watershed of Japanese economic development. It looked then as if the two mechanisms of Japanese economic growth for the preceding 20 years had foundered. The cheap and abundant supply of energy and other resources from abroad for refueling Japanese manufacturing halted abruptly. The subsequent economic recession replaced favorable conditions of easy access to basically expanding markets of the industrialized and industrializing worlds for Japanese exports of manufactured goods with increasingly stiff competition and creeping protectionism. These changes led some to conclude that the Japanese miracle had come to naught and that the Japanese future would be bleak at best. Contrary to this somewhat prematurely pessimistic view, however, the Japanese economy from the first oil crisis through the second oil crisis demonstrated that it was still robust and resilient, though not without problems and some important changes in its structure.[98] Various indicators of economic performance for the major industrialized countries clearly show that Japan's performance was among the best; inflation was effectively curtailed; real economic growth rate, though half of what it had been, still ran at a respectable 3–5 per cent on average; the unemployment rate doubled, but remained the lowest in the OECD (see Table 4).[99]

In monetary policy, the foremost policy emphasis after the first oil crisis was overcoming inflation.[100] The already overheated economy of the

TABLE 4
Major Economic Indicators for Selected OECD Countries, 1976–1987

Indicator	1976	1977	1978	1979	1980	1981
			JAPAN			
Nominal GNP	12.4	11.0	9.9	8.0	8.7	5.9
Real GNP	4.6	5.3	5.2	5.3	4.0	3.3
CPI	9.5	6.9	3.8	4.8	7.6	4.0
Unemployment	2.0	2.1	2.2	2.0	2.1	2.2
Current account						
($100 million)	47	140	119	−139	−70	59
Official interest						
rate	6.50	4.25	3.50	6.25	7.25	5.50
			UNITED STATES			
Nominal GNP	11.5	11.7	13.0	11.5	8.9	11.7
Real GNP	4.9	4.7	5.3	2.5	−0.2	1.9
CPI	5.8	6.5	7.7	11.3	13.5	10.4
Unemployment	7.7	7.1	6.1	5.8	7.1	7.6
Current account						
($100 million)	4.2	−145	−154	−10	19	63
Official interest						
rate	5.25	6.00	9.50	12.00	13.00	12.00
			UNITED KINGDOM			
Nominal GNP	17.3	15.2	15.4	15.8	16.0	8.9
Real GNP	2.6	2.6	2.8	2.7	−2.2	−1.2
CPI	16.5	15.8	8.3	13.4	18.0	11.9
Unemployment	4.5	4.8	4.7	4.3	5.4	8.5
Current account						
($100 million)	−17	−2	19	−15	68	125
Official interest						
rate	14.25	7.00	12.50	17.00	14.00	14.375
			FRG			
Nominal GNP	9.4	6.5	7.7	8.1	6.3	4.0
Real GNP	5.6	2.7	3.3	4.0	1.5	−0.0
CPI	4.4	3.6	2.7	4.2	5.4	6.3
Unemployment	4.6	4.5	4.3	3.8	3.8	5.5
Current account						
($100 million)	39	41	92	−60	−157	−52
Official interest						
rate	3.50	3.00	3.00	6.00	7.50	7.50
			FRANCE			
Nominal GNP	15.5	12.3	13.6	14.1	13.4	12.3
Real GNP	4.9	3.1	3.3	3.2	1.4	0.6
CPI	9.6	9.4	9.1	10.8	13.6	13.4
Unemployment	4.3	4.8	5.2	6.0	6.4	7.8
Current account						
($100 million)	−34	−4	71	51	−42	−47
Official interest						
rate	10.50	8.875	6.375	12.125	10.75	15.125

TABLE 4 (cont'd)

Indicator	1982	1983	1984	1985	1986	1987
JAPAN						
Nominal GNP	4.9	4.3	6.7	5.9	4.4	4.6 est.
Real GNP	3.2	3.7	5.1	4.3	3.0	3.5 est.
CPI	2.6	1.9	2.2	1.9	0.5	1.6 est.
Unemployment	2.5	2.7	2.7	2.6	2.8	—
Current account ($100 million)	91	242	370	550	880	770 est.
Official interest rate	5.50	5.00	5.00	5.00	2.50	—
UNITED STATES						
Nominal GNP	3.7	7.6	10.5	6.2	5.2	6.5 est.
Real GNP	−2.5	3.6	6.4	2.7	2.5	3.1 est.
CPI	6.1	3.2	4.3	3.6	1.9	3.0 est.
Unemployment	9.7	9.6	7.5	7.2	7.0	6.7 est.
Current account ($100 million)	−91	−466	−1,065	−1,177	−1,406	—
Official interest rate	8.50	8.50	8.00	7.50	5.50	5.50 est.
UNITED KINGDOM						
Nominal GNP	8.7	9.3	7.6	9.6	5.4	—
Real GNP	1.5	3.4	2.8	3.4	2.6	3.0 est.
CPI	8.6	4.6	5.0	6.1	3.4	3.75 est.
Unemployment	9.8	10.7	11.1	11.3	11.5	—
Current account ($100 million)	69	47	16	45	−5	—
Official interest rate	10.00	9.00	—	11.3125	10.8125	18.875 est.
FRG						
Nominal GNP	3.4	5.1	5.0	4.8	5.5	4.0–4.5 est.
Real GNP	−1.0	1.8	3.0	2.5	2.4	2.5 est.
CPI	5.3	3.3	2.4	2.2	−0.2	1.0 est.
Unemployment	7.5	9.1	9.1	9.3	9.0	8.5 est.
Current account ($100 million)	41	41	70	132	358	—
Official interest rate	5.00	4.00	4.50	4.00	3.50	3.00 est.
FRANCE						
Nominal GNP	14.7	10.5	8.9	7.5	6.9	5.7 est.
Real GNP	2.0	0.8	1.6	1.6	1.9	2.0 est.
CPI	11.8	9.6	7.4	5.8	2.7	2.5 est.
Unemployment	8.7	8.8	10.0	10.2	10.5	—
Current account ($100 million)	−121	−47	−8	−2	37	—
Official interest rate	12.75	12.00	9.50	8.75	7.25	7.75 est.

SOURCE: Same as Table 1, 1987 ed., pp. 150–51.

early 1970s was conducive to further inflation created by the first oil crisis. In 1974, Japan's inflation rate was the highest of the major industrialized countries. The hyperinflation of 1974 was, however, effectively tamed by 1976 through the fairly tight money supply policy pursued by monetary authorities. Since 1974, money expansion in terms of M2 and CD has averaged about 11 per cent.[101] The major considerations that led the monetary authorities to adopt this policy line were (1) the disappearance of the built-in economic discipline of the balance-of-payments ceilings since abandonment of the fixed dollar-yen exchange rate in 1973 and (2) the relative ineffectiveness of interest rate manipulation and public works spending in the stagflated economy.

On the whole, this "price stability first," or deflationary, policy set the tone of economic management for the decade after 1974. For the most part, however, business activities still remained sluggish. The economic upturns of 1977 and 1978 were not full-fledged. The second oil crisis triggered another recession, although consumer price stability was on the whole maintained. The policy thrust has undoubtedly been to preserve internal equilibrium even at the cost of leaving intact much of the external equilibrium, thus arousing further international complications. Such disturbances as trade surpluses and wild exchange-rate movements were considered to be of secondary importance and were handled more or less on an ad hoc basis.

In fiscal policy, on the one hand, there has been a steady accumulation of government debts because of the sudden large-scale decrease in tax revenue (especially corporate tax revenue), a steady increase in social welfare spending since the enactment of the social security reforms of 1973, and the consequent large-scale government bond issues, especially since 1975. On the other hand, Keynesian economic management has been perceived as ineffective.[102]

The continuing expansion of government expenditures during the high growth period (1952–73) did not pose much of a problem to the government because GNP expanded more rapidly than government expenditure. The sudden advent of an economic recession in 1974, however, meant that government revenue was far below government expenditure, which was already structurally committed and thus difficult to alter. Most serious was the steady increase in social welfare expenditures, which was the direct result of the 1973 social welfare laws and the aging of the population. The most dramatic revelation of this imbalance appeared in 1975 with the issuance of the so-called deficit bonds. Although this was not a new practice, the enormity and severity of the revenue-expenditure gap in 1975 were unparalleled and encouraged the fiscal authorities to go ahead with the scheme. By 1985, the cumulative total of government bonds reached more than 42.3 per cent of GNP.[103]

Since government bond issues themselves do not cause inflation, this pattern of fiscal management was most convenient and most comfortable to the government, at least in the short run. Efforts to cut expenditures started only in the 1980s. Prime Minister Zenko Suzuki commissioned the Provisional Council on Administrative and Financial Reform, instituted into law in 1981. It presented its proposal to the cabinet in March 1983 after intensive study and discussion. The reform efforts represent a cumulative policy package and aim to change expenditure patterns and underlying policy priorities.

The economic authorities thought that Keynesian demand management would be ineffective in their attempts to stimulate demand in the stagflated economy and would only aggravate both inflation and unemployment. Rather, as summarized above, a tight money supply policy became the key policy instrument. Even when internal and external criticisms against the tight economic policy were raised in 1976–78, Keynesian management was not wholeheartedly adopted. The major thrust of fiscal policy is directed not at Keynesian macroeconomic management but at resource allocation and income redistribution. Again, this represents the primary preoccupation with internal equilibrium. Price stability and provision of largely divisible public goods are two of the major concerns of the Ministry of Finance.[104]

Two changes in the Japanese economy take on special significance because they are directly related to, if not necessarily caused by, the two macroeconomic policy thrusts outlined above. The ratio of government outlays to GNP increased from 12.7 per cent in 1973 to 17.7 per cent in 1980.[105] In 1985 it reached 16.8 per cent. Though still low compared with comparable figures for most West European countries, the Japanese figures document the rapid expansion of the government's role in the economy over the past decade as an inevitable consequence of the government's accommodation of various public demands during the high growth period. The most important factor was a disturbingly steady increase in the amount of social security–related expenses. The welfare reforms enacted early in 1973 before the first oil crisis guarantee an automatic expansion in social welfare as long as the weight of the nonworking elderly population among the total population increases, which is indeed the case in the post–high growth period.[106] Moreover, although in 1969 the Diet passed a law prescribing a ceiling on the number of central government personnel, this did not limit the expansion of local government personnel, which increased in the 1970s with the expansion of educational and social welfare expenditures at the local level.

The second change is the increasing importance of foreign demand vis-à-vis domestic demand. Until the early 1970s, two features kept foreign trade from accounting for a large percentage of Japan's GNP: a large population with a high income level and Japan's effective isolation as a latecomer industrializing country. These two features caused a limited integration of the Japanese economy into the world economy in terms of the ratio of foreign trade to GNP, which belies the conventional image of Japan's reliance on exports. The figure was 22.2 per cent in 1970 and 26.1 per cent in 1980.[107]

However, the Japanese economy has become increasingly exposed to the world economy. The primary factor in this has been the saturated domestic demand since 1974. Deflationary economic policy, de facto tax increases, and semi-forced savings have all contributed to economic conservatism and made domestic demand sluggish. One extreme example of this is automobile sales. In January 1984, the domestic market accounted for 28.9 per cent of Japanese automobiles sold and the foreign market for 71.1 per cent.[108] A secondary factor is the liberalization of the Japanese economy. Macroeconomic management primarily oriented at maintaining internal equilibrium led manufacturers to rely increasingly on exports, but consumers were not much lured by less appealing, foreign-manufactured goods. Hence, growing external disturbances, such as criticisms of export drives as exporting unemployment and of high trade surpluses as originating from nontariff barriers against foreign products, have been almost inevitable.[109] In the mid-1980s, the aggravation of external economic frictions virtually forced the government to tackle such issues as the trade surplus and economic liberalization.

The Politics of Restructuring

Political management is the second facet of internal equilibrium. The predominantly internal preoccupation of the Japanese government throughout the 1970s was perhaps inevitable not only because of the economic recession but also because of the concurrent political problem of a possible loss of power to the opposition. The conservatives focused on restoring the internal equilibrium in their favor.[110]

Perhaps reflecting the complexity of problems facing incumbents, changes in government were far more frequent after 1972 than before throughout the democratic world. Japan was not an exception. Six prime ministers have ruled since 1972, whereas the decade before 1972 saw only two. The overall lower figures of public support for the LDP reflected the enormity of these problems. It looked during most of the 1970s as if the government might change hands at any moment. Nothing of that sort happened. Instead, support for the LDP started to increase in the late 1970s. Since Nakasone's ascension to power in 1982, the LDP has enjoyed extremely high opinion poll support. The most recent evidence of this high level of support was the landslide victory of the LDP in the elections for both Houses on July 6, 1986.[111]

Public support for the LDP reached a nadir in the 1970s. A series of external disturbances in the first half of the 1970s shocked, bewildered, or at least reinforced the feeling of uncertainty about the government. In addition, domestic upheavals were also pronounced. Accelerated inflation in the early 1970s was a major political issue for both Prime Ministers Sato and Tanaka. Environmental deterioration in the early 1970s enabled the opposition to gain control of many local governments. The Lockheed scandal and related malaise of the LDP delayed most major policy initiatives that needed to be tackled immediately. Intraparty conflicts within the LDP were aggravated by the handling of the issue of political ethics. The economic recession after the first oil crisis was prolonged until 1977. These unpleasant issues and concerns, along with the management of various external constraints and disturbances, dominated political developments in the first half of the 1970s. It is not surprising that public attitudes toward the incumbent party were not favorable.

Although external events occasionally gave cause for disquiet and uncertainty and the internecine struggle within the LDP was reinforced rather than resolved, political developments in the latter half of the 1970s and into the 1980s were more stabilizing and reassuring from the viewpoint of the incumbent party. As business conditions picked up slowly in 1976–77, the incumbent party steadily regained public support. Although the second oil crisis delayed a fuller business recovery, the public's attitude toward the economy changed unmistakably during 1977–78 to quasi satisfaction verging on resignation with the status quo. With per capita income reasonably high, inflation effectively tamed, and annual real economic growth registering a respectable rate, the public increasingly exhibited economic conservatism.[112]

The perception of economic improvement in the recent past and the expectation of economic improvement in the near future tended to converge year by year. Economic conservatism seemed easily channeled into political conservatism. Public support for the LDP reached a high level in the early 1980s. The strong internal equilibrium evident in the political developments of the 1970s and the early 1980s, assisted very much by economic resilience, seemed to restore the composure of the incumbent party. Nonetheless, to a remarkable degree the conservatives seemed to achieve this not so much by longer-term design as by short-term muddling through.[113]

The primacy of restoring the internal equilibrium in the conservatives' favor can be seen in public policy as well.[114] Farmers and small-business owners represent the two most loyal and trustworthy constituencies of the LDP. Their support, however, declined considerably and reached a nadir between 1973 and 1976. Regaining the strong support of traditional conservatives was of utmost importance to the LDP. The instinctive LDP response was to favor these groups by passing laws that channeled the benefits of public policy to them or to protect them from internal and external structural forces by not changing laws in a more market-conforming direction.

The LDP's selective and differential wooing of different social groups was particularly pronounced in the decade after the first oil crisis. At this time, the agricultural population was declining rapidly, and food (except rice) was increasingly imported from abroad. By 1982, Japan exceeded the Soviet Union in the total amount of food imports. Small businesses found it increasingly difficult to resist competition and penetration by supermarket chains, department stores, and other kinds of stores run by big business. Small family-owned factories have been subject to competitive pressures from big business, especially when economic conditions were not favorable. Although small-business owners have not dwindled in number as rapidly as farmers, their number is more or less stable.

Specific target policies seem to have helped the LDP regain the support of the majority of farmers and small-business owners. For 1976–79, the average rate of increase in the Ministry of Agriculture's budget was 11.1 per cent. For small-business budget items, the average increase for 1974–79 was 19.8 per cent. These groups' support for the LDP increased by 8 per cent and 4.3 per cent, respectively, between 1976 and 1980.[115]

The LDP's adaptation in the new policy areas of social welfare and the environment was remarkable. Contrary to its previous policy priorities, in the 1970s the LDP geared its policy emphasis to these new areas. In 1971 the Environment Agency was established, and since 1972 social welfare expenditures have received a strong emphasis. Overall, social welfare expenditures annually registered a 24.5 per cent increase (1973–79), and environmental expenditures (facilities and equipment for an amenable living environment) a 25.6 per cent increase (1973–79).[116] By 1980, Japanese social welfare standards had reached a level roughly on a par with those of the major OECD countries, and Japanese environmental regulation was among the strictest in the world.[117] Many factors favored the LDP's pursuit of these policies, including a still respectable economic growth rate and a favorable demographic age profile.

A major consequence of this policy for the LDP was to dissipate criticisms from the opposition parties, who had gained control of many local governments by pointing to the central government's neglect of social welfare and the environment. The result of this unabashed policy adaptation was unequivocal. Among the social groups that showed the strongest interest in these two issues, LDP support increased significantly.[118] In support of the government's emphasis on social welfare were the jobless, the elderly, and managers and professionals; supporting its policies on environmental issues were white-collar workers, urban residents, and youth.

The reincorporation of traditional clients into the LDP camp and the winning over of those social groups agitated by the opposition characterized government-public relations in the 1970s. Consequently, the restoration and restructuring of internal equilibrium dominated political developments during this decade. Overall economic resilience helped the government, although the government's macroeconomic policy may be given equal credit. Internal equilibrium between the government and the public was restored, and although political concerns were focused primarily on domestic issues, exogenous disturbances helped the government in a small way to retain public support since the people tend to rally around the government during a time of foreign pressure and national crisis.

Meeting External Requirements

That the basic orientation of government is toward internal equilibrium is not uncommon. By and large, the primary concerns and daily preoccupations of most central governments are about internal economic and political affairs. Japan is, however, an extreme example in its orientation toward internal affairs.

During the period of crisis absorption and management in 1973–78, the government was primarily concerned with assuring a stable supply of energy and nonenergy resources and with securing and expanding export markets around the world. During this period, the government favored the notion of "economic security";[119] that is, security involved protecting and consolidating economic efficiency in light of the unstable international business environment. This notion fitted nicely with the then-prevailing mood in Japan that (1) national security is economic in nature and (2) national security is ensured by paying costs that do not derive from economic considerations alone. The government's efforts were largely confined to consolidating the Self-Defense Forces slowly but steadily within bureaucratic and political constraints, without directly articulating its strategy.

In the period of initial recuperation and restructuring in 1979–83, the government focused on the intricate matrices of economic, political, and military aspects of the global transformation. The notion of "comprehensive national security" became a favorite during this period.[120] The emphasis was national security, relying on all conceivable resources, albeit with an undeniable emphasis on economic power. Although the government increasingly recognized the need to tackle national security issues squarely, it was painfully aware of Japan's shortcomings in military power and, at the same time, of the foolishness of publicizing this fact. Clearly influencing the thinking of the government were the Vietnamese invasion and occupation of Kampuchea, the Chinese invasion of

Vietnam, the Soviet invasion and occupation of Afghanistan, the Iran-Iraq war, the Israeli and Syrian occupation of Lebanon, the U.S. military involvement in Nicaragua and other Central American republics, and the Soviet downing of a Korean Airline aircraft.[121] In addition, the increasingly stern economic and business environment clearly disturbed government and business leaders. Particularly worrisome were the rash of protectionist bills introduced in the U.S. Congress, growing agitation in the EC against Japanese imports, the arresting of several Japanese nationals on charges of technological spying, and unfriendly takeovers of Japanese subsidiaries in the United States.

The path from economic security to comprehensive security was not linear. Rather, it involved a zigzag course reflecting the solid pacifist-isolationist sentiments of the public.[122] Furthermore, because of its strong internal preoccupation, even during this period it was necessary for the government to overhaul its whole range of public policies in order to redirect its foreign policy. Two actions are noteworthy.

The first was Prime Minister Ohira's creation of nine policy study groups on the future of Japanese culture, urban living, family life, lifestyle, science and technology, macroeconomic management, economic foreign policy, Pan-Pacific solidarity, and comprehensive national security.[123] Many of these groups attempted to grasp the nature of global and national transformations to help develop ways of restructuring national policies. Three of them directly addressed the question of Japan's foreign policy. In addition, there was a subtle stress on Japaneseness in the proposal: reevaluation of Japanese culture, Japanese family life, post-industrial society in Japan, Japanese urban life, and Japanese macroeconomic management.

The second action by the government, the administrative and financial reform, was initiated by Prime Minister Suzuki and continued under Prime Minister Nakasone.[124] The major goals of this reform package were the restructuring of administrative and financial patterns to fine-tune them to changing policy priorities and the retention of the grand conservative coalition of 1955 by not causing excessive strains on the public during implementation of transformed policy priorities.[125]

Administrative reform and the redressing of financial difficulties had several thrusts. First, they were intended to slash the excesses of previous expenditure patterns, especially in social welfare, education, public works, and personnel salaries, in favor of such items as defense, foreign aid, and science and technology. These high policy priorities were very significant in conjunction with the ceiling imposed on budget requests. The increases in defense and foreign aid spending are outstanding. Although these cuts are not enough to decrease the accumulated government deficit drastically, at least the direction of policy emphasis seems to have been set unequivocally.

Second, the reforms were aimed at reorganizing the state bureaucracy to facilitate high-level policy management to handle crises and emergencies of a higher order than was customarily envisaged earlier. Although the initial attempt at creating a comprehensive management agency directly under the prime minister did not materialize in the final proposal, bureaucratic functions of coordination and management and of policy analysis and planning were stressed.

Third, the reform emphasized the nonintroduction of a large-scale tax increase, which the government wishes to avoid for electoral reasons. Prime Minister Ohira's careless allusion during the 1979 election campaign to the possibility of a tax increase and the subsequent loss of votes seem to be behind this decision. With the LDP's landslide victory of 1986, tax increases are likely to become slightly more manageable. Even without a large-scale tax increase, the income tax has been increasing because of bracket creep. Even with these substantial de facto tax increases, however, the government debt cannot be reduced much for the rest of the 1980s.[126]

The period since 1984 has been characterized by the government response to intensified U.S. pressure for economic liberalization and international burden sharing. Two programs constitute the core of meeting and adapting to pressure from outside. One is a series of economic liberalization measures symbolized by the Action Program, announced in July 1985 for implementation by 1987. The other is the Self-Defense Forces' New Defense Capability Consolidation Plan for 1986–90. Both aim at overcoming the previously strong image of Japan as an economic spoiler and military free-rider and at creating an image of Japan as an economic and military supporter. The Action Program is expected to end much of Japan's activities as a high-tariff mercantilist state, and the new defense plan is expected to place Japan in the category of a nonnegligible military power supporting the United States in the Pacific region.[127]

During this most recent period, the administrative and financial reform packages have still been on the government's agenda. This has meant continuing budget austerity, with only foreign aid, defense, and science and technology targeted for more expansion and with socioeconomic, nonindustrial infrastructure set aside as a secondary policy priority—a continuation of the pattern since the 1950s.[128]

Conspicuous in these government attempts to reorient Japan's course are mobilization of the public by utilizing a wide spectrum of leaders for the articulation and deliberation of policy and the translation of many policy-related ideas into legislation and budget items. In this, bureaucrats have played an important role. These two features and the steady progress in implementation are a demonstration of the government's strength. Although not all of the proposals were implemented, the whole self-searching process seems to have set the basic tone of Japan's internal and external management.

However, because the exacerbation of major issues such as government debt, trade, and defense issues was partly the result of the government's previous semi-exclusive preoccupation with restoring internal equilibrium, primarily at the sacrifice of external issues, any policy reorientation must start by overhauling a whole range of public policies, which makes the task more difficult. Yet the government's promise not to increase taxes, together with the basic anti-inflationary preferences of the majority of the governmental actors and people, has effectively nullified a more fundamental budgetary restructuring than that necessary to accommodate all the internal and external problems.

Thus, the government's efforts to cast a Japanese image of an economic and military supporter have not been wholly successful in large part because domestic factors have inhibited or postponed otherwise timely and effective actions. When the United States, Japan's major ally, faces the tasks of enhancing its economic competitiveness and military buildup while plagued by trade and budget deficits of extraordinary proportions, it is inevitable that the United States is no less strongly pulled by concerns for its internal equilibrium. When the two largest economies put their externalities on the other's shoulders, it exacerbates their overall relationship. As one newspaper put it, "It is as if both actors push their garbage into the other's garden in order to clean up their own garden." [129]

Looking Ahead with Caution

Japan's rapid transition over the past decade in terms of macroindicators has provided Japan with complex and often conflicting images. The strength of the economy, the adaptability of industry, and the swiftness of technological innovation are sometimes contrasted with political-military passivity. Yet the same images of economic strength and efficiency are sometimes combined with a potential for political-military assertiveness. In between lies the ironically uneasy image of the increasing contribution of healthy economic growth and political resilience to general global welfare. Underlying these conflicting images are the increasingly wide policy options that Japan and the rest of the world have come to envisage and entertain for the future, even if only vaguely. These policy options have not been articulated often in the recent past.

Policy options in the economic sphere are basically divided into trilateralism and regionalism. This policy choice hinges on the degree of protectionism that develops in Western Europe and North America and the speed of economic development in the Western Pacific region. [130] If the protectionism that has developed in the EC over the past decade continues, it will leave de facto the multilateral free-trading system of GATT, and Japan will be forced to find other markets far more vigorously.[131] If in addition U.S. protectionism further develops in the same direction and if the United States substantiates its free-trade bilateralism with countries such as Canada and Israel, then Japan's policy choice will slide further toward regionalism.[132]

Yet the protectionism that has developed in Western Europe is not of a kind that would lead immediately to vicious political and economic conflicts reminiscent of those of the 1930s. Rather, it represents a combination of benign mercantilism and regionalism.[133] It is not likely that Western Europe will degenerate into a malign political and economic bloc reluctant to have economic transactions with others, even if it further develops its current version of protectionism. It is, after all, the largest economic bloc in the world and is sufficiently open in terms of trade relations, technological cooperation, and capital transactions. It would benefit the United States and Japan to do more for Western Europe in terms of technological cooperation and overseas direct investment in exchange for continuing West European membership in the GATT system.

Although protectionism has been gaining strength in the United States, especially in Congress, the U.S. government is determined to maintain the multilateral free-trade system and has been working hard to extend GATT coverage to the service, agricultural, and high-tech areas.[134] Although the United States has been generating its own version of sectoral protectionism, it is not likely that it will succumb to overall protectionism in principle. Sectoral protectionism is a rather temporary, limited device to appease maladjusted sectors affected by the rapid inroads of Japanese products and to facilitate the recovery and readjustment of the U.S. economy in the 1980s. For the largest economy and the greatest technological power in the world to pursue protectionism as it becomes increasingly interdependent with the rest of the world would be suicidal. Bilateral deals in trade, finance, technology, and weapons represent new tactics to enhance U.S. bargaining power with other kinds of influence over its negotiating partners.[135]

The economic size of the Western Pacific region is far from sufficient to compensate Japan for the loss of North American and West European markets.[136] Even if their economic growth rates were high, the Pacific countries are in a different development stage from Japan, let alone from America and Europe. Even if their income levels were to become roughly comparable to Japan's, the lack of a geoeconomic core in the basin may prevent Japan from developing a policy line for the area in isolation from other lines. Yet the Pacific Basin idea has been kept alive as insurance. Furthermore, the Western Pacific region as a whole is fairly evenly interdependent with the United States, Japan, and the EC. Japan is not economically predominant in the region. For example, Japan and the United States compete almost evenly as the largest trade partners. More important, the EC is a close third in international trade, and foreign direct investment in the region (excluding Japan for the moment) has been on the rise since some of the region's economies reached the status of the NICs or an even higher stage.

Whereas the Western Pacific line gravitates toward Southeast Asia, Northeast Asian regionalism will encompass Japan, the two Koreas, China, the USSR, and Outer Mongolia. The two dynamic forces, Japan and South Korea, might develop the kind of economic relations with their socialist neighbors that West Germany has developed with Eastern Europe.[137] If recent trends continue, Northeast Asian economic relations will become substantial in the future.[138] In addition to the already strong linkages with each other, Japan, the United States, and Hongkong have been enhancing their economic ties with China quite significantly, and Taiwan and South Korea have been strengthening their subterranean links with China.[139] However, the conceivable difficulties associated with strengthening trade and resource dependence on socialist countries might discourage Japan from pursuing this line very far.

In this regard, the USSR poses a far graver problem to Japan than China does. It is unlikely that Japan will be lured into the embrace of the USSR for such reasons as resources or anti-American nationalism. Most of the natural resources in the Soviet Far East and Siberia are available in other parts of the world. The question about China is whether the policy line of economic modernization and relative openness will continue. Although the Japanese government is basically optimistic about the steadfastness and stability of the current Chinese policy line, it is not quite certain about it.

Thus, for the foreseeable future, it seems that nothing fundamental will change. Basic trilateralism will continue as the core of Japanese economic interactions with the rest of the world; the regional components, both Southeast and Northeast Asian, will acquire more weight, but most likely will not surpass that of the trilateral components in the 1980s.[140]

There are basically two policy choices in the security sphere: a continuing link with the United States or the ending of this link. Crucial to Japan's policy choice are the cost-benefit calculations associated with the Japan-U.S. security ties and the geopolitical conditions constraining Japan's choice. It is not necessary here to recount the reasons why the current mode of Japan-U.S. security ties seem likely to last for the foreseeable future. However, if the inclusion of Japan in a U.S.-led joint action against the USSR threatens to make Japan a target of Soviet nuclear and nonnuclear attacks without involving U.S. forces throughout the rest of the world, Japan will think more than twice about the desirability of continuing Japan-U.S. security ties. Intermittently intense economic pressure from the United States based on its security hegemony would also encourage Japan to reconsider.

However, departing from the Japan-U.S. security relationship is easier said than done. The joint deterrence formula can be questioned in light of West European experiences with U.S. introduction of theater nuclear weapons, which enable the United States to decouple itself from Western Europe in case of a Soviet attack.[141] Thus, Japanese nuclear armament combined with the Japan-U.S. security relationship is a possibility.[142] But this formula has increasingly high costs of overcoming various easily aroused forces both at home and abroad. Most serious is the U.S. reaction to a nuclear Japan. Would the United States allow Japan to take policy steps that might lead to Japan's becoming more than a second-rate power?

The departure from the Japan-U.S. security relationship could take various forms. It might follow the French pattern of an independent military command with a close economic and security relationship with the United States. It could follow the Indian pattern of nonalignment and the resulting high prestige despite its weaker economic bases. It could also take a nonnuclear pattern. A Japan without nuclear weapons yet protected by extremely powerful antinuclear forces that render nuclear weapons antiquated is theoretically possible. Such a possibility still awaits a major technological breakthrough. Should Japan dissociate itself from the security relationship with the United States, Japan may well be lured into membership in a group 99, namely, a group of countries not strictly under the umbrella of either of the two superpowers.[143]

This is not the place to discuss all these and other policy options in detail. The task would require a book-length treatment. For the foreseeable future, however, Japan's security policy seems to rest on security ties with the United States. Despite all the discussions about the hegemonic decline of the United States, U.S. hegemony, if in a somewhat reduced form, will continue to be sufficiently robust for the foreseeable future. As Edward Gibbon wryly noted of the decline of the Roman Empire, "This intolerable situation lasted for about three hundred years."[144]

The main point here, however, is to show that Japan and the rest of the world have come to envisage Japan's options more widely than before. This is precisely because of Japan's growth and the altered configuration of power in the international system of which Japan is a part. This suggests that Japan's policy choice could affect the world far more strongly than was possible before.

It is widely believed that social systems, whether groups, firms, states, or empires, always face major difficulties because past successes encourage them to adhere tenaciously to the methods that brought about those successes. Japan today is a case in point. The once-astute policy mix of a low profile in high politics (security and money) and a high profile in low politics (production and trade) has now become more difficult to sustain because of its previous admirable success. By flying low in the community of nations, Japan has achieved peace for the past forty years. By single-mindedly pursuing economic growth and prosperity, it has achieved worldwide status as a first-rank economic power. These are admirable achievements for a country that had no choice but to surrender unconditionally to the Allies. Yet success does not breed success forever. Japan's successful adaptation to the turmoils of the 1970s and 1980s has made obvious both the positive and the negative aspects of Japan's policy mix.

On the positive side, Japan has performed respectably in the area of economic growth, inflation, employment, social welfare, and environmental control.[145] It has contributed to the growth of global welfare by sustaining stable economic growth, making developmental loans, and thus helping to prevent many from following the vicious cycle of a zero-sum game.[146] Moreover, Japan has increased its share of international responsibilities in such areas as defense, aid, and contributions to international organizations, in a remarkably resolute and steadfast manner.

On the negative side, the maldevelopment of the socioeconomic infrastructure, seen most prominently in housing, roads, and sewers, is highlighted by the accumulation of savings, which creates nothing other than interest income for savers and financial institutions purchasing foreign bonds and stocks. The economic surplus in trade that Japan has recorded intermittently has been seen as constraining industrial adjustment and macroeconomic management in the deficit countries.[147] And Japan's economic success has encouraged less adaptive countries to criticize Japan for its lighter burdens in the management of the international politico-economic system.[148]

These three externalities of the Japanese miracle are not in the forefront of the Japanese consciousness. In the short term, Japan will probably adhere to the policy line it has followed since 1945. But it would not take much reading in Japanese history to realize that the opposite of "plus ça change, plus c'est la même chose" better fits the Japanese reality, namely, "change and metamorphosis come about under the disguise of continuity and constancy."

What we have seen since the first oil crisis is the stable process of change, internally patching this or that without losing sight of the overall balance among the various social sectors and externally adjusting to disturbances with a clear sense of national purpose and international environmental direction. Looking at a deeper level of public policy for the past decade enables one to fathom more clearly the extent of Japanese adaptation in an age of transition. Rather than meticulously setting details for a long-term strategy, which is difficult in a time of transition, Japan seems to set its course by selectively following the overall U.S. policy line in the security and economic spheres and yet leaving its options open as much as possible. In the security area, U.S. prodding for a Japanese defense buildup and technological cooperation helps Japan strengthen itself. In the economic area, U.S. pressure for economic liberalization helps Japan become more competitive.

Yet on matters deemed essential or crucial to the Japanese future, Japan is consistently tough and resistant. Communications equipment, fighter bombers, and space shuttles immediately come to mind, to name but a few of the high-tech products that Japan tenaciously refuses to buy abroad. Since the first oil crisis, Japan has diversified its sources of natural resource supplies such as oil and iron ore. Japan's increasing imports from China of such grains as corn and beans are designed to mitigate excessive dependence on the United States for food supplies as well as to reduce China's bilateral trade deficit with Japan.[149] Cooperative business arrangements with technology and capital exports as key elements have been a Japanese answer to the rising protectionism and nationalism of the past few years.

All these represent adaptation, Japanese style, to an age of transition from an assured U.S. hegemony to a disorganized and disquieted U.S. hegemony. This has not been easy since the world now looks at Japan with jealousy and enmity; because the United States, by reasserting its hegemony, is causing major disturbances for its friends and foes; and, no less important, because the robustness of Japan's internal logic—both ideas and structures—makes drastic restructuring efforts look more tardy and more superficial than many wish to see, at least in the shorter term. Japan's efforts to be accepted fully as an economic and military supporter have been significantly hindered by domestic factors. But any policy restructuring not supported by internal logic is bound to be ineffective. Japan's policy restructuring may be slower but steadier and longer lasting than many are inclined to think. The title of a newspaper article aptly catches Japan's mood, "Japan: Uneasy on World Stage."[150] Japan is cautiously, and with such ad hoc improvisation, searching for its proper role in the world, knowing its capabilities and constraints and living with its aspirations and apprehensions. Assessment of the virtues and vices of the Japanese restructuring over a longer term remain a task for the future.

Shumpei Kumon and Akihiko Tanaka

From Prestige to Wealth to Knowledge

It is often argued that the current period is one of decline in U.S. hegemony. In 1980, a blue-ribbon study group appointed by the late Prime Minister Masayoshi Ohira made recommendations on "comprehensive national security" based on the premise that "the most fundamental fact in the changing international situation in the 1970s is the termination of clear American supremacy in both military and economic spheres."[1] Has a similar situation existed in history, and if so, how does it compare with the current situation? The most frequently cited precedent is the British experience in the late nineteenth century. Using a world-systems approach, several authors have attempted an explicit comparison between the two instances of hegemonic decline.[2] George Modelski is attempting to construct a theory that will facilitate comparison not just between nineteenth-century Britain and the twentieth-century United States but also between the "world power" of each century since the sixteenth-century Portugal.[3] The hegemonic stability theory explicitly links shifts in hegemony with the stability and the instability of international political economy.[4]

In this paper, instead of focusing exclusively on hegemonic power, we attempt to construct an alternative framework to explain change in the modern world system. We call it the theory of "social games." Although we have not worked the theory out fully, we are convinced that it can shed light on the current world system. We also briefly characterize Japan's role and national objectives at different stages of the world system. We believe that the theory of social games provides a larger context for examining Japan's role.

The Theory of Social Games

If social systems are to survive, they must be managed. One possibility is centralized management. Nation-states adopt this form, as do most domestic organizations. The other possibility is decentralized management, of which there are many types. One example is a social system managed largely by traditional taboos and precedents. Large numbers of primitive societies were, and are, managed in this fashion. The modern world system, however, though a decentralized social system par excellence, has not been managed by taboos.

We argue that the modern world system instead has been managed to a considerable degree by social games. By "social game" we mean a game in which at least some members of the social system compete to obtain conventionalized prizes by conventionalized means, and by their competition, as if by "an invisible hand," the needs of the social system as well as of its members are more or less fulfilled.[5]

For a social game to be possible, we argue that at least the following conditions are necessary.

1. Four "basics" should be conventionalized: the basic players, the basic values, the basic rights, and the basic activities. In other words, there should be conventions, implicit or explicit, that answer "Who gets what by what means by what right?"

2. Two "fields" should be established: the field of basic activities and the field for evaluating basic activities. A commodity, for example, is produced in a field called a "factory" and evaluated in a field called the "market."

3. For some activities to become conventionalized enough to be considered basic, technological and psychological revolutions are necessary to make these activities easily conducted repeatedly without overloading the social system.

Although our concept of social game overlaps the concept of "game" in mathematical game theory and the concept of "regime" as used in standard international relations literature,[6] it also differs from them. "Game" in game theory is an extreme abstraction and devoid of much consideration of the social setting within which it is being played; it can be applied to any decisional situation. In contrast, our concept of social game is a social category that differentiates a certain set of activities from others. Some activities may be "plays" in a social game, but others may not. Each activity in a social game may be represented as a game situation in game theory, but the entirety of a social game may not.[7]

Stephen Krasner defines "regimes" as "sets of implicit or explicit principles, norms, rules, and decision-making procedures around which actors' expectations converge in a given area of international relations."[8] In this sense, a social game may be regarded as a type of regime. But not all regimes are social games. First, activities managed by a social game are competitive. A social game is, therefore, a regime to manage competitive activities. Second, in a social game no agreed collective purpose is necessary. It is not a problem-solving scheme. In general, social games are found and explained rather than created and used. Third, the players' sense of freedom of action in a social game is maximal and their sense of being regulated is minimal. Although the actual levels of freedom and regulation are difficult to measure, the subjective level of freedom and regulation can at least conceptually be used to distinguish a social game from other types of regime.

In the modern world system, we argue, at least two different social games have been played in sequence, though with considerable overlap. Both games have not only the characteristics of social games discussed above but also analogous life cycles. One, which we call the "prestige game," corresponds roughly to the working of the states system in the sense of ordinary international politics; the second, which we call the "wealth game," to the working of the capitalist world economy.

We do not use conventional terms such as the "states system" (or the balance-of-power mechanism) and the "world economy" (or the market mechanism) mainly because of our conceptualization of social systems and social games. Our conceptualization is two-tiered, with social games over a social system. A decentralized social system may exist without social games being played on it. But, we argue, a decentralized social system exists more easily if social games are being played. The conventional conceptualization vertically divides the modern world system into the states system and the world economy. Even though analysts may consider interactions between the two systems, this vertically divided image of the modern world seems to make analysis either unnecessarily rigid or extremely ad hoc.

What we want to achieve by introducing the concept of social games is to create a higher-level concept to compare two sets of activities hitherto treated separately and then to treat them as subcategories of that higher concept. If the workings of the states system and the world economy are subcategories of a social game, then we may be able to find other social games. In this sense, creating a higher-level category facilitates discovery of new subcategories.[9]

In our conceptualization, a rough outline of the modern world system runs as follows. Primitive forms of both the prestige game and the wealth game arose with the birth of the modern world system in late-fifteenth-century Europe. The prestige game was the first to be played widely. It reached its prototypical form in the eighteenth century, was transformed in the nineteenth century, and declined in the twentieth century. The wealth game, on the other hand, grew slowly and spread rapidly only following the Industrial Revolution. The game was played in its prototypical form in the nineteenth century and is being transformed in the twentieth century. The declining phase of the wealth game has not arrived yet.

The spread of the prestige game may also be characterized as the diffusion of the organizational form called "states," characterized by territoriality and functions performed by specialized government personnel—a bureaucracy and a standing army.[10] Likewise, the spread of the wealth game may be characterized as the diffusion of the organizational form called "firms." In other words, the basic players of the prestige game are states, and the basic players of the wealth game are firms. As the name of each game suggests, the basic values of the respective games are prestige and wealth. To pursue their respective basic values, players in both games must be guaranteed their basic rights. The state is guaranteed its sovereignty; the firm is guaranteed its property rights. Based on these basic rights, the state has the freedom to maximize its prestige, and the firm the freedom to maximize its wealth. In terms of the effect on the world system, the prestige game is supposed to preserve the political stability of the world system, and the wealth game to achieve the economic efficiency of the world system.

In addition, the basic activities are conventionalized: wars in the prestige game and industrial production in the wealth game. Wars are fought on battlegrounds and evaluated in the field of diplomacy;[11] commodities are produced in factories and evaluated in the field of the market.

For each game to be widely played, a technological revolution, as well as a psychological revolution, was required. In the case of the prestige game, the technological revolution was the military revolution as well as the dramatic innovation in ocean transport in the sixteenth to seventeenth century,[12] and the psychological revolution was prepared by such doctrines as the divine right of kings. In the case of the wealth game, the technological revolution was the Industrial Revolution in the late eighteenth and the nineteenth centuries, and the psychological revolution was prepared by such movements as the Enlightenment, which contributed to the establishment of individualism. Both technological revolutions were radical changes in the production fields of the prestige game (battlegrounds) and the wealth game (factories). Both psychological revolutions brought radical changes in people's conception of the world: who they are and what role they play in relations with whom. In other words, these revolutions prepared the conditions by which both games are regularly played.

As we discuss below, the Industrial Revolution was not the only precondition for the wealth game. The existence of the prestige game was also crucial to the spread of the wealth game.

The prestige game and the wealth game are structurally similar. We further argue that they have analogous life cycles. The first phase of both games is the laissez-faire phase. Each player is encouraged to follow its

TABLE 1
The Prestige Game and the Wealth Game

Attributes of social games	Prestige game	Wealth game
Basic players	States	Firms
Basic value	Prestige	Wealth
Basic right	Sovereignty	Property rights
Basic activities (means)	Wars	Industrial production
Field of basic activities	Battlegrounds	Factories
Field of evaluation	Diplomacy	Market

own self-interest to maximize its basic value utilizing its basic activities, while the overall needs of the system are believed to be satisfied by an invisible hand or, to put it differently, by a synergetic process as opposed to a cybernetic process.[13] The second phase of both games is that of transformation. In this phase, the players realize that laissez-faire does not necessarily produce good results and that some regulating mechanism may be needed. And finally, even with regulatory mechanisms, the game does not function as prescribed, and it enters its declining phase (though this is not yet completely certain vis-à-vis the wealth game). In this phase, the legitimacy of the basic rights and activities is severely tarnished, if not completely lost. Also in this phase, involution may occur, and derivative games may emerge (see Table 1 for a summary of the four basics and the two fields of the prestige game and the wealth game).[14]

Prestige Game

A social game is not designed and created by a single architect. At first, its participants repeat certain patterns of action without realizing that those patterns may constitute a social game. Their awareness of playing a game comes after a certain period of participation. The emergence of the prestige game is no exception. Its basic actors, the modern states, emerged in the sixteenth and seventeenth centuries. Its basic activities, wars among states, were frequent in the sixteenth and seventeenth centuries. Jack Levy lists 49 wars involving at least one Great Power between 1495 and 1648.[15] Quincy Wright lists 78 wars and 37 "balance of power wars" between 1480 and 1650.[16] Thus, by the eighteenth century, the conduct of war, according to a perceptive observer in the early nineteenth century, "became a true game, in which the cards were dealt by time and by accident. In its effect it was a somewhat stronger form of diplomacy, a more forceful method of negotiation, in which battles and sieges were the principal notes exchanged. Even the most ambitious ruler had no greater aims than to gain a number of advantages that could be exploited at the peace conference."[17]

The invisible hand regulating this power game was the mechanism of the "balance of power."[18] We argue that the balance-of-power mechanism worked most perfectly from the late seventeenth to the eighteenth centuries—at least so it was believed then.[19] As Martin Wight writes, in the eighteenth century, the balance of power "was the political counterpart of Newtonian physics. The sovereign states followed their ordered paths in a harmony of mutual attraction and repulsion like the gravitational law that swings the planets in their orbits. Perhaps no statesmanship was needed."[20]

According to Karl Polanyi, the balance of power as a historical law was "first stated in modern thought by Hume. His achievement was lost again during the almost total eclipse of political thought which followed the Industrial Revolution. Hume recognized the political nature of the phenomenon and underlined its independence of psychological and moral facts. It went into effect irrespective of the motives of the actors, as long as they behaved as the embodiments of power. Experience showed, wrote Hume, that whether 'jealous emulation or cautious politics' was their motive, 'the effects were alike.'"[21]

Rousseau pointed out the automatic character of the balance of power more explicitly in his *Abstracts of the Abbe de Saint-Pierre's Project for Perpetual Peace* (1761):

We may fairly say that the political order of the continent is, in some sense, the work of nature.

In truth, we must not suppose that this much vaunted balance is the work of any man, or that any man has deliberately done anything to maintain it. It is there; and men who do not feel themselves strong enough to break it conceal the selfishness of their designs under the pretext of preserving it. But, whether we are aware of it or no, the balance continues to support itself without the aid of any special intervention; if it were to break for a moment on one side, it would soon restore itself on another.[22]

In the second phase of malfunction and organizational revolutions, it was realized that the prestige game did not always produce desirable results. The single most important incident in this realization was the Napoleonic wars. It was no accident that during these wars Friedrich von Gentz wrote in his *Fragments upon the Present State of the Political Balance of Europe* (1806) that the "whole of this excellent system has now at length, like all the works of man, seen the hour of its fall approach."[23]

Partly to cope with these undesirable effects, players tended to transform their organizational structures. Players of the prestige game seriously tried to transform themselves into nation-states. As Samuel Finer says, "With the French Revolution and its Napoleonic aftermath, statebuilding received a new emphasis while the concept of the nation and of the nation-state became full blown."[24] Especially important in terms of war-fighting capability was the adoption of universal conscription. The rise of the United States (1865), Italy (1870), Germany (1871), and Japan (1877) as important nation-states demonstrated this trend.

On the level of the overall working of the game, the concept of laissez-faire was gradually abandoned for a "semiautomatic" or "manually operated" mechanism.[25] Since no superior authority exists above the players in the prestige game, some players have to assume the role of regulators if the game is to continue. A single player acting as the regulator is called the "balancer" in the prestige game; multiple players acting as the regulators are called the "concert of powers." Both mechanisms were in fact tried in the nineteenth century. The Concert of Europe is argued to have existed from 1815 to either 1823, 1853, or as late as 1913. Our argument, however, is that from 1823 to the 1870s the prestige game was maintained not by the Concert but by Great Britain's (the balancer's) interventions. In the late nineteenth century, however, "most Englishmen had by now accepted Cobden's doctrine that events on the Continent were not their business."[26] From 1870 to 1913, peace in Europe was brought about by the Concert (the Bismarckian system) and, probably more important, because "all the Great Powers except Austria-Hungary found a safe channel for their exuberance in expansion outside Europe."[27]

However, two devastating world wars severely tarnished the legitimacy of the prestige game. This is most clearly underlined by the reemergence of "just war" theories in international law—the League of Nations Covenant, the Kellogg-Briand Pact, and the U.N. Charter.[28] It is significant that formal declarations of war have rarely been made since World War II. The Korean war, the Vietnam war, and other major wars simply occurred; no country formally declared them. This, of course, does not mean that the likelihood of armed conflicts has declined. In fact, according to one account, more than 100 wars occurred between 1945 and 1977.[29] But they have rarely been justified as a legitimate means of sovereign action except as defense. It is no accident that preparation of a war-fighting capability is most commonly justified in terms of deterrence. In other words, with a few possible exceptions, most states have ceased to be players of the prestige game in the classical sense.

The decline of the classical prestige game did not create a vacuum of politics among states, however. Relations among states in the post–World War II period have not been totally without regulatory mechanisms. We argue that three derivatives of the classical prestige game emerged and offered arenas for competition among states: the super-power game, regional prestige games, and the development game. But before examining the nature of these games, we discuss the evolution of the other dominant social game in the world system, the wealth game.

Wealth Game

The wealth game does not simply mean commerce; commerce has existed throughout history in one form or another. For production and commerce to become part of the wealth game, the first prerequisite is commodification of the factors of production. It is necessary that profit calculations be made about the factors of production: land, labor, and capital. Second, the price and supply of these factors of production must be determined by the market, as they are for other commodities. Pure capitalism as described by Kozo Uno in his attempts to reformulate Marxian economics or Thomas T. Sekine, for example, represents an ideal type of the wealth game in our sense.[30]

As the prestige game was believed in the eighteenth century to be regulated by the automatic mechanism of the balance of power, the wealth game was believed in the nineteenth century to be regulated by the automatic mechanism of the market. The rise of a "self-regulating system of markets" in the nineteenth century, as Karl Polanyi points out, was entirely unprecedented: "Previously to our time no economy has ever existed that, even in principle, was controlled by markets."[31] The official doctrine of nineteenth-century players in the wealth game was based on Adam Smith:

Every man, as long as he does not violate the laws of justice, is left perfectly free to pursue his own interest his own way, and to bring both his industry and capital into competition with those of any other man.

He [a participant in the market] generally, indeed, neither intends to promote the public interest, nor knows how much he is promoting it. . . . he intends only his own gain, and he is in this, as in many other cases, led by an invisible hand to promote an end which was no part of his intention. . . . By pursuing his own interest he frequently promotes that of the society more effectually than when he really intends to promote it.[32]

In the laissez-faire period, the players of the wealth game were mostly family firms or small partnerships. They were the driving forces of the Industrial Revolution and an extremely powerful "social species." But they were not born and raised in a vacuum. They spread so widely and so rapidly probably because a suitable social niche for them existed. Although we cannot discuss the process of industrialization in this paper, the existence of the modern state was at least one important condition that facilitated the birth and growth of industrial firms. With its police and armed forces, especially the navy, the state allowed firms to concentrate on industrial activities. Without this guarantee of security, any organization has to spend considerable amounts to secure its survival. The Dutch and the British East India companies, for example, were situated in a very different social environment from that of industrial firms; they often had to protect their commercial activities with their own armies and navies. The effective functioning of the modern state, and hence the prestige game, was a precondition for the gradual emergence of the wealth game in the modern period.[33]

In addition to its security-guaranteeing function, the modern state contributed to the increased popularity of the wealth game by withdrawing from economic activities. This change in state activities was brought about mainly by pressures from increasingly powerful industrial firms. And this further expanded the niche for industrial firms. In the international sphere, the role of the British state was important. British industrialists pressured the British state to open the market in the periphery of the world system, by force if necessary.

In the nineteenth century, at least subjectively, the players in each game acted independently of those in the other game after the formative period. But the results of each game's basic activities were closely connected. Industrial production, although conducted without the meddling of the state, reinforced the state's war-fighting capability. Wars and related activities, though often conducted independently of the will of industrialists, enhanced the interests of players of the wealth game. This virtuous cycle appeared most typically in relations between the British state and British firms.[34]

During this period, industrial production multiplied, but the defects of the wealth game became increasingly apparent. The most serious of these were cyclical downturns in the economy. Several attempts were made to gain more security from cyclical downturns and to acquire more capital to expand business. The ascendancy of incorporated businesses was one such attempt.[35] In England, limited liability became applicable to the stock of most types of businesses in 1855 and 1856.[36] Most firms in the cotton industry adopted this organizational form in the 1860s, as did most firms in the steel industry in the 1880s.[37]

The great depression of 1873–96 accelerated this trend. Especially in the United States, the merger of firms into giant corporations characterized the economy in the late nineteenth century. This "merger process began in the 1880s in the refining and distilling industries (Standard Oil) and then spread to manufacturing industries and, by the 1920s, to large retailing outfits. By the 1920s the organizational format of the modern corporation was by and large set."[38]

In the wealth game, the twentieth century has been the semiautomatic or manually operated period. Here the analogy with the prestige game breaks down in one important respect. In the prestige game, the players of the game carried out the manual operation. In the wealth game, states were called in. No firm acted as the balancer. Nor did firms make serious efforts to form a concert.[39] The states were available. "Increasingly business, in one way or another, called on the state not only to give it a free hand, but to save it."[40]

The initial attempt to use the state was made in Germany in the late nineteenth century, based on the theories of economist Friedrich List. "The German tariff of 1879 was long remembered as the first modern 'scientific' tariff—a piece of economic manipulation in the interests of national policy."[41] But in this period, although "protective tariffs remained everywhere except in Great Britain, international trade was otherwise free. There was no governmental interference, no danger of debts being repudiated. The gold standard was universal."[42]

In the twentieth century, especially in the 1920s and 1930s, however, a decisive change occurred in the role of the state. The Great Depression was the single most dramatic event promoting this trend. First, the state began to control more and more economic activities in the wealth game. Second, to enhance welfare, the state began to redistribute goods originally handled within the wealth game. Third, the state itself sometimes began to enter the wealth game as a player by, for example, nationalizing firms. Fourth, an increasing number of states began to utilize Keynesian policies to affect overall economic trends. All in all, the state came to be considered responsible for the management of the economy.

The wealth game, if confined to the domestic market, may be able to function under state management. But to the extent that international trade was an integral part of the wealth game, some kind of international regulatory mechanism was required. We argue that the United States assumed the role of international manager of the wealth game. The boom in the world economy in the 1950s and 1960s was possible because of the United States' effective management, with the IMF and GATT being the most important institutional frameworks. The United States, in a sense, was the balancer in the wealth game.

As business in other states grew rapidly, it became more and more costly to the United States to play the role of balancer of trade and payments. Thus, in the late 1970s and the early 1980s, in order to continue the wealth game, the players appear to have sought to form a concert. The summit meetings among leaders of Western industrial nations, it may be argued, constitute the Concert of the Developed.

Three Derivatives of the Power Game

In the twentieth century, especially after World War II, war as a means of achieving state policy came to lack legitimacy. The prestige game in the classical sense no longer functioned as a social game. But in its place, three derivatives of the prestige game appeared: the superpower game, the regional prestige game, and the development game. These three games are derivatives of the prestige game in the sense that their basic actors are states and that the participating states strive to maximize their prestige. But they have clear differences from the classical prestige game (see Table 2).

The superpower game differs from the classical prestige game in several aspects. First, the only players are the United States and the Soviet Union. No other states have the capability or the intention to join them. Second, wars between them are practically ruled out mainly because of the "crystal-ball effect" of nuclear weapons.[43] Instead, they compete in armaments and intervention capabilities in their respective spheres of influence, as well as in Third World areas. Third, the legitimacy of the arms buildup and intervention may not be as clearly established as wars were in the classical prestige game. And fourth, it is not clear whether there is an automatic stabilizing mechanism in the superpower game. Only a few people would recommend laissez-faire in this game. But the fact that for 40 years the world has not been destroyed by a nuclear holocaust, even without any rigid regulatory mechanisms, suggests a certain level of stability in this game.[44]

Regional prestige games are conducted by states within a limited region, mainly in the Third World, such as the Middle East and southern Africa. These regional prestige games seem to retain most of the basic characteristics of the classical prestige game, except for their indirect and limited effects on the entire world system. Sometimes, however, the

TABLE 2
Three Derivatives of the Prestige Game

Attributes of social games	Superpower game	Regional prestige game	Development game
Basic players	U.S. and USSR	mainly Third World states	states
Basic value	global prestige	regional prestige	economic prestige
Basic right	sovereignty	sovereignty	sovereignty
Basic activities	arms race, intervention	wars	economic development
Field of basic activities	global strategic field	battlegrounds	national economy
Field of evaluation	superpower diplomacy	regional diplomacy	economic diplomacy

overall effect of a war in a regional prestige game can be great. For example, the Yom Kippur War certainly had a tremendous effect on the world system, mostly through the oil crisis that it triggered. It was a catalyst rather than a prime mover, however.

The development game is a mixture of the prestige game and the wealth game. But we argue that it is a derivative of the prestige game rather than of the wealth game. Its basic players are states rather than firms; its basic value is enhancement of states' prestige rather than simple wealth maximization. Its only difference from the classical prestige game is its basic activity—economic development. The development game substitutes economic development for war.

This game became possible only recently. In the period of the classical prestige game, no systematic indexes existed to measure the level of economic development of a state independent of military power, which was virtually synonymous with economic development. Under these circumstances, one cannot differentiate the development game from the prestige game.

Crucial to the birth of the development game was the transformation of the wealth game. As we discussed previously, the state was called in to manage possible and real malfunctions of the wealth game. State interventions in the 1930s were desperate efforts. But once the crisis was over, the state found in economic management a new arena of competition with other states. Maintaining a high and stable economic growth became one of the central concerns among states.

In a sense, the conventionalization of the concept and measure of such vital statistics as GNP had a revolutionary effect. With GNP, one can measure the level of economic development of a country independent of its military strength. States now can compete on a different dimension from war-fighting capability. The currently dominant category of states—developed countries, developing countries, newly industrializing countries—symbolizes the spread and popularity of a competition measured essentially by the GNP statistics.

To use an analogy with ball games, the capitalist state is a fairly strong referee (or a commissioner) in the wealth game in its domestic market and a cheerleader and sometimes a manager in the international wealth game. The socialist state, on the other hand, bans the wealth game internally, but acts as a player of the wealth game internationally. How a state mixes these roles and how it conducts these roles determine its capability to compete in the development game.

At least until the mid-1960s, the legitimacy of economic development was clear. In a sense, laissez-faire in development prevailed; if each state devised its development strategy freely and did its best, world economic development would be realized. The emergence of the North-South problem, however, posed a serious challenge to the legitimacy of the development game; the development of the states in the North was faulted for producing the "development of underdevelopment" in the South.[45] The increase in interdependence among the developed countries posed another challenge to the development game, and the recent growth in trade friction challenges the assumptions of the development game that a state is free to devise any type of development strategy and to do its best.[46]

The Evolution of the Present World System

In the previous sections, we discussed the life cycles of the prestige game (and its derivatives) and the wealth game separately. In this section, to gain an understanding of the current world system, we discuss the overall world system in the nineteenth and twentieth centuries in terms of the life stages of the power game and the wealth game. Since the nineteenth century and the twentieth century are usually referred to as the centuries of the Pax Britannica and the Pax Americana, respectively, we discuss the respective roles of Britain and the United States in our framework. And since the theme of this volume is Japan's relations with the international society, we discuss how Japan tried to cope with the different phases of the world system.

Britain

The nineteenth century witnessed the transformation phase of the prestige game and the laissez-faire phase of the wealth game. Simply put, a balancer or a concert was required to manage the prestige game, whereas, in principle, no interventions from states were required in the wealth game.

It is certain that in the nineteenth century Britain played an important role in the birth of the wealth game. Britain deregulated and opened up its internal market and, if necessary, forced open the market in the periphery of the world system. But once the wealth game was well established, its working was maintained by the self-regulating market and the international gold standard. The role of the state was limited to that of a referee at most. Thus, as long as this self-regulating mechanism worked, the decline of British hegemony did not produce a severe malfunction in the wealth game. In fact, international trade increased until World War I, and the international gold standard worked most effectively in the very period often designated as the period of British decline.

But more crucial to the world system in the nineteenth century was the British role as the balancer in the prestige game. As already discussed, the working of the prestige game in the nineteenth century was guaranteed either by the British balancer or by the Concert of Europe. Up to 1890, the concert or the British balancer worked fairly effectively. But after the demise of the Bismarckian concert, Britain could not act as an effective balancer; British support for the Franco-Russian alliance could not contain the war started in August 1914. If the decline of British hegemony was important, it was important not as a malign factor in the wealth game but as a damaging factor in the prestige game. The wealth game might have been able to function in its laissez-faire phase for some time, if World War I had not broken out.

The United States

The world in the twentieth century is characterized by the almost total demise of the classical prestige game, the transformation of the wealth game, and the emergence of the three derivatives of the prestige game. In our framework, Pax Americana means (1) U.S. superiority in the super-power game, which further means a U.S. lead in the arms race and superior U.S. capability in intervening in wider areas of the world; (2) U.S. capability of containing the global effects of regional prestige games; (3) U.S. superiority in the development game; and (4) U.S. capability to provide management mechanisms for the wealth game and the development game.

The second feature is a corollary of the latter part of the first feature; the U.S. capability to intervene guarantees containment of regional prestige games. And this second feature, in turn, constitutes a background condition for the fourth feature; unless regional prestige games are contained, both the development game and the wealth game cannot function smoothly.

But the fulfillment of the second feature is not sufficient to guarantee the smooth functioning of the development game and the wealth game. After the total disaster in the world economy in the 1930s and 1940s, the wealth game was reestablished mainly by the efforts of the United States. (This was so not just in the case of international finance and trade but also in the cases of the European and Japanese domestic economies.) The wealth game after World War II, in contrast to the wealth game in the nineteenth century, depended heavily on governmental interventions domestically and U.S. involvement internationally. Without the United States as the balancer of international trade and payments, the wealth game could not have functioned effectively.

The role of the United States in the development game has been tremendous, both materially and ideologically. U.S. economic aid provides other states necessary, if insufficient, resources for development. U.S. economics textbooks provide other states convictions that they, too, can join the development game and compete for higher status.

Setbacks occurred in all four of these features in the late 1960s to the 1970s. The Soviet arms buildup in this period reached the point that U.S. superiority can no longer be assumed. The Vietnam and the Yom Kippur wars revealed U.S. impotence to prevent regional prestige games from exerting, however indirectly, a global impact. Although the United States' position as leader in the development game was still intact, it found in Japan a serious contender. And in 1971, the United States had to abandon its role as the balancer of international trade and payments.

These crises in the Pax Americana have not ended with disasters comparable to World War I or the crash of 1929, however. The relative decline of U.S. hegemony has not brought chaos to the world system. But the management of both the wealth game and the development game has become increasingly more difficult.

Compounding the difficulty arising from the relative decline of the United States' management capability is the current nature of relations between the wealth game and the development game. We have already pointed out that the wealth game is in the transformation period. But in addition to this general characterization, which has held since the 1920s, a more recent development deserves attention; namely, the recent spurt of internationalization of firms and their activities. Multinational corporations (MNCs) have been around for some time. But until very recently they were mostly American, and their activities were oriented to the overwhelmingly large U.S. market. This dominant pattern still exists. But new trends are emerging, including (1) the increase in MNCs of non-American origin, (2) the increase in non-American elements in MNCs of American origin, both in physical location and in marketing decisions, (3) the increase in multinational production, and (4) the increase in international cooperation among MNCs. It is increasingly more difficult to tell the exact nationality of firms and their products. In other words, the arena of the wealth game is becoming further integrated. The management of the wealth game in this highly integrated market requires a systemwide approach.

But this requirement is not entirely consistent with the renewed popularity of the development game. In the late 1960s and the 1970s, the development game was challenged by North-South problems and slow economic growth. But the recovery of the world economy in the mid-1980s and the emergence of the newly industrializing countries brought a renewed conviction that competition in economic development is possible and normal.

If the wealth game is increasingly more integrated globally, however, the management of the development game becomes proportionally more difficult because one state's economic policy affects other states more directly. It seems that a choice is necessary between the two games.

If the wealth game is to be managed globally, some of the basic assumptions of the development game have to be sacrificed; and if the basic attributes of the development game are to be preserved, further globalization of the wealth game has to be checked. The former implies further liberalization of the world market through coordination among states; the latter New Protectionism.[47]

Japan

After the turmoil of the Meiji Restoration, Japan found itself in the midst of the transformed prestige game and the laissez-faire wealth game.[48] But Japan was not ready to participate in the prestige game as a full-fledged player; the major and immediate concern of Meiji leaders was preserving the independence of Japan.[49] But after this immediate danger passed, the following objectives were formulated in the mid-Meiji period: (1) to construct a modern state by introducing Western institutions and civilization (*bunmei kaika*); (2) to participate in the prestige game as an active player and to become one of the powers (*rekkyō*); and (3) to construct a wealthy nation and a strong military (*fukoku kyōhei*) in order to achieve the above.

Although the Meiji state was active in promoting industry (*shokusan kōgyō*), it was not playing the development game. On the one hand, states were still playing the prestige game in the classical sense; the natural concern of state leaders was competition in the prestige game. On the other hand, the wealth game was still in the laissez-faire phase; there was little knowledge on which to base state intervention.[50] Economic development in itself could not have constituted the most important national goal then; *fukoku* (to make the nation wealthy) was considered necessary to create *kyōhei* (a strong military). "It cannot be denied that the Meiji government strongly held the view that railroads, telecommunications, and modern industries were all for *kyōhei*."[51]

The nature of social games in the world system changed in the twentieth century. Defeat in World War II gave the Japanese a devastating realization of that change and forced them to reformulate their role in the world system. The goals formulated in the immediate postwar period were (1) to construct a democratic society based on strong industries; (2) to succeed in the development game while abandoning participation in the prestige game ("renunciation of war"); and (3) to facilitate the working of the wealth game internally, to encourage exports (*bōeki rikkoku*), and to create systems to distribute the fruits of the wealth game as equally as possible in order to achieve the above. The international aspect of the above are what Kenneth Pyle, in his paper in this volume, calls the "Yoshida Doctrine," and the domestic and industrial aspect of the above is what Chalmers Johnson calls the "developmental state."[52]

Both the Yoshida Doctrine and the concept of the developmental state signify the Japanese shift in participation from the prestige game to the development game. In fact, Japan was the creator and exemplar of the development game. It is no accident that our description of the development game fits Japan best.[53]

It is also no accident that difficulties arising from the current nature of the development game and its relations with the global integration of the wealth game as described above are most apparent in Japan's relations with other countries. Laissez-faire in the development game seems to produce an endless series of trade frictions, not just between Japan and the United States but between most countries in the development game. Japan's success in the development game seems to have become unbearable and even threatening to other players; if one player always wins, most of the other players become fed up with the game.

The Twenty-first Century: The Knowledge Game?

We have described the development of the world system mainly in terms of the life cycles of the prestige game and the wealth game. But do these two games still provide a sufficient framework to speculate on the future of the world system? With only a few exceptions, prestige maximization by military means has been delegitimized among states; wealth maximization is still a legitimate principle of action among firms. But something new seems to be evolving among actors other than states and firms.

Are the prestige game and the wealth game the only possible social games? In principle, no. But it is not easy to conceive of a new social game that can function as well as the prestige game in the eighteenth and nineteenth centuries and the wealth game in the nineteenth and twentieth centuries. It would have been extremely difficult to conceive of the prestige game in the sixteenth and early seventeenth centuries and of the wealth game in the seventeenth and early eighteenth centuries.

We argue, however, that a new social game analogous to the prestige game and the wealth game is now in its embryonic stage. We call it the "knowledge game." Prophets of this game, in fact, abound. Hermann Hesse's *The Glass Bead Game* was probably the earliest prophecy.[54] In more recent years, some have called this game the "post–industrial society"; others call it the "information society"; and still others the "Third Wave."[55] The Japanese Ministry of Finance calls it the age of "Softnomics."[56] Common to these prophesies is the central place of information or knowledge in the broadest sense of the term, including arts and religion, in the now-evolving future. Can a social game be constructed with knowledge as its basic value? We believe that theoretically it can. As we have argued, four basics and two fields must be conventionalized for a social game to function: the basic value, the basic players, the basic rights, the basic means, the field of production, and the field of evaluation. The basic value is influence based on knowledge, and the basic means is research. Many people value knowledge and the influence derived therefrom and conduct research already.

But who are the basic players? States are not maximizing knowledge; nor are firms. We argue that the basic players maximizing knowledge are either individuals or small-scale teams. We opt for the latter because some sort of collaboration is still useful. Is there a social niche for them? Some people have tried to maximize knowledge from time immemorial— scholars, artists, and philosophers, for example. But their activities have been extremely limited and not all-pervasive throughout the world system. But just as the establishment of modern states prepared the social niche for firms concentrating on industrial production, it may be that the establishment of firms is now preparing a social niche for teams to concentrate on research without worrying about their financial security. We may find embryonic forms of teams in the current emergence of venture businesses.

What is to be the basic right to be guaranteed in the knowledge game? The copyright and patents are certainly the natural candidates. But probably a more general concept is called for; it should include the rights of free creation, use, and disposition (including restriction) of information in one's information space. Since this type of right is currently discussed under the rubric of "privacy" and no better term seems to exist, let us use *privacy* as the basic right in the knowledge game.

For a social game to be widely played, some technological revolution should take place in the field of basic activities. For the knowledge game to be possible, the field of research should be revolutionized. Something like Alvin Toffler's "electronic cottages," or "meditatories" to coin a new word, should spread on the basis of a highly advanced information infrastructure facilitating massive communication flows among them. This, we believe, is very likely in the not-so-distant future.

Probably the most difficult condition to conceive in the knowledge game is the field of evaluation. Information produced in the meditatory must be evaluated in some field according to some convention to become "knowledge." For want of a good name, we call the field of evaluation in the knowledge game the "schole," or the network of people or teams capable of creating and competitively disseminating knowledge; it is in a sense a universalization of the various academic disciplines. Various localized marketplaces existed in the world before the wealth game was being played; the various localized schools may be the foundation of the knowledge game. Networks of various schools may evolve into what we here call the global schole.

In any case, the knowledge game is currently in its embryonic stage, if it exists at all. It is not certain when it will be born. But to have a long-term perspective, we should not write off this possibility simply because it sounds like a wild speculation. Particularly important are the implications of the current information explosion for the wealth game and the derivatives of the prestige game. The current spurt of globalization of the wealth game owes much to the development of information technology. Just as firms pressured states to leave them alone in the early nineteenth century, will teams try to achieve nonintervention from firms or states? Just as the activities of firms and the activities of states reinforced each other's interests in the nineteenth century, will the activities of teams and the activities of firms reinforce each other's interests in the twenty-first century? What role will the state have? Will it serve as the "night watchman" in the knowledge game? Will it intervene in the knowledge game almost at its inception? Will it substitute knowledge acquisition for economic development in the development game? Or, will it simply become obsolete?

And what will Japan do? What role will the Japanese state play? Will it use knowledge accumulation as a means to enhance its prestige and to help create a further derivative of the prestige game (knowledge development game)? Will it facilitate the spread of the knowledge game played by teams by eliminating rigid state regulations? [57]

What will the Japanese firms do? Do they still need the state to play the development game, which may not be entirely consistent with their interests? What role will Japanese firms play in the possible spread of the knowledge game? Can they play a role similar to that played by the British state in the late eighteenth to the early nineteenth centuries with regard to the spread of the wealth game? [58]

And what will the Japanese do? Are they creative enough to form many teams for the knowledge game? But, in the age of the knowledge game, what will we mean by "nationality"? Can the knowledge game spread as long as the state barrier is intact and the concept of nationality remains rigid within people's minds?

These and many other questions can be raised and should be answered. But we are not ready to answer these questions in this paper. The purpose of this paper is fulfilled if our discussion and speculation encourage and provoke further speculation about the future possibilities of the world system.

Bruce Russett

U.S. Hegemony: Gone or Merely Diminished, and How Does It Matter?

Prognoses for stability and cooperation in the international political economy depend heavily on assessments of changes in the relative power of the United States, Japan, and other major powers. Has U.S. hegemony declined greatly over recent years? Much of the recent literature on "hegemonic stability" has been devoted to explaining the effects of a decline in U.S. hegemony on the international system since the highpoint of U.S. dominance immediately after 1945. In a variant of the theme, scholars have searched for ways to maintain the international regime established during that hegemony. Others have perceived an ethnocentric bias in some of this angst.[1]

The premise of a major decline in U.S. hegemony has, however, gone largely unexamined, and it rests at the heart of any consideration of Japan's role in the international system. I suspect that my Japanese colleagues, especially, will give some credence to my conclusion in this paper that the decline in U.S. hegemony is easily exaggerated. If so, I further suspect that will in part be because of the great sensitivity of Japanese (and other non-American analysts) to the dual and interlinked domains of international political economy and security.

In this paper, I make the familiar but crucial distinction between power base and power as control over outcomes. I am much readier to concede decline in the former—though it, too, can be exaggerated, especially by selecting an unusual baseline for evaluating later developments—than in the latter. Simple power variants of hegemonic stability theory predict that power base and control over outcomes would decay simultaneously. For reasons made clear below, collective goods theory— a key component of the hegemonic stability literature—seems to predict both that the achievement of these goods will decline and that they will be achieved only to suboptimal degree. Turning then to control over outcomes—the achievement of various goods in the global system and the regimes by which those goods are achieved—I distinguish between security goods and economic goods. A sensitivity to demands and achievements in the domain of international security helps to temper assessments, based primarily on political economy, that the decline has been great. I evaluate the degree to which achievement of those goods has in fact declined in the past three or four decades, and I try to develop some assessment, against some reasonably explicit baseline, of the degree to which the results can be judged suboptimal. I conclude that the decline has been substantially less than would be expected if those goods had been collective ones, and less than many variants of hegemonic stability theory would predict.

This substantial continuity of outcomes must be explained. First, I acknowledge the variants of hegemonic stability theory that emphasize institutionalization as a partial explanation. But I then argue (1) that many of the gains from hegemony have been less collective goods than private ones, accruing primarily to the hegemon and thus helping maintain its hegemony; (2) that this applies to short-term as well as to long-term gains; (3) that the costs of achieving these goods (both collective and private) have not been borne so unequally, by the hegemon, as might be the case had they been relatively pure collective goods; and (4) that one important gain—cultural hegemony—has proved a major resource to the hegemon in maintaining its more general hegemony. These gains have helped the United States both to maintain its power base in ways not readily measured by standard indicators and to continue to control outcomes. Specifically, the international system was structurally transformed, largely by the United States. The transformation of preferences and expectations continues to produce the goods (for example, free trade) needed by the United States and the dominant elements of the rest of the world (especially the other industrialized noncommunist states) to maintain a compatible international system. Thus, the United States does not have to exert such *overt* control over *others* to maintain control over *outcomes*. In the conclusion, I attempt a balanced evaluation of the nature and degree to which U.S. hegemony has really declined and speculate about its implications for the international system in general and Japanese-American relations in particular.

Power Base and Control

The perception of a significant decline in U.S. power over the past two decades is widespread, indeed virtually universal. Many observers, writing from diverse perspectives, characterize the decline in strong terms. Richard Rosecrance, for example, says the U.S. "role as maintainer of the system is at an end"; Kenneth Oye speaks of "the end of

American hegemony"; and George Liska repeatedly applies the word "dissolution" to the state of the "American empire."[2] People on the Left applaud the decline; many on the Right lament it. The perception of a U.S. decline is particularly common, however, in the literature on international regimes; that part of the literature identified with "hegemonic stability" theory is the most straightforward. Strong characterizations of that decline are frequently associated with Robert Gilpin, Stephen Krasner, Charles Kindleberger, and even Robert Keohane.[3]

To be sure, most of these characterizations are nuanced and change as the world and theorizing about it change. Nearly everyone recognizes that the United States retains great power in the economic sphere; at least, it is a greater power than any other state. These same writers typically carefully note a continuing degree of U.S. pre-eminence. The decline is relative to past U.S. power or perhaps to the amount necessary for a hegemon to maintain essential elements of the world economic order; the United States has not declined to a position of utter impotence. My purpose in this paper is not to criticize individual authors, but to point out the assumptions and consequences of emphasizing the decline rather than the continuity and to show that there is still much to be said for continuity.

The standards used to measure the decline are seldom clear. Part of the difficulty stems from the lack of agreement on how much power is necessary to produce hegemony. Unless there is some rather sharp stepwise jump at which hegemony comes into existence or is lost (and what that level may be has never been specified), one is necessarily talking about a continuous distribution of relative power, and there is always room for argument about whether a given degree of superiority is enough to produce particular (and also rarely well-specified) results. This is a basic theoretical problem.

A second and related difficulty is a lack of agreement on the relevant dimensions and indicators of power. In some amorphous manner, of course, our senses do not deceive us. The United States' power, as measured by various power base indicators, surely has declined. The litany is too familiar to require full recitation, and some examples will suffice: loss of strategic nuclear predominance; decline in conventional military capabilities relative to the USSR, especially for intervention, and in military capability generally (with effects compounded by perceptions of "helplessness" in the Vietnam and Iran traumas); diminished economic size (relative GNP), productivity, competitiveness in foreign markets, value of the dollar on foreign exchange markets, and terms of trade with some commodity producers (principally oil until recently); the loss of a reliable majority over the unruly in the U.N.; and the loss of assured scientific pre-eminence in the "knowledge industries" at the "cutting edge" and even in the numerical and financial base that enabled U.S. scholars to dominate global social science.

Even with the power base indicators, however, it is not quite a case where "all the instruments agree" that it is a dark, cold day. President Reagan's rhetoric about "a definite margin of superiority for the Soviet Union" had to be corrected the next day by the director of the Bureau of Politico-Military Affairs at the State Department and his remarks about a "window of vulnerability" by the Scowcroft Commission. Reasonable (if, on both sides, rather ideological) people can debate the relative importance of warheads versus throw-weights versus "kill ratios," the proper exchange rates for comparing Soviet and U.S. military expenditures, and the true balance of conventional forces between NATO and the Warsaw Pact. The United States' economic and industrial predominance in the world looks slightly less impressive if one considers its share of world GNP rather than its share of world manufacturing production. Although virtually all of these as well as other power base measures would show a clear decline in U.S. predominance over the past forty years, they do not reveal an equal rate or depth of decline. A few would show the United States slipping to second place; more would merely show a shrunken lead.[4]

It also makes a great difference where in time one begins measuring the power base indicators. If one begins with 1945, all of them show a significant, though never precipitous, decline in the U.S. power base over the subsequent four decades. That much is not really arguable.[5] But 1945 represents the summit of U.S. relative strength. The old powers—Europe and Japan—were physically and economically devastated, and the United States unscathed. That situation could not continue. Indeed, the United States hastened its passing, and by 1955 the former powers had recovered significantly. The first postwar decade, the era of the sharpest decline in U.S. predominance, represented a substantial return to normalcy. The immediate postwar years look even more peculiar if one starts the series in 1938 or earlier years. The United States' military pre-eminence dates, without question, only from World War II. Its military predominance in 1945 over all other states (even, at that point, the Soviet Union) was unprecedented for any power at least since the time of Napoleon. Since then, the Soviet Union has achieved parity, but the Soviet and U.S. dominance over all other powers, including those of the Western alliance, remains. The name of the Soviet-U.S. military game is duopoly. A long-term perspective on economic power makes clear the unusual degree of U.S. superiority in that power base as well.

Table 1 provides a historical perspective on hegemons' ability to dominate three of the most common dimensions of a national power base. GNP is the most fungible of resources, usable for many kinds of influence efforts; it also represents market size, whose attraction can give im-

TABLE 1

Four Leading Powers Indexed to "Hegemon," 1830–1984: Gross National Product, Military Expenditures, and Manufacturing Production

Year	\multicolumn{8}{c}{Country and percentage of "hegemon's" value}

Year	Largest		2d largest		3d largest		4th largest	
	\multicolumn{8}{c}{GROSS NATIONAL PRODUCT}							
1984	U.S.	100%	USSR	51%	Japan	34%	W.Germany	17%
1950	U.S.	100	USSR	29	U.K.	19	France	13
1938	U.S.	100	Germany	37	USSR	37	U.K.	27
1913	U.S.	306	Russia	123	Germany	113	U.K.	100
1870	U.S.	117	Russia	117	U.K.	100	France	86
1830	Russia	132	France	105	U.K.	100	Austria-Hungary	87
	\multicolumn{8}{c}{MILITARY EXPENDITURES}							
1984	U.S.	100%	USSR	100%	China	18%	U.K.	15%
1950	USSR	106	U.S.	100	China	18	U.K.	16
1938[a]	Germany	657	USSR	481	U.K.	161	Japan	154
1913	Germany	129	Russia	125	U.K.	100	France	99
1872[b]	Russia	127	France	119	U.K.	100	Germany	68
1830	France	148	U.K.	100	Russia	92	Austria-Hungary	54
	\multicolumn{8}{c}{MANUFACTURING PRODUCTION}							
1983	U.S.	100%	USSR	52%	Japan	30%	W.Germany	16%
1950	U.S.	100	USSR	24	U.K.	19	W.Germany	13
1938	U.S.	100	Germany	40	U.K.	34	USSR	29
1913	U.S.	235	Germany	109	U.K.	100	Russia	26
1870	U.K.	100	China	75	U.S.	51	France	37
1830	China	319	India	185	U.K.	100	Russia	59

SOURCES: 1984 GNP data from OECD, *Main Economic Indicators* (May 1985); USSR total is estimated. Other GNP data from Paul Bairoch, "Europe's Gross National Product, 1800–1975," *Journal of European Economic History*, Vol. 5 (1976), pp. 273–340; and U.S. Bureau of the Census, *Historical Statistics of the United States: Colonial Times to 1970* (Washington, D.C.: Government Printing Office, 1975). 1984 military expenditures from *World Armaments and Disarmament: SIPRI Yearbook, 1985* (London: Taylor & Francis, 1985). SIPRI lists Soviet military expenses as 71 percent of the U.S. figures, but U.S. government sources (CIA and DIA) give Soviet expenditures as exceeding those of the United States. I have set the two countries as equal. The estimate for China, given by SIPRI and used here, may be somewhat low. Military expenditure data for previous years are from the Correlates of War national capabilities data provided by Professor J. David Singer. Manufacturing production data from Paul Bairoch, "International Industrialization Levels from 1750 to 1980," *Journal of European Economic History*, Vol. 11 (1982), pp. 269–333. Data for 1870 are extrapolated from Bairoch's figures for 1860 and 1880. 1983 data from *U.N. Monthly Bulletin of Statistics* figures applied to Bairoch's 1980 data.

NOTES: The "hegemon" of the time is underlined; there was no hegemon in 1938, but I have arbitrarily used the U.S. values as the base.

[a] The United States ranked fifth.

[b] Data for 1872 were used since the figures for French and German (Prussian) military spending were inflated in 1870 and 1871 by the Franco-Prussian War.

portant advantages in international trade negotiations. It represents the basis of structural power; that is, the ability to define the context within which others must make decisions. Military expenditures give a good if hardly perfect indication of relative military strength. Manufacturing production is a basic source of both economic and military strength.

Several facts are apparent from these data. First, the United Kingdom was *never*, even at its peak in the nineteenth century, the dominant power as measured by either GNP or military expenditures. The wealth provided by its industrial strength was always overwhelmed in GNP terms by the demographic base of its sometimes less wealthy but more populous chief competitors; its military expenditures were always markedly below those of one or more of its continental rivals. Only in manufacturing production, and for that matter only rather briefly, did it lead the world. (For purposes of this analysis, however, we probably should discount the surprising manufacturing capacity of China and India since they were hardly great powers in the world system.) These data should encourage a cautious interpretation of Britain's hegemonic power during this era. Britain's commercial power (which would be reflected in trade or financial indicators) was not evident in other important power base indicators. Second, despite slippage since filling the immediate post–World War II void, the United States retains, on all these indicators, a degree of dominance not reached by the United Kingdom at any point and comparing well with the U.S. position in 1938. (U.S. military expenditures for 1950, not yet reflecting the Korean war, are artificially low for the cold war period.) The basis of U.S. hegemony may have declined, but it has hardly vanished.

Other indicators are imaginable, but many of the data are not available for a long time span, and that length of historical perspective is essential to the argument. Moreover, the meaning of some potential indicators is not entirely clear; for example, does a large volume of foreign trade indicate market dominance or vulnerability?[6] Nevertheless, any truly scientific assessment requires more, and more rigorous, measurement than Table 1 provides, as well as some agreement on appropriate baselines for temporal comparison. With conceptual and theoretical clarity, one could establish appropriate rules for measuring a decline in a power base. Until that time, it would be well to remember Galileo's experiment with falling bodies: to explain their velocity, one must first determine the velocity. In this instance, to be persuasive, the hegemonic stability literature demands better measurements.

The more important question, however, is "so what?" In what ways has this decline produced (been reflected in?) a decline in U.S. power as control over outcomes; that is, in the "ability to prevail in conflict and overcome obstacles"?[7] Surely it is control over outcomes that really interests us. The *Oxford English Dictionary* defines *hegemonic* as "capable of command, leading," and *hegemony* as "leadership" as well as "predominance, preponderance." If we are to have a question worth investigating, we must at least identify hegemony with success in determining and maintaining the essential rules, not merely with power base or resource share. Like Robert Keohane and Joseph Nye, we must see hegemony as a condition in which "one state is powerful enough to maintain the essential rules governing interstate relations, and willing to do so." We must avoid making a tautology out of Stephen Krasner's statement that "the theory of hegemonic leadership suggests that under conditions of declining hegemony there will be a weakening of regimes."[8]

Rather, we should ask, under conditions of declining power base predominance, is there either a weakening of the basic regime (the network of rules, norms, and so forth) or of the ability of the preponderant state to determine those rules? Weakening of the network is difficult to investigate empirically with precision, although good efforts have been made, especially with aspects of the trade regime. Here, however, I address the influence of the preponderant state and emphasize the distribution of *desired outcomes* as a result of the rules, in conformity with Krasner's formulation of a causal chain from "basic causal factors" to regimes to outcomes and behaviors.

It is widely acknowledged that the United States occupied a position of hegemony in the international system immediately after World War II. Its enemies were defeated and its allies exhausted. The productive base of the U.S. economy alone escaped wartime devastation; indeed, it was enormously expanded by the war effort. The United States was the world's foremost military power, and it alone had the nuclear "winning weapon." Although the United States' preponderance was not so overwhelming as to enable it to set all the rules for the entire world system, its power did permit it to establish the basic principles for the new economic order in the over 80 per cent of the world economy controlled by the capitalist states and to organize a system of collective security to maintain political and economic control over that 80 per cent. Although its power fell short of that necessary in an ideal case of hegemony, virtually all analysts of the regimes school agree that the United States circa 1946 came closer to meeting the criteria of global hegemony than has any other state in world history. Indeed, to quote Timothy McKeown and Robert Keohane, one should have important reservations about the "supposed hegemonic leadership" of nineteenth-century Britain and wonder whether Britain was hegemonic in any meaningful sense.[9]

One can also have some reservations about the scientific status of a "theory" of hegemonic stability derived in large part from a single case that attempts to explain behavior in that same case. (Proponents of this theory frequently acknowledge the problem, but I shall not be greatly concerned with it here.) One can appropriately, as many have done, seek to extend insights and test propositions by looking at various "issue-area" regimes within the overall set of rules and by looking at the behavior and outcomes of actors in various arenas (for example, in small groups or in shifting coalitions within organizations) where degrees of hegemony may be examined, compared, and even manipulated. Empirical tests of the theory of collective goods have been made in just such arenas, and with care their findings can be extended to the global situation. The questions addressed are important and should not be evaded because the set of cases is small or problematic. Nevertheless, the necessity to make extensions from arenas where global conditions are but crudely approximated should force the analyst to look closely at such key assumptions as whether the goods provided by a regime truly meet the definition of collective goods,[10] of behavior by unitary actors,[11] and of "fairness" in the distribution of costs and benefits.[12]

Achievements, Goods, and Regimes

In the years immediately following World War II, the United States emerged as a hegemonic power, perhaps following the path George Modelski characterizes as occurring at roughly hundred-year intervals.[13] The United States provided the world with a variety of goods (some of them collective goods), including security, international organization, and a framework for international economic relations. The idea of a hegemon providing collective goods to permit peace and prosperity within a wider area is an old one; in fact, Karl Deutsch's work on integration anticipated much of what emerged in the regimes literature of the 1970s.[14]

Another perspective on the provision of goods in the postwar international system is a radical one. It recognizes the existence of a Pax Americana and identifies the following achievements (not necessarily identified as collective goods):

The pacification of capitalist interstate relations and the imperial guarantee against nationalization created a reliable world legal framework which reduced the risks of transnational expansion; decolonization opened up the entire periphery to primary transnational expansion based on comparative advantage rather than on the monopolistic privileges and restrictions with which rival metropolitan states had increasingly enmeshed their colonial possessions; the gold-dollar standard restored the possibility of capitalist accounting on a world scale, thus enhancing secondary transnational expansion, which depends decisively upon reliable calculations of the cost advantages of alternative locations of production.[15]

Two kinds of achievements or goods are encountered in this quotation from Giovanni Arrighi: security (peace) and economy (prosperity). Each can be broken down further, and we can ask what conditions or regime made possible those achievements.[16]

In the passage quoted above, Arrighi speaks of the "pacification" of relations among capitalist states. At least since 1945, there have been no wars between the developed (capitalist) industrial states. Whether this is attributable more to the spread of advanced industrial capitalism or to the spread of representative democracy in the world is hard to say because the two potential explanatory variables are so closely correlated. All the correlations may be spurious, although various arguments do not necessarily agree on the direction of causality.[17] Nevertheless, the fact of no interstate war is indisputable. Moreover, by fairly early in the postwar era, even the preparation for, and expectation of, war among these states quickly diminished nearly to the vanishing point. By the end of the 1950s, one could say with reasonable confidence that a "security community" or "stable peace" had been established nearly everywhere in the OECD states, even between traditional enemies.[18] Nor have there been any civil wars (1,000 or more deaths) within any of the advanced capitalist countries or any serious expectation of such. (There has been fear that the violence in Northern Ireland and the Spanish Basque country could escalate above this threshold.)

One could argue that the absence of war between democracies has been a fact of life for the almost two centuries since the end of the Napoleonic era,[19] but the recent extension of stable democracy and (therefore?) of a "zone of peace" to various industrialized countries where it was previously fragile (for example, Germany, Italy, Japan) is surely a major achievement. It is, moreover, an achievement that can be credited in some degree to the United States, either as a result of enforced suppression of hostilities[20] or, in Arrighi's terms, by provision of a "cohesive political and ideological framework."

Stable peace has not, however, been achieved in the Third World and its capitalist states. Virtually all post-1945 wars have been fought on the territories of Third World states, between or within Third World states or between Third World states and intervening First or Second World states. Open insurgency was often avoided only because of the threat of direct foreign intervention or the establishment of powerful coercive states within Third World countries, usually with strong external support. It is all too often a "peace" based on threat, either mutual (deterrence) or one-sided (dominance).

From the point of view of Third World peoples, the achievement of stable peace is doubtless suboptimal. From the viewpoint of the United States, however, the judgment must be less certain. The wars have been fought in Third World countries and the civilian casualties incurred there. The costs of maintaining coercive states have been largely borne by Third World peoples. The result has been sufficient pacification to provide a reliable legal framework for transnational corporate expansion and to discourage most large-scale nationalization without "fair" compensation. Parts (some countries, some classes) of the Third World have shared fully in the resulting prosperity; others have not. But overall by historic standards (even compared with the colonial era of direct control), the results show not a bad ratio of costs and benefits for the United States.

If *stable peace* has been achieved among and within many capitalist countries, it surely has not been achieved between capitalist and communist countries. Instead, we can speak only of *containment* or deterrence and the ability of U.S. hegemony to achieve stable boundaries between the capitalist and communist spheres. The United States was able to erect, in the first decade after the war, a *cordon sanitaire* around the Soviet Union that held from the "loss" of China to the accession of Castro, with some breaches thereafter. It is a "peace" maintained by deterrence, initially somewhat one-sided (the U.S. nuclear monopoly, though compensated by Soviet conventional superiority in Europe) and becoming increasingly based on a system of mutual threat. Although there are many flaws and dangers in this system, the facts of substantial success for containment and the avoidance of superpower war should not be dismissed.

Other goods or achievements relate to the economy and are embodied in various regimes.[21] The second gain Arrighi identifies from establishment of the Pax Americana is decolonization and consequent entry of the United States into previously closed trade and raw materials markets. As the price of U.S. assistance for postwar reconstruction, the former colonial powers were required to accede to the demands of their colonial peoples for independence. Clear-cut examples include (but are hardly limited to) the experience in 1949 when the threat of a cutoff in U.S. economic aid halted the Dutch military operation to restore control over the Dutch East Indies (Indonesia), U.S. pressure in 1962 that helped impel the Dutch effectively to cede West New Guinea (Irian Jaya) to Indonesia, and the U.S. refusal to approve an urgent IMF loan that forced the British and French to retreat from their effort to reoccupy the Suez Canal in 1956.[22]

The U.S. goal was more than mere nominal independence for the colonies. Dismantling of the formal and informal barriers that had largely restricted colonies' trade to their former metropoles was to follow. Britain, for instance, was strongly pressured to give up the structures of Commonwealth Preference and the Sterling Area, which had provided it with a relatively closed, secure market. Britain was also required, most notably as part of the settlement of the Anglo-Iranian oil nationalization in 1953, to give U.S.-based multinationals a dominant share of Middle Eastern oil supplies. Decolonization as an ideology was attractive to Americans; it cost them almost nothing (the only American colony was the Philippines) and created enormous economic opportunities. With its then-dominant technology and industrial organization, the United States was in position to move into these hitherto closed markets. Decolonization meant acceleration of the introduction of advanced capitalism into the Third World—and the United States was the most efficient capitalist. The postwar international trade and finance regimes brought worldwide prosperity, not least to the United States.

Continuity and Distribution of Gains

These achievements, often embodied in regimes, are important products of U.S. hegemony. Moreover, they represent a continued achievement of outcomes desired by the United States, even at a time of a discernible decline in standard power base indicators. If one shifts perspective from narrow issue-area regimes to broader aspects of the post–World War II international environment, one has to be impressed by the degree to which perceived U.S. interests, not just the interests of other states, were served. One also should be impressed by the strong elements of continuity, of sustained reward, characteristic of these achievements. These two elements—the fact of important gains to the United States itself and their continuity—are interlinked.

First, the matter of continuity. Over the past decade we have seen a breakdown in détente, by which we mean a breakdown in the rules and norms governing Soviet-U.S. behavior. "Prompt hard-target kill" weapons have been acquired, in numbers and capabilities formerly avoided; troops have crossed some of the implicit boundaries between East and West; and continued adherence to formal agreements like SALT and the ABM treaty is in doubt. Yet the rules and norms, built up over the decades, have not entirely been abandoned. Some vestige of a regime in East-West relations remains.

More dubious is the continuity of containment, but even there I suggest that the argument of drastic decline is readily exaggerated. The United States' strategic nuclear predominance is gone, forever in my opinion. (Members of the Reagan administration may disagree about the "forever.") Most of us feel less secure about maintenance of the balance of terror than we did, especially about the risks of a low-level political or military conflict spiraling into something like Armageddon. But the risks of deliberate Soviet nuclear attack still seem remote and are likely to remain so indefinitely, barring either gross U.S. provocation or gross U.S. negligence in providing a secure nuclear deterrent.

Despite some breaches, the *cordon sanitaire* around the Soviet Union still looks quite effective. Counterbalancing the effects of Soviet gains in Afghanistan, Vietnam, and Africa has been the Soviet loss of China, once its foremost ally. By any standards of resources or population, the reentry of China into the world economy and the reorientation of Chinese foreign policy more than compensate for "free world" losses elsewhere. The United States' losses in the Middle East have by no means been translated into Soviet gains (witness Iran).[23] The biggest switch in that part of the world (Egypt) was from "them" to "us." Soviet penetration of Latin America since Cuba still remains more of a threat than a major reality (and the Soviet accession of Cuba occurred despite U.S. nuclear predominance at that time).

Continuity also applies to the United States' relations with the industrialized countries. The hegemonic stability literature does not give sharp predictions on whether and, particularly, how much the achievement of goals will decline as the relative power base of the hegemon declines. Except as a "crude theory,"[24] it emphasizes the mediating and conditioning roles of, for example, international institutions and the characteristics of domestic political systems. Nevertheless, some decline, particularly in light of the sharp decline in U.S. military power, might be expected. But it has not happened. By no reasonable criterion has there been any decline in the achievement of stable peace among the advanced capitalist countries. They hardly are able to solve all their common problems, but—and this is no small achievement—war among them is now less thinkable than ever. War among them became no more thinkable during the 1970s era of détente when their apparent common threat, the Soviet Union, became less threatening. And although wars in the Third World remain common, there is no discernible trend toward greater frequency.[25]

If U.S. predominance (hegemony) vis-à-vis the Soviet Union is gone, U.S. nuclear predominance (hegemony) over all other states remains and is perhaps stronger than ever. There is little sign that it will erode in the future. Europe seems unable to put together a substantial deterrent of its own. In a nuclear world, U.S. military hegemony over its allies may never end. And that kind of hegemony provides the United States with some fungible resources for maintaining a degree of hegemony in other areas. ("Open up your domestic market more, or Congress may tire of keeping our military commitment.")

In the economic realm, the structure of a relatively open world economy (GATT, the various rounds of trade liberalization, and so forth) remains substantially intact. Despite the spread of some measures like "voluntary" export restraints and many observers' anticipation of a major relapse into protectionism, the sky has not fallen. It is significant that world trade fell only in 1982, and then by only 1 per cent, after a decade of increased protectionist efforts. The inflation-adjusted increase in world trade between 1973 and 1983 was between 6 and 7 per cent, as contrasted with a 28 per cent drop from 1926 to 1935. Progress in opening up the biggest protected capitalist economy outside the United States (Japan's) continues to creep forward.[26] Currencies remain convertible. The United States can use the attractiveness of its financial markets and its high interest rates to finance its military buildup with other people's money (especially Japanese money).

It would be perverse to deny that there has been some demonstrable (if less easily measurable) decline in the United States' ability to get others to do as it wished in recent decades. That decline has been well documented in the regimes literature, although I consider the decline often to have been exaggerated. Since I have quoted Arrighi to illustrate the gains achieved by the United States by its world predominance, it is only fair to quote a long passage where he considers both the persistence and the decay of those gains:

> In general, the U.S. government has simply exploited, in the pursuance of national interests, the core position that the U.S. national economy still retains in the world-economy. Its internal reserves of energy and other natural resources, the sheer size of its internal market, and the density and complexity of its linkages with the rest of the capitalist world imply a basic asymmetry in the relation of the U.S. economy to other national economies: conditions within the U.S. state's boundaries influence, much more than they are influenced by, conditions within the boundaries of any other national economy. This asymmetrical relation, though independently eroded by other factors, has not yet been significantly affected by the undoing of the U.S. imperial order. What has been affected is the *use* made by the U.S. state of its world economic power: while in the 1950s and 1960s the national interest was often subordinated to the establishment and reproduction of a world capitalist order, in the middle and late 1970s the reproduction of such an order has been subordinated to the pursuit of the national interest as expressed in efforts to increase domestic economic growth.
>
> In such a sense, this redeployment of U.S. world political-economic power in the pursuit of national interests has been a major symptom of, and factor explaining, the state of anarchy that has characterized international economic relations since 1973. It is important to realize, however, that at least insofar as the advanced capitalist countries are concerned, this state of anarchy in interstate relations has been strictly limited to monetary and budgetary policies and that it has yet to undermine the two main "products" of formal U.S. hegemony: the unity of the world market and the transnational expansion of capital. These substantive aspects of U.S. hegemony have survived the downfall of the U.S. imperial order; and their operating reach throughout the world capitalist economy has, if anything, been continually extended.[27]

As will shortly be apparent, I disagree on several counts with Arrighi's assessment. I contend that the U.S. national interest was served, not subordinated, even in the short run, by the policies of the 1950s. I also regard his characterization of a "state of anarchy"—even as applied only to monetary and budgetary policies—as much too strong. A literal "absence of government" is not necessarily synonymous with chaos, as Hedley Bull and others have urged.[28] (It is worth emphasizing that, once the world capitalist order was established, the tasks of maintaining and reproducing it became far easier.) The strengths of Arrighi's argument, however, include its emphasis on asymmetries (versus simplistic uses of "interdependence") and hence the remaining power of the United States to influence others and its emphasis on the substantive aspects that remain.

If the fact of significant continuity is accepted, then it must be explained. The institutions for political and economic cooperation have themselves been maintained. Keohane rightly stresses the role of institutions as "arrangements permitting communication and therefore facilitating the exchange of information."[29] By providing reliable information and reducing transaction costs, institutions can permit cooperation to continue even after erosion of a hegemon's influence. Institutions facilitate opportunities for commitment and for observing whether others keep their commitments. Such opportunities are virtually essential to cooperation in non-zero-sum situations, as explicit attention to gaming experiments demonstrates.[30] Declining hegemony and stagnant (but not decaying) institutions may therefore be consistent with stable provision of desired outcomes, although the ability to promote new levels of cooperation to deal with new problems (for example, energy supplies or environmental protection) is more problematic. The institutions provide a part of the necessary explanation.

Collective or Private Goods?

The nature of the institutions themselves must be examined. They were shaped, in the years immediately after World War II, by the United States. They, and the regimes of which they are a part, have significantly endured. The U.S. willingness to establish those regimes and their institutions is sometimes explained in terms of the theory of collective goods. It is commonplace in the regimes literature to argue that the United States, in so doing, was providing not only private goods for its own benefit, but also (especially?) collective goods desired by, and for the benefit of, other capitalist states (nations?—but one should be particularly careful here in equating state interest with "national" interest). Thus, not only was the United States protecting its own territory and commercial enterprises, it was also providing desired military protection for some fifty allies and almost as many neutrals. Not only was it ensuring a liberal, open, near-global economy for its own prosperity, it was providing the basis for the prosperity of all capitalist states (and even for those states organized on noncapitalist principles willing to abide by the basic rules established to govern international trade and finance). Although it would not be quite accurate to describe such behavior as selfless or altruistic, certainly the benefits—however distributed by class, state, or region—did accrue to far more peoples than just to Americans.

Coupled with this is the implication that the United States paid substantial costs in the immediate postwar period to set in place the basis for the accrual of long-term benefits for itself and others.[31]

If this were a case of provision of a collective good, several conclusions would follow. First, collective goods theory predicts that, in the absence of a strong central authority able to coerce members to pay appropriate contributions, the collective good will be supplied only to a suboptimal degree. Second, the costs of providing the good will be borne unequally and by the hegemon. Implicit in the assessment of *inequality* in burden sharing is usually an assumption of *inequity* or unfairness; that is, the ratio of costs to benefits weighs against the hegemon, implying that although the hegemon bears disproportionate costs, the nonhegemonic powers desire the good as much as, or almost as much as, the hegemon does. (This proposition should make us critical of the prior assumption, and its consequent normative implications, that the principal goods provided truly are collective ones. If the goods are largely private goods for the benefit, and at the desire, of the hegemon, then it is hardly fair to berate the smaller states for an unwillingness to pay an equal share of the costs.)

A corollary is a serious doubt about the willingness, and even the ability, of the hegemon to continue to pay the costs. It is argued that the short-term costs were so heavy, and the benefits distributed so widely to those who never paid the costs, that a weakening of the United States, and loss of its hegemony, was thus inevitable. So, too, except as it could be retarded by such factors as institutionalization, was a weakening of the regimes that the United States had established and sustained.

As so applied, collective goods theory would predict the very weakening whose existence I have contested. Yet paradoxically, the absence of that weakening can, in fact, be understood by a different application of collective goods theory. It requires a careful examination of the goods provided and an awareness of the degree to which they were not collective but private. To the degree that they were private goods—benefits to the United States itself—they have brought important if sometimes obscured resources to the United States, resources that help it to maintain regimes and to obtain for itself a variety of private goods.

A collective good must meet the two standard criteria of nonrivalness and nonexclusiveness. By the first is meant that one's enjoyment or consumption of the good does not diminish the amount of the good available to anyone else; by the second, that it is not possible to exclude any party from enjoyment of the good, as a result of which many actors may be "free-riders" unwilling to pay any of the costs for providing the good. Few goods ever fit these criteria perfectly; one can usually find some possibilities of rivalness and exclusion,[32] but judgments of less and more are perfectly feasible. I argue, on the basis of an examination of each of the major goods identified above, that they do not primarily meet the criteria for collective goods, but that in many ways they represent private goods accruing heavily to the United States. If that judgment is accepted, the conclusion that exercise of hegemony necessarily weakened the United States does not follow. And if the United States has not been severely weakened, we need not be surprised at its continued willingness, and ability, to secure these goods.

The first of the goods at issue is "stable peace," particularly among the industrialized states. It probably satisfies the criterion of nonrivalness, although some radical critics contend that peace within and among the industrialized states is achieved only at the price of exploiting (through dominance, military threats, and military intervention) the Third World. Whatever one thinks of that assessment, clearly peace does not meet the criterion of nonexclusiveness. It certainly is feasible to exclude various countries or areas from stable peace with oneself if one so wishes—by attacking or invading—and even for "peace" by dominance one can choose boundaries to the area one pacifies.

Many Western observers would probably judge containment to be largely a collective good. It was desired by *most* of the citizens of all the countries protected, not just by the United States. The unanimity of this desire has weakened recently, however, as many of its beneficiaries, notably in Western Europe, increasingly doubt the reality of a Soviet military threat to their security or way of life. Containment is achieved both by deterrence and a willingness to defend. It is neither entirely nonrival or nonexclusive. As the distinction in the alliance literature makes clear, deterrence satisfies the criterion of nonrivalness well and that of nonexclusiveness reasonably well, but defense is another matter.[33]

Fortifying one area may, by requiring the adversary to concentrate troops there, actually enhance the defense of other areas. Or, by drawing the hegemon's resources away from other areas, it may indeed prove to be "rival" by leaving weak spots elsewhere in the perimeter. (In the Korean war, many American analysts feared too great involvement there would divert needed forces from the European theater.) One may attempt to exclude "unimportant" countries or uncooperative governments from one's defense or deterrent umbrella, although, as with South Korea in 1950, it is not always possible to stick to one's resolve to exclude them. Since defense is significantly a private good, there are strong incentives for small or large states to provide substantial military capabilities of their own. Other important goods can be derived from military forces, such as technological knowledge, prestige, and internal security.[34]

Prosperity, as provided by an open world economy, is also somewhere on the continuum between a private and a collective good. It is partly nonrival and partly rival. General gains accrue from prosperous and expanding markets, yet a capitalist economy lives by competition. One sells at the expense of a competitor. (The mixed-motive game characterization is appropriate.) As the Soviet Union has been, states can be formally excluded from the most-favored-nation system, the system that provides much of the basis of international prosperity.[35] Within the system, the rules of the international trade and finance game prohibit many kinds of discrimination (exclusion from benefits), but many loopholes can be found, for example, the various preferences, restrictions, and common-market arrangements.

I have already argued that the United States was well positioned, in the immediate postwar years, to reap *at least* a proportionate share of the collective and private gains that were obtainable from the prosperity induced by decolonization and a more open world market. Of course, there were costs. Postwar reconstruction entailed immediate costs in the high military expenditure the United States carried in the interests of containment, in the Marshall Plan, and the trade concessions to Japan, which largely substituted for heavy grant assistance to that country. The United States, in accordance with the liberal free-trade regime it was sponsoring, had to open its own previously protected markets. But these costs were, during the first decades after World War II, recouped many times over from the general prosperity stimulated by a relatively open world market, and specifically by U.S. access to others' previously closed markets. These, of course, included the metropolitan countries of Europe as well as markets in the Third World. The United States mitigated EEC discrimination against U.S. trade by insisting that EEC trade and investment barriers be low, and save for agricultural products, it succeeded in gaining access on terms not much worse than those accorded to intra-EEC enterprises.

The gains from an open global economy surely exceeded the costs to the United States. Despite what ultimately proved to be important burdens shouldered by the United States to maintain that open economy, when compared with the costs other powers accepted in decolonization, the balance sheet for Americans does not look at all bad. (For example, the costs associated with maintaining the dollar at a fixed price in gold eventually became too great, but for a long time they were substantially balanced by the gains from seigniorage and autonomy.) Indeed, the gains from decolonization helped shield the United States from what might have been a *rapid* deterioration of its relative and absolute economic position. The two defeated powers, Germany and Japan, did quickly close much of the per capita economic gap between them and the United States—as a consequence of the deliberate U.S. policy to build strong pillars of containment on either end of the Soviet Union. But the major power whose decolonization occurred *after* the war—Great Britain—was in no way able to close the gap.

The United States had a large surplus productive capacity after World War II, making the costs of overseas economic assistance not very onerous. Furthermore, given that excess capacity, the postwar U.S. prosperity was dependent on foreign economic expansion in a climate of worldwide prosperity. Had the European or former colonial economies been allowed to stagnate, almost surely the U.S. economy would have done likewise. Most major currencies became convertible with the dollar by the mid-1950s, at stable exchange rates, thus in Arrighi's terms "reducing the risks to capital of, and so favoring, the expansion of international trade and investment."[36] Again, the United States was superbly positioned to capture its full share of those gains. It is also worth remembering that although this open world economy did not, especially in the first decades, include the communist countries, when those states did seek partial global economic integration (Eastern Europe beginning in the 1960s, the Soviet Union and China somewhat later), the terms were largely set by the initial U.S. specifications, for example, most-favored-nation status.

Nor is it any more correct to describe the costs of obtaining non-economic goods as disproportionately borne by the United States. This can be seen even in the instance most often cited, the cost of containment. In purely economic terms (share of GNP, a cost that the wealthy United States could most easily bear), the burden sharing has been skewed so as to fall more heavily on Americans. But non-Americans have consistently provided the real estate and the personnel. For example, the United States' formal allies in Europe and Asia have maintained twice as many soldiers under arms as has the United States. They did so immediately after the war as well as in recent years, many of them with compulsory national service.

Thus, a careful toting up of costs and benefits to all parties, coupled with a rigorous application of the criteria for collective goods, casts much doubt on the proposition that the United States provided disproportionate benefits to others. Most of the major goods provided by the postwar U.S. hegemony ("stable peace" within much of the non-communist world; a *cordon sanitaire* around the major perceived security threat; a relatively open, expanding, and largely predictable world economy) were obtained in degrees that were not markedly suboptimal from the U.S. point of view. The burdens were not distributed in such a way as to be grossly unfair to the United States, relative either to the gains of the United States or to the burdens borne by many other noncommunist countries. Indeed, by many radical and even liberal perspectives, U.S.

aid and rearmament expenditures—both in themselves and as a stimulus for a wider, and more open, world economy—prevented a postwar repetition of the Great Depression. It was the ideal outcome; the United States did well by doing good.

Cultural Hegemony

How do we explain the United States' ability to achieve and maintain a rather favorable balance sheet of costs and benefits? An answer, found in a few versions of the hegemonic stability literature, asserts that in the early years, at least, the United States was such a powerful hegemon that it could skew the division of private goods in its favor and *enforce* "adequate" burden sharing for the collective goods on other noncommunist states. By this interpretation, the United States in effect provided something functionally equivalent to the coercive mechanism of central government that ensures the provision of collective goods within nation-states.[37] In this sense, the U.S. hegemonic regime (or regimes, as one prefers) was essentially imposed and maintained by politico-economic coercion and not largely by the threat or fact of physical violence. I would not dispute that other countries' bargaining position and ability to resist U.S. demands in the immediate postwar era were weak, and I acknowledged that—at least in comparison with the period before World War II—relatively strong international institutions, dominated by the United States, were created. But the qualification of "strong relative to what went before" is an important one, and I find it hard to believe that the institutions provided the basis for the coercive, tax-collecting power necessary to enforce near-optimal (from the U.S. point of view) provision of collective goods at a distribution of costs that was not, overall, unfair to the United States. Coercive hegemony is at best challengeable,[38] and another answer must be sought.

Another major gain to the United States from the Pax Americana, perhaps less widely appreciated, nevertheless proved of great significance in the short as well as the long term: the pervasive global cultural influence of the United States. By *culture*, I mean, following Clifford Geertz, a set of symbols that conveys meaning about the beliefs, values, and aspirations of a group of people.[39] This dimension of the power base is often neglected. After World War II, the authoritarian political cultures of Europe and Japan were utterly discredited, and the liberal-democratic elements of those cultures revivified. The revival was most extensive and deliberate in the occupied former Axis powers and especially Japan, where it was nurtured by imposing a democratic constitution, building democratic institutions, curbing the power of industrial trusts by decartelization, building trade unions, and imprisoning or discrediting most of the wartime leaders. Liberal ideas from the United States largely filled the cultural void. The effect was not so dramatic in the "victor" states, whose regimes were reaffirmed (Britain, the Low Countries, and Scandinavia), but even there the United States and its culture were widely admired. The upper classes often thought it too "commercial," but in many respects the spread of American mass-consumption culture was the most pervasive dimension of the United States' impact. American styles, tastes, and middle-class consumption patterns were widely imitated, in a process that has come to bear the label "coca-colonization."

Altogether, the near-global acceptance of so many aspects of American culture—consumption, democracy, language—quickly laid the basis for what Gramscians would call cultural hegemony.[40] It paid off in immediate benefits in markets and the willingness of many people to bear significant burdens to establish and maintain the *cordon sanitaire*. In longer-term ways, it shaped people's desires and perceptions of alternatives, so that their preferences for international politics and economics were concordant with those of Americans. (The rationalization of hegemony itself is part of this process.) The structure of pervasive American cultural influence was part of a structural transformation of the international system. It meant that in many cases Americans would be able to retain substantial control over essential outcomes without overtly exerting power over others.[41] Rather, others' values were already conditioned to be compatible with American wishes in ways that would benefit Americans as well as themselves (antiauthoritarianism and, with limits, acceptance of free-market economics).[42]

Gramscian ideas of influence are notoriously difficult to operationalize because by definition they leave no traces in events (overt persuasion, much less coercion, is usually unnecessary). But they should not be dismissed.[43] The mushrooming expansion of U.S. television, film, and printed media in the world, often in spite of other governments' efforts to reinforce their cultural boundaries, supports a Gramscian kind of interpretation.[44] It is truly a worldwide phenomenon, not just one limited to the European and Japanese industrial states, and mightily facilitated by the use of English as an international language.[45] The internalization of Western (but especially American) norms by the rulers and middle classes of the Third World forms a constant theme in *dependencia* writing. It has not noticeably diminished over the years. To the contrary, a Mitterrand or a de Gaulle can offer but ineffectual resistance in an industrial country; only the draconian measures of Khomeini bring much success in an underdeveloped one.

The international institutionalization associated with regime building facilitates the spread of common cultural and political norms, especially among governing elites. This helps to achieve consensus on what problems must be solved, and how. Norm-creating institutions broaden individuals' self-images; institutions may change the "decision criteria—members may become *joint* maximizers rather than just self-maximizers."[46]

The spread of American (democratic, capitalist, mass-consumption, anticommunist) culture has laid the basis for innumerable U.S. economic and political gains. The spread of American culture has been a collective good in the sense of being nonrival. (More strongly: to the degree one state in the global system becomes more Americanized, others are influenced to become more, not less, so.) It also is a good not readily capable of exclusion. If one regards it normatively as a "good," then all parties are beneficiaries. But the private benefits to the United States itself can hardly be ignored, and since many would have liked to exclude American culture more than they were able to do, it was hardly to them an unalloyed "good." It was appropriate that the Americans—who have reaped so many gains from that dominance—should pay whatever extremely modest costs it may have entailed. It forms a structure of long-term influence that persists, deeply, to this day. It is among the primary reasons why a decline in material power–base dominance has not been reflected in an equivalent loss of control over outcomes.[47]

Conclusions for Japanese-American Relations

These observations begin, I think, to untangle a central puzzle often posed in the hegemonic stability literature. Two empirical assumptions at the hard core of the hegemonic stability research program depart so far from reality as to have seriously misleading effects. First, the characterization of a hegemonic United States as predominantly supplying itself, and others, with collective goods is inaccurate, and for those goods that can correctly be called collective, the United States has not paid disproportionate costs. Second, the description of U.S. hegemony as having declined is also a gross overstatement, particularly when one looks at the military and cultural, as well as economic, elements of hegemony.

Clarity about the past and present is essential to any comprehension of the future, although forecasting is hazardous even with the best of models and information. Having refuted more-sweeping claims about hegemonial decline, we now are in better position to evaluate soberly the effects of what deterioration has occurred. Although reports of the demise of U.S. hegemony have been greatly exaggerated, surely some decline is unquestionable. The question is whether the decline represents a terminal illness or merely normal aging compounded by a few minor ailments.

It is useful to think of competing hegemonic systems (a U.S.-led one and a Soviet-led one), but even so the degree of change in U.S. dominance, and the importance of the Soviet Union, differs across military, cultural, and economic dimensions. The United States' *military* dominance over the Soviet Union is gone and will not return. But over the next decade or two, it is not likely that U.S. decision makers will allow "essential equivalence" to deteriorate. If anything, the Reagan administration's efforts will reverse the slow decline of the 1970s. The United States has the economic and technological base to do that, and its leaders seem to have the will. Only the United States and the USSR have the capacity for global power projection; China does not, nor, now, does even Britain. Barring true European unity, *only* the United States and the Soviet Union can run the nuclear race. Any Soviet and U.S. success in constructing space-based antimissile systems will have the effect—and perhaps the intent—only of reinforcing their nuclear duopoly. A working superpower SDI would drastically reduce the effectiveness of small, less sophisticated missile forces. Moreover, if the Soviet Union had an effective SDI, the U.S. nuclear umbrella, as a means of covering its allies, would be thoroughly degraded: a U.S. threat of first use of nuclear weapons would lose its last shred of plausibility. No Japanese eminence in high-tech electronics or rocketry can, without truly enormous expense, allow Japan to compete in that league. At best, non-superpowers can produce some modest shifts in the conventional military balance in their areas; they cannot, in this century, hope to play the nuclear game against the leaders.

The United States' cultural hegemony is not amenable to the precise measures familiar in the strategic literature, but I fail to see powerful signs of its imminent decline. (The conference from which the papers in this volume resulted, conducted in English and centrally concerned with the concepts and hypotheses of American social science, attests to its continued vitality.) American culture will continue to assimilate the elements of other cultures and so will become more international, but the solid rooting of that culture in American political, social, and economic norms will remain.

The most substantial, though not precipitate, decline is likely to be in the realm of international economics. The United States is caught in a scissors between the growth in Soviet military might and the rise of Japan and the EC as economic competitors; the effect is to reduce U.S. ability to pay the military costs. Ultimately an economic decline will erode the military and cultural dimensions as well. Conversely, the decay of U.S. economic dominance is likely to be hastened by efforts to retain great military power. Military expenditures at 6 per cent or more of U.S. GNP (as compared with 1 per cent for Japan) must sap U.S. economic vitality by diverting funds from productive investment and scientific endeavor from the fields of high-technology civilian needs in which Japan can effectively compete.[48] The long-term unsustainability of such heavy U.S. military expenditures makes it imperative, if Japanese-American cooperation is to be maintained, that Japan find some way of increasing its contribution to Western security. Perhaps that can be largely through development assistance if a much greater Japanese military role is not politically acceptable.

The Soviet Union has never quite been a top-level player in the economic realm. In fact, the impact of the United States' relative economic decline in the world at large has been cushioned by Soviet economic failures. The United States' hegemony has been too substantial for bipolarity or multipolarity to be an adequate representation of reality. Perhaps for this reason, cooperation among major states has been more apparent, and conflict more muted, than in the realm of military affairs. If so, a continued U.S. decline may portend a greater increase in conflict. The decline cannot be so severe as to produce equality of Japanese and American GNPs until well into the twenty-first century, even at very disparate growth rates (for example, 5 per cent per annum for Japan and 1 per cent for the United States). But continuing disparate rates of economic growth, even if not dramatically different, will bring approximate equality of the two big capitalist economies.

At some stage, the continued decline of U.S. hegemony will begin to have severe effects on the international system. There will be a lag in the relationship between declining power base and declining influence over outcomes because it is easier to maintain a system or regime than to establish it in the first place and because many elements of contemporary international regimes are quite robust.[49] Moreover, we do not know how the decline will be manifested or what the functional relationship will be. A smooth, relatively linear relationship between power base decline and influence decline would give decision makers time to adjust and to try to construct alternative regimes or alternative means to sustain existing regimes. If, rather, there is a distinctly nonlinear relationship or a reasonably sharp inflection point, the results would be much more unsettling. Talk of the relationship between those two variables alone ignores the potential shocks from other kinds of international change. A regime that was weakened by a steadily changing power relationship could be thrown sharply into disarray by a shock it might earlier have absorbed. Such imaginable, if not likely, shocks include a close Sino-Soviet rapprochement, a major U.S. military intervention or political defeat somewhere in the world, and a severe disruption to Middle Eastern oil supplies at a time when oil is in short supply.

It becomes important, therefore, to ask how the effects of declining hegemony may be managed, both by the declining hegemon itself and by its nearest "challenger," Japan. In this context, the term *challenger* is not really appropriate. Japan may challenge the United States' economic leadership, but it is unlikely to challenge its military superiority. Japan and the United States do not have sufficient conflicts of interest for us to imagine them, in the foreseeable future, as military antagonists. Their interests converge more than they conflict. Each has an enormous interest in maintaining an international order organized around liberal political and economic principles—democracy and free-market open-trading economics. They will not always interpret those principles identically, nor will their national systems converge totally. But the basic, and overwhelming, convergence of interests is apparent.

To say that they share great common interests is not to say that they necessarily will be able to cooperate enough to serve those interests. We have *some* theory and experience concerning the possibility of "power transitions" in international politics, but the notion of power transition has dubious relevance to this case. Most power transitions have come as the result of war, either from a challenger's defeating a hegemon or a new hegemon's arising when both former hegemon and former challenger are exhausted from war. Another Japanese-American war hardly seems likely, and if there should be a Soviet-U.S. war, the matter of subsequent power transition would be of little interest—the destructiveness of such a war would make our concepts of the international system utterly obsolete.

Largely peaceful power transitions in international politics are rarer; even at the point early in this century when the United States passed Britain, that passage was assisted by the cost of British exertions in World War I. As I noted above, an exchange of first and second economic positions between Japan and the United States is less likely, in peacetime, than is an extended period of approximate parity marked by coexistence, muted though not absent competition, and some active cooperation in pursuit of shared goals. The historical precedents for such an experience are meager. (Soviet-U.S. détente was stillborn; the Concert of Europe after 1815 was largely a multilateral rather than a bilateral détente.) The lack of fully appropriate models should be sobering; the situation has probably been rare because it is not easy to achieve and maintain.[50] Such a situation is poorly captured by terms like *leader* and *challenger* or by standard theories of multipolar systems. Cooperation is not anticipated by the usual "realist" theories of international relations. Collective goods theory and game theory emphasizing situations like the prisoners' dilemma also point to difficulties in the way of cooperation.

Yet there also are theoretical reasons not to dismiss the possibilities too readily. Constructive influences ignored in most "realist" analyses— like ties of communication and community—can be encouraged by deliberate effort. Game theoretic analyses stressing conditions of repeated interaction, and thus the strategic rationality of actors, give grounds for encouragement. States may anticipate that although free-riding may provide them with short-term gains, their noncooperation will induce collapse of the regime, and so they may continue to cooperate. Goods once provided by a large power who dominated all other powers may later be provided by collective action among the two or three largest members.[51] If, therefore, the decline in U.S. hegemony results less from a markedly slow U.S. growth rate than from a relatively rapid Japanese growth rate, the prospects for cooperation may be more promising. The potential benefits from cooperation are worth further theorizing, a search for relevant evidence, and planning.

Koichi Hamada and Hugh T. Patrick

Japan and the International
Monetary Regime

The international monetary regime, the set of rules that governs the monetary mechanism of international trade and investment, is one of the foundations of the world economy. The development of every national economy is conditioned by the way the international monetary regime is arranged, and every major economy has contributed, though with different degrees of importance, to its evolution. The Japanese economy is no exception. This paper reviews the postwar development of the international monetary regime and Japan's growing involvement, evaluates the efficacy and viability of the current flexible exchange-rate regimes, and speculates on the possibility of the future reform of the international monetary regime as viewed across the Pacific.

The United States played the dominant role in the postwar evolution of the international monetary regime. In the Bretton Woods system, particularly in its practice, the United States was such an important leader that, before Nixon's New Economic Policy in 1971, the Bretton Woods system was called the "dollar standard." However weak it was, the link between the value of currencies and gold remained a link between the dollar and gold. The dollar was the major, if not the only, vehicle currency. This U.S. leadership role declined after the breakdown in 1971–73 of the Bretton Woods regime, that is, the old IMF regime. European countries have come to play an increasingly important role, and in the past decade Japan has played a relatively significant role. The United States, however, continues to be the leader in the sense that changes in rules cannot occur without its cooperation. The best example of this is the intervention after September 1985 of the Group of Five (the United States, Great Britain, West Germany, France, and Japan), which was organized under the leadership of the United States and reflected a major shift from the earlier policy of nonintervention in currency markets.

The United States has also been an important actor over the past several years in a different respect. The dollar was overvalued for several years (from 1980 to at least mid-1986), in terms of trade flows and of the structure of the U.S. economy, largely because of the domestic macroeconomic policy of a highly expansionary fiscal policy combined with a restrictive monetary policy, which led to high real and nominal interest rates. Excessive spending in relation to production (typically stated in macro-terms as more investment than saving but more precisely a reflection of the immense and rising federal budget deficits) created high interest rates and a huge and growing current-account deficit that had to be financed by huge capital inflows. This caused serious concern in many parts of the world. The United States is still special in the world economy because of its leadership role, because of its huge size, and because, unlike every other country, foreigners were and are still willing to hold large amounts of their wealth in dollar-denominated financial claims, even though they assume substantial foreign exchange risks in the process.

For its part, Japan was a negligible player and passive accepter of the international monetary system in the 1950s and 1960s. Then, in the early 1970s, Japan emerged as a country with some destabilizing impact on the system and even as a catalyst for change. In the 1980s, Japan has become one of the major actors in the system, given its immense financial involvement in the rest of the world and burgeoning current-account surpluses and concomitant net capital outflows. Joint intervention to affect the value of the dollar (particularly vis-à-vis the yen) now requires the support of the Japanese monetary authorities as well as the U.S. authorities.

In 1949, during the Occupation, Japan fixed its exchange rate at $1 to ¥360. Under the old IMF adjustable-peg system (the Bretton Woods regime), Japan adhered strictly to this exchange rate until 1971, when President Nixon announced the New Economic Policy that cut the already weakening link between the dollar and gold completely. In addition, for the Japanese economy, which relies almost completely on foreign energy sources, the formation of OPEC's petroleum cartel was a heavy blow. The Japanese economy coped with these environmental changes by energy saving programs and by contractionary macroeconomic policies, although at the cost of a substantial slowdown in output growth since the mid-1970s in comparison with the superfast growth of the 1950s and 1960s. These relatively successful adjustment processes were accomplished under the flexible exchange-rate regime. Now Japan, like many other nations, seeks a better international monetary regime, though that will be difficult to devise.

The general attitude of the Japanese government as well as the Japanese public toward the international monetary regime has been rather passive. After the wartime destruction, the Japanese economy occupied only a tiny place in the world. It was generally conceived of as an economy closely associated with, and often subordinate to, the U.S. economy. The favorite phrase was When the United States sneezes, Japan catches pneumonia. Japan was completely under U.S. hegemony in the economic as well as the political sense.

During the period of rapid economic growth in the 1960s, the relative importance of the Japanese economy increased substantially, although the Japanese public still perceived of it as lagging behind.[1] However, Japan's sudden and large balance of payments current-account surplus and the reluctance of the Japanese government to revalue the yen were among the main factors that triggered Nixon's drastic adoption of the New Economic Policy. Because of its increased role in the world economy, Japan functioned as a pivotal element in this critical change in the international monetary regime.

In this sense, not only has Japanese economic development been supported by the international superstructure or overhead capital (namely, the international monetary regime), but the growing presence of Japan has influenced the evolution of the international monetary regime. This observation is reinforced by the effect of the Group of Five's interventions in September 1985, whose impact on exchange rates, particularly that of the yen, was much greater than anticipated. Subsequently, the Japanese began to recognize the extent of the repercussions of their own domestic policymaking on the world economy.

The methodology utilized in this paper is an extension of the political-economy approach of Hamada.[2] First, we specify the cost-benefit structure that an international monetary regime brings to participating countries and explore the questions What kind of international monetary regime do participating countries desire, and what kind of international monetary regime is likely to be realized, given the potential cost-benefit structures implied by various regimes? An international monetary regime, and more generally any international regime, can be regarded as a public good. The main goal of this approach is to study how to create the mechanism for providing an international monetary regime with proper incentives for participating countries.

In the first section, we briefly describe the development of the postwar international monetary regime. We discuss why the adjustable-peg system collapsed, and how this collapse affected the development of the Japanese economy. Then, we describe how the flexible exchange-rate regime among major industrial countries has worked in the past decade and how Japanese monetary authorities conducted their intervention (or occasionally nonintervention) policy in the exchange market.

In the second section, we provide a general assessment of the ongoing flexible exchange-rate system. Much can be said in favor of the partly managed flexible exchange-rate system. Unlike the adjustable-peg system, the system has not led to many crises in foreign exchange markets. Pressures in foreign exchange markets have not resulted in increasing controls on capital flows or on trade flows, as was often the case under the old IMF regime. Accordingly, the system has supported a relatively open international trade system as well as an open international financial system. Thus, the current system may be judged as satisfying the minimum requirement for an appropriate international monetary regime. However, movements in real and nominal exchange rates have been highly volatile, and some economists point out the possibility of misalignment from reasonably defined equilibrium exchange rates. They suspect that the degree of observed volatility may be greater than that required to accommodate smooth resource allocations through trade and capital movements. Moreover, misalignment and the huge trade deficit have resulted in substantially increased protectionist pressures in the United States. Determining the actual situation—whether and how much the market exchange rates have been misaligned—is, however, difficult.

In the third section, we discuss, as a digression, some of the short- to intermediate-run policy measures the Japanese government could take. We examine the pros and cons of various devices to cope with the currently pressing issue of Japan's accumulating current-account surplus, including import liberalization, exchange rate policy, expansive fiscal policy, and more focused incentives to increase investment.

In the final section, we explore the possibility of future reforms in the international monetary regime. There would be little merit in returning to the adjustable-peg system or to a stricter fixed exchange-rate system or to a gold standard. However, there may be some room to realize alternative ideas for reforms: for example, (1) to stabilize exchange rates and price levels by coordinating monetary policies among the major nations; (2) to oblige monetary authorities to pursue interventionist policies to contain exchange rates within a prescribed zone; or (3) to let monetary authorities compete in making profits by (presumably) stabilizing interventions. Then, we apply a political-economic analysis (the calculus of participation) to speculate what kinds of regimes or reforms, if any, are more likely to be adopted, and we consider the role of Japan in this political process.

Historical Development

The Bretton Woods adjustable-peg system prevailed in the postwar international economy until 1971. In May 1971, the German and Dutch monetary authorities abandoned fixed parity for the mark and guilder and moved to floating exchange rates. The Japanese monetary authorities strongly resisted revaluating the yen, despite Japan's accumulating large surplus in its balance of payments. In August, President Nixon announced his New Economic Policy, which cut the already weakening link between the dollar and gold and placed a 10 per cent surcharge on imports to the United States, notably imports of manufactured goods. This policy was widely seen as aimed particularly, though by no means exclusively, at Japan.

The basic principles of the Bretton Woods regime as originally conceived were as follows.

1. Exchange rates were normally fixed but could be changed up to 10 per cent. A country could adjust its exchange rate by more than 10 per cent if its balance of payments was judged as being in a "fundamental disequilibrium," which was not formally defined.

2. The dollar was linked to gold at a fixed parity. The confidence in the dollar was supported by this link. The United States supplied the liquidity for international transactions and for the growth of foreign exchange reserves by providing dollars by increasing its short-term liabilities to the rest of the world. In this sense, this was a gold exchange–standard system, based on the dollar rather than on the pound as had been the case before World War I and in the 1920s.

3. The adjustment of the balance of payments was primarily conducted by macroeconomic policies of the nonreserve countries (namely, all countries other than the United States) and supplemented by the occasional realignment of exchange rates.

Early on, Robert Triffin pointed to the liquidity dilemma as the fundamental instability in the Bretton Woods regime.[3] To satisfy the increasing demand for international reserves, the United States would eventually undermine foreign confidence in the dollar because its gold-liability ratio would decline. The link between the dollar and gold was broken de facto during the 1960s. The dollar-based gold exchange system turned into a dollar-standard system where the dollar was valued not because it was supported by gold but because it functioned as a medium of international payments.

An implicit principle of the dollar-standard system was that the United States would maintain domestic price stability, which would result in international price stability. In other words, the implicit quid pro quo for an increase in the U.S. dollars held by foreigners was a U.S. commitment to price stability. Robert Mundell advocated the following assignment of policies under the dollar standard: the United States adjusts its money supply so as to stabilize the international price level, and Europe and Japan (the rest of the world) adjust their money supplies to maintain balance-of-payments equilibrium.[4] This application of his celebrated principle of policy instruments works well so long as these rules are observed.

In the context of this policy-assignment argument, the degree of price stability in the United States was thus regarded as desirable by, or at least as acceptable to, the rest of the world. Those countries that, for whatever reasons, adopted policies of higher rates of inflation were able to devalue their currency from time to time under the adjustable-peg system (as, for example, France and Italy did). The problem, however, was West Germany in the 1950s and 1960s; it wanted a lower rate of domestic price increases, and its macroeconomic policies combined with good growth performance to generate substantial current-account surpluses and increases in foreign exchange reserves. There was strong pressure on Germany to expand its domestic macroeconomic policy, but the Germans resisted. This "German" problem spread to other countries in the late 1960s as the United States financed the Vietnam war through inflationary means and as Japan's current-account surpluses grew substantially. Moreover, de Gaulle and France were unwilling to finance the United States by holding dollars since France, too, had started to run current-account surpluses and came to insist increasingly that it be allowed to convert dollars into gold. The United States exercised moral suasion on other countries, particularly on Japan and to some degree on Germany, but this brought to the fore the problem that had worried Triffin earlier. To some extent, it reflected an unwillingness to go along with U.S. macroeconomic policy, not only for reasons of price stability but for political reasons over the United States' use of its assets to engage in the Vietnam war.

Thus, the question was whether there were sufficient incentives for national authorities to pursue the set of policies implicitly assigned to them in the Bretton Woods system. For Japan (or the rest of the world), incentives existed to adopt contractionary policies when the balance of payments was in deficit, and accordingly the system was binding. However, Japan, or more empirically relevant Germany, did not always have an incentive to adopt expansionary policies when the balance of payments was in surplus. Nor did the United States necessarily have the incentive to play the role of a benevolent leader by adjusting its macroeconomic policies to keep the world price level constant.

In fact, two of the major reasons why the Bretton Woods regime collapsed are that the rest of the world did not play the game symmetrically with respect to booms and recessions and that the United States, particularly after its involvement in Vietnam, came to be concerned not so much with world price stability as with its own national policy objectives.[5]

Japanese policymakers were strongly committed to the fixed exchange parity before Nixon's New Economic Policy. Japanese government officials were proud that since 1949 Japan had not changed the exchange parity to the dollar. Japan was, and liked to think of itself as, an "honor student" in the (old) IMF regime. Japanese policymakers apparently never conceived of using changes in the exchange rate as an instrument of balance-of-payments policy until such action was forced on them after 1971. After all, although some of Japan's balance-of-payments deficits in the 1950s and 1960s resulted from an overheated economy, there were occasions when the deficit was a consequence of changes in the external environment (world recession, the Suez crisis). It might have been reasonable at those periods for Japan to devalue rather than slow down the growth rate through restrictive policies. One reason for this was a sense of prestige: a successful, civilized country did not engage in exchange rate devaluations (though France had, and indeed England had in 1949). Another reason might have been an acute realization that Japan was beginning to expand in world markets, that it had had difficulty obtaining access to foreign markets (many countries continued to restrict Japanese imports under the GATT Article 35 exemption), and that any Japanese devaluations would have been taken as a beggar-my-neighbor policy and were not politically desirable because of the possibility of retaliation.

At the beginning of the 1970s, the adherence of the Japanese government to the fixed parity of $1 to ¥360 was too extreme. The mere discussion of flexible exchange rates was virtually a taboo in the mass media. Even Japanese economists, including one of us, went no further than a lukewarm proposal of a crawling peg for the yen. Whereas most countries that had been under the fixed exchange rates immediately closed their foreign exchange markets on President Nixon's announcement and shifted to floating exchange rates a week or so later, Japan alone kept its foreign exchange market open. As a result, the Bank of Japan bought about $4 billion at the overpriced exchange rate of ¥360, incurring a huge loss for Japanese taxpayers. Finally, the monetary authorities gave in, and the yen was allowed to float and appreciate. Some policymakers seemed to believe that trying to support the old dollar value would be appreciated as conduct faithful to the principle of the (old) IMF regime.[6]

Careful consideration is necessary to clarify the welfare effect of this purchase of dollars during fall 1971. At that time, Japan imposed severe exchange controls that prohibited foreigners from purchasing yen assets with dollars; only Japanese corporations (mainly trading companies and the shipbuilding companies, which had huge dollar claims outstanding through deferred sales of ships) were allowed to do so. Under such circumstances, the exchange rate policy was a measure by which the Japanese government deliberately shifted the costs of exchange rate appreciation from private business engaged in international trade to the government. One might argue that this was not wrong since those companies had been operating under a set of rules of the game they believed to be inviolate that were suddenly changed. Moreover, a number of trading companies might have otherwise gone bankrupt, with serious spillover effects on the domestic economy as well as on Japan's foreign trade capabilities. In this sense at least, the policy of shifting the burden from the private sector to the government might well have been stabilizing. (Note that this occurred only at a time when a major change in the rules of the game was completely unanticipated.) Needless to say, however, the taxpayer eventually had to bear the burden shifted to the government.

There was a short interlude of new fixed exchange rates (with a new parity of $1 to ¥308) with a wider band of permissible fluctuations. Known as the Smithsonian system, this regime lasted from December 1971 to February 1973. The momentum toward flexible rates had already passed the point of no return, however. The resurgence of financial crises in Europe and the increased demand for the yen made it necessary for Japanese monetary authorities to join in adopting flexible exchange rates in February 1973. Japan adopted the flexible exchange-rate system over a weekend, at a time when all the other major countries were taking the same action. This action demonstrated that monetary authorities could act swiftly when forced to by external events. At that time, it would have been senseless for Japan to keep the yen pegged to the dollar or to any other currency.

As Mundell argued, some monetary coordination was indispensable to the proper functioning of the fixed exchange-rate system. The Bretton Woods regime failed because the system did not have sufficient incentive mechanisms.

Because of the cost-benefit structure of the game of choosing an international regime, crisis often becomes the catalyst for financial reforms.[7] In the game of choosing or agreeing on a rule, the present system or status quo continues as long as there is no agreement. Institutional reforms are realized when the current status quo becomes intolerable for the participating countries. Richard Cooper has argued that rule changes frequently come about de facto as a result of gradually changing economic circumstances.[8] Only later are those changes in the implicit rules specified and codified. Many international monetary crises between 1971 and 1983 brought on the change from the dollar-standard system to flexible exchange rates.

The adoption of flexible exchange rates was not the result of a coordinated, planned, and deliberate decision of the participating countries. Rather, it was a necessary escape from an impasse and a measure against an emergency. Only in 1976 in Jamaica did the IMF interim committee agree on the basic rules of the international monetary system and allow adoption of flexible exchange rates. The flexible exchange-rate sys-

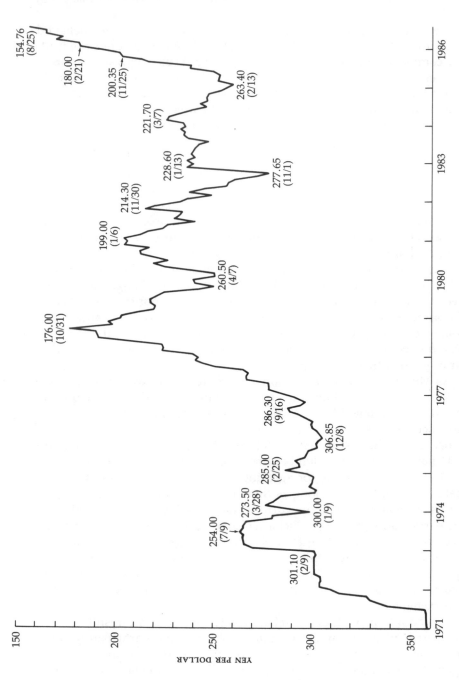

Fig. 1. Yen-dollar exchange rate (spot-closing rate in the Tokyo market), 1971–1986.

tem itself does not, at least prima facie, call for any cooperation between governments. The direct link among price levels in the participating countries that had existed under the adjustable-peg system was ended by the adoption of flexible exchange rates. Except for more subtle linkages,[9] the primary economic linkages resulting from synchronized price levels were virtually severed. Each national monetary authority recovered substantial control over monetary policy. The rules of the game do not bind participating countries very tightly. As a first approximation, the flexible exchange-rate system can be termed a "nonsystem."[10]

Needless to say, the system adopted by the major industrial countries after February 1973 is not a freely floating exchange-rate system. Of the different kinds of floating systems, one is that of the clean float (completely flexible exchange rates) in which supply and demand determine the exchange rate without intervention by the monetary authorities of any country and without exchange rate controls. Another is very short-term intervention when markets are disorderly; typically the stabilizing intervention lasts only for a matter of hours or at most a few days. In the managed float system, central banks systematically intervene in the market to affect the exchange rate; intervention either results in an undervalued currency (beggar-my-neighbor) or maintains an overvalued currency. The monetary authorities of most industrial countries have intervened to smooth out short-term fluctuations and occasionally to influence the direction of exchange rates. If various national monetary authorities simultaneously engage in foreign exchange interventions, then the monetary interdependence observed under fixed exchange rates reappears to some degree and creates the possibility of strategic interaction.[11]

As it evolved in the 1970s, the flexible exchange-rate system was at first a floating arrangement among the major nations: the United States, Great Britain, Japan, Canada, and the European Community. The European Community tried to establish a fixed exchange-rate mechanism among their currencies (or at least an adjustable-peg system) in the form of the European Monetary System, such that their rates floated against non-EC currencies but not against each other's (except within the band in which the snake danced). Finally, most of the developing countries chose to peg their exchange rate to that of a major trading partner, to the IMF-based special drawing rights (SDR) unit, or to a trade-weighted basket. Some of the countries pursued flexible or crawling-peg rates (for example, Brazil) because of internal circumstances, particularly when internal inflation rates were high.

Since 1971, the yen-dollar exchange rate has fluctuated widely, and the level of international reserves held by the Japanese monetary authorities has tended upward (see figs. 1 and 2). Has intervention by the

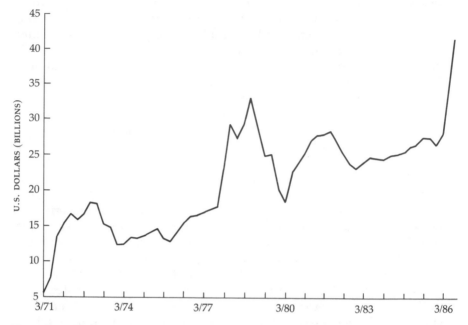

Fig. 2. Japan's international reserves, 1971–1986.

Japanese monetary authorities helped stabilize the value of the yen? Since interest payments accrue to international reserves, the reserves should increase slightly even without intervention. With this minor caveat, the increase (or decrease) in reserves implies net buying (or selling) interventions. Thus, Figure 2 adequately reflects the general trends and fluctuations of interventions.

For government interventions to be stabilizing, they should normally be profitable; that is, a government should purchase its own currency (sell foreign currency) when its own currency is appreciating and should sell its currency when it is depreciating. The massive purchase of dollars during the disorderly period of 1971 was definitely destabilizing.[12] Some sales during 1973 may have been destabilizing as well. Since that time, however, the Japanese monetary authorities have often engaged in stabilization by selling the dollar when it reached a peak and buying when it reached a trough. From 1974 to 1976, the movement of the yen exchange rate was moderate, and the intensity of interventions was weak. From the latter half of 1977 to late 1978, however, the monetary authorities bought dollars (sold yen), even though the yen was appreciating. This "leaning against the wind" caused controversy with the United States since Japan's global and bilateral current-account surplus increased sharply and unexpectedly.[13] However, the appreciation eventually became excessive. When the dollar hit a record low in 1978, Japan's international reserves reached a historical high. After an announcement of joint action by the Japanese and U.S. monetary authorities, the exchange rate changed direction. This movement toward lower values for the yen was reinforced by the second oil crisis. The pattern of buying the dollar at a trough and selling it at a peak generally continued until 1983.

It is not easy to determine whether interventions are stabilizing or not. Much depends on whether currencies come to be misaligned because of changes in fundamental factors or whether the exchange rate movements represent overshooting beyond an equilibrium rate. It is not always clear whether the monetary authorities should be reinforcing the direction of change ("leaning with the wind") or resisting it ("leaning against the wind").

Based on the familiar argument by Milton Friedman, Dean Taylor calculated the profits and losses accruing to interventions by monetary authorities and contended that monetary authorities were destabilizing the foreign exchange market. His dictum for private agents was to bet against the central bank in order to make profits and indirectly contribute to economic welfare.[14] Helmut Mayer and Hiroo Taguchi questioned the appropriateness of using profitability as the main criterion. They argued that the criteria for stabilization should be whether interventions help exchange rates approach the moving average trend of exchange rates and whether interventions, viewed *ex post*, succeed in leaning against the wind. They concluded that most of the interventions by Japan, Germany, and the United Kingdom had a stabilizing impact.[15]

To understand the movements among multiple exchange rates, where there are multiple sources of real and nominal disturbances and where expectations of market participants change endogenously in response to the rules of interventions—let alone to be able to identify the contribution of government interventions in the exchange market—one needs to develop analytical models further. It also should be emphasized that some important turning points in the yen-dollar exchange rate were induced by the announcement of joint actions by central bankers. By October 1978, for example, the value of the dollar had fallen to ¥176, less than half the ¥360 rate that had prevailed for more than 20 years before the collapse of the Bretton Woods regime. It seemed clear that the dollar was undervalued and the yen was overvalued. On November 1, 1978, the United States announced a policy package to defend the value of the dollar, based on separate consultations with West Germany, Switzerland, and Japan. Simultaneously with the U.S. announcement, the governor of the Bank of Japan held a press conference, at the unusual hour of 11:00 P.M., and announced an increase in the magnitude of a swap agreement between the United States and Japan as well as his intention to engage in a dollar-buying operation. These mutual announcements had a dramatic and immediate effect on the yen exchange rate.

This joint action seems to have been successful because it was a joint decision involving action by both Japan and the United States and because private participants in the foreign exchange market perceived that the yen was indeed overvalued. The market was very susceptible to a signal from the monetary authorities reinforcing its concern that perhaps the yen had appreciated too much. Certainly, the unusual degree of appreciation of the real exchange rate was a factor that made market participants suspicious of the existing market rates.

In some instances, however, coordinated interventions have not had much impact. In early August 1983, for example, joint intervention did not halt the strengthening of the dollar. The reasons for this failure require further research. At the time, the movement of the real exchange rate was not marked. In fact, the real exchange rate as computed by various indexes showed a more mixed picture than it had in 1978 when every dollar index had moved downward.

During 1983 and 1984, exchange rate movements became less volatile, and there is little evidence of substantial interventions. Until September 1985, the United States enunciated a policy of nonintervention. After 1983, the Japanese monetary authorities appeared to have shifted from a managed float to almost a clean float.

During 1982–86, however, Japan's overall current-account surplus, the United States' overall current-account deficit, and Japan's bilateral current-account surplus with the United States began to grow to huge levels (see Table 1). By 1985, the United States was no longer willing to accept its intolerably large and rapidly growing trade and current-account deficits, and not surprisingly it associated much of its trade problems with Japan's burgeoning success. The macroeconomic sources of these deficits and surpluses can be classified into (1) differences in respective phases in the business cycle; (2) changes in relative prices of exports and imports as reflected in an increasingly overvalued dollar and undervalued yen; and (3) changes in production and spending behavior and policies (private and public spending, savings, and investment) in the two countries.

In our view, the fundamental cause was the basic structural and policy situation in each country (the absorption approach); the fluctuations in nominal and real exchange rates were of lesser importance.[16] Indeed, exchange rates can be viewed as largely reflecting underlying structural conditions and respective macroeconomic policies and the expectations of market participants regarding the future course of these factors; even so, an overvalued dollar and undervalued yen surely made the huge

TABLE 1
*United States and Japan, Balance-of-Payments Surplus or Deficit
and Government Budget Deficit, 1970–1986*
(U.S. $ billions)

	Global current account				U.S. current-account deficit with Japan		Central government budget deficit (per cent of GNP)	
	Japan		U.S.		Current account surplus	Per cent U.S. deficit	Japan	U.S.
	Amount	Per cent GNP	Amount	Per cent GNP				
1970	$1.97	1.0%	$2.331	0.2%	$−0.857	*	−0.5%	−0.3%
1971	5.797	2.5	−1.433	−0.0	−2.750	191.9%	−1.5	−2.2
1972	6.624	2.3	−5.795	−0.5	−4.782	82.5	−1.3	−2.0
1973	−0.136	−0.0	7.140	0.5	−1.631	*	−1.6	−1.2
1974	−4.693	−1.0	1.962	0.1	−1.048	*	−1.6	−0.4
1975	−0.682	−0.1	18.116	1.1	−1.372	*	−3.6	−3.5
1976	3.68	0.6	4.207	0.2	−5.286	*	−4.3	−4.3
1977	10.928	1.7	−14.511	−0.7	−8.149	56.2	−5.2	−2.8
1978	16.534	1.9	−15.427	−0.7	−11.676	75.7	−5.2	−2.7
1979	−8.693	−0.8	−0.991	−0.0	−8.6	867.8	−6.0	−1.6
1980	−10.746	−1.1	1.873	0.1	−9.1	*	−5.9	−2.8
1981	4.770	0.4	6.339	0.2	−14.1	*	−5.0	−2.6
1982	6.850	0.6	−8.051	−0.3	−15.8	196.2	−5.2	−4.1
1983	20.799	1.8	−45.994	−1.4	−18.3	39.9	−4.8	−6.3
1984	35.00	2.7	−107.358	−2.8	−37.7	35.1	−4.3	−5.0
1985	49.169	3.7	−117.7	−2.8	−45.2	41.3	−3.9	−5.4
1986	86.970	4.2	−140.6	−3.3	−55.9	39.8	−3.8[a]	−4.8[b]

SOURCES: Various issues of Bank of Japan, *Economic Statistical Annual* and *Balance of Payments Monthly*; *Economic Report of the President*; U.S. Department of Commerce, *Survey of Current Business*.
NOTES: An asterisk in the sixth column indicates opposite relationship; a minus sign indicates current-account deficit. Japan-U.S. bilateral current account based on U.S. data; Japan's surplus is equivalent to the U.S. deficit.
[a]Ministry of Finance estimate.
[b]Office of Management and the Budget estimate.

trade imbalances that developed in the 1980s even more extreme. More precisely, Japan's current-account surplus was a consequence of the tendency for private saving to outstrip private investment demand while government budget deficits, so large in the latter half of the 1970s, were being reduced. With low interest rates at home, Japanese were eager to accumulate net wealth abroad. In the United States, the major change in the domestic macroeconomic balance lay in the rapidly increasing and ultimately immense federal budget deficit, far beyond the capacity of domestic savings to finance if it were also to finance domestic private investment. Monetary policy achieved price stability, in part by maintaining relatively high interest rates, especially in real terms; those interest rates attracted foreign capital to finance, indirectly at least, up to one-half the federal budget deficit, with a concomitant inflow of imports of goods and services in excess of exports.

Many economists place greater, and more direct, emphasis on exchange rates, arguing that the huge U.S. trade deficit and Japanese sur-

plus resulted from the overvaluation of the dollar, that is, the misalignment of exchange rates. As shown in Figure 3, the yen's real exchange
rate vis-à-vis the dollar tended to depreciate from 1980 until 1985. This
tendency was stronger in terms of the wholesale price index than of the
consumer price index. Compared with the 1975 level, the real exchange
rate in terms of unit labor costs declined sharply. This suggests that Japanese manufactured products gained substantial competitiveness during
1975–85.

Then came the fascinating experiment of the Group of Five. The finance ministers of the five countries announced their intent to intervene
in the foreign exchange market (the Plaza Agreement of September 22,
1985). As a result, the value of the dollar dropped by 37 per cent from
¥243 in September 1985 to ¥153 in September 1986.

The effects of the intervention on various currencies were uneven.
During the year after the joint intervention, the British pound appreciated only a little against the dollar. The West German mark appreciated
substantially. The yen appreciated by some 59 per cent against the dollar

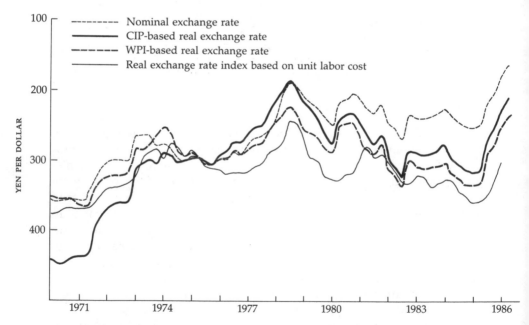

Fig. 3. Japan's real exchange rates, 1970–1986 (yen/$). CPI, WPI, and the unit labor cost
(relative normalized unit labor cost) are expressed on base 1975 = 100. Sources: International Monetary Fund, *International Financial Statistics*; Bank of Japan, *Economic Statistics
Annual*.

(viewed from the perspective of the yen). To what extent this revaluation of the yen was caused by the joint intervention remains unclear, and the reasons for the effectiveness of this intervention have yet to be explored. Here, we consider several possible reasons for the apparent success of the coordinated intervention since it is important not only for itself but also for what it tells us about the possibilities of successful intervention in the future.

First, the announcement was made in such a way as to maximize the feeling of surprise in the market. Joint actions were prepared in secrecy and announced on the weekend, when markets were closed. Japanese trading companies and financial institutions had been warned against excessive speculation in the form of accumulating credits in dollars, but whether they took this as a sign of future interventions is not clear. In any case, the announcement came as a surprise and indicated strongly that the Reagan administration had abandoned its policy of benign neglect by refraining from intervening in the market.

The amount of currency used in interventions by the Japanese central bank and other central banks has not been well publicized. Sam Cross, vice-president of the New York Federal Reserve Bank, revealed some fragmentary evidence on the magnitude of currency interventions by several governments.[17] According to him, from September 22 to the end of October 1985, U.S. monetary authorities sold about $3.2 billion, of which $1.4 billion was used to purchase yen. Other members of the Group of Five sold about $5 billion, and the other countries in the Group of Ten (the Group of Five plus Canada, Italy, Sweden, Belgium, and the Netherlands) intervened with about $2 billion. The currency composition of those interventions has not been reported.

Figures 4 and 5 show the movement of exchange rates and the changes in international reserves held by the Japanese monetary authorities in 1985 and 1986. If we neglect the accrual of interest payments, the changes in international reserves can be regarded as the amount of intervention. During September 1985, Japanese foreign exchange reserves decreased by about $1 billion. Cross described the sentiment of the Tokyo market after September 22:

During the next few days, there was some skepticism in the market that the lower dollar levels would be maintained, and a number of commercial customers responded to the apparently attractive rates by buying dollars. This phenomenon was most dramatic in Tokyo where, when the market opened on Tuesday, September 24, after a three-day weekend, dollar demand from corporations and investors spurred the largest turnover on record for spot dollar/yen trading. The Bank of Japan responded with massive dollar sales. . . . Following these and other operations in subsequent days by the Japanese and other G-5 central banks, market participants came to believe that the authorities were firmly committed to the joint effort and upward pressure on the dollar abated.[18]

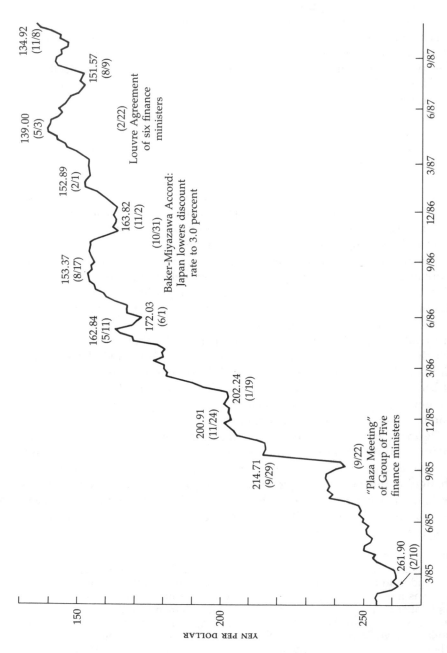

Fig. 4. Yen-dollar exchange rate (spot-closing rate in the Tokyo market), 1985–1986.

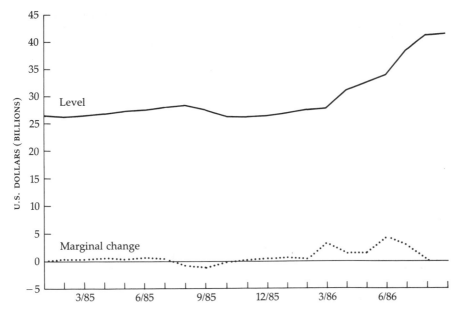

Fig. 5. Japan's international reserves (level and marginal change), 1985–1986.

Another factor in the success of the intervention was that the Bank of Japan did not adopt a policy of sterilizing the intervention. On the contrary, it maintained its contractionary monetary policy during 1985. On October 24, it let short-term interest rates on bonds jump from 5.6 per cent to 6.3 per cent, causing a panic in the newly established futures trading market in government bonds.

The strength of the leadership of the governor of the Bank of Japan after September 1985 was impressive. He (and perhaps the finance minister) strongly signaled their intention to let the yen appreciate and *not* to reduce interest rates until the yen had appreciated significantly and until interest rates in the United States had declined sufficiently to narrow the interest differential. The several shocks to the Japanese financial markets—the initial strong intervention, the October 24 decision to allow interest rates on bonds to climb, and other measures taken to heighten uncertainty—clearly had a severe impact on expectations. The uncertainty concerning the price range and the timing of the Bank of Japan's interventions made it difficult for the renewed capital outflow that one might expect, given the continuing (real) interest rate differentials between Japan and the United States, to occur.

In view of the strong impact compared to the relatively small scale of intervention, the effect was quite dramatic. The apparent efficacy of interventions can be explained only by taking into account its effect on the expectations of private agents. Presumably, the joint announcement after the secretive planning was made just at the time when the general public's belief in the strength of the dollar was about to erode. There had been many predictions of a sudden or gradual fall of the dollar, which had peaked in early March 1985, but market sentiment had not followed these predictions, until September when the Group of Five intervention provided a new impetus.

Once the balance of bearish and bullish expectations changed, the Japanese monetary authorities were able to ease their stance. On January 29, 1986, the Bank of Japan reduced the official discount rate from 5 per cent to 4.5 per cent. The value of the yen was not much affected, and it even showed some signs of a slight appreciation. Market participants seemed to consider that betting against the monetary authorities was too dangerous.

Moreover, the drastic decline in oil prices in late 1985 and the improvement in the terms of trade for Japan effected a further appreciation of the yen. Takatoshi Ito convincingly demonstrates, through an examination of hourly changes in exchange rates during a global business day of 24 hours, that the dominant determinants were the U.S. attitude toward exchange rates in September 1985, the Bank of Japan's high-interest-rate policy in late October, and the sharp decrease in oil prices after December 1985.[19]

General Assessment of the Present System

Despite its imperfections, the present system of flexible exchange rates does, in our opinion, provide an international monetary framework that satisfies minimum standards. The present system allows sufficient freedom to monetary authorities to pursue their own policies almost independently of the activities of the monetary authorities of other countries. We use the word *almost* because there are some positive or negative spillover effects even under the freely floating regime.[20] The intensity of interdependence, however, is indirect and of a second order compared with the intensity of interdependence in the fixed exchange-rate system, in which national price levels are directly linked. After the adoption of flexible exchange rates, the world economy came under the strong attacks of real disturbances, notably the two oil crises. Nonetheless, the present flexible exchange-rate system survived these disturbances without the financial panics experienced under the adjustable-peg system and without the imposition of exchange controls.

This recent experience has taught us, however, that the flexibility of exchange rates is not by itself a deus ex machina that can solve all external imbalances. Most of the earlier advocates of flexible exchange rates seemed to think that flexible exchange rates would balance current accounts; presumably, they assumed a world in which capital flows were not particularly large. In contrast, in the present world where capital mobility is nearly perfect, the flexibility of exchange rates does not equilibrate current accounts. Whereas goods markets are sluggish in adjusting, the foreign exchange market is a volatile market where the excess demand for outstanding stocks of foreign-denominated financial assets clears instantaneously. Moreover, goods markets are usually constrained by the past course of prices, but foreign exchange rates jump around in response to changes in expectations of future exchange rates and underlying macroeconomic variables. These differences are quite likely to give rise to a situation in which nominal exchange rates as well as the corresponding real exchange rates are quite different from the value that would balance current accounts.

The often-cited wide discrepancy between the real exchange rate and the rate that purchasing power parity theory predicts probably implies this kind of divergence. Divergence can occur when exogenous disturbances shift the equilibrium rate and asset markets react to them quickly while goods markets adjust only slowly.[21] In this case, even if the public were to find the right convergent path intuitively, the initial jump of the exchange rate would still be considerable. Divergence can also occur when the path diverges from the converging path to a "bubble path," where only instantaneous arbitrage conditions are set and transversality conditions[22] are not fulfilled.

The existence of a trade or a current-account surplus by no means implies a misalignment of exchange rates. If two or more nations have different ratios of time preferences and accordingly different saving ratios, the equilibrium growth path may imply continuing trade or current-account surpluses (or deficits). For example, in light of Japan's high personal savings ratio and the low U.S. savings ratio, a continuing Japanese current-account surplus and U.S. deficit is a plausible phenomenon, at least analytically if not politically (see below).[22]

Japan's current-account surplus and the United States' current-account deficit should be examined in global terms, not just in terms of the bilateral imbalance, because the efficient allocation of resources should be achieved globally rather than bilaterally and should be reflected in the global balance-of-payments position of each country. Moreover, it is not simply the difference in savings rates between two countries but the differences in rates of return on new investments that make it attractive to invest in one country or the other. Further complicating the case of the United States has been the Reagan administration's commitment to increasing total budget expenditures substantially, mainly for military purposes without a concomitant increase in tax revenues.

In any event, the difference in the speed of adjustment between goods markets and asset markets and the possibility of bubbles are often believed to make actual exchange rates diverge from the exchange rates that would govern some normal flow of international trade and investment. John Williamson utilizes the concept of a fundamental equilibrium exchange rate (FEER); that is, the exchange rate that would generate a current-account imbalance equal to the underlying net capital inflow or outflow.[24] This rate is presumably determined by fundamental factors. According to his calculations, in the first quarter of 1983 the U.S. dollar was overvalued by about 23 per cent and the Japanese yen was undervalued by 10 per cent from the FEER.[25] By early 1985 these deviations were substantially wider. He considers these misalignments to be even more important than the high degree of volatility in exchange rates.

According to Williamson, the costs of these misalignments and volatility are uncertainty in trade, distortion of consumption patterns, adjustment costs, unemployment, excess capacity, and pressures for protectionism. His argument would probably be true if some person or government could specify precisely the degree as well as the direction of misalignment. If that were possible, then the case for some form of managed float could easily be made.

The basic difficulty intrinsic to this problem is, however, that it is hard to determine very precisely whether the exchange rate is divergent from the level that the fundamentals would predict. There have been times, for example, 1982 or early 1985, when many people considered the yen-dollar exchange rate to be misaligned. During these periods, however, the yen remained relatively weak and the dollar strong. Market participants were aware of possible misalignments, but the market exchange rate did not change.

Another factor of importance is the ongoing and large difference in long-term interest rates between the United States and other countries, notably Japan. Added to that was the liberalization in Japan of portfolio restrictions on life insurance companies and pension funds to allow long-term investments in foreign assets. In early 1985, a portfolio manager for a Japanese life insurance company stated that his company focussed on the long-run yield over 20 years, to balance its requirements for payout periods, and that he regarded it as extremely unlikely that the yen would appreciate 5 per cent a year on average over 20 years, which was the difference in interest rate returns on long-term financial assets in Japan and the United States. His was apparently a good long-run investment strategy. However, it turned out to be a poor short-run investment strategy since the yen appreciated so much after Japanese insurance companies started purchasing dollar financial assets. (These losses were fortuitously offset in part by higher bond prices as U.S. interest rates declined.) Nonetheless, it does suggest that if the substantial interest rate gap for long-term assets persists, Japanese long-term financial institutions will continue to enter the market and demand dollars.

Needless to say, in international monetary matters that involve political negotiations, governments know what private agents do not know. If a government can use extra information to narrow deviations of its exchange rate from the FEER, then it could use its informational edge in interventions, thereby giving the right signals to market participants uncertain about the appropriateness of current exchange rates. The reason why the joint announcement of the Group of Five worked well in fall 1985 was probably that there was sufficient doubt about the continuing trend.[26] This also suggests interventions are most successful in extreme conditions, such as in November 1978 or September 1985, when expectations can easily be influenced.

The exchange rate system cannot be evaluated in isolation from its impact on other systemic components of the international economic system. Although perhaps not the fault of the flexible rate system—since the same imbalance might well have occurred under a fixed exchange rate or some other system—the large U.S. trade and current-account deficits in the 1980s (see Table 1) have profoundly adverse implications not only for the U.S. economy and for U.S.-Japan economic relations but for the international economic system as a whole. The two major systemic effects are the increase in protectionist sentiments and policies in the United States and the shift in the United States' position from the world's largest creditor nation to its largest debtor. During the same period, Japan emerged as the largest creditor nation in the world; most of its foreign assets are held in U.S. bonds and short-term financial instruments, but investment in equities, direct investment, including real estate, and other dollar-denominated claims are increasing. Although Japan began to be a creditor nation in the early 1970s, the tendency was masked by the two oil crises. Its emergence as a creditor nation in the 1980s was amplified and accelerated by the U.S. deficits.

The increase in United States protectionist sentiment and actions in the 1980s stems from many causes, analysis of which is beyond the scope of this paper. Surely the immense trade deficits contributed substantially to perceptions—correct or not—in the United States, particularly in Congress, that the U.S. economy was being seriously hurt and that the foreign trading system somehow did not treat U.S. participants fairly. In fact, the burgeoning trade deficits of the 1980s were primarily the unintended consequence of domestic macroeconomic policies, notably the tax cuts and the expansion of the federal budget after 1981. In retrospect, it was a profound policy error. One great danger is that the United States will shift to a substantially more protectionist position in trade policy by the end of the 1980s. That would have significantly adverse effects on the international trading system.[27] The experience of the 1980s raises a fundamental systemic question: Is it economically and politically possible to have both a free trading system and a system of free international financial flows? If the consequence is extreme trade imbalances (in amounts and as percentages of GNP) among the major participants, especially the United States, the answer may well turn out to be no. However, the problem is not the system of exchange rates and trade and capital flows per se but the underlying macroeconomic policies and structural conditions in each country.

The longer-run implications of the United States' becoming a huge debtor nation—say, $600–1,000 billion by 1990—and of Japan's becoming a major creditor nation—say, $450–600 billion by 1990—are only beginning to be understood. It is unclear how long and in what amounts these respective foreign debts (current-account deficits) and assets (current-account surpluses) will accumulate. What is clear is that even if these imbalances are eliminated completely, the adjustment process will take time, and at the minimum the respective debtor and creditor positions will be absolutely very large. Moreover, it is likely that a great preponderance of Japanese claims will be in dollars, and on the United States.

The interest, dividend, and profit income to be paid by the United States and received by Japan will become substantial and will affect the structural composition of merchandise and service trade in each country. Manufactured goods production and exports in the United States will grow rapidly relative to GNP, and manufactured goods production in Japan will slow down, with potentially significant effects on the structure of domestic production in each country. How much will depend on the cumulative size of the net debt or assets, foreign investment income flows, and the degree to which current-account imbalances persist.

The continuing net outflow of Japanese capital and the accumulation of such a large net foreign asset position will mean that both the Japanese government and Japanese private financial institutions will become a dominant player in world financial markets, a rapid quantitative and qualitative expansion of trends begun in the early 1980s. The yen will almost inevitably become an increasingly important reserve currency and transaction currency. Japanese financial institutions will have certain competitive advantages in assuming the management of these financial assets.

Such a large U.S.-Japan debtor-creditor position will inevitably make the bilateral relationship more complex and its management more complicated. A new, rather blunt, policy instrument will have been added to bilateral governmental negotiations. The situation will be fraught with danger because the possibilities of mutual damage are so great. A Japanese withdrawal of capital from the United States could precipitate a crisis in the United States of very high interest rates, recession, and a sharply declining dollar-yen exchange rate, but Japanese investors would concurrently take immense exchange losses. Actions by the United States that reduced the value of Japanese assets—by inflation, freezing, or other acts—would much reduce U.S. credibility. Even the threat to take such actions would sharply reduce confidence. Recognition of these costs might even result in greater cooperation in the bilateral bargaining game between the United States and Japan; the symbiotic relationship in defense and trade will gain a debt dimension. At any rate, this new debtor-creditor relationship almost certainly will become an important new element in the interrelationships among bilateral issues of trade, finance, investment, exchange rates, macroeconomic policies, and perhaps even defense.

Short-run to Intermediate Policy Alternatives for Japan

There are several policy areas in which the Japanese government may be able to contribute to the solution of current and intermediate-run problems.[28] The national income–accounting identity shows that the current-account surplus is a measure of the net surplus savings of the national economy as a whole; that is, the sum of private net savings and government net savings. Thus, an immediate and effective measure to reduce Japan's trade surplus would be to increase government expenditure or to reduce tax revenue, unless private net savings increase to offset completely the increase in government net absorption. Although some neo-Ricardian economists maintain that private spending offsets government action more or less completely (the rational expectations approach), we do not think that complete offset is a reality for either the Japanese or the U.S. economy. Accordingly, the Japanese current-account surplus will be reduced if Japanese fiscal policy becomes more expansionary. Changes in the exchange rate and terms of trade promote adjustment by affecting consumption as well as investment decisions. For example, substantially cheaper prices for imported goods encourage greater consumption and less saving by private savers. Nonetheless, the main point of our argument still remains; namely, changes in exchange rates and terms of trade do not reduce current-account surpluses unless they effectively influence the net surplus savings of the national economy.

Moreover, a policy of trade liberalization, including politically difficult sectors such as agriculture and services, should be welcomed for its own sake in order to promote efficiency and to benefit consumers. We certainly do not underestimate the importance of trade liberalization, but unless liberalization efforts affect the terms of trade strongly enough to change the net savings pattern of the national economy, the impact of such measures on Japan's current-account surplus will be modest.[29]

Foreign exchange interventions combined with contractionary monetary policy can have a considerable effect on the exchange rate, as exemplified by the Group of Five's interventions. However, by the same reasoning, in the case of trade liberalization, the effect on the current-account surplus will be limited without drastic real appreciation of the yen.

Of course, it is one thing to say that fiscal expansion is effective; it is quite another to say whether the political environment in Japan enables or forces the government to adopt more expansionary fiscal policies. Since 1981, Japan as an integral element of its administrative reform program has been undergoing a fiscal consolidation by reducing deficit financing in the budget; resistance to the misuse of resources in the government sector is strong. The Ministry of Finance has been reluctant to introduce any measures that would increase the general budget deficit. Unless foreign pressures for macroeconomic expansion counteract this resistance or unless Japan falls into a severe recession, Japanese fiscal measures are unlikely to be substantially expansionary. Moreover, during most of the early 1980s, the domestic need for fiscal stimulus was not obvious. After the Group of Five's intervention, the situation became somewhat different because of the slowdown in growth.[30] It is quite possible to imagine a scenario in which Japanese growth declines sharply after 1986 (to substantially less than 3 per cent) and business pressure builds for some expansionary fiscal policy—tax cuts or expenditure increases. Under these circumstances, the Japanese government should implement measures that minimize revenue losses and maximize the impact on domestic demand, in addition to the more conventional and straightforward macro fiscal policy instruments of tax cuts and increases in expenditures.

First, the corporate tax system could provide more incentives for new investment; for example, tax reductions for incremental investment increases used would encourage domestic investment with only moderate losses of tax revenues. Second, Japan could implement accelerated depreciation allowances to encourage domestic investment; the present Japanese corporate tax system does not provide particularly attractive investment incentives; early indications suggest the proposed tax reform legislation of 1987 is not likely to provide direct investment incentives either. (The first two measures are revivals of the supply-side policies—Japanese-style—of the early 1960s.)[31]

Third, some encouragement for consumer loans in the personal taxation system could be implemented, in particular, tax benefits for interest payments for residential construction to stimulate housing investments.

The tax code of 1985 allows only very minor deductions (below $750 per family a year) for the repayment of mortgage debt.

In summary, in the intermediate future, fiscal policy could be instrumental in reducing Japan's current-account surplus. The most desirable forms of fiscal expansion would not increase fiscal deficits excessively, even though some short-term deviation from the fiscal discipline of reducing budget deficits appears essential in order to expand domestic demand.

Thus, the solution to the current-account problem lies not so much in trade policy or exchange rate policy as in fiscal policy. The quest for a more stable exchange regime should be carried out for its own sake and not primarily for the purpose of solving the imbalance in the current account. This evaluation applies, mutatis mutandis, even more strongly to the United States, though of course the desirable direction of fiscal policy is the opposite.

The Possibility of Future Reform of the International Monetary Regime

What, then, is the scope for long-range reform of the international monetary regime, and what role can Japan play? We first list several alternative schemes for possible reforms and discuss the desirability of each. We then conclude by considering the feasibility of these schemes in the light of benefit-cost structures that they impose on the participating countries.

The current regime. Major industrialized countries float their currencies; small countries typically peg their currencies to that of a large trading partner or to some weighted average of exchange rates of major trading partners.[32] There are no fixed, agreed on rules for exchange interventions. Monetary authorities let market forces determine the values of their currencies in many instances, but occasionally intervene in exchange markets as an individual country or through joint actions. Sometimes these interventions have been effective in changing the tide of exchange rate movements. Sometimes they have not. As we argue above, the current system could be regarded as satisfying the minimum requirements for an international monetary system; in a sense, each country is allowed to take a reasonable max-min strategy by choosing its own relatively independent monetary policy.

Return to the adjustable-peg system. The history of the collapse of the Bretton Woods regime reveals the problems of the adjustable-peg system. The adjustable nature of the system works against the creation of credibility for the currently fixed parity; pegging intrinsically makes the smooth adjustment of the balance of payments difficult. The development of completely free international financial markets in the 1980s has made even easier not only the flow of capital but also the possibilities of speculation in foreign exchange markets whenever rates appear to be unrealistically pegged by governments. There is no desirable way to return to this old system.

Intervention based on profit motives. Friedman states that monetary authorities intervening in the exchange market according to the profit criterion normally serve to stabilize the path of flexible exchange-rate movements. According to this view, governments should intervene in such a way as to maximize their profits from intervention. As Mayer and Taguchi argue, however, there are several conceptual problems as well as difficulties of measurement with this proposition.[33] Nonetheless, this approach appears worth pursuing. Some ideal intervention schemes may help stabilize the yen and internationalize it, possibly by a competitive process.[34]

Coordination of monetary policies. The idea of attaining stable exchange rates by coordination of monetary policy among the major nations has been raised in a stimulating proposal by Ronald McKinnon.[35] He maintains that a nation's price level correlates more with the aggregate world money supply than with its own national money supply. Even though his empirical claim is not fully convincing, it is quite natural in the presence of currency substitution that a nation's price level correlates not only with its own money supply but also with those of other currencies. McKinnon argues that by stabilizing the weighted sum of the money supplies of major currencies—namely, the dollar, the mark, and the yen—price stability in the world economy as well as stability in exchange rates can be attained. He suggests, though with some reservations, that the stabilized exchange rate achieved under such a tripartite money agreement might eventually lead to a system close to the fixed exchange-rate system; interventions in the exchange market would eliminate short-run volatility of exchange rates within, for example, a 2 per cent band of the parity.

Since exchange rate determination depends strongly on the money supply process, regardless of the system, McKinnon's proposal reflects basic economic logic. Problems remain, of course: Why are three countries sufficient? How are the weights in his global monetarist formula to be calculated? How are real disturbances that affect the composition of the currency basket to be handled? And are the three governments willing to give up national monetary autonomy for the sake of tripartite monetary stability? Despite these problems, his proposal contains interesting elements that continue to stimulate thinking on the ideal monetary system for the future.

Interventions to maintain a target zone. Based on his diagnosis of the reasons for the misalignment of exchange rates of major currencies, John Williamson proposes that governments identify, in consultation with the IMF, the set of fundamental equilibrium exchange rates (FEER) and publicly declare their support for a system of crawling target zones with soft margins.[36] This target exchange-rate zone should be supported by governments through concerted interventions and a combination of suitable monetary policies. This kind of system would be desirable if the specific measurement of the FEER is easy. The difficulty in the real world under uncertainty is that diverse opinion may exist concerning the true value of the FEER.

Whereas the McKinnon proposal is limited to control of the money supply from a monetarist point of view, Williamson takes a broader perspective that includes fiscal as well as monetary policy. Indeed, much of the discussion in the mid-1980s about the possibility of macroeconomic coordination focuses on budget issues, in terms both of expenditures and of the nature of the tax system, as well as on the money supply. A further key question is to what degree the structural differences in the investment and savings rates of countries should be incorporated into this type of analysis of the FEER. The United States in the 1980s can be regarded as a special case because it has pursued a policy based not on a structural gap between domestic savings and investment but on a deliberate pursuit of high expenditures relative to production, made possible by historically high real interest rates, capital inflows, an overvalued dollar, and an excess of imports over exports.

Finally, we move from the normative question of what regime is desirable to the positive question of what kind of regime is likely to be realized. As explained in our introduction, the ongoing system will most likely continue unless the present situation deteriorates enough to make any important participant willing to give up the benefits of the status quo. So long as the current half-managed float is rendering imperfect but tolerable service, a drastic change of regimes will not take place.

From this perspective, the likelihood of a drastic reform in the intermediate future seems small. Among the alternative schemes listed above (other than the status quo), a return to the adjustable-peg system does not seem realistic, and intervention based on profit motives contains some conceptual difficulties. Moreover, there may be political or psychological resistance to the idea that a government or a central bank should behave primarily according to profit criteria.

The fourth alternative, the coordination of monetary policies, is a provocative idea. However, achieving agreement on the proper weights for the currency composition of the global money basket or on the proper distribution of the costs of monetary expansion (or contraction) among the participant countries will not be easy.

The fifth alternative, the announcement and observance of a soft target zone, appears desirable, but realizing it would require very substantial international coordination and agreement. First, countries would have to agree on some reasonable ways of calculating the FEER. Then, they would have to agree on the desirable degree of concerted actions in interventions. Even after agreement on evaluation of the current situation and on the possible remedy is achieved, the question of which countries should engage in interventions will have to be negotiated. The major countries have a long way to go to achieve all of these. The Baker-Miyazawa (U.S.-Japan) agreement of October 1986 was a step toward a target zone system, but it is unclear how long this agreement will last. Exogenous shocks are inevitable, but usually difficult to predict; they are likely to interrupt any system of a crawling exchange-rate zone.

In sum, the adoption of flexible exchange rates essentially ended the necessity of parallel movements in price levels, although there still exists more subtle interdependence among countries. Thus, the current system enables monetary authorities to enjoy a greater degree of monetary autonomy compared with the Bretton Woods regime. Each country has more freedom to choose its own price level since it is less affected by the policies of its major economic partners. In this sense, one may heuristically state that the "max-min" solution under flexible exchange rates provides relatively attractive solutions to participating countries, or that the noncooperative Nash equilibrium in the policy game under flexible exchange rates diverges less from cooperative outcomes, as compared with game solutions under the Bretton Woods regime. In the game of choosing or agreeing on a new exchange rate regime, it would be difficult to find payoffs under a new system that exceeded those of the status quo solution. Accordingly, this cost-benefit structure may give the present system a much longer life span than many have expected.

The dissatisfaction expressed in the mid-1980s with the current managed float regime does not justify a return to the old system. Even though participants in the present system seem to desire some degree of cooperation, cooperation is not crucial. Under the fixed exchange rate, cooperation was inevitable, but the incentive structure to realize cooperation was inadequate. The old system lacked coherent incentive compatibility, in addition to being vulnerable to speculative attacks.

A system based on a single global currency and a single monetary authority might be an economic ideal. But without world government, the achievement of a single currency system with full public-goods benefits would be extremely difficult, if not impossible. The loss of national autonomy in monetary policy during the process of attaining such a system would be immediate and concrete, whereas the potential benefits would accrue only when the final stage of world currency unification was reached. The realization of a completely fixed exchange regime without the possibility and defects of rate adjustment would be even more politically than technically difficult.[37]

The existence of considerable trade or current-account imbalances does not necessarily imply the misalignment of nominal exchange rates. In the year of continuing devaluation of the dollar following September 1985, for example, Japan's current account continued to increase substantially in dollars though its growth slowed down in yen. Although this is in part a short-run J-curve effect, the evidence suggests that structural mechanisms related to savings and investment behavior may be embedded in the world economy such that certain countries accumulate considerable current-account surpluses or deficits. Although the United States may in time eliminate its deficit, we anticipate a Japanese tendency to surplus for the foreseeable future.

Where will Japan stand then? Japan's economy now occupies a substantial share of the world economy—about one-tenth. Its trade structures and wage and price determination mechanisms are quite different from those of the United States and Western Europe as well as from those in developing countries. It seems therefore that the optimum currency area for Japan is Japan itself.[38] In addition, there seem to be many factors in Japan that obstruct the achievement of international reforms in the direction of stabler and quasi-fixed exchange rate regimes. Even though some former government officials apparently feel nostalgic for the Bretton Woods regime, it seems quite unlikely that sufficient political momentum based on economic interests will come about to motivate Japan to pursue a drastic reform. The only likely exception would be if protective pressures from outside Japan become stringent. This catastrophic situation might make a drastic reform possible, even though exchange rate reform by itself will not solve balance-of-payments problems unless accompanied by appropriate changes in macroeconomic fiscal and monetary management.

Thus, a realistic role in the monetary regime for the foreseeable future is for Japan to continue to be passive and to practice a managed float. Sometimes it will let the yen exchange rates be freely determined by the market; sometimes it will intervene unilaterally or multilaterally if the Japanese government feels the yen is misaligned. Depending on its ability to influence public expectations, intervention policy will or will not be successful.[39] In order to be realistic and not engage in wishful thinking, we are obliged to end this paper on this skeptical note.

Robert G. Gilpin

The Implications of the Changing Trade
Regime for U.S.-Japanese Relations

The future of U.S.-Japanese relations in the area of international trade will be determined largely by significant and continuing changes in the overall character of the international trading regime. Although it is much too early to forecast the precise effects of these developments, their nature and probable consequences are increasingly evident. In this paper, I analyze these shifts in the structure and practices of the trading system. They include the rise of the New Protectionism, the increased importance of domestic economic policies, and the changing significance of oligopolistic competition. The analysis begins with an examination of the General Agreement on Tariffs and Trade (GATT) system.

The GATT and Its Challenges

The GATT has provided the institutional basis for trade negotiations in the postwar era. Established in 1948, the fundamental purpose of the GATT was to achieve "freer and fairer trade" through the reduction of tariffs and the elimination of other trade barriers. In pursuit of this goal, the GATT has operated on the basis of four principles: (1) nondiscrimination, multilateralism, and the application of the most-favored-nation principle (MFN) to all signatories; (2) expansion of trade through the reduction of trade barriers; (3) reciprocity—that is, concession for concession—as the basis of trading relations; and (4) the establishment of a world trade regime or set of universal rules for the conduct of commercial policy.[1]

From the very beginning, there were important exceptions to these principles, such as the British Commonwealth, the permissibility of common markets or free-trade-area agreements, and Article XIX (safeguards provision) of the GATT. These exceptions recognized special economic relationships or encouraged countries to take the risk of moving toward more completely free trade. Under the formula of what John Ruggie has termed the "compromise of embedded liberalism," countries could accept the obligations of the GATT without jeopardizing their domestic economic objectives.[2] Moreover, the Eastern bloc never signed the GATT and did not accept GATT principles, and a number of countries never completely fulfilled their GATT obligations. Nonetheless, the basic principles of the GATT provided the basis for the postwar liberalization of world trade.

In the 1980s, these principles have come under increasing attack. Structural changes in the world economy have weakened the legitimacy of the GATT and its principles. New challenges have raised the issue of whether the GATT or some functional substitute can continue to maintain the regime of liberalized trade and, if not, what form or forms of economic nationalism and politically "managed" trade might possibly replace it.

The Transformation of World Trade

Following World War II, successive rounds of trade negotiations within the framework of the GATT led to an astounding decline of tariff barriers and the growth of world trade. As a consequence of numerous GATT negotiations in the early postwar period, the Dillon Round (1960–62), and, most significant of all, the Kennedy Round (1962–67), the merchandise trade of industrial countries grew from 1950 through 1975 at an average rate of 8 per cent a year, twice that of the growth of the global GNP.[3] The growing network of international trade began to enmesh national economies into a system of economic interdependence, leading some observers to speculate that a tightly integrated world economy was inexorably emerging. Then the balance between the forces of liberalization and economic nationalism began to shift; by the mid-1970s, the scales had tipped toward economic nationalism.

Although the volume of world trade expanded rapidly until the recession of 1974, trade liberalization was put on the defensive as early as the 1950s with the formation of the European Economic Community (EEC). The Dillon Round was initiated by the United States to counter the threat of the EEC's external tariff and Common Agriculture Policy (CAP). The sectoral or item-for-item approach of these negotiations had meager results. By the early 1960s, tariff reductions were beginning to impinge on key industrial sectors and the interests of powerful groups.[4] It became clear that a new approach to tariff reduction was required.

A new method of tariff negotiations in the Kennedy Round produced an across-the-board tariff cut of 35 per cent on 60,000 products, incorporated an anti-dumping agreement, and provided for food assistance to the LDCs. Yet the Kennedy Round failed in three important respects: it did not deal with the increasing problem of nontariff barriers (NTBs), the special problems of the LDCs, or the problem of agricultural trade (most important from the perspective of the United States).[5] Despite these failures, the Kennedy Round was the high point of the postwar movement toward trade liberalization. One authority has compared it to the Cobden Treaty of 1860, which appeared to have brought the world to "the threshold of free trade."[6] Yet, as in the late nineteenth century, the forces of economic nationalism continued to gain strength.

By the mid-1980s, the GATT regime and liberal world trade were on the defensive. In the words of the Economic Report of the President for 1985 by the Council of Economic Advisers, "The world is moving away from, rather than toward, comprehensive free trade. In major industrialized countries, for example, the proportion of total manufacturing subject to nontariff restrictions rose to about 30 percent in 1983, up from 20 percent just 3 years earlier."[7] Although the total volume of world trade continued to expand into the 1980s, the spread of protectionism increasingly affected the nature of the trading system and the international locus of industrial production.

Several developments accounted for the revival of protectionism. The OPEC revolution in winter 1973-74 and the massive increase in the price of world energy triggered a significant reversal in the movement toward free trade. The resulting wealth transfer, which amounted to approximately 2 per cent of the world gross product, had a twofold and contradictory impact on the international economy. First, it was highly inflationary because of the central role of petroleum in the modern economy as both a fuel and an industrial raw material. Second, the price increase also acted as a huge excise tax on the world economy, absorbing financial resources and depressing economic activities. The increase in the rate of inflation, the shift to recessionary monetary policy, and the consequent global stagflation accelerated the spread of trade protectionism.[8]

The relative decline in the size and competitiveness of the U.S. economy also contributed to the slowing of world trade and the rise of protectionism. Between 1953-54 and 1979-80, imports as a share of GNP more than doubled, from 4.3 per cent to 10.6 per cent.[9] This increased openness began to change the United States' relations with its major trading partners. Previously the West European and Japanese economies had pursued aggressive export policies while simultaneously importing U.S. goods to rebuild their own war-torn economies. In the 1970s, the relatively smaller, less competitive, and more open U.S. economy became highly sensitive to these imports at the same time that other economies began to import relatively fewer U.S. goods. Of perhaps greatest importance, the Reagan budget deficit and consequent highly overvalued dollar led in the mid-1980s to a huge influx of imports and increased unemployment. As trade competition became more intense, it stimulated protectionist pressures in the United States.

Yet another cause of rising protectionism has been the enlargement and increasing closure of the European Community. Over much of the postwar period, the development of the Common Market has been one of the most significant causes of the overall expansion of world trade. Since the mid-1970s, however, the Europeans have attempted to protect their traditional industries and their level of employment against threats from imports from Japan and the newly industrializing countries (NICs). Furthermore, the tendency to turn inward has been enhanced by the enlargement of the Community with the incorporation of the Mediterranean peripheral countries, the strengthening of ties with the European Free Trade Association, and the association with the community of a number of LDCs through the Lomé Conventions. The West European market in manufacturing and temperate agricultural products (especially foodgrains) has become more closed, and the EC has negotiated more and more as a unified bloc with outside powers. In short, Western Europe has increasingly operated as a regional trading system.

In the 1970s and 1980s, other broad changes began to erode the GATT system of trade liberalization.[10] As tariff barriers within the GATT have fallen, nontariff barriers in most countries have risen. This trend has been especially pronounced since 1974 due to stagflation, the shift to flexible exchange rates, and worldwide overcapacity in such industrial sectors as textiles, shipbuilding, steel, consumer electronics, automobiles, and petrochemicals. Cartelization and "orderly marketing agreements" (OMAs) have spread rapidly in these sectors. The closure and enlargement of the EC has encouraged regionalization of world trade. Barter or countertrade has grown rapidly, especially with respect to the LDCs.

Furthermore, the state has become an important actor in trading relations not only in command economies like those of the Soviet bloc but also in developed and less developed economies as well; from the sale of armaments to the negotiation of tied-aid packages and international cartels, the role of governments in commercial relations has greatly expanded, and industrial policies have increasingly influenced trade patterns.[11] The ratio of managed to total trade has increased sharply in the 1980s.[12] If one includes intrafirm trade associated with the expanded role of the multinational corporations in world commerce, the ratio would be much higher. Of all these developments, the spread of NTBs has had the most profound impact on world trade. Therefore, special attention is given below to the increased use of NTBs and the ineffective attempts to deal with the problem beginning with the Tokyo Round of tariff negotiations.

The Multilateral Trade Negotiations (Tokyo Round), begun in 1973 and completed in 1979, constituted the first and foremost effort of the major trading nations to find new ways to deal with many of these changes and the movement toward managed trade. Whatever its long-term significance for the regime of liberalized trade, the Tokyo Round transformed the basic framework for international negotiations over trading relations. One writer aptly entitled his evaluation of the agreement: "Tokyo Round: Twilight of a Liberal Era or a New Dawn?" [13]

The Tokyo Round, 1973-1979

The Tokyo Round was the first systematic attempt to resolve the developing conflict between the increasing economic interdependence of national economies and the growing tendency of governments to intervene in their economies to promote economic objectives and domestic welfare.[14] The Tokyo Round also dealt with a growing agenda of U.S. complaints against its principal trading partners. The United States particularly desired a return to the early postwar commitment to a multilateral trading system, the codification of international rules to govern domestic policies, and the elimination of discrimination against U.S. exports by the EC and the Japanese.[15] Among the vast array of subjects discussed in the Tokyo Round were the following:

1. Violations of the nondiscrimination or MFN principle through preferential trading arrangements (for example, the Lomé Conventions between the EC and certain LDCs) and the resultant increased fragmentation and regionalization of the world economy.

2. Resolution of issues related to unilateral imposition of import restrictions in cases of serious injury to domestic industry (Article XIX of the GATT) and the increased use of OMAs or "voluntary export restraints" (VERs).

3. Overall tariff reductions and the removal of NTBs.

4. Liberalized trade in agriculture and increased access to the EC and Japan for U.S. agricultural products.

5. Consideration of commodity agreements in wheat, coarse grains, dairy products, and meats.

6. Establishment of codes of conduct in a variety of areas, such as public procurement, export subsidies, and various types of government standards.

The primary goal of the Tokyo Round was to stabilize trading relations among the advanced OECD countries. This meant reformulating Article XIX, creating new codes for export subsidies, regulating countervailing duties and public procurement, and eliminating NTBs. The concerns of the LDCs for "special and differential" treatment, embodied in their demands for a New International Economic Order (such as the extension of "generalized preferences," access to developed countries for their manufactured exports, and formulation of commodity agreements) were partially recognized. During the 1970s, the United States and other developed countries did adopt the Generalized System of Preferences (GSP), which lowered the duties on a number of LDC exports in manufactured products, and it was generally assumed that the LDCs would benefit from measures that ensured a stable growth of world trade. The highest priority in the negotiations, however, was to overcome the expanding agenda of trade problems among the advanced countries themselves.

The Tokyo Round succeeded in several areas, including a further reduction of tariff barriers on industrial products of the major countries.[16] Its most important accomplishment was the establishment of a number of codes regarding NTBs. These codes of good behavior apply to such NTBs and trade promotion policies as restrictions on government procurement, the granting of tax benefits, and the use of export credits. The purpose was to make NTBs at least visible if not to eliminate them entirely, to decrease the uncertainties generated by government intervention in the market, and thereby to stabilize the trading environment.[17] In short, the codes were designed to limit a return to mercantilist trading practices and "beggar-my-neighbor" policies.

The Tokyo Round also extended trade rules into new areas such as government standards and government procurement and clarified international norms in older areas such as the use of industrial subsidies, anti-dumping regulations, and the use of countervailing tariffs. "Buy American" provisions were weakened. In areas covered by the codes, it introduced new dispute settlement procedures. In general, it made more "transparent" and available to international scrutiny those NTBs and other national practices associated with what is called below the New Protectionism.

In a number of important areas, however, the Tokyo negotiations failed to reach agreement. These areas included a number of the special problems of the LDCs; the agriculture issue, which was of great concern to the United States; the provision for dispute settlement; issues of foreign investment related to trade; and the expanding trade in services and high technology. The growing use of NTBs since the Tokyo Round indicates that the most serious shortcoming of the negotiations was its failure to revise the safeguards clause, which permits a country to restrict imports in order to protect an economic sector. This escape clause had been established to encourage the removal of trade barriers and to limit the damage to the regime of free trade if a nation imposed emergency protections to deal with actual or threatened serious injury to an industry from imports. Article XIX requires, however, that several preconditions be met: damage has to be demonstrated, the affected exporting countries have to be consulted and compensated, and any restrictions have to conform to the GATT principle of nondiscrimination.

In the Tokyo Round, the West Europeans wanted the right to apply restrictions selectively to the exports of particular countries (Japan and, to a lesser extent, the NICs), a modification that would have entailed a violation of the nondiscrimination principle. Japan and the NICs, needless to say, were intensely opposed, while the United States was generally indifferent. This fundamental controversy has not been resolved, and individual governments and the EC have imposed OMAs and VERs more frequently. The use of VERs is outside the GATT framework and violates the requirements of the safeguards principle. This practice has had a growing impact on the character of the international trading system.[18]

In retrospect it seems remarkable that the Tokyo Round succeeded as much as it did. The 1970s were a decade of economic upheaval. The problem of hyperinflation, the OPEC revolution, and the collapse of the Bretton Woods system strained international economic relations severely. With the spread of global stagflation after 1973, pressures mounted for trade protectionism. Under these circumstances, the Tokyo Round and its many years of intense negotiations were indicative of the transformed nature of the international trading regime.

The Tokyo Round occurred during a global trend toward economic nationalism. Although its development of new codes helped to limit arbitrary government behavior and thereby arrested the proliferation of NTBs, the new codes clearly acknowledge the extent of the retreat from international norms and the setbacks to previous GATT tariff reductions. Thus, whereas the several GATT agreements of the 1950s and 1960s were negotiated multilaterally and followed the MFN or nondiscrimination principle, since the Tokyo Round the "rules" of international trade have increasingly been set unilaterally, negotiated bilaterally, and, in some cases, have involved only the OECD countries. Particularist domestic interests in the advanced industrial countries have become increasingly significant in the determination of these rules. Furthermore, the Tokyo codes apply only to signatory countries and in general have been rejected by the LDCs. This could well lead to a two-tier system of world trade composed of the OECD countries with their trading partners on the one hand and all the rest on the other hand. Despite its achievements, therefore, the overall success of the Tokyo Round was limited in important ways.

Emergent Trade Issues

Although the Tokyo Round was by far the most complex and wide-ranging trade negotiation ever, it nevertheless left untouched many complex and difficult problems of increasing significance in international economic relations, such as the expanding global role of services and of high-technology industries, particularly finance and telecommunications.[19] (The increasingly important service sectors were never a part of the GATT.) One can rightly argue that the Tokyo Round was the last trade negotiation of the old industrial era and that since the Tokyo Round, the far more intricate exchanges of the "information" economy and the "knowledge-intensive" industries have become the key subject of trade negotiations. At the very least, the changing environment and patterns of world trade suggest that future trade negotiations will have to be vastly different from those of the past.

Emergent trade issues in the service and high-technology sectors have important characteristics that enhance their economic and political significance and will make them especially difficult to resolve. First, these industries will be the primary growth sectors for the advanced economies. At the same time, a growing number of NICs such as Brazil, India, and South Korea have targeted these sectors for development and are protecting them from foreign competition. Since these sectors are rapidly becoming the commanding heights of the contemporary world economy, competition and conflict are destined to be fierce. Second, they (in addition to agriculture) comprise the expanding export markets of the United States and hence are of intensifying concern to U.S. policymakers; thus, the removal of West European, Japanese, and LDC restrictions against U.S. service industries has become for U.S. policymakers the litmus test of future trading relations. Third, the service industries (finance, communications, and information processing) permeate domestic social relations and institutions, creating strong resistance to outside pressures for change and the opening of national markets; U.S. demands on Japan to open its economy in these areas are resisted because they are perceived to threaten Japanese cultural values and national self-sufficiency in strategic sectors.

Finance, data processing, and the like are infrastructure industries that affect the overall control and international competitiveness of the economy. Since they are central to the way in which an economy operates and to its basic mode of production, these sectors tend to be nationalized or highly regulated. Understandably, then, negotiations for increased economic liberalization in the service industries are extremely sensitive politically and raise the issue of whether a greater harmonization of domestic societies is necessary. Thus, whereas the United States believes strongly that harmonization is required to enable U.S. corporations to operate successfully in Japan and the LDCs, the latter denounce U.S. pressures in this direction as a new form of imperialism and a violation of national sovereignty.[20]

In the service sectors as well as other sectors, the 1980s have witnessed a growth in the conflict between the ideal of trade liberalization and the desire of nations to protect domestic priorities and preserve historically established business practices. This clash emerged from the existence of formal and informal barriers to trade that are intended to promote domestic social or political objectives or are simply an inherent aspect of the way that a particular society functions. For these reasons, it is doubtful that these issues can be treated by the multilateral and MFN approach of the GATT; instead they will have to be negotiated bilaterally and without reference to the traditional MFN principle.

The clash between further trade liberalization and domestic economic practices has presented itself most forcefully in the case of Japan. Although Japan has reduced most of its formal trade barriers (with the major exception of agriculture), what foreigners characterize as the illiberal structure of the Japanese economy, the "administrative guidance" role of the bureaucracy, and the economic behavior of the Japanese themselves make the Japanese market difficult to penetrate. A case in point is the highly restrictive and inefficient (at least by Western standards) Japanese distribution system, which is intended in part to protect small stores and the integrity of neighborhoods. Other examples of informal Japanese barriers are also frequently cited. The existence in Japan of industrial groupings and long-standing business relationships as well as the Japanese preference to do business with one another and to "buy Japanese" constitute formidable obstacles that limit foreign entry into the market. Pressures from the United States on the Japanese to harmonize their domestic structures with those of other countries and to open up their economy, especially when Japanese formal trade barriers are lower than U.S. barriers, obviously contribute to economic conflict.

Although deregulation and privatization have become important themes of contemporary economic discourse, state intervention to protect domestic values continues to be the universal norm. Further, it is exceptionally difficult for trade liberalization to proceed when resistance to increased economic openness is located in the very nature of a society and in its national priorities. Under these circumstances, it may be impossible to remove trade barriers, at least through the traditional means of multilateral negotiations. The existence of a liberal trade regime in a world composed largely of "illiberal" states is highly problematic.

Developments in the 1980s suggest that the postwar era of successive rounds of multilateral trade negotiations ended with the completion of the Tokyo Round. In each of the three dominant centers of the international economy—Western Europe, the United States, and Japan—strong resistance has developed to further removal of what others at least regard as trade barriers. Although changes in national attitudes and defined interests do not necessarily mean the termination of efforts to eliminate tariff and nontariff restrictions, they do suggest that the nature and pace of the freeing of trade have undergone a significant shift; in some cases national policies entail an actual retreat from the achievements of the past several decades. All major industrial economies are being pressed to reassess their commitments to the regime of liberalized trade because of the increased costs of adjustment to rapid changes in comparative advantage, the heightened impact of trade liberalization on employment, domestic institutions and social values, and the intensification of security concerns.

New Trading Patterns

In the 1980s, transformations in global patterns of international trade were apparent in the New Protectionism, the growing effects of domestic economic concerns on trading relations, and the increasing significance of oligopolistic competition. In addition, the rapid rise of Japanese and NIC trade competitiveness and the increasingly dynamic character of comparative advantage have severely strained the system. In turn, these developments have stimulated new theorizing on the determinants of global trading patterns and increased speculations on the future of the international trading regime.

The New Protectionism

Most aspects of the "old protectionism," especially the high tariffs left from the economic collapse of the 1930s, were eliminated by successive rounds of GATT negotiations. However, a proliferating array of NTBs and other devices have created a New Protectionism, which has become a major obstacle to the further liberalization of world trade. This New Protectionism of the 1980s consists of (1) the erection of a series of NTBs, including such measures as import quotas, VERs, exchange controls, domestic-content legislation, and a host of other negative and restrictive measures; and (2) governmental attempts to expand exports and support specific industrial sectors through such policies as export subsidies, credit guarantees, and tax incentives to particular industries.[21] In short, the New Protectionism entails expanded governmental discretionary powers to influence trade patterns and the global location of economic activities.

As Max Corden has pointed out, the New Protectionism is especially difficult to affect through traditional techniques of trade liberalization.[22] It is even difficult to assess the actual extent of trade protectionism because of the lack of openness or transparency. In many cases, it is even difficult to distinguish between NTBs and legitimate activities such as customs inspection, performance requirements, and other government regulations. Another complicating factor is the move from firm rules to administration discretion in measures ranging from government procurement policies to exchange controls. The return to bilateralism also aggravates the situation.

The foremost manifestation of the New Protectionism has been the use by governments of VERs and OMAs (or what the French euphemistically call "organized free trade"). Through the imposition by importing countries of quotas on exporting countries, trade has become managed and market shares have been greatly affected by state policies in a number of industrial sectors. By one estimate, in the early 1980s, nearly one-third of the U.S. and some European markets in manufactured goods were covered by NTBs.[23] Although the total percentage of world trade covered by VERs remains relatively small, their impact has been magnified because they tend to cluster in several critical sectors such as textiles, electronics, leather goods, steel, and, especially, automobiles.[24]

The controlled sectors tend to be characterized by global overcapacity and to be heavily unionized industries that are major sources of blue-collar employment.[25] The comparative advantage in these labor-intensive sectors, which have been sources of economic growth in the advanced countries, is rapidly shifting to the NICs; these industrial sectors constitute the major export opportunities for the NICs.[26] New Protectionism is also spreading to the service sectors and to the high-technology industries that are believed to be strategic sectors and the future growth industries of the advanced countries. Because of the economic and political importance of these areas, the major industrial powers have engaged in heated negotiations and unilateral actions to protect or improve their relative market shares.[27]

The first and most important effort to divide up the world market and parcel out shares was the Long-term Agreement on Cotton Textiles of 1962, later extended to become the Multi-Fiber Agreement of 1974.[28] Similar cartel-like arrangements have spread to the automobile, steel, and other industries. The United States and Western Europe have forced Japan and the NICs to limit their export of particular goods "voluntarily"; Japan has behaved similarly toward the Asian NICs. Further, developed countries are beginning to enact or to threaten to enact domestic-content legislation; that is, requirements that locally produced components be incorporated in foreign goods.

Although there is general agreement that NTBs are an important determinant of global trading patterns, it is difficult if not impossible to measure their extent or their effect with any precision. NTBs and VERs have existed for a long time, but their importance has increased because other tariff barriers have been lowered or eliminated. Their significance has increased because the items covered have shifted from light-industrial to higher-technology products such as automobiles, color televisions, and specialty steel products. The fact that the targeted exporter has most frequently been Japan also intensifies the political impact. It is clear that, at the least, NTBs and VERs are altering the structure of world trade; the New Protectionism has affected who is trading, who is left out, and what is being traded. However, the extent to which the New Protectionism is affecting the total volume of world trade remains unclear.

The actual extent of NTBs is difficult to gauge because by their very nature they are hidden from view. In many cases, even the identification of an NTB is subjective; what is a NTB to one person is a legitimate activity to another.[29] Yet it is quite certain that in the 1980s a sizable and growing percentage of world trade lies outside the GATT and is governed by NTBs, especially by bilaterally negotiated VERs. One estimate is that more than half of Japan's exports in the mid-1980s were limited by formal or informal agreements.[30]

As the OECD, in perhaps the most authoritative report on the growth of protectionism notes, a strong tendency exists to discount the significance of the New Protectionism because the volume of total trade and the manufactured exports of countries most affected by the restrictions have continued to grow.[31] Much of the New Protectionism, skeptics contend, has been in the form of political rhetoric and has not been translated into economic policy. A strong tendency has existed, therefore, to dismiss the actual extent of new protectionism.

According to the OECD report, however, mounting evidence suggests a significant transformation in the trading regime. In a relatively small but growing number of sectors, accounting for more than a quarter of the world trade in manufactured goods, important trade restrictions and government interventions exist. They include traditionally protected sectors such as textiles, steel, and footwear as well as previously unaffected sectors such as automobiles, consumer electronics, and machine tools. The mechanisms of government intervention in these areas are high tariffs, NTBs, and distorting subsidization.[32]

Conservative estimates suggest that between 1980 and 1983, the share of restricted products in total manufactured imports of the United States increased from 6 per cent to 13 per cent; for the EC, the rise was from 11 per cent to 15 per cent. For the major economies as a whole, the product groups subject to restriction jumped from 20 per cent to 30 per cent of total consumption of manufactured goods. As the OECD report states, "Within the protected sectors, the scope of protection has both deepened and widened," with the "absolute number of non-tariff barriers" quadrupling between 1968 and 1983. For example, the trade in automobiles among the OECD countries (excluding trade within the EC) affected by discriminatory practices increased from less than 1 per cent in 1973 to nearly 50 per cent in 1983! Significantly, the revival of economic growth in the early 1980s did not reverse this protectionist trend.[33]

Another major aspect of the New Protectionism has been its effect on the structure of international trade and the location of industry worldwide. The primary targets of NTBs and VERs have been Japan and the Asian NICs. Between 1980 and 1983, the share of their exports affected by discriminatory restrictions increased from 15 per cent to over 30 per cent.[34] These restrictions have had two effects. The first has been to force these countries to move up the technological ladder in a product line to higher value-added exports. For example, VERs on Japanese automobiles have caused the Japanese to shift their exports in the direction of luxury models. The second has been the dispersion of the industry, especially through direct investment by multinational corporations, to new locations in the developing countries not yet subject to VERs or OMAs. For example, restrictions on the Japanese have forced production in electronics, steel, and other products to shift to the Asian NICs and, as these NICs themselves have become subject to VERs and OMAs, to LDCs. Ironically, the consequence of this dynamic is that VERs and OMAs tend to spread to higher levels of technology and to increasing numbers of exporting countries and to encourage the growth of extensive regulations to prevent transshipment as governments and pressure groups attempt to catch up with these developments and limit imports. The result is an increasing global surplus capacity in a growing number of industrial sectors and a continuous encroachment of the New Protectionism on products and countries covered.

A third effect of the New Protectionism has been to alter the mechanisms of trade negotiations and to increase the overall extent of discrimination in violation of the unconditional MFN principle. As the OECD reports, there has been a significant shift away from GATT Article XIX (applied on a nondiscriminatory basis) toward bilateralism and discrimination.[35] As VERs and OMAs create lucrative economic rents to be shared by privileged foreign exporters and protected domestic industries, they have greatly intensified the politics of international trade and the issue of who benefits from these practices. The major losers, of course, have been the consumers in importing countries.

The New Protectionism has probably slowed and distorted but certainly has not prevented the global shift in the locus of industrial production and the consequent change in trading patterns.[36] Indeed, one of the most noteworthy features of the international political economy in the mid-1980s is the relative decline of the United States and Western Europe and the rapid rise of Japan and the NICs as producers and exporters of manufactured products. This process of rapid industrialization is generally concentrated in the smaller NICs of the Pacific Basin and in a relatively few large countries of immense potential such as India and Brazil. This historic transformation of the international division of labor parallels the changes that accompanied the industrialization of the United States, continental Europe, and Japan in the late nineteenth century.

The earlier transformation occurred in an age when the doctrine of laissez-faire still had force, at least in the declining hegemonic economy of Great Britain. At the end of this century, however, the United States and Western Europe are strongly resisting the operation of market forces. The multinational corporation and international production have also profoundly altered the international political economy. As comparative advantage has shifted to Japan and the NICs, U.S. and other multinationals have shifted their locus of production to other countries. Governments have responded by encouraging inward direct investment. These developments are resulting in a complex web of economic alliances and production sharing among corporations of differing nationalities and national governments that may mitigate the political conflicts generated by the New Protectionism. Finally, the continuing military supremacy of the United States and the security ties among the dominant economic powers serve to moderate divisive economic conflicts. These novel and contradictory features of the international political economy make it difficult, however, to extrapolate guidelines from past experience to illuminate the present.

As the New Protectionism continues to spread, a number of questions should be asked regarding its effects on the economics and politics of the emergent international political economy: (1) Which firms and which countries will be included in the trading regime and the cartelized world markets? (2) Who will share the economic rents and who will get left out? (3) On what political or other basis will these determinations be made? (4) Will the powerful countries seek to reward their friends and punish their enemies in the determination of VERs and OMAs? (5) How can trade-offs be determined and international agreements be negotiated successfully given the inherent difficulty of measuring the extent and welfare costs of NTBs and the benefits of eliminating them? (6) Does the New Protectionism inevitably mean a collapse of the world economy similar to that in the 1930s or merely its transformation into an economically more stable, albeit less efficient, and politically more sustainable set of global economic relations? The answers to these important questions will only be revealed over the course of the next several decades.

The Effects of Domestic Policies

The domestic economic policies of national governments and the interactions of these policies are important determinants of the volume and direction of international trade. Paradoxically, as international economic interdependence has increased, national policies have grown in their significance for trading relations. The shift from fixed to flexible exchange rates was expected to decrease the significance of domestic policies but has intensified it instead. The effect of macroeconomic policies on international trade is complex and pervasive and a matter of intense controversy among several competing schools of economic theory, including the Keynesians, traditional monetarists, and the rational expectations school. At the least, it is certain that both fiscal and monetary policies strongly influence, if not determine, the several economic variables that in turn (along with commercial policy) set the world's trading patterns.

In the postwar era, U.S. macroeconomic policies greatly influenced international trading relations. The United States' expansionary economic policies stimulated world trade, and the U.S. economy served as an engine of growth for other economies. The outflow of dollars through foreign aid, foreign investment, and trade imbalances provided the world with a noninflationary source of international liquidity that lubricated the channels of international trade. The United States' Keynesian policies were the key to unprecedented global economic growth and the expansion of world trade.

With the escalation of the Vietnam war in the mid-1960s, this relatively benign role of U.S. policy began to change. The massive outflow of dollars required to fight the war, the simultaneous launching of the Great Society programs, and the failure to raise taxes gave a powerful inflationary push to the world economy. Subsequently, the extraordinary rise in energy prices, the shift to flexible exchange rates, and the increasing importance of international financial flows for exchange rates further transformed the functioning of the international economy and enhanced the significance of macroeconomic policies in general and U.S. policies in particular.

Although the West Europeans and the Japanese share some of the responsibility for the difficulties of the international economy and trading system in the 1980s, the burden must be borne principally by the United States and its policies. The macroeconomic policies of the United States exert a powerful effect on global economic activities because it is the world's dominant economy and because the dollar continues to play a central role in the international monetary system. During the 1970s and 1980s, the alternation in the United States between expansionary and contractive economic policies produced wild fluctuations in exchange rates and international liquidity that affected national trade balances and rates of economic activities and exacerbated the global debt problem. The massive contraction of the U.S. economy during the initial years of the Reagan administration and then the even more massive expansionary policies that began in late 1982 (at the same time that the United States' major economic partners were pursuing restrictive policies) are only the latest and most dramatic examples of the roller coaster effects of macroeconomic policies on the international political economy.

The resulting massive trade and payments imbalances of the United States have given a powerful impetus to protectionist sentiments. There has been a prolonged period of cyclical global economic activity, and this boom and bust behavior of the world economy has accelerated the spread of protectionism through its devastating impact on specific economic sectors and its more general effect on economic expectations. Individual economies try to cushion the internal impact of external forces over which they have so little control. Protectionist pressures will no doubt increase unless the problems created by domestic macroeconomic policies and their interactions can be resolved through international policy coordination among the dominant economic powers.

Microeconomic policies also influence the patterns of international trade. The most important and controversial development in this area is the expanded reliance of a number of advanced economies on industrial policy. Although industrial policy means different things to different people, "it basically involves the active participation of the state in shaping the industrial pattern of development."[37] The means employed range from financial assistance to specific industries to governmental determination of production levels.

Sometimes used to aid senile or dying industries, industrial policy is also intended to create new industries, especially export industries in emergent high-technology sectors. By picking winners and targeting particular industries for development and financial support such as export subsidies, governments are attempting systematically to develop comparative advantage and to promote international competitiveness. In almost every market economy, there is an important partnership between government and corporations for the purpose of promoting exports and capturing world markets. Although this partnership is quite explicit in some economies, it is more indirect and subtle in others. For example, in the United States (as West Europeans correctly charge), expenditures on military research and development constitute an important subsidization of technologies with commercial significance.

Systematic intervention by a state in its economy and industrial development is obviously not new. In the late nineteenth century, the Germans were the first to transform their economy and capture world markets through the adoption of such interventionist policies.[38] Fascist Italy in the 1930s and Soviet Russia are more recent examples. Since World War II, however, Japan has most systematically implemented industrial policies that are credited with having propelled that island-nation from crushing defeat to the status of the world's first, or at least second, most competitive economy.[39] The success of "Japan, Incorporated," has spurred one country after another to adopt industrial and related policies to improve its economic and trading position, even though the Japanese are abandoning many aspects of their industrial policy and are moving toward greater liberalization of their economy.

The New Protectionism and the perceived success of Japanese industrial policy are changing the rules of the game in important ways. Whereas the primary purpose of the old protectionism was to protect threatened industries and to support an import-substitution strategy, a major purpose of the New Protectionism and industrial policy is to create comparative advantage and internationally competitive industries, especially at the high value-added end of the industrial spectrum, and to promote an export-led growth strategy. More and more states seek to establish their predominance in the production and export of "product cycle" goods; that is, products characterized by the use of high technology. This growing practice of "industrial or technological preemption" by which states attempt to jump over their competitors into higher levels of industrial technology is discussed below.

The increased importance of technology, technological change, and technological diffusion for international competitiveness and the consequently more arbitrary nature of comparative advantage in determining trade patterns are leading to new forms of technological protectionism and government interventionism. Nations are attempting to slow the diffusion of their own technology while forcing other countries to share theirs. Governmental restrictiveness regarding technology transfer for commercial reasons is extended by the enhanced importance of "dual technology" for both commercial applications and national security.[40] The trading of market access for technology transfers, the role of technology sharing in intercorporate alliances, and related practices reflect this enhanced importance of industrial technology in economic relations.[41] Without question, technological issues are becoming among the most important ones in the international political economy.

The development of new modes of state interventionism such as the reliance on nationalized firms and the crucial role in most advanced countries of joint research ventures financed and organized by the government reflect a number of changes in the economic and political environment: increasing global economic interdependence and openness of economies to foreign goods; the innovation of a broad array of policy instruments through which states can intervene in and influence industrial developments; and, as discussed below, the growing role of oligopolistic competition in the determination of trading patterns. Throughout the world, an awareness is growing that economic development requires the functioning of efficient export industries; governments (wisely or not) are responding by resorting to industrial policies to achieve this goal.[42] Since Japan is the foremost model for these efforts, its policies and an evaluation of their success will be the focus of the following discussion on government interventionism.

Government intervention in the economy may be categorized in terms of macro, compensatory, or adjustment policies.[43] Each type has had varying degrees of success both in Japan and in its imitators; these policy types, their different rationales, and their relative successes should be distinguished. Frequently, such distinctions are not made; indeed, there is a tendency to place them all under the heading of industrial policy and consequently to give industrial policy per se credit that it does not deserve.

Macropolicies refer to the various efforts of the state on an aggregate level to facilitate the smooth operation of markets and the accumulation of the basic factors of production. They include not only fiscal and monetary policies but other general policies such as the support of education, the financing of basic research and development, and the encouragement of high rates of national savings. For example, postwar Japan has maintained a level of national savings and investment twice that of the United States. Its policies have encouraged rapid productivity growth, moderate wage increases, the importing of foreign technology under licence rather than through direct investment, and the transfer of labor from agriculture to more productive industrial sectors. Internally, the Japanese government has stimulated intense competition in crucial industrial sectors, while the Ministry of International Trade and Industry (MITI) has discouraged fractious competition overseas. In short, Japan, with some major exceptions, has been more of an example of Adam Smith's ideas than those of John Maynard Keynes in its overall economic policies.[44]

Another type of economic policy may be called compensatory policies. In every economy, ongoing economic activities produce winners and losers. Although no society could afford to compensate all the losers, in times of rapid change the costs may be especially painful and harmful to particular groups and therefore necessitate government assistance. For example, the government may enact programs to retrain workers whose skills have become obsolete because of shifts in national comparative advantage. Such compensation policies have become an integral feature of the modern welfare state.[45]

A more controversial type of state interventionism is found in so-called structural adjustment or industrial policies designed to affect the ways in which the economic structure, that is, the national organization and composition of economic sectors, reacts to outside forces or tries to assume international leadership in an industry. Such policies may include the targeting of specific industrial sectors for research intervention and of particular industries and technologies for commercial development. With the exception of a few areas where market failure or a collective good may exist, say, pollution control or public health, most economists believe that such policies are probably not necessary in a market economy.

The Japanese and certain NICs have been exceptionally successful in their use of macropolicy. These economies have pursued remarkable growth-oriented fiscal and monetary policies, have made substantial investments in education, and have encouraged exceptionally high rates of national savings. The thrust of these policies has been to accumulate the basic factors of production and increase the overall efficiency of the economy. It is correct to conclude, therefore, that this type of macro-industrial policy and state intervention works. Additionally, Japan and a number of other societies have also pursued compensatory policies with a considerable degree of economic success.

The record regarding the efficacy of structural adjustment policies (what is most meant by industrial policy) is unclear, and it is difficult, if not impossible, to reach any definitive conclusion. It is doubtful, for example, that the stunning success of Japan in one product area after another can be attributed to the perspicacity of MITI and Japan's economic managers. Indeed, it is not certain that MITI and its industrial policies have outperformed the market. But it is not sufficient to retort, as skeptics do, that Japanese bureaucrats and businessmen simply looked around the world to see what others were doing and then took advantage of Japan's accumulated factors of production and comparative advantage in the low-cost mass production of standardized products. MITI and its policies should be given credit for encouraging and enabling Japanese corporations to climb the technological ladder.[46]

At best, available evidence regarding the efficacy of Japanese structural adjustment policy is mixed. Some attribute Japan's success primarily to its macropolicies, undoubtedly the world's best example of the application of "supply-side" economics.[47] Others draw attention to the high cost of those mistaken industrial policies that have caused over-expansion and surplus capacity in a number of industrial sectors such as shipbuilding, steel, and textiles. These Japanese policies have led to excessive concentration in particular industrial sectors and consequent generation of exports that have stirred foreign resentment. Judgment regarding the ability of Japan or any other state to pick winners and to guide the structural adjustment process appropriately should be suspended for the moment. At the least, it can be said that the Japanese have succeeded remarkably in improving and marketing the technological innovations of other societies, much as did the United States during its ascent to industrial pre-eminence a century ago.

The most important lesson to be drawn from the success of Japan and other rapidly rising industrial powers relates to the changing conception of comparative advantage and to its implications for national policy, trading practices, and, ultimately, for economic theory. These countries have unquestionably demonstrated that comparative advantage in a macro-sense can be created through appropriate national policies that facilitate the accumulation of the factors of production. Economists have, of course, long acknowledged the dynamic nature of comparative advantage; the competitive performance of Japan and the NICs in the 1970s and 1980s, however, has given new meaning and significance to this qualification of trade theory.

Regardless of how one evaluates these developments, there is no doubt that industrial policy (whether poorly or intelligently conceived) and trade policy (whether liberal or protectionist) are becoming more tightly integrated. As economists have noted, trade and industrial policies are being used to create the particular type of industrial structure desired by a government.[48] Nations are utilizing both import protection and export promotion to safeguard traditional high-employment industries while attempting to secure a strong position in the high-technology industries of the future.

These new types of policies differ from earlier forms of protectionism and state interventionism in that they are usually selective rather than across the board and are intended to protect or promote particular industrial sectors. Protectionism and industrial policies of all types are on the increase in the mid-1980s. Their fundamental objective is to protect and stimulate those economic sectors that political leaders consider most relevant to domestic welfare and the nation's political ambitions.

International Oligopolistic Competition

Trade patterns are also being affected by the growing importance of oligopolistic competition. As a number of economists have observed, the international economic environment is characterized by oligopolistic competition and strategic interaction.[49] In the perfectly competitive world of orthodox trade theory, the number of actors is too large and their individual size too small to determine economic outcomes; in such a market, economic decisions are based principally on variables such as the price, quality, and characteristics of goods. A strategic environment is composed of a relatively few large actors, and in such an imperfect or oligopolistic market, powerful actors can significantly influence market outcomes. Such a situation requires that each player give greater attention to the policies and reactions of other actors.

By 1985, strategic interaction had gained significance in the international political economy because of the expanding global role of the multinational corporation (MNC) and the growth of economic interdependence among national economies. The novelty of this situation was not the rise of oligopolistic competition as such; it has long existed. Rather, what was new was the enhanced importance of nonprice factors in competition, the emergence of powerful MNCs of competing nationalities, and the enhanced role of the state in assisting domestic corporations and affecting the "rules of the game."[50] Consequently the orthodox liberal model of atomistic competition where individual consumers and producers are assumed to be price-takers and the state is not a participant has become less relevant in a number of economic sectors. In many industrial sectors, especially in high-technology areas, international trade has become dominated by huge multinational corporations (frequently supported by the state) that can powerfully influence relative prices, trade patterns, and the location of economic activities.

An oligopolistic market composed of very large firms permits superprofits to exist. Individual producers can exploit a technological or other advantage to increase their economic return. As governments recognize that the international market is really one of imperfect competition rather than the ideal competition of liberal theory, they may well reason that it is far better for their own firms, rather than the firms of other countries, to enjoy the resulting high profits.[51] It is this real world of imperfect competition and multinational corporations that tempts governments to support a country's national economic champions and to develop a so-called strategic trade policy to shift profits to national firms.[52]

In this evolving oligopolistic environment, international trade and international production by multinational corporations have become closely intertwined. Intrafirm trade, subcontracting, and joint ventures have become important aspects of the international political economy. Trading patterns and the global location of industrial production have been strongly influenced by corporate strategies intended to minimize taxes, skirt trade barriers, and take advantage of global shifts in comparative advantage. For example, components made in a subsidiary or under contract in one or more countries may be sent to another country for final assembly into a finished product and then exported to yet another country where the product is ultimately marketed. Nearly 50 per cent of U.S. imports in 1977 consisted of intrafirm transfers.[53] This integration of trade and foreign production, frequently within the confines of a single corporation, is creating a more managed and increasingly complex global economy.[54]

Liberal economic theory presupposes an ideal world in which the internationalization of industrial production and the integration of national markets would pose few problems. International trade and foreign production would be alternative means of reaching world markets. Trading patterns and the location of production would be determined primarily by criteria of economic efficiency, and the international economy would increasingly resemble the integrated national markets that characterize advanced industrialized societies. At the international level, such a competitive market would create a situation in which the rate of profit would be held down by the interplay of market forces. Entrepreneurial profits would be quickly dispersed by the entry or the threat of entry of new producers. This is not, however, what is occurring in the real world of the 1980s.

Instead, the process of economic integration is being carried out by national firms in an increasingly interdependent world of competing states. The oligopolistic corporations that have become more influential in the determination of trade patterns and the global location of economic activities are not truly *multi*national; they are *not* divorced from a particular nationality. Home governments not only have the incentive but also may have the power to fashion commercial and other policies designed to benefit their own "multinationals" at the expense of competing firms and other economies. The tactics available to achieve this objective include government support of joint research ventures, predatory dumping, export subsidies, export cartels, domestic market preemption for domestic firms, and the use of import barriers as a means to export promotion.[55] In short, states and corporations ally themselves with one another to increase the national share of world markets.

Among available tactics employed by states to promote their own corporations one of the most important is what might be called "industrial pre-emption." Practiced most systematically by Japan and some of the NICs, this sophisticated form of infant-industry protection entails the denial of market access to foreign and in particular U.S. producers until "a Japanese producer achieves international cost and quality levels."[56] At the point of competitive equivalence, the Japanese market is opened, and Japanese firms begin their export drive for overseas markets. This has occurred in electronics, computers, and other areas of high technology. Although this practice does not determine Japan's overall trade balance (which is determined by macroeconomic factors), it most certainly does affect the structures of national economies and foreign trade. In thus reversing the product cycle, Japanese and NIC corporations are able to reap a significant fraction of the benefits and value-added of foreign innovations, which, of course, leads to intense negative reactions in the United States and the other innovating economies.

In the closing decades of the century, global trading patterns, the distribution of economic benefits, and the national location of production are strongly affected by strategic interactions among oligopolistic firms and national governments. The Tokyo Round and its codes of proper behavior failed to bring this emerging world of strategic interaction and intergovernmental bargaining under international control. The possibilities for nationalistic conflict over market shares and the distribution of corporate profits are considerably enlarged with the increasing importance of oligopolistic competition, the availability to governments of a wide array of policy instruments to assist national corporations, and the weakening of international leadership.

Trade patterns and the location of industry in a number of economic sectors have become significantly affected by the exercise of power and by international negotiation over market shares. How many cars Japan may export to the United States or how much U.S. beef Japan will buy have become matters of high politics. Although this politicization of the international division of labor does not mean a complete transcendence of market or efficiency considerations, it does mean that price competition has become a less important factor influencing the flow of trade. The New Protectionism, the industrial and trade policies of individual states, and the strategies of multinational corporations affect international trading relations in important ways. The intensified interplay of market, state, and corporation will largely influence, and in some cases determine, the future of international trade.

The renewed U.S. emphasis in the mid-1980s on reciprocity in trading relations and related shifts in U.S. trade policy should be considered against this background. The Japanese and NIC strategy of industrial pre-emption, the increasingly arbitrary nature of comparative advantage, and the relative decline of U.S. industry have encouraged the United States to be more aggressive in its trade policy. A major motive behind these policy changes is to prevent foreign economies from appropriating U.S. technologies and the monopoly rents generated by innovation, without which there would be little available capital or incentive to invest in scientific research and technological development. Thus, however poorly conceived the policy of reciprocity may be, it should be seen in part as a reaction to the policies of foreign governments that appear to threaten the basis of the United States' capacity to compete in world markets.

The changes in U.S. and other national trade policies are causing a metamorphosis of the global trading regime. The shift is clearly in the direction of negotiated market shares, bilateral bargaining, and the conditional MFN principle (that is, the granting of a trade concession only if one is granted in return). These more nationalistic approaches to international trade are displacing to a considerable degree the basic GATT principles of nondiscrimination, multilateralism, and the unconditional MFN principle as the governing features of the international political economy. Thus, the advanced economies and the NICs are fashioning a new international economic order, but not the one desired or envisioned by the large majority of the LDCs.

The Rapprochement of Liberal and Nationalist Theories

By the mid-1980s, the patterns of world trade had diverged significantly from the generally accepted theory of international trade based on natural endowments, perfect competition, and immobile factors of production. As Richard Cooper has noted, the gap between the theory and the reality of international economic relations has widened considerably since World War II.[57] Economists are, of course, attempting to narrow, if not close, this widening gap between liberal trade theory and the realities of international trade. Three recent developments are especially challenging to received trade theory: the significance and changing nature of oligopolistic competition; the increasingly dynamic, if not arbitrary, character of comparative advantage; and the enhanced role of the state in trading relations. The consequence of having to come to terms with these developments has been a significant convergence of the liberal and nationalist theories of international trade.

Traditional trade theory assumes the existence of a competitive market in which atomistic buyers and sellers are price-takers. Although it has long been appreciated that countries with a monopolistic or monopsonistic position could improve their terms of trade through tariffs or other devices, observers have assumed that individual firms were unable to influence terms of exchange at the international level because of the play of competitive forces. The rise of oligopolistic multinational corporations has altered this situation, and trade theory is attempting to adjust to the changed reality of imperfect competition.

The factors impacting on the nature of the international economy and international trade in the late twentieth century are similar to those that previously transformed the structures of domestic economies. For a century or more, every advanced economy has witnessed the partial displacement of competitive markets composed of many small firms by imperfect markets in which immense concentrations of corporate power exist. With the decline of trade barriers and increasing economic inter-dependence, a similar phenomenon has appeared at the level of the inter-national economy as a few large U.S., Japanese, and European firms (as well as those of some NICs) have grown in importance in world markets and as the world economy has become characterized by oligopolistic competition.

Advantages of scale are important in the increased power of many multinationals. The nature of modern productive technology, the impor-tance of learning by doing, and the possession of managerial and techni-cal skills frequently give a decided advantage to large firms in a number of industrial sectors. The competitive importance of scale will undoubtedly grow as tastes and technologies become more homogeneous throughout the world. It is increasingly anachronistic to postulate closed national markets and traditional tastes served by indigenous firms employing home-grown productive technologies; instead, the era of the global mar-ket served by global corporations appears to be emerging.[58]

Financial, technological, and other conditions in a large number of market sectors limit the entrance of new competitors into the market and thus encourage the growth of global oligopolistic competition.[59] Fre-quently, established firms adopt strategies that reinforce and elevate the barriers, and governments pursue industrial and strategic trade policies to benefit their own multinational corporations while controlling or ma-nipulating the entry of foreign corporations into particular markets. The tactic of industrial pre-emption discussed above is one example.

Moreover, intrafirm (as distinct from intraindustry) trade—the ex-change of goods and especially components across national boundaries but entirely within the same corporate entity—has grown in impor-tance. Oligopolistic corporations are compartmentalizing the industrial process and concentrating production and assembly of components to take advantage of resource location, market conditions, and government policies. In the 1970s and 1980s, multinationals rationalized global pro-duction as they redistributed manufacturing and the stages of produc-tion throughout the world.

The traditional concept of comparative advantage is also changing. The dynamics of factor accumulation, technological change, and the im-pact on international competitiveness of factor movements (through such mechanisms as foreign direct investment and technology transfer) have become more significant. As the economist John Williamson as-serted in 1983, the traditional conception of comparative advantage has become much less applicable, although it does retain usefulness in the definition of the limits within which trade can develop.[60] For example, despite the remarkable advance in technology over the past century or so, it is improbable that the advantages of soil, climate, and other natural conditions will cease to be relevant. It is hardly conceivable that England will ever surpass Portugal as a producer of wine or that Alaska will one day export bananas. Indeed, one might speculate that, as global levels of technological competence equalize, national resource endowments could reassert themselves as the primary determinants of trading patterns. Thus, the agricultural and raw material wealth of the United States has increased in importance at the same time that its former technological advantages have diffused to other countries; these natural endowments remain a major source of U.S. exports.

Whatever the long-term reality, for the moment both trade theory and trade practice must take into account the increasing importance of "arbitrary comparative advantage," characterized by William Cline as follows:

In some manufacturing products, the traditional bases for trade specialization—such as differences in relative national availabilities of labor, capital, skilled labor, and technological sophistication—may no longer dominate (as industrial and some developing countries become more similar in these attributes), while other traditional determinants of trade (such as natural resource endowment) may not be germane. In such products, the pattern of trade specialization may be arbitrary, and factors such as noncompetitive firm behavior and government intervention may determine which country prevails.[61]

The fact that comparative advantage is increasingly arbitrary and the result of corporate strategies and government policies leads to another major challenge to trade theory: the enhanced role of competitive national policies. By the mid-1980s, almost every advanced industrial country had begun efforts to emulate Japan's industrial policies, including such practices as government support of industrial development, encouragement of collusion among national and—in some cases—foreign firms, and governmental targeting of specific sectors or firms for financial or other support. Such government interventions will no doubt continue to spread.[62] Although the effectiveness of government policies is debatable and depends largely on the structure of the market and on relative national power, governments and their corporate champions are cooperating in a significant number of economic sectors to create comparative advantage and thereby to increase the national share of world markets.

These changes have raised serious problems for trade theory. Relative market shares, the terms of trade, and the composition of national imports and exports become strongly influenced by bargaining and negotiations among the relevant actors since relative efficiency, prices, and demand are not sufficient to determine outcomes. This indeterminacy will increase as the power and negotiating skills of multinational corporations and national governments grow. Trade theory will then become subordinate to bargaining theory, and trade policy will emerge from the development of a national industrial strategy and bargaining tactics.

The transformation of the nature of trade practice and theory has important implications. Liberal and nationalist trade theories have, at least with respect to trade in a wide range of manufactured goods, converged to a considerable degree (more than some economists may acknowledge). Over the past century, in fact, liberal trade theory has moved in the direction of nationalist contentions. In the classic Ricardian formulation, trade was based on fixed and immutable factors such as climate, natural endowments, and relative abundance of labor; international migration of the factors of production did not take place. Subsequently, the neo-classical reformulation of the Heckscher-Ohlin model (in agreement with Alexander Hamilton's *Report on Manufactures*) postulated trade patterns as more flexible and based on differences in *total* relative factor abundance, comparative advantage as more dynamic, and productive factors as diffusing via foreign investment and other means. In the early postwar period, product cycle, product differentiation, and other theories attempted to account for a world in which temporary technological advantages largely determined trade and investment patterns, comparative advantage diffused rapidly from more to less developed economies, and intraindustry trade based on differing tastes, economies of scale, and related factors characterized trade among advanced countries. More recent theorizing attempts to encompass a world in which comparative advantage is increasingly arbitrary and the interactions of powerful actors significantly affect trade patterns. Most economic nationalists would be quite comfortable with this analysis of the determinants of world trade.

The evolution of liberal trade theory suggests that liberal economists have begun to give more credence to the basic nationalist contention regarding the arbitrary nature of comparative advantage. They have had to come to terms with a world in which comparative advantage, international competitiveness, and the international division of labor result in large measure from corporate strategies and national policies rather than from natural endowments. Admittedly, the wrong conclusions may be drawn by nationalists and these changes may lead to ill-conceived protectionist and industrial policies, but it is not enough for economists to respond that it makes no difference whence comes comparative advantage as long as it exists. In a world where who produces what is a crucial concern of states and powerful groups, few are willing to leave the determination of trading patterns solely to the market.

In the mid-1980s, both trade practices and liberal theory have shifted remarkably in the direction of the nationalist conception of the dynamic and arbitrary nature of comparative advantage. Liberals and nationalists continue to differ regarding the extent of the shift and its significance for economic policy; whereas nationalists tend to believe that comparative advantage can be created by sector-specific industrial policies, liberals stress general macropolicies designed to foster the accumulation of the basic factors of production and to leave commerical developments to the market and the private sector. Liberals are more apt than in the past to stress the role of state policy in the creation of comparative advantage, but they also emphasize its inherent dangers and warn against the over- all efficiency losses of economic conflict. Furthermore, liberals have in- creasingly acknowledged the important role of economic power and strategic bargaining in the determination of international economic rela- tions but doubt their practicality. Nevertheless, the liberal emphasis on the superiority and the welfare benefits of an international division of labor based on free trade and economic specialization remains very dif- ferent from the ideas of economic nationalists.[63]

The Prospects for the Liberal Trade Regime

Most economists believe that the New Protectionism and related de- velopments entail a significant loss of economic efficiency and pose a threat to the liberal trading regime. The tendency to substitute condi- tional MFN for the unconditional and multilateral MFN of the GATT (that is, to make trade concessions only if one receives equivalent and bilateral concessions in return) has slowed the postwar movement to- ward free trade. Many fear that the Tokyo codes, because they apply only to signatories, could lead to a multitier system of trading relations dividing nations from others that do or do not ascribe to particular codes. Discrimination and preferential treatment based on the NTBs and VERs of the New Protectionism could cause a return to the aggressive nationalistic policies of the interwar era. At the least, these practices penalize emergent efficient producers of industrial goods, retard the ad- justment of advanced economies to ongoing global shifts in comparative advantage, and thereby prevent the transition to a new structure of international economic relations. Such developments will aggravate and prolong the economic crisis of the late twentieth century much as the old protectionism did in the 1930s. Some liberal economists believe that the regime of free trade, like a bicycle, is "dynamically unstable" and will fall down if it does not continue its forward momentum.[64] Such a col- lapse of the international economic order could give rise to economic conflicts threatening to world peace.

Others who are more sanguine about the prospects on an open trad- ing regime have a generally positive view of the New Protectionism and other changes in the trading regime. They argue that negotiated and bi- lateral arrangements constitute the best and in fact the only way to ex- pand trade in a world of increased uncertainty, greater emphasis on do- mestic economic security, and an unprecedented rapidity of change in comparative advantage. Susan Strange has written that the doctrine of free trade requires that states subordinate all other national values such as freedom, order, and justice to the goal of increased efficiency.[65] Bilateralism, the use of the conditional MFN principle, and what Robert Keohane has called "specific reciprocity" can and have been trade creating.[66]

These changes are held to be a new way of making rules and not the collapse of international rules. The exchange of explicit concessions in specific sectors and the creation of a "web of contracts" approach to trade liberalization, Strange argues, enable a state to safeguard other values and protect itself against the free-rider problem. According to this formulation, only those willing to accept the obligations become participants in the system. It is believed that as the historical barriers of time and space disappear because of advances in transportation and communication, NTBs and VERs constitute a necessary means to cushion the disruptive effects of the expansion of world trade and the continuing diffusion of industrial technology and comparative advantage to Japan and the NICs. Through interstate negotiations based on cooperation and mutual interests, the trading regime can be preserved in a much more nationalistic world. From this perspective, the New Protectionism is less a restriction on total world trade than a means of controlling the untoward effects of unregulated trade.

Whatever the ultimate outcome of the debate between the critics and the supporters of the changes in the nature of the GATT system, the New Protectionism, domestic policies, and oligopolistic competition are altering the nature of the international trading regime. The world is witnessing the rise of an interlocking network of bilateral and regional relationships. The principle of the conditional MFN has begun to replace the unconditional MFN, specific reciprocity has become more important than diffuse reciprocity, and trade is taking place increasingly outside the GATT framework. In fact, the legitimacy of the GATT principles themselves are being challenged. These developments suggest that new rules and norms may soon be required to govern trading relations in a much more interdependent world.

Violations of GATT principles and challenges to the legitimacy of these principles suggest that continuation of the multilateral trade regime will require increased international cooperation and a greater harmonization of domestic institutions and national policies. It is possible that a new set of internationally accepted rules applying directly to the internal workings of societies, rather than the removal of formal import barriers, is needed. For example, the United States, by breaking up the American Telephone and Telegraph Company and deregulating its own telecommunications industry, removed a significant barrier to foreign entrance into the U.S. market. This unilateral domestic policy decision conveyed an economic benefit to the rest of the world for which the

United States was not compensated. Yet, most other countries continued tight government control of the industry. This example demonstrates the incongruity of considering domestic policy decisions in isolation when trade has made them highly interdependent. Reform of the trading regime must recognize this fact. International rules to regulate imperfect competition may have to be established, and national practices such as antitrust policies and government support for research consortia must be made more uniform across national boundaries.

At the national level, a reordered trade regime might also have to determine what are and what are not legitimate governmental policies and interventions in the economy. The positive and negative effects of domestic policy changes on other nations would have to be weighed and decisions reached regarding the need for appropriate compensation or reciprocal actions. It may be necessary to coordinate and harmonize national practices to prevent governmental intervention in the market and the establishment of policies giving unfair advantages to national firms. Since national and corporate behavior significantly influence the pattern and outcome of trading relations, rules of the game are needed to limit harm to weaker nations and prevent a breakdown in the trading regime through the pursuit of nationalistic policies.

Most economists believe that the harmonization of domestic policies and practices is not necessary for a liberal trade regime to function effectively. In economic theory, nations are regarded as black boxes, and all that is required for mutually beneficial trade is that the exchange rates among the boxes be in equilibrium. However, as the history of the EC seems to demonstrate, at some point the process of economic integration and growing interdependence necessitates increased international cooperation and greater harmonization of national practices to prevent distortions and cheating.[67] At the global level, in the absence of cooperation and greater harmonization of national practices, it is likely that international economic conflicts will intensify as each nation seeks to improve the relative position and competitive advantage of its own multinational corporations.

Even if economists are correct that economic institutions do not matter and the harmonization of domestic practices is unnecessary, the more relevant consideration is that states and powerful groups believe that domestic institutions and practices are important in determining trade. Whether the structural features of the Japanese economy do serve as nontariff barriers to keep foreign products out, most Americans and West Europeans believe that illiberal aspects of Japanese society do constitute formidable obstacles to their exports and therefore hold them to be illegitimate.[68] As trade negotiations have reduced the barriers between national economies and the world has become more interdepen-

dent, the issue of the legitimacy and harmonization of domestic structures, as Gary Saxonhouse points out, has moved to the forefront of
international economic and political relations:

The increasing appreciation of how barriers in the international movement of
capital and technology, and discriminatory domestic microeconomic policies can
undermine the global benefits resulting from liberal agreements on trade in
goods has meant much expanded rules of the game for participants in the international economic system. If domestic policy instruments can always be good,
functional substitutes for the foreign economic policy instruments which are the
traditional objects of international diplomacy, it seems that liberal domestic economic policy by all rather than just some of the major participants in the international economic system, is a necessary prerequisite for the continuing legitimacy of that system. Thus, the thrust of international economic diplomacy has
already moved from tariffs to quotas and from quotas to standards, subsidies
and government procurement. The agenda for international economic harmony
is now demanding that much of the domestic economic affairs of participants in
the international system be governed by fully competitive open bidding and
contractual relationships. The history of postwar international economic diplomacy has shown that implicitly, but not yet explicitly, the increasingly difficult
task of maintaining the legitimacy of the international economic system requires
not just nondiscriminatory treatment of foreign goods in national markets, but
also a more far-reaching *harmonization of microeconomic institutions* [italics added].[69]

Unless this legitimacy issue can be resolved or somehow transcended,
economic nationalism and regionalism will make deeper inroads into
the postwar regime of liberalized trade. What this intensifying problem
demonstrates is that a liberal international economic order must rest
on a firm political and ideological base. The United States and its conception of a liberal order dominated the postwar era. With the relative
decline of U.S. power and the rise of economic powers with different
conceptions of legitimacy, the future of the liberal world economy has
become severely threatened.

The most likely outcome of these developments is a "mixed" system
of trading relations. It is improbable that the trade regime will collapse
as it did in the 1930s; there is enough momentum to keep the bicycle of
trade liberalization from falling over. Yet, it is equally improbable that
there will be a return to the liberalizing trends of the early postwar decades. Although strong elements of multilateralism based on GATT
principles will continue to characterize many facets of world trade, they
will be joined by bilateral, cartelized, and regional arrangements. The
GATT regime with its emphasis on universal rules will remain at odds
with the increased importance of government discretion and interventionism to promote national interests and domestic priorities.

Undoubtedly the most prominent feature of the emergent trading regime and the most significant departure from historical patterns will be
the expansion of sectoral protectionism.[70] In a substantial and growing

number of services, basic industries, and high-technology areas, governments and corporations negotiate market-sharing agreements. Involving principally the advanced economies and the NICs, such horizontal accords are intended to gain market access, acquire strategic technologies, and preserve employment. Although an international trading regime based in large part on negotiated market shares would be highly inefficient and characterized by gross inequities, powerful forces continue to push the world economy in that direction.

Conclusion

The GATT system of trade liberalization was based on the concepts of nondiscrimination (most-favored-nation principle) and of national treatment and on permitting the market to determine the international location of economic activities. Trade barriers have fallen, and the total volume of world trade has greatly expanded on the basis of these liberal precepts. The very success of this ongoing process of trade liberalization, however, has raised a host of new and troubling issues. In many societies, the domestic social costs of adjustment to changing patterns of comparative advantage are believed to outweigh the advantages of further trade liberalization. The relatively perfect markets in which equilibrium solutions were possible have been displaced to an indeterminate degree by strategic bargaining among corporate entities and national authorities.

The various codes instituted by the Tokyo Round to regulate government intervention in the economy constituted an attempt to deal with the new and uncertain international economy in which strategic interaction and bargaining among states and corporations have become increasingly the norm and where industrial policy and trade policy have become merely different sides of the same coin. Although it has increased global efficiency, trade liberalization has impacted seriously on those societies and has even raised the question of whether it can continue without greater harmonization of national societies. Is it possible for trade liberalization to continue in a world composed of societies with vastly different social and economic structures? In the emergent world economy, the determination of trade patterns is no longer simply a matter of lowering tariff barriers or of "letting the market decide." Instead, shares of exports and imports for particular countries and corporations and the location of industrial production are determined as much by political as by economic factors.

There are thus several conflicting developments in international trade in the mid-1980s. Although the pace of trade liberalization has slackened because of cyclical and secular factors, the dominant economic powers continue to favor the elimination of tariff and nontariff barriers. Yet, the New Protectionism, economic regionalism, and illiberal domestic structures constitute trade restrictions and lead to international conflict in a proliferating number of economic sectors. A highly ambiguous situation exists in which there is an ebb and flow from trade liberalization to economic protectionism rather than the continuously expanding trade liberalization of the 1950s and 1960s or a nationalism leading back to the chaos of the 1930s.

This mixed trade regime is the product of the interaction of two opposed tendencies. On the one hand, never before has trade been more nearly free and economic interdependence so great. Tariff barriers have declined dramatically during the postwar period, the foreign sector in most economies has expanded, and international competition has increased. On the other hand, this greater openness has given rise to and is paralleled by powerful countertendencies: economic closure in the form of the New Protectionism, economic nationalism embodied in industrial policy, and the temptations of strategic trade policy made possible by the enhanced importance of oligopolistic competition. The ultimate balance between these forces in determining the nature of the international trading regime is as yet undefined.

The challenge posed for U.S. and Japanese trade relations is to adapt to this set of economic developments. In making this adjustment, both societies are constrained by their commitment to the principle of free trade, which is no longer realistic in the present circumstances. Indeed, attempts to achieve what Americans conceive as "fair" trade by pressuring the Japanese to open their markets and harmonize their domestic structures may even be counterproductive in that they create powerful negative reactions. Bilateralism and similar arrangements, though having their own dangers, may be the only way to move even haltingly in the direction of a more open trading system.

Part II

Japan in the
International System

Ryutaro Komiya and Motoshige Itoh

Japan's International Trade and Trade Policy, 1955-1984

The purpose of this paper is to review the evolution of Japan's international trade and trade policy from the time of Japan's accession to GATT (General Agreement on Tariffs and Trade) in 1955 up to the present, to assess their impact on the Japanese economy, and to explore their likely development in the near future. More specifically, we investigate several questions. (1) How has the pattern of Japanese trade evolved, and what types of trade policy measures did the Japanese government take? What were the theory and philosophy behind such policy measures? (2) How have trade relations developed between Japan and other countries, especially the major developed countries? (3) What role did Japan play in the arena of world policy formation? (4) How did the Japanese government's trade policies and international agreements affect Japan's international trade? After studying these questions, we attempt to assess the future outlook for Japan's trade and for the world trade regime on which Japan's economic development critically depends.

We divide the three decades under review into three periods.

The first period: 1955–67. In 1955, Japan became a member of GATT and thereafter gradually began liberalizing imports (in the preceding period imports had been severely restricted). By the end of this period, a large number of import quotas had been removed. The Kennedy Round of tariff negotiations under GATT was held in the last part of this period, and the tariff rates of developed countries were lowered substantially.

The second period: 1968–75. This was an intermediate, transitional period between the first period, in which Japan was a relatively small country exporting primarily labor-intensive goods, and the third period, in which Japan became a large, dominant actor in the world economy exporting largely sophisticated machinery. During this transitional period, Japan and the United States engaged in prolonged and painful negotiations over their bilateral trade in textiles and apparel. In the second half

of this period, the world economy underwent a series of economic upheavals: the collapse of the Bretton Woods regime, the first oil crisis,
worldwide inflation, and a deep depression for the first time in the postwar period. Each of these events had a substantial impact on the Japanese economy.

The third period: 1976–84. The second oil crisis broke out in 1979, and
the world economy fell into a long stagnation. During this period,
Japan's shares of world industrial production and world trade became
much larger, and trade frictions with the United States and the European Community became a serious economic policy issue for Japan. In
the midst of this unfavorable environment for free trade, the Tokyo
Round—another GATT round of multilateral negotiations on tariffs and
nontariff barriers initially proposed by Japan in 1971—was successfully
concluded in 1979.

Accession to GATT and Trade Liberalization, 1955-1967

Japan's Trade During the Mid-1950s

In 1955, when Japan joined GATT, its exports amounted to only 2.4 per
cent of total world exports (excluding centrally planned economies), and
its exports of industrial products amounted to 4.2 per cent of total world
exports of industrial products (see Table 1). These shares were much
lower than in the 1930s: Japan's share in world exports was about 5.3 per
cent in 1938.

In 1955, Japan was gradually recovering from the destruction and dis-

TABLE 1
Japanese Exports, 1955–1982
(per cent)

As share of	1955	1960	1965	1970	1975	1980	1982
Total Western exports[a]	2.4%	3.6%	5.1%	6.9%	7.1%	7.1%	9.1%[b]
Total Western exports of manufactures[c]	4.2	5.9	8.1	10.0	11.3	11.8	12.5
Total Western exports of machinery[d]	1.7	3.9	6.7	9.8	12.5	16.3	18.4

SOURCES: Bank of Japan, Statistics Office, *Kokusai hikaku tōkei* (International comparative statistics)
(Tokyo, various issues).
[a]Japan's exports/Western countries' exports × 100.
[b]Figure for 1983.
[c]Japan's exports of manufactures/Western countries' exports of manufactures × 100.
[d]Japan's exports of machinery/Western countries' exports of machinery × 100.

TABLE 2
GNP, Selected Countries, 1957–1984
(U.S. $ billions)

Country	1957	1962	1967	1972	1977	1981	1984
Japan	$30.8 (339)	$52.8 (554)	$115.0 (1,148)	$300.1 (2,806)	$693.5 (6,095)	$1,139.2 (9,684)	$1,261.0 (9,917)[a]
U.S.	441.1 (2,565)	554.9 (2,974)	785.0 (3,942)	1,155.2 (5,532)	1,899.5 (8,704)	2,937.7 (12,783)	3,662.8 (14,093)[a]
U.K.	62.1 (1,207)	78.9 (1,441)	94.4 (1,713)	146.6 (2,627)	247.2 (4,419)	504.3 (9,032)	465.0 (8,140)[a]
FRG	51.6 (1,001)	88.8 (1,666)	120.9 (2,020)	259.1 (4,202)	515.6 (8,373)	682.8 (11,072)	642.5 (10,673)[a]

SOURCES: Same as Table 1.
NOTE: Figures in parentheses are per capita GNP in U.S. dollars.
[a] Figure for 1983.

order resulting from the defeat in World War II. It was still a small, latecomer industrializing country, with a GNP per capita and a wage level much lower than those of the developed countries (see Table 2). Its main exports were labor-intensive products produced by cheap labor using out-of-date equipment. Its imports were largely limited to such necessities as industrial raw materials, fuel, and foodstuffs.

Japan's industrial structure was changing rapidly, however, as a result of a high level of investment in plant and equipment and imports of advanced technologies. The capacity of the steel industry had already been sufficiently expanded and the technologies sufficiently advanced to make exports possible. In 1956, the shipbuilding industry had a share exceeding 20 per cent of total world orders, the first place in the world. In the machinery and chemical industries, a large number of new products were being produced, and levels of production were increasing rapidly.

Trade Policy in the Era of High Economic Growth

In December 1955, the year of Japan's accession to GATT, the Japanese government announced and implemented the Five-Year Plan for Economic Independence (*Keizai Jiritsu 5-ka-nen Keikaku*), the first of a series of national economic plans. The announced purposes of the plan were: economic independence and full employment. Economic independence meant, first, to achieve a balance-of-payments equilibrium without economic aid from the United States and without the help of foreign exchange receipts from "special procurements" (*tokuju*), the purchases of Japanese goods and services by U.S. forces in Japan, which had increased sharply during the Korean war; and second, to launch the economy on a steady growth path.[1] Since Japan had to import increasing amounts of raw materials once it got on the path of economic growth, a steady expansion of exports was considered vital to economic independence.

The plan specified four principal policy objectives: modernization of industrial plant and equipment; promotion of international trade; an increase in self-sufficiency; and curtailment of consumption. The second and the third goals may appear contradictory to students of the standard theory of international trade. The authors of the national economic plan and policymakers at the time seem not to have understood fully the notion of gains from free trade based on comparative advantage and efficient resource allocation through international trade and the competitive price mechanism. These two apparently contradictory policy objectives may have been behind Japan's persistently large balance-of-payments deficits from the 1950s to the mid-1960s.

The official exchange rate of 360 yen to the dollar set in 1949 overvalued the yen during this period compared with the exchange rate that would have brought the balance of payments into equilibrium without import restrictions and export promotion measures. This substantial overvaluation played an important role in determining trade and other economic policies in the 1950s and the 1960s. Japan had to promote exports zealously and restrict imports in order to balance its international payments. This was no easy task for the government since economic growth was impossible without increasing amounts of imported raw materials and fuel. The slogan "Export or die" was not too much of an exaggeration for Japanese policymakers in this period.

The government apparently did not consider depreciating the yen to balance Japan's international payments. In general, government policymakers and leading businessmen did not believe in the role of the price mechanism in equalizing supply and demand. For example, the Ministry of Finance and the Bank of Japan maintained the so-called low interest rate policy, artificially keeping the interest rate at a much lower level than the one that would equate the demand and supply of funds in the financial markets. Japanese policymakers preferred to operate a disequilibrium system in which there existed either excess demand or excess supply.

One can better understand the intentions of the policymakers if one interprets "promotion of trade" as "promotion of exports." This was the first pillar of the trade policy system from the 1950s until the late 1960s. On the one hand, exports were promoted by such policy measures as subsidies, provision of low-interest loans for promising export industries, and preferential tax treatment of income from exports and for exploration of new export markets. These measures were meant to lower costs for exporters and to give incentives to export.

On the other hand, since imports would naturally increase along with economic growth, they had to be restrained as much as possible. Imports of raw materials and machinery essential for domestic production were given priority, whereas imports of consumption goods and goods that could be produced domestically had to be severely restricted under the disequilibrium system. This is what was meant by the slogan "making the economy more self-sufficient."⁷ As a result, the government subsidized imports of raw materials and machinery under the overvalued yen exchange rate since firms purchasing these goods paid less in terms of yen than they would have had to pay under an equilibrium exchange rate.

The second pillar of Japan's trade policy system in this period was to develop in Japan modern manufacturing industries that existed in Europe and the United States. Catching up with the West had been Japan's earnest wish since the Meiji era. It was expressed by the two renowned slogans of the Meiji era: *fukoku kyōhei* (to enrich the country and to strengthen the army) and *shokusan kōgyō* (to foster industries and to promote enterprise). The Japanese people's ambition to have a strong military force resulted in the disastrous defeat in World War II, but their desire to catch up with the West in economic wealth and modern industries was not abandoned but strengthened after World War II. Slogans like "modernization of firms' equipment," "rationalization of industries," and "promotion of heavy and chemical industries" were very popular in the 1950s. In the New Long-run Economic Plan (*Shin Keizai Keikaku*, 1958–62), and the Plan for Doubling National Income (*Kokumin Shotoku Baizō Keikaku*, 1961–70), which followed the Five-Year Plan for Economic Independence, "strengthening the foundation of industry," "sophistication of the industrial structure," and "heavy and chemical industrialization" (*jūkagaku kōgyōka*) were the top-priority policy objectives.

Policymakers thought that only those industries that the highly industrialized countries had successfully established and that appeared to have good prospects for development in Japan should be nurtured and protected in their early stages of development. Although the government did not like the term "infant industry" for several reasons, what the government pursued under the slogan of "heavy and chemical industrialization" was essentially the protection of promising infant industries. As a means of protection, the government, on the one hand, granted infant industries various subsidies (although the amounts of the subsidies were generally limited), preferential tax treatment for depreciation and for incomes from "important new products," and low-interest loans through government-affiliated banks (especially the Japan Development Bank) and, on the other hand, protected them from foreign competition by import quotas and tariffs and by restricting domestic investment by foreign competitors.³

GATT and Japan

Japan acceded to GATT provisionally in 1953 and was admitted as a contracting party in 1955. There were several anomalies, however, in the relationship between Japan and GATT.[4]

In 1955, 14 countries, including the United Kingdom, France, the Netherlands, Belgium, Australia, India, and New Zealand, which accounted for about 40 per cent of Japan's exports to GATT members, refused to have GATT relations with Japan by invoking Article 35 (which allows member-states to refuse to have GATT relations with another member-state). Among the major trading nations, only the United States, Canada, West Germany, Italy, and the Scandinavian countries accepted Japan as a full member of GATT and gave it most-favored-nation (MFN) treatment, at least formally. This is one of the rare cases where Article 35 was applied among GATT members: no country besides Japan has ever been so widely discriminated against in the GATT system, whether legally or illegally. Moreover, many countries, mostly former colonies of the United Kingdom and France, that joined GATT later applied Article 35 to Japan.[5]

These countries had bitter memories of the rapid expansion of Japanese exports of textiles, sundries, chinaware, and other labor-intensive products in the 1930s, utilizing "cheap labor" or "social dumping" as a leverage, according to their perception. These countries feared, or argued that they feared, that cheap Japanese products would flood their domestic markets and those of their ex-colonies. "Underlying these [fears] was the knowledge that Japan was a country with a large and talented population relative to its other factors of production, . . . that Japan must import huge amounts of food and raw materials. . . . Japan was therefore seen as almost certain to be a particularly aggressive, international competitor in labor-intensive manufactured goods."[6]

The United Kingdom ceased to apply Article 35 to Japan in 1963, and other European countries followed. By 1972 among Western European countries, only Austria, Ireland, and Portugal still invoked Article 35 against Japan. Many European countries continued to discriminate against Japanese exports, however. Most of them requested Japan, as a condition for their withdrawal of the application of Article 35, to accept their discriminatory import policies against Japan or to agree not to bring the case to GATT even if they violated GATT by impairing Japanese exports. Moreover, Italy, West Germany, and the Scandinavian countries, which had never applied Article 35 to Japan, also practiced discriminatory import restrictions against Japanese exports that were not allowed under the GATT. A large number of European countries still impose discriminatory (nonmultilateral) import quotas and import embargoes against Japan.[7]

The United States was eager to establish a normal GATT relationship with Japan and helped Japan obtain full membership.[8] In fact, Japan's accession to GATT was made possible mainly by the strong leadership of the United States. The United States' support for Japan's accession should be viewed in the broad perspective of the overall U.S. policy toward Japan.[9] During the Occupation period, one of the United States' basic policies was to weaken Japan's economic power, especially that of *zaibatsu* groups, in order to prevent Japanese militarism from reviving. But this policy stance soon changed as East-West relations deteriorated. The outbreak of the Korean war in 1950 contributed significantly to this change. After the Chinese Communist Party took over mainland China, the threats of the Soviet Union and China in the Western Pacific evidently increased, and U.S. policy shifted swiftly from weakening the Japanese economy to promoting its reconstruction and development. A strong Japan would not only lessen the burden of economic aid for the United States but also make Japan a bridgehead of Western democracy in the Far East, an area where East-West tension was high. From the United States' point of view, it was necessary to provide Japan with ample opportunities to engage in worldwide trade. For this purpose, it was essential to give Japan a position in GATT equal to that of Western countries.

Given the basic U.S. policy toward Japan in the mid-1950s, it is ironical that the United States has asked Japan to impose "voluntary export restrictions" (VERs) on certain exports to the United States. The request resulted from the U.S. executive branch's compromise with Congress. Japan had occasionally used VERs in the late 1930s. Japan's exports of certain textile products and other light manufacturing products to the United States often increased sharply within short periods beginning from around 1955. Confronted with a sharp increase in such imports from Japan, the United States chose an informal approach of asking the Japanese government or industries to "voluntarily" restrict exports of the products in question to the United States for a certain time period rather than making use of formal procedures such as those under GATT Articles 19 (emergency action on imports of particular products) or 28 (modification of schedules). The Japanese government complied with most of these requests.[10] For one thing, Japan was then strenuously carrying on diplomatic negotiations, with the support of the United States, for the removal of the application of GATT Article 35 to Japan.

Although VERs are currently practiced, at the request of their trading partners, by a number of other countries (mostly by developing countries), few countries besides Japan were asked to institute VERs until the late 1960s. Although no statistics are published even today, Japan undoubtedly has a dominant share of the amount of trade under VERs. After Japan, the newly industrializing countries (NICs) conduct large shares of their trade under VERs. Developed countries other than Japan have rarely practiced VER; the export of steel by the European Community (EC) countries to the United States may be one of the few exceptions.[11]

The Kennedy Round and Japan

The Kennedy Round (KR, 1964–67) of tariff negotiations under GATT was an epochal event in world trade in the postwar period, or, one might say, since the beginning of the nineteenth century. The tariff rates of the major industrial countries, especially those on manufactures, were lowered substantially. As far as the developed countries were concerned, the world entered an era of unprecedentedly low-tariff trade.

It is often thought that the free, multilateral world economic regime of the Western nations after World War II, with the International Monetary Fund (IMF) and GATT at its center, was created and developed under the leadership of the United States and was an important part of the so-called Pax Americana. As far as GATT is concerned, however, this is a doubtful view.

Immediately after the war, there was an ambitious plan to establish an International Trade Organization (ITO), but the U.S. Senate refused to ratify the ITO treaty. After several years of unsuccessful attempts to persuade the Senate, the U.S. government had to accept GATT as an administrative agreement, not as a treaty, because of the strong Senate opposition. The United States' position toward GATT was asymmetric with that of most other GATT members, including Japan, in that other members ratified GATT as an international treaty. The asymmetry has been a frequent source of problems. The U.S. Congress takes the position that it is not restricted by GATT; a large number of bills inconsistent with GATT such as the Burk-Hartke bill, various recent "reciprocity" trade bills, and the so-called local-contents bills on automobiles have been introduced in Congress.[12]

Although it is not quite unambiguous whether the United States has been the foremost leader of GATT, no one would deny that the success of the KR owed much to the initiative of the United States, especially to the leadership of President Kennedy. The United States was forced, so to speak, to embark on the KR by the formation of the European Economic Community (EEC) and the challenge of a market without tariff barriers encompassing a population of over 250 million. At the time, it was thought that the United Kingdom might join the EEC.[13]

The United States, followed by the EEC, played the most important role in the KR. Canada played an important role at the beginning, but it soon retired from the main arena when it decided not to be a "linear cutter." The United Kingdom, after deciding not to join the EEC in the early stages of the KR, was also a leading player, as was the Nordic

Group (Denmark, Finland, Norway, and Sweden), which banded together during the KR in order to strengthen their bargaining power. Japan was perhaps the fourth or fifth most important actor.

In the beginning, Japan was not enthusiastic about participating. In hindsight this may appear strange, but the Japanese government was still inclined toward protectionism, especially for manufacturing industries, and its economic policy stance was not close to the principles underlying GATT and the IMF. The Japanese government seems to have felt somewhat uneasy about participating in the KR. Japan had been moving toward strengthening tariff protection for agriculture and some manufacturing industries, in order to cope with an impending liberalization of import restrictions and foreign exchange controls because of a change of Japan's status in the IMF to an Article 8 member (which forbids a member-state from restricting payments and transfers for international transactions on current account). (Japan's tariff policy in this period is reviewed in the next section.) The expectation that Japan's participation in the KR would force Japan to reduce its tariff rates made the Japanese government hesitant to take an active role in the early stages of the KR. Japan presented a large number of exceptions to the linear cutting of tariff rates for manufactures, primarily to protect newly emerging industries.

Since the KR was prolonged by a number of troublesome problems such as those concerning EEC agricultural products, not only did the international competitiveness of Japanese manufacturing industries improve considerably, but also the negative tendency of Japan's balance of payments was mitigated. These changes induced Japan to shift from a defensive stance with an emphasis on protecting domestic industries to a more liberal one of mutually lowering tariffs in the hope of expanding exports.

It is clear that Japan profited from the successful conclusion of the KR. On the one hand, the reduction of tariff rates on manufactured goods by its major trading partners contributed to an expansion of Japanese exports, directly as well as indirectly through the expansion of world trade. On the other hand, there is no evidence that Japan's manufacturing industries suffered much from Japan's own tariff reductions.

Trade Liberalization Program

Around 1960, the major West European countries reestablished their currency convertibility and became IMF Article 8 and GATT Article 11 members (such states are forbidden to use quantitative restrictions on imports for balance-of-payments reasons). Lagging only a few years behind, Japan embarked on a liberalization of import restrictions and foreign exchange controls. Japan became an IMF Article 8 member in 1964. Before this, in January 1961, the government adopted the Outline of the

Plan for Trade and Foreign Exchange Liberalization (*Bōeki Kawase Jiyūka Keikaku Taikō*). The plan called for increasing the "trade liberalization rate" (the percentage share of imports not covered by import quotas in total imports) from 40 per cent in 1961 to 80 per cent by June 1963 and for removing all restrictions on foreign exchange transactions relating to the current account and gradually relaxing controls on capital-account transactions as well.

Import quotas were removed or relaxed considerably from 1960 to 1963. Import quotas on 1,837 commodities (BTN four-digit classification) were removed; at the end of 1963, 192 items were still subject to import quotas, among which 155 items were "residual quotas," that is, quotas other than those allowed under various articles of GATT. This was still much more than those of other major countries. From 1964 to 1968, when the KR was in progress, trade liberalization made little headway in Japan; residual import quotas were removed on only 35 items during this period. After the conclusion of the KR, however, trade liberalization once again accelerated: quotas on 88 items were removed between 1969 and 1972.

The "trade (imports) liberalization" program and the "capital (inward direct investment) liberalization" program that followed a few years later constituted an important change in the Japanese government's economic policy.[14] These revolutionary policies transformed the Japanese economy, until then a relatively closed one. The liberalization policy distressed Japanese industries and firms; it was often likened to the visit of Perry's "black ships" in 1853 that led to the opening of Japan to foreign commerce.

Japanese industries and firms had been protected from foreign competition since the late 1930s. Trade liberalization forced them to compete in the open market. Government officials responsible for protective policies, representatives of individual industries, and advocates of protectionism such as some academic economists and journalists were generally opposed to the liberalization measures. The situation was described as *sōron sansei, kakuron hantai*; that is, people agreed on the desirability of liberalization in principle and for the Japanese economy as a whole but found it unacceptable for some special reasons in their own industry or the field that they supervised or had a special interest in.

The economic policy dominant in Japan until then was quite different from the ideal of free and multilateral international trade, foreign exchange transactions, and international investment underlying GATT, the IMF, and the Organization for Economic Cooperation and Development (OECD). In Japan the dominant economic policy was to view exports as a virtue and imports as a vice.[15] Also, there was a strong desire to protect manufacturing industries that used sophisticated technologies. It is not an exaggeration, perhaps, to say that in the 1950s and 1960s Japan's policymakers strongly desired to protect most modern manufacturing industries.

Tariff Policy

Before the trade liberalization program, the Japanese government revised its tariff schedule extensively in 1961. This revision was mildly protectionist. Japan raised, through the tariff negotiations under GATT, rates on many manufactures, such as machinery, heavy electric machinery, and computers, and on some agricultural products, such as dairy products, beans, and seaweed, in exchange for reductions on certain other commodities. Seven principles were announced as basic guidelines for the revisions.

1. To set low tariff rates on primary commodities (agricultural products and minerals) and increase rates with the degree of processing.
2. To set low rates on producer goods and high rates on consumer goods.
3. To set low rates on those goods that could not be produced domestically or only in limited quantities with no possibility of expanded domestic production in the future, and to set high rates on those goods whose potential domestic supply was elastic and either was or would be competing with imports.
4. To set high rates on the products of those industries with good prospects for development, especially on the products of newly established industries.
5. To set low rates both on the products or raw materials of well-established export industries.
6. To set rates on the products of stagnant industries, industries with no prospects for future development, or declining industries high enough and on their materials low enough to facilitate a smooth and gradual transfer of employment to other sectors.
7. To set low rates on necessities and high rates on luxuries, and to set low rates on imports for such purposes as education, culture, and health.[16]

A policy of protective tariffs and tariff escalation is visible in guidelines 1 through 5 and in the second half of guideline 6.

The Japanese Administrative System

The Japanese administrative system was another source of potential conflicts with the free-trade principles of GATT and the IMF. For each industry, there is a corresponding government office, department, or section of a ministry in Japan. Such an office is called a *genkyoku* in Japanese government jargon.

In the heyday of "industrial policy" in the 1950s and 1960s, the *genkyoku* (the bureau or authorities in charge of an industry) was in general strongly biased toward protectionism, particularly in the early postwar years.[17] Each *genkyoku* tended to introduce various measures to regulate new entries in the sector under its supervision and a licensing system to control the activities of firms such as new plants or branch offices, introduction of new products, imports of foreign technologies, and joint ventures with foreign firms. A *genkyoku* was generally considered responsible not only for supervisory matters prescribed by laws and ordinances but also for guidance, suggestion, direction, and consultation on an informal basis (*gyōsei shidō*) with respect to a wide variety of activities by firms in the industry. In particular, the *genkyoku* generally considered it desirable to eliminate "excessive" competition, making an industrywide plan for production, investment, and sales and, if possible, by regulating (formally and informally) prices (including fares, fees, interest rates, and commissions) when necessary. By these means, the *genkyoku* attempted to establish and maintain an "orderly" system in which each firm could secure a certain stable level of profits. The *genkyoku* further wished that the firms under its jurisdiction did not run into financial difficulties and even tended to dislike a change in the rank order of firms according to the market share.

Genkyoku officials held (and some still hold) such attitudes or policy orientations for several reasons. First, if the industry in question encountered problems, the officials were held responsible or even accused of mismanagement and had to expend much effort to help the industry recover. Second, bureaucrats enjoy authority, and it is natural for them to maintain and expand their authority. Third, paradoxically, when a regulatory system has existed for some time, it is often quite convenient and comfortable for the industry itself, especially for its leading firms.

During the 1930s, the Japanese government not only approved but sometimes promoted and even forced cartelization of industries. During World War II and the immediate postwar period, rigid and extensive controls on production and distribution of a large number of commodities were enforced. Antitrust law was introduced into Japan during the Occupation period, but since it conflicted with Japan's traditional economic policy, it took much time to take root.

Why, then, did the Japanese government want to join international treaties and organizations such as GATT, IMF, and OECD, given its traditional mercantilist philosophy as well as an administrative system for economic policy quite different from the basic philosophy and principles underlying such treaties and organizations? Our view is that it was not so much because the Japanese political leaders and government officials then in charge of economic policy thought that free competition and liberalization of trade, investment, and exchange transactions were the best arrangements for Japan. Rather, these leaders and officials wanted to secure export markets around the world by joining these treaties and organizations. They wished Japan to become a full member of the international economic community and to play a major role there in the future. Furthermore, they expected that Japan could utilize the financial facilities of the IMF and the International Bank for Reconstruction and Development (IBRD). Liberalization of imports, inward direct investments, and foreign exchange controls were thought of as a "necessary cost" or a "sacrifice" that Japan had to pay in order to secure membership in the international club of major industrialized countries.

Summary of the Trade Liberalization Process

The process of trade liberalization and capital liberalization in Japan in the 1960s had several basic features. First, politicians, officials, and businessmen did not quite understand, at least in the early stage, the theory that liberalization would benefit the Japanese economy by improving resource allocation and promoting competition. Rather, they thought that liberalization of imports and inward direct investment were a necessary sacrifice for Japan to become a member of the international economic community and especially of the club of major industrialized countries of Western Europe and North America.

Second, the government took great care not to trigger rapid change in resource allocation, especially in those areas much affected by the liberalization program. Liberalization proceeded in a gradual and piecemeal fashion; liberalization measures were introduced first in those areas where political and social opposition was weak. It took a long time, therefore, for trade liberalization, capital liberalization, and liberalization of foreign exchange controls to be nearly completed or to finish the first stage.

Third, the pace of liberalization was much influenced by the strength of external pressure for liberalization. In those areas where liberalization was requested by a foreign country with a strong negotiating power vis-à-vis Japan, and in periods when such pressures were strong, liberalization proceeded relatively fast. There were strong tendencies in Japanese society to resist foreign pressures and to preserve the status quo as much as possible unless forced to give it up.

Fourth, liberalization was carried out gradually and in a piecemeal fashion in order to avoid disorder in the areas affected. Policy measures were often meticulously designed down to minute details. This was made possible by the *genkyoku* administrative system and the many competent and honest bureaucrats operating it. For example, sometimes the government liberalized only several subgroups of commodities under a BTN four-digit group. Or it introduced a tariff-quota system, a new mechanism adopted in the 1961 revision of the tariff law, when abolishing an import quota, setting a second-stage tariff rate at a quite high level for imports over a given amount. Also, the government gave various forms of adjustment assistance to industries adversely affected by liberalization.

Fifth, there were few cases where liberalization was reversed after implementation. This is because liberalization was cautiously and meticulously prepared and was implemented in stages. To our knowledge, the government has only rarely reversed the liberalization of trade by reintroducing import quotas or other restrictive measures in view of a rapid increase in imports. Japan's liberalization of imports and inward direct investment was slow but steady.[18]

From an Improving Balance of Payments to the First Oil Crisis, 1968–1975

Development of Japan's Trade

Throughout the 1960s, the Japanese economy experienced what is called "high growth" and a rapid expansion of both exports and imports. It is not correct to characterize Japan's economic growth as export led since throughout the 1960s the growth rate of domestic private investment in plant and equipment was much higher than the growth rate of exports. Moreover, including both goods and services, Japan's exports and imports expanded almost at the same pace. There is no room for doubt, however, that the favorable international environment in the 1960s was one of the most important conditions for Japan's high growth: it made possible a higher growth rate of exports and hence of imports than that of GNP for Japan and a much higher rate of economic growth for Japan than the world average (see Table 3).

During the 1960s, three important changes took place in Japan's international trade. First, Japan's share of world trade rose substantially. Second, the composition of Japan's exports changed markedly; the share of products heavily dependent on cheap unskilled labor such as textiles, miscellaneous light industry products, sewing machines, and inexpensive cameras declined, and the share of products of heavy engineering industries such as steel, various kinds of machinery, and automobiles

TABLE 3
Ratio of Exports and Imports to GNP, Selected Countries, 1955–1983
(per cent)

Country	1955	1960	1965	1971	1976	1981	1983
				JAPAN			
Exports of goods, services, income	11.5%	11.6%	11.1%	12.3%	14.4%	16.6%	15.8%
Exports of merchandise				10.4	12.0	13.3	12.3
Imports of goods, services, income	10.6	11.2	9.9	9.7	13.7	16.0	13.9
Imports of merchandise				8.6	11.6	12.6	10.5
				UNITED STATES			
Exports of goods, services, income	5.0%	5.4%	5.8%	6.4%	9.9%	12.5%	10.2%
Exports of merchandise	3.9	3.9	3.9	4.1	6.7	8.0	5.9
Imports of goods, services, income	4.5	4.6	4.7	6.0	9.7	11.6	10.4
Imports of merchandise				4.2	7.2	9.3	8.1
				UNITED KINGDOM			
Exports of goods, services, income	26.1%	24.5%	23.3%	25.1%	31.3%	31.3%	30.5%
Exports of merchandise				16.1	16.8	20.5	20.8
Imports of goods, services, income	26.8	25.2	22.9	22.8	31.4	28.1	28.8
Imports of merchandise				17.3	20.4	20.2	22.5
				FRG			
Exports of goods, services, income	20.3%	21.2%	19.0%	22.6%	27.8%	32.1%	32.3%
Exports of merchandise				18.1	22.9	25.8	26.2
Imports of goods, services, income	18.0	18.8	19.0	20.6	25.3	31.4	30.0
Imports of merchandise				10.0	19.8	24.0	23.6

SOURCES: Same as Table 1.

rose substantially (See Fig. 1). As for imports, the share of raw materials for textiles declined, and that of fuel (primarily petroleum and coal) increased, even before the oil crisis. The share of machinery in imports increased slightly during the 1960s (but it declined from 1965 to 1975) (see Fig. 2). Japan was apparently in a transition between the stage of a latecomer, newly industrializing country having a comparative advan-

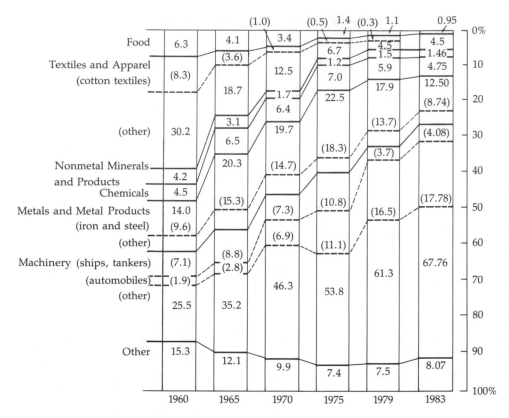

Fig. 1. Composition of Japan's exports, 1960–1983.

tage in labor-intensive products and the stage of a highly developed industrial country having a comparative advantage in high value-added engineering products utilizing sophisticated technologies.

The third change was in the balance of payments: Japan's balance of payments in its current account gradually freed itself from persistent pressure toward deficits around 1968. Since then, the current-account balance has generally been positive. This improvement resulted from the greater stability of wholesale prices—especially of manufactured products—in Japan than elsewhere, although consumer prices, including those for services and fresh food, were rising secularly in Japan. The pattern of technological progress in Japan (including introduction of new products and development of overseas marketing networks) was strongly biased toward raising productivity in "tradable" industries

(industries producing exports and import-competing goods), and it brought about stable wholesale prices and stable or even declining prices for exports, although consumer prices were rising.

After the period of unprecedentedly high economic growth in the 1960s, both the world economy and the Japanese economy experienced a series of upheavals in the early 1970s. The old IMF system collapsed in the summer of 1971 as a result of a unilateral action of the United States in violation of both the IMF Agreement and GATT, and major countries had no choice but to shift to the floating exchange-rate system in the beginning of 1973. The first oil crisis broke out in the autumn of 1973, imparting a heavy blow to oil-importing countries and the world economy, which had already begun to become unstable because of simultaneous booms in many countries and worldwide inflation. In the summer of 1974, there arose widespread, though temporary, financial uneasiness in the Eurodollar market as a result of a few bank failures, and for some

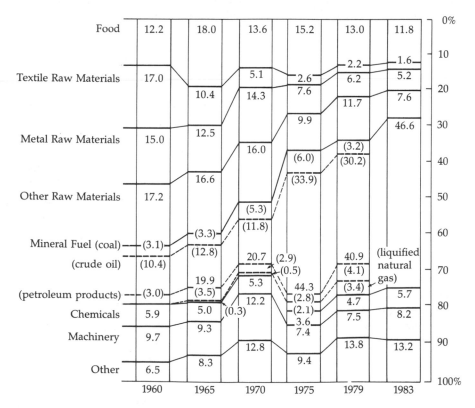

Fig. 2. Composition of Japan's imports, 1960–1983.

time Japanese banks had difficulties in rolling over their short-term borrowings. These unexpected events had severe impacts on the Japanese
economy, which was heavily dependent on imported oil as a source of
energy. Following these events, the world economy fell into the deepest
and most prolonged depression and the severest inflation of the postwar
period.

In spite of these unfavorable events, Japan was one of the earliest
countries to recover from the stagflation following the first oil crisis.
Japan succeeded in stabilizing wholesale prices by 1975 and consumer
prices by the beginning of 1976. Early adjustments of oil- and energy-
related prices and a determined tight-money policy were major factors
contributing to the successful price stabilization. Although the rate of
growth in real GNP turned negative in 1974, production began to pick
up from the latter half of 1974, led by an expansion of exports. By the
latter half of 1975, the Japanese economy was launched on a fairly steady
growth path, with an annual growth rate of about 5 per cent. Although
this was only about half the growth rate of the 1960s, it was still distinctly higher than those of other developed countries.

Foreign Requests for Import Liberalization and Japan's Response

After the late 1960s, when Japan's balance of payments began to turn
positive, foreign countries, especially the United States, frequently requested Japan to increase imports of manufactures and agricultural
products. They have strongly requested the removal of remaining import quotas and reductions of tariff and nontariff barriers, a revaluation
of the yen exchange rate, and relaxation of foreign exchange controls.

The Japanese government responded to these requests by removing
some import quotas and reducing tariff rates, to the extent that these
measures did not create serious difficulties for the domestic producers
concerned and did not obstruct the development of important infant industries. But it strongly resisted requests to revalue the yen.

After all, the yen had appreciated from the old IMF parity of 360 yen
per dollar before 1971 to 265 yen in 1973. Partly because of this substantial appreciation (approximately 36 per cent) and partly because of the
quadrupling of the oil prices, Japan's balance of payments in its current
account showed an unprecedentedly large deficit in 1974. Because of
this, external pressure for import liberalization subsided from the latter
half of 1973 to 1975, and at the same time liberalization halted.

Trade Liberalization Policy

As already mentioned, few import quotas were removed during the
KR period. After the conclusion of the KR, a large number of import

quotas were removed: the period from 1969 to 1972 saw a second spate of import liberalization measures. The Japanese government introduced a series of Yen-Defense Policy packages in order to reduce the balance-of-payments surpluses, and the removal of import quotas was part of these packages. As a result of this second spate, the number of items under "residual"—that is, illegal under GATT—import restrictions decreased from 122 in April 1968 to 40 in February 1972 to 33 in April 1972 and finally to 27 at the end of 1975 (see Table 4). Among these 27 items, only four items were manufactures (leather products) and only one was a mining product (coal). The removal of residual import restrictions on manufactures and mining products was practically completed during this period. These figures do not include the quantitative import restriction quotas acceptable under GATT; namely, import embargoes and quotas on (1) rice, wheat, sugar, silk, and certain types of dairy products whose prices were supported by the government or whose trade was controlled by the government, (2) goods such as weapons and gunpowder whose trade was restricted for national security reasons, (3) narcotics and anesthetics; and (4) radioactive substances and atomic hearths. Such items under nonresidual import restrictions numbered 37 in 1968 and 55 in 1975.

Import quotas on the following items were removed between 1968 and 1975: antibiotics and color film (January 1971), automobile engines and soda ash (June 1971), steam turbines and telephone exchange equipment (November 1971), auxiliary equipment for computer systems excluding memory apparatus and terminals, small airplanes (February 1971), high-capability computers and electric cash registers, and integrated circuits with less than 200 elements (December 1975). As a result of these liberalization measures, at the end of 1975 products affected by residual import restrictions were mostly agricultural.

Tariff Rates

After the tariff reductions agreed on in the KR were implemented, the government further reduced tariff rates in several steps. It put into effect the generalized scheme of preference (GSP) for developing countries in advance of other nations as part of the Yen-Defense Policy package in June 1971. Also, it unilaterally reduced tariff rates on a few commodities in May 1971. In December 1972, it reduced tariff rates on all (with few exceptions) processed agricultural products, manufactures, and mining products by 20 per cent. These tariff reductions were intended to reduce the current-account surplus. By these measures, Japan decreased its tariff rates substantially and mitigated the tendency toward tariff escalation, lowering the effective rates of protection on processed goods considerably.

It is not easy to compare average tariff rates at different points of time

TABLE 4
The Process of Import Liberalization in Japan, 1960–1981

Year	Month	Total number of items under import restrictions	Nonresidual import restrictions (number of items)	Residual import restrictions[a]			Selected items liberalized
				(1)	(2)	Total	
1960	Apr.	1,443					
1965	Oct.	161	39	55	67	122	
1968	Apr.	165	43	54	68	122	
1970	Jan.	161	54	50	68	118	
1971	Apr.	141	44	39	59	98	
	Jan.	123	44	31	49	80	
1972	Feb.	86	47	12	28	40	Auxiliary equipment for electronic computer systems, radar for aircraft
	Apr.	79	47	9	24	33	Ham and bacon, kerosene, fuel oil (reduction in the number of items because of a revision in the Tariff Rate Law)
1973	Apr.	83	52	8	24	32	High-quality desk calculators, electronic computers, integrated circuits (with less than 200 elements)
1974	Dec.	83	55	7	22	29	Integrated circuits (with more than 200 elements)
1975	Dec.	82	56	5	22	27	Electronic computers and auxiliary equipment
1977	Apr.	80	54	5	22	27	Tobacco
1980	May	78	52	5	22	27	(An increase of 5 items because of the Washington treaty)
1981	Dec.	79	53	5	22	27	(An increase of 1 item because of the Chemical Substance Regulation Law)

[a] (1) Manufactures and minerals, (2) agricultural and fisheries products.

TABLE 5
Ratio of Tariff Revenue to Imports, Selected Countries, 1970–1983

Year	Japan	U.S.	EC*a*	FRG	France	Italy
1961	5.8%	6.7%		7.1%	5.5%	7.4%
1965	8.0	6.8		4.1	6.4	
1970	6.9	5.7	7.4 (3.8)	5.9 (3.3)	5.8 (2.9)	7.5 (4.6)
1974	2.7	3.1	4.2 (2.1)	4.0 (2.0)	2.6 (1.5)	2.8 (1.7)
1979	3.1	3.9	3.9 (1.9)	4.0 (2.0)	2.3 (1.2)	1.8 (1.0)
1983	2.5	3.5	2.7			

SOURCES: Ministry of Finance, *Zaisei kin'yū tōkei geppō* (various issues).
*a*The figures for the EC include the surcharge on agricultural imports. Figures in parentheses are the ratio for total imports including imports from the other EC members; figures without parentheses are for imports from countries outside the EC. The EC includes Belgium, France, Italy, Luxembourg, the Netherlands, and West Germany before 1977, and these countries plus Denmark, Ireland, and the United Kingdom in 1979 and 1983.

or between different countries. Essentially this is an index number problem, that is, a difficulty in determining the appropriate weights in calculating the average. But judging from statistics on the "import burden ratio" (the ratio of total tariff revenues to the total value of imports, or to the total value of imports on which tariffs are levied), the changes in tariff rates on individual items during the KR and thereafter, and the implementation of the GSP, it seems that (1) the tariff level in Japan was about as high as those of the United States, the United Kingdom, and the EC and slightly higher than those of the Scandinavian countries and Switzerland before the start of the KR; (2) it declined substantially and more than any other country's between 1968 and 1975 (especially from 1973 to 1975); and (3) by the middle of the 1970s, it was lower than those of the United States, the EC, and the United Kingdom. By the early 1980s, officials in charge of the trade affairs of the major countries generally agreed that Japan's tariff rates were the lowest among them (see Table 5 for the average tariff levels of various industrial countries).

Trade Conflicts and the Japan-U.S. Textile Negotiations

Beginning from the late 1950s, the U.S. government occasionally asked the Japanese government to establish VERs on textiles and other labor-intensive, light-industry products. This situation continued into the 1960s. Diplomatic negotiations between Japan and the United States on such bilateral trade issues became prolonged and increasingly difficult in the case of textiles toward the end of the 1960s.

The rapid increases in Japanese exports to the United States of certain textile products and other light-industry commodities in the 1960s tended to induce protectionism in the United States. Generally speaking, this took one of the following forms: (1) the U.S. government acting at the request of private firms or groups adversely affected sometimes applied antidumping regulations, the escape clause, or countervailing duties; (2) VERs or export quotas based on intergovernmental agreement were introduced after diplomatic negotiations between the two countries; or (3) the U.S. Congress threatened to pass new laws restricting imports. In Japan, this situation or the process leading to restrictions on trade has been called "Japan-U.S. trade (or economic) friction (or conflict)" (*Nichi-Bei bōeki* [*keizai*] *masatsu*). This description applies to friction or conflicts over Japan's exports, but there are other conflicts over Japan's imports.

Among the trade conflicts over Japanese exports to the United States, those concerned with light-industry products like textiles and miscellaneous goods may be termed "old-type trade friction," whereas those concerned with color television sets, automobiles, motorcycles, machine tools, and integrated circuits can be called "new-type trade conflict." Trade conflicts over steel and special steel products may be considered an intermediate type.

The earliest round of Japan-U.S. textile negotiations resulted in the Short-term Agreement (STA) on the cotton textile trade in 1961. The negotiations continued intermittently until the first comprehensive Japan-U.S. agreement on the textile trade was concluded in 1971. This was a typical case of an old-type trade conflict. This was the first serious postwar trade conflict, and the diplomatic negotiations became increasingly troublesome and painful for the two countries. Here it is not necessary to discuss the details of the textile negotiations, but a few remarks from the viewpoint of the history of international trade policy are appropriate.[19]

When Japan and the United States agreed to conclude the STA as an administrative (intergovernmental) agreement in 1961, nobody thought that this was the beginning of widespread, detailed controls on trade in all kinds of textiles covering many countries. The quantitative restrictions on Japan's exports of cotton textile products to the United States was thereafter extended first to exports from Hong Kong, Taiwan, and South Korea and then to exports from all developing countries. On the side of the importing countries, import restrictions spread to European countries, Canada, and Australia.

The bilateral agreement on cotton trade, which was relatively informal in the beginning, became more and more formal, rigid, and multilateral. It also became highly complicated and more or less permanent. The STA on the cotton textile trade (1961) and the Long-term Agreement (LTA; 1962) were legally recognized by GATT and twice extended (1967, 1970). The United States was then threatened by a rapid expansion of Japanese synthetic fiber and woolen textile exports, and the wave of protectionism in the United States became overwhelming. The negotiations between Japan and the United States were prolonged, and unfortunately from the viewpoint of economics and world trade, the process became entangled in the U.S. presidential election and the restoration of Okinawa to Japan. Finally, the textile negotiations became so tense that the Japanese government had no choice but to accept the Japan-U.S. Textile Agreement in 1971, covering all textiles. The repercussions were great for all members of GATT. The Multi-Fiber Agreement (MFA) concluded in 1974 covered the worldwide trade of all textiles.

Textile products are important exports for many developing countries. The world trade in textiles today is regulated by rigid quantitative import restrictions under the MFA. Recently, some of the importing countries party to the MFA requested the developing countries exporting textile products to forgo even the modest (5%) annual increase in the quotas agreed on under the MFA. Nobody in favor of free and multilateral world trade would deny that MFA is an unfortunate precedent for formalized worldwide trade control that is strongly detrimental to the economic development of low-income (hence low-wage) developing countries and that it is a serious breach of the basic principles of GATT. It is, however, true that the transfer of the labor force from the textile industry to other industries poses a serious unemployment problem in the developed countries importing textiles since the textile industry is generally labor intensive and textile workers are either relatively unskilled or their skills are not of much use in other industries.[20] Most developed countries, the core members of GATT, felt at the time of the STA and LTA that it was difficult to observe the GATT rules strictly in regard to textile imports. Perhaps something like the STA, LTA, and MFA was necessary to maintain GATT as a more or less effective international agreement. Yet the benefits from these aberrations from free-trade principles are of doubtful value. Although fairly large-scale textile industries still exist in the United States and Western Europe, they have not recovered their international competitiveness. Much of the textile industry in the United States, Western Europe, and Australia is still essentially weak and viable only because of extensive import quotas and high tariffs.

Why did Japan readily accept the request of the United States to institute VERs on textile products at the beginning of the process described above? And why did the Japanese textile industry later strongly resist the U.S. request for export restrictions during the negotiations in 1968–71 for the Japan-U.S. Textile Agreement? The answer to the first question may be that Japanese political leaders felt obliged to accommodate the U.S. request in return for U.S. support for Japan's accession to GATT, as well as for the overall U.S. policy toward Japan. In any case, Japanese political leaders at the time did not want to create troubles in Japan-U.S.

relations. Another factor was that VERs, which allowed Japan to control exports, were considered more advantageous for Japan than other U.S. import-restriction measures.[21] VERs were considered the lesser evil and less likely to become permanent than more formal measures such as import quotas, tariffs, or tariff-quotas. The distribution of the rent element inherent in any quantitative restriction measure is more advantageous to the export industry under VERs than under import quotas or tariffs. Furthermore, the industries affected in the early stage—from the late 1950s to the early 1960s—were overwhelmingly small or medium-size firms with little political power.

The situation in the later years of the Japan-U.S. textile negotiations differed considerably. The leaders of the Japanese textile industry felt that they had long been suffering from the extensive voluntary export restraints since the late 1950s. They thought that the industry could not develop further if export restrictions were further strengthened and that there was no room for accepting an intergovernmental agreement freezing the status quo. Although small or medium-size firms dominated the production of many textile exports, there were large firms in the industry taken as a whole. When a majority of firms in the industry were united, their organizational and political power was considerable. Moreover, the cotton-spinning industry as well as several other major textile industries were centered in the Kansai region (the area around Osaka, Kyoto, and Kobe, and west of these cities) and had a tradition of free-trade beliefs dating from the Meiji period. Many leaders of the major Kansai-based textile companies were more independent and more liberal than the leaders of business circles in Tokyo, who were closer to the government and tended to favor government regulation.

Despite the industry's resistance, Japanese political leaders judged that it would be unwise to leave a major trade issue unsettled for long. The U.S. government succeeded in ending the long-running negotiations on the textile trade by strong, unilateral actions (including abolishment of the gold convertibility of the U.S. dollar and an across-the-board 10 per cent import surcharge), actions known in Japan as the "Nixon shock."

Since 1971, the Japanese textile industry has been losing its comparative advantage because of the rise in domestic wages and the growth of textile industries in the NICs. The share of textile products in Japan's total exports has been declining rapidly, and some of Japan's export quotas to the United States under the MFA have gone unfulfilled recently. It is even said that the rigid MFA now works to promote exports of Japanese textile products since the MFA restricts exports from the NICs to Europe and the United States, where Japanese exports have to compete with them.

Industrial adjustment in the Japanese textile industry has been relatively easy since its labor force is predominantly young female workers, who usually stay in the labor market only until they marry. Most young women now work in other industries, such as electric appliances, electronics, precision machinery, retail and wholesale trade, and service. Their wages are much higher not only absolutely but also relative to the average wage level for manufacturing or the economy as a whole than the wages young women received in the textile industry two or three decades ago.

Trade Conflicts in Other Areas

From 1968 to 1972, Japanese exports, especially to the United States, expanded rapidly, and Japan's overall balance of payments in its current account showed sizable surpluses. Trade friction tends to become more frequent and serious when the U.S. economy is in recession and Japan's balance of trade is positive, both overall and bilaterally with the United States. The period from 1968 to 1972 was the first such period. Japan experienced then what can be called the "first wave" of the Japan-U.S. trade conflict.

Among the more serious trade frictions were steel exports to the United States. A few years earlier, there had arisen a strong protectionist movement in the United States to restrict steel imports from Europe and Japan. A bill to establish import quotas for steel was introduced in Congress in 1967. Fearing that a formal quota system would be established, the Japanese steel industry set up a voluntary export restraint system in 1966, which was strengthened in 1969. A third VER was enforced from 1972 to 1974. During this period, the EC also introduced a VER on its steel exports to the United States. Meanwhile, Japanese steel exports to the EC increased rapidly from 1969 to 1971, and Japan has enforced a VER on its steel exports to the EC since 1972, with the exception of 1975.

We have characterized trade conflicts in the steel trade as an intermediate type. Japan once had a strong comparative advantage in textiles and other light-industry products based on cheap and efficient labor, whereas the strong international competitiveness of the Japanese steel industry is based on modern and sophisticated technology, locational advantage, and the large size of the domestic market. The steel industry is representative of heavy manufacturing, which policymakers of prewar and early postwar Japan as well as those of many developing countries until recently regarded as having central and symbolic importance in a modern industrial economy. The ability of the Japanese steel industry to compete successfully even in the North American and European markets since the middle of the 1960s indicated that the Japanese economy had reached a new stage of industrialization.

During this second period, trade conflicts arose over footwear and metal tableware (old type), special steel products, sheet glass, and fasteners (intermediate type), and electric and electronic machinery and parts and color television sets (new type). The response of the Japanese color television producers to the trade conflicts is worth noting. They partially replaced exports of their products by direct investment and production in the United States. They also invested in some MICs and exported sets produced there to the United States. The trade conflict over color television sets was solved in this way. This shift to foreign production in response to trade conflicts is becoming common in several other industries such as video tape recorders and motor vehicles.

The Post–Oil Crisis Period, 1976–1984

The economies of many developed countries heavily dependent on imported petroleum as a source of energy were hard hit by the first and second oil crises and experienced serious stagflation. The impact of the oil crises and stagflation soon spread worldwide, including the developing countries and Eastern Europe. Whereas the impact of the first oil crisis was limited mostly to the developed countries, the stagnation following the second oil crisis was more widespread. From 1981 to 1983, the value of world trade dropped from the previous year's level for the first time since World War II. The sharp increase in petroleum prices as well as stagnation following the second oil crisis depressed world demand for petroleum and resulted in a fall in petroleum prices in 1982 and 1983. This contributed to a decline in both the volume and value of world trade since trade in petroleum made up a large portion of world trade by then.

Stagflation hovered over the world economy in the late 1970s and the early 1980s. Unemployment increased annually and led to the rise of protectionism in many countries. The volume of exports of primary commodities and light manufacturing products from developing countries to developed countries generally declined. The international debts of developing countries rose rapidly. Many countries experienced difficulties in servicing their debt and were forced to reduce imports. It thus became increasingly difficult for the world economy to maintain the regime of multilateral free trade.

Despite this unfavorable international environment, the performance of the Japanese economy was good in comparison with that of other major developed countries. Although the inflation rate in Japan during the first oil crisis was among the highest of the major developed countries, the price level stabilized quickly. Inflation during the second oil crisis was well contained and short-lived. Although much lower than in the 1960s, Japan's growth rate was a fairly stable 4 to 6 per cent, a respectable rate much higher and much more stable than that of most other developed countries. The relatively satisfactory performance of the Japanese economy—its containment of inflation, low unemployment, stable growth, and a rapid increase in productivity and technological progress in manufacturing industries—attracted the attention of many developed countries as well as of developing countries such as China. Japan's position in the international economic community improved remarkably. With this rise in status, foreign countries have come to expect much more from Japan than in earlier times, and Japan has received more and more criticism from other countries.

Changes in Japan's Structure of Trade and Balance of Payments

An extensive change has taken place in the composition of Japan's trade since the first oil crisis. Because of the rise in energy prices after the first oil crisis, the share of mineral fuel in the total value of Japanese imports increased sharply, from 20.7 per cent in 1970 to 44.3 per cent in 1975 to 49.8 per cent in 1980 to 50.6 per cent in 1981. This occurred even though the ratio of energy consumption to real GNP fell substantially because of economizing in energy consumption in individual sectors and the shift in Japan's industrial structure in response to high energy prices. Furthermore, the ratio of domestic supply of food to total consumption has fallen year by year: the share of food in total imports has been in the range of 12–15 per cent since the beginning of the 1970s. In addition, raw materials for manufacturing industries amount to about 20 per cent of total imports. Thus, by the early 1980s, these three groups accounted for some 80 per cent of total Japanese imports. Despite extensive import liberalization, imports of manufactured goods, especially those of finished products, remain low, both relative to GNP and as a proportion of total imports. The low level of imports of finished products has become a focal point of the trade conflict with the European countries and the United States.

The largest change in Japanese exports was a rise in machinery products from 46.3 per cent of all exports in 1970 to 53.8 per cent in 1975 to 67.8 per cent in 1983. The shares of various types of machine goods, automobiles and other transportation equipment, and precision machinery and apparatus all rose conspicuously. Exports of labor-intensive products such as textiles declined sharply. Industries producing intermediate materials such as steel were also losing their comparative advantage as a result of increasing energy costs and a rise of competitors in the NICs.

Japan's terms of trade deteriorated greatly as a result of the two oil crises; from 100 in the base year of 1970, the terms of trade declined to around 60 in 1981. The balance of payments in the current account recorded large deficits of about 1 per cent of GNP in 1974 and 1980, the peak years of the two oil crises. In each case, however, the balance of payments improved promptly. Especially since 1982, Japan has recorded large and increasing current-account surpluses, larger than those from the late 1960s through 1972 and 1976 through 1978, relative to GNP. This has become another major focal point of foreign criticism of Japan.

Comparative Advantage in Japan

The change in the structure of Japanese exports since 1975 reflects the changing pattern of comparative advantage of the Japanese economy during the turbulence the world economy has experienced since the beginning of the 1970s. Japan has been strongly competitive in the world market since the latter half of the 1970s in industries with the following characteristics: (1) processing industries, especially the fabricating and assembly–type manufacturing industries with production processes consisting of parts production and assembly; (2) use of technology for mass production of standardized products, reflecting the large domestic market in Japan; (3) strict quality control to obtain uniformity of quality, a low proportion of deficient output, and relatively problem-free use; (4) differentiated products, requiring a marketing and service network and "fine-textured" maintenance services for users; (5) fields in which continuous cost reductions are made by accumulating small improvements in production process and product design; (6) product planning and development and accumulation of small improvements of products responding to the needs and preference of users and to changes in their preferences; (7) organizational skills in arranging stages and steps of production and in closely coordinating the timing of production and transportation; and (9) cooperation and coordination among firms in different fields and of different sizes (including the subcontracting system, but not necessarily restricted to it) and among engineers specializing in different areas.

Typical industries with these characteristics are automobiles, electronics, electric machinery, motorcycles, cameras, pianos, audio equipment, communication equipment and apparatus, machine tools, and machinery with electronic controls. These industries are strongly competitive in the world market. The shipbuilding industry lacks the second characteristic, and parts of it also lack the fourth characteristic, yet it satisfies the other conditions, especially 5, 6, and 7. The steel industry does not meet the conditions 1 and 4; but it does meet the other conditions. A part of the textile industry producing high-quality products satisfies 4, 6, 8, and Japan still enjoys a comparative advantage there.

Japan does not have a comparative advantage in all manufacturing industries, especially those with the following characteristics: (1) fields in which R&D plays an important role and R&D itself; (2) industries requiring large-scale fixed plant or apparatus (the exception may be the steel industry); (3) industries closely linked with natural resources; (4) industrial machinery and machine tools based on special technology, especially large-scale machines, with small production runs; (5) industries consuming a large amount of energy;[22] and (6) industries requiring a large amount of unskilled labor.

Airplanes, the chemical industry in general, pharmaceuticals and other specialty chemicals, petrochemicals, paper and pulp, and nonferrous metals are examples of manufacturing industries that satisfy some of the above characteristics and in which Japan does not have a comparative advantage. Condition 5 became more salient after the two oil crises. Aluminum refining, petrochemicals, and some basic chemicals are now declining industries in Japan. By contrast, although not yet prominent industries, Japan has long traditions in fermented products and in ceramics. Japan may well attain a prominent position in the world market in products based on biotechnology and in new ceramics. The production technologies in which Japan has a comparative advantage have wide applicability, and manufacturing industries based on such characteristics have and will continue to have a strong and quite versatile basis in our view.

Until recently, Japan did not have a comparative advantage in R&D and depended heavily on the United States, the United Kingdom, West Germany, France, and Switzerland for new technologies and new products. Japan's payments of royalties on patents and processes far exceed receipts. Japan receives the major portion of its royalties from developing countries.

Patented technology or the possession of patented technology is not crucial for superior business performance in such industries as shipbuilding, steel, automobiles, electronic products, and machine tools, in which Japan has had or now has a comparative advantage.[23] Japan depends on foreign countries for basic technology and has a comparative advantage in production engineering, control of production processes, improvement of production processes and products, quality control and marketing, all of which depend on the versatile ability characterized by the items in the first list above. This pattern of comparative advantage has resulted in a rapid expansion of machinery exports since 1975.

As many engineering firms in Japan achieved success, however, their R&D expenditures increased steadily, and in recent years many firms have developed their own new technologies. In some firms, receipts of royalties from abroad exceed payments abroad. But it will take some time until Japan's overall balance of payments for technological royalties turns positive.

The Second and Third Waves of the Japan-U.S. Trade Conflict

The first wave of the Japan-U.S. trade conflict occurred in 1968–72. The second wave took place in 1976–78, and the third has been ongoing since 1981. During each of these periods, Japan experienced a large trade surplus, and the United States a large trade deficit. Many European countries ran trade deficits as well. Exports of manufacturing goods, especially machinery, from Japan to industrialized countries in North America and Europe increased sharply in these periods. In the countries to which imports of specific products increased rapidly from Japan, especially the United States, movements arose aimed at restricting imports from Japan, and the issue of a bilateral trade deficit with Japan became politicized. Because of this, the second and third waves of the trade conflict between Japan and the United States became far more serious than the conflicts of earlier years, as did trade conflicts between Japan and some European countries. It is no exaggeration to say that the Japan-U.S. trade conflict has been a chronic disease since the beginning of the 1980s.[24] The focus of foreign complaints against Japan has shifted from labor-intensive, light manufacturing products, through an intermediate phase, to sophisticated differentiated products of the medium- to high-technology industries, such as color television sets, automobiles, numerically controlled machine tools, integrated circuits, and video tape recorders.

The politicization of trade conflicts also involves Japanese imports. The United States and the European countries have requested Japan to reduce its overall and bilateral trade surpluses and to increase its imports, especially of manufactures from the United States and Europe. The major focal points of discussions on Japanese imports in the third wave have been agricultural products such as beef, oranges, and cigarettes; leather products; the problem of government procurement, especially procurement by Nihon Telephone and Telegraph Corporation; the problem of standards for metal baseball bats and communication equipment; and tariff rates on certain wood products. Foreign countries further criticized the low ratio of imports of manufactures both to total imports and to GNP and the supposedly closed system of distribution and industrial organization, which were considered the cause of the low import ratio.

The diplomatic negotiations on trade conflict issues between Japan and the United States were similar to the earlier textile negotiations in that they were prolonged, complicated, and painful. Unlike usual trade negotiations, in the Japan-U.S. discussions on trade frictions in the second- and third-wave periods, the United States simply pressed Japan to liberalize imports in which the United States has interests, primarily in view of Japan's large overall and bilateral balance-of-trade surplus. Usually trade negotiations between two countries take the form of give-and-take, but in these negotiations, which have been going on almost continuously from 1976, the subject matter has been simply how much and how soon Japan would make concessions, with the United States offering little if anything in exchange. Moreover, during this period the United States has been raising its barriers to imports from Japan in various forms; for example, by requesting Japan to introduce VERs on color television sets and automobiles and by raising tariffs on small commercial vehicles and motorcycles.[25]

Japan's VER on automobile exports was one of the most important trade-conflict problems in the third wave. Although Japan had previously agreed to institute VERs on various products, the VER on automobiles was special in several respects. First, automobile exports constitute a large portion of Japan's exports to the United States and elsewhere. Second, the United States has long been the world leader of the automobile industry. Third, this industry has long been a key industry in the United States. Fourth, the automobile market in the United States is highly concentrated, and its products are considerably differentiated. Under such conditions, the VER on Japanese exports enabled U.S. producers to raise prices. Under free trade, U.S. producers must take into account a possible shift of demand to Japanese products when they raise prices, whereas under a VER they can raise prices without fear. Even if the export ceiling under a VER is equal to the level of exports that would be achieved under free trade, the VER leads to a substantial price increase.[26] This change in the behavior of U.S. producers could benefit Japanese producers unless the ceiling under the VER is much lower than the free-trade level.

Automobile prices in the United States rose substantially after the VER was introduced. Although a part of this increase can be explained by the upgrading of the quality of Japanese exports, a considerable portion of the price increase was essentially the result of cartelization. No one would deny that U.S. consumers were hurt by the VER.[27]

The Tokyo Round

Japan played a leading role in the Tokyo Round (TR) of GATT, the first large-scale, multilateral trade negotiation (MTN) after the KR, in which a record number of 99 countries participated. The Japanese government proposed the TR at the general meeting of GATT in November 1971, and its implementation was announced at the Tokyo meeting of the Ministerial Council of GATT in September 1973. However, its actual start had to await U.S. legislation enabling the president to negotiate with other countries on tariffs and other trade policy matters.[28] After passage of the legislation in January 1975, the negotiations began in February of the same year. Since 1974 and 1975 were a very inopportune time, there were many difficulties and the negotiations took much time. The TR was successfully concluded in December 1979. The main results of the TR were as follows.

1. Tariff rates levied by developed countries on manufactures were reduced by about 33 per cent on the average.

2. Tariffs on agricultural products were substantially reduced. The value of international trade in agricultural products on which tariffs were reduced amounted to about $15 billion in 1976. The KR had not covered agricultural tariffs.

3. Although the main theme of the KR was tariff reductions, the TR covered both tariffs and nontariff barriers and considered them as equally important subjects. Agreements on nontariff barriers such as antidumping regulations, government procurement, subsidies, countervailing tariffs, and standards were successfully concluded.

4. The principle of not expecting reciprocity from developing countries was carried over from the KR, and several agreements were reached about the legal basis of GSP and other preferences granted to developing countries.

Issues on which agreement were not reached that were left for future negotiations were (1) safeguards; (2) certain special problems of developing countries; (3) further liberalization of trade in agricultural products; (4) dispute-settlement procedures; (5) the trade in services; (6) trade-related international investment; (7) problems related to high-technology industries; (8) illegal products; and (9) adoption of a unified international classification system.

Japan took the initiative in beginning the TR negotiation and was, together with the United States, the most active participant. Japan offered tariff reductions on the largest number of items and was the first state to ratify all the agreements. Moreover, in March 1978 the Japanese government carried out the first round of tariff reductions in advance of the agreed time schedule, partly to express its enthusiasm for the successful conclusion of the negotiations and partly in response to a sharp rise in Japan's trade surplus in 1976–78.

It is clear that Japan held a much more influential position in the international economic community than at the time of the KR. The Japanese recognized much better than in earlier times that Japan benefited from worldwide multilateral free trade and that Japan should play a leading role in preserving and strengthening the multilateral free-trade regime. Such a change in Japanese perceptions was behind Japan's leadership in the TR.

Given the number of participating countries, the list of agreed tariff reductions, the number of the agreements on nontariff barriers, and their contents, one might conclude that the TR was a remarkable achievement. Many would agree that it was epochal in that it furthered the substantial reduction of tariffs achieved during the KR and reached agreement on a wide range of issues concerning nontariff barriers.[29]

On the other hand, the TR took a long time from announcement to conclusion. Many participating countries encountered difficult economic conditions during the negotiations because of the first oil crisis, the ensuing balance-of-payments difficulties, severe inflation, and the deepest depression since World War II. It was natural under such circumstances that protectionism rose in many countries and support for free trade weakened. Despite these problems, however, the TR continued and was successfully concluded, although the participants could not reach agreement on certain issues.

A system for international cooperation like GATT resembles a bicycle: it stops unless efforts are continuously made to keep it going. In this sense, the TR was important in preserving the multilateral free-trade system during the period of severe difficulties for the world economy. The Japanese government apparently realized this and took the initiative in the TR. For the same reason, it has played an active role in opening another new round, the Uruguay Round.

Changing Trade Policy Philosophy

Throughout the 1970s and early 1980s, the international environment surrounding Japan changed drastically, and Japan's industrial capability was strengthened remarkably. The status of Japan in the international community rose substantially. However, the relatively good performance of the Japanese economy after the two oil crises and the success of the Japanese machinery and electronic industries in the world market began to cause an increasing number of trade frictions, and strong tendencies toward protectionism have developed in many major industrialized countries against the expansion of Japanese exports. Foreign requests that Japan open its domestic market have become stronger and more frequent.

In keeping with these basic changes, the dominant philosophy among Japan's economic policy authorities and the Japanese public has changed considerably. The philosophy that free trade is basically the most desirable policy for the Japanese economy, although there could be exceptions such as agricultural protection, has gained recognition among policymakers, leading businessmen, and knowledgeable people. Japan's trade policy, which in the past tended toward mercantilist strategies of promoting exports and restricting imports began to change toward freer trade. At the same time, Japan's regulation-oriented economic policy philosophy has gradually been evolving toward a free-competition, market-oriented philosophy.

One manifestation of the new free-trade philosophy was the extensive tariff reduction put into effect in March 1978 in advance of the conclusion of the TR. The reduction covered some 125 items, including automobiles and main-frame computers. After the conclusion of the TR, other tariff reductions were implemented in April 1980 in advance of the agreed schedule. The extent of Japan's tariff reductions under the TR was generally greater than those of other countries, and Japan's average tariff level after the complete realization of the TR tariff concessions will be considerably lower than the corresponding levels of other major developed countries. Officials in charge of trade affairs in other major industrialized countries now generally agree that Japan has the lowest import tariffs.

As mentioned above, most of the residual import restrictions on manufactured goods were removed in the previous period. During the third period, partial liberalization (liberalization of import restrictions on some BTN 4-digit items) was put into effect for a number of items in April 1978, and "nonresidual" import restrictions on ten items were removed in January 1980. It is difficult to assess the height of various nontariff barriers in different countries, and the extent of changes in them. Yet Japan completed the necessary procedures for acceptance of all the MTN agreements on nontariff barriers concluded in the TR in advance of all other signatories. As of September 1980, Japan was the only country that had accepted all agreements unconditionally and completed the necessary legal procedures. In addition, Japan simplified customs inspection procedures, sent delegations abroad to promote exports to Japan, and implemented several import promotion measures. Furthermore, after 1980 the Japanese government renewed its effort to liberalize foreign exchange controls and began deregulating domestic financial markets and the telecommunication system.

Another manifestation of the newly emerging free-trade philosophy in Japan is that at the Bonn summit meeting (1985) and in the preparatory meetings for it, Japan jointly with the United States eagerly advocated a new GATT round to further remove trade barriers among the major countries.

Agricultural Protection

Japan's trade policy on agricultural imports is a major exception to its newly emerging free-trade policy. Residual import quotas still remain on 22 agricultural products and on a number of items under nonresidual import quotas for the purpose of protecting domestic agriculture. The gap between world prices and domestic prices of cereal products, which is an approximate measure of the strength of protection, is generally higher in Japan than in the EC and in the United States.[30] Japan's dependence on cereals and other food imports is, however, much higher than that of the EC or of the United States.

The political and social forces behind Japan's agricultural protectionism are complex and cannot be explained briefly. Although the policy authorities or agricultural economists who favor agricultural protectionism have rarely stated its purpose explicitly, the principal purposes of Japan's agricultural protection appear to be (1) maintaining a certain degree of domestic self-sufficiency in food supplies or preventing a decline in that degree; and (2) securing opportunities for farmers to earn income, especially those in agricultural prefectures in which there are few alternatives to agricultural employment. The second purpose may be interpreted as serving two further goals: promoting the transmission of basic agricultural technology in farm families in order to maintain some self-sufficiency in food supplies, and sustaining the level of income of farmers, who are now predominantly older persons.

The majority of farmers are now so old that they are reluctant to move to other parts of Japan, and it would be quite costly to move them. Once thrown out of agriculture, they could scarcely work and earn income. Keeping them on the farm may well be a second-best policy, even from a purely economic point of view. Most farmers in agricultural prefectures—the periphery of Japan in relation to the prosperous, industrial center—lack easy access to income-earning opportunities other than agriculture or agriculture-related activities or organizations such as food processing, meat packing, feed mixing, and agricultural cooperatives, which pursue not only agricultural, but also commercial, financial, and political activities. If farmers could gain easier access to alternative income-earning opportunities, the pressure for agricultural protection would be much weakened. It is now much more difficult to provide alternative income-earning opportunities for farmers than in the high growth period, not only for the obvious economic reason, but also for demographic reasons.

Is Japan's Domestic Market Really Open?

In the United States and European countries, the notion that Japan's domestic market is very closed remains prevalent, even though it is widely recognized that the average level of import tariffs is much lower in Japan than in other major developed countries; that, as far as manufactures are concerned, residual import quotas remain on only four items (leather products); and that Japan was the first of the TR signatories to implement all of the codes on nontariff barriers (the Standard Code, Government Procurement Code, Customs Valuation Code, and Import Licensing Code). But has Japan really liberalized imports of manufactures and has Japan's domestic market really become an open one? Or compared with other developed countries do visible and invisible barriers to imports still remain?

It is not easy to find the correct answer to these questions. Knowledgeable foreigners cannot deny that Japan's tariffs are generally lower than those of other major industrialized countries, and foreign complaints about the closedness of Japan's domestic market are concerned mainly with nontariff barriers.[31] Although tariffs and quantitative restrictions on imports (quotas and embargoes) can be identified readily and compared internationally—with some difficulties—nontariff barriers other than quantitative restrictions are difficult to identify, measure, and compare. Most nontariff barriers are not even objective entities: whether a certain governmental measure or institutional arrangement constitutes a nontariff barrier depends on subjective judgment and can be controversial. For example, from an importing country's point of view, an import quarantine for a vegetable or animal may be absolutely necessary to protect against dissemination of certain diseases; from an exporting country's point of view, it may be an unnecessary nontariff barrier since there is no danger of dissemination, especially when proper care is taken. Various standards and approval systems for safety and consumer protection, importing procedures, and government procurement policies that are necessary for some legitimate purposes and not intended to favor domestic products or domestic suppliers may have characteristics foreigners consider discriminatory against imports. It is exactly in these areas where foreign complaints about Japan's nontariff barriers concentrate. It is difficult to know the facts about what are said to be nontariff barriers, to judge whether they are unnecessary barriers to trade, and to compare them with similar institutions in other countries. Moreover, the actual treatment of imports often differs from the official rules or announced policies in this area.[32]

Since the Meiji period, the Japanese government, as the government of a small, latecomer developing country, has pursued policies to develop domestic industries and modernize the country. From the beginning of industrialization until the late 1960s, Japan's balance of payments has tended toward a deficit, except for a short period around World War I. As a result, government regulation of economic life tends to be pervasive, and institutions tend to give preference to domestic industries over imports and foreign suppliers. It is no wonder that foreigners have had difficulties understanding and dealing with the Japanese economic system. Considering the historical legacy, institutions and a traditional mentality unfavorable to imports and foreigners doing business in Japan remain despite policies since the 1960s to liberalize imports and direct foreign investment.

Since the last years of the 1960s, however, the Japanese government has almost consistently pursued policies of reducing nontariff barriers and promoting imports. In 1981, when the large current-account deficits resulting from the second oil crisis were disappearing, it renewed efforts to reduce import barriers, and from 1982 through 1984 it announced and implemented a series of "packages" of comprehensive import-promoting measures. These include reduction or elimination of tariffs, removal of quotas, improvement of importing procedures and other regulations, dispatch of import promotion missions abroad, and opening of import fairs in Japan.

Beginning in February 1982, the Japanese government reviewed about a hundred rules regarding importing procedures, standards, testing, and so on that had been subject to foreign criticisms and took measures on three-quarters of them. In 1982, the Office of Trade Ombudsman (OTO, later expanded to the Office of Trade and Investment Ombudsman) was established to expedite complaints from foreign and Japanese businessmen about importing procedures and government regulations. The OTO received a total of 159 complaints by the end of August 1984 and instituted improvements or corrected misunderstandings in 117 of them.

Admittedly, these are no answer to the questions posed at the beginning of this section. Yet the serious efforts of the Japanese government to reduce what are thought to be barriers to imports must be taken into account when evaluating the openness—or closedness—of Japan's domestic market.[33]

The Low Level of Imports of Manufactures

The low level of manufactured goods in Japan's total imports as well as relative to GNP can be explained as follows. The share of minerals, fuel, raw materials, and food in the total imports of Japan is quite large because of its poor endowments of natural resources and land. Japan has a strong comparative disadvantage in natural resources and agriculture and an equally strong comparative advantage over a wide range of manufactures. Moreover, Japan has no neighboring countries that are similar in language, culture, and income level.[34]

The last condition seems to be an important aspect of the low level of import of manufactures. In order to enjoy a good reputation with consumers and firms in Japan, foreign firms must develop products that conform to the way of living of the Japanese people, the dimensions of their bodies, and their tastes and must provide stable supplies and careful follow-up services. Because of the barriers of language, customs, and distance, few firms have succeeded in taking deep roots in Japan's domestic market, although there are now quite a few—and a growing number of—exceptions.

Political Background of Trade Policy

In the post–oil crisis period, it became increasingly obvious that Japan's prosperity depends critically on the world multilateral trade system. In earlier periods Japan was nearly a free-rider on the world trade system, but as it emerged as the second largest highly industrialized free-market economy in the world and as its share in world trade, especially trade in manufactures, became conspicuously large, Japanese policymakers came to recognize the necessity of positive actions to maintain and strengthen the world free-trade system. For that purpose, Japan had to adhere faithfully to the free-trade principles of GATT. But in any country with parliamentary democracy, a move from protectionism or mercantilism toward free trade is politically a rough and rugged path.

Trade policy during the third period has evolved under the balance of power between a group aiming at freer trade and another group trying to maintain the status quo. The former consists of the leaders of the government, the Ministry of International Trade and Industry (MITI), excluding some *genkyoku* sections dealing with specific industries; the Ministry of Foreign Affairs; parts of the Ministry of Finance; and the leaders of the *zaikai* (the industry and business world), who are in a position to consider Japan's overall economic welfare and its position in the international community. The Economic Planning Agency and the Fair Trade Commission are also liberal, free trade–oriented offices. The other group consists of the leaders of a wide variety of industries (including agriculture) and interest groups that suffer or are supposed to suffer from trade liberalization; *genkyoku* sections in the ministries and agencies that superintend such industries; and politicians, especially in the Liberal Democratic Party, representing the interests of such industries or regions where such industries are located. The government offices that tend to be protectionist are the Ministry of Agriculture, Forestry, and Fisheries, the Ministry of Public Welfare, the Ministry of Transportation, some *genkyoku* sections in MITI, and the Ministry of Posts and Telecommunications. This group often resists implementation of trade-liberalization measures contemplated and planned under the initiative of the first group. The trade policy of Japan during this period evolved as a steady but piecemeal advancement toward freer-trade policies; the advancement was rapid in some times and in some areas and slow in others.[35]

The political background of Japan's agricultural protectionism is illustrative. Japan is similar to other developed countries in that farmers are well organized politically and their representation in the parliament is disproportionately stronger than those of other groups, such as urban residents, consumers, and export industries. This is partly the result of the distribution of parliamentary seats, which has favored rural districts. Urban residents (and, strange as it may seem to foreigners, even consumers' groups sometimes) in Japan are, however, generally sympathetic to farmers. This sympathy is partly based on the general public's uneasiness about Japan's heavy dependence on imported food supplies. Furthermore, most urban families are only one or two generations removed from farming, and they still have strong ties with relatives in rural communities. Thus, urban residents and consumers do not consider their interests as directly opposed to those of farmers, who are often parents, brothers, sisters, or cousins.

In our view, the year 1973 was the turning point in the history of Japan's agricultural protection policy. Until then, a majority of Japanese did not feel uneasy about depending on imported food supplies. This was one factor behind Japan's sharply increasing dependence on imported food throughout the 1960s. (In fact, Japan's current dependence on food imports is markedly higher than that of other major industrialized countries. Although the United Kingdom, Switzerland, and Sweden are also heavily dependent on food imports, the size of Japan's imports of cereals and foodstuffs is strikingly large.) In 1973, a series of events, including the oil crisis, sharp worldwide rises in food prices, and the U.S. embargo of soybean exports to Japan, shook the so-far complacent Japanese. Suddenly they came to realize the vulnerability of the Japanese economy to external shocks and began to think that a further increase in the degree of dependence on food and energy imports would be unsafe and undesirable. This change in attitudes strengthened the political basis of agricultural protectionism.

In regard to import liberalization in other areas, the political power of consumers is weak in Japan, as it perhaps is in other countries. To have a job and to have a position in an organization through which one can exert influence appear to be much more important than small reductions in the prices of some goods.

Intensification of Japan-U.S. Economic Conflicts

Since 1983, the Japan-U.S. trade conflicts have been aggravated as the U.S. overall current-account deficit, Japan's overall current-account surplus, and the Japan-U.S. bilateral trade imbalance all increased to unprecedented levels. On the Japanese side, the ratio of the current-account surplus to GNP rose to over 1.8 per cent in 1983 and 2.9 per cent in 1984 (the highest figures in the past were 2.3 per cent in 1971 and 2.2 per cent in 1972; it never reached the 2 per cent level from 1973 to 1982); on the U.S. side, the ratio of the current-account deficit to GNP increased to 1.0 per cent in 1983 and 2.6 per cent in 1984 (the highest figures in the past were 0.5, 0.7, and 0.6 per cent in 1972, 1977, and 1978 respectively).

In the United States, the notion spread that such a large balance-of-payments deficit was detrimental to the economy, that the large U.S. deficit was caused by the closedness of Japan's domestic market and the resulting large surplus in Japan's balance of payments, that the Japanese government's trade policy was aimed at increasing the trade surplus or at least keeping imports from increasing, and that if Japan's domestic market were opened by abolishing or reducing artificial trade barriers, U.S. exports to Japan would increase enough to eliminate or substantially diminish the U.S.-Japan bilateral trade imbalance as well as the overall U.S. deficit. These notions arose partly because export expansion in Japan more than compensated the deterioration in Japan's terms of trade, Japan's export expansion tended to be concentrated in a limited number of product areas, and Japanese exports replaced the products of the import-competing industries in the United States.

From an economic point of view, the large imbalance in the balance of payments in the current account reflects the large saving-investment gap between the United States and Japan. Unless gross national saving is increased and investment reduced in the United States, its trade deficit cannot be reduced. The appropriate policy for the United States is to reduce the government budget deficit—that is, to reduce the dissaving in the government sector—and to increase household saving. Also, from 1982 to 1985, the overvalued dollar discouraged and promoted imports. This, in turn, suppressed domestic production and reduced income and saving. In order to reduce the U.S. balance-of-payments deficit, it is apparently necessary to reduce the budget deficits. But many U.S. politicians pay no attention to this simple fact and continue to blame Japan for the trade imbalance. The general mood in Washington toward Japan has worsened rapidly since the beginning of 1985.

Initially, Japan-U.S. bilateral negotiations revolved around trade issues, but as time went by they became more diverse. Since around 1976, the U.S. government has extended bilateral negotiations to a wider range of economic policy issues, such as the yen-dollar exchange rate, Japan's macroeconomic policies, liberalization of foreign exchange controls, domestic financial deregulation, Japan's industrial policy, and internationalization of the yen. Thus, since the second half of the 1970s, the Japan-U.S. *trade* conflict has turned into a Japan-U.S. *economic* conflict.

An Overview: The Past and the Near Future

There have been a number of unexpected events in Japan's trade since 1955, and both Japan's trade and the Japanese government's trade policy have changed much over the past three decades. At the beginning of this period, Japan was a small, newly industrializing country that depended chiefly on cheap-labor products to earn foreign exchange. Japan is now one of the largest trading nations in the world and plays a leading role in the arena of international trade diplomacy. In the following, we summarize what we consider some of the most important findings from the previous sections, evaluate Japan's current international trade relations, and speculate on prospects for the future.

Favorable International Environment for Japan

The rapid development of Japan's trade since the 1950s was one of the most important factors behind its successful industrialization and high growth rate. World trade developed steadily and fairly rapidly throughout the past three decades except for the past few years. The international economic environment was favorable enough for Japan to achieve a very high rate of growth of imports and exports as well as of real GNP.

The gains from international trade for Japan have not been restricted to gains from a better allocation of already existing productive resources. In the past thirty years, the composition of Japan's exports has changed greatly: many new products unknown at the beginning have emerged in the list of exports. Japan's productivity, technology, the industrial capabilities of the Japanese people, and the managerial capacity of Japanese firms have improved remarkably, and both the level of wages and per capita income have risen greatly. The human resources of Japan (knowledge, technologies, skills, and managerial ability) have expanded greatly through Japan's active participation in international trade.

Changing Comparative Advantage

At the beginning, Japan had a comparative advantage mainly in labor-intensive products depending on cheap yet high-quality labor and a comparative disadvantage in most primary products closely related to natural resources and land and certain types of machinery and chemicals using sophisticated technologies and requiring large amounts of capital. As time went by, wage levels and technology rose, and the pattern of Japan's comparative advantage shifted toward processing and assembling–type manufacturing industries that depend on mass-production methods and medium to high technologies.

Japan's comparative advantage today is based on such factors as organizational and managerial skills, intelligent and cooperative labor, an efficient use of information, and flexibility in shifting resources from one sector to another. Such technologies in a wider sense are of a versatile character and can be applied over a fairly wide range of manufacturing industries. It appears that Japan will lead other countries in this kind of technology and hence in a fairly wide range of sophisticated manufacturing industries for some time to come.

Since such technologies can be applied to many new industries in which technological innovation is taking place or for which the world demand is increasing rapidly, and since Japan has a severe comparative disadvantage in industries dependent on natural resources and land, free multilateral world trade will be most advantageous for Japan. Thus Japan will remain strongly in favor of free multilateral trade.

Discrimination Against Japan Within GATT

Japan has been discriminated against in several ways in the GATT system and in trade among the major industrialized countries. The forms of discrimination include the application of the Article 35 against Japan, discriminatory import restrictions on Japanese products, and VERs requested by importing countries. Japan is the only member-country of GATT subjected to these forms of discrimination by a large number of other member-countries and over a wide range of products. Gerald Curzon and Victoria Curzon wrote in 1976 that when Japanese wage levels approached European and North American levels, discrimination against Japan would cease.[36] Even today, however, when Japan's wage levels exceed those of several European countries, including the United Kingdom, a wide range of discriminatory practices by European countries against Japanese products still remains. Moreover, discrimination against Japanese exports has intensified in recent years.

Despite this wide range of discriminatory practices, however, Japan's exports increased at a much higher rate than that of the whole world, even in recent years. This implies that although there were barriers and discrimination against Japan, a majority of the countries under the GATT system imported increasing amounts of Japanese products. Thus, Japan enjoyed wide opportunities for trade by participating in the GATT system, despite discrimination against it within the system.

Changing Economic Policy Philosophy

The theory or philosophy of trade policy prevalent among Japanese government officials and leading businessmen has changed considerably during the past three decades. At the beginning, they held a mercantilist philosophy of exporting as much and importing as little as possible and of controlling even the smallest activities of private enterprises. Along with the development of Japanese industry and worldwide trade, however, the philosophy of free trade and free enterprise have become increasingly dominant.

On the one hand, after the two oil crises, the relatively favorable performance of the Japanese economy attracted the attention of many other countries, and the role of Japan in the world economy and in world trade became more prominent. On the other hand, the trade surpluses in 1976–78 and since 1983 have been considered as a major disturbing factor in the world economy, although such a view is doubtful from an economic viewpoint. Hence, the pressure on Japan for trade liberalization became stronger. Moreover, both foreigners and Japanese now expect Japan to play a more active and constructive role in the maintaining and strengthening the world free-trade regime. As a result of such changes and pressures, the dominant philosophy of trade policy in Japan has been changing steadily. It was in response to such a change that Japan, together with the United States, played a leading role in the Tokyo Round of GATT and is now eagerly supporting another round.

Of course, the resistance of protectionist groups in Japan has been, and is still, quite strong. Industries and specific regions that are supposed to suffer from import liberalization and market deregulation strongly resist such policy changes. But government leaders, MITI (excluding some *genkyoku* offices), the Ministry of Foreign Affairs, and business leaders now fully recognize the importance of the world free-trade system to Japan and are quite eager to contribute to maintaining the free, multilateral trade system. Japan's trade policy has been evolving under the balance of power between these two groups.

The Process of Import Liberalization

As Japan's balance of payments improved and as requests for import liberalization by foreign countries, especially by the United States, became increasingly strong, Japan's import liberalization proceeded rapidly at some times and in some areas and slowly in others, but it has advanced steadily and more or less continuously since the late 1960s except during the two oil crises. Roughly speaking, the pace of tariff reduction and the removal or relaxation of quotas and other nontariff barriers were directly related to the strength of outside pressure and the size of the balance-of-payments surplus. In contrast, in areas where domestic interest groups strongly resisted, as in agriculture, import liberalization made little progress. The pace of import liberalization also depended on the development of multilateral trade negotiations.

There have been few cases where trade liberalization policy was reversed; that is, where an import quota was reinstituted.[37] This is quite different from the situation in the United States and European countries, where progress toward freer trade has often been reversed, especially since the first oil crisis.

As a result of steady import liberalization, Japan now has perhaps the lowest tariffs among the major countries. Japan's nontariff barriers are also perhaps among the lowest of major industrialized countries, although international comparison in this area is difficult. The barriers to imports of manufactures in the United States and European countries cannot be said to be lower than Japan's if one takes into account import restrictions under the Multi-Fiber Agreement, discriminatory import restrictions against Japan, and VERs that these countries formally or informally ask Japan and developing countries (especially NICs) to implement. But there still remains a myth among politicians, policymakers, and businessmen as well as among the public in Europe and North America that Japan's domestic market is relatively closed and artificially insulated from import competition by tariff and nontariff trade barriers.

Agricultural protection is an important exception to Japan's free-trade policy. Such factors as low agricultural productivity because of the scarcity of land, the rapid aging of the agricultural population, and the Japanese people's strong attachment to their ancestral land have retarded the shift away from agricultural protectionism in Japan. Moreover, the two oil crises and the worldwide food shortage in the early 1970s made the Japanese people realize their vulnerability to external shocks because of their heavy dependence on imports of energy and food supplies. Considering the domestic political situation and the strength of public opinion in favor of agriculture, there seems no prospect in the near future of a drastic change in this area.

The Japan-U.S. Economic Conflict

The Japan-U.S. trade conflict began in the period of the textile negotiations in 1968–72 and became more and more serious and expanded into wider areas in 1976–78. In the 1980s, it became the Japan-U.S. economic conflict.[38] Viewed as a series of diplomatic negotiations over trade and economic matters, the Japan-U.S. economic conflict is unusual in several respects. First, unlike usual negotiations over trade or other economic issues in which both parties engage in give-and-take, in the Japan-U.S. negotiations, the United States nearly unilaterally requests Japanese concessions. The main question of the negotiations has been how much and how soon Japan would agree to concede, with the United States' offering little if anything in return.

Second, beginning in 1976 the United States steadily widened the subject matter of the negotiations from trade issues to government policy problems that are thought to affect directly or indirectly trade flows between the two countries. Thus, the United States requested that the agenda include such topics as the yen-dollar exchange, Japan's macroeconomic policies, financial deregulation, internationalization of the yen, and a wide variety of the Japanese government's regulations and standards related to safety, health, telecommunications, and so on.[39]

Third, since most of these subjects are traditionally considered as belonging to the domain of internal affairs of a sovereign state, the attempt by the United States to make these topics the subjects of Japan-U.S. negotiations and to force Japan to take certain policy measures in these areas gave an unfavorable impression that the United States was trying to encroach on Japan's internal affairs.

U.S. pressure on Japan accelerated the liberalization of import restrictions, foreign exchange controls, and regulation of financial markets. Hence, it can be argued that the U.S. pressure has helped make the Japanese economy not only more open but also more efficient and rational. In fact, some Japanese welcomed such U.S. pressure for liberalization. But the unilateral and high-handed way in which the U.S. government demanded concessions from Japan has aroused resentment in Japan.

Why Japan Made Concessions

In the diplomatic negotiations over economic conflict issues, the Japanese government has made numerous concessions one by one in response to foreign requests in the areas of trade problems and nontrade areas. This passive and piecemeal approach gave the unfavorable impression to government officials and the general public in the United States and other foreign countries that the Japanese government was using delay tactics to evade as much as possible what it should have undertaken by itself.

One might wonder why the Japanese government made concessions at all to such one-sided requests from the United States. First, Japan's overall balance-of-payments surplus and bilateral trade surplus vis-à-vis the United States were especially large when the trade or economic conflict was intense, and the performance of the Japanese economy was relatively good. Japanese government officials perhaps thought that Japan was "guilty" and could afford to accommodate some of the U.S. requests, especially when the United States strongly demanded that Japan cooperate in reducing the large U.S. deficit. But in retrospect this is strange since many members of the IMF with balance-of-payments deficits have been held responsible for mismanaging their economies and have been requested to take corrective actions. No country except the United States has ever requested other countries to take actions to correct its own balance-of-payments deficits.[40]

Second, it may be argued that the U.S. government requested Japan to take actions to correct the imbalance between the two countries to prevent protective legislation. It is a constructive step, therefore, to request Japan to cooperate in countering an incipient rise of protectionism. We think that there is some truth in this view. But if one accepts this view, then a major cause of the Japan-U.S. economic conflict is a lack of political leadership in the United States. Whether such an approach has been successful is a moot question since one could argue that the approach has had at least some effect in fanning the flame of protectionism.

Third, Japanese officials may have feared that the United States would retaliate if Japan did not concede to the United States and thought that concessions were helpful in calming protectionist sentiment in the United States. Although there still remain strong protectionist groups in Japan, the free-trade philosophy has been gaining force among officials and businessmen. More and more Japanese have become convinced that the preservation of the world's free-trade regime is essential for the economic prosperity of Japan. It is not surprising that they thought they should cooperate with the United States as much as possible in eliminating an imbalance they considered detrimental to the maintenance of the free-trade regime.

Fourth, although it has never been mentioned in official documents, the Japanese and American officials in charge of trade negotiations may have considered the bilateral trade and other economic problems as a part of overall—not only economic but also political, security, and cultural—relations. More specifically, Japanese officials felt indebted to the United States for Japan's national security, and U.S. officials were also conscious of the United States' heavy burden as a protector of Japan and as the leader of the Western countries. Such a feeling and perception may have been reflected in Japan's unilateral concessions in trade and other economic relations vis-à-vis the United States.

In this period, the United States strongly requested an expansion of Japan's defense expenditures. Japan acceded to this request to a limited extent, but generally speaking the Japanese government did not want to involve Japan much in defense cooperation because of domestic political considerations. Under these circumstances, the Japanese government tended to consider that it was necessary—and easier—to make concessions in trade and other economic issues.

Economic Conflict in a Wider Perspective

Viewed in a wider and longer-run perspective, several conditions have given rise to the Japan-U.S. economic conflict. First, Japan and the United States have become more and more closely integrated as a result of reductions in tariff and nontariff barriers to trade and in costs of transportation and communication. Not only in merchandise and invisible trade but also in technology, information, finance, and cultural, scientific, and educational exchange, the two countries now depend on each other more heavily than ever before. Second, economic and social forces in the two countries are still very different because of differences in incomes, demography, culture, and customs. These give rise to market forces leading to sudden changes in the pattern and levels of trade flows. Third, both countries are parliamentary democracies, in which decision making on economic policies takes time, with various interest groups participating actively. When a new development is thought prejudicial to a vested interest, the pressure group representing it moves to resist the change, and sometimes such resistance becomes highly politicized.

Fourth, the United States behaves as a superpower and a center country and tends to believe that its social, legal, and administrative institutions are universally superior and should be adopted by other countries. This belief often leads to an imperial or imperialistic manner in economic negotiations with other countries with different cultural traditions. One of the major factors behind the recent flare-up of anti-Japanese feelings in the U.S. Congress is the deficient American understanding of Japan and Japanese culture. Judging from the newspaper reports, U.S. politicians generally seem to have a distorted view of Japan and the Japanese. The extent of Americans' understanding of Japanese culture, language, and social institutions is perhaps much more limited than the Japanese people's understanding of contemporary American culture and social institutions and the English language. This is a great handicap for the United States in marketing its products in Japan and in negotiating effectively with the Japanese.

Fifth, Japan was long isolated from the mainstream of international economic affairs, and Japan's social, legal, and administrative institutions are largely legacies from the time when Japan was a small, latecomer developing country and are not appropriate to Japan's current position in the world economy. The Japanese people's mentality has generally been a small-country one, always thinking about taking advantage of advanced technology and free markets in the outside world, especially in developed countries, but jealously trying to protect their own industries and various vested interests at home. Moreover, the flow of information and exchange of views have been largely one way: that is, from the outside world into Japan. Generally, the Japanese people have made little effort to make themselves well understood by foreigners and to express their own views and ideas. This Japanese failing has been a substantial handicap in Japan's diplomacy.

Of these basic conditions, the first three will remain unchanged in the near future, and the last two will change only slowly. Hence, the Japan-U.S. economic conflict will persist for some time. The subject matter of the conflict will change from time to time, as it has in the past ten years or so, but it is unlikely that the wellspring of friction and tension will dry up in the near future.

Erosion of the GATT System

The GATT system, which is the core of the world's multilateral free trade, has been strengthened since the 1960s by the KR and the TR and by an increase in the number of member-countries. But it has been weakened in some other aspects. In our view, it should be a matter of grave concern that the proportion of the trade among member-countries that is strictly in conformity with GATT declined throughout the 1970s and the first half of the 1980s.[41]

Even in the 1960s, there were some symptoms, such as the agreements on cotton textiles and VERs on certain products, but deviations from the GATT norms became much more visible and numerous in the 1970s. The Multi-Fiber Agreement of 1974 nearly froze the textile trade among GATT members. Bilateral trade in certain products between exporters such as Japan, Korea, Taiwan, and Hongkong and importers such as the United States, Canada, the United Kingdom, France, Italy, and other European countries has been restricted by formal or informal agreements, such as VERs, the trigger price mechanism (TPM), the basic price system (BPS), and orderly marketing agreements (OMAs). In some sectors such as shipbuilding, world trade has been regulated by attempts at "international coordination" in the OECD. In an effort to protect domestic agriculture, many industrialized countries including Japan, France, and the United States restrict imports of agricultural products by quotas and other administrative measures, some of which are illegal under GATT, although this aberration from the norms of GATT was largely carried over from the beginning of the GATT system.

Apart from these deviations from the principles of free multilateral trade, developing countries have restricted imports of a wide range of products under Article 12 of GATT (which allows import restrictions for balance-of-payments reasons); they have never implemented free-trade policy and hence never participated fully in the GATT system. About the only major obligation they have fulfilled as GATT members is to enforce import restrictions on a nondiscriminatory basis. For GATT members in Eastern Europe (Czechoslovakia, Poland, Romania, and Hungary), the multilateral free-trade principles of GATT or even the tariffs themselves mean little since their trade is under strict state control. Thus, even before the MFA and various VERs, the GATT articles embodying the free-trade principles had real meaning only for a limited number of countries with Article 11 status (West European countries, the United States, Canada, Japan, and a few others). These are the countries that removed, in principle, import restrictions for balance-of-payment reasons. During the 1970s, even among these countries the proportion of international trade under restrictions inconsistent with the basic principles of GATT probably increased.

From the late 1970s to the early 1980s, exports to the United States of textiles, steel, special steel products, color televisions, automobiles, and several others were under restrictions inconsistent with GATT principles. According to some estimates, this proportion reached about a quarter of the total in the case of imports from Japan.

Although some of the arrangements inconsistent with the basic GATT principles were established under the auspices of GATT (STA, LTA, and MFA), most of them were made outside GATT through bilateral negotiations between the governments concerned. Some of the measures restricting bilateral trade have been negotiated and implemented primarily by industry representatives of the two countries concerned, with government officials participating only marginally. Moreover, some of these are little known to the public. These developments indicate a serious and increasing erosion of the GATT system as a world trade regime. It is no exaggeration to say that the GATT system is now covered with wounds and that the role of GATT as the norm for world trade has diminished substantially.

A Repeat of the 1930s?

What is the future of the world trading system and how will it change, say, in the coming five to ten years? It is always difficult to predict the future, but it is particularly difficult to predict the future of the world trading system given the uncertainty about economic, social, and political trends in most major countries. The following is no more than highly speculative conjecture.

In the first half of the 1980s, the dark cloud of stagflation continued to cover a large part of the world economy. Today inflation and unemployment rates are still quite high in many developed countries, and a majority of developing countries are suffering from balance-of-payments difficulties, rapidly accumulating debts, and stagnant exports. It is not surprising that a strong tendency toward protectionism has developed in many countries. Many fear that if current conditions persist, protectionist tendencies will be strengthened and protectionism increased in many countries. The world economy may disintegrate into a few regional economic blocs, each encircled by a wall of trade barriers, as it did in the 1930s.

This is indeed a bleak picture. If this happens, the volume of world trade will dwindle, with disastrous consequences for Japan since it depends heavily on multilateral world trade and has little prospect of forming a largely self-sufficient bloc of its own or joining some regional bloc on favorable terms.

A Moderately Optimistic View

Yet present conditions in the world economy appear to us considerably different from those prevailing in the 1930s. First, the economies of the industrialized countries are much more closely integrated with each other. Despite the erosion of GATT described above, the major industrialized countries are now generally much more open. The ratio of imports to GNP has risen substantially in most countries. They are more heavily dependent not only on international flows of merchandise and services, but also on those of technology, information, and knowledge. For industrialized countries, the internationalization of economic and social affairs is an irreversible secular trend.

In such a mutually internationalized world economy, protectionism cannot constitute an advisable permanent solution for any industrialized country to the economic difficulties it now confronts. To protect a medium- to high-technology industry from increasing import competition nearly amounts to defeatism if there is no prospect of getting rid of the protections within a few years. If an industry cannot compete effectively with imports from another country even in its domestic market, it will not be able to compete with other countries' industries in a third country's market. In a world in which colonial empires are a thing of the past, developing countries wishing to import medium- to high-technology products or seeking foreign direct investment into their country for producing such products under joint ventures will turn to those developed countries that produce such products most efficiently. In the case of a labor-intensive, low-productivity light industry as well, it is obvious that protectionism fails to provide a solution over a long run. Protecting such an industry from foreign competition means entrapping a larger proportion of the labor force in a low-productivity sector. It will be a burden for the national economy as a whole. It is much better to shift labor and other resources from such a sector to more promising sectors or to any sector that can survive without protection.

Second, from a political point of view, the international relations among the major industrialized countries of the West are basically different from what they were in the 1930s. The world's primary political and military confrontation today is between the two superpowers, the United States and the Soviet Union, and not among Western industrialized countries. In this East-West confrontation, Western countries are by and large tied by common interests and cannot but cooperate in economic and social affairs, although the extent of cooperation may differ in different areas and at different times. The North-South confrontation is also severe at times. In this confrontation, too, the Western countries have common interests in maintaining the liberal, market-oriented economic order and at the same time in assisting the developing countries and mitigating the North-South conflict.[42] From a worldwide political context, it is clear that the major countries of the West have far greater common interests than opposing ones.

The GATT system has been subject to erosion by formal and informal arrangements inconsistent with its basic principles, as pointed out above, yet in the near future there seems to be no international economic system to supersede the free, multilateral, market-oriented economic system of GATT, the IMF, and the OECD. The so-called New International Economic Order proposed by those who profess to represent the interests of developing countries appears to amount to no more than an expression of dissatisfaction with the status quo and of dreary desires. It does not seem to constitute a set of principles for a workable international system in which a large number of countries will participate willingly. It is unlikely that some of major countries, including the United States, will withdraw from GATT, the IMF, the OECD, or other major international economic organizations or even cease to play an active role in them.

Although its leadership and economic power have been declining, the United States is obviously still the leader of the Western countries in the international economic community and will remain so for many years to come. The role of Japan, which is now perhaps number two, is to cooperate with the United States and other leading countries in maintaining and strengthening the liberal, multilateral world economic order. Japan can never be in a position to contest with the United States or any other country for hegemony over the world economy or some part of it. Japan— or any other country for that matter—would gain little by pursuing such a struggle but would lose a great deal.

Ambition on the part of Japan to be the leader in world affairs is out of the question not only in view of its much restricted military role but also in view of the Japanese economy's high vulnerability to external shocks. If Japan and the United States were vehemently opposed over economic matters and decided to fight an economic war using trade and other economic measures, the United States could inflict severe damage on Japan—of course, at a substantial cost to itself—but Japan could not inflict much damage on the United States. We believe this is well understood by those in charge of international economic affairs in the two countries.

Economic difficulties confronting countries today, such as international payments imbalances, high inflation, unemployment, protectionist tendencies, accumulation of debts, and stagnation cannot be overcome easily. Improvement in these matters will take much time. Yet it seems to us that the world economy is considerably more stable than in the 1930s. It will not as easily disintegrate as it did in the 1930s. We hope that Japan will adhere to the free-trade principle and play a more active role in maintaining and strengthening the free, multilateral, and market-oriented order of the world economy.

Gary R. Saxonhouse

Comparative Advantage, Structural Adaptation, and Japanese Performance

The postwar international trading system continues under great attack. The success of this system, which has led to an almost entirely unforeseen forty-year explosion in international trade, has created conditions that are threatening its foundations. Many of the problems of the international trading system reflect the difficulties associated with structural adaptation to changing comparative advantage. In the first section of this paper, I review the role of structural change in the economic performance of the advanced industrialized economies, giving particular attention to the character of Japanese structural change. Has Japan had a pattern of success in structural adaptation that differs not only from that of the advanced industrialized economies in the West but also from that of the so-called China-periphery civilizations, such as might be found in Korea?

To the extent that this structural change is related to an economy's participation in the international trade in goods and services and to the international movement of factors of production and technology, I pay particular attention to whether a watershed is approaching in international economic relations. Specifically, whatever Japan's past performance, are the advanced industrialized economies becoming sufficiently alike that less rather than more interaction among them can be expected in the future? As Japanese, Western European, and U.S. endowments converge, will international commercial relations come to be more important or less important as a source of structural change than they have been during the first forty years of the postwar period?[1]

The future role of international trade and factor mobility provides an important perspective on the continued viability of concepts such as national treatment as organizing principles for the international trading system. For trade to be mutually beneficial, there is no particular requirement that trading partners have identical domestic economic institutions. However, as it becomes increasingly clear that concessions on trade barriers at national borders can be undermined by domestic economic policies, demands for the harmonization of domestic economic institutions among trading partners have mushroomed. In the fourth section of this paper, I review the intellectual origins of the national-treatment concept and the economic basis for replacing it with ideals that are particularly intrusive on traditional notices of national sovereignty.

Japanese Structural Change in Comparative Perspective

The years since the end of hostilities in 1945 have witnessed an unprecedented growth in the world economy. As shown in Table 1, of the advanced industrialized economies, Japan's economy grew almost twice as fast between 1960 and 1980 as those of other countries.

In theory, structural change is not necessary for rapid economic growth. Nor does rapid economic growth in an open economy necessarily alter an economy's comparative advantage.[2] For example, consider the extremely simple case of a closed economy with homothetic preferences, no economies of scale, and neutral technological change. If all factors of production are inelastically supplied and grow at the same rate, GDP can grow without any interindustry transfer of resources in either the absolute or the relative sense. In the more likely case that capital accumulates more rapidly than labor and the other factors of production, structural change still need not occur, if, for example, technical change augments the non–capital factor by the same degree that the growth of capital stock exceeds the growth of the other factors of production.[3]

In reality, for many economies, rapid growth goes hand in hand with dramatic structural transformation. Table 2 presents measures of the transformation of trade structure at a variety of levels of disaggregation for three different time periods for ten economies. Tables 3 and 4 present

TABLE 1
GDP of Selected Countries as Per Cent of Japanese GDP, 1950–1980

Country	1950	1960	1965	1970	1975	1980
U.S.	1,000%	625%	500%	345%	313%	286%
Canada	70	50	45	31	34	29
France	150	113	90	72	69	63
FRG	160	163	130	97	84	77
Italy	80	69	55	45	38	37
U.K.	180	106	80	52	47	40

SOURCE: U.S. Department of Commerce, Bureau of the Census, *Statistical Abstract of the United States* (Washington, D.C., 1982), p. 868.

TABLE 2

Percentage Changes in Trade Structure, Selected Countries, 1960–1980

Country	Standard International Trade Classification	1960–73	1973–80	1960–1980
		EXPORTS		
Japan	2 digit	30.9%	23.0%	43.1%
	4 digit	49.6	37.6	62.3
	6 digit	73.2	41.8	83.8
U.S.	2 digit	14.6	9.3	20.2
	4 digit	28.2	17.3	34.7
	6 digit	44.3	28.0	56.4
FRG	2 digit	11.6	8.2	16.9
	4 digit	26.0	15.1	30.3
	6 digit	41.5	26.7	51.8
France	2 digit	19.3	14.0	26.4
	4 digit	35.8	27.3	41.5
	6 digit	57.2	41.1	63.9
Italy	2 digit	24.3	17.3	34.2
	4 digit	43.8	29.5	51.0
	6 digit	61.6	36.2	74.8
Canada	2 digit	16.3	7.2	21.6
	4 digit	32.7	15.2	38.2
	6 digit	48.0	27.8	59.8
Belgium	2 digit	12.7	7.1	16.3
	4 digit	29.3	16.5	31.8
	6 digit	48.1	24.9	55.5
Netherlands	2 digit	18.5	13.3	27.1
	4 digit	33.4	26.9	40.3
	6 digit	53.2	38.5	65.2
U.K.	2 digit	9.8	22.5	29.7
	4 digit	20.1	31.7	37.0
	6 digit	36.5	39.9	51.4
ROK	2 digit	37.5	28.6	55.6
	4 digit	53.1	40.3	74.8
	6 digit	83.3	47.1	90.1

Country	Standard International Trade Classification	1960–73	1973–80 Non-energy	1973–80 Total	1960–80 Non-energy	1960–80 Total
		IMPORTS				
Japan	2 digit	19.3%	14.8%	29.0%	29.5%	45.9%
	4 digit	37.4	25.7	43.6	49.6	61.7
	6 digit	53.9	37.5	65.2	71.4	88.6
U.S.	2 digit	23.9	22.3	34.8	36.3	52.9
	4 digit	45.2	41.8	58.5	55.0	70.4
	6 digit	69.7	63.1	77.4	79.3	87.4
FRG	2 digit	19.6	17.9	27.4	31.2	38.4
	4 digit	33.1	29.8	39.6	46.8	52.5
	6 digit	56.2	46.1	50.2	60.9	70.6

TABLE 2 (cont'd)

Country	Standard International Trade Classification	1960–73	1973–80 Non-energy	1973–80 Total	1960–80 Non-energy	1960–80 Total
		IMPORTS				
France	2 digit	22.5%	20.5%	36.2%	33.2%	49.6%
	4 digit	40.7	34.6	59.4	48.6	67.3
	6 digit	61.8	58.2	72.1	74.9	83.1
Italy	2 digit	26.4	16.7	35.4	34.6	50.7
	4 digit	43.2	36.8	63.1	53.2	62.3
	6 digit	67.9	61.3	80.4	76.7	89.0
Canada	2 digit	24.5	19.6	22.3	33.7	36.8
	4 digit	40.9	37.2	39.5	45.0	48.9
	6 digit	65.3	52.7	54.7	62.0	67.4
Belgium	2 digit	22.8	18.3	27.4	32.7	42.3
	4 digit	39.5	29.1	45.2	49.1	63.8
	6 digit	63.8	52.3	59.5	68.4	77.6
Nether-lands	2 digit	17.5	16.3	19.2	36.3	39.9
	4 digit	35.2	36.5	41.6	45.8	56.2
	6 digit	57.3	46.8	55.1	60.3	71.5
U.K.	2 digit	26.3	24.3	26.5	43.5	55.8
	4 digit	39.0	41.1	43.8	59.7	73.6
	6 digit	57.6	67.4	71.7	73.6	89.3
ROK	2 digit	28.7	17.1	36.3	39.7	53.1
	4 digit	43.1	27.6	52.5	63.5	73.5
	6 digit	70.9	39.9	73.8	80.0	91.6

SOURCES: United Nations, *Commodity Trade Statistics*, various issues.

NOTE: $\Delta = \left\{ 1/2 \sum_i \left(\frac{X_{i2}}{X_2} - \frac{X_{i1}}{X_1} \right) \right\} \times 100$ where

X_i refers to the trade flow of each of the i sectors,

X refers to total trade, and 1 and 2 are time periods.

measures of the structural transformation of production and labor force allocation for nine of these ten economies.

Among the advanced industrialized economies whose performances are measured in Tables 2, 3, and 4, Japan has undergone the most profound structural transformation. This appears to have been true both before and following the first oil crisis. Rapid economic growth has been accompanied by a dramatic shift in the relative importance in production of the various sectors of the Japanese economy.

Along with changes in production, changes in labor force allocation and changes in export structure have been greater for Japan than for any of the other seven industrialized economies for which data are presented. In one area—import structure—however, the pattern is more

TABLE 3
Percentage Changes in Real Value Added Originating by Sector, Selected Countries, 1960–1979

Country	1960–73	1973–79	1960–79
Japan	24.7%	13.6%	30.2%
U.S.	11.3	5.8	14.5
FRG	12.6	4.1	14.2
France	14.4	4.8	16.7
Italy	18.6	11.1	25.0
Canada	15.1	3.9	16.4
Netherlands	11.7	4.6	15.0
U.K.	11.9	4.9	15.3
ROK	32.1	17.9	43.4

SOURCE: Adapted from Dale Jorgenson, Laurits Christensen, and Diane Cumming, "Economic Growth, 1947–1973: An International Comparison," in J. W. Kendrick and B. Vaccara, eds., *New Development in Productivity Measurement and Analysis* (Chicago: University of Chicago Press, 1980). The 26 sectors are agriculture, forestry, and fisheries; mining; construction; food and beverages; textile products, pulp, and paper; publishing and printing; synthetic fibers; oil and paints; pharmaceuticals; miscellaneous chemical products; petroleum products; rubber products; ceramics; iron and steel; nonferrous metals; fabricated metal products; general machinery; household electrical appliances; telecommunications equipment; other electrical equipment; automobiles; other transportation equipment; precision instruments; other manufacturing; electricity and gas; other.

NOTE:
$$\Delta = \left\{ 1/2 \sum_i \left(\frac{X_{i2}}{X_2} - \frac{X_{i1}}{X_1} \right) \right\} \times 100 \quad \text{where}$$

$X_i \equiv$ value added in the ith sector, $i = 1, 2, \ldots, 26$,

$X \equiv$ GDP, and 1 and 2 are time-period subscripts.

TABLE 4
Percentage Changes in Employment by Sector, Selected Countries, 1960–1979

Country	1960–73	1973–79	1960–79
Japan	33.4%	15.9%	43.7%
U.S.	14.5	7.6	18.1
FRG	13.3	6.4	16.5
France	18.2	7.0	21.3
Italy	26.6	12.1	34.0
Canada	17.2	4.4	19.2
Netherlands	14.3	4.1	15.7
U.K.	12.2	5.3	14.6
ROK	42.0	25.3	57.1

SOURCE: Same as Table 3.

NOTE:
$$\Delta = \left\{ 1/2 \sum_i \left(\frac{X_{i2}}{X_2} - \frac{X_{i1}}{X_1} \right) \right\} \times 100 \quad \text{where}$$

$X_i \equiv$ employment in the ith sector,

$X \equiv$ total employment, and 1 and 2 are time-period subscripts.

complicated. If petroleum and other energy-related imports are included and measured in current prices, Japan's import structure has experienced much the same change as the import structures of the United States, France, Italy, Belgium, and the United Kingdom. If we ignore energy imports, however, or if we focus only on the period before the first oil crisis, Japan may have experienced the smallest transformation in import structure. Indeed, for non-energy imports for the period 1973–80, this is true without exception. For the entire period, it is true at the highest levels of aggregation. At a more disaggregated level, the situation is somewhat different. At the Standard International Trade Classifications (SITC) four-digit level, only the Federal Republic of Germany and the Netherlands exhibit less structural change than Japan. And at still more finely disaggregated levels, Canada and Belgium also appear to have experienced less change than Japan.

Tables 1–4 clearly reveal that Japan's rapid economic growth was accompanied by dramatic shifts in the allocation of resources. But is Japan's extraordinary capacity for structural adaptation in any sense unique? If, for example, we compare it with a middle-rank industrialized economy, such as that of the Republic of Korea, Japan's performance no longer looks particularly distinctive. Korean economic growth has been faster than Japanese economic growth, and Korea has experienced an even more profound sectoral reallocation of its production, labor force, and trade structure than has Japan. Moreover, rather like Japan and unlike the United States and Western Europe at the most aggregated level, Korea's import structure appears to have undergone rather less change than might be expected, given the other dramatic changes in its economy.

Although the example of Korea does suggest that unique premodern Japanese social institutions have little interpretive role to play at the level at which comparative economic analysis is generally conducted, it should not be supposed that broader constructs such as "Confucian cultural area" explain the pattern of structural adaptation much better. If, for example, we remove Japan from the list of advanced industrialized economies examined in Tables 2–4, virtually all the superlatives applied to Japan could be applied to Italy. With Japan excluded, Italian growth between 1960 and 1980 was more rapid than that of any other advanced industrialized economy. And again, the sectoral reallocation of its production, its labor force, and its export trade during this same period exceeded the performance of the other advanced industrialized economies.

Japanese Imports of Manufactured Products

The comparatively small change in the structure of Japanese non-energy imports between 1973 and 1980 (and later) deserves closer scru-

tiny. These data are increasingly being taken as evidence of the closedness of Japan's domestic market to competing foreign manufactured
products (see Table 5).[4]

Ironically, since the early 1970s, Japan has maintained few formal barriers on foreign manufactured products. The average level of Japanese
tariffs for manufactured products is lower than U.S. or European Community tariff levels.[5] And what is true for tariffs is also true for quotas
and other nontariff barriers (NTBs), such as export restraints imposed
on trading partners, variable levies, minimum price systems, tariff quotas, and similar restrictive techniques of import surveillance. By comparison with other advanced industrialized economies, including the
United States, Japan makes little use of such protective barriers (see
Table 6).[6]

Unlike its policy toward manufacturing sectors, the Japanese government does use such barriers to protect its agricultural sector. Whether
Japan is number two after Switzerland on the list of dishonor regarding
protection of its agricultural sector, whether it provides somewhat less
formal protection than virtually all members of the European Community, or whether its position is somewhere in between depends critically
on how the burden of protection is measured.

In examining the question of foreign access to the Japanese market,
we should, of course, not confine ourselves to the barriers erected at the
Japanese border. If a government so chooses, domestic sectoral policy
instruments such as taxes and subsidies can be good functional substitutes for tariffs and quotas. In fact, however, close examination of
Japan's sectoral subsidy policy and calculation of the so-called effective
Japanese corporate tax-subsidy rates by sector suggest exceedingly spar-
ing use of such instruments since the early 1970s. With the exception
of agriculture, no major Japanese sectors have received significant subsidies from the Japanese government since the mid-1970s. And quite
unlike the U.S. and Western European governments, the Japanese gov-

TABLE 5

Imports of Manufactures as Per Cent of Nominal GNP,
Selected Countries, 1962–1985

Country	1962	1973	1982
Japan	2.8%	2.8%	2.7%
U.S.	1.3	3.4	6.5
FRG	6.0	9.1	15.0
France	4.8	9.5	13.1
U.K.	4.7	12.0	16.3

SOURCES: Bank of Japan, *Kokusai hikaku tōkei* (International comparative
statistics), various issues.

TABLE 6
Extent of Industrial Countries' Nontariff Barriers by Product Category and Country, 1983
(own imports coverage ratio; all exporters)

Industrial country market	All products	All, less fuels	Fuels	Agriculture	Manufacturing	Textiles	Footwear	Iron and steel	Electrical machinery	Vehicles	Rest of manufacturers
EEC	22.3	21.1	24.4	36.4	18.7	52.0	9.5	52.6	13.4	45.3	10.3
Belgium-Luxembourg	26.0	33.9	10.0	55.9	33.6	38.3	12.3	47.4	19.5	54.3	30.6
Denmark	11.7	15.9	0.0	28.5	13.2	46.5	13.6	49.9	6.7	35.0	5.4
France	57.1	28.1	91.0	37.8	27.4	48.4	6.6	73.9	41.7	42.9	19.4
FRG	12.4	18.3	0.0	22.3	18.5	57.0	9.7	53.5	6.8	52.0	6.6
Greece	13.4	23.2	0.0	46.4	20.4	21.8	22.8	54.5	13.5	65.5	8.5
Ireland	13.4	15.0	0.0	24.8	13.8	31.7	8.8	23.0	0.5	65.8	6.6
Italy	6.9	14.6	0.0	39.9	9.3	37.2	0.2	48.6	7.1	10.2	2.6
Netherlands	25.5	28.0	22.0	51.9	17.8	57.3	12.0	35.5	4.0	49.7	10.7
U.K.	14.3	17.5	0.0	34.9	14.8	59.6	12.2	42.1	12.7	44.3	6.7
Australia	34.1	24.1	98.0	36.1	23.6	30.9	50.0	55.6	48.7	0.7	21.6
Austria	4.9	6.0	1.0	41.7	2.4	2.2	0.1	0.0	0.0	2.9	3.0
Finland	34.9	9.2	94.0	31.5	6.7	31.0	68.8	43.9	0.0	0.0	0.4
Japan	11.9	16.9	7.0	42.9	7.7	11.8	34.1	0.0	0.0	0.0	7.7
Norway	5.7	5.8	5.0	24.2	4.1	42.9	5.4	0.1	0.0	0.2	0.4
Switzerland	32.2	23.6	94.0	73.4	17.6	57.4	0.0	3.9	28.1	1.1	14.6
U.S.	43.0	17.3	100.0	24.2	17.1	57.0	11.5	37.7	5.2	34.2	6.1
All 16 markets	27.1	18.6	43.0	36.1	16.1	44.8	12.6	35.4	10.0	30.4	8.8

SOURCE: Julio J. Nogués, Andrez Olechowski, and L. Alan Winters, "The Extent of Non-tariff Barriers to Industrial Countries' Imports," World Bank Economic Review, Vol. 1, (1986), pp. 181–99.

ernment does not use its tax code to discriminate among sectors by implicitly protecting them from foreign competition. By comparison with the United States and Western Europe, the cross–industrial sector variance of the effective corporate tax in Japan is very small.[7]

It is commonly suggested in the United States and Europe that the traditional measures just reviewed do not really address the issue of whether the Japanese market is open or closed. In 1982, U.S. Senator Russell Long, when discussing "reciprocity legislation," found that "no lesser mind than that of Deity itself can keep up with all the subtleties and rules of Japanese import trade which are so effective in excluding American products."[8] It is at this somewhat less tangible level that foreign concern is now directed. The alleged lack of transparency in the regulatory environment created by the Japanese government, both at the border and domestically, it is argued, underwrites still more subtle understandings among Japanese firms, which limit the access of foreign products to the Japanese market.

Unhappily, it is difficult to evaluate the impact of these kinds of trade barriers, if that is what they are. For many Japanese citizens, foreign complaints about lack of access to the Japanese market over the past decade must be incomprehensible. He (or she) can patronize McDonald's or Kentucky Fried Chicken even at remote stops on Tokyo's commuter lines. He may work at a company that uses an IBM mainframe computer and on weekends may drink Scotch whiskey or Coca-Cola, lounge in U.S. designer jeans, and take his children to Tokyo Disneyland. In all these cases, domestic substitutes are available, but he will choose a foreign product or a foreign-licensed product. Of course, at the same time, on the basis of a foreign trip, he will grumble at the high price and poor quality of beef in Japan.[9]

Against this sophisticated Japanese perspective, there is an enormous store of anecdotes by U.S., European, Korean, Taiwanese, and Hong-kong businessmen who claim to have been unable to sell their products in Japan even when offering a superior item at a price well under that of competing Japanese firms. Such anecdotes are at the heart of Japan's current problems with its trading partners. How much these anecdotes reflect uniquely restrictive behavior by Japanese firms and government officials and how much they are simply a now-sanctioned response to marketing failure in a culturally, but not necessarily economically, bewildering context is a matter of considerable controversy.[10]

Perhaps the best-known anecdote is told by Lionel Olmer, former U.S. under-secretary of commerce for international trade. While employed by Motorola, Olmer attempted to sell high-quality, inexpensive pager phones to Nihon Telephone and Telegraph (NTT). Despite offering a phone that was qualitatively identical to that supplied to NTT by its affiliate NEC, at a price well below what was being charged by his competitor, it took Olmer's company many years to conclude a sale. This is a good story, but it does not describe a uniquely Japanese phenomenon. For example, it is only within the past few years that General Motors has bought cheaper overseas steel. Throughout the 1950s, 1960s, and much of the 1970s, General Motors was unwilling to purchase West German and Japanese steel even though it could be delivered at many of its plants at prices well under what U.S. steel companies were charging.[11]

The closed Japanese market argument has been buttressed by citing evidence (such as in Table 7) on Japan's distinctively large current-account balance on international transactions. Superficially, the current-account data may be seen as reinforcing the anecdotal evidence. Informal, uniquely effective Japanese restrictions are seen as holding down imports of manufactured goods and consequently as enlarging Japan's current-account surplus. In fact, as should be well known, there is little relationship among these elements. Of course, the current-account balance is a macroeconomic phenomenon reflecting the balance between domestic investment and domestic savings. Moreover, it is not a trivial matter to show that an increase in trade barriers enlarges the gap between savings and investment. The opposite might more likely be the case.[12]

If trade barriers affect primarily the structure but not the size of the current-account balance, the question remains, Are there informal Japanese barriers whose removal will result in more imports of manufactured products?[13] It is quite difficult to model what cannot neatly be characterized. The very informality of these alleged restrictions makes it difficult to attempt to estimate their impact. No real analogue to incorporating a tariff rate in a structural equation of import demand is possible if Senator Long is correct and only God can specify the structural equation of Japanese import demand.

Even if it is impossible to characterize the mechanism of alleged Japanese trade barriers neatly, there are still ways to measure their impact. For example, it might be possible to measure the price impact or quantity impact of informal barriers against some reference measure that charac-

TABLE 7
Current-Account Balance on International Transactions,
Selected Countries, 1987
($ billion)

Country	Balance	Country	Balance
Japan	+88.1	France	−1.0
U.S.	−161.4	U.K.	−2.9
FRG	+42.1		

SOURCE: Nomura Research Institute, *Nomura Investment Review*, Jan. 1988.

terizes what the price or quantity might be in the absence of Japanese-style informal barriers.[14]

There is no great mystery to this. The prices of particular goods in the Japanese market can be compared with the world market prices of these same products. Under some familiar assumptions, the differential can be viewed as the tariff equivalent of Japan's informal NTBs, and the analysis can proceed by analogy with the treatment of tariffs.

This is usually the way measurement of NTBs proceeds. But empirically minded scholars in the field of international trade are quick to point out the stringency of the assumptions that are required if the domestic price–foreign price differential is taken as the NTB tariff equivalent. It is necessary to assume that perfect competition exists and that domestically produced goods are a perfect substitute for foreign goods. As a framework for empirical analysis, such assumptions should not be troubling. If trade in general is being discussed and a great many products are under consideration, as opposed to any particular product, this is clearly the best way. The more pertinent problem is that although the world market price seems the natural reference point, in practice the connection between domestic price and world market price is not easily made. The categories for which Japanese domestic price data are collected are not directly comparable with international market price data. This is a general problem, not just a problem of Japanese price data. And this problem affects not only price data but also quantity data.

All this suggests that the search for a natural point of comparison, whether using price or quantity as a reference point, will fail. The alternative approach is obvious. We must elaborate a formal model of trade structure and examine trade under the assumption of no special Japanese barriers and then compare this model with the actual pattern of trade.

Explaining Changes in Economic Structure

Assume that an indirect trade utility function exists that expresses the maximum level of utility an open economy can attain as a function of a vector of prices for commodities, a vector of factor endowments, and the balance of trade.[15] The indirect trade utility function can be defined concretely in terms of the ordinary indirect utility function and the GNP function (or variable profit function). When this is done, an extension of Roy's Identity can be developed that allows the easy generation of net export functions by differentiation. If it is assumed that commodity prices are equalized by trade and that technology is homogeneous and identical across economies up to multiplicative quality differentials in factors of production, then these net export functions can be written in a form that is linear in the parameters that need to be estimated econometrically. If the generalized Leontief form is imposed on both demand and supply functions, the following general form of net export function emerges:[16]

$$X_i = \sum_{j=1}^{J} B_{ij} (a_j L_j) + \sum_{j=1}^{J} \sum_{k=1}^{K} C_{ijk} (a_j L_j)^{\frac{1}{2}} (a_k L_k)^{\frac{1}{2}} \qquad (1)$$

where $i = 1, \ldots , N$; $X_i \equiv i$th good; $L_j \equiv j$th factor of production; and $a_j \equiv$ quality of jth factor. If it is also assumed that the factor price equalization theorem holds up to a multiplicative quality differential term, then international trade equalizes factor prices per unit of factor quality and the term C_{ijk} in equation (1) equals zero.[17] This simplifies (1) to the extent that[18]

$$X_i = \sum_{j=1}^{J} B_{ij} (a_j L_j) \qquad (2)$$

where $i = 1, \ldots , J$. Equation (1) or (2) can be used as a framework to explain structural change in an economy's international trade.[19] Like the direct comparisons made above with Italy and Korea, (2) can be used to demonstrate that there is nothing particularly distinctive about the pattern of change in Japan's trade structure. I have estimated (2) with data taken from nine countries (Australia, Canada, France, Germany, Italy, Korea, Netherlands, the United Kingdom, and the United States) for 113 internationally traded commodities for the years 1962, 1964, 1967, 1969, 1971, 1973, 1975, 1977, and 1979. The seven factors treated as central to the explanation of changing trade structure are directly productive capital stock, labor, educational attainment, petroleum reserves, iron ore resources, arable land, and distance. I removed Japan from the sample in estimating (2). Some of the results are reported in Table 8. Note that 105 of the 113 equations estimated proved to be statistically significant.

The estimated equations in (2), together with the Japanese values for the right-hand explanatory variables and quality terms, allow an ex post forecast on the changing pattern of Japanese trade. In order to test the null hypothesis that the ex post forecast on the extra sample values of Japanese trade structure do not differ significantly from the historical values, the test statistic

$$S = \sum_{i=1}^{654} [(\hat{X}_i - X_i) / S_{\hat{x}_i}]^2$$

is utilized.[20] On the null hypothesis, S is distributed X_{654}^2 since approximately $(\hat{X}_i - X_i) / S_{\hat{x}_i} \sim N(0,1)$. Since the calculated value of S is 678.5 and the critical value at 5 per cent is 784.1, the null hypothesis cannot be rejected.

TABLE 8
The Explanation of Trade Structure

Commodity	Capital	Labor	Educational attainment	Petroleum reserves	Iron ore reserves	Arable land	Distance	F-test
Meat and meat preparations	*	*	—	—	—	*	*	3.8**
Dairy products and eggs	*	*	*	—	—	*	*	3.7**
Fish and fish preparations	—	*	—	—	—	—	*	6.2**
Wheat (unmilled)	*	—	—	—	—	*	*	6.4**
Rice	—	—	*	—	—	—	—	0.41
Maize (unmilled)	—	—	—	—	—	—	*	10.5**
Other cereals	*	—	—	—	—	*	*	3.7**
Bananas and plantains	—	—	—	—	—	—	—	1.6
Other fruits and nuts	—	—	—	—	—	—	—	4.2**
Tobacco and tobacco manufactures	—	—	—	*	—	*	—	4.3**
Hides, skins, and furs	—	—	—	—	—	—	—	1.2
Soybeans	*	—	*	—	—	*	*	12.4**
Oilseeds, excluding soybeans	—	—	—	—	—	—	—	8.6**
Crude and synthetic rubber	—	—	—	*	—	*	*	6.5**
Saw-veneer logs—conifer	—	*	*	—	—	*	*	10.1**
Saw-veneer logs—nonconifer	—	—	—	—	—	*	*	9.6**
Shaped wood	—	—	—	—	—	*	—	7.0**
Pulp and waste paper	*	*	—	—	—	—	*	10.6**
All other wood—lumber and cork	—	—	—	—	—	—	*	14.8**
Silk	—	*	—	—	—	—	—	0.62
Wool and animal hair	—	—	—	—	—	—	—	2.3**
Cotton	—	—	*	—	—	*	—	1.7
Synthetic regenerated fibers	—	—	—	*	—	—	—	0.39
All other waste fibers	—	—	—	*	—	—	*	0.26
Crude fertilizers	—	—	—	—	—	—	—	3.9**
All other fertilizers and crude materials	—	*	—	—	—	*	*	3.8**
Iron ore concentrates	—	—	—	—	*	—	—	2.9**
Iron and steel scrap	*	—	*	—	*	—	—	3.3**
Copper ores and concentrates	—	—	—	*	—	*	*	2.8**
Nickel ores and concentrates	—	—	—	—	—	*	*	4.2**
Zinc ores and concentrates	—	—	—	—	—	*	*	5.8**
Manganese ores and concentrates	—	—	—	—	—	*	*	7.1**
All other metalliferous ores, concentrates	—	—	*	—	*	—	—	6.0**
All other crude concentrates	—	—	—	—	*	—	*	5.3**
Coal, coke, briquette	—	*	—	*	—	—	—	7.1**
Crude petroleum	—	—	—	—	—	—	—	11.0**

TABLE 8 (cont'd)

Commodity	Capital	Labor	Educational attainment	Petroleum reserves	Iron ore reserves	Arable land	Distance	F-test
Petroleum products	*	*	—	*	—	*	—	12.5**
Natural gas and manufactures	—	—	—	*	—	—	—	14.1**
All other minerals	—	—	—	*	—	—	—	2.1**
Organic chemicals	*	—	*	*	—	—	—	3.2**
Inorganic chemicals	*	—	*	*	—	—	—	7.5**
Manufactured fertilizers	*	*	*	*	—	—	*	6.3**
Plastic materials	—	—	—	*	—	—	—	7.9**
All other chemicals	—	*	—	*	—	—	—	6.2**
Leather, pressed fur	—	—	—	—	—	—	—	8.0**
Rubber manufactures	*	—	—	—	—	—	*	9.1**
Cork manufactures	*	—	—	—	—	*	*	2.8**
Veneer plywood	—	*	*	*	—	*	*	4.1**
Paper, paperboard, and manufactures	*	*	*	—	—	—	*	7.5**
Gray cotton yarn	—	—	*	—	—	—	*	2.6**
Yarn, synthetic fibers	—	—	—	*	—	—	—	8.2**
Cotton fabrics, woven	*	—	—	—	—	—	—	11.3**
Silk fabrics, woven	—	*	—	—	—	—	—	6.1**
Wool fabrics, woven	*	*	*	—	—	—	—	13.5**
Cement	—	—	*	*	—	—	—	10.2**
Glass	—	—	—	—	—	*	*	19.2**
Glassware	—	—	—	*	—	*	—	8.1**
Pearls, precious and semiprecious stones	—	—	—	—	—	—	—	7.8**
Pig iron	—	—	—	—	*	—	*	12.1**
Iron and steel, primary forms	*	*	*	*	*	—	*	14.2**
Iron and steel, bars and rods	*	*	*	*	*	—	*	27.1**
Iron and steel, universal plates and sheets	*	*	*	*	*	*	*	35.3**
Iron and steel wire, excluding wire rod	*	*	*	*	—	—	*	30.1**
Iron and steel tubes and pipes	*	*	*	*	*	—	*	33.4**
All other iron and steel	*	—	—	—	—	—	—	19.1**
Silver and platinum	—	*	—	—	—	—	—	7.6**
Copper	—	—	—	—	—	—	—	10.7**
Nickel	*	—	—	—	—	—	—	17.5**
Aluminum	—	—	—	—	*	—	—	12.3**
Lead	—	—	—	—	—	—	—	26.1**
Zinc	*	—	—	*	*	—	—	29.2**
Tin	—	—	—	*	—	—	—	26.3**
All other basic manufactures	*	—	—	—	—	—	*	13.4**
Aircraft engines	*	*	—	*	—	—	—	22.1**
Piston engines	—	—	*	*	—	—	*	17.6**
Nuclear reactors	—	—	—	*	—	—	—	13.2**
All other engines	*	—	—	—	—	—	*	21.8**

TABLE 8 (cont'd)

Commodity	Capital	Labor	Educational attainment	Petroleum reserves	Iron ore reserves	Arable land	Distance	F-test
Agricultural machinery	*	—	*	*	—	—	—	42.3**
Office machines	*	*	*	—	—	—	*	47.1**
Machine tools for metal	*	*	*	—	—	—	—	110.2**
Textile machinery	—	*	*	*	—	—	—	142.1**
Sewing machines	—	*	—	—	—	—	—	147.9**
Other clothing equipment	—	—	—	—	*	—	*	25.1**
Paper mill machinery	*	—	*	—	—	—	—	37.2**
Printing and binding machinery	*	*	—	—	—	—	—	9.3**
Construction and mining machinery	—	*	—	—	—	—	—	19.2**
Heating and cooling equipment	*	*	—	*	*	*	*	16.5**
Pumps and centrifuges	*	—	*	—	—	—	—	23.2**
Balls, rollers, bearings, etc.	*	*	*	*	—	—	*	19.5**
Electric power machinery	*	*	*	—	—	—	—	32.1**
Switch gears	*	*	*	—	—	—	—	34.5**
Electric distribution machinery	*	*	—	—	—	—	—	29.5**
Radio	—	*	*	*	—	—	—	22.6**
Television	—	*	*	—	—	—	—	87.6**
Other sound equipment	—	*	—	*	—	—	*	53.1**
Domestic electrical equipment	*	*	*	*	—	—	—	57.1**
Transistors, valves	*	*	*	*	—	—	—	63.2**
Railway vehicles	*	*	*	*	—	*	—	71.7**
Passenger motor vehicles	*	*	*	*	*	—	—	63.3**
Lorries, trucks	*	*	—	*	—	*	—	101.3**
Motor vehicle parts	*	*	*	*	—	—	*	97.0**
Motorcycles	—	*	*	*	—	*	—	92.1**
Aircraft and parts	—	*	*	*	—	*	*	80.3**
Ships and boats	*	*	*	*	*	—	—	71.5**
Clothing	—	*	—	—	—	—	—	132.6**
Footwear	—	—	*	—	—	—	—	131.0**
Optical equipment	—	—	*	—	—	—	—	146.7**
Photographic equipment	—	—	—	—	—	—	—	91.4**
Medical instruments	—	—	—	—	—	—	—	67.1**
Photo, cinema supplies	—	*	—	—	—	*	—	72.5**
Pianos and other musical instruments	—	*	*	—	—	*	—	40.8**
Printed matter	—	—	—	—	—	—	—	37.3**
Fishing, hunting, and sports equipment	—	—	—	*	—	*	—	10.1**

NOTE: — Statistically insignificant; * Statistically significant at 5 per cent level; ** F-test statistically significant for 5 per cent at (7,73) degrees of freedom.

This analysis suggests that the distinctive elements in the pattern of Japanese trade structure since 1960 can be explained by drawing on the experience of the other advanced industrialized economies and the Republic of Korea. In this sense, Japan has not exhibited a distinctive pattern of structural adaptation. Industry analysis confined to a single country, or even a simple bilateral comparison, can be misleading. Japanese structural adjustment is mundane in light of the changes in its economy. At the same time, it is difficult to demonstrate a significant causal chain running from sectoral-specific structural adjustment to changes in economy-wide factor endowments.

The economy-wide features that have shaped Japanese structural adjustment include Japan's poor natural resource endowment, its distance from the other large advanced industrialized economies, and its size. The natural resource wealth of the United States and the natural resource poverty of Japan make it unlikely that structural adaptation in the United States will follow the Japanese pattern. Similarly, the proximity of the resource-poor Italian economy to other large industrialized economies makes unlikely a full Italian convergence to Japanese patterns. Finally, the relatively small size of the Korean economy means that it will likely always have a larger foreign sector than will Japan.

The importance of economy-wide characteristics might better be appreciated by examining, for example, what might happen to the Japanese and the U.S. trade structure if the United States were to give Alaska to Japan.[21] A Japanese Alaska would mean a 7,000-fold increase in Japanese oil reserves, a several hundred–fold increase in Japan iron ore resources, and a Japan whose center of gravity is much closer to its major trading partners. The results of such a simulation are presented in Tables 9 and 10.

Assuming that Alaska had been given to Japan at the same time as the

TABLE 9

Percentage Change in the Structure of Non-energy Imports,
Selected Countries, 1973–1980

Country	Change	Country	Change
Japan with Alaska	31.9%	France	28.2%
Japan without Alaska	20.3	Italy	23.5
U.S. without Alaska	33.6	Canada	29.7
U.S. with Alaska	31.7	Belgium	27.2
		Netherlands	32.8
		U.K.	38.5
		ROK	29.3

SOURCES: Same as Table 2.
NOTE: Based on 113 commodities.

TABLE 10
*Imports of Manufactures as Per Cent
of Nominal GNP, Selected Countries, 1973*

Country	With Japanese Alaska	Actual
Japan	4.1%	2.8%
U.S.	3.1	3.4
FRG	9.1	9.1
France	9.5	9.5
U.K.	12.0	12.0

SOURCES: Table 5 and simulation.

reversion of Okinawa, the peculiar lack of change in the structure of Japanese non-energy imports between 1973 and 1980 vanishes, and the Japanese performance is virtually identical with the character of changes taking place in many European countries and the United States. With a better natural resource base, the ratio of manufactured goods imports to GNP rises for Japan. By the same relationship, the ratio of U.S. imports of manufactured goods to GNP falls when Alaskan resources are removed from the U.S. national endowment.

Although the role that manufactured goods play in Japan's import structure rises when Alaska is added to Japanese resources, this role is still modest in comparison with the experience of many European economies. Suppose now that Southeast Asia and non-Japanese East Asia had the same economic size as Europe and that Japan retains Alaska. The ratio of manufactured imports to Japanese GNP rises to 6.7 per cent.[22]

Trade and Structural Evolution

The empirical framework just developed is useful not only for explaining how the growth of domestic resources may alter trade structure, but also for ascertaining how trade may affect the reallocation of domestic resources. Suppose, in the analysis developing equations (1) and (2), a GDP function is used instead of a trade utility function.[23] This substitution gives amended equations (1) and (2) as a framework for explaining industrial structure rather than trade structure, but otherwise the analysis proceeds as before.

$$X_i = \sum_{j=1}^{J} B_{ij^*} (a_j L_j) + \sum_{j=1}^{J} \sum_{k=1}^{K} C_{ijk^*} (a_j L_j)^{\frac{1}{2}} (a_k L_k)^{\frac{1}{2}} \qquad (1')$$

where $i = 1, \ldots, N$.

$$X_i = \sum_{j=1}^{J} B_{ij^*} (a_j L_j) \qquad (2')$$

With equations (1') and (2'), industrial structure can now be explained as a function of national endowments and commodity prices. Commodity prices are assumed to be given by international trade. In equations (1') and (2'), these prices are embedded in B_{ij^*} and C_{ijk^*}, and it is primarily for this reason that these coefficients vary over time. Necessarily, as with trade structure, industrial structure is determined by comparative advantage. In terms of equations (1') and (2'), changes in national endowments, with B_{ij^*} and C_{ijk^*} unchanged, explain changes in industrial structure under the small-country assumptions of no changes in global endowments. Symmetrically, changes in B_{ij^*} and C_{ijk^*}, with national endowments unchanged, reflect changes in industrial structure induced exclusively by the changing global scarcity of the various factors of production. Table 11 reports the results of employing this analysis for decomposing changes in industrial structure into their domestic and foreign sources for two periods and 22 sectors averaged over ten countries. Although the evidence in this table is certainly not uniform and the fit of the underlying regressions is inevitably crude, it does appear that the role of international trade in goods, services, and factors of production as a determinant of change in the industrial structure of the advanced industrialized economies has increased since 1960.

In the perspective of the standard theories of international trade, the preceding result may at first glance appear surprising. These theories suggest that as the factor endowments of economies converge, gains from international trade decline and the basis for mutually beneficial trade is removed. In 1960, German and Japanese aggregate capital stocks together equaled 20 per cent of U.S. capital stock. In 1980, they were together almost equal to the U.S. stock. In 1960, the Japanese aggregate capital–labor ratio was 15 per cent of the U.S. ratio. In 1980, it was 80 per cent. In 1960, the German aggregate capital–labor ratio was one-third the U.S. ratio and more than twice the Japanese ratio. In 1980, the German ratio was equal to the U.S. ratio and only 25 per cent above the Japanese ratio.

Such data do suggest declining foreign-induced structural change, rather than more such structural changes, as has actually been experienced in recent years. Of course, it is at least theoretically possible that the foreign-induced structural changes that have been identified resulted from the loss of export markets abroad and increasing import substitution at home. Such changes might simply represent the rocky road to less international interchange. In fact, this is most unlikely. Most of the world's trade occurs among the advanced industrialized economies, and this trade has been increasing secularly at an extremely rapid rate. The share of the foreign sector in GNP has increased dramatically for all advanced industrialized economies since 1960.

TABLE 11

Foreign and Domestic Sources of Changes in Industrial Structure
for Ten Countries, 1962–1980

(per cent of total change)

Sector	1962–73		1973–80	
	Foreign source	Domestic source	Foreign source	Domestic source
Agriculture, forestry, and fisheries	7.1%	55.5%	12.3%	46.4%
Mining	4.8	67.5	9.1	53.8
Construction	8.0	49.6	5.5	47.2
Food processing	3.7	43.9	7.2	44.6
Textiles	6.2	76.1	4.7	73.0
Pulp and paper	9.6	60.1	15.1	53.6
Chemicals	7.7	68.0	12.1	64.6
Petroleum and coal products	16.4	61.2	36.1	48.4
Ceramics	4.8	69.2	3.7	43.5
Primary metals	6.7	69.2	4.6	77.7
Fabricated metals	3.1	80.4	3.6	76.1
General machinery	5.2	71.4	4.9	68.2
Electrical machinery	9.1	70.3	13.3	67.4
Transportation equipment	12.6	75.0	15.2	66.9
Precision equipment	7.1	72.1	7.0	69.8
Other manufacturing	6.0	55.1	7.2	48.5
Electric, water, gas utilities	5.8	63.4	18.4	60.2
Transportation and communications	8.3	45.3	10.1	44.0
Wholesale and retail trades	5.0	46.1	4.9	42.8
Finance and insurance	3.8	40.6	5.2	39.6
Real estate	4.1	53.3	5.7	48.2
Other nongovernmental services	3.6	60.1	3.1	58.4

SOURCES: Same as Table 2. This table has been constructed using the method of finite differencing. In some instances, attributed changes and actual changes diverge quite substantially because of the imperfect fit of the estimated underlying regressions and to rounding error. The underlying regressions, but not the decomposition presented here, originally appeared in Gary Saxonhouse, "Services in the Japanese Economy," in Robert P. Inman, ed., *The Services Economy: Prospects and Problems* (Cambridge, Eng.: Cambridge University Press, 1985).

NOTE: $\Delta X_i = F(B_{ij}{}^* + \Delta\, B_{ij}{}^*,\ L_j + \Delta L_j)$.

How can this paradox be explained? Can increasing intimacy among the advanced industrialized economies be expected? Or has the secular acceleration of the past decade been an aberration brought on by special circumstances that are unlikely to recur?

The standard theories of international trade embodied in the framework used here to identify and explain structural changes do not allow for economies of scale or for a wide diversity of taste either within an economy or across economies. If we allow for both these related possibilities, a positive relationship between international trade and the increasing similarity in economic size between two economies becomes plausible.[24] It is generally assumed that a disproportionate amount of the trade among advanced industrialized economies is in similar products. If tastes are sufficiently finely discriminating, then most products will be produced in markets characterized by monopolistic competition where full economies of scale are not achieved. In such a world, when two large, advanced economies trade, intraindustry specialization will yield gains from trade. Indeed, the greater the similarity between the economies, the larger the gains from trade and the greater the amount of trade.

If this analysis is correct, it may well be that no watershed is at hand and that intimacy among the advanced industrialized economies will continue to grow. In common with the more standard treatments of international trade, the intraindustry specialization framework does rest on fairly restrictive assumptions about preferences and technology. Indeed, it is still not well established that most trade among advanced industrialized economies is in goods roughly similar in character. The bold assertion commonly made that intraindustry trade may account for something like 75 per cent of all trade among industrialized economies remains largely unsubstantiated.[25] Since economists do not have a good definition of industries, or at least definitions that correspond anywhere closely to the Standard Industrial Classifications (SIC) or SITC classifications, the large body of empirical work on intraindustry trade indicates only that the importance of this phenomenon varies obviously and closely with the level of SITC aggregation chosen.[26]

Suppose, for the moment, that a relatively high level of SITC aggregation is considered appropriate and considerable intraindustry trade is identified. It is by no means clear that such trade should be attributed to product differentiation and economies of scale. Surprisingly, the few empirical efforts to incorporate scale economies have not yet produced good evidence that this is an important determinant of trade.[27]

Much of what has been identified as intraindustry trade is more likely some form of border trade. As such, distance is probably a much more important determinant of such trade than the other attributes of product differentiation and/or economies of scale. Indeed, the failure of Japan to participate in intraindustry trade might properly be attributed to its distance from its major markets and could follow directly from the analysis presented in the preceding section.[28]

Quite apart from distance, it has been shown that factor intensities can vary almost as much within three-digit SITC categories as between them.[29] This means that much of what passes for intraindustry trade can be explained on the basis of more mundane theories of international trade.[30]

This argument should caution against a too ready acceptance of plausible new theories with new implications in place of more familiar analyses. It may be that it is still reasonable to suppose that a convergence of national factor endowments will remove the gains from all but border trade. It should be recalled, however, that the increasing similarity of capital–labor ratios among advanced industrialized economies does not necessarily mean a convergence of national endowments. With radically different natural resource endowments, it may well be that a converging capital–labor ratio will make these economies more, rather than less, unlike and create increasing opportunities for mutually beneficial trade.[31] This may explain the pattern of recent years and suggest that there is no particular reason not to expect a continuation or even an increase in economic intimacy among the advanced industrialized economies.

National Treatment, Harmonization, and Japan's Position

If, at the most general level, there is no particular economic reason to expect a decline in the role of the international trading system as a force for inducing structural change in participating advanced economies, can it be expected that the system will continue to persist much as it has during much of the postwar period?

Where once an advanced industrialized economy might have been considered a pillar of the international economic system for simply maintaining nondiscriminatory tariffs and refraining from overt quotas, the agenda for international economic harmony is now much more complicated. The greatly increased role of trade in the advanced industrialized economies has reinforced two seemingly self-canceling tendencies in international economic diplomacy.

The increased tempo of international trade has increased the number of industries seeking and getting protection, outside of the GATT framework, from the consequences of liberal trade. But at the same time that protectionist pressures have introduced new product-specific voluntary and involuntary restrictions, such complaints have also encouraged a further extension of the liberal practices of the international economic system. In the interest of bolstering a crumbling structure of legitimacy, many practices that had been implicit, if not formally accepted, as part of the GATT framework have been singled out and made the subject of bilateral and multilateral negotiations.

An increasing public appreciation that barriers to the international movement of capital and technology and discriminatory domestic microeconomic policies can undermine the global benefits resulting from liberal agreements on trade in goods has forced an expansion of the rules of the game on participants in the international economic system. If policy elites and wide segments of public opinion in major trading economies view domestic policy instruments (especially those of other countries), sometimes rightly and sometimes wrongly, as good functional substitutes for the foreign economic policy instruments that were the traditional methods of protection, the harmonization of many elements of traditional domestic economic policy by all the major participants in the international economic system may be a necessary prerequisite for the continuing legitimacy of that economic system.

Thus, the thrust of international economic diplomacy has moved from tariff to quotas and from quotas to standards, subsidies, and government procurement. The agenda for international economic harmony seems now to include the demand that much of the domestic affairs of participants in the international economic system should be governed by fully competitive, open, and contractual relationships.

Japan's position in the international economic system as a large, rapidly growing, resource-poor market economy with an increasing share of world exports has inevitably meant, as the reciprocity discussions make clear, that many of the complaints about the increasing costs of participation in the international economic system name it as the culprit. Much of the expanded agenda of international economic diplomacy (in particular, much of the interest in the harmonization of domestic economic practices in the name of transparency) has been motivated by the desire to get Japan to harmonize its institutions for allocating goods, capital, labor, and information with those of its major trading partners.[32]

Unfortunately, the very great success of the Japanese economy, particularly relative to American performance, has left many among the Japanese policy elites increasingly resentful of continual demands that Japan conform in increasingly intimate ways to the full liberal paradigm. Indeed, many elements of Japanese government and industry have gone to great effort to convince Japan's political and economic elites and the broader body politic in its trading partners that it is the rest of the world, and not Japan, which should be adjusting economic institutions to improve global performance. Visitors returning from Tokyo tell all who will listen that there is an alternative, if possibly illiberal, Japanese way of conducting economic affairs and that many of Japan's trading partners' problems could be solved if only they would learn from rather than lecture Japan.

From an American, if not from a Western European perspective, Japan's distinctive but not necessarily liberal way of conducting economic affairs might include (1) a major government role in formulating and facilitating a high-profile industrial policy; (2) special government impact on the financial system through an enormous volume of government-controlled postal savings and through nonmarket forced placement of government debt; (3) the continued existence of large back-centered industrial groups and the underdevelopment of venture capital markets and related financial institutions; (4) the existence of very large industrial-group-associated general trading companies, which dominate important sectors of Japan's foreign trade and important elements of Japan's distribution system; (5) legislation and administrative regulations that continue to reinforce, notwithstanding great changes in recent years, Japan's highly inefficient distribution system; (6) frequent use of cartels as an anti-recession device and longstanding lax enforcement of American occupation-derived anti-trust statutes; (7) despite recent epochal changes, some continuing limitations on the terms and forms by which capital liabilities and assets can be acquired; (8) treatment of Japanese labor as a fixed cost rather than as a variable cost over the course of the business cycle; (9) incomplete and delayed implementation of competitive bidding practices for public sector procurement; and (10) incomplete and delayed liberalization of service sector transactions.

For each distinctive Japanese institution, it is possible to hypothesize dynamic benefits accruing to the Japanese economy. Some of these benefits may have been important during the adolescence of the Japanese economy, but may not now be important even though the market-distorting institution generating them persists. In other instances, the benefits are as important today as they were in the 1950s. In still other instances, they have never been important. Regardless of benefits, past or present, each distinctive practice may cause major static distortions that are transmitted through Japan's international transactions to the global economy. The resulting losses and gains may be distributed quite unevenly between Japan and its trading partners and within these economies (between various productive sectors, between owners of physical and human assets, and between consumers and producers). The only general conclusion that might be drawn from an analysis of the impact of these many market distortions is that their overseas impact almost certainly is not self-canceling and that almost certainly these impacts are not politically neutral.

Many of Japan's distinctive institutions may involve the creation of market power or the alteration of the terms under which pre-existing market power is exercised. The theory of international trade would conventionally suggest that where such market power results in nontrivial distortions, intervention of some kind by trading partners is justified. (A nontrivial distortion is one that significantly changes the terms under which goods and services are offered for sale either in Japan or abroad.)

Does this mean that there is no place in the international economic system for Japan's distinctive economic institutions? There is surely no legal basis for intimate harmonization. In particular, Article III of GATT, which discusses the so-called national-treatment obligations, specifically rejects the harmonization of national microinstitutions and simply requires that imported goods be accorded the same treatment as goods of local origin with respect to matters under government control, such as regulation, taxation, and government procurement.[33] As Immanuel Kant and John Stuart Mill noted in their writings on international trade, international trade creates common ideals and understanding, but such common ideals are not a precondition for trade.

However tolerant Article III may be of national differences in practices that may create the differences in national endowments that create the basis for mutually beneficial trade, many other GATT provisions start from the premise that "by controlling and reducing the degree of governmental interference with the transactions of private trading enterprises, these transactions will result in a better allocation of international resources (through trade) and therefore will increase the economic welfare of the whole world."[34] This is the principle behind Articles VII–X (customs, administration), XVI (subsidies), and XVII (state trading and monopolies) and the Subsidies Code and the Government Procurement Code of the Tokyo Round.

It is ironic but not historically unusual that the issue of whether the Western economies will remake themselves in the Japanese image, however unwise that may be, or whether Japan will embrace the fully liberal market paradigm promoted by the United States will be decided on grounds that have little to do with the relative efficacy of the two alternative paradigms. It is also ironic because the case remains to be made, as noted earlier, that Japanese institutions do, in fact, create the kinds of distortions that invite Japan's trading partners to demand changes! Japan's distinctive institutions may well have accelerated its economic growth without unfairly advantaging any particular Japanese sector.[35]

Yoichi Shinkai

The Internationalization of Finance in Japan

The global role of Japanese finance has recently been attracting consider-able attention. At the end of 1986 the Japanese international assets on a net basis stood at $180.4 billion, making Japan the world's largest creditor. The U.S. international position at the same time was *minus* $263.6 billion, making the United States the world's largest debtor. Since the bulk of Japan's international assets are in the United States, it is not too mislead-ing to think of the U.S. debt in terms of the influx of Japanese capital; without the availability of Japanese capital, the present U.S. debt could not have reached such unprecedented levels.

This is not to imply that Japan has been responsible for making the United States the world's largest debtor. Japan's creditor position is partly a result of its domestic macro-policies, but largely reflects the lib-eralization of Japanese finance, a process in which the United States played no small part. Indeed, the deliberations of the U.S.-Japan Yen-Dollar Group,[1] which were touched off by the U.S. demand for more internationalization and liberalization of Japanese finance, and which ended in an agreement in May 1984, paved the way for Japan's financial developments for several years. In a sense, the present global role of Japanese finance is a direct outcome of the U.S.-Japan financial dispute.

What is the nature of this dispute, and what implications will it have for broader politico-economic relations between the two countries? The dispute arose in the context of the growing trade imbalance, which re-inforced the U.S. perception of a closed Japanese market. Financial liber-alization was a natural extension of the U.S. demand that Japan open its market. Moreover, the U.S. was said to have expected that internation-alizing the yen would lead to an increase in its value and thus to an al-leviation of the trade imbalance.

It is doubtful that internationalization of the yen will raise its value, and the U.S. perception of regulated finance in Japan may have to be modified. There can be no doubt, however, that the stakes of the recent financial dispute are high. If the liberalization measures implemented by the Japanese authorities are not effective and U.S. financial institutions fail to gain a larger share of the Tokyo market, U.S. frustration will be difficult to contain. Moreover, at an annual rate of $100–150 billion, the growing trade imbalance means that in several years Japan will have accumulated a huge net credit position, and the United States a huge net debt. A figure of $500 billion for Japan as against a $1 trillion debt for the United States in 1990 is not inconceivable.

I am not persuaded that things will go that far; under the flexible exchange rate system, trade imbalances of this order of magnitude will not last long. But many economists regard these numbers as likely, and if things turn out that way, the economic and political implications will be serious. Take the projected U.S. debt and note that the total combined debt (intermediate and long-term) of the less developed countries (LDCs) is less than $1 trillion. Again, take the projected Japanese net credit position and note that at the height of U.S. economic dominance, its net position was about $20 billion (at the beginning of the 1940s, when the U.S. GNP was about $100 billion). In the post–World War II period, the U.S. credit position was much smaller in proportion to its GNP. Is it imaginable that the U.S. and Japan, their present political and military positions unchanged, can accommodate themselves to such lopsided economic positions? Or will their political and military roles have changed by then? I am not going to discuss these larger issues in what follows. It is apparent, however, that the recent financial developments point to a possible outcome with important implications.

It is against this background that I will discuss the internationalization of finance in Japan. As the foregoing suggests, I will touch on three topics: the internationalization of finance, liberalization of finance, and internationalization of the yen. These are interrelated, of course, but they are not the same thing, as is sometimes implied.[2] For example, a number of LDCs with heavy external debt are by definition financed internationally, but no one would claim that their currencies are internationalized. Internationalization of finance means only that the country in question has a large foreign debt or a large foreign credit. Internationalization of a currency means that it is widely used by foreigners. At present the only truly international currency is the U.S. dollar. In contrast to these two concepts, financial liberalization simply means that financial transactions are not regulated and that the terms of transaction (interest rates in the broad sense) are determined by the market.

It is quite possible that Japan's financial system is already internationalized but that the internationalization of the yen is far from a reality. I argue that the Japanese financial system is far more liberalized than is commonly perceived, in part because of the U.S.-Japan dispute but primarily because of the economic pressures at work for the past several years. The purpose of this paper is to distinguish the three issues of the Japanese financial system and examine the present state and near-term prospects of each one separately.[3]

The Pressures for Liberalization

Foreigners doing financial business with Japan may perceive that its market is heavily regulated, and their perception is right for some important sections of the market. It is true, nevertheless, that strong pressures have been at work that will make deregulation inevitable, although opinions differ about how fast liberalization will proceed. In this section I examine how multiplying government debts, developments in external trade, interest-rate-sensitive firms and individuals, and U.S.-Japan disputes have contributed to these pressures.

Multiplying Government Debts

The Japanese central government is heavily in debt, as heavily as the U.S. government. At the end of 1985 the outstanding national debt stood at ¥134 trillion or 42 per cent of GNP; a comparable figure for the U.S. was about 45 per cent. One remarkable thing about the Japanese government debt is that the bulk of it has been accumulated during the relatively short period since 1974. Briefly, the major factors behind this rapidly multiplying debt were anti-recession public outlays after the oil crisis, large social expenditures initiated during the high-growth period of the 1960s, and low tax revenues in the slow-growth period of the 1970s.

Annual issues of government bonds have been on the order of 5 to 6 per cent of GNP. The bulk of newly issued bonds are sold to primary dealers or "syndicated underwriters," at regulated prices, meaning prices that are higher (and interest rates lower) than would prevail under free bidding. At least this was how things stood until 1982. Among the underwriters the city banks play a major role (their share in 1982 was 35 per cent), but until April 1983 they were prohibited from selling the bonds to their own customers. Portfolio management considerations sometimes (perhaps often) dictate that banks unload their government bond holdings, and unless the Bank of Japan purchases them (as it sometimes does), the city banks are forced to sell them in the secondary market, not infrequently at a loss (at least until 1982).

If the volume of bonds involved were small, the banks could absorb the government-debt-related inconveniences and losses. As it is, the developments described above have brought about a measure of liberalization in the Japanese capital market. At first the banks could not sell bonds even in the secondary market, but since 1977 they have been able to unload any bonds a year after issuance. Now they can sell bonds after three months. The secondary market has been deregulated, and the volume of transactions has increased rapidly (from ¥32 trillion in 1974 to ¥1,629 trillion in 1985). The prices there are free-market prices, and it is natural that the banks (and other underwriters) exert strong pressure on the Finance Ministry to "respect the market rate" when issuing new bonds. The ministry has yielded to the pressure grudgingly; the prices of new issues are now revised frequently to reflect market rates, and some medium-term bonds are floated by free bidding.

Another development that should be noted is that the amount of so-called close-to-maturity bonds will soon increase. The majority of Japanese government bonds mature in ten years. Since the large deficits started after 1974, a large number of bonds in the secondary market are approaching maturity now. Thus there is already a free market in de facto short-term government securities, and the Finance Ministry has to refinance matured bonds in large quantities. These developments have an important implication for the liberalization of short-term finance in Japan (see the third section below).

Large Current-Account Balances

Developments in Japanese foreign trade since the first oil crisis also merit a brief discussion. Largely because of increased oil-import bills, the ratio of exports and imports combined to GNP has risen steadily. The ratio was 23 per cent in 1970, but rose to 28 per cent in 1975, and to 29 per cent in 1985. Though these numbers are still small compared with those for West European countries, it is undeniable that the Japanese real (i.e. nonfinancial) sector is more internationalized than is commonly perceived. A larger foreign trade, which amounted to $430 billion in 1986, implies larger trade finances. The bulk of Japanese trade is transacted in U.S. dollars. This fact is usually cited as evidence that the yen is not internationalized, which is correct. But it also means that Japanese trade is internationally financed. In fact, Japanese finance has long been internationalized as far as trade finance is concerned.

Turning to trade balance or the current account balance of payments, the annual figures fluctuated widely during the 1970s and early 1980s. Japan's current account balance was (in billions of U.S. dollars, fiscal years): −13.9 in 1974, −7.0 in 1975, 24.2 in 1983, 37.0 in 1984, 55.0 in 1985, and 93.8 in 1986. Not only do these balances fluctuate widely, but they have reached a stage where large surpluses are normal, at least in the eyes of some economists. Whether such a stage has been reached is still controversial, but the sizable surpluses accumulated in a few years do have important implications for the Japanese financial system. (This issue is discussed in more detail below.)

The Interest-Rate-Sensitive Japanese

During the high-growth 1950s and 1960s, Japanese firms and households were not particularly conscious of interest rates. For one thing, nearly all interest rates were regulated, and pegged to low levels. For another, the accumulation of financial assets was small, and firms were more interested in the amount they could borrow than in the terms of borrowing. But the situation has changed fairly rapidly. The high inflation of 1973 and 1974 taught the Japanese that their financial assets could easily lose purchasing power if they were indifferent to interest rates. And the stakes have become higher with much larger assets on hand; the financial assets of Japanese households, for example, stood at ¥526 trillion or 160 per cent of GNP at the end of 1985.

Thus Japanese firms and households have been ready to take advan-

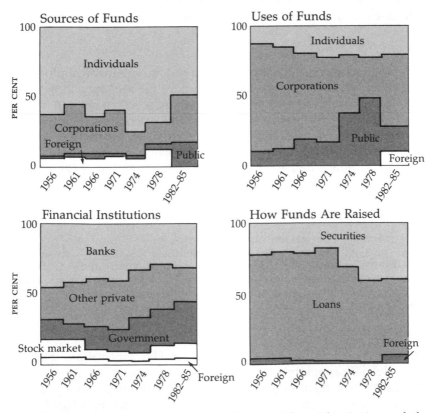

Fig. 1. Sources and uses of funds by sectors, and shares of financial institutions and of securities. Source: Hiromi Tokuda, "Kinri gyōmu no jiyūka to ginkō keiei no shōrai" (Liberalization of interest rates and banking and the future of bank management), *Shūkan Tōyō keizai, rinji zōkan, kin'yū to ginkō*, Apr. 13, 1984.

tage of better terms in managing their portfolio if they are offered the opportunity, and financial institutions have been competing to offer better instruments. The result has been remarkable. The share of firms' portfolios invested in instruments with market-determined interest rates (CDs, bonds, foreign currency deposits) rose from 10 per cent in 1978 to 63 per cent in 1985. In household portfolios, the share of bank deposits whose interest rates are regulated declined from 63 per cent in 1981 to 11 per cent in 1985, when computed in incremental terms. Households are now more and more interested in such securities-related instruments as government-bond funds and financial bonds.

As illustrated in Fig. 1 the demand for funds by the public sector has increased dramatically, the share of banks has declined, and securities have gained importance vis-à-vis loans. The only item that may belie these trends is the share of the foreign sector as a source of funds. Recent developments in the foreign sector imply that it uses (demands) large sums to finance its deficits (surpluses as seen from Japan).

Pressures from Abroad

Most Japanese agree that liberalization and internationalization will be accelerated because U.S. financial institutions are seeking a larger share in the Japanese market and in the Euroyen market (see below). In addition, the United States reportedly expects that internationalizing the yen will result in an appreciation of its value. Politically, the motive for this is understandable: the U.S. government can blame its large trade deficits on Japanese unwillingness to internationalize the yen. Economically, however, it is not clear to me why the yen should appreciate when it is more widely used.[4] I will return to this topic later.

Jeffrey Frankel seems to corroborate these remarks:

When it became more evident that the fruits of the U.S. campaign would not include a major impact on the value of the yen, some Treasury officials sought to deny that the exchange rate had ever been the primary motivation. . . . But two pieces of evidence attest to the importance attached by Treasury to the exchange rate objective. First, the name of the Sprinkel-Oba committee was, after all, the Working Group on Yen/Dollar Exchange Rate Issues. Second, some very busy senior U.S. officials spent much valuable time, on airplanes to Tokyo and elsewhere, to pursue this enterprise. This suggests a certain sense of urgency.[5]

If appreciation of the yen was the primary U.S. motivation, the result was a deep disappointment. For more than a year after the May 1984 agreement the yen stayed low, and it was only through concerted intervention in the foreign exchange market in September 1985 that the yen was started on its recent ascent. These developments seem to corroborate my view that internationalization of the yen has little to do with its value.

Internationalization of the Japanese Financial System

Economy-wide Portfolio

Perhaps the most representative numbers for our purpose are Japan's foreign assets and liabilities. The assets at the end of 1986 amount to $727 billion (40 per cent of GNP) and the liabilities $547 billion (31 per cent). To see these numbers in historical and international perspectives, and also how their composition has changed, the reader is referred to Tables 1 and 2.

The left panel of Table 1 gives Japanese foreign assets and liabilities at the end of 1986. Note that assets are fairly diversified, whereas on the liability side two major items, foreigners' holding of securities and the Japanese banks' short-term borrowings (including deposits), predominate. It should be noted in passing that Japanese banks' short-term assets (not shown in the table) are $128 billion, making the net short-term

TABLE 1
Japan's Foreign Assets and Liabilities, Year-end 1986

Components	Balance		Average balances (per cent of totals)			
	U.S. $ billion	Per cent of total	1972– 74	1975– 77	1978– 80	1980– 83
Assets						
Direct investments	58.1	8.0%	9.3%	14.9%	12.5%	12.3%
Deferred payments for exports	33.4	4.6	13.0	11.7	8.0	7.3
Loans	102.8	14.1	14.7	16.9	20.4	19.3
Securities	257.9	35.5	6.8	6.7	12.8	18.3
International reserves	43.3	6.0	30.1	25.5	19.2	10.9
TOTAL	727.3					
Liabilities						
Direct investments	6.5	1.2%	6.4%	4.9%	3.4%	2.2%
Securities	183.7	33.6	20.9	24.7	34.4	40.4
Banks' short-term liabilities	322.2	58.9	58.5	61.3	59.4	56.2
TOTAL	547.0					
Net assets	180.4					

SOURCES: Japan, Ministry of Finance, *Kokusai Kin'yūkyoku nempō* (Annual report of the International Finance Bureau) (Tokyo, various issues); and Nomura Research Institute, "60-nendai no kin'yu shihon shijō no tembō" (Finance and capital markets after 1985), *Zaikai kansoku*, May 1984.
NOTE: Some items are omitted, and entries do not add to totals shown.

TABLE 2
An International Comparison of Foreign Balances
(per cent of GNP)

Country	Assets and liabilities	Year-end 1975	Year-end 1980s
Japan 1986	Assets	11.7%	40.9%
	Liabilities	10.3	30.8
	Net assets	1.4	10.1
U.S. 1986	Assets	19.0	25.4
	Liabilities	14.2	31.7
	Net assets	4.8	−6.3
FRG 1982	Assets	31.5	36.6
	Liabilities	21.5	32.5
	Net assets	10.0	4.1
U.K. 1982	Assets	88.1	147.6
	Liabilities	89.6	133.7
	Net assets	−1.5	13.9
Switzerland 1980	Assets	209.7	249.1
	Liabilities	112.9	149.8
	Net assets	96.8	99.3

S O U R C E S : Japan, Economic Planning Agency, *Nihon keizai no genkyō, Shōwa 59 nen, bunseki kenkyū hen* (The present state of the Japanese economy, 1984: Supplemental analyses and studies) (Tokyo: MOF Printing Bureau, 1984). Japanese figures for 1986 by the author.

position of the banks and monetary authorities combined about *minus* $91 billion. Japan has not been building up large liquid reserves through its current account surplus. Its net assets are mostly in the form of long-term securities, direct investments, and loans.

The right panel of Table 1 shows how the composition of Japan's assets and liabilities has changed over the past decade. On the asset side, the shares of export finance and official reserves have declined, and those of loans and security holdings have risen (the former very moderately). On the liability side, the share of securities held by foreigners has increased. These developments may be taken to indicate that on both sides Japan's foreign balance sheet reflects the portfolio diversification that is a feature of the internationalization of finance.

What about the scale of Japan's internationalization? Table 2 compares five leading countries with respect to their foreign assets and liabilities and net positions in relation to GNP. Not surprisingly, Britain and Switzerland are far more internationalized financially than the others. Japan's position is comparable to those of the United States and West Germany. Note, however, that these figures reflect residents' position vis-à-vis the rest of the world, and that the bulk of Eurodollar deposits, for example, is not taken into account in the U.S. figure. The latter is related to the internationalization of currencies, to be discussed below.

Other Indicators of Internationalization

The internationalization of the Japanese financial system should be reflected in the assets and liabilities of financial institutions, firms, and individuals. At present only fragmental data are available.

On the asset side,[6] in mid-1983 the shares of foreign securities holdings in the total securities holdings of financial institutions were 5.4 per cent for banks, 4.1 per cent for trust banks, 19.8 per cent for life insurance companies, and 10.9 per cent for property insurance companies. The share of direct investments is still small (see Table 1), and Japan lags behind Britain, the United States, and West Germany in terms of the ratio of direct investments to GNP. The floating of foreign bonds in Tokyo has been increasing, but at about $3.5 billion annually, the level is about half that of the United States and a third that of Switzerland.[7]

On the liability side, Japanese bonds floated abroad amounted to about $13.9 billion in 1985, with about half placed in Switzerland and about a quarter in the Eurodollar market. Compared to domestic issues worth $25.6 billion,[8] Japanese firms' dependence on foreign capital markets is very large. As for short-term financing, the foreign share of *gensaki* (short-term sales of bonds with repurchase agreements) balance was 9 per cent in 1984, and of bank deposits was about 1 per cent. In short, the Japanese financial system is internationalized, but in a skewed way; raising long-term funds and investing short-term funds in Japan seem to have been restrained.

Finally, a few words on the activities of Japanese banks abroad and foreign banks in Japan. Foreign branches and affiliated outposts of Japanese banks numbered 716 as of 1985, and their foreign assets amounted to about 10 per cent of total domestic assets. It is estimated that in 1985, Japanese banks accounted for 26 per cent of international loans, and for over 30 per cent of foreign bank loans in the U.S. market. The presence of foreign banks in Japan is much less visible. Their share of loans (balance) is about 3 per cent and of deposits 1 per cent. Since foreign banks account for 21 per cent of loans in the United States, the U.S. complaint of a closed Japanese market is understandable.

Internationalization of Currencies

Data on the use of the yen in international transactions are fragmentary (see Table 3). It is undeniable that the yen is far from being internationalized. Even for the Japanese exports, the ratio of yen-denominated transactions is about one-third, and for imports 10 per cent. These numbers are well below those of European countries, not to mention U.S. figures. As for financial transactions, yen-denominated bonds play a fairly significant role, but yen-denominated loans lag behind.

TABLE 3
Uses of the Yen in International Transactions, 1986

Uses	Per cent of total
Trade	
Japanese exports	36.5%
Japanese imports	10.3%
Third-party trade	probably 0
Issues or new loans	
Yen-denominated bonds	10.0% of international bond issues
Yen-denominated loans	5.6% of international loans (exclusive of short-term loans).
Balances[a]	
Euroyen deposits	2.3%
Official reserves[a]	7.6%
Loans	5.5%

SOURCE: Ministry of Finance (Okurasho), *Annual Report of the International Finance Bureau of MOF* (Kokusaikinyukyoku Nenpou), 1986, 1987.
[a]Year-end 1985

We are thus led to the conclusion that the Japanese financial system is internationalized but the yen is not. This means that the bulk of financial transactions are conducted in U.S. dollars, Swiss francs, and various other currencies. Does this state of affairs need changing, and will the change come about? Why should foreigners worry about the use of their currency in financial dealings with Japan? After all, it is the Japanese who bear the exchange risks to the extent that hedging is difficult. The U.S. government insists that Japan should share the cost of having its currency used internationally. But my understanding is that the benefits of owning an international money outweigh its cost,[9] economically as well as politically.

The fact that Japanese now bear exchange risks will probably lead to greater international use of the yen. When assets and liabilities are more or less in balance, it is possible to hedge against exchange risks. As we have seen, however, it is possible that Japan's net assets will grow rapidly. In that case Japanese creditors will find it impossible to hedge, and they will try to denominate their foreign assets in yen.

Japanese finance is internationalized in the sense that its foreign assets and liabilities are diversified and on a scale comparable to those of the United States and West Germany. The Japanese make active use of foreign markets to raise funds, whereas foreigners make less use of the Japanese market. This may be because the Japanese current account surplus was not large until 1982, and the Japanese capital market is regulated. Foreign holdings of short-term Japanese instruments are limited.

In other words, the yen is not internationalized, though this situation may change fairly rapidly.

Deregulation of Finance

In this section I briefly describe the present state of financial deregulation in Japan and cite some empirical evidence of the effects of liberalization on the market. I will then summarize the reports of the U.S.-Japan Working Group and the Foreign Exchange Council and assess their impact on the Japanese financial system.

Present State of Deregulation

The foreign perception of the Japanese financial market (including the Euroyen market) is that it is heavily regulated. Anecdotal reports of foreign frustration in dealing with Japan abound. Aside from the notorious phenomenon of "administrative guidance,"[10] for which data are difficult to obtain, the state of regulation is as follows. In financial transactions financial institutions must adhere to rather strict rules, but otherwise exchange controls are absent except in the cases noted below. Interest-rate

TABLE 4
Japanese Regulations on Interest Rates

Regulated	Gray zone	Free
SHORT TERM		
Deposits	Loans[a]	Call rate,[b] bills
Treasury bills[c]		CDs
		Gensaki
		Yen-denominated foreign loans
LONG TERM		
Deposits	Loans[a]	All bonds in secondary markets
Financial bond[d] issues		Yen-denominated foreign loans
Government and corporate bond issues[d]		

[a]Short-term and long-term prime rates are regulated to some extent, though effective loan rates are said to be flexible.

[b]The Japanese equivalent of U.S. federal funds. It can be argued that the Bank of Japan manages the call rate.

[c]Treasury bill issue rate. There is in effect no secondary market for treasury bills.

[d]Interest rates "respect" the market rates. The interest rates on convertible bonds are free.

regulations on deposits and on the long-term loan and bond-issue markets remain in effect, but are virtually nonexistent in other markets. The more important regulations of international financial dealings include (1) limits on banks' net foreign exchange position;[11] (2) regulations on banks' issue of CDs abroad (now eased substantially); (3) limits on the amount of foreign assets held by institutional investors; (4) regulations on long-term Euroyen loans (to be eased soon); and (5) qualification standards for Euroyen bond issues. In addition to these regulations, the authorities regulate interest rates, for example, on yen-denominated bonds issued by foreigners.

Interest-rate regulations are summarized in Table 4. Investors of both short-term and long-term funds in the secondary market enjoy free interest rates. There is little regulation of transactions here, even for banks and foreigners.[12] Second, though interest rates on bank deposits are regulated, banks can accept dollar-denominated deposits, on which interest rates are market-determined. (Recall that the share of bank deposits in yen has declined as a percentage of financial assets.) Third, regulations on general-purpose loans from abroad, called somewhat oddly "impact loans," have been liberalized. Thus only on domestic loans and domestic bond issues do some regulations on interest rates remain in existence. It could, of course, be argued that these are the most important aspects of the Japanese financial system.

Arbitrage Transactions

Even where regulations are in effect, the authorities have had to consider demand and supply pressures; a notable example is provided by government bonds, as discussed earlier. In fact, most of the interest rates classified as regulated category in Table 4 have changed quite frequently in the past few years. In these circumstances we should observe lively arbitrage transactions across markets and a tendency for the yields of various instruments to be equalized. An obvious but often neglected point in international finance is that the yield from a foreign investment is not the foreign interest rate but the foreign interest rate minus the appreciation rate of the domestic currency. Hence spreads between spot and forward exchange rates are equal to interest rate differentials.

For Eurodollar and Euroyen deposits, the interest-parity condition has been satisfied almost exactly, at least since 1980.[13] This means that interest rates on Euroyen deposits are free because of lively arbitrage transactions between them and Eurodollar deposits, which are unquestionably free instruments. Euroyen and *gensaki* rates have been almost equal, at least since April 1979. This implies that *gensaki* rates are free, and that short-term funds move freely between domestic and European markets. The interbank bill rates differ slightly from Euroyen rates, but the difference between bill rates and *gensaki* rates has shrunk since 1981. It appears that arbitrage transactions through impact loans and foreign-currency deposits have worked to narrow that difference. In any case, interbank bill rates are substantially free now.

As for yields on long-term instruments, on the one hand European and Japanese monetary authorities complain that they find it difficult to decouple their rates from U.S. rates.[14] Indeed, during the 1980s when U.S. rates were high, the interest rates of other countries were also generally high. On the other hand, some U.S. economists emphasize that U.S. and Japanese real long-term rates have differed, and argue that this fact testifies to insufficient liberalization of the Japanese capital market.[15] What is the true situation? Do long-term funds move so freely that interest-rate decoupling is difficult, or do they move so slowly so real interest rates differ markedly?

Over a long enough period, during which expected real appreciation could be ignored, one can argue that real interest rates should tend to be equalized. Otherwise, real rates would diverge, as can be seen from the recent U.S. and Swiss figures.[16] Moreover, since real long-term rates tend to be equalized only in the long run, if the U.S. real rate fluctuates widely, there is no reason to expect consonant movements in the Japanese rate.[17] In short, judging the openness of the Japanese capital market by comparing the real long-term rates of Japan and the United States is misleading.

Available evidence on the relation between the U.S. and Japanese long-term rates suggests that arbitrage transactions have been lively. According to several studies of yen-dollar exchange rates,[18] deviations of exchange rates from some norm can be explained by, among other things, differences in the U.S. and Japanese real long-term rates. This implies that long-term funds tend to move freely, say, from Japan to the United States, and thus depreciate the yen against the dollar. This also means that comparing interest rates without taking exchange rates into account leads to the wrong conclusion.

The U.S.-Japan Agreements

In the recent financial disputes between Japan and the United States, the United States argued for direct U.S. investments in Japan, access to the Japanese market, liberalization of the Japanese market, and liberalization of the Euroyen market. Of these four the first two are to my mind relatively unimportant so far as the future performance of the Japanese financial system is concerned. The Japanese market is potentially very competitive, and easier access for foreign institutions will not in itself improve its performance. The latter two points, however, directly involve the liberalization of the financial system, and the agreements reached so far will have important consequences.

Among the more significant items agreed on by the Working Group were: (1) financial market liberalization (regulations on banks' spot exchange positions were lifted, regulations on CD issues were relaxed, and interest rates on large deposits will be liberalized, a yen-denominated BA (bankers' acceptance) market will be established, and regulations on yen-denominated foreign bank-loans were liberalized); and (2) Euroyen market liberalization (in addition to foreign governments and international organizations, foreign private agents will be able to issue Euroyen bonds, with some restrictions, Japanese agents can issue Euroyen bonds, Euroyen CDs were permitted, and regulations on short-term Euroyen loans were liberalized. Of the items that were *not* agreed on, the more significant to my mind were establishment of a treasury bill (TB), qualification standards for Eurobond issues, and liberalization of long-term Euroloans (begun in 1985).

Deliberations at the Foreign Exchange Council

Since the U.S.-Japan agreement, some liberalization measures have been implemented. Meanwhile, there have been fairly intensive deliberations on this matter at the Foreign Exchange Council, whose interim report, "On the Internationalization of the Yen," was delivered to the Finance Minister in March 1985.

The council's deliberations at the Council typify Japanese policy-making. Council members, except for a few neutral (and therefore unimportant) academicians and journalists, are representatives of interest groups. In this particular instance, the members represent the city banks, the Bank of Tokyo (a foreign-exchange specialist), the long-term-credit banks, security houses, manufacturing firms, trading companies, and so on. Representatives of foreign financial institutions were invited as "witnesses" to express their opinions. These members and witnesses air their grievances against the present system or contemplated changes in it. They propose changes that would benefit their groups. Arguments are sometimes bitter, but after a number of formal sessions and backstage lobbying efforts by ministry officials, a consensus emerges, which may, however, leave some thorny points unresolved. The result is a report by the Council, drafted by ministry officials and approved (in most cases unanimously) by the members.

The March 1985 interim report consisted of three parts: a basic stand on yen internationalization, liberalization of the Euroyen bond market, and liberalization of long-term Euroyen loans. The first part occupies a large portion of the report but is relatively unimportant: it is long on principles but short on the specifics that count at this stage of financial liberalization. The first part does, however, recommend that a short-term financial market open to non-banks be established, and approves the idea of a Tokyo offshore market. The former implicitly favors establishing a free TB market. (The Bank of Japan, an advocate of a TB market, has been selling TBs in large quantities, paving the way for a secondary TB market.)

The second part, on the Euroyen bond market, notes a few important (though hardly dramatic) measures that were agreed upon. It recommends that the withholding tax on earnings from Eurobonds issued by residents be abolished, a recommendation subsequently implemented. Since other major countries have implemented the same measure, the Japanese action was not remarkable but it was a victory by the "internationalists" over the domestic tax authorities. The report also recommends that variable-interest bonds should be introduced in the Euroyen market, though with the usual provision that this should be done without disrupting the domestic market, and that the qualifications for nonresidents be relaxed.

As for medium- and long-term Euroyen loans, the report recommends (and the ministry subsequently implemented) the liberalization of such loans to nonresidents. It also notes that it is desirable for loans to residents to be liberalized as soon as possible. The funding side of the long-term loans (that is, liberalization of the long-term Euroyen CDs) is one of the thorny questions the report leaves unresolved. If the city banks are allowed to issue long-term CDs, it argues, the interests of the long-term-credit banks, whose primary source of funding is long-term bonds, will be seriously compromised.

The last example suggests that the unresolved questions concern the so-called fences, or the segmentation of financial institutions in Japan. Not only are banks and security houses divided by a fence (by the Japanese equivalent of the U.S. Glass-Stegall Act), but banks are subdivided into city banks, trust banks, long-term-credit banks, and so on. These barriers are expected to remain more or less intact for some time. I would submit, however, that segmentation can go hand in hand with liberalization of interest rates. Segmentation is a ban on side businesses, and it has nothing to do with a pricing rule; prices may be regulated or market-determined irrespective of the ban on side businesses.

Taken together, the U.S.-Japan agreement and the Foreign Exchange Council report imply that short-term lending and interest rates will be virtually free in the near future. In addition to the liberalization of interest rates on large deposits, Euroyen loans with unregulated interest rates to residents will do much to liberalize lending rates in Japan. A BA market will help, too. What remains to be done is to provide short-term investors with diversified instruments. The instruments available are CDs and *gensaki*, but TBs will be conspicuously absent, though close-to-maturity government bonds will substitute for TBs to some extent. Long-term funding, especially bonds, are yet to be completely deregulated. Yen-denominated bank loans will perform this function to some extent, but bond issues will still be subject to regulations on qualification standards. Pressure for liberalization of bond issues will come from the mounting government debt, as well as from U.S.-Japan disputes.

Recent agreements between the United States and Japan mean that Japanese short-term transactions and interest rates will soon be unregulated. An important issue yet to be settled is the establishment of a TB market. Few economists would deny that for well-functioning short-term financial markets a free market for short-term government bills, open to nonbanks, is essential, as it is for increasing foreign holdings of yen-denominated assets and liabilities.

Investments in long-term Japanese instruments by foreigners and in long-term foreign instruments by Japanese are free, as are Japanese interest rates. What is yet to be completely deregulated is Japanese capital, especially bonds. Whether regulation in this area makes sense is problematic given Japan's large current account surplus and the belief of some knowledgeable economists that for the near future it will continue to be large.

Supply of Capital by Japan

The large surpluses in Japan's current accounts have recently been the object of widespread complaints. At the same time, Japan is often mentioned as a potential supplier of capital to countries that need it. But commentators sometimes ignore the fact that a net supply of capital by Japan is by definition equal to the surplus in its current accounts. That is, Japan cannot both reduce its surplus *and* increase its export of capital.

Supply of Savings

An easier way to see the relation between capital exports and current-account surpluses is in terms of supplies of savings. For example, in 1985, the excess of (gross) Japanese savings over domestic (gross) investments was 3.8 per cent of GNP; the excess savings of the household sector was 9.8 per cent; of corporations 5.6 per cent, and of the government −0.8 per cent (with a statistical error of 0.4 per cent). Since government and corporate investments did not fully absorb excess household savings, the rest was exported through the current-account surplus. The bulk of the surplus was with the United States, where excess of investments over savings was on the order of 3 per cent of Japan's GNP.

The bulk of Japan's excess savings was invested in the United States. High U.S. interest rates no doubt played an important role, but the undervaluation of the yen against the dollar also played a role in realizing Japan's excess of exports over imports. That is, the supply of savings by Japan to the United States, the high U.S. interest rates, the cheaper yen, and the trade imbalance are all aspects of the same phenomenon: a Japanese supply of capital to the United States. If liberalizing the Japanese financial system leads to higher Japanese interest rates and appreciation of the yen, as some commentators have suggested, and thus wipes out the trade imbalance, then the Japanese supply of capital will disappear as well.[19]

The situation is politically difficult. A Japanese export surplus hurts U.S. industries, such as the steel and auto industries, that compete with imports, and they blame Japan's surplus. A stronger dollar would hurt U.S. export industries, and they would blame Japan's closed financial markets. But an increase in the Japanese supply of capital would mean more business for U.S. financial institutions; at present the bulk of capital exports is dollar-denominated. The demand for a freer capital market should imply more capital exports. I wonder if these U.S. complaints are consistent, but perhaps economic consistency is irrelevant in the political context.

Japan as Capital Exporter

The current-account surpluses in 1985 and 1986 were large, but will the trend continue? Some knowledgeable economists believe that Japan has become a capital exporter. I am somewhat skeptical; I have argued elsewhere that in the past one hundred years Japan's current accounts were more or less balanced despite such shocks as four major wars and two oil crises. In the present context the difference between these other economists and myself is rather small. One representative economist argues that normally the Japanese surplus will be 1.0–1.5 per cent of GNP.[20] My position is that the surplus has been 1 per cent or less of GNP. I do not exclude the possibility that it may exceed 1 per cent or deny that a surplus of about $150 billion is large in absolute terms.

To what regions has Japan been exporting capital? Japan's foreign-asset figures (see Table 1) are not broken down by region, but we can get a rough idea summing regional trade balances. The result for 1966–85 is (in billions of dollars): United States 168.1; other OECD countries, 62.4; non-oil-exporting Asian countries, 101.4; other LDCs, 26.4; oil-exporting countries, −237.0; and a total of $141.7 billion. According to these figures, two main recipients of Japanese capital were the United States and the non-oil-exporting countries of Asia, followed by other OECD countries—a picture that is hardly surprising and to be repeated in the future.

Asian NICs are natural recipients of Japanese capital. As economies undergoing rapid industrialization, they are capital-hungry, and savings imported by them are likely to be used productively. If Japan has entered the capital-exporting stage, Asian NICs are at the capital-importing stage, and the two regions make a natural pair, economically as well as geographically. But is there an equally convincing reason why Japan should export capital to the United States? The latter is after all one of the richest countries in the world, and moreover there is some suspicion that capital imported there will be used unproductively. As a mature capital importer, the United States should be repatriating the fruits of past investments, but it is not doing so.

Implications for the Japanese Financial System

To the extent that Japanese current-account surpluses are large in absolute terms, Japan is exporting large sums of capital. It will become increasingly difficult to concentrate investments in dollar-denominated liquid assets. For one thing, the share of plant and engineering exports and technology-related knowledge (service) exports will increase, and direct investments or long-term export financing will accompany them. For another, this type of financing will have to be yen-denominated because the exchange risks involved are difficult to hedge.[21] We should observe a steady rise in direct investments or yen-denominated long-term financing.

At present Japanese net long-term foreign assets are mainly in direct investments and dollar-denominated loans (*net* security holdings are not large). My comment above implies that direct investments will play a larger role, and that loans and bond issues will tend to be yen-denominated. It is even conceivable that direct investments may be yen-denominated in the sense that a resource development project abroad with a commitment of yen-denominated imports into Japan can be financed in yen. In short, if Japan becomes a capital exporter, it will tend to hold its foreign assets in yen-denominated instruments. At the very least, this is what one infers from the experience of Britain and the United States.

But will debtors be willing to owe yen-denominated debts? With Japan's net foreign assets growing, other countries can be expected to bear larger exchange risks to the extent that Japanese resort to yen-denominated loans. There is no logical solution to this dilemma. One way out would be for Japan to provide diversified short-term debt instruments. They serve to facilitate foreigners' management of long-term debts; a foreign long-term debtor may try to hedge by maintaining a short-term portfolio. This is one reason why I would like to see a TB market develop.

Financial Intermediation

I have argued that Japan cannot export capital unless it has a current-account surplus. But a country can export long-term capital in exchange for short-term debt without running a current-account surplus. This is what amounts to international financial intermediation. A number of economists have pointed out that the United States as world banker was practicing "borrow short-term, lend long-term" in the 1960s. There is no reason, then, why Japan cannot be another world banker, quite apart from the size of its current account surplus.

At present, short-term yen borrowings are small; Euroyen deposits and domestic nonresident deposits account for about 2 per cent and 1 per cent, respectively, of the totals. In addition, nonresidents account for less than 10 per cent of the *gensaki* balance. Increasing yen-denominated short-term debt may not be easy; this would depend on foreign supply of yen-denominated short-term funds. Here again it is important to provide diversified instruments at unregulated rates of interest. Thus the liberalization of short-term markets (including the Euroyen market) would be desirable.

But would it be desirable for Japan to serve as a financial intermediator? Note that in principle no net capital need be exported from Japan; its current accounts can be balanced. Note also that the world's largest banks (including some Japanese banks) now engage in this business in dollars (and to a lesser degree in Deutsch-marks and Swiss-francs). Even if financial intermediation in yen is encouraged, it will at most play a supplementary role. I doubt it would do much to solve the debt problems of LDCs, for example. Still, one can argue that providing an array of yen-denominated instruments would help the world financial markets.

Japan's large current-account surpluses, at least in absolute terms, are likely to persist. This will satisfy foreign demands that Japan provide more capital to the rest of the world. But large current-account surpluses go hand in hand with a weaker yen; it is illogical to expect both a stronger yen and large capital exports from Japan.

If Japan becomes a capital exporter, Asia's NICs are natural recipients, and they have received a large share of capital in the past. Another main recipient has been the United States, but there is some doubt that it is a natural candidate. The financial implications of this development are that Japanese foreign assets will tend to be yen-denominated and that Japan will be obliged to provide diversified short-term yen instruments, including TBs, so that foreign borrowers can better manage their debts. Providing short-term instruments is also important if Japan is to serve as a world banker.

Implications for Future Financial Development

So far I have been concerned with recent developments and the near-term prospects of the Japanese financial system. I now turn to discussions of a more speculative nature, namely, how far financial liberalization will and should proceed, prospects for internationalization of the yen, and the impact of these financial developments on the domestic and foreign economies.[22]

Liberalization

As I wrote at the outset, internationalization of finance, internationalization of the yen, and liberalization of finance are different issues. Which aspect of the Japanese financial system is the most important? It is not surprising that Japanese finance is fairly internationalized. The financial systems of a number of developed countries are more or less internationalized, as are the financial systems of some LDCs. Internationalization of the yen is an important issue, which I take up below.

This leaves liberalization as the key issue. Partly because of economic pressures and partly because of political pressures (which culminated in the U.S.-Japan financial agreement), the Japanese financial system has been, and will continue to be, liberalized more speedily than anyone expected a few years ago. This is especially true of its international aspects.

I have argued that the Japanese capital market is yet to be deregulated, and that the long-term Euroyen market will be deregulated, especially for bond-floatation. This does not mean, however, that the yen capital market is more closed than the financial markets of most developed countries. For bank loans, yen-denominated foreign lending from Japan has been liberalized, and short-term Euroyen loan are also unregulated, which means that revolving short-term loans can substitute for long-term Euroyen loans. The remaining regulations on bond issues both in Japan and in the Euroyen market are qualification standards, not outright regulations on interest rates or the amounts that can be issued. By my lights the Japanese domestic market ranks next to the American, British, and Swiss markets in openness, and the Euroyen market will soon rank just after the Eurodollar market.

Does financial liberalization spell trouble for the conduct of monetary policy? It is often argued that Japan's traditional monetary policy, which relied on official discount rates and "window guidances," will lose its effectiveness once liberalization is in full force. I agree with this view, but I am optimistic about the effectiveness of monetary policy in an internationally liberalized environment. My optimism stems more from the U.S. experience with disinflation than from a detailed examination of the future Japanese market, which is not easy. As is well known, U.S. monetary authorities succeeded in curbing inflation, despite the existence of the vast, unregulated Eurodollar market and the absence of exchange controls. There is no reason why Japanese monetary authorities should not do as well, once Japan's short-term market is equipped with such instruments as TBs.

Domestic Liberalization and Sound Banking

My argument becomes much murkier when it comes to liberalization of the Japanese domestic market. It is not that liberalization of interest rates is in doubt; there are strong pressures working toward liberalization, as I and we will see substantially free rates fairly soon. What is murky is the extent to which regulations on the "segmentation" of financial institutions and on banking practices will or should be lifted.

Japanese financial institutions are classified into fine segments. Not only may banks not engage in security transactions, as in the U.S., but they are classified into mutually exclusive city, long-term, regional, and trust segments. Insurance companies and consumer credit businesses as well as security houses are similarly segmented from one another. Some of these segmentations may be irrational; all banks could be grouped together if transitional problems were surmountable. As it is, it will be quite some time before regulations on segmentation are substantially eased. Moreover, segmentation between banks and security houses may be rational; witness the recent shift of U.S. opinion after the Continental-Illinois incident. Banks, after all, are suppliers of all-important money, and sound banking should always be their first principle.[23]

Few economists would advocate complete laissez-faire in banking policy, but the proper extent of bank regulation is a difficult question. I for one am unable to give an answer. Some regulations on reserve ratios, foreign exchange exposure, and securities transactions are necessary, but I cannot specify to what extent. In fact, I doubt that economic theory can help answer this question. Protection of depositors is another area in which some regulation is needed. At present it is widely conceded that the Japanese deposit insurance system is poorly equipped to handle liberalization, but few agree on what should be done and what the role of the regulators should be. We can expect a fairly long period of trial and error in the process of domestic liberalization.[24]

Internationalization of the Yen

I have already touched on this and argued that although international-ization of the yen has a long way to go, there are factors that may shorten the process. Ryutaro Komiya has argued in his discussion of my paper that the process may be more speedy than I imply because the Japanese economy is large, making its financial market "deep"; the value of the yen has been stable; and the Japanese financial market will soon be very sophisticated. Although it seems to me that he somewhat underestimates the forces of inertia, on the whole I have no quarrel with his arguments.

What are the implications of internationalization of the yen for the Pacific nations? Trade and capital transactions with Japan will be easier to conduct when agents can avoid using a third-party currency (i.e., the U.S. dollar). From the point of view of portfolio diversification, agents will be able to deal in yen in addition to dollars and pounds, which should be welcome. But offshore financial centers such as Singapore and Hongkong may be eclipsed by the Tokyo market; those offshore centers have thrived mainly because of regulations in Japan. Once the Japanese financial market is internationalized and liberalized, the factors Komiya mentions will inevitably make it a dominant market.

Impact on Nonfinancial Sectors

Two questions have been raised with regard to the impact of financial liberalization on consumers and producers. One is the level of interest rates and profits of financial institutions. Although there seems to be no assumption about which way interest rates will move, it is reasonably certain that the profits of financial institutions will be squeezed after lib-eralization. This will be good news for consumers and producers. What remains to be seen is whether this efficiency can be achieved without undue volatility in interest rates, as in the United States. (One might call the U.S. situation a speculative bubble).

The other question concerns the relations between banks and busi-ness firms. In the past Japanese firms were predominantly financed by banks, with a house bank (called in Japan the "lead bank") sometimes playing a supervisory role. With financial deregulation and interest-rate consciousness on the part of firms, will the situation change, and will the long horizon of Japanese firms be replaced by American-style fas-cination with quarterly bottom lines? Here again I have no definite an-swer, but I am inclined to believe that a firm's time horizon depends on other factors as well as on finance—how chief executives are selected, for example. To the extent that Japanese business firms continue to have long horizons, they will also retain special relations with their house banks. In the long run, a firm may experience hard times, in which case it would certainly miss a house bank if it had dispensed with one.

In this last section I have touched on quite a few topics without reaching firm conclusions. And this is as it should be. Financial liberalization is Japan's first experience with an unregulated financial system in more than fifty years.[25] (Japan had a laissez-faire financial system in the 1930s.) Moreover, the U.S. experience with financial deregulation has yet to produce a definite precedent, even given the obvious fact that the U.S. economy differs from the Japanese. I may thus be excused for raising questions without answering them.

It may nevertheless be appropriate to conclude with a few remarks on the probable effects of Japanese financial developments. The Japanese financial system has already been internationalized, and its liberalization has been and will continue to be accelerated. Given the large savings its economy provides every year, the Japanese financial system will exert an enormous impact on the outside world. The world's financial institutions will be busy dealing with Japanese clients. A number of countries, including the United States, will come to depend on the long-term funds supplied by Japan. Tokyo will emerge as one of the financial centers of the world and probably eclipse Hongkong, Singapore, and other lesser markets.

In brief, Japan will become a financial giant as it already is a manufacturing giant. It is by now painfully clear that Japanese manufacturing has outgrown Japan's political and military status. In a few years so will the Japanese financial system. This is so even if one does not accept the figures I cited at the outset. A political and military dwarf with the economic might of Japan will be a strange sight. One has only to remember nineteenth-century Britain and the twentieth-century United States to be reminded that such a Japan will be an unprecedented, and perhaps destabilizing, phenomenon.

Domestic Institutions and Policymaking

Peter J. Katzenstein

Japan, Switzerland of the Far East?

In gauging Japan's achievements, admirers and critics during the past decade have compared it either to the United States or to the medium-size welfare states in Western Europe: Britain, France, and West Germany. The battle for technological and commercial supremacy in the twenty-first century, it is argued, justifies the first comparison; the evolution of a new-style capitalism the second. A paper that compares what General MacArthur reportedly called the Switzerland of the Far East with the real thing in the Alps requires some justification. Why complicate matters by comparing two anomalous cases?

One reason is the great, though differing, economic success of these two states. In the 1970s, Japan's growth record measured in terms of increase in real GDP was the best among the major OECD countries, whereas Switzerland's was the worst. Conversely, Switzerland had the lowest inflation rate in the 1970s, whereas Japan had one of the highest. Finally, for different reasons both countries have consistently registered some of the lowest unemployment rates in the OECD. Japan and Switzerland were exemplars of success in the 1970s. And their relative performance has been as strong in the 1980s.[1]

This strong performance has not led to direct competition in the bilateral trade between the two countries. In the early 1980s, Japan exported automobiles, machinery, appliances, and optical instruments to Switzerland, and the Swiss shipped chemical products, machinery, and watches to Japan. Because of the high technological quality of their products, these two societies increasingly use each other as test markets for new products. After the United States, Switzerland was the second largest investor in Japan in 1980. And through the Swiss capital market in the late 1970s, Japan financed half of its total debt in international capital markets.[2]

Each country's strong economic performance, furthermore, can be traced back to some striking similarities in policy and politics. Since 1945 Japan has behaved like Switzerland and other small industrial states in adjusting to many of the world's currents rather than seeking to dominate them. Like Switzerland, Japan is acutely aware of developments in world markets. Both have institutional mechanisms that limit markets; yet in both societies the principle of market competition is enshrined deeply. And both countries are distinguished by strong conservative political regimes that have constrained the growth of a public welfare state.

I argue in this paper that these similarities in performance, strategy, and structure are deceptive. Japan adheres to a strategy of market domination, whereas the Swiss are content to discover market niches. In their domestic politics, Switzerland and Japan differ in the extent and character of accommodation between business and labor. Specifically, Swiss politics is more inclusionary than Japanese politics. It accommodates more fully the labor movement and the Left. Finally, the Japanese view themselves, as do the Swiss, as occupying an exposed and vulnerable state and emphasize the need for harmony in a dangerous world. But because of the size of its economy, the disruptions Japan causes in the global economy are much greater. The strategy of a free-rider that Switzerland has followed so well and that the Japanese find so attractive is of decreasing use to "Asia's new giant."[3]

Industrial Adjustment in Switzerland and Japan

Japan's and Switzerland's political strategies of industrial adjustment have similarities and differences. Both countries see their own existence as tied closely to an open international economy. Both thus favor economic interdependence and are strong opponents of protectionism. And both are flexible in exploiting the opportunities of world markets and in adjusting to their pressures. At the same time, for reasons of size, Japan typically adopts a strategy that aims at domination of global markets. Switzerland in contrast is typically content to search out profitable market niches for selling high-quality, customized products. In the language of Michael Piore and Charles Sabel, Japan approximates the paradigm of mass production, Switzerland the paradigm of crafts production.[4]

Switzerland

Switzerland went through a sharp process of deindustrialization in the 1970s with little more than a token industrial policy.[5] In the 1970s, Switzerland's industrial work force decreased by 240,000, and the number of employees of Swiss multinationals increased by 140,000.[6] At home, service sectors such as finance and insurance showed the highest growth rates in employment, and the service component in industry—organized around an activity that the Swiss call industrial problem solving—increased greatly in importance. Swiss industry is decentralized both regionally and in terms of the average size of its industrial plants. The process of ownership concentration, which, in Switzerland as elsewhere, has been under way for decades, has done little to change this basic feature of Swiss industry.

Furthermore, Swiss industry has always been receptive to developments in world markets. During the past thirty years, the share of GDP earned abroad has increased from 25 to 40 per cent, and Swiss exports have grown at a faster rate than did world trade. The search for high-value-added products and product niches in international markets with inelastic demand is reflected in Switzerland's specialization in research-intensive products requiring a highly skilled labor force. In contrast to Japan, a strategy of mass production is not part of the typical repertoire of Swiss industry. The process of industrial specialization has occurred within an industrial structure that has not undergone any drastic large-scale change in the past thirty years. Unlike Japan, Switzerland was lucky in being particularly well positioned in those sectors of industry that experienced dynamic growth in the 1950s and 1960s.

In advanced industrial states, the textile industry typically is threatened by foreign producers and is marginal in domestic politics. The political responses to economic change that one might expect, therefore, are a variety of trade restrictions and relatively small amounts of government assistance. Switzerland does not confirm these expectations. Instead, Switzerland has remained resolutely committed to a free trade policy. Industrial adjustment in the textile industry relied primarily on the responses of different segments of the business community, as well as of the unions, to the requirements of a flexible adjustment policy. Scores of firms found it economically relatively painless to exit from the industry in the pursuit of real estate profits, which diminished political pressures for a policy less accommodative to market trends. So did the fact that half of the industry's work force is foreign. This provided the industry with a large cushion of female, migrant labor left defenseless against layoffs. Both factors facilitated a flexible adjustment, as did the assistance the industry received from the banks on the question of export finance and from the unions on the question of organizing the elimination of jobs. In the eyes of both business and unions, the process of retrenchment could not be resisted. And retrenchment was piecemeal and incremental.

Flexible industrial adjustment is not an automatic response in Switzerland to changing market conditions. Adjustment results from policies that are responsive to both the economic and political requirements of change. Concern over declining profits and endangered jobs alarmed businessmen and workers in declining industries such as textiles and watches. A reactive policy was the dominant response in both industries. Where the opportunities for shutting down production were good, as in textiles, firms closed in relatively large numbers, thus easing the process of adjustment. But even under such relatively advantageous conditions, adjustment is costly and painful for business and workers. Furthermore, Switzerland's commitment to full employment was not readily apparent in its economic policies. But during the past three decades, full employment for the Swiss has been largely protected by the influx of a foreign labor force that acts as a shock absorber for the Swiss economy. With official unemployment rates below the 1 per cent mark throughout the 1970s, Swiss workers who lost their jobs in large numbers in the textile and watch industries normally could find other work.

Since the textile industry is not as central to the general economic health of Switzerland as is the watch industry, the process of industrial adjustment in textiles did not exhibit the urgency and activity at the highest levels that distinguished the adjustment process in the watch industry. The interventions of Swiss banks in the rescue of the two largest Swiss watch firms remained a private affair. High-level intervention in Switzerland is thus not easily documented. But the largest financial reconstruction in Switzerland's corporate history occurred in the watch industry in the early 1980s. It was probably discussed fully by the country's economic and political leadership.

Like the textile industry, the Swiss watch industry experienced adverse economic change in the 1970s. But, in contrast to textiles, the change occurred in an area of relative strength. The Swiss watch industry dominated international markets. The industry also occupied a more influential position in Swiss politics than did the textile industry. Situated along the only ethnically contested line in Swiss politics in the 1970s, the watch industry commands influence because of the politicization of the Jura region, the industry's size, its contribution to the Swiss balance of payments, and its importance to the very self-conception of what it means to be Swiss. The political response to change that one might expect in such conditions is protectionism and massive assistance to achieve structural transformations. But Switzerland's adjustment policies do not confirm these expectations.

Switzerland's adjustment policy in the watch industry was largely market driven. In the 1960s and 1970s, producers paid a heavy price for incorrectly judging market trends that forced quick reactions from those firms that maintained their international competitiveness. Because of its total reliance on export markets as well as its growing internationalization of production, the watch industry remained strongly committed to free trade. Although adjustment was market driven, the issue of compensating some of the costs of change remained vital in political as well as economic terms. The banks provided compensation through special credit facilities for exporters; the federal government did the same through a modest and carefully constructed program of assistance. Finally, aware of a severe shortage of labor in Switzerland, the unions did not obstruct the elimination of jobs in uncompetitive firms but aided in making what the industry regarded as inevitable cuts in employment. Between 1970 and 1984, employment declined from 90,000 to 30,000. The initial resistance to acknowledging economic change was followed by quick industrial adjustments that excluded policies of planned structural transformation.

In sum, Switzerland's policy of adjustment in textiles and watches relied primarily on the responses of different segments of the business community, as well as of the unions, to the requirements of a flexible adjustment policy. Although the textile and watch industries experienced adverse economic change, politics either did not impede a shift in the factors of production or did so in a manner that contributed to a flexible adjustment policy. Although adjustment was forced primarily through the institution of the market, it was aided by a special effort by Switzerland's banks to assist producers through a variety of financial measures granted at preferential rates. Unique to Switzerland was the calibration of economic flexibility with political compensation. Switzerland's adjustment policy encourages economic flexibility while making concessions to the need for compensation. In linking flexibility closely with compensation, Switzerland has chosen to live with the costs of change rather than seeking to pre-empt these costs through policies of structural transformation.

Japan

Japanese businessmen and state officials favor a process of domestic industrial adjustment in which the government assists firms in exploiting long-term market developments. Because foreign investment by Japanese corporations was low throughout the 1960s, the preferred mode of adjusting to economic change was through government industrial policy, including protection. Japan's policy is geared to anticipating structural changes in markets by assisting firms to become competitive in particular industry segments or product lines. Comparative advantage is conceived as a result not only of market forces but also of political action that affects competitiveness. A number of Japanese industries reveal this policy pattern. For example, the emergence of Japan's steel industry as the most efficient producer in the world depended on a variety of innovative policies, including administrative guidance, recession and rationalization cartels, and the socialization of risk through various financial arrangements. Armed with these policies and favored by the climate that U.S. policies had created, Japan succeeded within two decades in creating an industry that no longer required protection or assistance. Similarly, Japan's computer industry became an important target of government attention in the 1960s and 1970s. Government policies helped either to narrow significantly or to close the gap between it and leading U.S. firms in the production of computer hardware. By the late 1970s, the industry had become largely independent of the need for protection. In these and several other cases, Japan's innovative industrial policy focused on long-term market development, relied on protection while establishing international competitiveness, and relinquished formal protection, often under intense foreign pressure, when competitiveness had been achieved.

Japan's industrial adjustment in textiles and watches must be seen in the context of a more general reorientation of Japanese industry.[7] The emphasis on knowledge-intensive domestic industries, which in the early 1970s emerged from a reassessment of Japan's position in the international economy, has been reaffirmed by the ambitious target of a 50 per cent increase in total R&D expenditures to 3 per cent of GDP by 1990. Japan's program for the 1980s expresses a renewed concern over the security of raw-material supplies and questions of energy policy. Numerous basic industrial sectors built up under government tutelage in the 1950s and 1960s were hit hard by the prolonged recession of the late 1970s and early 1980s. Depressed industries legislation passed in 1978 gave the Ministry of International Trade and Industry (MITI) the support of the Fair Trade Commission in reducing capacity and rationalizing production structures in 14 industries, including shipbuilding, synthetic fibers, electric furnaces, and aluminum. In the area of research and development in high-technology sectors, Japan's industry confronts greater uncertainty and unaccustomed challenges. For the first time, the Japanese government is being pushed to confront risky choices of allocating venture capital to projects that do not have proven commercial value. Finally, there are industries like steel, automobiles, or consumer electronics where the policy successes of the past leave the government without essential tasks in the near future.

In textiles Japan's industrial policy is a far cry from a touted story of success.[8] While the industry was still the world's leading exporter, the Japanese government initiated several programs in the 1950s and 1960s designed to reduce capacity. But in the hothouse atmosphere of high economic growth in the 1960s, these attempts were condemned to failure. Japan's textile industry grew and prospered. And it was so powerful that it contributed its fair share to the acrimonious "textile wrangle" that divided the United States and Japan between 1969 and 1971. The government attempted, halfheartedly, to fashion a long-term policy of structural transformation. But it did not succeed.

With economic growth rates declining sharply after 1973, however, government and industry objectives have converged. This is reflected, for example, in legislation such as the Structurally Depressed Industries Law of 1978, which was designed to assist large firms to reduce capacity in a number of energy-intensive industries, including synthetic fibers. But the government also passed five special laws between 1976 and 1979 designed to help smaller and medium-size firms to modernize.

Politically, the most intriguing aspect of Japan's industrial adjustment strategy in textiles is how government policy self-consciously exploits changing conditions in international markets to advance the objective of sectoral transformation. The international context has always been an important determinant of the Japanese textile industry. In sharp contrast to the United States, the internationalization of production after 1945 began with technologically backward industries such as textiles. For a variety of reasons, in the 1950s small and medium-size producers moved part of their production to neighboring countries such as South Korea and Taiwan. Differences in wage levels were probably less important than the prospect of rapidly growing markets in countries less developed than Japan that were then embarking on a strategy of import substitution and protection. Furthermore, various trade restraints imposed after 1957 on Japanese textiles, first by the United States and later by other OECD members, made relocation an attractive option compared with the prospect of being shut out of Western markets. Finally, the financial incentives of host governments in countries like South Korea, Taiwan, and Thailand provided an additional incentive for moving overseas.

Throughout the 1950s and 1960s, the Japanese government encouraged overseas expansion, although with little foresight of how such a policy might eventually affect the textile industry in the 1980s. In the late 1970s, Japanese textile producers were, for the first time, experiencing dramatic increases in imports from newly industrializing countries such as South Korea. The existing evidence does not permit us to distinguish clearly between two different possibilities. Are low-cost imports from neighboring countries pressing the many thousands of uncompetitive firms producing for Japan's domestic market? Or are Japanese producers who moved abroad in the 1950s and 1960s, together with their foreign competitors, invading Japan's large domestic market, thus forcing a fight between one segment of the Japanese industry and another?

The proud insistence of Japanese government officials that they have not interfered with changes in the international division of labor through the adoption of U.S.- or European-style protectionist policies is thus open to two different interpretations. If Korean producers are now shrinking Japan's textile industry, the government is relying on market pressures to succeed in the 1980s where it had failed in the 1960s. Market change is thus being exploited to serve the political objectives of the government. If Japanese producers who moved abroad in the 1950s and 1960s have recently begun, for whatever reasons, to re-export their products to Japan, the government is standing aside while the internationally oriented, stronger segments of the industry are undermining the domestically oriented, weaker ones. In this case, the government is now exploiting market changes that conceal a constellation of potentially explosive political forces. In either case, Japan's strategy of sectoral transformation is not, as in the 1960s, being undermined by market dynamics. Instead, that strategy exploits market developments in order to reach thousands of firms in a highly fragmented industry.

Finally, it is quite plausible that the "industry conversations" so typical of Japan's manufacturing industries have spread to include Korea and other highly competitive producers now threatening the Japanese market. Informal, privately arranged orderly market arrangements between Japan and some of its competitors may play the same role as the government-to-government negotiated orderly market arrangements between the United States and Japan. In any case, state power and market change, far from being contradictory, are made compatible by the way the state has defined its political objectives.

Although Japan's watch industry dates to the late nineteenth century, the origin of its present-day rivalry with Switzerland's industry arose less than a generation ago. By the end of the 1950s, the industry had recuperated not only from the losses incurred during World War II, but had also retooled and upgraded the quality of its product.[9] During the 1960s, output trebled to 24 million units. Whereas exports had been negligible in 1960, ten years later, because of the beginning saturation of the home market, half of Japan's production was destined for export markets, primarily Hongkong and the United States. Southeast Asia was a natural export market. It was close to home and offered a chance to displace Swiss producers from one of their traditional strongholds. And as suppliers of inexpensive movements and parts for assembly by U.S. producers, Japanese firms were also pulled into the U.S. market.

In contrast to Switzerland's fragmented industry, Japan's watch industry is highly concentrated. Four firms control virtually all of Japan's production, with Seiko and Citizen accounting for 90 per cent of the total. These firms adopted a mass-production strategy geared to the medium-price range of jeweled-lever watches. More expensive timepieces and cheaper pin-lever watches were left deliberately to Swiss watchmakers and to Timex. Instead, in a market large enough for mass production, Japanese producers succeeded in matching Swiss watches in quality and features while undercutting Swiss prices. What impressed Seiko's managers most when they visited the United States in the 1950s were the assembly lines in Detroit. Manned by cheap, unskilled labor, Japanese producers focusing on standardized watches achieved cost advantages ranging from 15 to 45 per cent over their Swiss competitors. Furthermore, unlike the Swiss, because of their large domestic market, Seiko and Citizen could afford to sell at or near their marginal costs in foreign markets. Government policy helped producers both indirectly and directly in this mass-production strategy. The National Income-Doubling Plan of the 1960s brought about an expansion of the domestic market that facilitated corporate strategies of achieving significant economies of scale. Substantial tariff protection and the government's strong support of a highly concentrated industry pushed in a similar direction.

But the continuation of the industry's explosive growth in the 1970s must be credited, in sharper contrast to the Swiss case, to its openness to adapting its production and marketing strategy to the era of the electronic watch, an innovation that revolutionized the industry. Between 1970 and 1983, production increased fivefold to about 120 million units, with a proportionate increase in export sales. Japan led the shift to digital quartz watches, which created, as had the transition from black-and-white to color television in the early 1970s, a new market both at home and abroad.

But in the new "watch war" shaping up in Asia, Japanese producers must now increasingly contend with Hongkong, in terms of volume the leading producer of watches in the world. Hongkong producers, using parts imported from Japan, are giving the Japanese serious price competition on the strength of Hongkong's low labor costs. In response, Japanese firms have rapidly shifted production abroad and are now automating their production lines at home. A disciplined and accommodating labor force that permits this degree of flexibility in the industry's adjustment is now as important to the industry's continued success as was its openness to new technological developments in the 1970s. The mass-production strategy aiming at the domination of world markets is as evident in this industry as in such others as textiles, steel, shipbuilding, automobiles, and semiconductors. But since the watch industry is still experiencing very high growth rates, it is too early to tell whether the government will pursue the same strategy of structural transformation through exploiting market developments as it evidently is doing in the declining textile industry.

In sum, these illustrations show that Japan is endowed with the means and the institutions to pre-empt the costs of change through a structural transformation of its economy. This strategy often requires protectionist policies, at least in the short and medium term, because it seeks to meet structural changes in the world economy head on. It is a political option for a large industrial state with power sufficient to exercise effective control over its own society. The Swiss state lacks that sort of control. It has chosen a different kind of response, one that does not fit easily into the dichotomous categories of analysis suggested by the large industrial states: competition or intervention, market or plan. Because of its small size and great dependence on world markets, protectionism is not a viable option. And its economic openness and domestic politics do not permit the luxury of long-term planning of sectoral transformation. While letting international markets force economic adjustments, Swiss elites choose economic and social policies that prevent the costs of change from erupting politically. They live with change by compensating for it.

The Left in Japan and Switzerland

In their domestic structures, Japan and Switzerland also exhibit similarities and differences. In Japan, business plays a central role in a broad coalition of social forces that one recent book has called a system of creative conservatism.[10] Business, especially big business, is at the center of the political coalition that has sustained the Liberal Democratic Party (LDP) in power for three decades of uninterrupted rule. After a brief period of explosive growth in the immediate postwar years, Japan's labor movement has never succeeded fully in escaping from the position of relative marginality in which the Left in postwar Japan has found itself. On the other hand, throughout the postwar period the Japanese state has been an important actor in the evolution of Japan's economy. The network linking the different actors in Japan's political economy is relatively tight. Japan's financial system traditionally was based not on autonomous capital markets but on a system of administered credit, which accords the state a prominent role in influencing investment flows in the economy. Government-business relations are integrated and cooperative. And labor, less close to the corridors of power at the national level, suffers from fundamental weaknesses on the shop floor. The political inequality between Right and Left and between business and labor is quite similar in different areas of Japanese politics.

In Switzerland as in Japan, business and banks are at the center of a conservative regime. And in Switzerland as in Japan, the state is deeply embedded in social relations, in the Swiss case relations centered around the citizen-soldier of Switzerland's militia army. But in contrast to Japan, Switzerland's Left has not been excluded from power. Since the 1950s it has been a central part of an all-party government. The Swiss trade unions are also an important actor in national politics. But on the shop floor Swiss workers lack political power. They are shielded from Japanese-type management techniques by law rather than by political organization. Compared with Japan, what is notable in Switzerland is the increasing equality in the distribution of power as one moves from plant-level to union and national-level politics. By the standards of Japanese politics, no great disparities exist in national politics.

Switzerland

Switzerland has arguably the most liberal market economy in Western Europe. Yet the strength of business and of political conservatism has not prevented the political inclusion of the Social Democratic Party and the labor movement. Indeed, I have argued elsewhere that this incorporation has occurred not in spite of but because of the weakness of the Swiss Left.[11] The logic of Swiss politics is to diminish rather than enhance political inequalities.

The political inclusion of Switzerland's Left is symbolized by the Federal Council, an all-party government that, since 1959, has included among its seven members two Social Democrats. The council acts like a collegial body. The office of chair rotates annually among its members. Eschewing an adversarial style of politics, it reaches unanimous positions on all issues. And in the 1970s, it left Social Democrats in charge of the Ministries for Foreign Affairs and Economic Policy. This pattern of political incorporation is characteristic of all levels of government. In the early 1980s, Social Democrats were part of coalition governments in 19 of the 26 cantonal governments and in 88 of the 96 communes.[12]

By European standards, Switzerland's labor movement is organizationally fragmented and lacks an ideologically committed rank and file. But by Japanese standards, Swiss unions are exemplary for their organizational unity and strength. Compared with Japan's 75,000 enterprise unions, Switzerland's approximately 170 unions are part of three umbrella organizations. In the early 1980s, Swiss unions organized about 38 per cent of the total work force. This figure is fairly low by European standards but high compared with the Japanese figure of under 30 per cent. The labor movement is institutionally fully represented at all decision nodes of Swiss politics.[13] Like all other groups, the unions participate in the elaborate process of consultation. And they rely on the implicit threat of challenging policies they cannot support through organizing a referendum, a common form of political decision making in Switzerland; this strengthens their position. But because they occupy a central political position, especially on questions of social policy that matter most to them, the unions do not rely on the referendum, a weapon for political outsiders. During the past 30 years, the unions have not launched a single major referendum drive. Furthermore, the unions avoid unilateral political initiatives. Their views are fully represented where they think it counts—in the pre-parliamentary consultation process that shapes all important policy initiatives.

At the level of the individual plant, collective bargaining agreements are the decisive force that defines the position of workers.[14] In industrial firms, work rules must conform to collective agreements. Collective bargaining in Switzerland is decentralized by European standards but not by Japanese standards. Industry-wide agreements covered about two-thirds of the work force in the 1960s and 1970s. But because of extremely tight labor markets, these agreements have provided only a floor to which plant-level agreements have typically added substantial benefits. The de facto indexation of wages to the cost of living is a notable feature of the Swiss system of collective bargaining. Although Swiss trade unions were eager in the 1930s and 1940s to establish their position as coequals to business in all matters affecting economic and social policy broadly defined, they were much more hesitant to demand the right of codetermination at the plant level that is so distinctive of West German and, to a lesser extent, of Austrian industrial relations. The Swiss Left posed the issue in 1971, and it was defeated in a national referendum in 1976. But collective bargaining in many industries has instituted works councils, which date to 1906 in Switzerland. The main purpose of Swiss works councils is to inform, discuss, and advise but not to decide. The right to take part in management decisions applies only to few issues "confined to questions about the organization of labor or, sometimes, about some kinds of dismissal."[15] Like those of Japanese workers, the institutional prerogatives Swiss workers enjoy in their plants are remarkably weak compared with those of workers in other West European states. Particularly striking is the contrast between the weakness of Swiss labor at the plant level and its much greater influence in national politics.

Japan

In sharp contrast to Switzerland, for the past 30 years the Left has been excluded from the corridors of power in Japan. In the immediate postwar period, the Japan Socialist Party (JSP) was one of the main contenders for power, based on its strength in Marxist labor unions.[16] The party won an important electoral victory in 1947, and Socialist Prime Minister Tetsu Katayama then led a coalition government. But the Left was weakened by U.S. policy and the Occupation's purging of Communists from all political and social organizations; and it was discredited by the Communists' violent tactics as well as the Korean war. In addition, the JSP's brief tenure in office was disastrous. The party's program expressed demands not widely held, such as the nationalization of the coal industry. And the Socialist government was saddled with the unpopular task of enforcing the austerity policy of the Occupation.

In the 1950s, U.S. foreign policy, fusing security and economic concerns, created an adverse international climate for Japan's Left. But only the merger of the Liberal and Democratic parties in 1955 created a dominant conservative bloc. This conservative coalition adopted successful and adaptable political strategies. With the end of the era of high economic growth in the mid-1970s, it looked for a while as if conservative rule could be extended only with the support of some smaller parties of the Left.[17] For a time Japan promised to look like Italy in the 1960s, when the *apertura sinistra* with the Italian Socialists in 1962 extended the era of political dominance of the Christian Democratic Party. However, the dynamics of change in Japan's mass society have reconsolidated the political base of the LDP. Because it has succeeded in broadening its social base substantially since the late 1970s, Japan's conservative camp appears to hold an unassailable position today, while the Left remains deeply divided.[18] Should, however, the LDP's electoral fortunes decline, most of the groundwork has been laid for building a coalition with the Democratic Socialists, thus securing the LDP's control over the committee system in the Diet.[19] Furthermore, such a coalition would solidify the support of the conservative, private-sector unions for the LDP and its approach to industrial policy.

Japan's labor movement grew at a phenomenal rate after the defeat in World War II.[20] The Trade Union Law of 1945 was imposed by the Supreme Commander for the Allied Powers. Within a year, under the leadership of the Communist Party, Sanbetsu (Confederation of Industrial Unions) had a membership of 1.6 million. And by 1947 the ranks of all unions had swelled to 5 million.[21] But a change in U.S. policy on the eve of a nationwide strike called for February 1, 1947, blocked labor's advance. From then on, the Occupation systematically curtailed left-wing militance in the union movement.

Unions organize about 30 per cent of the Japanese work force, which is low by Swiss standards. But the relative weakness of the unions is also a product of their fragmentation.[22] The national union movement is split into different organizations. Sōhyō (General Council of Japanese Labor Unions), long the largest union federation, is divided into two ideological factions. Private-sector unions are divided from public-sector unions. And the national federations have virtually no control over the 75,000 enterprise unions that exist in the 1980s. The innate weakness of Japanese unions, in contrast to Switzerland's, is reflected "in the unions' tendency to rely almost totally on protections embodied in the law—what might be called their excessively legalistic attitude—rather than to develop their own 'muscle' to increase their bargaining power."[23]

It is thus not surprising that unions have effected little change in the structure of Japanese politics and that their militancy, which does not help them to articulate reform strategies, has had a diminishing impact on the political consciousness of union members. "Japanese employees," influential union official Akira Yamagishi said, "are more likely these days to think less like workers and more like company managers."[24]

Michio Muramatsu and Ellis Krauss argue in a series of important papers that Japan's "patterned pluralism" is noteworthy because it has substantially broadened the social base of the LDP (see their paper in Volume I of this series).[25] Labor unions and civic as well as political groups that have remained excluded from the coalition of social forces sustaining the LDP in power have, however, by no means been denied total access to the bureaucracy. Unsurprisingly, the groups excluded from the dominant coalition ranked the second and third lowest in having favorable policies adopted. But, these groups ranked first and third among all interest groups in veto power over objectionable policies. "It appears that despite their lack of support for the dominant party, interest groups close to the opposition parties are able to influence policymaking, although they are more successful at vetoing proposals; whereas interest groups closer to the LDP are more successful at having favored policies adopted."[26] In elaborating the point in an unpublished paper, Muramatsu and Krauss conclude that "opposition groups are not excluded from influence on policymaking under the contemporary Japanese dominant party system . . . [and] the opposition parties' influence on policymaking at both the prelegislative and the legislative stage may be greater than most models of Japanese politics under LDP rule have expected."[27]

It is less clear whether the system of enterprise unions in and of itself has necessarily doomed Japan's labor movement to a relatively marginal position. At least one recent comprehensive assessment of Japanese scholars is divided on this point.[28] Both Ronald Dore and Kazuo Koike look to Japan's delayed and rapid industrialization as an explanation for the cooperative, flexible pattern of enterprise unionism. Although their explanations emphasize, respectively, "welfare corporatism" and a distinctive pattern of "skill acquisition," they both point to the far-reaching equality between white- and blue-collar workers in Japanese enterprises.[29] Enterprise unions engage in a fair amount of consultation with management on a wide variety of issues. A survey conducted in 1972 concluded that 90 per cent of large firms (with more than 1,000 employees) and 56 per cent of medium-size firms (with 100–299 employees) had workers' advisory committees.[30] This figure makes the situation in Japan look quite comparable to that in Switzerland. Direct labor participation in management does not exist on any issue.[31] Taishiro Shirai draws the following balance between the advantages and disadvantages of Japan's system of enterprise unions: the rapid increase in unionization, the enlarged scope of collective bargaining, the successful organization of white-collar workers, sound union finances, easy communications between rank and file as well as with management, unity, and the establishment of appropriate solutions to specific problems versus the dispersal of union resources, the barriers against a possible development of a united labor movement, the unwillingness to organize unorganized workers and to defend the interests of retired workers, administrative and financial inefficiencies, susceptibility to interference and pressure by employers, and relative weakness in bargaining with employers, including the government.[32]

That weakness was cemented in the 1950s, the crucial decade for understanding the evolution of Japan's political economy since 1945. More important than Occupation policies in the 1940s and the phenomenal growth rates of the 1960s were the decisive battles against the labor movement that Japanese businessmen, aided by the state, won in the 1950s. In the immediate postwar years, one of the most pervasive rebellions against the status society of prewar Japan was the "democratization of management."[33] This rebellion largely succeeded. But for management, it symbolized a potentially dangerous attack on the right to manage that needed to be redressed. Japanese scholars differ in their assessment of these crucial years. For Hideo Otake, Prime Minister Shigeru Yoshida's (1946–47, 1948–54) economic liberalism provided the political climate and backing for an aggressive campaign by business to combat radical unions. "From its formation until about 1953, Nikkeiren [Japan Federation of Employers Associations] devoted its energies to destroying the most combative unions. . . . The Nikkeiren line was not a reactionary return to prewar management policies but an endorsement of the rationalism needed for free competition."[34] Haruo Shimada, in contrast, views the rise of a moderate economic unionism as "the spontaneous choice of the working mass under the perceived economic crisis."[35] Whatever the political interpretation, there is widespread agreement that in a series of dramatic confrontations in the 1950s business gained substantial control over the shop floor. It then proceeded in the 1960s and 1970s to perfect a system of industrial relations that has tied the interests of subordinated unions indelibly to those of management. Because it closed an era of confrontation and symbolized the collapse of the most powerful, militant union in Japan, the coal miners' strike of 1960 is worth particular attention.[36]

Growing competition from cheaper petroleum had created a structural crisis; Japan's coal industry and government responded with a far-reaching rationalization (*gōrika*), subsidies, and special manpower policies. By 1959, about 85,000 jobs had been lost, and the industry anticipated closing up to 200 mines and laying off another 100,000 miners. Tanrō, the coal miners' union, was the largest and most powerful private-sector union, as well as one of the largest affiliates of Sōhyō. "The Miike Coal Miners' union was regarded at the time as the strongest union in Japan and as a model of 'workshop-struggle' activity."[37] Its policy prescription—rationalization on the basis of capacity expansion—was disregarded by government and industry. Tanrō charged with some justification that the price for rationalization was being paid solely by the workers. Matters came to head when the largest of Japan's coal companies, Mitsui Mining Company, announced the layoff of 5,000 employees. The Sankōren (Mitsui Coal Miners' Federation) local at the Miike mine in Kyushu refused to come up with its full quota of volunteers for "early retirement." The company then dismissed 1,277 miners, including 300 union activists.

The ensuing ten-month struggle pitched business and government against Tanrō and the Miike local of Sankōren. At stake was nothing less than management's prerogative to plan for rationalization. The extreme bitterness of the strike belies the notions of Japan's consensus culture. The union demanded the reinstatement of dismissed workers, and the company responded with a lockout. Management was evidently trying to break the power of Tanrō and thus of Japan's labor movement.[38] Other coal companies agreed to supply Miike customers. "A number of electric utilities and manufacturing companies opted to forego a recent ¥250 ($0.70) per ton coal price reduction. Instead they contributed the difference to a fund for Mitsui Mining."[39] And the Japan Federation of Employers Associations mobilized business nationwide. Tanrō's allies were not as powerful as Mitsui's. Sōhyō mobilized labor support, including financial contributions and manpower to strengthen the picket lines at Miike. The Japan Socialist Party advocated the cause of the miners in the Diet and in the press.

But Japan's system of enterprise unions left only limited strike funds in the hands of workers. Mitsui exploited the financial hardships of the strikers. It withheld year-end bonuses in other mines and thus encouraged the defection of 4,000 miners, one-third of the total local work force, from Sankōren. They then formed a pro-company union that in pitched battles eventually reopened the mine. Since the strikers continued to control the shipping facilities, Tanrō twice requested mediation by the Central Labor Relations Commission. On both occasions, the commission came down squarely on the side of business in supporting the original list of 1,277 dismissed workers and the $83 in severance pay per worker. Financially exhausted and politically defeated, Tanrō and the Miike local eventually accepted the settlement. In sum, the coal strike of 1960 "is a graphic example of corporatism without labor—industry and government working together in charting industrial policies while labor is excluded." [40]

In the 1950s, the bitter struggle over the pace and content of rationalization occurred not only in declining industries like coal mining but in industries that later were to dominate world markets. In 1953, the "100-day strike" at Nissan Motors destroyed a powerful left-wing union and crippled the entire labor movement in the automobile industry. A new enterprise union emerged with goals and tactics largely indistinguishable from those of management. [41] Rationalization in the steel industry led to unsuccessful steel strikes in 1958 and 1959 in which management resorted for the first time to a new technique in collective bargaining, the one-shot reply, in which management replies to the union's demand only once and refuses to negotiate further. The purpose of this kind of ultimatum or show of force is to demonstrate that wage increases are given at the discretion of management and not because of worker pressure. [42] Indeed, between 1955 and 1975, collective bargaining in the form of the annual *shunto* ("spring offensive") was a way of coordinating labor's decentralized demands. It secured for Japanese workers their share of the dividends of growth, especially in the 1960s. At the same time, the union's shop-floor power was broken by successive rationalization drives. Large wage increases for workers were thus traded for management prerogatives on the shop floor. The system of labor relations that emerged from this bargain left much power in the hands of management and sapped the strength of labor. Research on the automobile and the steel industries illustrates five mechanisms that produce this result. [43]

First, workers were trained for multiple functions in the productive process. Traditional teams of workers organized around a foreman who was typically a union member were dissolved. Frequent transfers of workers tended to undermine worker solidarity and build company solidarity. Workers are trained to intervene in a broad range of work stations and are motivated to assist their fellow workers because of the stringent production quotas that they all have to meet.

Second, production in Japanese firms rests on the principle of organized competition among workers. A worker's wage is composed in about equal parts of a "basic wage" and a "capacity wage." The basic wage is tied to seniority, the capacity wage to efficiency. Here, as with questions of promotion, management evaluation of worker performance is decisive. Wages are thus not related, as in Switzerland or other Western countries, to jobs. "By disconnecting the wage system from the work assignments, Japanese management has . . . developed an independent system of wage careers that promotes ambition and competition among the workforce without requiring any changes in the skill pyramid."[44] Evaluation rests on the workers' proven willingness to work to their maximum level. In this system of labor relations, work time is utilized better than in any other country. Absenteeism is low, and the workers typically do not use all vacation time to which they are entitled. In fact, collective bargaining provides for no restriction on the work load of Japanese workers. The Japanese system of just-in-time delivery (*kamban*) has an analogy in a deliberate understaffing of the assembly line. Any assembler unable to keep up with the speed of the line turns on a yellow light to signal a demand for help from one of the roving master assemblers. Many yellow lights would be a sign of trouble in a Swiss factory. But in Japan, "plant management is pleased when many yellow lights are on, yes, on. As one Kawasaki manager put it: 'When the yellow lights are on, it means that we are really busting ass.'"[45] The system of organized competition leaves Japanese workers unprotected against speedups determined at the discretion of management.

Third, the widespread practice of subcontracting has integrated the dualism of Japan's industry into the structure of the firm.[46] This has reinforced the differences between the higher wages, better social benefits, and lifetime employment of core workers in larger firms and the lower wages, inferior social benefits, and lack of employment security in smaller firms. Since the unions have had no influence over this extension of the firm's "internal" labor market, they have had no choice but to accept this segmentation of the work force inside the firm.

Fourth, the combination of high quantitative output with high qualitative performance pushes the logic of Fordism to an unanticipated new terrain that researchers have dubbed Toyotism. In this new system, atomized workers are unprotected by a solidaristic labor movement against speedups and integrated into a production process organized around the no-buffer principle. Workers competing against each other thus push for further rationalizations of production. What from the perspective of cultural or management approaches looks like the search for solutions that benefit workers and managers alike striving for the collective, microeconomic good is also the consequence of a distinctive system of industrial relations that distributes power unequally at the level of the plant and in national politics.

Finally, the traditional paternalism that characterizes Japan's industrial relations is reinforced by modern personnel-management techniques that enhance workers' satisfaction and involvement with the firm. Bonus pay is linked to productivity and profitability; opportunities for retraining and skill enhancement exist; salary differentials between white- and blue-collar workers as well as between managers and workers are relatively low. A substantial fraction of the male labor force enjoys job security. In the words of Robert Cole,

The various dimensions of the Japanese work ethic rest ultimately on a fundamental power relationship that brooks no misunderstanding. Among corporate management in the industrialized market economies, there is no doubt that it is the Japanese managers, above all, who maintain most of their traditional managerial prerogatives and hold firm to the reins of power. Worker participation, worker commitment, company training, and so on, must all be understood in this context. For those committed to democratizing the firm this hardly represents an ideal to be emulated . . . [the] assertion that Japan, by a peculiar set of historical circumstances, is riding the high tide of evolutionary development in its acceptance of welfare corporatism seems strangely archaic.[47]

The loss of power and militancy on the shop floor undoubtedly was influenced by two decades of exceptionally high economic growth and the enterprise unions' identification with the economic conditions of their firm in hard times. But its roots were the political struggles that crushed labor in the 1950s and the institutional innovations Japanese business introduced subsequently. Since the mid- to late 1950s, a more conciliatory system of labor-management relations has spread.

Having reinforced managerial authority and secured exclusive leadership for top executives, management felt that the time was ripe for soliciting workers' all-out cooperation in raising productivity. Thus with Dōyūkai's [the Japan Committee for Economic Development] support, the Japan Productivity Center was born. The result in practice was the creation of labor-management consultative bodies and cooperative management committees in the private sector, especially in companies that had unions affiliated with Dōmei [Japan Confederation of Labor] . . . [which] gave the productivity movement its full backing.[48]

The erosion of shop-floor power in the 1960s, later reinforced by changes in the international economic climate, blunted much of the edge of the spring wage offensive. Sōhyō lost many of its private-sector members to Dōmei and other conservative unions. In the harsher economic climate of the 1980s, a new "corporatist labor movement" is emerging.[49] The National Private Sector Union Council (Zenmin Rōkyō), with its five million members, represents the big unions in the private sector that have emerged since the 1950s and that have actively supported the rationalization programs of Japanese industry. Although Zenmin Rōkyō unions are still members of other labor federations, including Sōhyō, the organization of this new council "has virtually robbed Sōhyō of its power in the private sector."[50] As for public-sector unions, the government's program of administrative reform targets has affected, among others, Japan National Railways, where Sōhyō-affiliated unions have kept alive a tradition of shop-floor militance. Although it is too early to tell, the threat of privatization is likely to enforce standards of private-sector efficiency in the public sector.

There can be little doubt that Japan's system of industrial relations is of crucial importance to its strategy of industrial adjustment. Chalmers

Johnson, for instance, argues that "nowhere does Japan achieve a greater comparative advantage over its competitors than in its utterly flexible, strike-free ways of avoiding labor conflict."[51] Management broke the hold of leftist unions in the 1950s and provided an enlarged career system for a substantial fraction of male blue-collar workers in a decentralized system of enterprise unions. Japanese business now deals with an accommodating labor force keenly aware that international competitiveness affects the economic well-being of individual firms, often quite content to accept labor-saving technologies because of career job security, and uninterested in projecting union power into politics. This lack of interest in political involvement is one of the reasons why Japan's industrial policy rests uncontested in the hands of the LDP, business, and the bureaucracy.

At first glance, the paternalism in both Swiss and Japanese industrial relations is striking. Although the labor movements in both countries are weak by international standards, in the 1970s and 1980s Switzerland and Japan had the lowest unemployment rates among the advanced capitalist states. The Swiss unemployment rate has been below 1 per cent in each of the past forty years.[52] The reduction in jobs in the face of declining demand after 1973 was based on a preference for national over foreign labor. Without that preference, the Swiss unemployment rate would have climbed above 10 per cent. In fact, the Swiss developed a full system of preferences favoring, in descending order, Swiss male workers, Swiss female workers, and foreign workers with permanent residence permits. Based on an ideology of social partnership subscribed to by both business and unions, the liberal Swiss state thus intervened strongly in labor markets to enforce a policy favoring Swiss labor.

Official Japanese unemployment statistics are unrealistically low (perhaps by as much as a factor of five), as Angelika Ernst has demonstrated exhaustively.[53] It is also clear that in the mid-1970s Japanese business contained the employment decline in manufacturing industries to one million workers (that is three times the corresponding Swiss figure in a country with 17 times the Swiss population) through such measures as reductions in overtime; a ban on recruiting mid-career workers as well as temporary, seasonal, or part-time workers; temporary suspensions; transfers to related companies; and the encouragement of voluntary retirements. Because of these policies, the number of employees laid off was only one-third of the U.S. figure, even though the reduction in total man-hour inputs was about the same.[54]

More noteworthy here are the differences in the position of the political and economic Left in Japan and Switzerland. Whereas the situation in the two countries is reasonably similar at the plant level, at the level of the national union movement and of the national party system, the

Swiss Left enjoys far greater strength than the Japanese Left. Since the differences are smallest at the level of the plant and greatest at the level of national party politics, Swiss politics tends to narrow power inequalities. Japanese politics does not.

I would suggest two reasons for this. The 1940s and 1950s were a period of political advancement for the Swiss Left, with its inclusion in the Federal Council in 1943, the constitutional amendment of 1947 cementing the position of the unions as a social partner, and the addition of a second Social Democrat to the Federal Council in 1959. By contrast, in Japan the impressive gains of the radical Left in the immediate postwar period were largely eliminated in the 1950s. Dualism, especially in labor markets, is strong in both countries. But because of Switzerland's large foreign labor force, which has no counterpart in Japan, Swiss labor is divided primarily along national and gender lines. In Japan, by contrast, besides gender there are numerous other divisions that separate different categories of workers. The flexible disposition of the Japanese work force is probably greater than that of the "nationally solidaristic" Swiss, but so is its weakness, especially in national politics.

Why Japan Cannot Be the Switzerland of the Far East

My analysis disagrees with a number of studies that, because of Japan's and Switzerland's economic success in the 1970s and 1980s, have grouped them together politically. The concept of corporatism is the analytical bridge for bracketing what many students of comparative political economy view as two anomalous cases. Manfred Schmidt, for example, agreeing with several other researchers, categorizes Japan in the 1970s, like Switzerland and (some other small European states), as one of the five countries that has a strongly developed form of corporatism.[55] Corporatism, in this view, can occur in settings where the composition of the government expresses bourgeois hegemony (as in Japan), bourgeois dominance (as in Switzerland), or social-democratic hegemony (as in Austria).[56] As part of his broader comparative findings, Schmidt focuses on the "corporatist and paternalist mode" of regulating society in these two "active market economies."[57] But Schmidt distinguishes between the "paternalistic capitalism" and "private corporatism" of Japan and the "social partnership" and "societal corporatism" of Switzerland.[58]

In Schmidt's analysis, that difference lies in history and in the methods adopted for avoiding mass unemployment in the 1970s.[59] Japan's political and economic leaders adhere to semi- and precapitalist rules of conduct and are willing to give selective aid to industry and people short of deliberately expanding employment in either the public or the private sector. The rules of conduct for Switzerland's political and economic leaders emerged in the 1930s. In the 1970s, full employment was maintained in part by exporting surplus foreign workers. These differences notwithstanding, the cases of Switzerland and Japan in the 1970s suggest a road to full employment that differs fundamentally from the one Scandinavia's social-democratic engineers designed.

Schmidt notes only in passing some of the similarities in political structure that have been the focus of other analyses: the comparatively weak role of labor unions, a decentralized system of industrial relations, and distinctive values shared by both employers and employees that inhibit the emergence of a strong solidaristic labor movement. Such factors are central in an important paper in which T. J. Pempel and Keiichi Tsunekawa pose the question "corporatism without labor?"[60] For them, "the Japanese case presents a curious anomaly: a high degree of corporatized interest mediation in many sectors, but virtually none in the important area of labor . . . such an anomalous situation—socio-economic success with a low level of corporatism in the area of labor—should surely command the interest of students of corporatism."[61] In describing a broad trend in Japan toward corporatism in a growing number of sectors after 1945, Pempel and Tsunekawa note that labor was consistently allied with the political opposition. They conclude that "Japanese labor has been dealt with piecemeal at the level of the individual enterprise while economic growth in the 'national interest' has been able to proceed without central regard to the specific demands of collective labor."[62]

Andrew Shonfield similarly argues that "effective corporatist organization has been at the root of successful economic and social performance. . . . It is no accident that it [Japan] has the most advanced *large* corporatist system."[63] Shonfield agrees with Pempel and Tsunekawa that in Japan's dual economy, labor plays a distinctive role.[64] The flexibility of Japan's labor market rests on a particularly large gap between the top of the economy and the underprivileged sectors. This sharp segmentation of the labor market is mirrored and reinforced by an institutional separation: unions exist overwhelmingly only in the public sector and the big-company sector. In Shonfield's view, unions are neither weak nor simply the stooges of bosses. But they do concentrate their energies on improving the welfare benefits of their own members rather than those of unorganized workers (temporary workers, women, the old, and those working in small firms). Since they are organized as enterprise unions, union leaders and members are more sensitive to variations in the business cycle and the trade-off between employment and wages.

Finally, in noting the difference between the wage explosion after the first oil price rise of 1973 and the decline of real wages after the second price increase of 1979, Haruo Shimada points to the importance of emerging corporatist arrangements in the 1970s.[65] In 1975, leaders of the

LDP and the business community were extremely anxious to prevent a repetition of the wage explosion that had occurred during the 1974 *shunto*. That explosion had caused in one year an unprecedented 7 per cent increase of labor's relative share in the entire economy. Before the 1975 *shunto*, the leading steel and shipbuilding corporations agreed on a common offer that fell within the guidelines recommended by Nik-keiren. "Many unions officially viewed their experience as a defeat. Union negotiators confessed that there were irresistible external pressures imposed upon them. . . . Whether unions were 'defeated' or not is not the point of our interest. It is significant that the new framework of *shunto* system has operated in such a way as to build up a complex structure of organizational interactions within which individual negotiators feel strong binding forces or pressures even in the absence of formal agreements." [66] For Shimada, Japan features not a structural corporatism organized around centralized interest groups but a functional corporatism facilitating information exchange and sharing.

This discussion reconfirms that corporatism is an ambiguous concept open to a variety of interpretations and definable in different ways. [67] For Schmidt, corporatism is based on a high degree of industrial consensus and wage restraint, especially during economic crises. It can be a process of equal exchange in countries with a powerful union movement strongly integrated into the policy network. Alternatively, corporatism can involve unequal political exchange. Then it implies strong social control over the labor movement, again based on consensus and wage moderation. In either version, corporatism is decisively affected by the values of industrial managers and the concessions they are willing to make to labor. Japan's strong paternalistic tradition and the strength of laissez-faire liberalism in Switzerland, for example, illustrate the range of variation of a bourgeois ethos. [68] For Pempel and Tsunekawa, corporatism is a specific pattern of interest intermediation that links state and society. [69] And for Shonfield and Shimada, contemporary corporatism is an organized dialogue between private and public interest groups that aims at reducing business fluctuations and creating a more predictable economic environment. [70] Although overlapping, these definitions emphasize three different aspects of corporatism: ideology (Schmidt), institutions (Pempel and Tsunekawa), and policy process (Shonfield and Shimada).

Many recent studies of advanced industrial states have given different labels to a phenomenon on whose existence most observers agree: the voluntary, cooperative regulation of conflicts over economic and social issues through highly structured and interpenetrating political relationships among business, trade unions, and the state, augmented by political parties. [71] *Democratic corporatism* is distinguished by three traits. It features an ideology of social partnership that mitigates class conflict between business and unions and integrates different conceptions of group interests into a vaguely but firmly held concept of the public interest. It features centralized and concentrated interest groups that frame and often resolve major political issues and thus determine which issues appear on the public agenda. Finally, political bargaining is voluntary, informal, and continuous, and thus it can coordinate political objectives among different political actors. The preferences of different sectors are often traded off against one another. The political predictability of the process increases the flexibility of actors.

In each of its three defining characteristics, democratic corporatism is tied to political parties and electoral politics. Competition for voters prevents suffocation under a consensus ideology. Close relations between parties and interest groups increases the centralization of domestic structures, especially on the Left. And parties and the perception of electoral gains or losses influence groups' willingness to coordinate their divergent objectives. All advanced industrial states share some of these characteristics, but none exhibits all of them. I have argued elsewhere that the small European states (Switzerland, Sweden, Norway, Denmark, the Netherlands, Belgium, and Austria), with their open and vulnerable economies, exemplify the political tendencies of democratic corporatism much more fully than do the large industrial countries with the possible exception of West Germany.[72]

In an unpublished paper extending his work on corporatism to Asia, Philippe Schmitter notes that Japan invalidates the assumption of structural symmetry between business and labor organizations that holds in Western Europe. Japan "has one of the most pluralist or least corporatist structures of interest intermediation, if viewed from the perspective of labor. From what I have been able to gather about employers' associations, however, Japan would appear to have one of the most centralized and monopolistic interest systems in existence."[73] Since national-level bargaining and implementation of contracts is not prevalent in Japan, Schmitter concludes that with its "enterprise corporatism" Japanese corporatism may well be comparable but not analogous to European corporatism.[74] Although one may quarrel with Schmitter's definition of corporatism, this is a sensible conclusion. Even though Japan's political economy does not typify the politics of democratic corporatism, it features collaborative arrangements that are reminiscent of those of small European states like Switzerland.

One common source of political collaboration in Switzerland and Japan is their openness to the international economy and a high degree of perceived vulnerability to it. I have developed elsewhere an argument that specifies the effect that international vulnerability has had on both the origin and the maintenance of democratic corporatism in small European states such as Switzerland.[75] An interlocking set of crises—the Depression, fascism, and World War II—forced political elites to develop new strategies and institutions eventually dubbed corporatist. Since the late 1950s, under U.S. leadership an increasingly liberal international economy has also forced political collaboration on actors often pursuing divergent objectives. In a similar vein, Pempel and Tsunekawa have pointed to the strong effect that international pressures have had on corporatist tendencies in Japan.[76] Although this is not the place to develop and test this explanation in great detail, I would like to establish its plausibility since it accounts for some of the elements common to political collaboration in both Japan and Switzerland.

In the early postwar years, for example, Japanese policymakers decided to improve Japan's standard of living and, subsequently, to achieve greater economic independence, "reflecting both a national crisis consciousness and a popular desire to catch up with the advanced Western nations."[77] The principal strategy chosen, Shimada argues, was export promotion through the rationalization of industries in the 1950s, which had far-reaching consequences for Japanese labor in subsequent decades. In the 1950s and 1960s, policymakers promoted key export industries, for example, through the allocation of limited foreign exchange and investment capital. "This structure has been reinforced by an 'indirect finance policy' involving capital and through fairly large wage differentials, according to industry size, for the workers. . . . The development of highly internalized labor markets in Japan is the product of this priority-resource-allocation system."[78] The internalized labor markets that Kazutoshi Koshiro and other labor economists refer to are what Schmitter has called "enterprise corporatism."

The effect of international pressure on Japan was evident subsequently. "The impact of the liberalization of international trade and direct foreign investment on Japan in the late 1960s and early 1970s generated a 'crisis consciousness' among employers and workers."[79] Quality control, zero-defect movements, and joint consultation arrangements between management and labor fed on that crisis consciousness. "It is noteworthy that most of the unions who are parties to consultation schemes are affiliated with Domei. . . . The only Sohyo union among them is Tekkororen (iron and steel workers), which has, in fact, shared Domei's philosophy of economic-based unionism since 1960."[80] And after the first oil shock of 1973 Japan responded as a nation in crisis. To give one example, the corporatist *shunto* reforms in the 1970s occurred primarily in industries with a particularly high export orientation.[81]

Japan's economic vulnerability is not well measured by its overall dependence on foreign trade. Japan is totally dependent on imports for many crucial raw materials: 100 per cent of its bauxite, nickel, wool, and raw cotton; 99.8 per cent of its petroleum; 99.6 per cent of its iron ore; 95.5 per cent of its copper; 95.2 per cent of its soybeans; 90.9 per cent of its natural gas; and 87.7 per cent of its lead.[82] It is thus no accident that the Japanese refer to their national security in both military and economic terms under the category of "comprehensive security."[83] Since no other industrial state is as dependent as Japan on imported raw materials, especially energy, none specializes as totally as Japan on exporting manufactured products. For its Western trading partners, the imbalanced composition of Japan's foreign trade has become a source of growing irritation as they find themselves locked out of Japanese markets by a variety of nontariff barriers ranging from government and corporate policy to social customs and local traditions. That irritation can easily feed protectionist sentiments, as it did in the United States in 1985, if in its bilateral trade balance Japan runs a substantial and growing export surplus. Despite the government's attempt to spur foreign imports, the proportion of imported manufactured products and services accounted for a smaller share of GNP in 1985 than it had in 1974.[84]

International vulnerability and a recurrence of episodes of crisis consciousness, I would argue, have left Japan with the semblance rather than the essence of democratic corporatism. If this argument is true, the collaborative arrangements that stem from international pressures should be stronger in sectors where vulnerability is perceived to be very great. Pempel and Tsunekawa, for example, argue that the internationalization of the Japanese economy during the past two decades has weakened collaborative arrangements between business and government in advanced industries while leading to the opposite effect in agriculture and the small-business sector.[85] Similarly, the two sectors that illustrate the logic of my argument best are the import of raw materials and the export of manufactured products. In both sectors, Japan's economy has internationalized rapidly in the past two decades. But on questions of resource policy, policymakers and businessmen have perceived Japan to be vulnerable while in manufacturing industries they by and large have not. Collaborative links between government and business thus grew tighter in the first sector and loosened in the second.

Since 1945, government and business have viewed the heavy dependence on foreign sources of raw materials as "a kind of unifying national challenge to the Japanese."[86] For two reasons Japan's postwar economic strategy required moving from light to heavy industry: the vast markets of mainland China were closed, as were the markets of the smaller states of East Asia, which began their own industrialization drives with light consumer industries. Japan's shift to heavy industry required stable and low-cost supplies of raw materials, specifically oil and minerals. During the 1960s, both the consumption and the import of raw materials increased at a high rate. "Concern among both governmental leaders and businessmen throughout the 1950s and 1960s increased, due to Japan's increased resource dependence. Japan's weakness, the lack of domestic resources, worsened in direct relation to its economic growth based on heavy industry."[87]

Faced with this challenge, Japan has followed, with occasional false starts and outright errors, a coherent line of policy. "Japan's policies and practices with regard to industrial raw materials, however, were not simply the result of its perceptions of high risk," Raymond Vernon argues, but resulted from distinctive institutions.[88] The Ministry of International Trade and Industry (MITI), in particular has been in increasingly close contact with the minerals industry. In the case of oil, the watershed was probably the Petroleum Industry Law of 1962, which eventually brought a substantial segment of the Japanese oil industry under national control. It gave MITI wide discretionary authority.

Looking back at this period, the various steps taken could easily be interpreted by foreigners as confirmation of the existence of a Japan Incorporated juggernaut, which enlisted the unquestioned support of all sectors of the Japanese economy and proceeded singlemindedly to overcome the foreigners. In fact, each such step encountered plenty of domestic opposition. . . . The ease with which the law was eventually passed is explained in part by the fact that such an open-ended grant of authority for the regulation of an industry was in no way offensive to the fundamental ideology of the country—indeed, was wholly in harmony with the ideology.[89]

By the early 1980s, despite some serious setbacks, government policy had reduced the dependence of the Japanese petroleum industry on a few international corporations. In minerals as in oil, between the 1950s and the 1980s, Japan moved from simple market purchases to loan-tied purchases to a variety of ways of directly developing foreign supply sources. In sum, Japan's resource diplomacy was framed in the context of an increasing vulnerability to international developments. And it furthered a broad array of far-reaching collaborative arrangements between business and the state.

Japan's advent as one of the world's foremost exporters of manufactured products has spawned internationalization of its economy and has required wide-ranging changes in Japan's legal system.[90] Internationalization, as Chalmers Johnson has argued, concerns governmental policy, not cultural mores. Since the mid-1960s, a number of the high fences that used to shield Japan from international influences have been dismantled. Average Japanese tariff levels are now below those of the United States and the European Communities. The Foreign Exchange and Foreign Trade Control Law was rewritten in 1979 to accommodate liberalization policies adopted since 1964. Without denying the government considerable leeway, the rules governing external transactions were changed from "prohibition in principle" to "freedom in principle."[91] In the 1980s, the main battleground has been financial liberalization. The Ministry of Finance is resisting pressures from the private sector and from abroad to dismantle the web of institutions and practices by which it exercised control in the past. But it is probable that internationalization will force an adaptation in the relationship between business and the state. The growing importance of export markets and the internationalization of financial markets have left Japanese corporations less dependent on the government and eager to operate autonomously from government interference. Internationalization in this instance has reduced rather than enhanced the perception of international vulnerability. And it has loosened rather than tightened the collaboration between business and the state.

But Japan's great economic success has also altered relations with its trading partners. Its commercial offensive has generated a protectionist reaction that now risks closing down export markets, till now the main stimulus for Japan's economic growth. Conquering growing world markets will intensify rather than alleviate Japan's political problems. Here the contrast with Switzerland could not be greater. Because of its small size, Switzerland's niche strategy makes it less vulnerable to the attention and political pressures of other states. Japan's strategy of mass production penetrates deeply into the markets of its foreign competitors and often aims at total domination. This strategy is a threat to which Japan's trade partners have become increasingly attentive. Its rapid economic growth has transformed it from a small and marginal player in the world economy to a large and central one. The Japanese may still perceive themselves as occupying a small and exposed position in the international system. But in economic terms, they loom large in so many international markets that they are increasingly perceived by others as an economic superpower. Domestic perceptions and the facts of international economic life match much better in the case of Switzerland than of Japan.

Japan's changing size is making new demands on its foreign policy.[92] Gone are the days in which Japan could conduct its foreign policy as one more small country interested in making a good living by exploiting the opportunities of the international economy without worrying about providing some of the material and ideological resources necessary to support and adapt an international regime so supportive of its prosperity and security. Pressure from the United States and an intense domestic debate about Japan's defense effort symbolize the change in Japan's political environment. How far a reluctant Japanese government will move down the path of an armaments strategy in a period of severe fiscal strain remains to be seen. But it is clear that the task of developing a new ideology and new rules for the international economy will be infinitely greater.

Many Japanese officials, especially the younger generation, expect Japan to be the dominant economic and technological power of the twenty-first century. Political and economic elites sense that the U.S. version of "laissez-faire liberalism" and European debates about "organized free trade" are either unworkable or inimical to Japanese interests. Yet Japanese society appears to have few institutional resources to foster a sustained debate from which new concepts for organizing the international economy might arise. Instead, every major organization in Japanese society insists on sending its "best and brightest" to U.S. business schools, from which they return imbued with an ideology and assumptions about how the world works that the Japanese themselves regard as increasingly irrelevant to the contemporary global economy.

A small country, like Switzerland, does not face this particular worry. It adopts instead a stance that seeks to depoliticize international relations, to be friends with everyone, and thus to create a climate in which it can trade. It is symptomatic of this conception of politics that Switzerland is not a member of the United Nations but the home of the Red Cross. The compatibility of neutrality with U.N. membership has been debated in Swiss politics for forty years. The U.N., rather than its technical agencies (in which Switzerland participates fully), is typically viewed as an ideological forum where countries must choose sides. History has taught the Swiss a different way. They host and largely fund the normal operations of the Red Cross because it reinforces Swiss neutrality and inviolability by providing valuable services for the international community.[93] The Swiss run the Red Cross as they do their own plebiscitary democracy. Until the 1970s, it "was controlled by a committee of 25 prominent Swiss, who coopted each other and had many formal and informal links with government circles."[94] The Red Cross is pragmatic, safe, and almost immune to politics. It stands for the kind of international politics that permits the unhindered pursuit of what the Swiss cherish most deeply: the industrious reaping of profit. Since 1945 Japan has discovered its Swiss avocation. But in its single-minded pursuit of a new calling, Japan will increasingly be denied safe, stable, pragmatic, and inexpensive international options.

In Switzerland, an important force for collaboration in domestic politics derives from the perception, widely shared among the Japanese, of occupying a vulnerable position in the modern world. But unlike Switzerland, Japan's sharply growing relative size now imposes the formidable task of contributing toward a partial reorganization of international structures.

Beyond the force of individual leadership, it remains to be seen what Japanese institutions can contribute to meeting this political challenge.

The image of Japan as a Switzerland of the Far East has had political appeal for others besides General MacArthur. Both Japan and Switzerland have enjoyed great economic success with their flexible export strategies, conservative political regimes, and political collaboration rooted in shared perceptions of international vulnerability. This image, I have argued in this paper, is misleading. Japan adheres to a strategy of market domination, features a domestic politics that is less inclusive than Switzerland's, and must address the political consequences of its growing size in the international political economy. Japan is moving into new and uncharted terrain in which its continued economic success will depend less on productivity and more on politics.

Daniel I. Okimoto

Political Inclusivity:
The Domestic Structure of Trade

Japanese trade behavior has become the target of mounting criticism as the country's surplus in merchandise trade has reached levels deemed unacceptable by its leading trade partners. Japan's trade surpluses with the United States and Western Europe, for example, began to balloon after the two oil shocks (1973–74, 1979–80), when Japan stepped up exports to pay for the higher costs of energy imports. By 1980, Japan's overall surplus had exceeded $25 billion—precisely at a time when the rest of the world was struggling to cope with severe problems of declining industries and double-digit unemployment. In 1986, Japan ran a trade surplus of $70 billion with the United States, which constituted the largest single component of the overall U.S. deficit of $170 billion. Since the public associates large deficits with the demise of industries and the widespread loss of jobs, countries running huge trade and current-account deficits with Japan (like the United States and Europe) have threatened to retaliate with protectionist legislation.

What makes the deficits especially hard for foreigners to bear is the perception that the Japanese do not abide by the rules of fair play.[1] Foreign complaints run the gamut from charges of dumping and predatory pricing to accusations of government-business collusion and obstructing access to Japanese markets.[2] The U.S. government has asked Japan to take a variety of steps to correct the bilateral imbalance, including acceptance of voluntary restraints in automobile, steel, and other exports, containment of the powerful impulse to flood foreign markets, and an opening of Japanese markets.[3] Foreign demands have even moved beyond the boundaries of merchandise trade into the closely related realm of industrial policy and macroeconomic management. It has been suggested that Japan abandon the practice of industrial targeting; that it lift oppressive regulations over financial services, telecommunications, and other sectors; and that policies be adopted to encourage greater consumption and less saving. Japan has complied with some of these demands, but not with others. The result? Bilateral deficits have continued spiraling upward.

To foreign leaders, Japanese trade behavior is hard to fathom. The glaring contradictions in trade policies defy explanation. On the surface, Japan seems to function as a homogeneous and unitary rational actor, advancing its national interests through skillful manipulation of its trade partners. Yet, if there is harmony of purpose, U.S. leaders wonder why is there overt conflict between farmers, who resist U.S. pressures to liberalize agricultural imports, and manufacturers, who want a rollback in agricultural protectionism? Why is it hard to make headway in negotiations over lumber, plywood, and processed wood products when the number of lumber mills is small?

U.S. officials realize that the Japanese farm lobby wields political power out of proportion to its numerical strength. But is this also true of tobacco growers, the medical profession, and managers of pension funds—areas reputed to be unfairly closed to foreign penetration? And what about such manufacturing sectors as telecommunications, pharmaceuticals, and medical instruments? How can protectionism in these areas be reconciled with the relative openness of other sectors like fast foods, consumer electronics, and precision instruments? How does one account for the puzzling and incongruous pattern of Japanese trade behavior, involving closedness and openness, accommodation and foot-dragging, nationalism and internationalism, export deluges and voluntary restraints?

One interpretation—widely adhered to outside Japan—is that Japan selectively protects those sectors incapable of competing against foreign producers.[4] How else can the U.S. inability to succeed in Japanese markets where it commands a clear comparative advantage be explained? Yet, as tidy as this view may be, it fails to account for Japan's relative openness in such industries as aluminum and petrochemicals, where comparative advantage has been lost. Unlike the United States and Western Europe, which heavily protect declining industries, Japan has relied less on protection and more on rationalization to deal with the loss of comparative advantage. Making sense of these and other incongruities in Japanese trade behavior clearly requires more than the attribution of conspiratorial closure. It calls for a broad, integrated framework of analysis, capable of placing what are otherwise puzzling contradictions into a readily understandable context of institutions, political interactions, and policymaking.

Japan's Political Economy: Competing Models

In the United States, at least three models of the Japanese political economy have been used to explain the peculiarities of Japanese trade behavior: "Japan, Inc."; pluralism; and bureaucratic statism.[5] The three correspond roughly to the three dominant paradigms in comparative politics: elitism; liberal pluralism; statism.[6] Other models developed out of the crucible of the Western industrial experience might also be applied, such as neo-corporatism and state monopoly capitalism,[7] but exploratory efforts at testing the applicability of, say, neo-corporatism have uncovered significant deviations that call into question the closeness of the fit between the theory and Japanese experience.[8]

Japan, Inc., can be viewed as a variant, sui generis, of the power elite model. In this sense other descriptive models, including the "ruling triad" concept, can also be placed within the power elite framework.[9] The essence of Japan, Inc., is the notion that power is concentrated in the hands of a select coterie of leaders from big business, the economic bureaucracies, and the Liberal Democratic Party (LDP).[10] Japan's power elites hail from highly homogeneous backgrounds and pass through the progressively narrow entrance gates of the nation's educational hierarchy.[11] The educational hierarchy serves as an effective screening device, provides a common base for elite socialization, and enmeshes everyone in an intricate web of human relationships spun out in ever widening circles, linking one sector to another. The power elite in Japan is thus said to possess the power to coordinate the various sectors of society so as to advance the national interest.

The Japan, Inc., model casts Japan in an overly simplistic light. It portrays Japan as a unitary, interest-maximizing, rational actor.[12] The "incorporated" metaphor is used to convey the image of a monolithic multinational corporation. It fails, however, to account for the deep-seated discord, clash of interests, and sectoral variations in government-business relations in Japan. It cannot explain why the Japanese auto industry accepted the government's plea that it voluntarily restrict exports to the United States when, nearly a decade earlier, the textile industry has stubbornly refused to cave in to government pressures; only grudgingly did textile producers agree to restrict exports, and only after the government bought them off by promising to provide compensatory subsidies.[13] If the Ministry of International Trade and Industry (MITI) functions as corporate headquarters for Japan, Inc., why was it unable to impose voluntary export restraints readily in both cases? Indeed, why is MITI's relationship with the steel industry strikingly different from its relationship with small and medium-size industries? Japan, Inc., fails to supply an answer.

The second model—for many years the prevailing paradigm for Western industrial democracies—is pluralism. Rejecting elitist assumptions concerning the cumulative concentration of power, proponents of pluralism argue that power has to be understood not in terms of some static and abstract structure, but, rather, in terms of its actual use in specific policy arenas.[14] Pluralists contend that the exercise of political power varies by issue area, with no single group or elite coalition controlling outcomes across all policy issues. Pluralism is built into democratic systems by the dispersion of political resources over a wide range of political actors. Policymaking thus features conflict and open competition within and among interest groups possessing diverse and intransitive power resources, differentially applied across individual policy domains.[15]

In contrast to the United States, where the pluralist paradigm is perhaps the reigning orthodoxy, it is not the dominant model for the Japanese political economy. Surprisingly few scholars have characterized Japan as pluralist in the sense that freewheeling competition among interest groups determines the outcome of public policies.[16] Ellis Krauss and Michio Muramatsu, who have applied the term "patterned pluralism" to Japan, justify the characterization by proposing that (1) influence is widely distributed; (2) multiple points of access to policymaking exist; and (3) interest groups are relatively autonomous from the state and compete against one another for influence.[17] They use the term *patterned* to suggest that interest groups in Japan function within an institutional setting consisting of strong bureaucracies that give structure to their political activities.

Although the pluralist paradigm helps to correct the simplifications of Japan, Inc., it does little to explain the government's ability to persuade private companies temporarily to suspend fierce rivalries, submit to voluntary export restraints, and apportion shares of export quotas among various manufacturers. If private actors vie for influence in a competitive political marketplace, then how can the state's binding power over certain policy domains or the private sector's capacity to cooperate be explained? Even under conditions of open competition, the model has limited power to predict winners and losers based on their different political resources. It cannot explain why export-oriented manufacturers, who have an overriding stake in free trade, were unable to force protected producers of plywood and finished wood products, possessing far less economic and political clout, to agree to an abolition of import barriers. Nor does pluralism offer compelling insights into Japanese-style consensus-building or the formation of temporary cartels in certain trade-oriented sectors. The problem with applying a single theory to Japan, be it elitism or pluralism, is that in a distressingly large number of cases, the model fails to fit empirical reality.

The third model, often referred to as the "statist" or "state-dominant" model, is probably the broadest in scope. It differs from elite and pluralist theory in positing the primacy of the state as an autonomous actor in the political arena.[18] The state is not simply an instrument of elite control, responsible for maintaining the status quo. Nor is it merely a neutral aggregator of pluralistic competition between interest groups. The state has its own set of interests and goals, its own repertoire of power resources, including administrative authority and an established legal order, and legitimate control over the instruments of coercion.

Individuals and interest groups thus operate within the framework of political institutions, under rules and norms laid down by the state. Unlike elite theory, which focuses on the concentration of power in the hands of a small, homogeneous cabal of leaders, or pluralist theory, which is concerned with the competitive processes in the allocation of resources, statist theory concentrates on problems of governance and the state's capacity to mobilize resources to meet a country's collective needs and interests. In its emphasis on Japan's pursuit of national interests and its assumptions of rational, goal-maximizing behavior on the part of the central bureaucracy, the statist model skirts the edges of—but does not overlap—the Japan, Inc., paradigm. The Japan, Inc., model sees the country as run by elite leaders from three more or less equal sectors—big business, the bureaucracy, and the LDP—but the statist model elevates the bureaucracy far above the other two in terms of its power to shape public policy.

Of the three, the model of bureaucratic dominance is probably the one most commonly applied to Japan. It has the virtue of parsimony and casts light on the central role of the state in all matters related to trade. Within a statist framework, certain types of behavior become understandable—such as industrial policy targeting and the formation of rationalization and antirecession cartels.[19] One can comprehend how Japan has been able to respond to foreign pressures in a number of areas. Since the early 1970s, Japan has lifted formal import tariffs and quotas, streamlined nontariff barriers, removed restrictions on foreign direct investment, and liberalized its financial markets (see the paper by Komiya and Itoh in this volume). None of these changes has been easy. In every instance, the government has had to overcome inertia and the entrenched opposition of interest groups with a stake in trying to preserve the status quo. That the state, under intense pressure from the United States, has managed to overcome domestic resistance is evidence of its enormous power.

As with the other two models, however, the fit between theory and empirical reality is far from perfect. Statist theory as applied to Japan, for example, fails to differentiate the bureaucracies in terms of their ties to the producer groups under their jurisdiction, the extent of their politicization, and their interactions with the LDP. The variations are striking. At one extreme stands the Ministry of Agriculture, Forestry, and Fisheries (MAFF), a domestically oriented, politicized bureaucracy anxious to protect the livelihood of Japanese farmers against the inroads of more competitive foreign producers. At the other extreme is MITI, an internationally oriented, nonpoliticized bureaucracy with a major stake in maintaining access to overseas markets. A model of Japan's political economy should provide an analytical framework capable of distinguishing among (and to some extent, within) the various government ministries. Without such a framework, it is impossible to understand the seeming inconsistencies of Japanese trade behavior.

Since Japanese trade behavior emerges from the interaction between the international environment and domestic institutions, an understanding of the regime characteristics of Japan's political economy is essential. The nature of the Japanese state is the logical place to begin since any model purporting to explain Japanese trade behavior must come to terms with the role of the state and its relationship to other sectors of society.

The Japanese State

Many perceptive students of Japan, from Robert Bellah to Masao Maruyama to Chie Nakane have stressed the overriding importance of the state in relation to the structure of society.[20] Bellah characterizes Japan as a society in which the collectivity, be it the family, the corporation, or the nation-state, takes priority over its individual members, and the polity (broadly defined) is given primacy over other sectors of society.[21] The emphasis on the polity and on political values means that Japan is oriented toward the achievement of collective goals, with a value system based on performance, particularism, and loyalty.[22]

The state's central role is to function as the guardian of the public's welfare. Its responsibility to serve the public by advancing the interests of the largest and most important collectivity—not its individual parts— is reflected in the enormous symbolic (though not always functional) importance attached to the head of the group, be it the father, the corporation president, or the chairman of a business association. State and society form mutually reinforcing parts of a whole. The state is not, as in some Western countries, simply an administrative appendage, superimposed on society, with the responsibility of allocating resources, laying down equitable rules and norms, and adjudicating conflict through the operation of the legal apparatus.

Perhaps the closest Western equivalent to the Japanese state is the concept of the "organic state," which emerges out of a time-honored philosophical tradition stretching back to Aristotle.[23] In Aristotle's view, the political community (*polis*), takes priority over individual citizens because the whole is of greater importance than the sum of its constituent parts. The state's central mission—indeed, its moral obligation—is to use its authority to advance the common good of the political community as a whole.

This moral obligation provides the normative underpinnings for a highly interventionist—if not authoritarian—state. Although there is no intrinsic reason why groups in the private sector cannot play vigorous roles, the organic state's attitude toward interest-maximizing private organizations is a far cry from Adam Smith's unshakable faith in the benefits of freewheeling politico-economic competition. Because the behavior of selfish interest groups can damage the welfare of the political community as a whole, the organic state bears the responsibility for stepping in and keeping private actors from rending the fabric of society. It is no accident, therefore, that corporatist and authoritarian states have sprung up from the philosophical soil of organic statism, especially in the Iberian countries and Latin America.[24]

The concept of the organic state is similar in some respects to the concept of the Japanese state. Both function within the framework of a collective community that takes priority over its constituent parts. Both symbolize, and have the functional responsibility to reaffirm, the basic solidarity of the national collectivity.[25] Both are expected to steer private interests away from the pursuit of narrow self-interest that would tend to undermine long-term collective objectives and national goals. Harmony, unity, pragmatism, and national interests constitute overriding values for both.

There are, however, some basic differences. One is the absence of universalistic principles underpinning the legitimacy of the Japanese state. Without a foundation of universalistic principles on which to base its raison d'être, the Japanese state has had problems establishing a higher ground from which to exercise autonomous power.[26] Instead, it has either had to stand on its record of superior performance or, failing in that, had to fall back on particularistic values to undergird its authority. There have been times—though historically the exception rather than the rule—that the Japanese state has been able to convert its particularistic underpinnings into authoritarian regimes. The period of militarism (1931–45) is probably the best known (and most extreme) example. The military regime practiced repression at home and aggression abroad, using ultranationalism to buttress its authoritarian rule.[27] But it can be argued that the prewar military state was never able to establish a stable base of legitimacy and that its emergence could be attributed to a concatenation of "abnormal" developments at home and abroad.

The Meiji (1868–1912) and early postwar (1952–1978) periods provide two more normal and intriguing eras of powerful governance from above. Unlike the prewar military regime, the Meiji and early postwar states were able to establish a strong basis of legitimacy to justify policies of government intervention. Measured by standard economic indicators, Japan's performance during these two periods under the auspices of what Chalmers Johnson calls the "developmental state" can be highly evaluated.[28] Do these two examples prove that Japan is a statist society? Or were the Meiji and early postwar experiences historical aberrations?

Bellah and Johnson (as well as all believers in the notion of Japan, Inc.) would take the former view—that the Japanese state is intrinsically powerful; but an argument can be made for the latter interpretation since the Meiji and postwar periods are among the few instances in the long history of Japan that the state has played a dominant and stabilizing role.[29] In both instances, the power wielded by the Japanese state can be explained by the convergence of extraordinary circumstances—the threat of foreign domination, potentially crippling industrial backwardness, the perception of national crisis, and the urgency of latecomer catch-up—all of which provided the backdrop for the assertion of strong, centralized authority.[30] For most other stretches of Japan's 2,000-year history, however, state power had been circumscribed by the absence of a legitimizing system of universalistic principles, making the assertion of autonomous state authority problematic.

By contrast, the philosophical tradition of organic statism is rooted in universalistic values associated with Aristotle, Roman law, and Catholic social thought. Curiously, this universalistic grounding both limits and at the same time strengthens state power. It is limiting in the sense that the organic state is itself accountable to strict standards of behavior based on such universally applicable values as democratic representation and legal justice. Yet, it is reinforcing in that state authority carries the powerful weight of universalistic values behind it. On balance, the net effect has been to strengthen the hand of authoritarian states.[31]

Because the Japanese state today is stable and actively involved in the management of the country's economy, the notion that it has traditionally had problems establishing an independent base of authority may be hard to believe. The statist model is, after all, the reigning paradigm for contemporary Japan's political economy. How can the notion of a state historically lacking in universalistic legitimacy and autonomy be reconciled with abundant evidence of a vigorously active, if not dominant, state? Perhaps the conundrum can be cleared up by placing the state in its broad, societal context.

If the state's authority is circumscribed, from whence does it derive its power? The answer can be found in a number of distinctive historical and institutional characteristics: the legacy of the Allied Occupation, a broad national consensus concerning industrial catch-up,[32] the clamp-down on militant labor and its organization into enterprise unions, the emphasis on *wa* (harmony) as an integrative principle of social organiza-tion, and the structure of Japanese society, which provides the frame-work within which the state functions. Chie Nakane characterizes Japan as a "frame society," composed of numerous vertically organized groups locked in fierce competition, with only weak horizontal links holding the groups together. Japanese society thus calls for, and facilitates, cen-tral coordination by a neutral entity, the state.

Characteristics of Japanese society assist in the development of the state political organization. Competing clusters, in view of the difficulty of reaching agreement or consensus between clusters, have a diminished authority in dealing with the state administration. Competition and hostile relations between civil powers fa-cilitate the acceptance of state power, and in that [the] group is organized ver-tically, once the state's administrative authority is accepted, it can be transmitted without obstruction down the vertical line of a group's internal organization.[33]

Although Nakane underestimates the strength of horizontal ties, she calls attention to the pivotal role played by the state in aggregating com-peting private interests through the vehicle of consensus formation. Consensus is an effective means of coordination not only in homoge-neous countries like Japan but also in socially fragmented countries like the Netherlands.[34] But since consensus is not always readily achieved among rivalrous groups, some central authority—the state—must act to bring it about.

The task of forging consensus or mediating private conflicts is facili-tated enormously by the emphasis placed on *wa*.[35] All persons and groups with a claim to authority use *wa* to buttress their capacity to take binding action. For the Japanese state, especially, the concept of *wa* pro-vides an indispensable source of power. The state would have an infi-nitely harder time fulfilling its oversight functions if the principle of *wa* did not carry such strong normative weight.

Effective power thus hinges largely on the state's capacity to achieve harmony—in terms of collective interests and national goals—amidst the cacophony of dissonant private interests. Consensus, the most com-mon manifestation of *wa*, is the concrete means by which Japan reaches agreement within the private sector and between the private sector and the government. As a neutral mediator and as the guardian of the public interest, the state is usually involved in coordinating the processes of consensus formation; and consensus, painstakingly arrived at, legiti-mates state intervention in the activities of the market economy.

In taking vigorous action, the Japanese state seldom threatens legal sanctions to bring recalcitrant groups into line. The exercise of brute power is considered neither desirable nor effective, particularly as a frequently used instrument of governance. Rather, the state prefers to rely on its ability to (1) maintain an aura of strict neutrality in relation to rivalrous interest groups; (2) keep the trust of groups with which it works; and (3) use persuasion and incentives to steer the private sector in desired directions. Its capacity to persuade the private sector to take voluntaristic action—which, the state usually argues, lies in their long-term, collective interests anyway—is the secret to its effectiveness. The state's capacity to wield power emerges, in short, out of the structure of its working relationship with other groups in society, particularly private corporations. It is far from absolute.

Perhaps Japan can be characterized as a "network," a "relational," or a "societal" state in the sense that government power is intertwined with that of the private sector. The government's power hinges on its capacity to work effectively with the private sector, with each side making an effort to take into account the needs and objectives of the other. Political power in Japan is thus exercised through a complex process of public–private sector interaction, involving subtle give-and-take, not frontal confrontation that results in the forceful imposition of one side's will on the other.

In terms of the state's capacity to force its will on society, the power of authoritarian states in Latin America and in parts of the Third World far exceeds that of Japan.[36] Indeed, throughout Japan's long history, the central government has almost never wielded absolute power.[37] Even during the heyday of prewar military rule, military cliques never possessed the absolute power of the fascist regimes in Germany or Spain.[38]

If state power is defined solely in terms of confrontational clout, even the U.S. government might be considered stronger than its Japanese counterpart; consider, for example, the many cases of U.S. government enforcement in the regulatory arena, antitrust, equal opportunity employment, and national security (for example, controls over the export of dual-purpose technology). Differences in the exercise of power by the U.S. and Japanese governments can be seen not only in the contrasts between the United States' arms-length, legalistic style and Japan's close-in, cooperative approach, but also in the frequency of, and reliance on, confrontational coercion in the United States versus persuasion, painstaking negotiation, and mutual accommodation in Japan.

To be effective, the Japanese government must maintain close working relations with the private sector since mutual trust is the sine qua non of cooperation and compliance. This implies that the state, like a parent, has to have the best interests of the private sector at heart, even when it seeks to reconcile parochial private interests with collective goals. It must listen to the views of private companies, taking them fully into account when formulating public policies—but without becoming merely the puppet of powerful private interests. For a societal state like Japan's to assume a strongly pro-business posture is, therefore, hardly surprising. This stance is perfectly in keeping with the way society is structured and the way political power is exercised.

The concept of a societal state implies that the lines of demarcation between state and society are blurred. Indeed, there is considerable overlap between public and private sectors. The exceptional organization of each side and the highly routinized interaction between public and private actors greatly facilitate policymaking.[39] In Japan, a vast network of "intermediate organizations"—neither entirely public nor strictly private—functions in what might be called the "intermediate zone" between the state and private enterprise. Included in this category are public corporations like the Japan Export-Import Bank, special nonprofit entities like the Japan External Trade Research Organization (JETRO), mixed public-private corporations like the Japan Electronic Computer Corporation (JECC), and a whole range of horizontal associations—industrial associations, business federations, government advisory councils, public policy study groups, and parliamentary caucuses. The networks of intermediate organizations link government officials with elites from industry, banking, the mass media, labor, and academia, permitting much public policy discussion, consultation, and implementation to take place.

Intermediate organizations, which extend the tentacles of state power throughout the private sector, perform a variety of vital functions for the political economy, including gathering and analyzing information regarding overseas markets, monitoring technological developments abroad, promoting and regulating exports, and facilitating overseas investments (to mention only some of the trade-related activities). For trade purposes, probably no country has utilized intermediate organizations as extensively or skillfully as Japan.

From the U.S. standpoint, the impact of Japan's intermediate organizations on bilateral trade has been mixed. On the one hand, they have increased Japan's penetration of the U.S. market, bringing to bear the combined resources of the public and private sectors. Some have also made the obverse—U.S. penetration of the Japanese market—more difficult by erecting a variety of nontariff barriers. The Japan Tobacco and Salt Monopoly is an example of how a public corporation, with bureaucratic turf to protect, has resisted U.S. pressures for import liberalization.

On the other hand, the maze of intermediate organizations has helped to resolve trade conflicts. They have been instrumental, for example, in implementing orderly marketing agreements (OMAs) and in slowing down "export deluges" during times of political volatility. Indeed, one reason Japan has been saddled with more voluntary export restraints

(VERs) and OMAs than any other OECD country (see the paper by Komiya and Itoh in this volume) may be that it possesses the kind of institutional structure—including a constant flow of communications between government and business and strong intermediate organizations—that is necessary for acceptance and implementation of VERs and OMAs. There is perverse irony in the relationship between the exceptionally large number of VERs imposed on Japanese industry and Japan's institutional capacity to accommodate foreign demands that VERs be practiced.

Whether the consequences of Japan's capacity to swallow VERs have been positive or negative from the standpoint of maintaining an open international trade regime is debatable. The paper by Komiya and Itoh in this volume implies that it has undermined the GATT trade structure, whereas the paper by Gilpin suggests that it has kept the GATT system intact, albeit at a price. Less controversial is the notion that Japan's acceptance of VERs has functioned as a coolant for "overheated" U.S.-Japan trade relations. Without VERs, a U.S.-Japan trade war might have been hard to avert, and the United States might have passed measures providing formal protection for its damaged industrial sectors.

Whether VER concessions will see the international system through the conflicts that lie ahead, however, remains to be seen. It may be that the discrepancy between what lies in the United States' short-term interests and what is desirable for long-term systemic stability may be widening, as U.S. economic prowess atrophies. If so, this could place Japan in a dilemma. It may have to choose between keeping bilateral relations harmonious or reinforcing the structure of the GATT system (even at the cost of conflicts with the United States).

The Support Coalition Behind the LDP

The LDP's Grand Coalition of Support

The most extraordinary feature of Japan's political regime is the LDP's domination of parliamentary power over most of the postwar period. No other party in any of the world's large industrial democracies comes close to matching the LDP's record of longevity in office. The LDP's staying power results from its ability to hold the loyalty of traditional support groups while continually incorporating new groups into its grand coalition. The coalition consists of a heterogeneous assortment of support groups, including farmers, small-scale businessmen, doctors, war veterans, religious groups, big businesses, financial institutions, industrial interests, the elderly, and housewives. Practically every segment of society is incorporated, though in varying degrees. Only a few major groups are conspicuously underrepresented, most notably blue-collar workers and organized labor.

The encompassing nature of the LDP's political coalition poses a striking contrast to the narrow, single-organization base of most opposition parties. The major support group of the Japan Socialist Party (JSP), for example, is the Sōhyō (General Council of Japanese Labor Unions); of the Democratic Socialist Party (DSP), the Dōmei labor union; of the Kōmeitō (Clean Government Party; CGP), the Sōkagakkai (religious sect); and of the Japan Communist Party (JCP), party members. The LDP is the only party in Japan that cuts across almost all occupational groupings. Its political inclusivity has had far-reaching consequences, affecting electoral stability, public policy,[40] interactions among the LDP, interest groups, and the bureaucracies, and the political configuration of power in each policy domain.

The inclusivity of the LDP's coalition parallels what is an even more comprehensive structure of interests encapsulation by Japan's "bureaucratic inclusivity."[41] The parallel levels of inclusivity—political and bureaucratic—have shaped a stable structure of public policymaking, divided into various policy domains. The boundaries of each domain are more or less determined by the division of jurisdictional authority among the bureaucracies. Which political actors get involved and how they interact within each policy sphere have become routinized over the years, even though the configuration is constantly changing in response to political developments. The LDP's relationship with each interest group differs, as is evident in the political goods and services they exchange. Similarly, the interaction between the bureaucracies, the LDP, and private producers varies substantially in terms of their relative influence and the degree of politicization by issue area.

Because the LDP is not effectively organized at the grass-roots level as a national party (in spite of the longevity of its postwar reign), it depends heavily on political resources contributed by the various interest groups in its grand coalition, particularly those groups capable of turning out the vote. The brunt of responsibility for voter mobilization is scattered among the hundreds of LDP Diet members, who must fend for themselves through the organization of personal support groups (*kōenkai*) in their local electoral constituencies.[42] Because of the single-vote, multi-member nature of electoral districting, many LDP Diet representatives must rely on their own personal support groups to deliver votes, often against fellow LDP candidates running in the same district. This means that the local interest groups attached to individual LDP members assume enormous importance at the grass-roots level. Notwithstanding the decentralized nature of voter mobilization, interest groups at the national level are also crucial to the staying power of the LDP. To hold its grand coalition together, the LDP must do all it can to satisfy interest group demands at both the local and the national levels.

This suggests that the LDP–interest group interaction within each policy domain is apt to be politicized. Presumably, this tendency is counterbalanced by the bureaucracy's technical expertise and commitment to safeguarding the country's collective interests.[43] In Japan, where a high premium is placed on the collective national good, constraints on selfish behavior can be binding, especially in combination with norms stressing the importance of government-business accommodation.

At the same time, however, Japanese bureaucrats—though custodians of the public's interests—do feel a responsibility for looking after the well-being of specific producer interests under their direct jurisdiction. There is natural tendency for *genkyoku* bureaucrats (those in divisions that deal with specific industries) to view the interests of groups under their regulatory jurisdiction as congruent with the national interests.[44] Since constitutional authority is vested in the legislative branch, however, the autonomy of the bureaucracies is susceptible to eclipse by a combination of private sector and LDP interests. Bureaucratic institutions, in other words, operate within an environment of complex, ever-changing political forces that affect their autonomy, power, and capacity to make public policy choices based strictly on technocratic desiderata and the public interest.[45]

The Bureaucracy

The bureaucracies in Japan play a key—sometimes decisive—role in the configuration of political power.[46] On trade-related issues involving conflicts with the United States, the bureaucracy often plays the central role, serving as the communications link between domestic and foreign groups, as mediator of domestic disagreements, and as coordinator of the overall negotiating processes. Lacking the expertise and experience to handle complicated, international trade negotiations, private producers and party politicians rely on MITI and other ministries to take charge but reserve for themselves the right of constant consultation and a say in the final decision.

The reasons for the Japanese bureaucracy's power are well known.[47] In addition to the universal sources of bureaucratic power—control over vital information flows, superior quality of civil servants, cumulative experience and expertise, regulatory power over the financial system—there are special circumstances that explain the unusual strength of the Japanese bureaucracy: the legacy of the Occupation, the LDP's continuous control over the Diet, the movement of ex-bureaucrats into key positions in the private sector and in electoral politics, and the sociocultural tradition of deference to bureaucrats on policymaking matters. It would be hard to find another market-based political economy where the bureaucracy has played a more pivotal role.

The extent to which bureaucracies shape public policies, however, varies over time, by issue area,[48] and according to bureaucratic jurisdiction. With the maturation and internationalization of Japan's economy and the LDP's longtime reign, the power of the bureaucracies has waned over time.[49] MITI has lost a number of powers, including its control of foreign-exchange rationing. The deregulation of Japan's financial system will surely lead to a significant erosion of the power of the Ministry of Finance (MOF). The two mightiest and most prestigious ministries in Japan, the MOF and MITI, have thus seen their power bases whittled away. Nevertheless, though no longer as dominating as it once was, "embedded" bureaucratic power in Japan is still considerable compared with that in most other countries.

But the notion of bureaucratic power needs to be disaggregated and refined—broken down by individual ministries and issue areas. There is an implicit hierarchy of bureaucratic prestige and power, just as there is in most areas of Japan's political economy. A crude rank-ordering of ministries, based on interviews with a small sample of government officials (N = 21) and supported (though far from perfectly) by the preferences of those who have passed the rigorous higher civil service examinations, clusters the leading trade-related bureaucracies into at least five groups:

1. Most powerful (by a wide margin)—MITI, MOF.
2. Very powerful (on local budgetary issues)—Ministry of Local Autonomy.
3. Powerful (in specific trade issue areas)—MAFF; Ministry of Posts and Telecommunications; Ministry of Health and Welfare.
4. Fairly influential (in terms of broad involvement)—Ministry of Foreign Affairs.
5. Weak—Ministry of Labor; Defense Agency; Science and Technology Agency; Economic Planning Agency.

The concept of power is hard to define and measure, as Robert Dahl has pointed out.[50] The list above is based on the subjective weighings of higher civil servants in terms of the capacity of relevant ministries to determine the outcome of trade-related policies at minimal costs to their political autonomy.

The validity of subjective interview data can be tested by comparing the results with those obtained from less obtrusive indicators. The reemployment of higher civil servants in high-level posts within the private sector (*amakudari*) is perhaps the best unobtrusive indicator of relative bureaucratic power, although the data must be interpreted with care. In 1976, for example, available statistics reveal that the number of *amakudari* officials from the MOF (45) far exceeded that for any other ministry by a factor of about three, with MITI (17) ranking second (see Table 1). The rank-ordering corresponds roughly with the hierarchy of power constructed from interview data, with the MOF and MITI at the top, followed by the MAFF and the Ministries of Health and Welfare and Posts and Telecommunications.

There are several reasons why so many retiring MOF officials find second careers in desirable private-sector positions. Personnel assignments within the MOF—especially service as head of a district tax office—offer ready-made springboards for the launching of second careers, either in the private sector or in elected office. The high quality of MOF officials can be attributed in part to the enticing second careers offered to retiring MOF officials. There is a mutually reinforcing, closed loop at work here: the capability of MOF officials, in turn, renders them attractive targets of recruitment by private-sector corporations. Finally, the enormous power once wielded by the MOF over taxes, budgets, and financial markets has promped private corporations to hire ex-MOF officials as a means of securing information and consolidating ties with the MOF.

Officials in the ministries in charge of functionally specific sectors—Agriculture, Forestry and Fisheries, Transportation, Health and Welfare, Construction, and Posts and Telecommunications—do very well in finding employment in the private sector, although the range of choices is much narrower than that of retiring MOF or MITI officials, owing to the narrower jurisdictional scope of these ministries. The regulatory responsibilities of these ministries are substantial, and the level of adhesion and mutual interdependence between these ministries and producer groups is high, thereby increasing the incentives for both sides to develop and maintain extensive relational networks through the mechanism of *amakudari*. Except for the MAFF, these ministries share with the

TABLE 1
Rank-Ordering of Ministries by Reemployment of Bureaucrats, 1986

Ministry	Number of reemployed	Ministry	Number of reemployed
Finance	44	Construction	10
MITI	17	Post and Telecom-	
Transportation	15	munications	9
MAFF	14	Labor	3
Health and		Education	2
Welfare	10	Foreign Affairs	1

SOURCE: Japan, National Personnel Authority, *Eiri kigyō e no shūshoku no shōnin ni kansuru nenji hōkokusho* (Annual report on private-sector employment of government personnel) (Tokyo, 1976).

TABLE 2
Private-Sector Employment of Ex-Bureaucrats, 1986

Industry	Number of reemployed	Industry	Number of reemployed
Construction	42	Electronics	8
Finance	34	Pharmaceuticals	7
Transportation	28	Chemical	6
Food and food		Timber and wood	
processing	8	processing	3

SOURCE: Same as Table 1.

MOF and MITI the common characteristic that the industries under their jurisdiction are vigorous, growing sectors of the Japanese economy, with expanding employment opportunities.

From the demand side, few of the industries that have hired former higher-level civil servants have close ties with ministries like Labor, Education, and Foreign Affairs or the Economic Planning Agency and the Defense Agency (see Table 2). Ex-officials from these ministries tend to be excluded from the annual migration of bureaucrats (although retired personnel from the Foreign Ministry appear to be securing a growing number of positions as consultants to major corporations involved in international trade). The low rate of *amakudari* for these ministries can be explained by the fact that none possesses supervisory authority over powerful producer groups like construction, pharmaceuticals, or food processing. Lacking powerful producer-group constituencies, these bureaucracies lack the reemployment opportunities that service in other ministries offers their retiring officials. This, in turn, diminishes the attractiveness of these ministries as places of employment for college graduates who have passed the higher civil service exams.

Not surprisingly, the lack of powerful producer constituencies also diminishes the clout that these government agencies can bring to bear. In the context of bureaucracy–producer group ties, therefore, it is easy to understand why MITI or the MOF often dominates the Foreign Ministry when they lock horns over trade-related issues. MITI and the MOF have mighty economic constituencies, with which they work closely and on which they base their power.

Some of the bureaucracies that rank low on the power scale, like Foreign Affairs and the Economic Planning Agency, deserve a higher prestige ranking. The two are considered desirable places of employment among those who have passed the higher civil entrance exam, especially compared with the Ministries of Education and Labor or the Defense Agency. Except for those two bureaucracies, power and prestige appear to be correlated.

The rank-ordering also reveals that bureaucratic prestige and power tend to be inversely related to the degree of regulatory—as contrasted to promotional—activities (although, here again, the inverse correlation is only rough). Except for the MOF (which is a special case, because it deals with finance instead of industrial production), the ministries involved primarily in regulatory work (Environmental Agency, Education, and Labor) tend to be located near the bottom of the hierarchy. The ministries clustered in the third category (powerful in specific trade issue areas)—Posts and Telecommunications, Construction, Transportation, and Health and Welfare—have substantial regulatory responsibilities; but their power derives more from the size of their budgets, the political importance of the interest groups under their jurisdiction, and the support they receive from LDP *zoku* ("tribes," or informal support caucuses) than from their regulatory authority. Ministries more involved in promotional activities, like MITI, Local Autonomy, and to a lesser extent, the MAFF, tend to enjoy high prestige and power.

Because of the nature of their tasks, the ministries involved primarily in regulation tend to be conservative, slow-moving, and organizationally rigid. The weight of inertia is often so heavy as to stultify bold new initiatives. In contrast to MITI, where young officials at the deputy division director level (*kachō hosa*, usually in their mid-thirties) have considerable leeway to take creative initiatives and dominate policymaking, the regulatory ministries permit much less scope for creative initiatives. Older, higher-ranking officials, who serve as liaison with the LDP, play a more prominent role. Such bureaucratic conservatism tends to undercut their power.

Interestingly, several of the middle-ranking ministries with significant regulatory responsibilities seem to be attempting to shift a greater proportion of their activities from the regulatory to the promotional arenas. Taking a cue from MITI, the Ministries of Posts and Telecommunications, Health and Welfare, and Transportation have begun to lay much greater stress on activities that go beyond regulatory tasks, presumably in order to consolidate their own institutional power bases.

The power of regulatory agencies in Japan tends to be limited to a rather narrow scope of jurisdictional authority. Even though, for example, the telecommunications industry is closely linked to other key industries such as computers, semiconductors, new materials, and data processing, the Ministry of Posts and Telecommunications' regulatory authority is restricted to the telecommunications field; and even there, it is trying to fend off territorial incursions by MITI.

As evident in the cases of the Ministries of Transportation, Construction, and Health and Welfare, several of Japan's regulatory ministries enjoy close working relations with the producer groups under their supervision. This closeness contrasts with the distance and antagonism between certain regulatory agencies and producer interests in the United States, such as the Occupational Safety and Health Administration and the Federal Drug Administration.[51] The closeness in Japan may be, in part, a by-product of ministries' responsibilities to promote industrial productivity and international competitiveness. Such promotional activities have had the effect of enhancing their embedded power—but at the cost of rendering them more vulnerable to capture by interest groups and partisan politicization.

A Taxonomy of the Political Processes

Political Exchange and Interest Configurations

Bureaucratic freedom from political interference, a critical factor not only for the substance of public policy[52] but also for the resolution of trade disputes, is dependent on the nature of the relationship between the LDP and interest groups under each ministry's jurisdiction. Specifically, it depends largely on the exchange of political goods and services between the LDP and its broad coalition of interest group supporters. The nature of the exchange, in turn, affects the extent to which LDP Diet members are motivated to tread on bureaucratic turf as lobbyists on behalf of parochial interests. The political goods and services routinely exchanged can be grouped into four types.

Type 1: Clientelistic votes. The LDP receives votes in exchange for favorable legislation and effective public policies. Private interests that take part in the exchange include traditional LDP support groups—agriculture, small-scale enterprise, the health profession, heads of local postal service, and so forth. The bureaucracies involved include the MAFF, Small and Medium Enterprise Agency (MITI), Posts and Telecommunications, and Health and Welfare.

Type 2: Reciprocal (pork-barrel) patronage. The spoils of public expenditures (public works, procurements, subsidies) are recycled back to the LDP in the form of financial contributions, often to individual LDP Diet members. Involved interest groups include a variety of traditional LDP supporters—local small businesses, and construction, transportation, and telecommunications interests. Recycling also takes place in the regulatory arena, with regulated interests contributing to the LDP in return for acceptable regulatory control (transportation, electrical power utilities, securities markets). The bureaucracies most often involved include Construction, Transportation, Posts and Telecommunications, Local Autonomy, and Defense.

Type 3: "Untied" general contributions. Various interest groups—big business, banking, business federations—give the LDP financial support, untied to specific expenditures or public policy favors. It can be understood as a general exchange based on the broad benefits that the business community receives from having a pro-business party in power. Big businesses' willingness to contribute what are usually large sums—in spite of the public goods nature of the contribution—perhaps can be understood as payment of an insurance premium by those most capable of paying. The bureaucracies under whose jurisdiction these donors fall are MITI and the MOF.

Type 4: Generalized voter support. As the size of Type 1 groups shrinks with economic maturation, the LDP has had to win support from a much broader and more diffuse cross section of voters: white-collar salarymen, housewives, young residents in metropolitan areas, citizens on welfare. These groups tend not to be politically well organized, identify themselves only weakly and conditionally as LDP supporters, and vote on the basis of broad policy concerns (the overall health of the economy, welfare, and pollution). The LDP tries to appeal to them through the implementation of public policies that improve the overall quality of life. Given the diffuseness of the groups and their concerns, no single set of ministries can be identified as principally involved.

The four types of political exchange can be viewed hierarchically in terms of level of politicization and the closeness of ties among the LDP, interest groups, and bureaucratic agencies: accordingly, Type 1 is the most politicized, with the closest adhesion (*yuchaku*) among the LDP, interest groups, and ministries; in Type 2 the politicization and adhesion taper off; Types 3 and 4 are the freest of politicized forces; relations between members of this interest configuration can be characterized as arms-length.

The typology of political exchange would suggest that most ministries—with the notable exceptions of MITI and the MOF—are politicized, vulnerable to LDP interference, and captured in varying degrees by the very groups they are supposed to regulate. A crude rank-ordering of ministries on the dimension of politicization is nearly the inverse of the power and prestige hierarchy:

1. Heavily politicized—Construction; MAFF.
2. Quite politicized—Transportation; Posts and Telecommunications; Health and Welfare; Defense.
3. Somewhat politicized—Local Autonomy; MOF.
4. Comparatively nonpoliticized—MITI (excluding the Small and Medium Enterprise Agency); Foreign Affairs; Economic Planning Agency.

Politicization is measured here in terms of the adhesion between the LDP and private interest groups and the degree to which LDP Diet members intrude into the bureaucracy's policymaking domain, either individually or through informal Diet member caucuses and formal LDP policymaking committees. It is also reflected in the bureaucracy's capacity to withstand (or accede to) politicized pressures from the LDP and special interest groups in the formulation of public policy.

As a very crude generalization, one can hypothesize that the chances that a ministry is heavily politicized tend to be greater, all things being equal, under the following conditions: (1) when the jurisdictional scope of the ministry is narrow and involves regulatory control over labor-intensive sectors, especially the primary sector; (2) when private interest groups under the ministry's supervision are politically well organized and possess the resources necessary to mobilize votes or funnel ample amounts of money to influential political leaders; and (3) when inefficient and internationally noncompetitive producer groups are heavily dependent on the government for import protection, subsidies, procurements, or specific favors. From a systemic standpoint, the barometer of politicization tends to rise under slow-growth macroeconomic circumstances—when fiscal constraints turn budgetary politics into a zero-sum competition for resources. It is not surprising, therefore, that the level of politicization has risen sharply in Japan since the end of the era of rapid growth (beginning with the onset of the first oil crisis in 1974).[53]

The Migration of Bureaucrats into the LDP

The close working relationship between the LDP and the bureaucracies has created an effective mechanism for interest aggregation. It has helped the LDP sustain its Diet majority for an unprecedented length of time while providing the bureaucracies with the political support and stability necessary to formulate and implement comparatively intelligent public policies. For certain bureaucracies, like MITI, the LDP-bureaucratic alliance has made it possible to retain an extraordinary degree of autonomy and insulation from partisan politics.

Various reasons for the closeness of the LDP-bureaucratic alliance can be cited; but among the most important—and distinctive—is the extraordinary phenomenon of ex-bureaucrats becoming LDP Diet members. Of all LDP representatives elected to the lower house from 1955 to 1984, 21 per cent hailed from bureaucratic backgrounds, an astonishing proportion given the limited number of officials leaving the higher civil service each year.[54] The LDP has enjoyed a virtual monopoly over the recruitment of ex-bureaucrats. Opposition parties have managed to recruit only a negligible share: only 3 per cent of all DSP representatives in 1955–84, 2 per cent of JSP parliamentarians, 1 per cent of Kōmeitō members, and no Communists.

For members of the JSP, the largest opposition party, the dominant occupational route to the lower house has been through organized labor;

some 37 per cent have risen through the ranks of Sōhyō labor unions. Over a quarter of the DSP representatives have come up through Dōmei, the private sector labor unions. The Kōmeitō has turned to its religious support group, the Sōkagakkai, for 32 per cent of its representatives. The JCP has dipped into party ranks for 34 per cent. By analyzing the career paths to elected office, therefore, one gets a sense of the stark contrasts in the core groups with which each party is closely allied.

For the LDP, the benefits of the large influx of ex-bureaucrats have been substantial. The bureaucracy has provided the LDP with its most fertile breeding ground of talent, and recruitment of ex-bureaucrats has facilitated interactions between the legislative and executive branches; this has extended the LDP's longevity in power. Owing to their policy-making experience and abilities, ex-bureaucrats have dominated the key positions within the LDP and cabinet. Most Japanese postwar prime ministers have come from the higher civil service. Moreover, in terms of all cabinets formed between 1948 and 1977, 183 of the 425 members (an incredible 43%) have come from the ranks of ex-bureaucrats.

Recruitment from the higher civil service has meant that the LDP has been the recipient of a critical and constant transfusion of talent. Ex-bureaucrats have infused into the ruling conservative party a high level of competence, intimate knowledge of the substance and processes of policymaking, quick access to rich sources of information in the bureaucracies, and extensive personal contacts with elites in both the public and the private sectors. It is hard to imagine how the LDP might have fared—or how the postwar history of Japanese politics might have unfolded—had this influx not taken place.

From an institutional and policymaking standpoint, this migration has had the effect of blurring the boundaries between the executive and legislative branches, breaking down some of the barriers to effective communications and coordination, and strengthening the capacity of the LDP-bureaucratic alliance to manage the country on a day-to-day basis. The LDP-bureaucratic union has allowed the comparative strengths of each side—the bureaucracy's administrative skills and technical know-how and the LDP's constitutional authority and electoral mandate—to be blended. Within this institutional framework, the LDP has been able to take advantage of the formidable prerogatives of majority-party status to sustain itself in power, servicing the needs of the vast array of support groups in its grand coalition.

It is widely assumed that the large representation of ex-bureaucrats strengthens the hands of the bureaucracies vis-à-vis the LDP and interest groups because it places loyal ex-officials in strategic posts within the LDP. The presumption is that these "old boys" maintain their loyalties to the ministries they once served. In many cases, this is true; but the influx of ex-bureaucrats also strengthens the hands of the LDP, if only because it gives the ruling conservative party the in-house expertise to formulate policy without having to depend so one-sidedly on the bureaucracies. In Type 1 and Type 2 political exchanges (see above), this enhances the LDP's capacity to align with interest groups and apply combined pressure on the bureaucracies. The influx of in-house experts has come to be reflected in the growing influence of LDP policy subcommittees dealing with such issues as agriculture, defense, and the budget. The influence of both sides is enhanced, and the LDP-bureaucratic alliance is strengthened.

Significantly, the ministries ranking highest in the power hierarchy— the MOF, MITI, MAFF, Local Autonomy, Construction, Transportation, Health and Welfare—tend to send the most officials into the LDP. For reasons already explained, the MOF has the largest contingent of "alumni" in the Diet (30 in 1985). Like the MOF, several Type 1 and Type 2 ministries—the MAFF, Construction, Transportation, Health and Welfare, Posts and Telecommunications—offer civil servants local or national springboards to elected office. Special interest groups under their jurisdiction—such as the medical profession and the heads of local post offices—are well positioned to mobilize support, deliver votes, or contribute campaign funds. Many ex-officials from Type 1 and Type 2 ministries join party and parliamentary policymaking committees, and some become in-house experts on Type 1 and Type 2 policy issues. Hence, the large representation of ex-officials from the MAFF, Transportation, and Construction has helped the LDP extend and consolidate its control over these policy domains. Here, in short, is another reason for the aforementioned hierarchy of politicization and for the political resistance to foreign pressures to liberalize import markets involving Type 1 and Type 2 industries.

Type 1. For the LDP, Type 1 is the most important form of political exchange. Its majority status hinges on stable support from groups that are well organized to deliver votes—agriculture, small and medium-size enterprises, heads of local postal services, local business interests, the medical profession, and war veterans. Because of the gerrymandered system of electoral districting, agriculture is overrepresented in the parliament. In the lower house, only 25 of the 130 districts are located in large metropolitan areas. Although the population in the metropolitan districts exceeds 40 per cent of the national total, they elect only 100 out of 511 seats in the Diet, or less than 20 per cent.[55] By contrast, eligible voters in the agricultural sector represented only around 20 per cent of the national electorate in 1984, but the districts in which they were located elected about 30 per cent of the Diet. In spite of its relatively small size, therefore, agriculture is critical to the LDP's majority. This makes it easy to understand why trade conflicts in agriculture are politically hard to resolve, and why the MAFF is among the most politicized. In return for electoral support, Japanese farmers receive huge subsidies as well as protection from foreign imports.

Small and medium-size enterprises (MITI), the heads of local post offices (Posts and Telecommunications), local organizations (Local Autonomy), and, somewhat surprisingly, the medical and health professions (Health and Welfare) are also well organized to deliver votes. Here, too, the bureaucratic agencies responsible for oversight tend to rank high on the scale of politicization. This suggests that the disaggregated analysis of the bureaucracy should be extended not just to the level of individual ministries but even in some cases to subunits within the ministries. Thus, although most bureaus within MITI are comparatively insulated from politicized interference, some are more vulnerable than others. Owing to the electoral clout of small-scale businesses, one of the LDP's key support groups, the Small and Medium Enterprise Agency is clearly more politicized than other MITI bureaus. What MITI officials can do to rationalize Japan's retail distribution industry, therefore, is constrained by the realities of electoral politics.

Retail distribution is one of the areas identified by the U.S. government as constituting a serious, structural nontariff barrier. American companies feel they have had a hard time getting their products through the maze of Japanese distributors. MITI officials would like to streamline the large number of "mom and pop" retail stores and create greater opportunities for large discount retail chains to extend their national networks—not only to enhance efficiency at home but also to placate criticisms abroad—but MITI's hands are tied by the veto power held by the multitude of small retail merchants located in neighborhoods across the country. Here, in short, is a classic example of how political entanglements obstruct the bureaucracy's leeway for change.

There are two subcategories of interest configurations involving voter support. Type 1 involves clientelistic ties between the LDP and the traditional electoral support groups mentioned earlier. Because the relationship has developed over decades of interaction, the political exchange is fairly well routinized and stable. What the LDP receives—decisive votes—is so valuable that it must supply goods and services of comparable value for its Type 1 support groups. In consequence, the LDP's package of political payoffs is very generous, the largest and most expensive in terms of the economic inefficiencies sustained. For agriculture, the package includes protection from foreign imports, price controls set far above production costs, generous tax breaks, and exorbitant land prices. For small-scale retail distributors, the payoffs include special, low-interest financing, favorable tax treatment, and veto power over the establishment of large-scale outlets in local areas.

In nearly all Type 1 cases, a stable alignment involving the LDP, the interest groups, and the bureaucracy has taken shape over decades of routinized interaction. Type 1 interest groups have organized themselves in ways that extract maximum value from the political resources at their disposal. Agriculture, telecommunications, small-scale enterprises, the medical profession, and so forth all have powerful LDP *zoku* behind them to lobby on their behalf, not only in the Diet but also with the relevant ministries. Since Types 1 and 2 regulatory ministries—the MAFF, Health and Welfare, Posts and Telecommunications—tend to be functionally more specialized than MITI, the interest groups under their jurisdiction tend to have more leverage than the manufacturing sectors have with MITI.

Type 4. Type 4 voter mobilization is very different. It involves large, diffuse, poorly organized sectors outside the LDP's traditional coalition—welfare recipients, young residents in metropolitan districts, housewives, white-collar workers, professionals. Since the concerns of Type 4 voters are not as narrowly focused on tangible rewards and since their relationship with the LDP tends to be distant and diffuse, the LDP has attempted to appeal to them through a combination of macroeconomic measures, aimed at maintaining a healthy economy, and "targeted" policies, aimed at correcting specific problems—environmental pollution, inadequate welfare programs, substandard social overhead infrastructure. By casting its net broadly—beyond the boundaries of its traditional coalition—the LDP has turned itself into what Yasusuke Murakami calls a "catchall" interest party.[56] This has enabled it to stem the decline in its popular vote. The only problem is that voter support from these Type 4 sectors is not nearly as reliable as that from clientelistic groups (Types 1 and 2). Type 4 supporters fall into the category of unpredictable "floating" voters: their voting preferences are not anchored in strong and stable party identification. How they vote, whether for or against the LDP, is contingent on their evaluation of how effectively the LDP has governed.

Type 2. The interest coalitions associated with Type 2, reciprocal patronage, are much closer to the patterns of Type 1 than to those of Type 4. The LDP–interest group symbiosis is not as great as in the case of Type 1 because these groups are not as well equipped to deliver votes, save for certain local districts. Nevertheless, they are part of the LDP's coalition of clientelistic supporters and, over the years, have worked out a mutually profitable relationship based on reciprocal patronage.

What the LDP offers its supporters in Type 2 exchanges are two types of political goods and services: procurements, public works contracts, subsidies, and other budgetary allocations; and acceptable regulatory practices, legislative support, and facilitation of administrative procedures. The Ministries of Construction, Transportation, and Posts and

Telecommunications are the most heavily involved in Type 2 exchanges. The availability of public largess gives the LDP an opportunity to engage in old-style pork-barrel politics or what Michisada Hirose calls the "political profit-sharing system" (*rieki haibun*).[57] The Ministries of Health and Welfare and Posts and Telecommunications and the Agency of Natural Resources tend to be heavily involved in regulatory matters that bring them into contact with the LDP.

Ministries with large public funds to dole out—such as Construction—tend to be especially close to the LDP. Indeed, the Ministry of Construction, for example, may be closer to the LDP, more thoroughly penetrated by the LDP, and therefore more politicized than any other ministry. All Type 2 ministries are oriented toward serving the interests of domestic producers. Within each Type 2 ministry, the voice of officials who can be considered "internationalists" is weak. These ministries tend to subordinate concerns about the international ramifications of public policies to domestic considerations and needs. Thus, the configuration of power, involving the alliance of bureaucracies, industries, and the LDP, is patterned in ways that contribute to trade tensions and complicate the resolution of conflicts.

Type 3. Although the LDP depends on big business for much of its money, the nature of the Type 3 power configuration—MITI, big business, the LDP—differs from the other two patterns.[58] MITI has little in the way of procurement budgets to offer. Its jurisdictional scope is so sweeping that no industry—no matter how big or powerful—is capable of capturing it. It is not the pawn of the steel industry, any more than it is the handmaiden of the electronics industry. The needs and interests of each industry are weighed against those of all others. Through internal mechanisms of aggregation, MITI balances the diverse spectrum of industrial interests under its broad jurisdiction. Moreover, its impressive track record, history of independence, and capacity to reach consensus with industry makes it more immune to politicization than most other ministries.

The big corporations under MITI's jurisdiction are also reluctant to move into too incestuous an embrace with the LDP because greater dependence on the LDP might entail larger donations. Hence, although big business pays far more than its share of political dues, it is not as a whole locked in a pork-barrel or clientelistic relationship. Nor is it as beholden to the LDP as construction or transportation for reciprocal patronage or as dependent on the LDP for specific policy measures. Its financial contributions can be viewed as generalized support for the LDP's pro-business posture. In spite of the massive concentration of money and its economic importance, therefore, big business under MITI's jurisdiction is not as inextricably entangled in a symbiosis with the LDP as agriculture, construction, and other Type 1 and Type 2 interests.

Impact on Trade

Trade Implications

Over the more than three decades of unbroken LDP rule, a complex structure of interest aggregation has formed from the dynamic interplay between electoral imperatives and the LDP-bureaucratic brokerage of interest group demands. The interest coalitions that have emerged in various policy arenas have had far-reaching trade ramifications. Probably the most noteworthy feature of the LDP's grand coalition is that key elements of the conservative party's support base come from comparatively inefficient, domestically oriented, protected sectors where Japan's international comparative advantage is on the wane. Agriculture, fisheries, forestry, and tobacco are sunset sectors. Retail distribution, medical services, the postal service, the national railways, housing construction, and public works are inefficient, domestically oriented, politicized industries in comparison with the well-known, export-oriented sectors like steel, automobiles, and electronics. In contrast to cases of infant-industry protection in Japan (like automobiles) where domestic competition has always been fierce (which explains why a number of Japanese infant industries have grown up and matured into world-class competitors), the protection given these highly politicized sectors tends to breed inefficiency.

Only some of the numerous politicized enclaves of economic inefficiency in Japan have been identified above. If the Japanese economy is in a state of general equilibrium, one would expect that the costs of inefficiency in sunset industries would be passed on to the efficient sectors. No doubt they have. But the overall health of the manufacturing sectors suggests that Japan has not suffered that much, perhaps because of the extraordinary efficiency of the manufacturing sector, perhaps because Japan has not had to shoulder some of the common causes of inefficiency in other economies, such as the heavy burden of military defense. Or it may be because the benefits of economies of scale achieved through exports outweigh the costs of domestic political patronage.

Whatever the explanation, the ruling coalition in Japan appears willing to pay the price of—or perhaps more accurately, seems locked into—economic inefficiency in certain sectors in exchange for preserving the political status quo. The LDP can hardly turn a deaf ear to the troubled pleas of clientelistic groups whose support sustains it in power. As long as the price is not prohibitively high, the economic cost of trade protection can be widely dispersed throughout society. No single group or sector is forced to absorb the full brunt.

The notion that the price of political stability should be distributed widely—a kind of compulsory political insurance premium—is perhaps the flip side of the economic concept of collective goods.[59] The use of implicit insurance premiums is widespread throughout Japan's political economy.[60] In the trade arena, probably its most graphic manifestation is the government's protection of labor-intensive producers in the primary sector. Curiously, the Japanese people, including consumer groups, appear perfectly willing to accept and disperse the costs of political insurance premiums. If the costs cannot be diffused, the dislocations tend to be sharp for specific industries and politically traumatic for the government in power.

Except in small countries of limited power, heavily dependent on foreign trade, which feel they have no choice but to adhere to principles of free trade,[61] reliance on de facto political insurance premiums is not uncommon. In a one-party-dominant political system like Japan's, where inefficient sectors are incorporated into the ruling coalition, the tendency may be especially pronounced. In such systems, however, the chances for a long-term solution—a gradual streamlining of inefficient sectors—may be relatively good if the dominant party has time to adjust by shifting its electoral base from Type 1 to Type 4. The problem, from the standpoint of Japan's trade partners, is that the rationalization process may take too much time. How Japan handles the problem will be one of its major political challenges.

Of the Type 1 and Type 2 sectors, only shipbuilding (Ministry of Transportation), telecommunications (Posts and Telecommunications) and parts of the construction industry (Construction) are sufficiently efficient today to compete in world markets. They are the only three that have managed to sell a measurable portion of their production abroad. But the successful exporters in both the telecommunications and construction industries tend to be those under MITI's jurisdiction, not that of Posts and Telecommunications or Construction.

Owing to the power configuration in inefficient but politically pivotal sectors, foreign competitors have encountered great difficulty breaking into Japanese markets. Not surprisingly, some of the bitterest U.S.-Japan trade confrontations have occurred in Types 1 and 2 areas: tobacco, beef, citrus, fruits, lumber, plywood, semiprocessed and processed wood products, paper and pulp, sugar, food processing, cosmetics, drugs, and procurements for Nihon Telephone and Telegraph (NTT), to name a few. In areas where the Japanese have a comparative advantage—like automobiles and consumer electronics—Japanese markets are open, but foreign manufacturers have trouble competing. It is frustrating for foreigners to be denied access to markets where they feel they possess a comparative advantage such as agriculture, lumber processing, telecommunications, value-added networks, software, personal computers, custommade semiconductors, artificial intelligence, aerospace, large jet aircraft, laser products, financial services, medical instruments, pharmaceuticals, industrial chemicals, construction machinery, or pesticides.

There are, of course, Japanese markets where foreign producers have garnered significant shares, but many of these success stories have occurred in nonstrategic, consumer, or specialized market niches and not at the expense of entrenched domestic producers: soft drinks (Coca-Cola), fast-food chains (McDonald's), wines (French), instant coffee (Nestlé's), razor blades (Schick), international credit cards (American Express), and disposable diapers (Procter and Gamble). Foreign firms have shown that they can succeed when they offer (1) famous brand-name products (Pierre Cardin); (2) specialized niches (Häagen Dazs); (3) resource-driven products—such as aluminum (where Japan lacks the low-cost raw materials to be able to compete); (4) the introduction of new products (manufacturing control devices); and (5) technologically advanced, state-of-the-art products (commercial jet aircraft).

Even if foreign firms establish a foothold in cases 4 and 5, their market advantage may be short-lived. There have been innumerable instances in which new or technologically more sophisticated products pioneered by foreign firms have been overwhelmed by second-to-market products developed by Japanese companies and adapted to suit Japanese tastes. This has been especially striking in "targeted" latecomer industries (often Type 3) in which big, blue-chip corporations have strained to overtake foreign competitors, with the assistance of the government. The point is that the configuration of political power makes Type 1 and 2 markets exceedingly hard to pry open, whereas the competitiveness of Type 3 industries makes those markets hard to crack.

The configuration of interests and the structure of power in Types 1 and 2 are so deeply embedded as to effectively rule out rapid liberalization. The LDP, clientelistic interest groups, and the politicized ministries have formed what amount to effective political cartels in a number of policy arenas. The strength of political cartels is indicative of the high stakes in preserving the status quo. Since most clientelistic groups export very little, they feel they have little to gain and much to lose by agreeing to free trade.

In the face of the closed Type 1 and 2 markets, the United States has applied strong pressures for liberalization. Many U.S. government officials believe that the application of firm pressure from outside is the only way of generating any momentum for domestic change. The status quo is so deeply entrenched that, absent foreign pressures, little is apt to change. Hence, the United States' approach has been to hammer hard on the fair-access issue. The tactic has yielded some results, although its effectiveness has been diluted by the inconsistent level of pressure applied over time (overbearing at times, nonexistent at others) and by the ever-shifting targets of pressure (from beef and citrus one year to baseball bats the next to NTT procurements thereafter). By keeping the pressure on, backed by threats of trade sanctions, it has been the U.S. hope that the free-trade interests in the LDP coalition would be galvanized into taking joint action, if only to protect their own interests.

A Free-Trade Coalition?

The notion that trade-oriented sectors with a high stake in maintaining international openness could be organized into a powerful coalition to force the inefficient sectors to bow to the inevitable seems inherently plausible because the economic power of trade-oriented sectors far outweighs that of protectionist interests. The idea of an emergent free-trade coalition fits into the pluralist framework of interest group competition. It assumes that the group or coalition able to mobilize the most resources will win the competition over trade policy in the political marketplace. One can conceive of a free-trade coalition as a rational, interest-maximizing act on the part of industries with a vital stake in free trade within a pluralistic political structure. Indeed, the boundaries of the coalition need not be limited exclusively to domestic producers; they can be extended to incorporate foreign actors in transnational coalitions who have a similar stake in open access to the Japanese market.[62]

Some observers believe that a free-trade coalition is not only taking shape but is beginning to exert itself in Japan.[63] The coalition is said to consist of such mainstream organizations as general trading companies, multinational corporations, and large retail chains, powerful business federations like Keidanren (Federation of Economic Organizations), and internationally oriented bureaucracies like MITI. In an industrial structure like Japan's that is constantly advancing, the power configuration of interest groups continually changes.[64] If, at present, the relative power of producer groups with a stake in open trade is greater than that of protectionist groups, then a free-trade coalition would not only make sense, it would be poised to impose its will on the rest of the country.

If one views the clash between open- and closed-trade coalitions solely in terms of pluralistic competition, the outcome would seem almost a foregone conclusion: the open-trade coalition possesses more than enough muscle to overwhelm the advocates of closed markets. Nor would the outcome predicted be any different if one changed the conceptual model from pluralism to statism. Since open trade clearly lies in Japan's long-term national interests and since MITI is, if anything, a rational, interest-maximizing actor, the MITI-dominant theory would predict that the proponents of free trade would easily carry the day.

The problem is that neither the pluralist model nor the concept of state dominance works. The mere fact that certain interest groups have a stake—even a decisive one—in open trade does not necessarily mean that they are motivated to contest the activities of protectionist groups, much less defeat threats to free trade. Sheer inertia keeps some inactive, the perception of unacceptable transaction costs may immobilize others; and still others may not even be aware that their own self-interests may be adversely affected. American producers of soybean, wheat, or other cereal products, for example, who rely heavily on exports to the Japanese market, have failed to take action against any of the proposed pieces of protectionist legislation, such as the local-content bills, submitted to the U.S. Congress.

In Japan's vertically organized society, where policy arenas tend to be segmented and self-contained, it is unusual for horizontal, public-interest coalitions to emerge spontaneously and browbeat other groups into submission. Few, if any, examples of cross-sector coercion can be found in the postwar history of Japanese trade. When a Keidanren subcommittee on agriculture recommended that markets be thoroughly liberalized and members of that subcommittee criticized farmers for protectionism in 1984, the Hokkaido Agricultural Cooperative demanded an apology and organized a boycott of products made by several of the companies—Ajinomoto, Sony, Daiei—whose heads sat on the subcommittee. The chairman of the subcommittee resigned and, together with the heads of Sony and Daiei, tendered apologies. The episode illustrates the deep-seated barriers against cross-sectoral coercion. Not even Keidanren, Japan's biggest and most prestigious business federation, whose membership includes virtually all blue-chip corporations, could trespass on the policy domain of a smaller, economically less central, but politically autonomous sector.

Segmentation of policy domains also limits the scope for bureaucratic accommodation. Unless a trade issue falls between the crevices, it would be difficult for one bureaucracy to trespass on the turf of another. Even in cases where jurisdictional boundaries overlap, there is no guarantee that the stronger bureaucracy will dominate. Indeed, Japan's vertically organized policymaking apparatus has trouble dealing with the problem of making horizontal adjustments to resolve territorial squabbles between bureaucracies.

More and more trade conflicts are falling untidily across bureaucratic boundaries. Consider the flap over telecommunications, for example. Telecommunications is a technologically complex industry that has developed in directions that have rendered the old bureaucratic division of jurisdiction obsolete. The convergence of computer and communications technology (C & C) has obliterated the old rationale that separated administrative responsibility between MITI (computers) and the Ministry of Posts and Telecommunications (MPT) (communications). In consequence, the two ministries have been waging an ongoing struggle for control over the telecommunications industry, a struggle that has complicated resolution of trade frictions. Using NTT's privatization as a lever, the MPT has attempted to expand and consolidate its power vis-à-vis MITI by gaining control over such policy issues as the administration of value-added networks and the specification of technical standards for the telecommunications industry. To counteract the MPT's maneuvers, MITI has used foreign pressures as a lever to loosen regulations and liberalize the industry, thereby containing the MPT's attempt to expand its territorial turf.

Similar struggles involving other ministries are bound to arise, if only because of the fast-moving nature of technological progress. It is the nature of high-technology industries that they defy tidy administrative categorization. Biotechnology, for example, cuts across the jurisdictional boundaries of Health and Welfare, MITI, Education, Science and Technology, and the MAFF. Unless a more orderly method of interbureaucratic coordination can be devised, unresolved conflicts, policymaking paralysis, politicization, and exacerbation of trade disputes may increase.

Hence, complicated trade issues that cannot be contained within a single policy domain pose potentially serious complications. When the bureaucracies cannot work out their differences by themselves, the matter usually has to be resolved at the cabinet level, often by the prime minister himself. It is no accident that, as the number of interbureaucratic trade disputes has risen, the prime minister and cabinet have been compelled to intervene. The need for intervention from on high is likely to grow as trade tensions intensify. What is worrisome, if this happens, is that the political circumstances may not be ripe for the assertion of more vigorous leadership by the prime minister. Indeed, given factional turmoil within the LDP, conditions within the party may be unfavorable for the emergence of a strong leader, a prime minister who possesses the power to steer the country through the many pitfalls that lie ahead.

It appears that Japan has had the good fortune or foresight to annoint prime ministers who have fit the country's needs at critical junctures in its postwar development—Yoshida during and after the occupation, Ikeda in the early 1960s, and Nakasone during the mid-1980s. Nevertheless, the "right man for the right time" succession may come to an end. Japan may face a dilemma: just when adversity in the external environment calls for the assertion of strong leadership, the political circumstances at home may complicate the exercise of such leadership.

Even if a strong leader or a succession of leaders should emerge, the involvement of politicians might accelerate the trend toward greater politicization. It might open the floodgates for electoral, as opposed to strictly technocratic, factors to dictate policy outcomes. Thus, there is a possibility that Japan's system of policy segmentation under a grand coalition may not function nearly as well as it has in a simpler past. Although the policymaking structure features many strengths, the international and domestic environments within which it functions are constantly changing. Whether it possesses the flexibility to adapt to a much harsher external environment remains to be seen.

Adaptability

Flexible Adaptation

Does this mean that a liberal trade posture is out of the question? Will a structural inability to adapt to a more adverse international environment cause the world to declare a trade war against Japan? To restore balance to what may seem like excessive pessimism at the end of the last section, it should be pointed out that since the mid-1970s, Japan has demonstrated that it can respond flexibly to foreign trade demands. Indeed, it has already done much to lift formal barriers against imports, foreign direct investments, and international capital movements.

To be sure, foreign skeptics can argue that the Japanese reforms have failed to rectify the trade imbalance. They can also contend, as many do, that Japan has not really opened its markets, that it has done only enough to avert immediate crises and major retaliation. Leaving aside the reduction of tariffs, the concessions receiving the most publicity have been voluntary export restraints (VERs) and liberalization of foreign direct investments, neither of which have hurt domestic producers much. Although VERs have imposed opportunity costs, Japanese exporters have continued reaping handsome profits under export ceilings.[65] It is easier to restrain a portion of exports than to permit foreign producers to seize shares of domestic markets. One can argue, in fact, that foreign consumers have had to bear the main costs of VERs. Moreover, VERs have also had the effect of accelerating Japan's structural shift to manufactured exports of higher value added.[66] Without belittling the significance of VERs as means of reducing trade conflicts, foreign skeptics can claim that Japan has actually lost little and has gained much in terms of maintaining its access to foreign markets.

The structure of domestic power configurations suggests that the greatest capacity for flexible adaptation lies in the Type 3 arena, which includes MITI, most of the manufacturing sector, and a sizable segment of the service sector. Indeed, political configurations in the Type 3 arena allow some sense of optimism that adjustments to trade conflicts can be made without irreparable damage to U.S.-Japan trade relations. The majority of past examples of successful trade adjustments—textiles, color televisions, energy, steel, and automobiles—have taken place in the Type 3 policy arena. Moreover, progress toward the resolution of conflicts has been faster in Type 3 sectors than in Types 1 and 2, where many long-standing differences continue to smolder.

There are many reasons for the adaptability of the manufacturing sector under MITI's jurisdiction. The first and most obvious is that unlike the labor-intensive sectors in Type 1 and Type 2, the manufacturing sector is where Japan's comparative advantage currently lies. Over the postwar years, as its economy has matured, Japan has done a remarkable job of moving up the ladder of value added, thus easing what might otherwise have been more serious problems of structural adjustment (see the paper by Saxonhouse in this volume).

Beyond the economic reasons, one must cite political factors involved in the Type 3 policy arena. Unlike the Type 1 and 2 bureaucracies, which tend to be more narrowly focused on a single sector or small interrelated cluster, MITI has authority over the broadest and most powerful spectrum of industries in the country. This enables it to treat the manufacturing sector as an interrelated whole, more or less in a state of equilibrium. Like the industries it oversees, MITI is far more internationally minded than its Type 1 and 2 ministerial counterparts. And just as the industries themselves have a more arms-length relationship with the LDP than Type 1 and 2 interest groups, MITI has a greater capacity to stand above political struggles.

Collective Cooperation: Cost Diffusion

The sociocultural emphasis on the collectivity and MITI's appointed role as guardian of the collective good are also major factors in Japan's flexibility to respond to foreign trade demands. This combination makes forms of collective cooperative possible in Japan that are impossible almost everywhere else. Selective cooperation in the midst of otherwise intense competition is graphically seen in two concrete areas: joint research of a precommercial, public goods nature and collective acceptance of unavoidable costs. In most other areas of politico-economic activity, cooperation is just as elusive in Japan as it is elsewhere.

From a trade standpoint, Japan's capacity to absorb what are deemed unavoidable costs is one of the main explanations for its compliance when confronted with U.S. and European demands for VERs (textiles, steel, color televisions, automobiles). It also helps to explain why Japan, almost alone among the large market economies, has managed to rationalize sunset and declining industries in the manufacturing sector—aluminum, textiles, shipbuilding, petrochemicals, and paper and pulp.[67] Both forms of collective cooperation—VERs and structural adjustments to the loss of comparative advantage—have served to smooth Japan's trade frictions with other countries, especially the United States.

But the capacity to reduce and share losses collectively—damage-limiting cooperation, so to speak—has also given rise to trade conflicts. There is a pervasive (and greatly exaggerated) perception outside Japan that collusion is rampant in Japan. Foreign competitors often accuse the Japanese of collusive behavior of almost every imaginable sort, ranging from coordinated closure of Japanese markets to price-fixing, oligopolization, and cartelization. No doubt some of the accusations are true. Certainly, the damage-limiting disposition of the Japanese, combined with relaxed antitrust enforcement, lies behind the profusion of antirecession and rationalization cartels that used to be practiced.[68] Although the number of legal cartels has diminished considerably, it is hard to monitor how many tacit cartels continue to be formed through the mechanism of unwritten administrative guidance.

The effectiveness of administrative guidance itself depends on the Japanese capacity to cooperate in the face of national crises. In the vast majority of cases, MITI uses administrative guidance to deal with zero-sum problems, especially the sharing of downside costs. MITI has found that administrative guidance in positive-sum situations, as in attempts to regulate investment in rapidly growing industries, or attempts at industrial restructuring to heighten the capacity of domestic producers to compete against foreign companies, is far less effective.[69] Companies are much less likely to agree to prescribed formulas for the distribution of rewards from positive-sum competition than they are to accept negotiated settlements, based on market-share calculations, for the diffusion of costs in zero-sum contingencies.

The distinction between upside, positive-sum benefits and downside, zero-sum costs is crucial. Making a habit of cooperating in positive-sum competition would severely damage the framework of incentives on which market competition rests. To be a net asset, collective cooperation has to be confined largely to the domain of diffusing downside costs; and even in negative-sum situations, it must be used only selectively. Excessive reliance on damage-limiting cooperation is apt to have stultifying effects if companies come to expect that downside risks will be taken care of. For this reason, MITI has tried to confine downside damage limitation largely to unanticipated, external contingencies bearing little or no linkage to normal kinds of corporate risk taking.

The capacity to diffuse risks and cushion downside costs is one of the most striking characteristics of the Japanese political economy. Institutional mechanisms for damage limitation not only link public and private sectors but also extend throughout the private sector: for example, the interdependence between parent company and subcontractors, banking-business ties, *keiretsu* organizations, and extensive patterns of intercorporate stockholding.[70] The mechanisms of collective damage limitation emerge from the interstices of organizations and markets.[71] On balance, they have helped to facilitate risk taking and maintain order and hierarchy in the private sector.

As pointed out above, the impact of collective damage limitation on matters of international trade is complex and mixed. It has helped to make Japanese enterprises more formidable competitors. But by giving shape to a maze of institutional mechanisms that have had the effect of impeding foreign penetration of Japanese markets, it has also contributed to tensions in the trade arena.[72] But because it enhances the private sector's capacity to adapt to foreign demands and external crises, it is also a potentially valuable resource for the resolution of trade disputes.

Conclusions

The analysis of political power configurations offers an alternative model to Western-based theories of Japan, Inc., statism, pluralism, and free-trade coalitions (a subcategory of pluralism)—static theories that fail, in their traditional form, to fit the Japanese case. The new framework proposed here might be called "political inclusivity and issue-area segmentation" because it uses, as the integrative framework, the LDP's grand coalition of interest support, with its bureaucratic division of labor and issue-specific power configurations that form dynamically into separate, semi-self-contained policy domains.

The model suggests that there may be deep-seated difficulties in integrating Japan into the international system. The difficulties go beyond the sociocultural barriers usually cited—language, legal system, business customs. They stem from something that may be harder to overcome: the structure of Japan's political regime.

In spite of evolutionary changes in the nature of Japan's political system, it can still give rise to, or exacerbate, trade tensions. The nature of the LDP's interest coalition leads to the political protection of a number of inefficient sectors. From the standpoint of the U.S.-Japan trade, the opening of these protected sectors would be unlikely to make much of a dent in the huge bilateral imbalance. This is the main reason why, after years of hammering and frustration, the U.S. government decided to shift its attention to financial liberalization and to more lucrative markets in high technology (for example, telecommunications) and services (management of pension funds). Nevertheless, from a political standpoint, those Japanese markets that remain closed for what appear to be indefensible reasons, such as plywood, and finished and semifinished wood products, continue to cause substantial symbolic damage.

The problem in the Type 3 arena is not the existence of residual formal impediments but the network of organizational links that keep barriers to entry high (for Japanese and foreign entrants alike). These include a strong propensity for long-term corporate relations between suppliers and customers (making it hard for foreign firms and new domestic entrants to break in); criss-crossing patterns of *keiretsu* and other forms of intercorporate stockholding; extensive vertical linkages between parent and subcontracting firms (making the sale of foreign intermediate goods especially difficult); the labyrinth of wholesale and retail distribution; and close banking-business ties. Although none of these barriers is insurmountable, they raise the level of difficulty facing foreign firms seeking to win shares of lucrative Japanese markets. Indeed, as obstacles to Japanese markets, the organizational or network barriers loom larger than formal trade barriers consciously erected by the government.

There are, as I have tried to suggest, strengths and rigidities built into the structure of Japan's political regime. Although it may not hold up under the strains of the changing international environment (including Japan's own evolving position), it may still be well suited to handle certain kinds of trade-related conflicts. Skeptics need only look at the manufacturing sector under MITI's jurisdiction, which has jettisoned nearly all vestiges of infant-industry protection; curbed the practices of dumping, predatory pricing, and export-led recovery from domestic recession; and resisted the temptation to impose orderly marketing arrangements on imports from the newly industrializing countries (NICs). Probably no other country has come so far, so fast, in reorienting its trade policies.

It is significant that these changes have taken place under the same basic coalition of interests aligned to the LDP. In how many other large industrial democracies have once-protectionist coalitions presided over trade liberalization? Japan's striking turnabout is attributable mainly to the convergence of two developments: the rapid emergence of Japan's manufacturing sector as a world-class competitor and mounting external pressures for the liberalization of infant-industry barriers.[73] As Japanese industry became increasingly competitive in world markets, foreign trade partners grew progressively intolerant of protectionism, particularly as international trade regimes founded on U.S. hegemony began to erode.

One would expect the manufacturing sector under MITI to be supportive of an open-trade regime, based on the Type 3 characteristics of issue segmentation: namely, an autonomous, powerful, relatively nonpoliticized, and internationally minded bureaucracy; competitive manufacturing industries with a large stake in overseas markets; and corporate groups that make donations to the LDP but do not organize blocs of votes for it.

Frictions in Type 1 and 2 arenas will continue to simmer, but for all the political heat generated, there is little likelihood that conflicts in these arenas will cause the U.S.-Japan alliance to disintegrate. The economic stakes are not large enough, alone, to bring down the alliance. Furthermore, over the decades of dealing with trade conflicts, Japan and the United States have learned how to handle most of the problems that arise in these arenas, as well as in heavy manufacturing. The most intractable problems for the future are likely to arise in the fastest growing sectors—high technology and the services—especially issues that cut across ministerial boundaries and affect producer interests across all four ideal types.

Trade: Outside and Inside the LDP Coalition

It is interesting that certain groups such as organized labor that have become powerful forces behind the protectionist movement in other countries, like the United States, have not lined up en masse on the side of closed trade in Japan. Organized labor is one of the few major interest groups not represented in the LDP's grand coalition. Unlike the UAW and AFL/CIO, Japanese labor federations have not tried to force NICs to swallow orderly marketing arrangements in most manufacturing sectors where Japan is losing comparative advantage. Nor have they tried to halt Japanese investment in manufacturing facilities overseas, even though massive capital investments overseas have the effect of moving jobs out of Japan. At the height of the U.S.-Japan automobile wrangle, Japanese auto union leaders even came out in favor of restricting exports to the United States.

The freedom the Japanese state enjoys from protectionist pressures exerted by organized labor is a significant factor in its ability to shift to (and sustain) a more open trade posture. Indeed, the lack of intransigence on the part of organized labor gives the state a much freer hand to implement a range of policies that reduce the pressures for protectionism. Since the oil crises, the unions have been comparatively flexible on wage demands. Here, again, is evidence of Japan's capacity to practice downside damage limitation in the face of external crisis. That labor, which is not part of the LDP's grand coalition, works in relative harmony with mainstream supporters of the status quo is a reflection not only of the absence of deep-seated class cleavages but also of the ruling coalition's ability to convert even excluded groups into de facto supporters of the status quo.

Although not formally part of the LDP's inclusive coalition labor has shared in the rich bounty of the country's economic growth. It was not so much that the ruling conservative coalition adopted policies to benefit labor; it was more a case of "spillover" or "coattail" effects, with labor benefiting, as nearly everyone else did, from an expanding overall pie.

Equity in income distribution helped, but, again, this grew out of policies that were not a direct response to labor demands.

Labor's acceptance of the status quo and the fact that it partakes in the fruits of growth reflect the importance placed on the well-being of all elements of Japanese society, not just those in power (though their slices of the pie are unquestionably larger). Although there is inevitably a bias toward rewarding those who faithfully support the party in power—big business, agriculture, the health industry, small-scale entrepreneurs—the bias does not completely crowd out the interests of groups not part of the ruling coalition. More than in other countries, there is a strong normative emphasis on distributing benefits to the *whole* collectivity. Inclusivity in this sense is not confined to just the governing coalition. It is supposed to embrace the entire body politic. Japan's value system places a high priority on equality. This emphasis is a central reason for the stability of Japan's political regime.

The Societal State

The remarkable normative strength of collective interests and goals continues to give the state (despite the erosion of bureaucratic power) a sturdy basis on which to deal with parochial private interests and politicized forces. The staying power of this collective orientation is evident in even the most highly politicized, domestic policy arenas. Progress is being made to resolve such longest-standing problems as agriculture, for example, and given enough time (a political question mark), the government may be able to make some headway on the rationalization of agricultural production. Under the right set of circumstances, therefore, the state still seems capable of rising above petty politics to take action in the public's and nation's best interests.

It retains this capacity, in part, because most interest groups in the LDP's grand coalition have no alternative party to which to transfer their support. If the LDP-bureaucratic alliance fails to respond as fully to their needs as they want, they cannot credibly threaten to shift their support to one of the parties in the opposition camp. Only a few of the opposition parties offer visible alternative policies. None stands much of a chance of expanding its narrow base of interest support sufficiently to dislodge the LDP. The only realistic alternative to LDP hegemony is either to whittle away at the LDP's majority, forcing it to enter into a coalition with one or more of the middle-of-the-road opposition parties, or to hope that factional divisions within the LDP will cause the party to rupture. Only the latter scenario can be considered a threat.

Short of a LDP breakup, Types 1, 2, and 3 interest groups are wedded to the LDP-bureaucratic structure. The lack of a viable alternative implies that the costs of "exit" (to use Albert Hirschman's terminology) will outweigh the potential gains.[74] The genius of Japan's current political regime is that all members of the LDP's grand coalition—including even some excluded groups like labor—have some stake in preserving the basic status quo. Although the system contains some seeds of its own possible demise, especially in the expansion of Type 4 groups, as Murakami points out, it also has built-in elements of stable governance.[75] As international and domestic environments change over time, the role and importance of Japan's political structure as the central mechanism for the mediation of internal-external conflict as well as for domestic conflict resolution will undoubtedly increase.

Donald C. Hellmann

Japanese Politics and Foreign Policy: Elitist Democracy Within an American Greenhouse

Japan stands at the threshold of a new era in international affairs, an era in which domestic politics will exert a more important and more unpredictable influence on the nation's role in the global political economy. The future foreign policy of Japan will differ fundamentally from that of the recent past because the Japanese can no longer remain at the periphery of international political or economic policymaking. This enhanced international role will occur even if it is not explicitly acknowledged and effectively regulated by new foreign policies of the Japanese government.

Three fundamental changes in the structure and dynamics of the international system will mandate an expanded international role for Japan: (1) the remarkable growth and mounting international economic importance of Japan (for example, by 1989 Japan's position as the world's leading creditor should approximate that of OPEC at its zenith) amid growing uncertainties about the future structure and stability of the global economy; (2) the precarious future of the U.S.-made "international greenhouse," in which Japan has flourished free from the costs and uncertainties of full participation in international political and security affairs; (3) the conspicuous dynamism and change in the East Asian region, in which Japan perforce must play a leading, but as yet undefined, role. Because these alterations in the international system are fundamental, the perimeters of Japan's international role throughout the remainder of the twentieth century can properly be understood only by looking beyond current policies and personalities and considering the impact on the Japanese of the basic structure and dynamics of the global political economy.

My primary purpose here is to identify and evaluate those aspects of Japanese domestic politics that most adequately explain its past international behavior and that will condition its future role. Another is to elaborate the growing importance of U.S. domestic politics in defining bilateral policy because of the critical importance of the United States in defining Japan's place in the world.

As is increasingly noted,[1] there is often a direct and causal relationship between the political character of the domestic regimes of specific states and the prevailing character and modus operandi of the international political and economic systems. This has been especially true for modern Japan. Accordingly, any effort to understand the dynamics of Japan's contemporary domestic politics (as well as its foreign policy) must encompass the international context within which the Japanese live. Analyzing the foreign policy–making process in its historical and international contexts yields several unconventional conclusions: (1) skepticism (rather than rose-tinted optimism) about Japan's capacity to participate fully and effectively in international affairs because of the character of its elitist democracy; (2) the enormous degree to which Japan's international role is dependent on international conditions beyond the easy reach of policymakers in Tokyo, and (3) the unique importance of the U.S.-Japan relationshp in defining Tokyo's role in the world and of recent fundamental political changes emanating from the U.S. side.

Since World War II, three extraordinary and integrally related circumstances have muted the impact of Japanese internal politics on foreign policy: the U.S. alliance, the continuous rule by a conservative elite, and a policy consensus on national purpose limited to economic development. The hegemonic alliance with the United States has not only spared the Japanese the material and psychological costs of participating in power politics, but assured them access to the free-trade bloc of the Western alliance while allowing them to restrict access to their own economy. The unbroken dominance of the conservative political elite (Liberal Democratic Party [LDP] politicians, upper-echelon bureaucrats, and leaders of the business world) created a stable configuration of political power—an elitist democracy that minimized the impact of domestically generated political pressures on the conduct of foreign policy.

These two conditions were critical to Japan's remarkable economic achievements and permitted the implementation of a long-term foreign policy consensus (sometimes designated the Yoshida Doctrine) that called for the separation of politics and economics and for the pursuit of unidimensional "economic diplomacy." Implemented under what Chalmers Johnson has called a "plan rational" governmental arrangement,[2] Japan's record of international achievement since 1952 is rightly seen as a brilliantly successful example of a "neo-mercantilist" foreign policy.

The continued success of this policy, however, depends not only on calculations by governmental leaders in Tokyo, but also on the persistence of an international greenhouse within which controlled choices can be made. However, the U.S.-Japan alliance, which provided the environment for controlled choices, has been significantly eroded by a series of crises beginning in the early 1970s—the collapse of the Bretton Woods monetary system, the Nixon "shocks," the oil crisis, the U.S. defeat in Vietnam, the chronic and enormous U.S. bilateral trade deficits, and the relative decline in the United States as the pre-eminent global economic power. At the same time, the political foundations of conservative rule in Japan have been complicated by problems of generational change, the persistence of factionalism within the LDP, and an apolitical national mood generated by prosperity.[3] These changes have not yet led to major alterations in either the domestic or the international position of Japan, but they have contributed to an ongoing debate over the future national purpose of Japan—whether to replace or modify the Yoshida Doctrine (see the paper by Pyle in this volume).

Because the future shape of Japanese foreign policy–making is unlikely to be simply an extension of the past, it seems appropriate to identify the forest before examining the trees. That is, before reviewing the capabilities and limitations of the Japanese political system in formulating foreign policy during the past three decades, it is necessary to delineate—from a fresh perspective and in a way that facilitates comparison with other nations—the fundamental structure and dynamics of the Japanese political system itself.

Japan as an Elitist Democracy

Japan is an elitist democracy. So, too, are all other modern "democratic" nations; the exigencies of life in an industrial, interdependent, and nuclear age require that crucial political decisions be made by a small number of leaders at and around the apex of government. What is distinctive about elitist democracy in Japan is its deep historical and cultural roots and the peculiarly effective web of connections—personal, economic, legal, social, political, and cultural—that circumscribe recruitment into the elite, define relations among its members, and regulate interaction with the masses (the society at large).

The scholarly consensus is that from the Meiji Restoration until the end of World War II, the Japanese political system was explicitly an elitist democracy and that government policies and institutions mobilized the citizens around the various themes of Japanese nationalism. Despite some notable exceptions, however, analyses of postwar Japan and speculations concerning the future shape of Japanese society have overwhelmingly been based on a pluralist-democratic model. Studies stress the fragmentation of power throughout the society and the central importance of public opinion and elections as determinants of government actions, but downplay the hold of culture and of nationalism and the highly visible elitist component of Japanese politics.

Despite the prevalence of pluralism as an ideology and as an analytical model among empirical American political scientists, many of the most noted political and social theorists in the West during the past half-century (for example, Joseph Schumpeter, Karl Mannheim, Harold Lasswell, Giovanni Sartori, John Plamenatz) find this version of political reality incomplete. Although their approaches vary in detail, all of these scholars find some kind of elitist pluralism the most appropriate framework for describing and analyzing modern democracies. Although they offer different analytical insights on the dynamics of modern society, all share a profound skepticism about the capacity of the masses to participate effectively in democratic government. Most would agree with Sartori that "distrust and fear of elites is an anachronism that blinds us to the problem of the future . . . that democracy may destroy its own leaders (. . . by electing mediocrities), thereby creating conditions for their replacement by undemocratic counter elites."[4]

If elitism is a central component of modern Western societies, then surely it is a feature of Japanese politics, with its cultural and historical legacies of hierarchy and nationalism. Accordingly, to evaluate the present and future impact of Japanese domestic politics on foreign policy, we must begin by delineating the broad features of the Japanese species of elitist democracy.

Elitism and statism have been conspicuous throughout the history of modern Japanese politics. The Meiji "aristocratic revolution" and the emperor system, which prevailed until 1945, are prototypes of what Western elite theorists such as Gaetano Mosca believed was essential for a nation: "to transform itself continually without falling apart" in the face of the revolutionary social changes and ideologies unleashed by the industrial age. Together, elitist and democratic principles and institutions assured restraint among elite groups and helped recruit new elites (representing new social forces in the society) while preserving the policy autonomy of the state. This process also involved furthering the international interests of the various nations.[5] In the case of Japan, international interests focused on catching up with the West. The collapse of the first version of Japanese elitist democracy in the late 1920s and 1930s involved not only a breakdown in the balance among the members of the elite coalition (the military, the political parties, the bureaucracy, and business), but an unprecedentedly severe international economic smashup, which then led to the radicalization of foreign policy.

The second, postwar, version of Japanese elitist democracy involves a balance between two discrete components, the highly democratic values and institutions embodied in the U.S.-authored constitution of 1947 and the Japanese values and practices that have persisted and flourished throughout the postwar era. Because this is truly the age of democracy and equalitarianism, because the excesses of militarism and defeat thoroughly discredited the prewar system, and because political institutions were explicitly democratic, the continuities between prewar and postwar Japanese politics (especially the elitist component) have been downplayed or ignored.[6]

Even a cursory inspection of the extensive scholarly literature on elitism, however, shows that it is extremely helpful in understanding the dynamics of postwar Japanese politics. The central role of the state in leading society, the remarkable continuity of traditional values and social structure in the face of sweeping economic change, the persistent importance of nationalism (especially cultural and economic nationalism), and the actual and theoretical compatibility of elitism and democracy resonate with generalizations by theorists of elitism such as Joseph Schumpeter.

Schumpeter (and others) stress the remarkable persistence of traditional values and social structures in the political systems of Europe in the throes of industrialization.[7] For him (as well as for Mosca), not only are democracy and elitism compatible, but their conjunction was a natural feature in the development of nonsocialist societies, one that was conducive to the preservation of liberty.[8] The classical liberal concept of democracy saw the self-realization of individuals as the essential end of the state, but for Schumpeter democracy is simply a "political method . . . a certain type of institutional arrangement for arriving at political decisions."[9] This is a startlingly appropriate description not only of the prewar emperor system but also of the modus operandi of the U.S.-conceived political order under which the Japanese have operated since World War II. Democratic components of Japanese politics have expanded and flourished since 1945, but not surprisingly, these developments have occurred side by side with elitist components.

Social change obviously has resulted in alterations in the political system and in the composition of the elite itself. "Circulation of elites" within Japanese society has created the elite meritocracy that is a conspicuous and much praised feature of modern Japanese politics.[10] Elite power in Japan is restrained not simply by the nature of relations with the masses, the institutional framework, or the balance of political forces within the elite, but also by an "elite consensus" regarding *both* the basic aims of national policy and the process of leadership through which this will occur.[11] In other words, because of the dual character (democratic and elitist) of Japanese politics, the dynamics of policymaking is extremely complex. It involves not only the balance of political forces at the moment and the immediate substantive policy considerations, but also encompasses the national political myth (democracy, the emperor system) that legitimates the way in which the elite leads the masses. In prewar Japan, the competition over the proper foreign policy between military and party leaders also involved the structure of the political system and the ideology of nationalism. Today the issue is whether the current political system can build a consensus that goes beyond the economic nationalism embodied in the Yoshida Doctrine to encompass a political and strategic posture that is domestically palatable and internationally acceptable. Consequently, an elitist approach to the dynamics of the postwar system places the record of the past three decades in a perspective that enormously facilitates considerations of the future international role of Japan and bares the dilemma within the Japanese system.

Because my primary purpose here is to analyze the structure and dynamics of Japan's domestic politics in terms of its impact on the formulation of foreign policy, the components of Japan's elitist democracy need to be sketched only in very broad strokes. There are three critical questions regarding the Japanese political system. First, what limitations does the comprehensive and personalized character of the elite that has grown up over the past four decades impose on a major shift in foreign policy? Second, in what ways will the democratic components of the political system affect the capacity of Japan to adopt a new and more orthodox international political role? Finally, how and in what ways has the international system affected the nature of Japanese domestic politics in the past and what are the implications for the future?

Japan is a functional elitist society, with those in power having a relationship to the citizenry that is benign and legitimate, not adversarial and exploitative. The pre-eminent role of the bureaucracy (especially the Ministry of Finance and the Ministry of International Trade and Industry) in formulating national policy and as a recruiting ground for conservative party leaders has rightly been seen as the most important component of the governmental process throughout much of the postwar era. It is only a part, however, and elitism in Japan goes beyond the functional dominance of this group in policymaking and recruitment of political leaders.[12] Individual access to the bureaucracy is overwhelmingly dependent on success in the world's most competitive and most structured educational system. Moreover, the prestige and status of working in the government (especially the elite ministries) have assured that the "best and brightest" move from the education ladder into government service.

Success in this meritocratic recruitment process is then supplemented by other practices that consolidate and personalize elite leadership. One of the practices central to this process is the arrangement of marriages among the offspring of upper ranks in the business, bureaucratic, and political worlds. The extent to which brokered or "quasi-brokered" marriages assures an overlap of personal and professional careers is manifested in an astonishing web of personal connections among the elite and has contributed to a continuity in leadership without parallel in the contemporary Western world.[13] One noteworthy by-product is the extent to which family ties are transformed into political capital; fully a third of all LDP Diet members are sons of former LDP Diet members.[14]

Other formal and informal practices that have assumed institutional and quasi-institutional forms since 1945 and that have helped consolidate the ruling group in Japan are better known. For example, *amakudari* ("descent from heaven") refers to the reemployment of bureaucrats in business and public corporations after they leave the government. The practice is found in other societies, but on nowhere near the same scale.[15] Other notable extra-institutional practices that surround and sustain the formal policymaking activities of the government include the extensive financial ties between businessmen and corporations and the conservative party (and its factions) and the semiformal relationship between the standing committees of the Federation of Economic Organizations (Keidanren) and the various ministries. The brilliant success of Japan's economic foreign policies can be understood only by placing the formal governmental processes within the context of this broader, informal, personalized, and culturally circumscribed elite system.

The capacities of such an elitist system to devise and implement coherent national economic policy in a flexible and effective way is universally acknowledged. But there are limitations. Perhaps the clearest is a functional limitation rooted in the fact that an astonishingly high proportion of the elite is cut from the economic-bureaucratic cloth. A technocratic elite is equipped to deal with internal and international problems of a peaceful and prosperous world, but not with the problems of a world in which politics and conflict are conspicuous features of domestic or international affairs. A second limitation arises from the comprehensive web of informal, personal, and cultural considerations that delimit membership in the elite, as well as the extended length of Japanese prosperity. The elite of Japan should be viewed not simply as the configuration of political and economic power of the moment but rather as an organic part of Japanese society.

Accordingly, for Japan to move to an expanded and political role in the world would, of necessity, involve more than a policy change. First, it would entail a redefinition of national purpose and a change in the assumption that the special economic interests of the elite ministries and the business world are identical with Japan's national interest. The newly established consensus would have to fulfill domestic nationalist aspirations and meet the needs of the international political system. Second, a Japanese foreign policy like that of an ordinary country (with greater symmetry between the economic and political dimensions of its international role) would entail an institutional revolution and challenge the institutional and informal practices sanctified by decades of success in purely economic matters and the web of personal ties that sustains the system. The tasks of redefining national purpose and undergoing an institutional revolution make internally generated change unlikely short of a major economic or political upheaval.

The challenge for Japan today is not unlike that faced by English society on the eve of World War I and American society in the late 1920s. It may properly be called a "peril of prosperity." This peril encompasses, among other things, a systemic inertia seen in the inability of the elite to recognize the need for a fundamental change in policy (especially vis-à-vis other nations), an inability worsened by institutional and procedural rigidities. Ironically, the centrality of the elitist component of contemporary Japanese politics to the nation's success during four decades of peace and prosperity impedes the capacity for fundamental change in foreign policy. If the elitist dimension is constraining, what then is the impact of public opinion, pressure groups, political parties, and the other democratic accoutrements of policymaking on the capacity of Japan to play a broadened role in the world?

Democracy and Foreign Policy

Japanese politics has a strong democratic as well as elitist component, and the history of the past four decades demonstrates how conflict, change, and political competition have flourished side by side with functional elitism. Many of the excellent recent studies of politics in Japan see the essence of the system as a kind of democratic (or "patterned") pluralism in which policy emerges as the product of a continuous process of interaction and compromise among competing groups, especially in elections.[16]

Although they vary on details, those who view Japan as a democratic-pluralist society share a belief that economic prosperity and political competition within the constitutional framework have constituted a process of "democratic homogenization." The main results of this process are seen to be (1) the attenuation or dissolution of cultural and ideological predispositions—creating individuals who are interest oriented and rational calculators—and (2) the creation of a number of diverse social and political groups who, through competition with each other, direct political pressure, and participation in elections, are critically decisive in establishing the direction of policy.

This approach is fully appropriate for one level of analysis of the Japanese political system, especially for understanding the twists and turns of electoral and interest group politics in the short run. It is clearly premature, however, to suggest that Japan has reached a state of democratic development that renders obsolete the elitist and statist elements of its political tradition—especially since the political system has evolved within an international greenhouse and has yet to experience a change in regime.

One feature of the institutional framework of the current political system creates a latent structural tension between the democratic and elitist elements of the society. The prime minister, in fact as well as institutionally, has primacy in decision making regarding major foreign policy issues. Some prime ministers (for example, Ichiro Hatoyama regarding the peace agreement with the Soviet Union in 1956 and Nobusuke Kishi regarding the security treaty with the United States in 1960) have used their office to force through policies. More important, a strong and articulate prime minister is positioned to circumvent the business-bureaucratic elements of the elite by appealing directly to the people to gain support for a bold new foreign policy with a political, presumably nationalist, appeal. As discussed below with regard to Prime Minister Nakasone, any such appeal not only would involve a shift in policy but also would pose a challenge to the basic modus operandi of the elitist-democratic political system—and could succeed only in the most extreme circumstances.

Public opinion in Japan, as in all Western societies,[17] has a very modest impact on the conduct of foreign policy. Many scholarly and almost all journalistic accounts of Japanese politics, however, exaggerate the importance of opinion polls (especially on matters of defense and nuclear weapons) and the largely oppositional views of the mass media in defining the perimeters of Japan's international role. This exaggeration is partly rooted in the appeal of democratic ideals and slogans first nurtured during the Occupation. Because public opinion provides a direct link between the people and specific political decisions, it seems to exemplify a basic democratic procedure and at the same time dignify these individuals by projecting them immediately into the governmental process.

Beyond the moral attractiveness of an influential populace, the exaggerated importance accorded public opinion in foreign policy is rooted in a somewhat simplistic and undifferentiated approach to the role of opinions in policy formulation. In assessing the role of the public, we must distinguish between "mass opinion" and "articulate opinion."[18] Mass opinion, or "the mass mood," includes broad and loosely structured opinions such as nationalism and isolationism as well as cultural and ethnic biases (for example, Japanese attitudes toward Koreans). It influences policymakers as part of the prevailing political and cultural climate of opinion (that is, it provides the context within which political leaders instinctively operate) and through the cumulative impact of overwhelmingly popular trends manifested in elections, polls, and the temper of the political dialogue.

The mass mood is important only in those few decisions that are of both dramatic and far-reaching significance, such as an immediate threat of war, but normally it has only an uncertain and indirect impact on governmental decision making. One reason for this is that the overwhelming majority of the public is uninformed about and indifferent to all but a few foreign policy issues. Pollsters normally create opinions by asking questions that respondents have never considered until they are asked.[19] This extreme lack of awareness and the amorphous nature of mass opinion assures that the public plays a passive role in the foreign policy–making process and that the Japanese government (that is, the current elite) has wide latitude for policy leadership.[20]

Articulate opinion, which consists of overt expressions on foreign policy issues by groups, individuals, and the mass media, does exert influence through direct access to decision makers (either through persuasive appeals or violent demonstrations) and by structuring the public debate on policy. Because the opposition parties have not been in power since 1948, the full range of their activities regarding foreign affairs can be seen as one dimension of articulate opinion. Moreover, with few exceptions, the mass media (especially the newspapers) remain part of an oppositional subculture chronically opposed to official policy. The existence of these forms of opposition are commonly and correctly cited as conspicuous democratic departures from the prewar Japanese political system.

However, the critical question is Has the existence of these groups been translated into influence on foreign policy? In all democratic politics, what ultimately determines the effect on policy of publicly articulated opinions is the responsiveness of decision makers to the public, a responsiveness dictated as much by the personalities of the leaders and the elite political culture as by the immediate political exigencies of the situation. The postwar political history of Japan suggests that government leaders react only to the most extreme demands of public opinion, especially regarding major foreign policy issues.[21] Nor is this likely to change unless there is a sharp change in the electoral strength of the parties. This means that Japanese decision makers, like those in the United States and other Western democracies, have wide latitude for policy maneuvering and leadership regarding foreign affairs.

In summary, the role of the public in shaping Japanese foreign policy has been and is likely to remain quite modest. Foreign economic policy has been successful because it has been kept almost wholly in the hands of the technocrats of the ruling elite and outside domestic politics.[22] The timing and substance of the critical political-strategic foreign policy decisions since 1952 have been in the control of the political elite, primarily the leaders of the conservative party. To be sure, public opinion and the opposition parties did shape the processes by which the decisions were made and the careers of the incumbent prime minister, but Japanese foreign policy, like that in other "open" societies, was neither directed nor significantly modulated by participation of the masses.

Indeed, one of the unsolved dilemmas of modern democracy is bringing meaningful, "democratic" participation in line with the responsibility of government to act in a rapid, decisive, and informed way in times of political-strategic crises. One of the ironies of the current democratic-equalitarian age is that the complex and changeable nature of the international political economy assures that effective control of foreign policy rests in the hands of government leaders. It is the Japanese elite that holds the responsibility for charting the nation's course in the world.

One of the more striking results of examining postwar Japan as an elitist democracy rather than as a pluralist democracy is analytical because it essentially reverses the most common approaches of scholars and commentators. Yasusuke Murakami's 1983 work *Shin chūkan daishi no jidai* (The age of the new middle mass), one of the most original and insightful books on postwar Japanese politics, exemplifies the socioeconomic approach at its best. From this analytical approach, which Sheldon Wolin has aptly labeled "the sublimation of politics,"[23] politics is seen as causally rooted in socioeconomic change. Therefore, analysis focuses on the ways in which the political attitudes and behavior of the public are derived from the current structure of society. What is important is societal change, and political leadership is cast largely in terms of response to these changes.

A second and more common analytical perspective is what can be called the "barefoot-descriptive" approach. Scholars in this school deal in a straightforward way with the most visible features of the Japanese political process (the relative strength of the parties, factional struggles, the personalities of leaders, the impact of public opinion and pressure groups), primarily through case studies or general descriptions of political systems.[24] Although such studies have enormously broadened understanding of the political process, they rarely try to see the whole as anything more than the sum of its parts and simply do not generate the kind of questions appropriate to a political system that (despite its stability) has experienced truly fundamental and revolutionary change since 1945.

In view of the scope of economic change that has occurred within the framework of political institutions devised by an occupying nation whose main purpose was to assure discontinuity with the past, the most distinctive feature of postwar Japanese politics has been the remarkable continuity, coherence, and effectiveness of the leadership the nation has had. It is this aspect of the system that deserves the most scrutiny.[25] Accordingly it is more appropriate to concentrate on the architectonic capacities of Japanese leaders; that is, to see mass political behavior as reflecting the inducements of those holding political authority rather than the other way around.[26] From this viewpoint, it is the political elite (not amorphous public opinion or an emergent social class) that will have to revise or replace the foreign policy consensus called the Yoshida Doctrine.

Japanese Politics and the International System

From the time Japan entered the modern world, the international system has had an extraordinary and enormous impact not only on Japanese foreign policy but on Japanese domestic politics. In an important sense, Japan was and is a passive actor, responding to the shifting configurations of international political power, adjusting to the changing distribution of economic activity and wealth, and adopting the prevailing international political mores (constitutionalism and imperialism in the prewar period, democracy and hegemonic alliance since World War II) that fit the needs of a resource-poor late arrival on the global scene.

The extreme degree of economic interdependence of the nation, especially with chronically unstable Third World nations, as well as the grossly underdeveloped capacities of the Japanese to develop an effective political-strategic role, make the nation extremely vulnerable to shifts in international conditions. Because the web of Japanese international economic ties is so large and so strong and because the nation is unusually dependent on the drift of international events beyond the control of its policymakers, it is doubtful that Japan can continue to remain aloof from power politics in a fluid, nation-centered world—especially since the capacity of both superpowers to project power has receded in relative terms on all levels except the nuclear.

Indeed, the two issues that are likely to remain at the center of Japanese foreign policy in the decade ahead, rearmament and nationalism, are likely to find their genesis in relations between Japan and the external world rather than in the dynamics of internal politics. This "outside-in" pattern of policy development contrasts with the prewar system and is abetted by the peculiar character of the postwar elitist democracy. Should, however, Japan be drawn more fully into the political-security dimension of international affairs, the monochromatic economic character of the postwar elite must be fundamentally altered.

One international relationship, the U.S. alliance, has totally overshadowed all others since World War II, and it holds the key to the future direction of Japanese foreign policy.

Domestic Politics and the American Greenhouse

Throughout the postwar period, Japan has flourished in an international greenhouse that was almost totally "made in America." The seven-year occupation was initially conceived as a multinational operation, but with General MacArthur in charge, these years have rightly come to be known as Japan's American interlude. The price for returning to international affairs included alliance with the United States in the cold war under a security treaty that effectively made Japan a defense satellite of the United States. This treaty (only slightly modified in 1960), the "no war" clause of the constitution, a U.S. policy that involved deployment of conventional and nuclear forces in East Asia, and U.S. participation in the Korean and Vietnam wars have kept Japan from real participation in international politics for almost four decades.

To be sure, foreign policy issues did feature prominently in electoral politics and in intraparty disputes throughout this era, but Japan alone among the major states was spared the material and psychological costs of active participation in power politics. That this period involved war, revolution, and continuous tension in East Asia only underscores the extraordinary and artificial character of this aspect of Japanese politics. The isolationist pacifism of Japan was not simply the product of unusually prudent or moral policies of the government; it was essentially the result of U.S. policy and international developments over which the Japanese had no control.

The extraordinary isolation of Japan from international turmoil contributed much to the internal political stability of the country during these decades. Most obviously, Japan was spared the divisiveness and disharmony that beset not only the United States but all other major nations actively involved in international affairs. Those few times when Japan did make modest but significant foreign policy choices (the Soviet-Japanese peace agreement, the revision of the U.S. security treaty) invariably touched off a political crisis and led to the political demise of the prime minister. Thus, as will be subsequently elaborated below, on those few occasions when the doors of the international greenhouse did open, the health of the Japanese political system itself was affected.

International political isolation did contribute to the economic prosperity of the country. Free from the uncertainties and challenges of political choices in foreign policy, the Japanese government found it much easier to develop and sustain a policy consensus focused first on economic growth and then on welfare—both of which had immediate and favorable domestic political payoffs. A single-minded concern with the social and economic well-being of its citizens is a luxury that no other major advanced industrial country could afford. During the 1950s, 1960s, and 1970s, all industrialized nations of the West (including West Germany) spent an average of 4.5 per cent to 9.0 per cent of their GNP for defense, whereas Japan averaged roughly 1.0 per cent. According to one authoritative estimate, had the level of Japanese defense expenditures roughly equaled the average of the Western nations during this period, by 1974 the size of Japan's economy would have been 30 percent less than it was.[27] Moreover, Japan benefited substantially in economic terms from the Korean and Vietnam wars and from the U.S. policy of procuring military supplies in East Asia to sustain U.S. military forces in the region. In fact, the economic shot-in-the-arm provided by U.S. expenditures in the Korean war initiated the momentum that led to the ensuing decades of economic growth. Finally, as part of the global effort to contain communism, the United States provided more than $2 billion in aid to shore up its main ally in the Pacific, gave Japan access to the U.S. market without insisting on reciprocity, and led the way to bring the Japanese into the Western economic bloc and the host of supporting international institutions. Consequently, in ways that are rarely noted, the security policy of the United States was critical to the economic prosperity of Japan and in this way, facilitated the stability and health of Japanese politics.

To be sure Japanese policy choices did contribute to the international incubator in which the country flourished. Throughout the 1970s, there was notably little evidence of fundamental differences among the elite over policy toward the United States because of the singular advantages of this arrangement and the personal deference to and respect for the United States by a generation for whom defeat in war and occupation were still vivid memories. The essential factor in keeping Japan outside international politics was, however, U.S. policy and the extraordinary international conditions that prevailed for more than three decades after World War II.

Japan was and still remains essentially a passive actor on the world political stage, more a trading company than a nation-state, a nation without a foreign policy in the usual sense of the word. It is critical to keep this in mind when reviewing the pattern of internal politics in postwar Japan since many of the extraordinary but purely domestic features of Japanese politics would not have developed outside this international greenhouse. Because of profound changes in the global political-economic conditions and in bilateral relations, the durability of the greenhouse is now in serious doubt.

U.S. Domestic Politics and Bilateral Relations

Before considering the impact of Japan's domestic politics on its foreign policy, some attention must be accorded the most important international reality shaping the Japanese role in the world, the degree to which bilateral relations have been caught up in U.S. domestic politics.[28] Congress and interest groups working primarily through Congress have more or less set the policy agenda since bilateral economic crises surfaced in the late 1970s. One way of understanding the evolution of U.S. policy toward Japan and its place in Japan's foreign policy–making process is to analyze this issue within the broader context of U.S. foreign policy since the onset of the cold war.

From the late 1940s, U.S. policy toward Japan was a central aspect of the strategic doctrine of containment. It was the perceived threat of the Soviet Union that led to a reversal of the initial idealism of the Occupation in order to pave the way for Japan to become an ally of the United States. As a result of the communist triumph in China and the Korean war, Asia was brought fully into the cold war. Accordingly, the San Francisco peace treaty was concerned as much with assuring Japanese alliance with the United States as with liquidating the legacies of World War II. The U.S.-Japan Mutual Security Treaty of 1951, together with a series of other security treaties signed in rapid succession (ANZUS, 1951; U.S.–Republic of the Philippines, 1951, U.S.–Republic of Korea, 1952, U.S.–Republic of China, 1954; and SEATO, 1954), was part of a general policy of containing communism on a global level. Because most discussions of bilateral Japanese-American relations tend to emphasize the special nature of the relationship and the enormous consequences of the Occupation for Japan, it is instructive to note that from the perspective of Washington, Japan was but a part, albeit an important part, of the U.S. policy of containment. The impact of U.S. domestic politics on its Japan policy must be understood within the context of the strategic consensus of the cold war.

The cold war consensus was not so much concurrence on detailed policies as a general ideological agreement shared by the general public on the one hand and the informed foreign policy elite, including those responsible for making and implementing policy, on the other hand. It was as much a consensus about who should make policy (the president and his advisers) and the procedures through which policy debate should move as it was an agreement about the substance of policy. There were two policy themes: to contain communism by any means required in order to create a peaceful and democratic world order and to promote international economic well-being through free trade (and aid). Both of these themes were rooted in the ideals of the U.S. diplomatic tradition, especially Wilsonian liberalism, and were facilitated by the global military and economic paramountcy to which the United States fell heir after World War II.[29] The specific policies that grew out of this consensus led to 25 years of Pax Americana and widespread and unprecedented economic growth in a U.S.-dominated world economy.

Of particular interest for our purposes is how this consensus shaped the process by which specific policies, such as those regarding Japan, were made. Because the consensus focused on national purpose, which above all related to the use of military force, those institutions in the government responsible for the establishment of national security goals, notably the Office of the President, the Department of Defense, and the Department of State, played the critical roles. In performing their roles, these institutions were effectively insulated from the pressure of partisan politics and domestic economic pressure groups.

The situation was analogous to a time of war—bipartisan support for the national interest was defined in specific terms by the president and his men. Congress played a purely advisory role, and the most prestigious congressional committee during this time, the Senate Foreign Relations Committee, served primarily as a conduit for explaining and defending policies formulated in the executive branch. What was devised was not just a set of individual policies; each of these policies was related to a national strategy ("containment") and was justified in terms of grand national purpose. It was a confident articulation of the universal relevance of the United States' national values *and* material interests. Our foreign policy, in the words of George Kennan, involved "a firm and unapologetic insistence on respect for our national dignity, not just as something we owe to ourselves, but as something we owe to our own possibilities for world usefulness." [30]

As long as policymakers and the general public accepted a strategic vision, the presidency was the institution that dominated foreign policy–making. In addition to the personality of the president, the policy professionals who personally advised him and others who held critical cabinet and subcabinet roles in the foreign policy departments and agencies played central roles in establishing national policy. There developed a continuum in policymaking that blurred the distinction between the public and private sectors. The government bore the responsibility for policies appropriate for the day-to-day conduct of diplomacy, but there was almost continuous review of the long-term strategies and objectives of the United States by organizations such as the Council on Foreign Relations and private institutions like the Rockefeller and Ford foundations. Their studies produced ideas that readily found a hearing within the government, and they served as a recruiting ground for the best and the brightest. Dean Rusk, McGeorge Bundy, Walt Rostow, Henry Kissinger, Cyrus Vance, and Zbigniew Brzezinski are but a few of the more visible recruits from these activities of the Eastern foreign policy establishment. This blending of knowledge and talent to establish and implement long-term national security policies does have some broad similarities to the now much-admired (and feared) system purportedly used by Japan to achieve its remarkable record of economic growth. In any event, during this era of consensus, the primary impact for U.S. domestic politics on foreign policy (beyond electing the president) came from the personalities and ideas of the foreign policy elite and the government officials who implemented the policies.

Throughout the 1960s, the international economic policy of the United States was, in the words of Marina Whitman, "primarily a stepchild of our national security objectives." The Marshall Plan and other aid programs, the posture of the United States in trade negotiations, the dollar-centered monetary system, and eventually the chronic trade deficits were all justified in terms of containing communist aggression. Accordingly, "the United States was frequently willing to subordinate its short-term economic interests, narrowly conceived, to long-term political and economic advantages of strengthening economies in other free-world nations and a viable trading and monetary system linking those nations."[31]

This approach to foreign policy, which subordinated specific economic interests to a clearly articulated general national interest, virtually eliminated the capacity of specific businesses and pressure groups to work through Congress and congressional committees to achieve limited economic benefits for themselves.[32] The intrusion of domestic interest groups into the conduct of foreign policy was further inhibited by the global economic paramountcy of the United States and the strong commitment to the doctrine of free trade.

The unraveling of the substance of this policy consensus and the domestic political practices on which it rested began with the Vietnam war. As frustration with the war escalated, the issue of national security was dragged into the maelstrom of domestic politics in ways that radically changed how the system worked.

The most important casualty of the war (and of the Watergate scandal, which was integrally linked to the domestic political turmoil caused by the war) was the capacity of the president to provide unquestioned leadership in foreign policy. Congress moved from being a largely passive supporter of the White House to being a focal point for opposition to foreign policy. It demanded an expanded and direct role in foreign policy–making and in 1973 passed the War Powers Act, which sought to curtail the capacity of the president to deploy troops abroad. In addition, doubts concerning the credibility and integrity of successive presidents were raised in extravagantly unrestricted terms by the media (for example, in the Pentagon papers incident) and also by the public at large—through disruptive demonstrations and acts of civil disobedience. Although these legal and existential limitations on presidential actions have been greatly attenuated by time, the presidents since Nixon have neither displayed bold leadership in foreign affairs nor developed a comprehensive and coherent strategic vision to replace the cold war consensus.

This lack of a new consensus partly results from the fragmentation and disarray that beset the foreign policy elite in the 1960s and 1970s and that still persists. Although many members of this elite did serve in the Carter administration (especially those connected with the Trilateral Commission), the critical task of defining a new strategic vision, and in this way laying the foundation for a new national consensus, has been largely abandoned. Indeed, in 1978 a high-ranking official in the State Department asserted: "The Carter approach to foreign policy rests on a belief that not only is the world far too complex to be reduced to a doctrine, but there is something inherently wrong with a doctrine at all."[33]

This view, that it is neither possible nor desirable to have a consensus, has found frequent expression among leading foreign policy intellectuals and marks the end of the serious efforts at long-term national security planning by institutions in the private sector.[34] No comparable group has replaced them either inside or outside of government. Lacking a coherent and realistic concept of national purpose, U.S. policy has drifted without clear priorities from one international crisis to another and has sought legitimacy behind undifferentiated assertions of themes from the early cold war consensus ("human rights" in the case of Carter, and "communist military containment" in the case of Reagan). For the moment, one of the most important positive influences of domestic politics on the direction of foreign affairs seen in the era of consensus has been lost.

At the same time that the heat of the Vietnam war was melting the consensus on national security, the economic component of the national consensus was dissolving as well. Various factors, some international and some related to the performance of the domestic economy, were involved: the gradual decline in the importance of the United States in the world economy; the severe costs to certain sectors (initially steel and textiles) of increased imports; repercussions from the collapse of the dollar-centered Bretton Woods monetary system; the oil crises; and the decline in U.S. economic performance, leading to trade disputes in the late 1970s and massive, seemingly chronic, trade deficits, which have made the United States a debtor nation for the first time in more than seventy years. The cumulative impact of these events had important results. First, the willingness of the government to sacrifice immediate economic interests at home on behalf of international economic stability was effectively erased. Second, qualified economic nationalism (fair trade not free trade) came to replace the virtually unconditioned free-trade commitment. Finally, as the foreign policy consensus disappeared, domestic politics became deeply entangled in international economic policy as various interest groups pursuing narrowly defined goals were able to work effectively through Congress and various government departments to shape policy. By 1980, the domestic political system had become the critical variable in most U.S. foreign policy decisions, and internal political pressures had contributed significantly to the linking of economic and national security issues.

U.S. Policy Toward Japan

From the perspective of Washington, until approximately 1970 U.S. policy toward Japan was a model of success—an example of how the American cold war consensus could be translated into a specific policy triumph. The Occupation had laid the basis for the democratization of the country, and this was then buttressed by a hegemonic alliance (effectively making Japan a U.S. defense satellite) and an astonishing prosperity, which was fostered within the international economic bloc dominated by the United States. Bilateral relations appeared prominently on the agenda of U.S. domestic politics only twice, at the time of the 1951 San Francisco Conference, which ended the war and established the security treaty as a preface to terminating the Occupation, and in 1960, when the Security treaty was renewed and President Eisenhower's visit to Tokyo was canceled because of Japanese demonstrations. These were, however, merely episodes in a quarter century of relations, and both were successfully resolved. In aggregate, the Japanese-U.S. alliance was a prototype of what the United States wanted to achieve in its diplomacy toward its allies. It was consensus foreign policy at its best.

Several operating features of this alliance are particularly worthy of note in terms of their relation to U.S. domestic politics. First, in large part because the issues involving Japan were of such little controversy or consequence against the *Strum und Drang* of war and confrontation that characterized these decades in international affairs, they were insulated from the turmoil of both partisan and pressure group politics. Decisions were handled almost entirely by the professional diplomats and foreign policy specialists in the State Department, the White House, and the Defense Department. In insulating economic issues from the growing pressures of interest groups in the late 1960s, the foreign policy professionals linked economics to politics and insisted that primacy lay with the grand, politically defined goals of the cold war. There are many examples of the State Department's or the White House's interceding in congressional hearings and invoking the obligations of the United States to its main ally in the Pacific to prevent a particular industry from gaining protection from imports. Indeed, the Japanese lobby in Washington (legally registered groups and individuals representing the interests of Japan) remained remarkably small, and the Japanese embassy was extraordinarily dependent on the State Department for representing its interests in the governmental process.[35]

As long as the domestic consensus remained in place and the United

States was the pre-eminent actor on the global stage, this arrangement worked well. However, a gap developed between U.S. domestic politics and policy toward Japan, which steadily widened in the early years of the 1970s and sowed the seeds for the subsequent intense politicization of Japanese policy.

The year 1971 is a landmark in postwar Japanese-U.S. relations, delimiting the honeymoon years of the cold war consensus from the era of recurring crises and uncertainty. It was the year of the two Nixon shocks to bilateral relations, with each shock representing a separate dimension of the alliance. The announcement in July 1971 that the United States had secretly cultivated an opening to China and that the president himself would visit Beijing stunned the Japanese, who had long claimed a special relationship with the Chinese and at the same time loyally supported the U.S. position on Taiwan. What was significant about this action was not the diplomatic affront to Tokyo or the short-term policy implications. Rather, it served as a graphic illustration of what presidential leadership in foreign policy could be. The decision to open relations with China was a strategic decision in the fullest sense of the word, a calculated move away from the doctrine of containment toward détente. It was a policy that the Japanese would like to have initiated, but it required a style of leadership that was clearly beyond the Japanese political system.

The second shock, an economic package that forced revaluation of the yen and the imposition of quotas on Japanese textile exports to the United States illustrated how economically generated domestic political pressures were directly shaping trade policy. The shock was the culmination of a series of events that began with a 1968 campaign promise by then-candidate Richard Nixon to Southern textile interests to establish quotas on imports from Japan. This was followed by a communication breakdown between President Nixon and Prime Minister Eisaku Sato over such quotas and a fiasco in which the Japanese directly negotiated an abortive settlement with Democratic Congressman Wilbur Mills *without* the knowledge of the White House.[36] All of this took place against the background of growing concern over the mounting bilateral trade deficit and the overall deterioration of the international economic status of the United States.

Again, the importance of the shock lies not so much in its immediate effect (it did force revaluation of the yen and the imposition of quotas), but in its inauguration of a still ongoing period in which bilateral relations center on economic conflicts. In terms of their impact on U.S. politics, these conflicts have worked like an inkblot. Issues concerning economic relations with Japan have progressively become embroiled in congressional and bureaucratic politics in Washington and in the increasingly aggressive and uncompromising activities of business and labor lobbies seeking various forms of protection to redress narrow and specific grievances. A polarized debate has developed among policy intellectuals centering on the issue "Should Japan be emulated, bashed, or both?" Japan was at the center of the controversy in the early 1980s over the need for a U.S. "industrial policy," which was seen essentially as an antidote to the international economic challenge. As the issues of relations moved more widely and deeply into U.S. politics, the overall problem became increasingly distorted and intractable.

Around 1970, Japan moved from being a special case on the international scene to become an ordinary country in the eyes of policymakers in Washington because it had passed a certain threshold of size and because the importance of Japan as an ally in "containment" was seen as diminished in the era of détente. Japanese economic issues becamed enmired in the morass of policymaking, involving the bureaucracies in Washington and the web of connections between them, the standing committees of Congress, and the domain of lobbyists and consultants, which are at the heart of the day-to-day operation of government. This removed the foundation of the bilateral alliance from the high politics of consensus to the low politics of the economic and bureaucratic world. It has foundered there ever since, and proposals for remedying the problem have focused overwhelmingly on tidying up the quagmire rather than bypassing it.

The growth in the relative weight of domestic structures in shaping U.S. foreign policy (with other nations as well as Japan) has provoked a wide range of explanations and reactions from scholars, policy intellectuals, and politicians. Scholarly reaction has led to a modest revival of old-fashioned political economy. It has properly focused on the fundamental features of the nature of states and international conditions, but has unfortunately been expressed in terms of grand theory with only tenuous ties to the real world. For example, it is suggestive to assert that the "politics of plenty" associated with periods of an orderly international political economy lead to a decline in the role of the state and a rise in importance of nonstate actors such as multinational corporations[37] or that in periods of hegemonic decline (such as the present) "the relative importance of domestic forces affecting foreign policy is increased."[38] To deal clearly and forcefully with issues such as Japanese-U.S. relations, however, somewhat more modest and concrete hypotheses are in order—it is necessary to understand the trees to delineate the forest.

The policy intellectuals, who regularly hew on the trees of policy, have the opposite problem—they have lost sight of the forest. Working essentially with models of decision making within bureaucracies and universalizing the American experience, the approach has emphasized that the complexity of foreign policy is such that full control is lacking to the central policy makers.[39] It is the bureaucrats and specialists, not political leaders, who are decisive. Accordingly, books such as *Managing an Alliance: The Politics of U.S.-Japanese Relations*, published in 1976 by the Brookings Institution, provide a kind of technocrat's manual on managing policy (understand institutional differences, avoid cultural misperceptions, and so forth) as the formula for effectively managing the alliance. Neither the political system, the leaders it produces, nor the international system is treated as a fully independent variable.

Policy intellectuals also tend to see all problems of the alliance as solvable by policy tinkering. For example, a widely quoted article in *Foreign Affairs* by Fred Bergsten claimed that the primary cause of economic conflict between Japan and the United States since 1971 was the misalignment of exchange rates.[40] Undoubtedly, this factor has played a critical part in the various economic crises, especially in 1971. However, to offer a monocausal explanation of the economic conflicts between Japan and the United States without a passing glance at the international and domestic political contexts within which they occurred is truly to walk on ground where angels fear to tread. Proposing solutions to these conflicts in purely economic terms may be satisfying to economic policymakers, but it is clearly inadequate as the basis for an enduring solution. The emphasis on technical policy adjustments in addressing the issues of the bilateral alliance flows mainly from the previously noted abandonment by foreign policy intellectuals of the quest for a broad political foreign policy consensus and from their willingness to separate economics from politics. For these reasons, the Bergsten article is representative of the mainstream dialogue in the United States on policy toward Japan and stands as a footnote to the times.

The reaction of U.S. politicians to the Japanese-U.S. economic crises of the past decade has been visceral, not intellectual, and it has been divided in ways that accurately convey the realities and confusion of the contemporary domestic scene. Except for the brief period in the early 1970s when John Connally was secretary of the Treasury, the executive branch has been dominated by presidents and economic advisers committed to free trade. It has been Congress that has supported protectionism and economic nationalism. The commitment of President Reagan and his advisers to the free-market concept is a matter of principle, not policy. This is mirrored in the Reagan administration's approach to Japan: to give national pep talks on the virtues of free trade while pressuring the Japanese to become more like Americans by enforcing antimonopoly laws more fully and liberalizing access to the Japanese market.

In contrast, the national labor federations have been protectionist since the early 1970s. With the growth of unemployment, their increased commitment to economic nationalism has led to so-called local-content legislation and to clamor for an "industrial policy"—a sort of internationalized New Deal modeled on and primarily directed against Japan. Responding to the pressures from labor and then from businesses hard hit by imports, Congress first funded and undertook a number of studies of Japanese trade practices (for example, the Jones Committee reports). In the face of chronic bilateral deficits, despite the Reagan administration's efforts to defuse all attempts at trade restriction, there has been a crescendo of congressional criticism of Japan, and more than 300 protectionist bills have been introduced since 1981.

Four aspects of these developments are of particular importance: (1) they are grounded in domestic circumstances and involve groups with clearly identifiable political values; (2) the circumstances themselves (unemployment, declining industries) are *not* amenable to short-term solutions; (3) rightly or wrongly, Japan now symbolically represents the main source of the grievances and will be the lightning rod in the future if an economic storm gathers; and (4) the peculiarly political quality of these pressures and the depth of emotions associated with them make it extremely difficult for the White House to terminate this domestication of foreign policy and reclaim leadership in foreign policy–making. Politics and economics are now inextricably entangled in U.S. policy toward Japan.

Since the Soviet invasion of Afghanistan and President Carter's discovery of the need to strengthen U.S. defense, the United States has pressured Japan to increase its share of the defense burden. The approaches adopted have been curious. Rather than privately indicating the desire for Japan to devise a new defense policy, the Carter administration publicly criticized Japan's failure to act, thereby insulting the government and the individuals involved and assuring that no action would be taken. Under the Reagan administration, the pressure has been private not public, but economic policy has not been linked with defense concerns in the broader context of the alliance relationship, thereby forgoing the utility of economic sanctions and maximizing the likelihood of conflict on the security issue. Although President Reagan has indicated a need for a broadened security role for Japan and the Defense Department has agreed, both the U.S. ambassador in Tokyo and the State Department have not uniformly supported this position.

The results have underscored the lack of a coherent general security strategy, exposed the divisions on the Japanese defense issue within the government, provoked counterproductive responses in Japan, and allowed the defense issue to be entangled in the anti-Japanese maneuvering over economic issues in Congress. Instead of recognizing that the real need is to establish an appropriate new strategic role for Japan, the United States has instead (following the lead of Tokyo) engaged in sterile arguments about the percentage of the national budget that ought to be spent for defense.

Indeed, the U.S. debate on Japanese defense has taken on an opera buffa character for those who listen closely to the music. On March 1, 1981, the assistant secretary of state for East Asian affairs stated that any "massive increase" in Japan's defense spending, such as doubling it (to 1.8 per cent of GNP), "would probably have destabilizing effects elsewhere in the East Asia region and cause severe political upheaval at home."[41] Apparently, the future of democracy in Japan and peace in Asia is at stake over a defense commitment less than half the size of that of any comparable industrialized nation. A serious article in a scholarly journal by a distinguished authority on East Asian affairs is premised on the notion that Japanese public opinion (as measured in various newspaper polls) imposes ineluctable limits on U.S. defense policies toward Japan.[42] That is, U.S. defense policy is fundamentally determined not by a calculation of national interest but by the public mood of the country toward which the policy is directed. Finally, at least one American congressman has suggested that the problem of defense burden sharing with Japan be solved by allowing the United States to provide the equipment and the forces and the Japanese pay for them through a tax formula linked to their GNP. American soldiers, among other things, will apparently become the Gurkhas of East Asia in the last years of the twentieth century.

The babel of voices concerning U.S. policy toward Japan and the inability of the White House to devise a new foreign policy consensus linking politics and economics has dragged bilateral relations deeply into U.S. domestic politics. Presidential leadership in policy toward Japan is now as much concerned with managing internal political considerations as with adjusting state-to-state relations.

Japanese Domestic Politics and Foreign Policy

The remarkable success of Japan in gaining international wealth and status has led to the almost unanimous conclusion that Japanese foreign policies have been shrewdly calculated responses to the realities of world politics. Accordingly, virtually all commentaries by Japanese and American international relations specialists assume that Japan's decision makers have selected and will continue to select the "appropriate" policy in terms of external realities and a given set of values. It is, however, especially important when considering long-term patterns of behavior to recognize that situational factors, both domestic and international, severely limit the options open to decision makers. Thus, a simple analysis of the policy debate (for example, reasons pro and con on armament) stands as an incomplete and misleading guide to the basic influences shaping *any* nation's role in the world.

This is particularly true in Japan, where the international conditions of the recent past have severely limited the range of options open to policymakers and where decision-making institutions have produced reactive, not active policies, regarding major *political* issues in foreign affairs. In a basic sense, Japanese foreign policy–making has been schizophrenic, with a record on major foreign policy decisions involving political considerations as bad as their record in conducting an effective international economic policy is good. Major decisions focused on political-strategic issues have been rare, but they offer a better window on the fundamental dynamics of foreign policy–making because Japan's future role in the world will have to have a political as well as an economic dimension and because these issues lay bare the pattern of relations among the components of the elite and their relation to the public.

Basic to all other questions about decision making in Japan are the electoral prospects of LDP. Despite sporadic and dramatic challenges to their role on specific issues (especially the alliance with the United States) and some electoral attrition through the 1970s, until recently the Liberal Democrats's control of the government was never seriously challenged. Several factors account for the party's prolonged success: (1) the highly successful policies of economic growth, which have steadily raised the standard of living; (2) a broad consensus on the goal of growth among the public as well as among political, business, and bureaucratic elites; (3) an overwhelming advantage in access to money, talented candidates, and political organization; (4) a divided, highly ideological, and politically inept opposition; and (5) a national culture stressing deference to authority and group loyalties, which moderated the societal tensions—and their reformist political by-products—involved in the massive socioeconomic changes of the period.

Although a number of these factors have been slightly modified since the early 1970s (notably the policy consensus on economic growth), these changes have been small. There is little likelihood of a challenge to conservative rule through a shift in election results.

The continued rule of the conservatives is in large part assured by the weakness of the opposition. Long-standing rivalries in and among the four opposition parties, rooted in personal conflicts as well as profound differences in policy and ideology, make cooperation difficult except on selected local candidates or an occasional more specific issues. Co-operation in parliamentary (rather than electoral) endeavors is possible (especially if the help of an "anti-mainstream" conservative group were forthcoming), and this would add another element of instability to government decision making. Nevertheless, any challenge of this sort would ultimately force a reconstitution of the LDP coalition, and this, in turn, would leave most of the opposition in its current divided minority status.

The virtually insurmountable division among and within the opposition parties is another basic impediment to significant political gains. The Socialists are badly faction-ridden and as likely to split as the LDP conservative coalition. Comprehensive cooperation between the Communists and the Kōmeitō (Clean Government Party) is all but unthinkable, and cooperation between the Socialists and the Democratic Socialists is barred not only by deep political differences but by divisions in the Japanese labor movement that have a definite political coloration. To envision success in dealing with problems of common candidates, party organization, and platforms in the face of these underlying problems is an exercise in fantasy.

A clear-cut party realignment directly affecting Japanese foreign policy is remote, but even if the opposition parties do not share power, they will continue to have an influence on foreign affairs. By virtue of their sizable popular support, the highly sympathetic mass media, and their direct access to foreign policy–making in the Diet, they occupy a strategic position from which they can articulate and press their views and thereby make conservative decision making more difficult.

Conservative Decision Making

In the immediate future, the LDP or a similar, conservative-dominated coalition will hold the reins of power, perpetuating the essentials of the current pattern of policy formulation centered in the intraparty decision-making process of the LDP. All other components of the political system—the opposition, pressure groups, public opinion, as well as other members of the elite—influence major foreign policy decisions primarily through access to this process. Formally, the prime minister is vested with the responsibility for policy leadership. In practice, however, his powers have been limited, primarily by the fragmented composition of the party and the close relationship between the formulation of policy on critical international issues and intraparty politics. Thus, the master keys to conservative foreign policy–making are the structure and dynamics of party politics.

Despite repeated efforts to create a unified party, the LDP remains a coalition of factions (*habatsu*). The factions, built around a single personality, are basically autonomous parties, having their own independent sources of finance, running their own candidates under the LDP label, and regularly caucusing for discussion of political strategy and, occasionally, of policy matters. Leadership within the party is recruited from those members of the Diet who can best operate in the complex and constricting world of the *habatsu*. In such circumstances, it is inappropriate to see the personalities of future Japanese prime ministers as shaping in any new and basic way the fundamental direction of Japanese diplomacy. There is no real possibility of an individual-centered, personalized style of leadership emerging in the LDP (or a conservative-dominated coalition) as a substitute for the faction-dominated, collectivist decision making that now prevails—barring a major political and economic breakdown of catastrophic proportions or the definition of a new national purpose.

In addition to assuring the recruitment of broker-type leaders, the commingling of factional politics with foreign policy–making imposes serious restraints on the prime minister's capacity for leadership. As head of a coalition, he must seek at least the agreement of the other faction leaders concerning not only the merits of policy but the current balance of power within the party. Beyond the usual constraints any coalition must face, the Japanese case is further complicated by a style of traditional authority that requires at least tacit consensus among all the responsible parties involved in policymaking, in this case the party faction leaders.

This limits the kinds of policies that are undertaken. Initiative tends to be confined to issues with minimum risk and controversy and with relatively calculable costs—which excludes all important international political matters. Moreover, by confounding domestic and international considerations, the policy debate unduly emphasizes the specific and short-term effects of each decision. Only in the special incubator conditions in which Japan has been able to operate can salutary results be produced by this style of policy formulation. Japanese foreign policy has been successful in the past because it was restricted to issues free from the imperatives of long-term strategic planning and decisive action required of a nation fully engaged in international politics.

The formal and informal organizations associated with strategic and military planning have to be thoroughly renovated if Japan is to play an expanded and significant role in international politics. Neither of the two main bodies set up to assist the prime minister to formulate and implement national security policy, the National Defense Council (crudely analogous to the U.S. National Security Council) and the Defense Agency, hold strong positions in the policymaking process. The council meets only sporadically and does not play a continuing and guiding role in devising policy. Although the Defense Agency is the centerpiece of security policy and Japanese military leaders have uniformly been of high caliber, the low status of the agency (it still is not a ministry), the domination of the budget-making process by the Finance Ministry (budgetary not strategic criteria are paramount), poor—but improving—connections between the military establishment and the LDP, and the extreme politicization of any issues related to defense have made formulating a coherent and effective defense program extremely difficult.

Since the late 1970s, there has been a remarkable proliferation of private think tanks and study groups concerned with defense (for example, the Research Institute for Peace and Security and the Japan Center for Strategic Studies), which together with established research organizations (for example, Nomura) and the activities of individual scholars, have begun to produce a more interesting and sophisticated defense debate. Nevertheless, these, too, remain on the periphery of the national policy dialogue. As long as the Yoshida Doctrine stands as the ultimate criteria for policy decisions and the dominant components of the elite remain the business-bureaucratic group, it will be difficult for any Japanese prime minister to lead the country to a significantly expanded strategic policy.

A review of all major Japanese foreign policy decisions since the end of the Occupation (for example, the peace agreement with the Soviet Union, the renewal of the Japanese-U.S. security treaty in 1960, normalization of relations with South Korea and with China) illustrates the inhibitions that this process of decision making has imposed on positive leadership in foreign policy. The decision to recognize Beijing in 1972 provides a superb illustration.

To a degree exceeded only by relations with the United States, China policy has been central to the foreign policy debate within Japan, and an extraordinary emotional and symbolic importance surrounds this matter for all politically articulate groups. Although formally adhering to the U.S. position, during the 1960s the Japanese developed a de facto "two Chinas" policy involving more extensive regular contacts with Beijing than any other country had. The government repeatedly asserted its special role in bringing China into international relations. Yet the Japanese remained on the sidelines until China was admitted to the United Nations, until almost all other major powers had recognized Beijing, and until the president of the United States had made a formal visit to the country.

Moreover, the decision to recognize the People's Republic was deeply colored by intraparty factional considerations. Kakuei Tanaka, a neutral on Chinese issues, became prime minister in mid-1972 by putting together a factional coalition including three pro-Beijing rivals (Takeo Miki, Masayoshi Ohira, and Yasuhiro Nakasone), all of whom made normalization a critical condition for their support. There is little to suggest that the dynamics of political and strategic decision making will break out of the immobilism seen in this case as long as the basic structure of the postwar party system persists.

Despite the vision of intimate business-government collaboration conjured up in the image of "Japan, Inc.," the specific role of business in decision making regarding foreign policy issues is ambiguous and varies widely from issue to issue. Business leaders are closely tied to the conservative party through overt and covert financial support, through a sharing of basic political values, and through continuous and intimate personal contacts. Ties between business and the Ministry of International Trade and Industry (MITI) and the other government agencies that exercise careful control over the day-to-day conduct of Japan's international economic activities are similarly close—inevitably so, given the overwhelmingly economic character of postwar foreign policy. Despite these conditions, and despite the establishment by the national business organizations of committees to deal with specific foreign affairs issues and continuing questions such as rearmament, there is no clear mutual understanding regarding the procedures through which business opinion should be brought into the policymaking process. Nor is there automatic agreement on the goals of the nation's foreign policy. The complexity and diversity of the Japanese business world is mirrored in the viewpoints of the various individuals and groups who speak out on international affairs. Consequently, if political and security considerations become involved in policies previously geared toward maximizing economic benefits, businessmen are as likely to become further divided as they are to rally round the flag.

The impact of organized business and individual businessmen on major Japanese foreign policy decisions has varied. Regarding diplomatic normalization with the Soviet Union in 1956 and the extension of the security treaty in 1960 (both issues involving essentially political questions), business did not influence the policy process in a decisive way. It played a somewhat more important part in the normalization of relations with South Korea and with China, but not in the critical political decisions involved. As the links between politics and economics grow (as a direct result of Japan's commercial stake in East Asia and the world) and Japan moves toward full participation in power politics, the relationship between the business world and the LDP will take on added importance *and* at the same time be placed under increasing strains—especially regarding security policy.

The structure and dynamics of Japanese foreign policy–making will not change much in the future, but the limitations of this process in providing suitable responses to the new international milieu will become increasingly evident. The groups constituting the policymaking elite for the past two decades (the LDP conservative coalition, bureaucrats, and businessmen) are likely to continue to interact through the same diffuse and essentially immobilist process of compromise and consensus that has characterized all past major *political* decisions regarding foreign affairs. This pattern of decision making, which virtually prohibits bold leadership, is not well suited to fluid economic and strategic international circumstances, which call for frequent and rapid changes of front. Purely reactive policies can hardly be expected to serve as well in the future as they did in the immediate past when Japan was on the periphery of a far more predictable international system.

Moreover, the efforts required to cope with recurrent external crises feed back into domestic politics and aggravate relations among members of the conservative elite and inevitably affect the electoral position of the LDP. Unless basically altered, the links between international politics and internal events are likely to have reciprocally negative influences, both on domestic political stability and on the development of a positive international role for Japan.

Economic Foreign Policy

In contrast to this record on political-security decisions, the Japanese record in devising and executing international economic policy has been routinely described as a "miracle" and as offering a model for all industrialized societies.[43] Most analyses uniformly treat Japanese performance as historically rooted, blending cultural values, bureaucratic efficiency, and political institutions and groups into a new species of national political organization (a developmental state, a corporate state) ideally suited for maximizing the country's well-being in the contemporary international political economy. Not surprisingly, these arguments tend to downplay the political imperatives, both internal and international, that constrain Japanese policy choices. In their most extreme form, they ascribe the kind of economic rationality to national behavior that nineteenth-century British liberals attributed to individuals.[44]

Three features of these highly successful policies are particularly noteworthy: the extent to which they were conducted with minimal domestic political pressures; the extent to which they were formulated and implemented in terms of long-term goals; and the dominant role of the bureaucrats in the overall process. In an important sense, Chalmers Johnson is right, the bureaucrats have ruled while the politicians reigned, and the main function of the Diet and the party system was to fend off interest groups and others who tried to distort the priorities of economic growth.[45]

However, such an analysis gives short shrift to political values and the political process at both the international and internal levels. Internationally, it ignores the special conditions, discussed above, that allowed Japanese foreign policy to be defined almost exclusively in economic terms and assumes that a policy of economic nationalism will not take on a political dimension in an interdependent, nation-centered, and conflict-prone international order. Internally, it assumes that the ends of national policy will remain economic in nature and that the bureaucrat-business elements of the elite will continue to dominate the policy process within roughly the same legal and party framework that has operated in the past. The basic changes in international economic and security conditions over the past decade (especially those challenging the neo-mercantilist policies of Japan) and the surfacing within the country of the issues of rearmament, constitutional revision, and relations with the United States suggest that the future agenda will extend to issues not fully within the domain of the bureaucratic-business components of the political elite.

Japanese foreign policy thus stands at a threshold in two senses: in terms of the political-strategic issues it will face in the future and in terms of the capacity of the political elite to formulate effective policies in this area. The effort to devise a new foreign policy consensus to deal with these issues has been largely a rearguard action to extend the Yoshida Doctrine.[46] Because the pressures to deal with political-strategic issues will come from outside the country, many Japanese visions of Japan's future role foresee a world (for example, an informational society) that is essentially apolitical with minimal international conflict.[47] This is not surprising since Japan is perhaps the most successful technocratic society in history, a kind of Asian offspring of the eighteenth-century European Enlightenment. It was the promise and the achievements of technology that led the idea of "progress" to take hold in the West, and this passage from J. B. Bury captures the spirit of the approach to the future taken by the Japanese bureaucratic-business elite: "In societies founded on technology, the warrior, the priest and the political leader sink into the background or at all events can operate only in accordance with economic realities produced by the machine."[48]

It is primarily those members of the political elite whose careers have been in political parties (for example, Prime Minister Nakasone) and whose popular appeals are often cast in terms of nationalism who have taken the lead in urging an expanded security role and a reconsideration of the U.S.-drafted peace constitution. These appeals have been concrete, not theoretical, and have stressed the need for an expanded defense budget, the Soviet threat, and the need for a revised relationship with the United States, as well as some sort of new nationalism in Japan. What is striking about this debate is that it has concrete political definition within the broad structure of the political elite. Any shift to a new policy consensus will, however, severely test the fundamental stability of the postwar political system. This is well illustrated by Prime Minister Nakasone's record during his first years in office.

Nakasone's Leadership: The Limits of the System

At the beginning of his administration in December 1981, it appeared as if Yasuhiro Nakasone would bring a new style of leadership to the office of prime minister, a style that was assertive, issue oriented, and personal—especially in the area of foreign affairs. His visits to South Korea, the United States, and Southeast Asia were dramatically successful, albeit primarily in symbolic terms. For the first time since the end of World War II, a Japanese statesman was playing a conspicuous role on the stage of international diplomacy. This performance strengthened his tenuous domestic political position, which from the beginning was almost totally dependent on the goodwill of Kakuei Tanaka. Nakasone actively cultivated public support, and he did so as an unapologetic nationalist: appealing for a significantly expanded defense budget, a strengthened U.S.-Japan alliance to make it more genuinely a security partnership, and eventual revision of the constitution to bring it in line with "the lofty ideals inherent to the Japanese people." [49]

This approach not only stressed international over domestic issues and political rather than economic matters, but bypassed the business and bureaucratic elite to appeal directly to the public in the style of U.S. presidents. These actions simply put into practice his long-standing beliefs in the need for direct popular election of the prime minister and referendums on major policy issues—a political philosophy reminiscent of the extensive powers of the president and plebiscitary features found in the Gaullist constitution of the Fifth Republic. For a brief period, Nakasone seemed to have single-handedly transformed the style of Japanese political leadership.

In adopting this leadership posture and this set of issues, Nakasone deviated sharply from all previous postwar Japanese prime ministers. The fragmented structure of the conservative party assures that those who achieve the prime ministership must more or less continuously act as power brokers to keep their intraparty factional coalition together. Sharp policy positions are normally avoided in the interests of maximizing the life of the factional coalition. Moreover, the culturally sanctioned style of consensual decision making inhibits bold policy statements until after a final choice is made.

Because Prime Minister Nakasone was at variance with virtually all of the basic norms of LDP foreign policy–making, he could expect to succeed only by vastly expanding his political power base. This did not happen. Because he cluttered the agenda with too many serious and controversial issues, immobilism quickly set in. Eventually, little remained beyond rhetorical flourishes to distinguish his policy posture from those of previous prime ministers.

What began as a bold new attempt at leadership in foreign policy has yielded meager results, except in preventing a major breakdown in U.S.-Japan relations. The debate over defense continues to involve sterile arguments over whether Japan should (or does) spend more than 1 per cent of GNP on security rather than on new and appropriate strategic goals for spending. Issues such as the transfer of military technology to the United States remain largely unfulfilled after being given dramatic attention at the outset of the Nakasone administration. Relations with Asian nations are, on the whole, good, but Japan continues to be a passive rather than leading actor in the region.

What factors underlay the transformation of Nakasone from his self-proclaimed image as a Japanese de Gaulle to that of an articulate but "ordinary" prime minister? Undoubtedly, it was partly the result of special circumstances involving intraparty politics, but the answer also lies in the fundamental structure of the Japanese political elite. As long as the LDP is divided into a coalition of factions struggling for political power, there is no real possibility for an individual-centered, policy-focused, and assertive style of leadership. In the summer of 1986, Nakasone personally engineered the most smashing LDP electoral victory in a quarter of a century; all he obtained was a one-year extension of his term as prime minister—an unenviable lame-duck consolation prize. Nakasone was right: short of a constitutional revision regarding the method of selecting the prime minister or perhaps a cataclysm that forces a basic alteration in the national mood or the electoral strength of the ruling party, Japan will not make bold moves in international politics. The problem of leadership in Japan is systemic not personal.

Another impediment to Nakasone's leadership initiatives came from the bureaucrats and the mainstream of Japanese business. Even if Johnson is wrong in his belief that the Diet and party politicians are a sideshow to keep the citizens happy while the bureaucracy rules, Nakasone's initial challenge to the authority of the bureaucracy as well as the to substance of their policies proved too much for the system to digest. Because of the obvious advantages of continuing to avoid increased expenditures on security at a time of huge deficits, the Finance Ministry and related supporting groups (including Japanese business) treated the entire question of strategy as a budget issue. They reluctantly yielded to U.S. pressure (but no more than was symbolically appropriate), and the rhetorical flourishes of the prime minister regarding defense remain empty words.

The bureaucratic and the business worlds were even more uncomfortable with the elevation of political issues (defense, foreign aid, and nationalism) over matters of economics, *and* this concern was exacerbated by Nakasone's appeal to the two constituencies over which they have the least influence—the Japanese electorate and foreign governments. Again, the challenge posed by the attempt at assertive leadership was contrary to the basic modus operandi of the postwar elitist-democratic system. Accordingly, the limitations placed on Nakasone's initiatives should be understood in part as a result of this, not simply in terms of short-term political events.

Despite extraordinary continuity in the basic features of the Japanese political system and remarkable success in fulfilling the foreign policy aims articulated at the end of the Occupation, it is far from clear that the achievements of the past have laid a foundation for future success. Partly this is because the policy choices of the past were made in the context of extraordinary international conditions created largely by the U.S. alliance, which relieved Japan of the costs and responsibilities of developing a strategic policy borne by all other nations in the Western alliance. Japan's record on political-strategic decisions is as bad as its record on international economic policy is good. Because Japan is an elitist democracy, the future impact of domestic politics on foreign policy will be shaped primarily by relations among the political elite and by their capacity to generate a new foreign policy consensus congruent with international realities and acceptable to the Japanese public.

Paradoxically, although Japan operates as a highly successful neomercantilist state, because future policies must encompass political-security issues as well as economics, their direction is likely to be dictated by the drift of international events (especially U.S. policy) and the tides of domestic politics over which the decision makers have little control. This immobilism in Japanese domestic politics regarding the political-strategic dimension of foreign policy has a final ironic implication. Despite the remarkable success of Japan and the relative decline of the United States, the definition of Japan's role in the world (the new concept of national purpose) may most felicitously come from outside the country, from American initiatives to revise and restructure the U.S. alliance in terms of partnership and reciprocity.

Part IV

Japan's Emerging World Role

Stephen D. Krasner

Japan and the United States:
Prospects for Stability

In the 1980s Japan clearly emerged as the second largest economy in the noncommunist world. Its growth rate has consistently exceeded that of its nearest rivals—West Germany and the United States.[1] Japan is a big player, but how will it play, particularly with the United States? A breakdown or alteration in the pattern of interaction between these two countries would have consequences for the world system as a whole. In economic affairs policy in Japan and the United States has been characterized by a commitment to a liberal, open global economy, at least rhetorically, and by a high and growing level of transactions. Neither Japan nor the United States has attempted to legitimate any alternative regime, although central decision makers in both states have engaged in illiberal activities. In the security area, Japan has accepted a subordinate role to the United States. It has not taken an active defense posture or tried to convert its formidable economic resources into military capability. Among the major industrialized countries, Japan's ratio of military expenditures to GNP is by far the lowest.[2]

Will these patterns continue? Do they even accurately describe the past? For both security and economic affairs, various arguments have been made regarding the stability of U.S.-Japanese relations. They can, for expository convenience, be classified according to whether they focus on systemic or domestic/national causes and whether they predict stability or breakdown.

Stability

At the systemic level several analyses pointing to stability and continuity have been presented. Some analysts have argued that the high level of economic interdependence in the global economic system engulfs both the United States and Japan. Current transaction levels could be limited, even substantially curtailed, but only at great costs in terms of economic utility for all actors. Moreover, in the contemporary system, economic ties link private as well as public actors in a dense web of interdependence. Private transnational interactions and relations between particular bureaucratic groups may be as influential as formal state-to-state intergovernmental decisions. These specific actors are likely to have a strong interest in at least some specific transnational flows.[3]

Others emphasize the significance of existing international regimes. Most of these regimes were established at the conclusion of World War II, largely on the initiative of the United States. They are based on liberal principles and norms—the belief that reductions in the barriers to the international movement of goods and factors benefit all states. Rules and decision-making procedures to facilitate the maintenance of a liberal order are formalized in a number of international organizations, including GATT, the International Monetary Fund, the World Bank, and the OECD. International regimes reduce transaction costs, provide information that facilitates monitoring and thereby increases trust, and define appropriate compensation for transgressions, thereby limiting the danger of self-defeating and pernicious retaliatory cycles. The effort needed to maintain regimes is less costly than the resources needed to establish them.[4] Thus, regimes both reinforce and define the substance of liberalism and establish procedures that promote the realization of these goals.

A third group stresses the rational utility maximizing calculations of state actors rather than international regimes or transnational interactions. A state's choice to follow an open or a closed policy is determined by its place in the international global economy. That place is defined by its level of development and share of world transactions. The ideal situation for a state is to act as a free-rider by, for instance, imposing an optimal tariff. If, however, a state's trading partners retaliate, then all states will be worse off. The probability of retaliation is a function of the distribution of power. In a world in which several technologically advanced states enjoy high and relatively equal shares of world trade, one rational outcome is for them to maintain open trading policies. They would all gain from an open system and would be subject to retaliation if they imposed trade barriers.[5] In sum, at the systemic level, arguments that point to transnational interactions, international regimes, and rational state calculations in a multipolar world all suggest continuing stability in U.S.-Japanese economic relations.

Agreements focusing on domestic factors suggest the same conclusion. Proponents of these arguments emphasize the flexibility and responsiveness of Japan's domestic system. One analyst has, for instance, praised Japan's positive anticipatory adjustment. Another has pointed to the extensive supportive pattern of interactions between certain elements of the business community and particular bureaucracies.[6] A state that can adjust to changes emanating from the international system is unlikely to feel compelled to alter existing relationships radically.

In the security area, there are also systemic and domestic-level arguments that suggest stability; Japan will continue to follow the United States' lead and to accept the U.S. nuclear umbrella. The Soviet Union is a major security threat to both the United States and Japan. This threat is a function of systemic characteristics: the United States and the Soviet Union are rival poles in a bipolar system, and Japan is geographically close to the USSR. Domestic characteristics (communism versus capitalism/democracy) need not be introduced. Both Japan and the United States are threatened by the Soviet Union. Japan's major defense contribution would be to prevent any major Soviet naval breakout into the Pacific, an objective that is equally valuable to the Unted States. Domestic factors in Japan that contribute to accepting a subordinate role to the United States include a disinclination among leaders and the public to pursue an ambitious foreign policy, the limited attraction of traditional nationalism, and Japanese values, which accept a hierarchically structured social order. The Japanese may not be discomforted by active U.S. leadership in the international system.[7]

Domestic considerations in the United States also suggest the continued stability and continuity of U.S.-Japanese relationships. The United States has strong interest-oriented and ideological commitments to international liberalism. Major segments of the U.S. economy are heavily involved in international transactions. Corporations in some import-competing industries, such as automobiles, have been able to establish equity interests in Japanese companies. (Others, such as steel, have not.) Japan is the largest market for U.S. agricultural exports. Japanese investments in the United States have increased, with some benefits for labor.

Central decision makers in the United States have also, since the conclusion of World War II, had strong ideological commitments to international liberalism. These commitments have been shared by Democrats and Republicans. No postwar president has been sympathetic to protectionism. The executive branch has generally resisted congressional efforts to restrict access to the U.S. market. These commitments reflect both enduring values and specific historical experience. Of all the advanced industrialized countries, the United States has been most strongly influenced by conventional liberal, market-oriented ideas. There has never been an enduring socialist movement in the United States. The prevalence of market-oriented institutions at the domestic level has not, of course, always been reflected in international economic policy. The

United States inclined strongly toward protectionism for most of the nineteenth century. The Hawley-Smoot Tariff Act of 1930 increased import duties to high levels and has been widely perceived as contributing to the global economic depression of the 1930s. The political, not just the economic, consequences of this depression have deeply influenced the ideas of central decision makers in the United States. The lesson of the 1930s was that economic and political breakdown went hand in hand and often led to international aggression and war. The desire to avoid a repeat of the 1930s influenced U.S. policy toward the postwar recovery of Europe and Japan and continues to provide a compelling image for U.S. policymakers. Hence, both interest-oriented and cognitive considerations suggest a continued U.S. commitment to open economic relations with Japan and other countries.[8]

Instability

Other arguments, again at both the systemic and domestic/national levels, suggest that the current pattern of U.S.-Japanese relations—liberalism in international economic transactions and Japanese acceptance of U.S. security leadership—is not sustainable.

At the systemic level, these arguments point to changes in the international distribution of power, especially a relative decline in the United States' capabilities and a rise in Japan's. In the area of international political economy, hegemonic stability theory suggests a deterioration in U.S.-Japanese relations resulting from a declining U.S. commitment to maintaining an open global economic order. This approach emphasizes the need for a hegemon not only to create new international regimes but also to sustain old ones. A dominant power can accept free-riders, at least for an extended period, thus easing the adjustment burdens of other states. As the power of the hegemon declines, its behavior is increasingly motivated by short-term interests rather than general principles. It becomes less tolerant of free-riding, or even lengthy adjustments, in other countries. It puts more pressure on its economic partners to make immediate concessions.[9]

The declining hegemon is also increasingly reluctant to ensure the global economy against shocks. The best-known exposition of this danger is Charles Kindleberger's discussion of the Great Depression. He argues that the failure of both the United States and Great Britain to act as a market of last resort for distressed sectors of the raw-materials trade and as a lender of last resort for transnational financial networks led to the collapse of the global economy. Such stabilizing interventions do provide a collective good: the benefits of stability enjoyed by one actor do not lessen the benefits available to others, nor can members of the liberal system be excluded from the benefits of stability. (It is, of course, possible to exclude certain countries from the liberal order altogether.) Kindleberger's basic argument is that such collective goods, like all collective goods, are likely to be provided at a suboptimal level, especially if there is no hegemon. In a multipolar system, it may be impossible to cope with a crisis (a situation that threatens important objectives, is not accurately foreseen, and requires quick action) because the large number of actors complicates bargaining.[10]

Hegemonic stability theory should be considered a specific case of a more general formulation—uneven growth generates tension. Uneven growth refers to the variation in the rates of growth of underlying power capabilities across states over time. A number of different dangers have been associated with uneven growth. One set arises when the relative power base of a challenger state increases. This state finds itself functioning in an international environment—defined by geographic boundaries and international regimes—delineated by choices made when the international distribution of power was different. A challenger state may find that it is disadvantaged by this environment; for instance, the resources it controls may not be transformed into influence or benefits as easily under existing regimes as they would under an alternative regime. Existing national boundaries or spheres of influence may deny a newly powerful state access to resources. (Had the distribution of colonies in Asia taken place in, say, 1920, Japan's access to crude oil would have been very different in 1939.) Depending on its underlying military capabilities, the challenger may be tempted to use force to alter existing regimes and boundaries. There is some evidence that major general wars are associated with such challenges.[11]

Uneven growth may also lead to instability because of disparities between underlying relative power capabilities and the perceptions and goals of central decision makers. Charles Doran argues that states follow a parabolic cycle of rising and declining power. Within this cycle, the most dangerous moments are at the turning points (maximum and minimum power) and at the two inflection points. The perceptions of central decision makers regarding the capabilities and objectives of their state are extrapolated from their past experience. At inflection points and turning points, however, past experience no longer provides an adequate guide to the state's present situation. There is a disparity between expectations of capability based on extrapolation of past development and the actual pattern of relative power distribution. At these points, policymakers confront great uncertainty and are prone to extreme reactions. "It appears that governments and societies find adjustment to new behavioral roles difficult and become vulnerable to hyperinsecurity and aggressiveness at critical points where the direction of the volutionary outlook changes pervasively." Doran applies his analysis to the outbreak of major wars, but the logic of his argument applies equally well to economic issues.[12]

Uneven growth also poses management difficulties for declining hegemons. Robert Gilpin argues that such states tend to allocate too much of their resources to consumption and defense and not enough to investment. In the long term, this further weakens the power position of the state and undermines its ability to manage the international environment.[13]

Other systemic-level arguments driven by the logic of uneven growth include Robert North's discussion of lateral pressure, in which differential rates of change of population, resource availability, and technology lead to pressures for external expansion, and, of course, Lenin's discussion of imperialism, in which he saw World War I as resulting from the inability of the European states to reallocate colonial territories to accommodate Germany's rising power.[14]

These arguments share a basic logic. Shifts in relative power capabilities, especially shifts involving major powers, are difficult to accommodate. Declining states tend to adhere to commitments they cannot defend. Rising states make demands that others refuse to accept. While power distributions are changing, the institutional characteristics of the international system—international regimes, territorial boundaries, and transnational legitimating myths—remain fixed. Ultimately, the pressure between changing relative power capabilities and static institutional structures leads to a convulsion. As with locked tectonic plates, the pressure between the distribution of power and global institutions can be released only by an upheaval. Theories based on uneven growth are implicitly or explicitly skeptical about the possibilities for incremental change, in which institutional characteristics are frequently altered to accommodate changes in the distribution of power.

Several domestic-level arguments also suggest instability in the relationship between Japan and the United States. Their common characteristic is the contention that policymakers lack the flexibility to adjust to changing external circumstances. Because of domestic constraints, they cannot accommodate either pressures from their economic and military partners or shifts in the global environment. With regard to Japan, such arguments have pointed either to the particular political needs of the ruling Liberal Democratic Party (LDP) or to consensus decision making. Daniel Okimoto argues that there are four distinct political policymaking networks in Japan: (1) the LDP and particular segments of the society, especially farmers, who exchange protection from international competition for votes; (2) the LDP and specific domestic sectors (for instance, construction), who trade favorable government policies for financial support; (3) large corporations and the central economic ministries, especially the Ministry of International Trade and Industry (MITI) and the

Ministry of Finance, who share a commitment to national economic goals; and (4) the LDP and the general public, which assesses the LDP's performance in elections. The third network is very flexible in its ability to respond to external pressures. Major corporations and the leading economic ministries have close working relationships, common objectives, and a shared insulation from political interference. So long as general economic performance is reasonable, the fourth network is also unlikely to constrain Japanese decision makers. However, the first network is much less flexible, and the second somewhat less. The LDP cannot accommodate pressures to open its domestic agricultural markets without undermining an important base of political support.[15]

Sociological and political analyses that emphasize consensus decision making in Japan also suggest a possible source of instability for U.S.-Japanese relations as well as larger global relations. Donald Hellmann argues that especially in the security area, Japanese policy has been reactive (see his paper, this volume). Passivity has been possible because of the protection provided by the United States. The factional party system has made it difficult for Japanese prime ministers to respond quickly to foreign policy crises. In the economic sphere, there has been consensus on basic objectives. But if conditions change dramatically, it will be difficult for Japan to adjust because of the central importance of consensus decision making. This decision-making style works effectively in a stable environment where issues are limited to tactics rather than strategies. If changes in the external environment make existing strategies ineffectual, then consensus decision making would make it difficult to explore and implement alternatives expeditiously. Japan would not be able to initiate new proposals because of the need for internal consensus and related assurances of external acceptance. This could lead to a breakdown in U.S.-Japanese relations, especially if qualitatively new demands were suddenly placed on Japan.[16]

There are also domestic factors in the United States that could lead to instability. Historically, U.S. attitudes and policies toward foreign relations have gone through cycles of involvement and isolationism. Louis Hartz argues that these cycles are driven by the dominance of Lockean liberal values in the United States. Because Americans have so little familiarity with competing value systems, they adopt a Manichaean view of the world. The opponent is seen as an "evil empire," as "uncivilized." Americans either have tried to remake the world in their own liberal image, leading to excessive involvement, or have rejected the world as sinful when these efforts at salvation failed, leading to isolationism.[17] The United States has, since World War II, been heavily involved in the international system. If the pattern of ideologically driven cycles continues, it will withdraw in the future.

The fragmented distribution of power in the U.S. political system may also be a source of instability for U.S.-Japanese relations. Disaffected groups can easily secure a hearing. Congress is highly attuned to constituency needs. Especially in the area of international trade, the costs of importing foreign products are concentrated in particular industries, whereas the benefits are diffused to the whole population. This suggests that societal pressures for protectionism will be more insistent than pressures for free trade. Thus, whereas interest group politics and consensus decision making in Japan may impede adjustment to external pressures, the fragmentation of power and ideological commitments in the United States may lead to the same result.[18]

A final consideration that may lead to instability in U.S.-Japanese relations cuts across the distinction between systemic and national-level arguments. The basic institutional structures and belief systems associated with the Japanese and U.S. political economies may be a source of difficulty simply because they are different. The distribution of variance in political economies matters more than their specific characteristics. Variations in national characteristics can lead to misperception and make international institution building, negotiation, and cooperation more difficult.

One key difference between Japanese and American society is the fluidity of personal and business relationships. In the United States, the basic unit of society is the individual (or perhaps the nuclear family). General practices and norms accept the right of individuals to frame their own preferences and strategies. The economic manifestation of this pattern is the auction market, in which exchanges are conducted at armslength and based solely on price. In contrast, the basic unit of Japanese society is the group, not the individual. Murray Sayle, an Australian journalist living in Japan, argues that as "the basic social unit the Japanese have neither the individual nor the family, but the village-like group who work together and, as the Japanese say 'share a common destiny.'"[19] Social relationships are less fluid in Japan than in the United States. Because of these differences in social organization and value, practices that Americans find laudable might be unacceptable to the Japanese and vice versa. For instance, Americans regard corporate takeovers as simply part of the game, whereas Japanese find such forays deeply offensive. It is less problematic for an American executive to move from one company to another than for his or her Japanese counterpart, who will almost certainly be male. Adjustments that are easy in one national environment might be difficult in another. It is easier for an American corporation to deal with market conditions by firing a large number of workers. A Japanese firm entering the U.S. market has only to offer a better economic package (price, service, marketing). A U.S. company entering the Japanese market may have to penetrate a dense network of relationships established over many years.[20]

TABLE 1
Prospects for Stability

Systemic-level argument	National/domestic-level arguments
STABLE OUTCOMES	
Economic interdependence links groups together.	Ability of some parts of the Japanese economy to adjust to external changes.
Rational national calculations in a multipolar international economic environment lead to liberal policies.	U.S. executive commitment to international liberalism.
Complementarity of Japanese and U.S. security goals in East Asia.	Japanese acceptance of U.S. leadership in the security area.
Hegemonic decline and power transitions resulting from uneven growth.	Adjustment rigidities in the United States and Japan because of interest group pressures.
UNSTABLE OUTCOMES	
Variations in national values and institutions.	Consensus decision making in Japan.
	Fragmentation of power in the United States. U.S. cycles of foreign involvement driven by ideological commitments.

Differences in domestic political economies may mean that international rules that are constraining for one country may impose no constraints on another. If state intervention in the economy is conducted through formal and explicit actions, such as public subsidies for export industries, it can be challenged under the provisions of GATT and other international agreements. If state intervention is accomplished through informal mechanisms, such as administrative guidance, it is much more difficult to establish the relevance of international rules. The various nontariff barrier codes negotiated during the Tokyo Round of the GATT trade talks are an effort to deal with this problem. Their impact remains to be seen. Thus, problems may arise not because one set of institutions is in some inherent way superior to another, but because the expectations of each party, based on its own national experience, diverge. (For a summary of the arguments in this section, see Table 1.)

Empirical Descriptors

Clearly there can be no simple empirical test of these arguments. There are too many variables and not enough cases. Moreover, many of the arguments are purely projective; they are efforts to predict the future

based on general theoretical considerations and extrapolations of existing trends. They do not, however, make claims about past events. In this
section, I present some information on general trends in underlying
capabilities, economic transactions, and military expenditures for Japan
and the United States.

Underlying Capabilities

One factor that emerges as an important consideration in many of the
arguments presented above is the relative power positions of the United
States and Japan. It is the prime mover for power-based systemic arguments. It is also relevant for domestic-level arguments that see such
changes as posing new environmental challenges. For instance, arguments based on consensus decision making emphasize the difficulty that
Japan would have adjusting to radically different systemic conditions.

Ratios of U.S. to Japanese capabilities can be measured for several different indicators of underlying power capabilities (see Table 2). Using
1950 as a starting point obviously exaggerates the rate at which the
power capabilities of Japan have changed relative to those of the United
States because of the greater wartime damage to Japanese productive capabilities. However, Japan's rapid growth (with GNP as a proxy for capabilities) is not limited to the immediate postwar period. Japan's economic
growth continued to be higher than that of the United States in the 1970s
and 1980s. A. F. K. Organski and Jacek Kugler have estimated that the
normal period of postwar recovery, the length of time it takes a state to
achieve the growth path extrapolated from prewar experience, is about
20 years.[21] Japan's relative power capabilities have been on a sharp upward trajectory since the end of the nineteenth century. Based on five
indicators of national power capabilities, Charles Doran and Wes Par-

TABLE 2
*Japanese Indicators as Per Cent of U.S. Indicators of Underlying National Power
Capabilities or Potential International Influence, 1950–1984*

Indicators	1950	1960	1970	Most recent	
GNP	8%	9%	20%	34%	(1984)
Manufacturing output	—	10	29	52	(1980)
Exports	17	18	39	81	(1984)
Military expenditures	—	1	2	6	(1982)

sources: World Bank, *World Tables*, 3d ed., pp. 238–39, 256–57 for manufacturing 1960–80; exports
1950–70; and GNP 1950–70. GATT, *International Trade, 1984/85*, tables A34 and A36 for exports 1984.
Military expenditures from U.S. Arms Control and Disarmament Agency, *World Military Expenditures
and Arms Transfers*, various years. All figures at current prices or factor costs. GNP for 1984 from *World
Bank Atlas*, 1986.

sons estimate that Japan's power capabilities as a proportion of the capabilities of all major powers in the international system rose from under 5 per cent in 1895 to about 10 per cent during World War II.[22] Hence, from a systemic perspective Japan and the United States have experienced uneven growth. Japan's power position in the international system, including its capabilities relative to those of the United States, has rapidly increased. There is no indication that this pattern will change.

If Japan's GDP growth rate for 1970–82 of 4.6 per cent and the United States' growth rate for the same period of 2.7 per cent are extrapolated into the future, it will take about 50 years for Japan's aggregate output to equal that of the United States. If growth rates for manufacturing output for the same period of 2.4 per cent for the United States and 6.6 per cent for Japan continue, it will take about 20 years for Japan's manufacturing output to surpass that of the United States.[23]

If systemic arguments based on uneven growth are correct, these patterns (if they persist) suggest that there is cause to worry about the future relationship between the two countries. Unfortunately, they do not say much about present relationships. As Bruce Russett has accurately pointed out, theories of hegemonic stability have not been very precise about the level of power necessary for a hegemon to be a hegemon. The present capabilities of the United States, even after a period of relative decline, exceed those of Great Britain at the apex of its power in the mid-nineteenth century.[24] Nevertheless, the arguments based on uneven growth, such as the incongruity between power capabilities and extant regimes and the disparity between perceptions and goals arising from extrapolations of past trends, suggest that U.S.-Japanese relations will be troubled in the future.

Economic Interactions

Japan and the United States continue to be important trading partners for each other, and in absolute terms trade has grown over time. Japanese exports to the United States increased about 5.5 times between 1960 and 1970 (in current dollars) and by about the same amount from 1970 to 1980. U.S. exports to Japan increased by about 3.5 times between 1960 and 1970 and by about 4.5 times between 1970 and 1980 (again in current dollars). Exports to Japan increased from about 6 per cent of total U.S. exports in 1960 to 10 per cent in 1970 and remained at the 10 per cent level through the 1970s. Japanese exports to the United States increased from 27 per cent of total Japanese exports in 1960 to 31 per cent in 1970, but fell to 24 per cent in 1980.[25]

A second measure of U.S.-Japanese interaction in the area of trade is relative acceptance indicators. Relative acceptance indicators show whether the trade between two countries is more or less than would be expected given their share of world trade. Relative acceptance indicators for U.S. exports to Japan, for example, equal the percentage of U.S. exports to Japan divided by Japan's percentage share of world imports. When trade between two countries is equal to what would be expected on the basis of size alone, the relative acceptance indicator is equal to 1.00; when trade is less than would be expected, the indicator is less than 1.00; when it is greater, more than 1.00.

What should one make of the figures for the United States and Japan shown in Table 3? Relative acceptance indicators did drop substantially during the 1970s. But trade between the U.S. and Japan is still larger than would be predicted solely on the basis of size. Export shares and relative acceptance indicators do not suggest a breakdown in U.S.-Japanese relations.

Other patterns, however, indicate more grounds for concern. More than that of any other major industrialized country, Japan's trade has been characterized by an absence of intrasectoral trade. Japan imports raw materials and exports manufactures. The sectoral trading patterns of the United States and Europe are much more difficult to classify because they import and export similar products. Moreover, the level of Japanese foreign direct investment is less than the level for the United States and Europe. Intrasectoral trade and direct foreign investment create cross-cutting political cleavages that weaken protectionist pressures. If Country A and Country B both import and export widgets from and to each other, it is unlikely that protectionist pressures would be effective. If A bans the import of widgets from B (to help its own producers), B could well ban the import of widgets from A (hurting these same widget producers). Widget producers in both A and B are unlikely to press for trade restrictions. But if A exports widgets and imports cars (a product that it also produces) and B exports cars and imports widgets (a product that it also produces), then car producers in A and widget producers in B have an incentive to press for trade restrictions. On the other hand,

TABLE 3
Relative Acceptance Indicators, 1960–1985

Flow of exports	1960	1970	1975	1980	1985
U.S. to Japan	1.97	1.68	1.26	1.22	1.54
Japan to U.S.	2.45	2.33	1.59	1.53	1.96

SOURCES: Derived from figures in IMF, *Directions of Trade*, various issues.
   NOTE: This is a somewhat different operationalization of relative acceptance indicators than the one originally proposed by Richard I. Savage and Karl W. Deutsch, "A Statistical Model of the Gross Analysis of Transaction Flows," *Econometrica*, Vol. 28 (1960), pp. 551–572.

TABLE 4
Trade Patterns and Protectionist Pressures

Trade pattern	Societal pressures for protection
Non–import competing trade: *A* and *B* trade goods that are not produced domestically.	Nonexistent
Intrasectoral trade: *A* and *B* export and import similar products.	Low
Intersectoral trade: *A* and *B* export and import different products; imported products do compete with domestic producers.	Higher
Bilaterally unbalanced trade: *A* imports products from *B* that compete with its domestic producers; *A* does not export to *B*.	Highest

if widget producers in *A* and car producers in *B* fear retaliation, they would oppose such measures. Finally, if *A* imports products from *B* that are also produced in *A*, but exports nothing to *B*, then there are no specific groups with a stake in maintaining openness, but there are specific import-competing groups that would favor protection. The possible patterns are summarized in Table 4.

Pressures for protection would also increase if aggregate trade were unbalanced. If *A* imports much more than it exports to *B*, pressure for protection would be greater than if trade were balanced since more import-competing industries are hurt by trade than export-competing industries are helped. Moreover, pressures for protection are greater during periods of macroeconomic recession because under such conditions capital and labor are more difficult to reallocate. High intrasectoral trade with robust macroeconomic performance would support the optimistic assertions about stability voiced by adherents of global interdependence. Bilaterally unbalanced trade is likely to lead to the skepticism typical of analyses focusing on societal pressures, especially those that emphasize the significance of fragmented power and interest group pressure in the United States.

The pattern of sectoral trade between Japan, the EC, and the United States is shown in Table 5. Japan's trade in manufactures with the United States and the EC is much more sectorally imbalanced than trade between the United States and the EC. Moreover, the overall trade balance between the EC and the United States (with EC exports to the United States exceeding U.S. exports to the EC by 3 per cent) was much more balanced than Japan's with the United States (with Japanese exports to

TABLE 5
Sectoral Trade Balances in Manufacturing Industries, 1983

Sector	U.S.–Japan	EC–Japan	U.S.–EC
Products	13.59 (U.S.)	2.74 (EC)	1.26 (U.S.)
Iron and steel	54.25 (J)	7.66 (J)	15.50 (EC)
Chemicals	1.84 (U.S.)	1.61 (EC)	1.50 (EC)
Other semimanu- factured goods	1.35 (J)	1.10 (EC)	2.02 (EC)
Machines for specialized industries	3.01 (J)	2.03 (J)	1.27 (EC)
Office and tele- communications equipment	4.30 (J)	17.50 (J)	4.35 (U.S.)
Road motor vehicles	106.71 (J)	8.35 (J)	7.47 (EC)
Other machinery and transporta- tion equipment	1.58 (J)	4.26 (J)	1.38 (U.S.)
Household appliances	33.68 (J)	47.77 (J)	1.00
Textiles	5.90 (J)	1.00	1.71 (EC)
Clothing	9.25 (J)	4.80 (EC)	4.53 (EC)
Other consumer goods	3.97 (J)	2.07 (EC)	2.65 (EC)
Total manufac- tured goods	4.32 (J)	3.47 (J)	1.15 (EC)
Total trade	2.01 (J)	2.87 (J)	1.03 (EC)

SOURCE: Derived from figures in GATT, *International Trade, 1983/84,* tables A23, A25, and A26.

NOTE: The table shows the ratio between *A*'s exports to *B* and *B*'s exports to *A* in the designated sector. The larger number is used as the numerator. The trading area with the largest exports is indicated in parentheses (J for Japan, U.S. for the United States, EC for the European Community). The indicator varies from 1.00 (equal intrasectoral trade) to infinity.

the United States exceeding U.S. exports to Japan by 101 per cent) or Japan's trade with Europe (with Japanese exports to the EC exceeding EC exports to Japan by 187 per cent). Interactions between the United States and the EC are characterized by high levels of intrasectoral trade; U.S.-Japanese interactions are characterized by intersectoral trade (the United States exports primary products, Japan exports manufactures); and EC-Japanese interactions can be described as bilaterally unbalanced trade. A pure interest group analysis of trading policy would suggest that there would be more pressure to impose protectionist measures against Japan, especially in Europe.

Static sectoral trade balances are, of course, only one indicator of the potential intensity of interest group pressure generated by different patterns of trade. A second indicator is the rate of increase in trade. If changes in export levels take place incrementally, trading partners have time to adjust. Labor and capital can be reallocated. If exports surge in short time periods, adjustment is more difficult (assuming no other changes, particularly with regard to macroeconomic conditions). Japanese exports of manufactures have often grown quite rapidly. For instance, in the period 1980–83, total Japanese engineering products exported to the United States grew by 42 per cent, with the subcategories of office and telecommunications equipment growing by 142 per cent, road motor vehicles by 4 per cent, and household appliances by 67 per cent. The same categories of exports from the EC to the United States increased by 16, 26, 4, and 7 per cent, respectively, and from the United States to Japan by 26, 49, 22, and 46 per cent, respectively.[26]

One factor that can reduce protectionist pressures is direct foreign investment. Outward direct foreign investment creates crosscutting cleavages for corporations that produce import-competing goods. For instance, U.S. automobile companies with a stake in Japanese firms have a more complex set of interests than those without investments in Japan. Outward investment is, of course, no help for labor. Labor in import-competing industries generally supports protection not only because it may reduce imports but also because it may induce foreign corporations to invest in domestic plants, thus increasing the demand for domestic labor. Domestic corporations with their own foreign investments are unlikely to oppose such inward investment since they would be subject to retaliation. Hence, direct foreign investment complicates calculations of interest, especially for corporations, and reduces the probability of sectorally cohesive domestic pressures for protection.

The level of U.S. direct foreign investment in Japan has been modest compared with U.S. activities in Europe. At year-end 1981, the total value of U.S. direct investment in Japan was $6,755 million, of which $3,236 million was in manufacturing. (The rest was almost all in either trade or petroleum.) The total value of U.S. direct investment in the EC was $80,646 million, of which $41,212 million was in manufacturing. Total investment in Japan was about 8 per cent of total investment in the EC, although Japan's gross national product in 1981 was equal to about 47 per cent of the EC's gross national product.[27] Total direct foreign investment in Japan has increased rapidly in the 1980s, however, and more updated figures may show a more comparable picture for Europe and Japan.

The level of Japanese direct investment in the United States has also been modest compared with European investment in the United States. As of year-end 1982, the total value of Japanese investment in the United States was $8,742 million, with 17 per cent in the manufacturing sector. The total value of European investment was $68,514, with 35 per cent in manufacturing. However, Japanese investment has been increasing much more rapidly than European investment, growing by 400 per cent from 1977 to 1982 while European investment grew by 190 per cent.[28]

Hence, in the area of direct foreign investment, U.S. relations with Japan are less intense than those with Europe. However, in contrast to the situation in trade, where Japan's sectorally imbalanced pattern of exchange has been a persistent feature of its international commerce, the level of direct foreign investment into and out of Japan has increased dramatically in the 1980s, a development that should, according to interest group and interdependence arguments, mitigate societal pressures to change existing U.S.-Japanese relationships.

Military Expenditures

Japanese military expenditures as a percentage of gross national product have been among the lowest of all industrialized countries. In 1982, only Iceland spent less than Japan in percentage terms (Iceland spent nothing). Japan and Luxembourg were tied at 1.0 per cent. Among the other major industrialized countries, Italy spent 2.6 per cent, West Germany 3.4 per cent, France 4.2 per cent, the U.K. 5.1 per cent, and the United State 6.4 per cent. Japan's military expenditures were also low compared to those of some neighboring Asian states. Taiwan committed 8.2 per cent of its GNP to the military, Thailand 4.0 per cent, South Korea 6.9 per cent, and Singapore 5.9 per cent. Japan's modest commitment of resources to the military has been a persistent characteristic of its postwar behavior.[29]

The United States has persistently spent a relatively high proportion of its GNP on the military. American behavior is consistent with an analysis that sees security as a collective good that is disproportionately provided by larger states. Japanese behavior is not.

Figure 1 plots the standardized residuals derived from the linear regression of the equation ME (military expenditures) = $a + b$ GNP against the predicted standardized value of military expenditures for the years 1972 and 1982 for all of the advanced industrialized market economy countries with the exception of Iceland, and for Taiwan, Thailand, South Korea, and Singapore. The points for the United States and Japan are labeled. The United States and Japan are the two outliers: the United States spends much more than would be predicted, Japan much less.

From a realist or structural perspective, this cannot be regarded as a stable situation. The Soviet Union is as much of a threat to Japan as it is to the United States. Japan has economic interests in the Middle East and East Asia. About 25 per cent of Japan's exports go to South and East Asia compared with 10 per cent for the United States. In 1982, Japanese military expenditures were about 2.5 times greater than those of South Korea, whereas its GNP was 18 times greater.[30] Japan is far more dependent on Middle East oil than is the United States; yet Japan has virtually

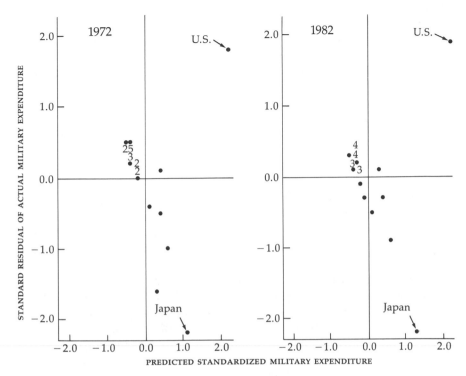

Fig. 1. Military expenditures, 1972 and 1982. Numbers indicate number of cases in that position. Derived from figures in U.S. Arms Control and Disarmament Agency, *World Military Expenditures and Arms Transfers, 1972–82* (Washington, D.C., Apr. 1984).

no military presence in that area, whereas the United States is heavily committed.

From other perspectives, however, the disparity in military commitment between Japan and the United States is much less problematic. Interdependence arguments see a world in which the connection between military power and economic interaction is low. In fact, Japan's modest military expenditures might be politically and economically stabilizing because they make Japan less threatening to its neighbors. It is, for instance, from South Korea's perspective more comforting to have U.S. troops on Korean soil than it would be to have Japanese. Given the geopolitical situation in East Asia, the present commitment of forces can be seen as rational since direct military threats to Japan are improbable.

At least one empirical pattern does emerge from this review of Japanese capabilities, economic interactions, and military expenditures—Japan is different. Japan is growing at a faster rate than the other industrialized states, and its trade is much more sectorally imbalanced. Direct foreign investment into and out of Japan has been more modest than inflows and outflows involving Europe and the United States (although the inflow and outflow of direct foreign investment in Japan have increased dramatically in the 1980s). Finally, Japan's military expenditures deviate from the empirical norm more than those of any other country.

For many of the theories discussed in the first section of this paper, these deviations suggest trouble in U.S.-Japanese relations, in the future if not in the present. Japan is growing quickly enough to challenge the United States in many specific issue-areas and even, in the long run, in terms of overall power capability. Although the level of aggregate economic exchange is substantial, some of the hallmarks of interdependence among other major industrialized countries, particularly a high level of intrasectoral trade and direct foreign investment, are not present for Japan. (This may, however, be changing for direct foreign investment.) Analyses emphasizing the importance of domestic interest group pressure in determining foreign economic policy suggest that U.S.-Japanese relations ought to be particularly difficult because of the imbalance of interests, at least in comparison with U.S. relations with Europe and Canada, its other major economic partners in the industrialized world. Japan's low level of military expenditures in comparison not only with those of the United States but also with those of its Asian neighbors is problematic from a systemic perspective, although here the actual pattern of causality is imprecise because many of the scenarios that would demand higher levels of expenditure from Japan seem farfetched. In contrast, the argument that links sectorally imbalanced trade with greater domestic pressure for protectionism, especially in the United States where political power is fragmented, is much more clearly worked out.

Finally, there is one theoretical argument that would draw optimistic conclusions from this review of aggregate trends—David Lake's contention that Japan and the United States will become mutual supporters of a liberal, open international economic regime. Lake's analysis, based on the rational self-interest calculations of two major trading states of relatively equal size and technological sophistication, draws optimistic conclusions about handling at least the first phase of any power transitions between Japan and the United States, a phase during which the two states would be more or less equal partners.[31]

However, the aggregate data presented in this section have no bearing on several of the arguments presented in the first part of this paper, especially those that see institutional structures, including national values, as basic determinants of policy. Intrasectoral trade flows do not tell us much about the world views of central decision makers, including their commitment to maintaining an open international economic order, a commitment that may be based on military and political calculations that supersede concerns about the economic consequences of commodity flows. An assessment of these arguments requires a more detailed investigation of the causes and resolutions of actual disputes between the United States and Japan.

Cases

There is no lack of examples of economic and political conflicts between the United States and Japan. In the typical pattern, the United States presses for change, Japan resists, and ultimately a specific agreement is reached. The United States appears satisfied for a time, but issues are rarely finally resolved. In the security area, the intensity of disagreements has declined since the 1960 renegotiation of the Japanese-U.S. Mutual Security Treaty. In economic affairs, the frequency, intensity, and variety of disputes has increased over time from isolated questions related to specific Japanese exports to the United States in the 1950s to a wide range of issues related to market access in Japan and the United States as well as to the coordination of macroeconomic policy and the functioning of Japan's financial system.

International Security

In international security, tensions peaked in the 1950s, culminating with the tumult associated with the conclusion of the Mutual Security Treaty in 1960. Once the basic rules of the game had been set, however, disagreements between the United States and Japan followed a predictable, even boring, pattern characterized by U.S. efforts to get Japan to make marginal increases in its level of military expenditures.

Such efforts began in the 1950s. The U.S. enchantment with the anti-military provisions of Japan's postwar constitution eroded as the level of tension with the Soviet Union increased. In the early 1950s, Secretary of State John Foster Dulles encouraged Japan to increase its military forces to 325,000–350,000 men. In 1955, Dulles rejected Japan's request for a revision of the security treaty between the two countries, arguing that Japan was not doing enough for its own national defense. Domestic conflict over the passage of a new security treaty in 1960 led to the resignation of Prime Minister Nobusuke Kishi and the cancellation of a scheduled visit by President Eisenhower.[32]

The events of 1960, which were traumatic for both the United States and Japan, led to a modus vivendi based on the rule that Japan would spend 1 per cent of its gross national product on defense. This rule was important in internal Japanese politics because it offered a salient solution around which expectations converged, leaving the LDP less vulnerable to political attack. The United States has not made any effort to change the basic thrust of Japan's fundamentally antimilitary stance, although U.S. officials have persistently urged Japan to make marginal changes in its level of security expenditures. The United States has also pressed for greater cooperation in the area of military technology. Japan has made various concessions, such as Prime Minister Yasuhiro Nakasone's decision to allow the export of military technology to the United States. Japan has also attempted to articulate an independent policy position based on a division of labor in the security area, with Japan attending to economic security by, for instance, providing higher levels of foreign aid, and the United States devoting its energies to military security by maintaining larger armed forces.

Developments in the security area give no indication of any major change in the pattern of U.S.-Japanese relations. There has been constant friction for the past 20 years, but the nature and intensity of this friction have not changed. Even the Vietnam war did not alter the basic characteristics of U.S.-Japanese interactions in the security arena, although the war caused great strains for the United States and was fought in an area geographically close to Japan. The United States did not, for instance, urge the Japanese to send troops to Indochina—a suggestion whose apparent bizarreness only emphasizes the extent to which the basic parameters of the debate in the security area have been limited. Nor, for example, have U.S. policymakers urged Japan to develop the capability to station a carrier task force in the area of the Persian Gulf. The United States has asked Japan to spend more money but not to alter the essentially passive and clientilistic role that Japan has accepted, even embraced, in the international security area.

Stability in the security area can be attributed to systemic factors and to domestic considerations in both the the United States and Japan. Bruce Russett has argued that the decline of U.S. hegemony is much exaggerated.[33] Without making a judgment about the general merits of this argument, it is clear that the Soviet Union and the United States continue to be the two dominant and unchallenged military powers. No Western country other than the United States, certainly not Japan, can project military capacity globally. No other Western state has nuclear capabilities that rival those of the United States. Unlike various economic issue-areas, the military dominance of the United States within the Western alliance has not been challenged. Nor is there any indication that such a challenge will occur in the future. As Fig. 1 indicates, the United States continues to spend a larger percentage of its GNP for defense than any other Western state. Hence, the lack of variance in U.S.-

Japanese interactions in security matters is consistent with an interpretation that points to the basic continuity of postwar structural conditions.

An explanation of Japanese security policy based solely on structural considerations can explain consistency, but it cannot explain the relatively low level of Japan's military commitments. Stable Japanese expenditures of 2, 3, or 4 per cent of GNP would be equally consistent with a structural explanation emphasizing the persistent bipolar distribution of postwar military power. In the final analysis, structural arguments are almost always about constraints rather than about specific behavior. In the postwar military arena so clearly dominated by the Soviet Union and the United States, Japan was constrained to be part of the U.S. security alliance, but its role within that alliance was not determined by systemic factors. A more complete understanding of the persistence of Japanese policy and its peculiar nature requires some discussion of domestic considerations.

Domestic factors in both Japan and the United States conspired to create and then reinforce a low level of military expenditures in Japan. As Kenneth Pyle argues in his paper in this volume, Japan adopted a strikingly antimilitary policy after 1945. The Yoshida Doctrine (named after Prime Minister Shigeru Yoshida, 1948–54) called for economic development, limited armament, and military bases for the United States. Japan explicitly rejected the possession or development of nuclear weapons. The Yoshida Doctrine has been the LDP's consensus position and has been widely accepted within the Japanese polity. Groups advocating either remilitarization or total disarmament have increasingly been pushed to the outer margins of the political spectrum.

Policymakers in the United States were sympathetic to the Yoshida Doctrine despite their persistent nagging about Japan's level of military spending. The primary concern of U.S. policymakers in the early postwar period (and even to the present) was to prevent the internal as well as the external spread of communism. The fundamental lesson that U.S. leaders drew from the experiences of the 1930s was that authoritarian regimes were a product of a breakdown in domestic economic and social order. Economic development was not just an end in itself, it was a prophylactic against political changes inimical to the most deeply held goals of U.S. leaders. Political instability arose from economic instability, and political breakdown implied the rise of authoritarian and probably communist regimes. But stable economic growth was associated with political development, which was identified with democracy.[34] Thus, the Yoshida Doctrine coincided perfectly with the basic world view of central decision makers in the United States, even though its intellectual origins were very different. Moreover, the political disorder associated with the revision of the security treaty in 1960 suggested to U.S. policymakers that extreme pressure on Japan could lead to developments in Japan that would undermine broader U.S. objectives. Thus, once a particular policy had been articulated, it was reinforced both by institutional relations, such as the weak bureaucratic position of Japan's Defense Agency, and by the expectations of political decision makers in Japan and the United States that the issue of increased military expenditures could have wider and potentially destabilizing consequences for internal and external Japanese politics.

The basic structural condition—the great military power of the United States—gave Japan considerable leeway in establishing its level of defense commitments, but once this level was more or less fixed in the early 1960s it was strongly reinforced by ongoing political routines. One of the few events that would disturb this routine would be an external crisis that demonstrated that the military capacity of the United States was inadequate to defend Japan's vital interests.

International Economic Relations

Economic interactions between the United States and Japan do not offer quite so sanguine a picture. As in the case of security disputes, the United States has been the *demandeur*. The frequency, intensity, and variety of U.S. demands have, however, increased over time. During the 1950s and 1960s, the major concern of U.S. policymakers was to limit selected Japanese exports. In the 1970s, U.S. policymakers began to raise issues related to the management of macroeconomic policy and access to the Japanese market. Such issues inevitably involved not only specific Japanese policies but also the institutional characteristics of Japan's political economy. The economic conflicts that have arisen between the United States and Japan reflect both changes at the systemic level, especially the dramatic growth of Japan's relative capability, and domestic factors involving parliamentary politics and differences in national values and institutions.

Access to the U.S. market. Import restrictions on Japanese products offer the most extensive set of cases in the economic area. The United States has imposed controls on a wide range of products. Developments associated with the first set of controls, which were adopted for some cotton textiles in 1955, have been repeated in a number of other sectors. In the case of textiles, central decision makers in the United States acted reluctantly and then only because they were pressured by powerful domestic interest groups. They refrained from imposing unilateral restrictions and opted instead for voluntary export restraints, which were at least proximately imposed by the Japanese. American policymakers endorsed this policy because they were afraid that unilateral action would undermine the wider international trade regime.[35] The Japanese acquiesced to U.S. pressure. In the mid-1950s, they felt that they had no alternative. Japan was dependent on the United States both strategically and economically. Loss of the U.S. market would have been disastrous for Japanese producers. MITI was able to orchestrate the allocation of quotas among Japanese firms. This same pattern of pressure from domestic producers in the United States, reluctant initiatives by the U.S. government, and ostensibly voluntary restraints by Japan was repeated for steel in the late 1960s and automobiles in the early 1980s.[36] The United States used other policy instruments as well, such as escape-clause actions and the imaginative trigger-price mechanism for steel, a device that was almost certainly designed to stave off domestic pressure without having much effect on Japanese imports.

These restrictions have been universally bemoaned by advocates of the liberal trade regime. Import barriers have been viewed as an unfortunate capitulation to interest group pressure. But the actual outcome of these measures has hardly been disastrous. Overall trade between the United States and Japan has continued to grow, indeed it has grown by leaps and bounds. The imposition of restrictive measures on specific products has not resulted in any general move toward protectionism. American actions have not led to incremental Smoot-Hawleyism. What has happened, though, is that the systemic change in the position of the Japanese economy—the increasing international competitiveness of more and more sectors of the Japanese economy—has led Japan's trading partners to abandon the pristine precepts and principles of the liberal international trade regime in favor of actions that are more responsive to the need to ease the burden of adjustment for import-competing industries. The United States has, however, been far more reluctant to impose restrictions than have the major European countries.

Import restrictions have become a focus of mutual recriminations in both the United States and Japan. On the U.S. side, there are persistent accusations that the Japanese are not playing by the same rules. On the Japanese side, there is the perception that Americans are tailoring their interpretation of the rules, if not the rules themselves, to suit specific circumstances. Such recriminations could be avoided, or at least decreased, if both U.S. and Japanese policymakers redefined their understanding of the central features of the postwar economic regime. In particular, issues related to Japanese exports to the United States could be handled more effectively if the postwar trade regime were interpreted as being based on what John Ruggie calls *embedded liberalism* as opposed to orthodox liberalism; if it were recognized that maintaining social stability as well as international openness is an integral part of the regime.[37] This would relieve Americans of the frequent need to prove that the Japanese are doing something wrong to justify import controls and would eliminate the need for the Japanese to defend themselves against charges that they are cheating.

Moreover, it is unlikely that accepting the legitimacy of some form of trade restraints would lead down a slippery slope to general protectionism. There is little empirical evidence from the postwar period that the slippery slope exists at all. Many areas of trade have been excluded from the liberal trade regime from the outset, most notably agriculture, without having any clearly adverse effects on the application of liberal precepts in other areas. The greatest danger arises not from the threat of mutual retaliation among relatively equal trading partners but from the ability of more powerful states to impose unilateral trade restrictions on weaker states. Power and weakness in such instances are a function of the relative opportunity costs of altering existing trading relationships.[38]

For instance, many European states have established substantial barriers against Japanese imports. Japan is not a significant market for European goods, and this makes it easy to impose restrictions because Japan cannot credibly threaten to retaliate. Vinod Aggarwal argues that the international texile regime has, in fact, become a device for restricting the exports of newly industrializing countries.[39] Here, too, there are tremendous asymmetries of power between exporting and importing countries. This is not the case for Japan and the United States because the level of trade is high even though relative opportunity costs are not the same (it would be more costly for Japan than for the United States if relations were broken or sharply curtailed), direct foreign investment is growing, and Japanese capital is becoming increasingly important for the United States.

Thus, neither past experience nor general empirical or even theoretical arguments suggest that U.S. restrictions on Japanese exports could destroy the international trading regime or undermine U.S.-Japanese relations. The kinds of measures that have been used in the past, such as the Multi-Fibre Agreement and voluntary export restraints, ought to be regarded as legitimate means of managing commercial conflict, not as aberrations that reflect the political clout of narrow-minded interest groups or the pusillanimity of political leaders. The growing economic competitiveness of Japanese industries has increased the number of disputes over U.S. restrictions on Japanese products, but it has not changed their basic character. The United States continues to be the *demandeur*, but its demands have generally been modest, designed more to mollify domestic interest groups than to close down economic transactions across the Pacific.[40]

The most challenging problem in handling conflicts over sales in the U.S. market is to prevent policy from being driven entirely by specific interest groups. The most notorious case of such a development was the textile dispute of 1969–71, which almost led the United States to invoke the Trading with the Enemy Act against Japan. President Richard Nixon became locked into a set of political commitments to the textile industry. Prime Minister Eisaku Sato was unable to honor a promise that he had made to Nixon because of resistance from both MITI and the textile industry.

Managing pressures from U.S. firms for greater protection and from Japanese firms reluctant to participate in export restraint agreements is politically difficult, even though both Japanese and U.S. industries might benefit from higher prices in a restricted market. Management is more likely to be successful when power is concentrated in the hands of central bureaucracies. This suggests that so long as MITI continues to be sensitive to the demands of Japan's trading partners, a sensitivity that developed during the 1970s but was not present during the textile wrangle,[41] that U.S. policymakers ought to welcome an active MITI role rather than applauding reports of its slow demise. In the United States, the fragmentation of power creates an endemic problem that has been somewhat alleviated only by the concentration of commercial policy–making in the executive branch since 1934.

Finally, the contrast between textiles and automobiles points to some lessons about the ease with which disputes involving market access to the United States can be handled. Because of direct foreign investment, there were more crosscutting cleavages in the area of automobiles. American firms had substantial interests in Japanese automobile companies. The American industry was not united; General Motors opposed quotas, whereas the UAW, Ford, and Chrysler supported them. Moreover, one consequence of the dispute was to encourage higher levels of Japanese direct foreign investment in the United States, a policy that was strongly supported from the outset by American labor. Direct foreign investment from Japan may benefit U.S. corporations and the U.S. economy more generally by facilitating the transfer of Japanese production technology to the United States. The joint General Motors–Toyota plant in Fremont, California, is an example of how such a transfer could take place.

The absence of any clear regime in automobiles, as opposed to textiles, may have made it easier to adopt relatively liberal short-term quotas rather than long-term quasi-permanent restrictions. When technology, interests, and actors are rapidly changing, it may be better to cut specific deals than to attempt to find some appropriate general rules. It is true that rules may grease agreements and constrain grossly self-interested behavior by more powerful states.[42] But U.S.-Japanese interaction is not characterized by gross disparities in power, and the experiences of the past 30 years have provided a rich repertoire of potential responses to market-access disputes. If there is a model for handling problems involving access to the U.S. market, it is offered by the automobile case of the early 1980s.

The automobile case is not, however, a model of liberal behavior. The United States did impose trade restrictions on Japanese manufacturers. MITI and the Japanese industry had to allocate shares in the U.S. market. Japanese companies did not decide to invest in the United States because of pure market considerations. Indeed, Nissan and Toyota were both skeptical of such investments because of their expectation that U.S. manufacturers would become effective competitors in the small-car market, leading to excess productive capacity.[43] The decision to invest was based on an assessment of political conditions in the United States. Nevertheless, a situation in which both production and trade cut across national boundaries is much more politically sustainable than one based on trade alone. The absence of any permanent regime in the automobile industry made it easier to change policies.

Since trade restrictions are a product of both specific industry concerns and macroeconomic conditions, especially the overall or bilateral U.S. trade deficit, the absence of institutionalized strictures is an advantage because it may make it easier to rewrite agreements that were prompted at least in part by overall deficits as opposed to the specific circumstances of a particular sector. Moreover, recognition of the need to follow different policies in different situations may moderate the mutual recriminations that have characterized some recent U.S.-Japanese disputes, where accusations of unfairness, of engaging in sin rather than merely pursuing self-interest, have exacerbated tensions.[44]

Access to the Japanese market. Disputes over access to the Japanese market will be more intractable than disputes over access to the U.S. market. The saliency of this issue has grown over time for a number of reasons. First, the bilateral trade deficit with Japan has made central decision-makers in the United States more sensitive to Japanese restrictions. Second, the declining position of the United States in the international system has made U.S. leaders less willing to accept economic costs in exchange for general and ill-defined political benefits. The postwar growth of Japan virtually eliminated the fear of economic collapse leading to political disorder. However, the uncertainty associated with an LDP electoral defeat must remain part of U.S. calculations. Third, domestic ideological commitments to liberal precepts have made U.S. leaders more willing to combat explicit restrictions on the sale of U.S. products than to offer protection to import-competing industries; the former activity represents the pursuit of virtue, the latter shows weakness of will. Fourth, despite the elimination of virtually all quotas in Japan and the sharp reduction in tariffs during the 1970s, it has still been difficult for a number of U.S. products to penetrate the Japanese market. This has led to accusations that the Japanese are using various informal trade barriers. Fifth, domestic structural constraints in Japan have made it difficult to respond to some U.S. complaints at either the legal or the behavioral level; Japan has not been able to eliminate all of its formal restraints, and even in cases where formal restraints do not exist, informal institutional structures impede the sale of U.S. products.

At the most basic level, the increasing attention paid to access to the Japanese market reflects changes in the distribution of economic capabilities in the international system. Japan has become the second largest market in the world. Barriers to entry into this market are much more economically significant now than they were 20 years ago. Moreover, the relative decline in the overall aggregate power of the United States, military as well as political, has made U.S. leaders less willing to tolerate restrictive policies in other countries. In the immediate postwar period, the United States accepted, even encouraged, Japanese protectionism because its primary concern was political development. As international economic costs and pressures, as well as benefits, have increasingly affected the U.S. economy, the preference structure of U.S. leaders has changed, and short-term economic benefits have come to occupy a more important position in their calculations.

However, the strategy adopted by U.S. policymakers to increase access to the Japanese market reflects their particular ideological and institutional proclivities. They have focused, or at least directed, their initial attention to formal trade barriers rather than to informal barriers or actual behavioral results. In recent years, they have paid an inordinate amount of attention to the few remaining formal Japanese trade barriers. These barriers are concentrated in the agricultural sector. Even if eliminated, the impact on U.S. exports would not significantly affect the overall trade deficit. American leaders have continued to focus on these measures because they are clearly in violation of the liberal rules of the game. Unfortunately, agriculture is one issue-area in which the Japanese find it extremely difficult to respond.

As Daniel Okimoto's paper in this volume points out, the decision-making network in the agrarian sector involves farmers, the LDP, and the Ministry of Agriculture, Forestry, and Fisheries. The basic pattern of exchange is farm votes for the LDP in return for policies that favor agriculture. Restrictions on imports are one such policy. Compromise in this area would weaken the electoral base of the ruling party. Hence, the ideological proclivities of U.S. central decision makers, their tendency to focus on formal trade barriers that can be treated in a legalistic way under either the rules of the GATT or U.S. law, has led them to emphasize the one economic sector in which Japanese policymakers are constrained by electoral considerations. Clashing domestic institutional structures and different belief systems make it more difficult to find a mutually acceptable modus vivendi, let alone a final solution.

Disputes over access to more technologically sophisticated sectors of the Japanese economy are also likely to present difficulties for U.S. actors. Here, however, the impediments to greater sales are not formal. Tariff barriers have been essentially removed in these industries. There is little hard evidence that the Japanese government is attempting to impose informal barriers. Private or public actors have made explicit efforts to increase foreign sales in Japan. The economic sectors involved, such as finance and communications, largely fall within Okimoto's third policy-making network in which central bureaucracies, especially MITI and the Ministry of Finance, are largely insulated from narrow sectoral pressures and in which there is a high level of cooperation and consensus between public and private actors. Yet there has not been a substantial increase in U.S. exports. The impediments to greater sales arise, at least in part, from the basic structure of Japan's political economy. The emphasis on the group, on the need for trust, on long-term rather than short-term business relationships, on survival rather than simply profit maximization, makes it difficult for foreign firms to penetrate the Japanese market. These impediments are not the result of official policy, and it is not clear that the Japanese government could do anything about them even if it wanted to.

At the present time, it is impossible to reach any definitive conclusion about market-opening efforts in manufacturing and service sectors. Nihon Telephone and Telegraph (NTT) did agree to open its procurement to foreign bidding after extreme pressure from the United States. The company has opened purchasing offices in the United States and even hired a major public relations firm to get out the message that it is interested in purchases from U.S. companies. Some specifications have been made more flexible, and technical requirements have been translated into English.[45] In the financial area, Japan introduced changes as a result of pressure from the United States. The Yen-Dollar Agreement of November 1983 liberalized capital flows, made the yen more of an international currency, and gave foreign financial institutions greater leeway to operate in the Japanese market. It also gave foreign banks the right to acquire subsidiaries in Japan, to manage trust funds, and to participate in underwriting syndicates for government bonds.[46]

It is too early to know if these arrangements will produce results. Failure is more likely to be the result of the informal institutional structures that govern economic relations in Japan rather than of any explicit or tacit action on the part of the Japanese government. Conventional U.S. liberal precepts, which focus on the activities of public as opposed to private actors, cannot adequately deal with this situation. Again, as in the case of market access for agricultural products, conventional liberal precepts will not work. Changes in the relative economic capabilities of Japan and the United States, coupled with differences in domestic attitudes and institutional structures, have created problems and challenges that cannot adequately be dealt with by simply invoking the market and urging an end to government intervention.

Conclusions, Necessarily Tentative

Too much is changing too quickly in U.S.-Japanese relations for any observer to claim great confidence in policy prescriptions or analytic conclusions. Theoretical arguments are often not completely worked out, and as the first part of this paper indicates, such arguments are not mutually compatible. The available empirical evidence is inconclusive if only because some patterns of behavior are changing so rapidly. Arguments firmly supported by this year's available information could be undermined by next year's national account statistics.

Given these disclaimers, what conclusions can be drawn about the theoretical arguments presented in the first part of this paper and their implications for stability in U.S.-Japanese relations? First, there is little support for the optimistic expectations of analysts who emphasize only the benevolent effects of economic interdependence or see problems as self-correcting. Transactions have grown, but in creating economic benefits, they have spawned political conflicts. In some cases, the political tensions generated by growing economic flows have compelled political decision makers to limit, if not cut back, the level of exchange. The involvement of more groups with more diverse interests has not produced a more benign political environment. Indeed, I. M. Destler argues that in some situations the multiplicity of actors leads to confused and contradictory signals, increases the chances of misperception, and makes it more difficult to resolve disputes.[47]

The one behavior that does support the benign vision of interdependence theorists is direct foreign investment in the United States. Such investment has created crosscutting cleavages. It is welcomed by American labor. If it occurs in an industry where U.S. firms have engaged in significant direct foreign investments themselves, especially if this investment has taken place in Japan, corporate opposition is unlikely. Japanese direct investment in manufacturing plants can facilitate the transfer of technology to the United States. By redirecting some imports to domestic production and providing local employment, direct foreign investment may alter the calculations of some members of Congress. It is not so obvious that direct foreign investment in Japan has the same benign effects. Such investment is not taking place in import-competing industries. It may be difficult for both Japanese corporations and bureaucracies to integrate foreign firms into the dense decision-making networks based on cooperation and trust that characterize Japan's political economy.

In sum, there is no substantial evidence that the growing economic exchange between Japan and the United States is any guarantee of stability; such interactions raise problems that they do not solve, except in the case of Japanese direct foreign investment in import-competing manufacturing sectors.

Systemic-level arguments, which emphasize the relative capabilities of Japan and the United States, are fairly well supported if such arguments are interpreted in issue-specific terms; that is, if relative capabilities are examined in specific issue-areas.[48] In the security area, there have been no basic changes in the overall distribution of power. The United States and the Soviet Union continue to dominate all other actors. The military capabilities of Japan's neighbors in East Asia have not changed in any substantial way. The stability of U.S.-Japanese interactions in the security area, with the United States pressing, but not pressing too hard, for higher levels of Japanese expenditure, has not altered significantly over the past thirty years.[49]

The extremely low level of Japanese expenditures (as opposed to the lack of variation in behavior in the security area) can, however, be explained only by the domestic considerations that led to the policy of limiting defense expenditures to 1 per cent of GNP. Once this choice was made, it was reinforced by the subsequent development of institutional structures and political expectations. Given the very loose structural constraints imposed on Japan by the contemporary international environment, dramatic change is likely only if some crisis demonstrates that the United States is unwilling or unable to protect Japan's vital economic and security interests.

In the economic issue-areas, some structural arguments are more pervasive than others. There has been a significant shift in the underlying economic capabilities of the United States and Japan. The dominance of the United States has eroded. Hegemonic stability theory, one example of structural analysis, suggests that such a shift would lead to a decline in trade. Such a decline has not taken place.[50] David Lake's arguments are more strongly supported by the available evidence. Japan and the United States can both be seen as supporters of the liberal international economic regime. The United States has not changed its basic commitments, although it has imposed restrictions in several specific issue areas. Japan has become an increasingly vocal advocate of international liberalism and has removed almost all of its formal trade barriers. In some areas, the Japanese government is actively promoting a more open attitude among Japanese businessmen. Nevertheless, even Lake's argument does not fully explain the pattern of protectionism and openness that has developed in recent years. Although the liberal regime has hardly collapsed, both institutional and legal arrangements and patterns of behavior have become more variegated across issue-areas.

Analyses that contend that variation in national values and institutional structures is the prime mover of conflict and cooperation between the United States and Japan provide clearer and more persuasive conclusions about the prospects for stability than do systemic-level perspectives. Such arguments suggest that even if U.S.-Japanese economic interactions have been based on liberal precepts and rules in the past, it will be harder to sustain such practices in the future. It will be extremely difficult for Japan to eliminate its remaining formal trade barriers because the LDP is dependent on the sectors involved for electoral support. Moreover, even in those areas of the Japanese economy where formal liberalization is complete, informal institutional structures will make it difficult for U.S. goods to penetrate the Japanese market. It is not clear that the Japanese government could have much influence on the practices that stem from these informal institutional arrangements even if it wanted to.

In the United States, the fragmentation of domestic political power inevitably generates protectionist pressures. The United States has responded to various sectoral dislocations by imposing restrictive measures (usually by asking Japan to impose "voluntary" restraints). This practice, only marginally consistent with the spirit of a liberal international regime, will become more prevalent if the range of import-competing Japanese products continues to grow. Calls for protection cannot be easily contained because there are so many avenues of access to decision making in the U.S. political system. The great bulwark against such pressures to date has been a strong ideological commitment on the part of central decision makers to liberal practices and norms, coupled with institutional arrangements that have concentrated trade policy in the hands of the executive branch, particularly the White House. If this commitment erodes or institutional arrangements are changed to give more power to Congress, then the level of U.S. protection could increase substantially.

Arguments that emphasize the consequences of divergent national values and institutions—and these are the arguments that offer the most precise and complete explanation of past developments in U.S.-Japanese relations in the economic issue area—suggest that the persistent genuflection to liberal precepts, norms, and rules does not offer the best prospects for stability. Central decision makers in the United States have pushed liberalism since the conclusion of World War II, a stance that reflects the basic lessons they drew from the experience of the 1930s.[51] In recent years, Japanese leaders have also become increasingly vocal supporters of the international liberal regime. If the domestic institutional arrangements of the United States and Japan were identical, such a mutual commitment to the same set of principles might be conducive to stability. But Japanese and U.S. institutions are very different. It is much easier to penetrate the U.S. economy because transactions are more frequently determined by relatively short-term market calculations than by stable long-term relations.

Although these differences have become almost a cliche in the literature on comparative politics, they pose real problems for a policy that is based, if only implicitly, on the assumption that similar government actions have similar effects. If the United States removes a trade barrier, competitive producers in Japan have a good chance of increasing their sales in the U.S. market. If Japan removes a trade barrier, it is not clear that competitive producers in the United States will be able to penetrate the Japanese market.

This situation more and more often leads to mutual recriminations—to accusations on the one hand that the playing field is not level and on the other hand that one party is simply not playing by the rules that it has itself supported. Absent some major crisis, this backbiting is not likely to lead to any major shift in policies. But in a crisis, which requires quick action and high levels of cooperation, trust, and understanding between the United States and Japan, the acrimony that has been generated by adherence to normative prescriptions that are inappropriate because of divergent national values and institutions could make effective cooperation difficult.

In a penetrating article, Susan Strange argues that the liberal international economic regime is a myth. She maintains that, in fact, the postwar international trading system has been maintained by what she terms a web-of-contracts. Specific agreements have been made in specific issue-areas. Behavior across sectors, time, and countries has not been consistent. World trade has grown because it has been mutually advantageous. The world trading system will not be brought to a crisis by any specific protectionist actions. The real danger stems from the monetary sector, not the trade sector. Only a breakdown in international financial arrangements could lead to the collapse of the world economic system. Specific trade actions can always be contained, but a financial crisis impacts simultaneously on the whole system.[52]

Web-of-contracts will produce mutually satisfactory outcomes only if there is reasonable symmetry in the power of the contractors. As Aggarwal's analysis of the textile regime has shown, contracts do not work well if one of the parties has little leverage. In the case of U.S.-Japanese relations, there is, however, a reasonable degree of power symmetry. The United States still enjoys a bargaining advantage because the relative opportunity costs of change are less for the United States; nevertheless, the absolute costs of a closure of trade would be high for both countries. The two largest economies in the world are not in a situation in which they can engage in mutual exploitation. Japanese and U.S. policymakers would be better off if they abandoned aspirations for virtue based on adherence to liberal principles and norms and instead legitimated policies that were more closely attuned to short-term and specific interests. Such interests are likely to drive policy in any event. Aspiring to virtue will only lead U.S. policymakers to continue to demand that Japan look more like the United States and Japanese policymakers to regard their U.S. counterparts as hypocrites. Japan will not become more like the United States, and U.S. policymakers cannot ignore protectionist pressures.

A reduction in mutual recriminations through an interest-based policy would leave the United States and Japan in a better position to meet the most important challenge in the contemporary economic environment: the ability of the world's two largest economic powers to act quickly, decisively, and effectively to cope with international crises. The proper analogy to the contemporary international environment is not the political and military conflict between the United States and Japan before World War II; rather it is the difficulty that Britain and the United States experienced in attempting to manage the international economic system between the two world wars. Britain had the desire and the institutional structures needed for effective management but lacked adequate resources; the United States had the resources but lacked commitment and institutional capabilities. As Japan's relative economic capability increases, it will become more important for Japanese and U.S. central decision makers to work effectively together. In crises, efficacy is related to trust. In U.S.-Japanese relations, trust is more likely to emerge from ad hoc procedures based on interests in specific issue-areas, a web-of-contracts, than on efforts to create and enforce general rules based on abstract liberal precepts.

Charles E. Morrison

Japan and the ASEAN Countries: The Evolution of Japan's Regional Role

The concluding paper in this volume describes Japan as a "supporter" country, buttressing the international systems dominated by the United States.[1] Other papers address the questions of whether the maintenance of the international security, political, and economic regimes of the non-communist world requires hegemonial leadership, whether the United States continues to have the capacity to provide this leadership, and what the implications for Japan's international role of a weakened U.S. power position are relative to those of other countries. In this paper, I provide a case study of Japan's interaction with the member-countries of the Association of Southeast Asian Nations (ASEAN)—Brunei, Indonesia, Malaysia, the Philippines, Singapore, and Thailand. The ASEAN group has been closely associated, politically and economically, with the West. How has the relative decline of U.S. global power affected the ASEAN countries and Japan-ASEAN relations? Has there been a significant erosion of the effectiveness of international trade and security regimes in the region? Have Japan's policies toward the group compensated for the U.S. decline? Has Japan established regional regimes under its own hegemonial influence? What problems and constraints exist in Japan's relations with its ASEAN neighbors?

Japan's policies toward the ASEAN member-countries are probably more indicative of the nature of Japan's evolving international role than are its policies toward other regions. The U.S. government has long urged Japan to accept greater international responsibilities and to play a larger economic and political role, especially in developing Asia. As early as October 1962, President John F. Kennedy told visiting Eisaku Sato, then out-of-office, that Japan should contribute more to the economic development of Southeast Asia.[2]

Japanese leaders have acknowledged a need to play a more active international role, and government statements, particularly since 1980, have become more and more explicit on this subject. In its 1981 Diplomatic Bluebook, the Ministry of Foreign Affairs stated: "Japan has now reached the stage at which it should participate, autonomously and in a positive way, in the maintenance and organization of international relations."[3] In a policy statement to the Diet in January 1985, Prime Minister Yasuhiro Nakasone said that he has sought "to develop Japan as an 'international country' actively taking part in the work of promoting world peace and prosperity."[4]

The first postwar Japanese efforts to establish an overseas economic and diplomatic role, however, began considerably earlier, and Japanese diplomatic relations are most highly developed in the ASEAN region. Japan has had long-standing economic and political interests in this region, which is significant to Japan as a source of raw materials, a market for Japanese manufactures, and an area through which many of Japan's fuels and products are transported.[5] In the early 1980s, the ASEAN countries accounted for approximately 15 per cent of Japan's imports, including most of its natural rubber, tropical timber, and palm oil, about half its liquid natural gas, and one-sixth of its petroleum. The region purchased about 10 per cent of Japanese exports. It stands astride major trade routes connecting Japan with fuel suppliers in the Middle East and iron ore suppliers in western Australia. Politically, the future ASEAN member-countries were the first in the developing world in which Japanese influence and presence was reasserted after the war. One scholar of Asian international relations has commented that "Japan's interest and involvement in Southeast Asia were barely interrupted by her failure to enforce her coprosperity policy during the course of the Pacific War."[6]

A legacy of bitterness and suspicion remains from the 1941 to 1945 occupation of the region, but the nature and impact of the memories of the war are by no means uniform. They have not inhibited some Southeast Asian leaders from asserting that Japan should have a special relationship with the ASEAN region as a leader, a donor, or as a model.

Singaporean prime minister Lee Kuan Yew said in a private interview in 1968 that "my generation and that of my elders cannot forget [the Japanese occupation] as long as we live." But, he added, "our population is by and large a hard-headed one. The policy of the government is not to allow the unhappy experiences of the past to inhibit us from a policy which can enhance our growth rates by Japanese participation in our industry. . . ." Lee has long been an advocate of a strong Japanese role in the region and once called for Japanese naval forces in Southeast Asian seas in association with U.S. and European naval forces.[7]

Boonchu Rojanasathien, a Thai politician and business leader, has urged Japan "to fill the role of leader in the ASEAN region," comparable to the role of the Soviet Union in COMECON or the United States vis-à-vis other Western democracies.[8] Other Southeast Asians have called for a prominent Japanese role in more cautious and general terms, usually interpreting leadership as requiring a special level of political and economic support. For example, former Indonesian foreign minister and later vice-president Adam Malik, for example, was among those who advocated a Japanese Marshall Plan for the region, and General Ali Moertopo, another leading Indonesian figure in the post-1966 New Order era, proposed a Japanese-Australian-Indonesian entente to maintain an Asia-Pacific regional order.[9] Explicit policies in the late 1970s and the early 1980s to "learn from Japan" in Singapore and to "look East" in Malaysia are indicative of another kind of Southeast Asian expectation of Japan— that it can provide a model for social and economic development.

Compared to such expectations, Japanese diplomacy in the region has appeared reticent. For much of the postwar period, Japan needed little in the way of an independent strategy for supporting its political and security interests in Southeast Asia and looked primarily to the United States for leadership in providing external support for maintaining stability in the ASEAN region. Nevertheless, as I argue below, the Japanese and ASEAN governments have had complementary interests in a stable regional order in East Asia, including the preservation of the basic social, economic, and political framework of the ASEAN societies. Changes in the international environment forced a more explicit recognition of these interests. American pressures as well as uncertainties about the U.S. regional role have raised the question of whether Japan must assume a more prominent regional role if it is to achieve its economic and political goals. Japan has become an important regional actor, and its fundamental foreign policy priority in its relationship with the United States has ensured that its activities in ASEAN generally have been supportive of the previously established political and economic order in the region.

In this paper, I first look at the evolution of Japan-ASEAN diplomatic and military relations during the period of U.S. withdrawal from the region and then examine elements of the economic and cultural relationships. Before turning to these subjects, however, it is useful to review the power disparities between Japan and ASEAN. A comparison of some basic indicators are listed in Table 1. Clearly, Japan is a much larger power than any of the individual ASEAN countries, but it must be remembered that despite the focus in this paper on the ASEAN group as a collectivity, it is from individual national perspectives that Southeast Asians see the power differences. Japan's greatest advantage lies in its economy, which is nearly six times that of all the ASEAN members combined. Although economic growth in most of the latter exceeds Japan's, projections made for Japan's Economic Planning Agency suggest that

TABLE 1
Basic Comparisons: Japan and ASEAN, 1980s

Country	Population (millions, mid-1985)	GNP/capita (U.S. $, 1984)	GNP (billions U.S. $, 1984)	Defense spending (billions U.S. $, 1982)	Size of armed forces (thousands, 1984)
Japan	120.8	10,390	1,248.1	10.4	245
ASEAN	296.9	780	215.3	8.7[a]	802[a]
Brunei	0.2	20,520[b]	4.3[b]	—	—
Indonesia	169.1	540	85.4	2.9	281
Malaysia	15.7	1,990	30.3	2.1	125
Philippines	56.8	660	35.0	0.9	105
Singapore	2.6	7,260	18.4	0.9	56
Thailand	52.7	850	42.8	1.8	235
Ratio: Japan/ ASEAN	0.4 to 1	13 to 1	5.8 to 1	1.2 to 1	0.3 to 1

SOURCES: Population Reference Bureau, *World Population: Toward the Next Century* (Washington, D.C., 1985); World Bank, *World Bank Atlas, 1986*, for GNP, GNP per capita; and International Institute for Strategic Studies, *The Military Balance, 1984–1985* (London, 1985), for defense spending, size of armed forces.
[a] Excluding Brunei.   [b] 1983.

even in the year 2000, the ASEAN gross national product will be about $750 billion in today's dollars, still only a third of what will then be a $2.18 trillion Japanese economy.[10] Because of the large economic disparity, ASEAN leaders know that theoretically Japan's military power could also be expanded to about the same range of difference. That Japan's defense outlays remain only slightly larger than that of the ASEAN countries combined provides some reassurance to those who fear potential Japanese hegemony.

Japanese-ASEAN Political and Security Relations

The Changing Regional Environment in the late 1960s and 1970s

The period from approximately 1967 to 1979 witnessed a major shift in large power relationships in Asia, affecting the underlying sense of security of the elites associated with governments in both Japan and in the ASEAN region, especially the latter. These shifts at first contributed to growing tensions in the Japan-ASEAN relationship, but ultimately they proved a source of mutual attraction.

After the 1966 establishment of the New Order in Indonesia, all the ASEAN countries were ruled by relatively conservative and staunchly anticommunist governments, some with a still insecure base of domestic political support. The Philippines and Thailand were linked by security treaty with the United States; Malaysia and Singapore were linked with the United Kingdom (thus indirectly with the United States); and the new government in Indonesia remained formally nonaligned but depended heavily on aid from the Western countries and Japan. During the 1950s and 1960s, Japan economic relations with these countries had grown rapidly, but there were relatively few reinforcing links in the political and cultural spheres. Little sense of political solidarity, apart from a utilitarian economic relationship, had been established, even in the case of Indonesia, where Japan had become a major source of economic assistance to the new regime after 1966.[11]

Thus in the late 1960s, the United States and Western European countries remained the main sources of both tangible assistance and psychological support for the ASEAN governments. The governing elites in the ASEAN societies were, however, deeply disturbed by what seemed to be a steady retreat of their major allies after 1966. Some milestones along the way were the 1967 British announcement that it would withdraw its military forces from Singapore; the 1969 Guam (or Nixon) Doctrine, which stated that the United States would look to its allies to take the primary burden in dealing with internal insurgencies; the United States' Vietnamization policy; the 1973 Paris Peace Agreements ending U.S. military intervention in Vietnam; the 1975 fall of the Lon Nol government in Cambodia and the Thieu government in South Vietnam; and the 1977–78 U.S. plans to withdraw ground forces from South Korea. To these must be added the significant rapprochement in Sino-American relations, whose implications were variously interpreted but which was frequently regarded in Southeast Asia as an effort by the United States to cover its retreat from the region. Finally, another disturbing element for some of the ASEAN governments was the growth of human rights concerns in the United States in the mid-1970s, at times accompanied by harsh political rhetoric directed precisely at the elites and governments that looked to the United States for support.

These events, of course, seemed to Southeast Asian elites to be the regional manifestations of a more general external and internal decaying of the postwar U.S. hegemon. The broader context included the visible social conflicts within the United States, the years of stagflation, the collapse of the postwar monetary system, the growing signs of protectionism, the inability of the United States to respond effectively to the Arab oil embargo, the decline of U.S. support for foreign aid, the ability of the Soviet Union to establish strategic parity with the United States, the collapse of bipartisanship in U.S. foreign policy, and the weakness of U.S. executive vis-à-vis the legislature for much of the time from the late Johnson administration through the Carter administration. In the wake of these larger global changes, there was little the ASEAN governments could do other than to adjust their foreign policies to the new international environment.

The relationship of the international environment with domestic politics in the ASEAN countries was an indirect one, but events such as the communal riots in Malaysia in 1969 and temporary suspension of parliament, frequent demonstrations in Manila prior to the September 1972 declaration of martial law, and political jockeying in Indonesia as the Soeharto government gradually entrenched itself occurred during the same period. At the domestic level, the November 1971 coup in Thailand, which result in the abolition of political parties and the National Assembly, and the declaration of martial law in the Philippines were justified in part by the need for a more controlled society during a more dangerous period of international affairs. Less dramatic events took place in Indonesia and Malaysia, but these, too, went in the direction of tightening governmental control. These efforts in turn caused dissatisfaction and set in motion counterpressures. Throughout the 1970s, there was considerable political tension within all the ASEAN societies. This political tension played a major role in the riots that occurred in Jakarta and Bangkok in January 1974 during Prime Minister Kakuei Tanaka's Southeast Asian tour.

The ASEAN countries' foreign policy adjustments to the changing and uncertain structure of the regional order included the creation of ASEAN in 1967 and its strengthening after 1976.[12] Another significant adjustment involved efforts by all the countries except Indonesia to diversify their foreign relations and especially to improve ties with China. Malaysia took the lead, emphasizing its nonaligned status in its 1970 proposal for the neutralization of Southeast Asia and normalizing its relations with Beijing in 1974, after a year's delay to mitigate Indonesian objections. The Philippines and Thailand waited until mid-1975 to establish relations with China, although they had begun the process two to three years earlier.

To summarize, the ASEAN governments, unsure of their political bases of support both externally and internally, sought in various ways to strengthen their positions. Their main efforts were directed toward consolidating control on the domestic level, strengthening regional solidarity, and diversifying their foreign relations. Especially in this latter context, they began to view Japan, an economic power whose interests and interaction in the ASEAN region had been rapidly expanding, as a potentially greater source of political support.

As in the case of the ASEAN countries, the premises of Japan's postwar foreign policy were severely shaken by the upheavals in the 1970s. During the 1950s and 1960s, the United States had been the dominant actor in Asian international relations; the Japanese government was uncomfortable with certain aspects of U.S. policy (for example, the extent of U.S. involvement in Vietnam and its hostility toward China), but it supported its main lines with minor variations. Where Japanese economic interests appeared to conflict with the political positions in part dictated by the U.S. alliance, Japan found a useful device in the "separation of politics from economics," initially used to permit a limited trade with China, but extended to some degree to Japan's foreign policy as a whole. As Japan's economic strength grew, it came under growing pressure from the United States to play a more active economic role in support of "free world" political goals, but in contrast to the later Japanese emphasis on "comprehensive security," the economic-political connections were downplayed. Japan's regional initiatives, including its prominent role in the establishment of the Asian Development Bank, its joining of the Asian and Pacific Council (ASPAC), and its initiative in establishing a series of Ministerial Conferences for the Economic Development of Southeast Asia (all occurring in 1966), heavily emphasized economic cooperation. Tokyo was especially sensitive to the charge, both domestically and abroad, that these initiatives were designed in collusion with the United States to build an anti-Beijing axis along the Pacific rim.

Several dramatic events in the 1970s demonstrated that the underlying conditions had changed and that new foreign policy approaches might be required. Aside from the shift in the U.S. posture in Southeast Asia, these events included the serious textile dispute with the United States in the late 1960s and early 1970s, which was the first major postwar U.S.-Japan trade conflict, and the "Nixon shocks"—the opening to China and the floating of the dollar. These called into question the degree of Japanese dependence on the United States. Another important event was the 1973 Arab oil embargo. Japan had developed a particularly energy-intensive pattern of industrialization, and it relied heavily on petroleum imported from the Middle East for energy. The embargo's short-term effects were enormous, bringing Japan's economic growth rate down from 9 per cent in 1973 to zero in the following year.[13] It brought home the fragility of Japan's economic base and illustrated the helplessness of Japan's principal ally—the United States—to help it cope with this resource crisis.

The riots during Prime Minister Tanaka's 1974 Southeast Asian tour followed closely on the heels of the oil embargo. These could be dismissed to some extent as reflecting Southeast Asian resentments dating from the Pacific war. They also, however, challenged some cherished Japanese notions: that Japan could serve as a bridge between Asia and the West, that Japan's economic growth in and of itself was appreciated as beneficial to the region as a whole, and that the separation of economics from other aspects of relations was a successful formula for avoiding political problems with Asian neighbors.[14] The demonstrations showed that Japan was alienated from some of its neighbors, whose importance as raw material providers had just been highlighted by the oil embargo.

It pointedly reminded Japan of the political fragility of Southeast Asia and reinforced an almost universal feeling among Japanese leaders that Japan itself needed to do something to strengthen stability in this nearby region.[15]

The Fukuda Doctrine

The changing, less secure structure of the international environment thus strengthened the affinity of interests between the Southeast Asian governing elites and their counterparts in Japan. Japan was one logical place for Southeast Asian governments to seek new sources of support. It was already the principal trading partner and aid provider for most of the ASEAN group, and although the growth of Japan's economic presence had created some resentments (discussed below), it had become a major supporter of the economic development programs that, by the late 1960s, had become a principal basis of governmental legitimacy for the ASEAN governments. Although the ASEAN governments were making accommodations with China and Vietnam, the purpose of these, at least initially, was to reduce potential threats rather than to seek additional support from those who shared complementary interests.

As Singaporean foreign minister S. Rajaratnam observed, Japan was the one large noncommunist power that could not withdraw from the Southeast Asian region. "So Japan has a very crucial interest in the survival of ASEAN. If ASEAN goes, she is completely cut off by a whole batch of communist countries."[16] This apocalyptic vision was not necessarily shared in Japan, but new concern for ASEAN stability and the continuing U.S. pressure for Japan to strengthen its regional role lay behind a major redefinition of Japan's Southeast Asian policy in the mid-1970s. The ASEAN efforts to reinvigorate relations among themselves by strengthening the ASEAN regional framework and with noncommunist governments outside the region through ASEAN "external dialogues" provided an opportunity for a Japanese initiative.

At the end of February 1976, at the first ASEAN summit conference, political cooperation among the member-countries was formally initiated, and the economic ministers were elevated to a role in the organizational structure more or less equivalent to that of the foreign ministers. Shortly afterward, Japanese Foreign Ministry officials concerned with Southeast Asia met in Hongkong and agreed that Japan should assist ASEAN in developing its own "resiliency" and encourage peaceful coexistence between the ASEAN and the Indochinese countries. In October 1976, Foreign Minister Zentaro Kosaka spoke publicly of Japan's interest in promoting an ASEAN-Indochina dialogue, and at the end of the year, Prime Minister Takeo Fukuda spoke of Japanese-ASEAN ties as being "a little alienated" and said that he would like to make contacts as soon as possible.[17] Plans for a Fukuda trip to the region were well under way by this time, and there were reports that Japan would step up its assistance in light of decreased U.S. and Soviet assistance.[18] In March 1977, the joint communiqué issued during Prime Minister Fukuda's visit to Washington reaffirmed the two countries' policies of assisting the ASEAN nations.

Japan's Southeast Asia policy was formally enunciated in August 1977 when Prime Minister Fukuda visited the ASEAN countries (as well as Burma) and attended the second ASEAN summit in Kuala Lumpur. In a celebrated speech in Manila at the end of his trip, Fukuda announced that Japan would not become a military power, that it would cooperate with the Southeast Asian countries in developing practical cooperation in the political, economic, social, and cultural spheres based on "heart-to-heart" understanding, and that Japan would assist in strengthening the solidarity and resilience of the ASEAN member-countries while fostering mutual understanding between them and the nations of Indochina.

The Fukuda Doctrine is regarded as a major turning point in postwar Japan-ASEAN relations in that it provided what Japan regarded as a statement of its political interests in the Southeast Asian region.[19] These interests not only were compatible with the new concept of "omnidirectional" foreign policy that generally characterized Fukuda's diplomacy, but also assumed a degree of Japanese political leadership in the region, to be based on economic and political initiative rather than on military strength. Japan's Southeast Asian diplomacy was explicitly cited as a Japanese contribution to the international order. Foreign Minister Sonoda explained that "it is the duty of Japan as an advanced country in Asia to stabilize the area and establish a constructive order."[20] Fukuda noted that "Japan should seek global affluence and peace to assure its own affluence and peace. We should seek even stronger ties with the Asian nations since they are closer to Japan racially, culturally, and economically."[21] He added that "Japan should take actions, reflecting its increasing responsibilities toward Southeast Asia."[22]

Radical critics of the Fukuda Doctrine came to much the same conclusions about Japanese aims from a different perspective. According to one Filipino, "Obviously, Japan is trying to assume the role of big brother to Asian neighbors. . . . The aim is to prevent the ASEAN countries from joining the ranks of the non-aligned and to maintain their economic dependence on U.S. and Japanese imperialism."[23] A Japanese Marxist commentator argued that the purpose of Fukuda's trip was "to maintain the 'political stability' of ASEAN and thus form an alliance responsible for maintaining world capitalism." He saw Japan being forced by the U.S. decline and the insecurity of the ASEAN elites "against her will into being a leader of 'counter-revolution' in East Asia."[24]

Japan's Diplomatic Role After the Fukuda Doctrine

Japan continued to define a more active diplomatic role in the region, but a somewhat different one from that envisioned by the authors of the Fukuda Doctrine. By the time the Fukuda Doctrine had been enunciated, the ASEAN governments were already well on their way to recovering their confidence. A number of other factors seemed to make an expanded Japanese diplomatic role in Southeast Asia less needed. These included the breakdown in relations between China and Vietnam, the development of close Sino-Thai ties assuring the security of ASEAN's "front-line" state against possible Vietnamese aggression, and the restoration of a more vigorous U.S. defense role. ASEAN, however, eagerly sought Japan's support on issues of great political importance to the member-countries, especially Vietnam's occupation of Kampuchea and the Indochinese refugee crisis. Rather than a leader, Japan became a sometimes reluctant supporter of ASEAN demarches on these issues.

The Fukuda notion of maintaining some kind of balance to facilitate understanding between ASEAN and Indochina fell by the wayside, along with the more general concept of omnidirectional foreign policy, in the late 1970s and early 1980s, as ASEAN or the United States insisted that Japan prove its friendship by supporting their causes on a variety of issues—Kampuchea, Afghanistan, hostages in Iran. Shortly before the Vietnamese invasion of Kampuchea, Vietnamese foreign minister Nguyen Duy Trinh visited Japan, and a new aid package was worked out. Neither this inducement nor Japanese encouragement of a political settlement had any effect on the Vietnamese. After the Kampuchean invasion, Japan froze aid to Vietnam, but under great pressure from ASEAN, which demanded that Japan show its political solidarity with the Southeast Asian group. By the beginning of 1980, Japan was coordinating its positions on Vietnam and Kampuchea closely with ASEAN, and since then, its positions have deviated only in minor details from those of ASEAN. There has been ambivalence within Japan about this situation. On the one hand, Japan can diplomatically support ASEAN at little cost to other Japanese interests, but on the other hand, some would prefer to improve ties with the Indochinese states and resent ASEAN's (especially Thailand's) ability to dictate the parameters of Japan's policies toward these third countries.

During 1978 and 1979, the high number of refugees fleeing Indochina was of great concern to the ASEAN governments, who sought assurances that the refugees would be guaranteed homes in countries of "ultimate asylum." In the United States, the interest provoked by this issue centered more on the plight of the refugees than on the social and political concerns of the ASEAN group, but nonetheless resulted in a variety of U.S. initiatives to deal with both the immediate and longer-term aspects of relief and resettlement. Japan initially seemed to have little to offer the ASEAN countries since it was unwilling to accept more than a token number of refugees. Under great pressure from both ASEAN and the United States, however, the Japanese government somewhat tardily carved out an important and appreciated role as the primary financier of the international refugee assistance effort in Southeast Asia.[25]

By the mid-1980s, Kampuchea and refugees had disappeared as issues regarded as serious threats to the stability of the ASEAN region. An issue of looming importance was the political crisis in the Philippines. The legitimacy of the government of President Ferdinand Marcos, in office since 1966, had been progressively undermined by a number of factors including military abuses, the 1983 assassination of opposition leader Benigno Aquino, Marcos's uncertain health, low prices for Philippine commodity exports, an international debt crisis, civil unrest, and a growing Communist insurgency. This crisis created concern within other ASEAN countries (it was referred to in a Suharto-Lee joint communiqué in April 1985 much to Marcos's chagrin) and resulted in a strong U.S. effort to push Marcos in the direction of political, economic, and military reforms, and eventually out of office. The Japanese government did not play a major political role, regarding U.S. interests in the Philippines as paramount. When Imelda Marcos passed through Japan in November 1985 following stops at the United Nations and Moscow and at a time of severe Washington criticism of the Marcos government, she was advised by Foreign Minister Shintaro Abe to talk to the Reagan administration "frankly" and maintain good ties with Washington for the good of Asia as a whole.[26] It was only after Corazon Aquino became president in February 1986 that Japan strengthened its assistance program, complementing U.S. policy initiatives. It was symbolic that President Aquino visited Washington first (September 1986) and then Tokyo (in October).

It was only on the marginal question of Pacific Basin cooperation that Japan became identified with a major regional initiative. Despite the skepticism of professionals in the Foreign Ministry, in late 1979 Prime Minister Masayoshi Ohira and his foreign minister, Saburo Okita, became enthusiastic about the concept, and it became imbedded in the rhetoric of subsequent Japanese prime ministers and foreign ministers, with the degree of political enthusiasm waxing and waning with perceptions of the degree of positive or negative echoes in Washington or ASEAN. The appeal of the concept of Pacific Basin cooperation is hardly new; the notion neatly combines the two principal axes of postwar Japanese diplomacy—relations with the United States and relations with noncommunist Asian countries.

On the concept of Pacific economic cooperation, ASEAN political sensitivities quickly asserted themselves. The initial reactions in ASEAN in 1979 and the early 1980s were cautious, and fears were expressed that a broader regional grouping would dilute ASEAN cooperation or would be dominated by Japan and the United States. Yet there were groups of some influence in the ASEAN region who saw an advantage for ASEAN if the enthusiasm for the concept in the more advanced Pacific Basin countries could be translated into increased attention or aid. In 1984 at the initiative of Indonesian foreign minister Mochtar Kusumaatmadja, the ASEAN countries agreed that the annual foreign ministers' meeting with their advanced country counterparts could include Pacific Basin economic cooperation as a specific agenda item. By putting Pacific Basin economic cooperation in the ASEAN dialogue framework, the ASEAN governments co-opted the government-to-government discussions of the dialogue and asserted their own control of the pace and substance of progress.[27]

The Military Dimension

The firm statement in the Fukuda Doctrine that Japan would not become a regional military power raises the question of whether a nonmilitary power can play a strong political role. This abjuration was intended to reassure Asians who feared that Japanese economic power would eventually lead to commensurate military strength and Japanese who were concerned that a political role might create pressures for an expansion of military power. In the context of U.S. military withdrawals from Asia and speculation that the United States would want Japan to assume U.S. "responsibilities," it was also intended to indicate clearly that Japan was not seeking to fill a previous U.S. role in Asian security.

The strong Southeast Asian sentiments against a significant expansion of Japanese military power are well known. Prime Minister Zenko Suzuki's 1981 promise to the Americans to increase the Japanese defense perimeter to 1,000 nautical miles along the sea lines of communication southward from Tokyo and Osaka occasioned considerable concern in the ASEAN region. In separate visits to Washington in 1982, Presidents Soeharto and Marcos expressed their reservations with a vehemence that surprised U.S. officials. There are two elements in these reactions; one is concern about a greater Japanese military presence in and of itself; the other, perhaps even stronger one, is that a greater Japanese role would serve as an excuse for the Americans to reduce further their own military commitment in the region.[28] The reactions of the U.S. and Japanese governments reassured the ASEAN leaders on these points. The United States was in the process of rebuilding its military strength, globally and in the air and sea in East and Southeast Asia. When Prime

Minister Nakasone toured the ASEAN region in April 1983, a constantly reiterated theme of his trip was that Japan's defense programs were being undertaken within the context of Japan's "peace" constitution.

Despite the opposition to a Japanese security role in Southeast Asia, the most important constraints on Japanese action are domestic rather than external. The conservative ASEAN governments do have some security needs that Japan theoretically could help fulfill. For example, in the early 1980s high-level Indonesian officials suggested that Japan could contribute more directly to Indonesian defense by supplying military aid, arms, and technology to ASEAN countries. Japan turned this down as inconsistent with its policy since 1976 of virtually prohibiting arms exports. As a front-line state, Thailand has had the most clear-cut external security needs of the ASEAN states. In the early 1980s, Japan increased its economic aid and refugee assistance to Thailand in line with a new policy of contributing to the "comprehensive security" of strategically important countries. This, as well as the freeze on aid to Vietnam and political support for ASEAN positions on Kampuchea, are appreciated in Thailand, but the Thais regard the informal alliance with China vis-à-vis Vietnam as more directly relevant to Thai security. It can be speculated that from the Thai perspective, a similar Japanese security role might theoretically be as acceptable as the Chinese one, although less credible in view of the distance.[29]

The articulation in 1980 of the concept of a Japanese role in promoting comprehensive security, including that of the ASEAN region,[30] does provide for expanding assistance based on security considerations, as noted in the case of Thailand. Perhaps a more important longer-term effect of this concept, however, will arise not so much because any particular Japanese aid might be justified with reference to its importance for the recipients' security, but because it can provide a basis for discussions between Japan and the ASEAN partners on security issues.

It could be argued that the growth of a Japanese diplomatic and political role in Southeast Asia has been hampered by the lack of effective leverage to support such a role, including the absence of a military presence in Southeast Asia or military aid. Despite Japan's failure to develop a strong political presence in ASEAN, the idea of Japan's having special responsibilities for encouraging political stability in the ASEAN region endures. Under the concept of comprehensive security, Japan has chosen, as it has throughout the past quarter century, to define its contribution in terms of economic cooperation, but it is now willing to acknowledge and even to emphasize the economic-political links. Habits of broad consultations have been built up, perhaps most visibly demonstrated by Japan's practice of consulting the ASEAN governments before and after the annual economic summits of the seven major industrial nations and its participation in external ASEAN dialogues. The prevailing regional order in Southeast Asia and Japan's interests in that order are not now being obviously threatened. Should there be renewed instability on a broad regional basis, a basis for nonmilitary cooperation on political and security issues has been laid.

Japan and the Economic Growth of ASEAN

The ASEAN governments have looked on their economic relations with Japan as vital to their economic growth and political survival. These governments all regard economic growth as a high political priority and give their past achievements and future promises prominent places in their internal rhetoric. Soeharto's New Order after 1966, Marcos's New Society announced in the wake of the 1972 martial law declaration, and Malaysia's New Economic Policy, which was a major long-term policy for redistribution of wealth announced after serious communal rioting in 1969, are all rooted in the promise of economic progress. Since the elites on whom these governments are based, including the successor Aquino government in the Philippines, are unwilling and unable to undertake serious redistribution programs, the only way of attaining their promises to alleviate the lot of the poor is to keep expanding the overall economic pie.

In this, the ASEAN group was outstandingly successful until the early 1980s. Between 1960 and 1982, per capita income increased at an average annual rate of between 2.8 per cent for the Philippines (the lowest) and 7.4 per cent for Singapore (the world's fastest growing economy after Saudi Arabia in these years). The three other major ASEAN economies grew at per capita average rates of between 4.2 per cent and 4.5 per cent annually. Economic growth has been accompanied by rapid structural change, with the industrial sectors accounting for an increasing share of production at the expense of agriculture (or in the case of Singapore, services). Although the larger ASEAN economies are relatively resource rich, they are also labor rich, and a process of continued expansion of more labor-intensive industries can be expected for years to come. This process is supported by demographic trends. All the ASEAN countries have achieved remarkable reductions in fertility rates during the past ten years, but the labor force increments through the year 2000 have already been born. For at least the next two decades, ASEAN labor forces will be growing rapidly, and a large share of new employment will have to be found in the nonagricultural sectors. Thus, despite their good economic growth performances, the ASEAN governments have never felt economically secure. Fears of serious economic problems or of unmet expectations with attendant serious political implications are always present. The fall of the Marcos government in 1986 and a slump in prices of ASEAN's major export commodities have increased these anxieties.

The international economy has played an important role in ASEAN growth strategies and in the plans of the ASEAN governments for meeting future employment problems and maintaining income growth. The international environment provides markets, a source of capital to help make up the gap between investment and domestic savings, and a source of technology. Japan is looked on as an important economic partner in all three respects.

The Japanese government regards the economic development of the ASEAN group as important to Japan's political and economic interests in the region. Japanese concerns about political instability in ASEAN have tended to focus more on potential internal political and economic failures than on external threats. Because of this, Japanese government officials believe that Japan's trade with ASEAN, its investments in the region, and especially its aid programs have important political implications. Moreover, Japan's definition of its evolving international role in a more general sense, including its support for the comprehensive security of developing countries, centers around economic policies.

Japan-ASEAN Trade Relations

Trade is the most significant economic dimension of Japan-ASEAN relations, reaching $32.7 billion in 1985. All the major ASEAN economies are highly trade oriented, with exports and imports as a percentage of GNP ranging from a low of 33 per cent for the Philippines to highs of 99 per cent for Malaysia and 302 per cent for Singapore (see Table 2). ASEAN prosperity and growth prospects thus depend critically on trade, and Japan's influence in the ASEAN region and its ability to support the ASEAN governments are in part a function of the benefits derived from Japan-ASEAN trade.

These benefits are not inconsiderable. Japan's trade with the ASEAN group grew extremely rapidly in the 1950s and 1960s, both as a percentage of ASEAN imports as well as a percentage of ASEAN exports. By the end of the 1960s, Japan had become the first or second largest trading partner of most of the countries. This trade relationship was based on the purchase of natural resource products by Japan and a vertical division of labor in manufacturing. Rapidly growing Japan had an enormous appetite for raw materials and primary products from Southeast Asia; it sold in return manufactured goods that displaced traditional imports from the United States and Western Europe. Undoubtedly, Japan's growth as a market for the primary products of ASEAN countries has been an important factor in their export earnings and growth. This, of course, happened less because of any conscious Japanese program to as-

TABLE 2
Direction of Trade Statistics, 1970–1985

Country	Trade as per cent of GNP 1983	Per cent of Exports to Japan		Per cent of imports from Japan		Per cent of exports to U.S.		Per cent of imports from U.S.	
		1970	1985	1970	1985	1970	1985	1970	1985
Indonesia	43%	41%	49%	29%	28%	13%	23%	18%	14%
Malaysia	99	18	25	17	23	13	13	9	15
Philippines	33	40	19	31	14	42	36	29	25
Singapore	302	8	9	19	15	11	20	11	13
Thailand	41	25	13	37	26	14	20	15	11

SOURCES: IMF, *Direction of Trade Statistics Yearbook*, various issues.

sist Southeast Asian development than because Japan's own rapid industrial development created (at least until 1973) new demand for raw materials and fuels. The ASEAN countries were willing suppliers, close to home.

Japanese government spokesmen frequently cite the high level of Japanese trade interaction with Southeast Asia, especially Japan's imports from ASEAN, together with its investment and aid, as a contribution to regional development and stability.[31] It has often been assumed that ASEAN trade with Japan will continue to grow, contributing to ASEAN economic expansion and perhaps providing the basis not only for enhanced Japanese political influence but also for increasing trade frictions.[32] Despite the continued growth in the absolute value of trade, however, Japan's share of the imports and exports of many ASEAN countries has been dropping since the mid-1970s (see Table 2).

Two factors have significantly changed the pattern of ASEAN export growth to Japan. The first is the reduced growth of demand in Japan for ASEAN primary products, a consequence of a much slower Japanese growth rate after 1973, structural change in the Japanese economy away from resource-consuming industries and toward less resource-intensive service and high-technology activities, and the success of energy and raw materials conservation efforts within the industrial sector. A second factor has been that as manufactured goods have become increasingly important in ASEAN exports, the ASEAN export structure has apparently become less complementary with Japan's import structure. Both factors have been a source of friction in Japan-ASEAN trade relations and, from the Southeast Asian perspective, have caused ASEAN doubts about Japan's value as an economic partner.

The first factor and its consequences for trade relations are illustrated by Indonesian petroleum, the largest single ASEAN export to Japan. Japan's trade deficit with Indonesia, mainly because of petroleum, has been so large ($7.7 billion in 1982, $6.9 billion in 1983) that it has overwhelmed its persistent surpluses with Thailand and Singapore, giving Japan a deficit for ASEAN as a whole ($4.7 billion in 1982 and $2.3 billion in 1983).[33] Because of recession and energy conservation, crude and partly refined petroleum imports from Indonesia have been decreasing in both value and quantity terms. Japan's petroleum imports from Indonesia decreased from 37.4 million kiloliters in 1977 to 36.6 million in 1981 to 29.4 million in 1983. The effect on export earnings was magnified by the sharp decline in prices.

The Indonesians have understood that the value of petroleum exports to Japan will drop with the decline overall in Japanese demand and the drop in prices. They have, however, been upset by the decline in the Indonesian share of the Japanese petroleum market from the traditional 15 per cent to 12 per cent. In contrast, despite the recession, Japanese petroleum purchases from China have increased slightly in quantity and thus more significantly in terms of market share.[34] Unlike Indonesia, which has been committed to defend prices set by the Organization of Petroleum Exporting Countries (OPEC), China has been able to price its crude more competitively. Some Indonesians believe that there was an informal understanding at the time of the oil embargo that Indonesia would continue supplying Japan in return for a long-term commitment to a 15 per cent share of the Japanese market, and they have asked that Japan guarantee this share. Japanese point out that oil purchases are made by private companies and the government cannot commit them to a certain share of the market. Moreover, as Japan began to develop a significant trade surplus with China in the mid-1980s, China put pressure on Japan to make larger petroleum purchases.

In the longer run, Japan's value as an ASEAN market will be increasingly judged in the ASEAN states by its purchases of manufactured products, and here is where the second factor comes into play. All of the ASEAN countries have adopted to varying degrees export promotion–based industrialization strategies, modeled after the successful policies of the newly industrializing countries (NICs). Manufactures now account for 25 per cent or more of ASEAN exports for all countries except Indonesia (and Brunei), whose exports of manufactured goods have been suppressed until recently by a "Dutch disease" problem (that is, high volume of resource exports helped maintain an exchange rate at which manufactures could not be competitive). Like the other ASEAN countries, however, Indonesia believes its longer-term growth prospects depend on the fortunes of its manufacturing sector, and it is now emphasizing diversification of its exports into relatively unsophisticated processed or manufactured goods such as textiles and plywood.

Japan's imports of manufactured goods from ASEAN are low, and they have not been expanding nearly as rapidly as industrial goods are expanding as a percentage of ASEAN exports. As a consequence, following a pattern established in the case of Japan's trade with more industrialized Taiwan and South Korea, Japan's share of total exports is declining for those ASEAN countries whose export structures are rapidly becoming more industrialized. This is in contrast to the United States and Western Europe, whose shares of ASEAN exports in the past fifteen years have remained about the same or even increased, primarily because these other advanced countries are large importers of labor-intensive manufactured goods.

These trade trends for several ASEAN countries and, for comparison's sake, Taiwan and South Korea, are shown in Fig. 1. For Thailand, industrial goods increased from 16.4 per cent to 35.3 per cent of exports between 1970 and 1980, but the share of all Thai exports going to Japan dropped from 25.5 per cent to 15.1 per cent. The share going to the United States, Canada, and Western Europe increased during the same years from 34.0 per cent to 41.6 per cent. In the case of the Philippines, the share of industrial goods in total exports increased in the 1970s from 7.6 per cent to 23.6 per cent. The proportion of total exports during the decade going to Japan decreased from 40 per cent to 27 per cent. In the Philippine case, the share sold to other advanced countries steadily dropped before 1975, but has been stable thereafter. Trade patterns with Indonesia and Malaysia, both of them oil-exporting countries, have been different, with the share of exports to Japan rising into the early 1980s.

The pattern of industrialization in East and Southeast Asia has been likened by some Japanese economists to "flying geese." Although the statistics just cited are very gross and there are undoubtedly different patterns in some product sectors, they do call into question whether Japan, despite its position as the lead goose, is helping the industrialization efforts of the others much in terms of providing demand for their principal export growth sector—manufactured goods. The whole pattern of export-oriented growth appears to depend largely on markets outside Asia, principally in the United States and Western Europe. The extent to which Japan's trade with developing Asian countries reflects an efficient division of labor based on comparative advantage and current factor endowments is not the question addressed here; the point is simply that in recent years the evolving ASEAN export composition appears to be moving in a direction more complementary to the import composition of countries, both developed and developing, other than Japan.

Japan's relative share of ASEAN import markets has also tended to decline since the early 1970s as ASEAN importers have diversified sources of supply (see Table 2).[35] Therefore, both export and import figures suggest that Japan's importance as a trading partner has declined in the ASEAN region, particularly for those countries where there is a strong

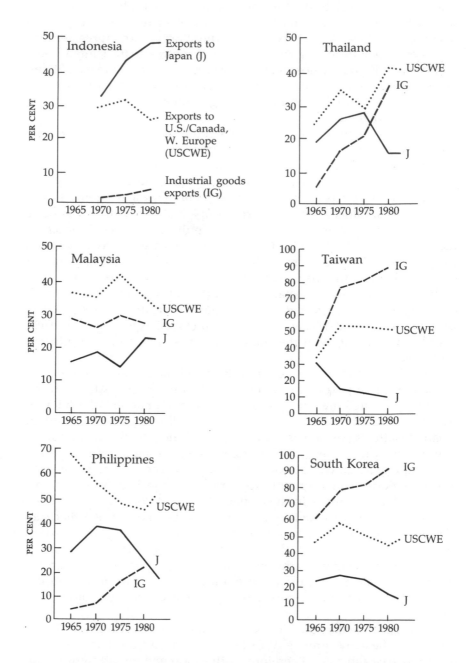

Fig. 1. Exports of industrial goods, exports to Japan, and exports to the U.S.–Canada–Western Europe as a percentage of total exports, 1965–1980. Adapted from IDE matrix tables.

upward trend in the share of manufactured goods in total exports. Trade policy changes in other advanced countries could reverse this decline. Until recently trade protectionism in the United States and Western Europe has primarily affected Northeast Asian rather than Southeast Asian economies. In recent years, however, the ASEAN countries have had to deal with U.S. countervailing and antidumping threats as well as increased controls on textiles and apparel imports. As ASEAN businessmen and trade officials become more concerned that they are reaching the limits of rapid growth of their exports to the U.S. market, they will be increasingly looking for alternative markets. Because Japan is a large, nearby market with greatly increased potential demand for ASEAN labor-intensive manufactures, there has been rising ASEAN pressure on Japan to improve market access for ASEAN manufactures. The appreciation of the yen after September 1985 makes these products more competitive in Japan.

The most bitter recent trade disputes have involved products such as boned Thai chicken and plywood made from tropical hardwoods where previous trade concessions to advanced-country trade partners for similar products such as chickens with bones (primarily a U.S. product) and plywood made from temperate softwoods have affected the terms of competition. ASEAN pressure for these items escalated in 1984 and 1985, producing a boycott movement in Thailand and occasioning Keidanren (Federation of Economic Organizations) and Liberal Democratic Party missions to the ASEAN region. Japan's Advisory Committee for External Economic Issues called for increased imports of manufactured goods from Asian developing countries in its report of April 1985.[36] At the June 1985 Second ASEAN-Japan Economic Ministers Conference, Japan announced a number of concessions as part of its economic action program. These included a promise of parity between Thai and U.S. chicken within three years, but Indonesia's main concern, plywood, was not addressed because of the depressed condition of Japan's domestic industry.[37]

The Future of Japan-ASEAN Trade Relations

Japanese trade friction with ASEAN is likely to continue into the future primarily over issues of ASEAN access to the Japanese market and ASEAN efforts to locate more higher value-added processing and manufacturing in their countries. Frustrated with the slow process of overcoming Japanese protection that escalates with the degree of processing, the ASEAN countries are increasingly resorting to blunt means of forcing exports of processed goods. The case of logs and plywood is an instructive one. To encourage their domestic industries, the ASEAN countries have progressively restricted log exports. As early as 1976, the Philippines limited unprocessed exports to 20 per cent of total log harvest. Indonesia has introduced similar restrictions and provided an incentive for logging companies to install plywood-making equipment. Malaysia banned all log exports from the peninsula in 1985, and the Kalimantan states of Sabah and Sarawak have quotas on log exports as well as export taxes.[38] Although these restrictions do cause some dislocations within the Japanese lumber industry, the ASEAN countries' efforts can be frustrated by Japanese and Korean customers relying on alternative log supplies from Canada and the United States.

"Countertrade" requirements are another industrialization strategy in some vogue in the ASEAN region that has created sharp disputes between ASEAN and Japan. Indonesia has been the leader, requiring after 1982 that for foreign enterprises to be eligible for all government procurements of 500 million rupiah or more, they must make or arrange counterpurchases of an equivalent amount of Indonesian non–oil and gas products. Moreover, these products must be in addition to traditional purchases from Indonesia.

ASEAN exports to Japan may increase as Japan loses its competitive advantage in a number of areas to the ASEAN group and other developing countries. For example, there has been already a considerable shift in resource processing away from Japan toward ASEAN to the apparent benefit of both areas. Before the first oil shock, Japanese policy encouraged the siting of resource-processing industries in Japan, but the oil price increases shifted the comparative advantage of such projects toward countries where energy costs were cheaper. Increased concern about pollution also encouraged this shift.

The large-scale Asahan hydroelectric power and aluminum-smelting project in Indonesia provides an example. Financed by five Japanese aluminum-smelting companies, seven trading corporations, and agencies of the Japanese and Indonesian governments, the project is providing aluminum ingots to Japanese fabricators, thus transferring the most energy-intensive part of the aluminum-manufacturing process to a site in Indonesia where hydroelectric power is in plentiful supply and assuring Japan's weakened aluminum industry of a secure supply of ingots. In this case, the Japanese government played the central role in financing the project, and Japanese business interests and Japanese foreign policy interests in cultivating relations with Indonesia were complementary.[39] Not all resource projects, however, work out so felicitously. Where smelting may be near the source of production but not in an energy-rich country (for example, copper smelting in the Philippines), the transfer of processing operations merely shifts the problem of importing energy (as well as pollution problems) to another country, one with fewer financial resources for dealing with the problem.

Japan's overall economic growth and the success of its structural adjustment programs will be an important determinant of how smoothly it can accommodate ASEAN demands for increased market access for industrial goods. Despite issues of the kind described above, there is reason to think that ASEAN trade friction with Japan, in comparison to Japan's trade friction with the United States and Western Europe, will be more mild.

First, the ASEAN countries, unlike the United States or Western European countries, feel that they can less afford to antagonize Japan. They are aid recipients and depend on Japan for technology and investment funds. Second, trade disputes can be inconvenient because in the less pluralistic ASEAN societies, as one ASEAN diplomat has commented, "the same [government] people who might raise problems are those who must solve them." ASEAN governments can, however, be expected to be more aggressive than in the past in insisting on access for their industrial products because as industries in their countries grow, they also acquire political power. These industries will increasingly lobby their governments to pressure Japan to provide more access, particularly if other markets look less hopeful. Third, from the ASEAN side, trade frictions with Japan mostly represent future opportunities rather than actual jobs in the economy that workers believe are being lost to foreign imports. Future benefits are not as politically emotional as perceptions of actual losses. Finally, it might be argued that the pathway into the Japanese market for industrial goods should have already been broken by Taiwan and South Korea and that many of the economic adjustments required of Japanese industry will have already been made. To some extent, ASEAN goods, therefore, should be displacing imports of more developed NICs. To date, however, there has been relatively little import penetration by NIC manufactured goods in Japan.

On the more pessimistic side, the extent to which ASEAN exports appear to be added to those of the NICs, China, or other developing nations, the prospect of a host of cheap-labor competitors could add to a siege mentality by Japanese industry and labor and increase resistance to trade liberalization. The Japanese government has been losing its ability to "guide" the business community and to force the kinds of adjustments that occurred in the aluminum industry. Moreover, the Japanese government often has protected even very small industries, and an altered balance of power between politicians and bureaucrats may make it even more politically difficult in the future to accept the demise of industries facing import competition from abroad. A more slowly expanding economy reduces the scope for smooth economic adjustment, and the rapid aging of the labor force may provide an additional social deterrent to the movement of workers from less competitive to more competitive sectors. Japan has not experienced the high levels of unemployment now characteristic of Western Europe and the United States, and if the budget austerity of the early 1980s continues, it will be difficult for Japan to finance the kinds of unemployment compensation that may be required for economic adjustment in a more slowly growing economy.

There seems to have been little conscious effort by Japan to use trade policy as a means of increasing Japanese political influence in the ASEAN region. As noted above, Japan has made trade concessions to ASEAN, for the same reason that it has to the United States—the desire to maintain reasonably good economic and diplomatic relations with countries deemed important to it. Nevertheless, these concessions have not come easily, and one of the most consistent complaints of ASEAN officials is that Japan is less solicitous toward and accommodating of their countries than it is of the OECD countries. In the United States, a sense of broader international political and security considerations has played a significant role in maintaining a relatively open market despite overwhelming public support for greater protection. Whether a similar definition of enlightened self-interest, including Japan's interest in ASEAN political stability, will play an important role in Japan's future trade policies is a crucial question relevant to Japan's ability to strengthen its political influence through trade.

Foreign Direct Investment

Approximately 20 per cent of direct Japanese foreign investment has gone to the ASEAN region. As in the case of trade, Japanese investment increased rapidly from 1967 to the mid-1970s, while the U.S. share declined.[40] By 1984, cumulative direct Japanese foreign investment was reported to be $11.7 billion, compared with approximately $8 billion in U.S. investments. Some factors behind this growth included the relaxation of investment constraints by the Japanese government, the need to gain secure access to resources and raw materials, and the desire to escape protective tariffs on manufactured goods that appeared with import-substitution industrialization strategies in ASEAN countries.

As in the case of Japan-ASEAN trade, Indonesia has tended to dominate the statistics of ASEAN-Japanese foreign investment. Sixty-five per cent of reported Japanese direct investment in ASEAN between 1951 and 1984 has been in Indonesia. Of the ASEAN countries, only in Indonesia, Malaysia, and possibly Thailand is Japan the largest single source of direct foreign investment, but the huge size of its investments in Indonesia makes Japan the largest supplier of direct foreign investment to the ASEAN region as a whole.

Two features of Japanese foreign investment that appear to be appreciated in Southeast Asia are the tendency of Japanese to prefer joint ventures (U.S. investors in contrast favor wholly owned subsidiaries) and the relatively high proportion of Japanese investment projects in small-scale manufacturing industries (except in Indonesia).[41] It can be argued that both these features facilitate technology transfers to ASEAN nationals.

Much of the criticism of Japan's economic role in the region has, however, focused on issues relating to foreign investment and technology transfer. Despite the high proportion of Japanese investment in manufacturing, the job-creating impact of these investments appears to be surprisingly small—approximately 50,000 jobs each in Indonesia, Malaysia, and Thailand.[42] Japanese investors, like those of other countries, are alleged to be reluctant to transfer the latest technology. Moreover, the limited amount of ASEAN manufactured goods being imported into Japan suggests to some Southeast Asians that little of this investment has been for the purpose of taking advantage of lower-cost labor and exporting finished products back to Japan. Much more of the manufacturing investment appears related to Japanese exports to ASEAN, for example, of motor vehicle parts to be assembled in the region and sold there.[43]

Another frequent complaint by Southeast Asian governments and businessmen is that joint venture contracts with Japanese firms often include restrictions on exporting. An informal Keidanren estimate is that 10–20 per cent of Japanese joint venture contracts in Thailand involve such restrictions. Japanese businessmen contend that host-government policies frequently give an incentive to import-substituting investment and that direct foreign investment would not occur in the first place without such contracts.

Finally, small-scale manufacturing ventures between Japan and ASEAN nationals are likely to involve overseas Chinese, whose economic role in many ASEAN nations is resented. In Indonesia, critics of the Japanese economic presence have frequently argued that this presence reinforces existing social inequities. Moreover, small-scale manufacturing activities are much more likely to be directly competitive with indigenous, existing manufacturing than large-scale resource or service activities.

The limited studies available of Southeast Asian workers in Japanese joint venture companies have found relatively favorable attitudes toward the Japanese on the whole.[44] General public attitudes toward foreign investment are less favorable, but there is little overt agitation against investments within the ASEAN elites at the present time. Khien Theeravit's massive study of Thai attitudes toward Japan in the mid-1970s found that 68 per cent of the Thai elite regarded Japanese trade and investment in Thailand as "economically imperialistic" in nature (21 per cent did not), and 63 per cent believed that Japan takes unfair advantage of Thailand, while another 32 per cent saw Japan as "the same as other nations" in respect to its economic activities in the country. Nevertheless, 48 per cent of the same elite thought that Japanese investments should be promoted and increased versus 20 per cent who wanted to restrict and reduce investments.[45]

In contrast to many other developing countries, direct investments account for a major share of the external capital flows to the ASEAN group.[46] Technology flows appear closely related to direct investment flows, with Japan a major provider of technology in countries where its investments are relatively large.[47] All of the major ASEAN countries maintain a variety of incentives designed to attract direct investment and technology. Although there have been persistent reports that some ASEAN governments have discriminated against Japanese investment and trade, preferring Western European or U.S. investors in order to diversify their economic relations,[48] ASEAN governments also express concern that Japanese investors favor China or that too large a share of new Japanese investment is going to other developed countries, especially the United States.[49] ASEAN governmental officials and business have complained of the slow growth of Japanese investment since the mid-1970s.

It can be argued that the complaints about investment practices and ambivalent and seemingly contradictory attitudes toward investment are exactly what one would expect to find in smaller countries whose economies appear to be dominated by a larger one and are comparable to Latin American complaints about U.S. companies.[50] The ASEAN government elites are both fearful of domination and its political appeal in mobilizing government critics, and they want to pre-empt criticism and threats of domination by diffusing sources of outside support. At the same time, investment is regarded as important to economic growth and thus regime survival. As a major source of investment capital, Japan helps underwrite the economic growth strategies of current ASEAN governments.

Foreign Assistance

The most impressive indication of Japanese interests in and commitments to the economic development and political stability of the ASEAN countries lies in its foreign assistance effort. Japan's foreign assistance programs grew out of reparations agreements with such countries as the Philippines and Indonesia, and ASEAN has continued over the years to be a heavy focus of Japan's overseas development assistance (ODA) activities. During the 1970s, more than 45 per cent of Japanese foreign aid went to ASEAN countries, and even in the 1980s, although all ASEAN countries had achieved "middle income" per capita levels of GNP (according to the World Bank's criteria), they continued to receive 30–35 per cent of Japan's ODA.

Japanese foreign assistance policies have been characterized as having two basic objectives: to establish markets for Japanese products and to secure raw materials and resources.[51] However, from the beginnings of "economic cooperation" (as Japanese aid programs are called), it was recognized that Japanese aid should help maintain the economic, social, and political stability of Asia, a prerequisite for mutually supportive economic activities.[52] Alan Rix argues that Japan has favored a concept of an "international division of aid labor" in which it concentrates on Asia, leaving other developing regions such as Latin America and Africa to donors with more familiarity and interest in those regions.[53] The growing emphasis on political objectives as opposed to commercial activities may be reflected in the emphasis in recent years on "human resource" development as opposed to large-scale industrial projects.

Japanese aid predominance in this region is reflected in its strong role in the Intergovernmental Group for Indonesia, where it is the largest donor country and traditionally provides Indonesia with a general target figure into which projects are then fitted rather than developing an aid budget based on specific projects. Japan's aid to Thailand rose dramatically in the early 1980s, when Thailand became important not only as an ASEAN member but as a front-line state where Japanese aid could be counted as assistance to security-sensitive countries (a consideration important in the U.S.-Japan context). Malaysia, with a per capita income of close to $2,000, would normally not be receiving ODA, but for political reasons, Japan continues to provide assistance to this country.

The large Japanese assistance programs are not always appreciated in Southeast Asia. A sober ASEAN view, as expressed by Snoh Unakul, a leading Thai economic planner, and Narongchai Akrasanee is that "despite its good intention," Japanese aid to Thailand reinforces an "unfavorable" trade and investment relationship between the two countries. They argue that existing aid programs focus on infrastructural development requiring additional imports from Japan and would prefer programs that concentrate on activities that more directly strengthen Thai export capabilities.[54] As in the case of private investment, attitudinal studies of Southeast Asia show that many more Southeast Asians believe Japanese aid contributes to Japanese self-interests than to mutual interests, but this does not inhibit them from believing that their countries should receive aid on better terms from Japan.[55]

Of course, the critics of current ASEAN governments look at another aspect of the aid relationship—how it reinforces existing regimes. This is perhaps clearest in the Philippine case prior to Marcos's departure. Senator Lorenzo Tanada, for example, appealed to Japan not to provide a loan to the Philippine government in April 1984, arguing that it would "tend to lengthen the life of the government and prolong the people's suffering." About the same time, Agapito Aquino, the elder brother of

TABLE 3
Comparative Figures for U.S. and Japanese Aid to ASEAN Countries, 1970–1984

ASEAN country	Source of aid	Total ODA gross (millions U.S. $ and per cent of DAC[a] bilateral total)			
		1970	1975	1980	1984
Indonesia	Japan	128.8 (27%)	209.6 (37%)	426.1 (42%)	286.3 (37%)
	U.S.	195.0 (42%)	98.0 (17%)	146.0 (14%)	114.0 (15%)
Total ODA gross		461.0	563.5	993.4	764.6
Malaysia	Japan	2.2 (7%)	64.6 (64%)	81.2 (62%)	270.5 (82%)
	U.S.	3.0 (10%)	2.0 (2%)	1.0 (0.7%)	—
Total ODA gross		28.2	100.5	129.0	330.6
Philippines	Japan	19.2 (44%)	72.1 (44%)	109.6 (48%)	190.1 (48%)
	U.S.	21.0 (48%)	65.0 (39%)	53.0 (23%)	137.0 (35%)
Total ODA gross		43.6	163.7	226.3	396.0
Singapore	Japan	5.8 (21%)	7.6 (67%)	8.0 (47%)	32.5 (72%)
	U.S.	—	—	—	—
Total ODA gross		27.2	11.2	16.9	42.5
Thailand	Japan	16.9 (23%)	44.4 (52%)	196.9 (61%)	260.0 (66%)
	U.S.	37.0 (50%)	14.0 (16%)	17.0 (5%)	36.0 (9%)
Total ODA gross		73.2	84.0	319.6	390.6
5 ASEAN country total	Japan	172.9 (27%)	398.3 (43%)	821.8 (49%)	1039.4 (54%)
	U.S.	256.0 (40%)	179.0 (19%)	217.0 (13%)	287.0 (15%)
TOTAL ODA GROSS TO ASEAN		633.2	922.9	1685.2	1927.0

SOURCES: Table constructed from data in OECD, Geographical Distribution of Financial Flows to Developing Countries, various reports, 1970–84.
NOTE: Total ODA Gross excludes U.S. military aid.
[a] Development Assistance Committee.

assassinated Senator Benigno Aquino, led demonstrators to the Japanese Embassy to demand that the loan be postponed until the government had "demonstrably responded to the demands of the Filipino people for the restoration of democracy." [56] The Japan Socialist Party expressed concern that aid strengthened the Marcos regime and that Japanese government policymakers were neglecting opposition voices. [57]

Whether the political order being supported by Japanese aid programs in ASEAN is "just" is a separate and debatable point, but there is little doubt that Japanese foreign assistance toward ASEAN has supported the growing economic and political interdependence of these countries with the capitalist world. Foreign assistance in general is not so important to the ASEAN countries as it once was, but it still is a significant factor in increasing their ability to close the resource gap between domestic investment and savings. Japan provides approximately half of all foreign economic assistance to the ASEAN region. The United States share has dropped to approximately 16 per cent (see Table 3). In the early 1970s, Japan replaced the United States as the largest source of foreign economic assistance for Indonesia, the Philippines, and Thailand. Here, clearly, onetime U.S. support has substantially been assumed by Japan, which continues to maintain fundamentally the same economic, political, and social order.

The Cultural Relationship

At the time of Prime Minister Fukuda's 1977 meetings with the ASEAN leaders following the Kuala Lumpur summit, Japan made a major commitment to strengthening its cultural relations with the ASEAN group. Fukuda remarked that "many key government posts were occupied by people who once studied in Japan." Because Japanese-ASEAN relations hitherto had consisted of "mainly material and monetary ties," Fukuda urged "the ASEAN leaders to take the initiative in promoting cultural exchanges" and promised Japanese support.[58]

Nevertheless, Japan has not succeeded in developing a cultural relationship with the elites or middle class of the kind that would support "hegemony" in the Gramscian sense. This weakness is reflected in survey data, in foreign student statistics, and in media coverage and attention. To cite some examples, a recent study of middle-class attitudes in the Philippines asked the respondents with which foreign country they felt most intimate. Not surprisingly in view of historical relations and migration patterns, 71 per cent cited the United States. Japan came second with 6 per cent, ahead of Western Europe and China at 5 per cent each.[59] A survey of Thai public opinion found that 65 per cent of the public and 61 per cent of the elite regarded the United States as the most friendly of five foreign countries; Japan came in third place (after Australia) among the public at 12 per cent, and fourth (after China but ahead of the Soviet Union) among the elite, cited by only 2 per cent.[60] Indonesian students, asked in a 1983 survey where they wanted to study abroad, cited the United States 91 per cent of the time; Japan was in second place with 8 per cent.[61] In fact, in 1979 of the 46,108 ASEAN students abroad, only 680 (1.5 per cent) were studying in Japan. In contrast, 17,258 were studying in Western Europe, 16,500 in the United States, and many of the remainder in Australia and the Middle East.[62]

Reciprocally, there does not appear to be a strong base of Japanese public interest in ASEAN on which to build a more intimate cultural relationship. Only 0.9 per cent of respondents to a 1982 survey on Japan's diplomacy cited one of the ASEAN countries as the most important overseas partner of Japan. When asked to choose up to three Asian countries with which Japan should have close relations, the Philippines was the most frequently cited ASEAN country at 12.3 per cent, far behind China (76.2 per cent), South Korea (45.7 per cent), and India (20.5 per cent).[63] In a 1985 survey, the percentage of the public citing ASEAN as the most important partner had slipped to 0.6 per cent.[64]

Undoubtedly Japanese-ASEAN cultural relations have been expanding, albeit on a small base. Youth ships have provided opportunities for Japanese and ASEAN students to meet and visit each other's countries. The Japan Foundation and the Toyota Foundation have been active in promoting exchanges of academics and translations of literature, although these are on a small scale compared with U.S. foundation activities in ASEAN. Tourist and visitor exchange rose dramatically in the 1970s; Japanese visitors to Singapore, for example, increased from 110,000 in 1974 to 381,000 in 1983, and Singaporean visitors to Japan increased more than eight fold in the same period (from 1,854 to 15,668).[65] It is estimated that more than 100,000 Japanese reside in ASEAN countries. There is increased use of Japanese programs on television; for example, a Japanese cartoon series about a cat, *Doraemon*, is one of the most popular children's television shows in Bangkok, and many Thais enjoyed a Japanese soap opera, *Oshin*, that was dubbed in Thai.

The official Learn from Japan campaign in Singapore and Look East policy in Malaysia have resulted in increased exchanges that may strengthen longer-term cultural relationships. Under the Singaporean program, there has been a significant increase in the number of Japanese experts attached to Singapore government departments, including those dealing with education, health care, traffic safety, labor-management relations, personnel administration, and broadcasting. Other effects of the program included the establishment of a Japan-Singapore Institute of Software Technology and the creation of a Japanese Studies Department at the National University of Singapore.[66] In Malaysia, management trainees have been sent to Japan as part of the Look East policy, but the main emphasis of Prime Minister Mohamed bin Mahathir's policy is to inculcate values such as hard work, discipline, and strong family ties.

Despite this trend, it will take a long time before Southeast Asian–Japanese cultural ties are fully developed. Two main groups of Southeast Asians have strong, outwardly oriented cultural links. One of these is the overseas Chinese, who, although cut off from mainland China for many years, may now be able to reinforce their affiliation. The other is the educated, upper-class elite, historically oriented toward the colonial powers, with whom they share many values. In contrast to these Western countries, Japan's occupation of Southeast Asia lasted long enough to provide a legacy of wartime memories, but not long enough to develop local elites with a strong cultural orientation toward Japan. In recent years, cultural relations with the West have been reinforced among the ASEAN elites and middle classes by other common values, including similar consumer tastes and popular culture. There are few, direct natural linkages for Japan in either the ethnic Chinese ASEAN populations or with the Western-oriented elites except through the intermediation of third parties, China, Hong Kong, or Taiwan in the first case, and the United States in the second.

Japanese Hegemony in Southeast Asia?

When the Japanese economic presence was rapidly expanding in Southeast Asia in the late 1960s and 1970s, U.S. economic, military, and political hegemony in the noncommunist part of the region was under great strain. That Japan might inherit the U.S. mantle was common speculation at the time; and U.S. pressure for Japan to rearm seemed to suggest that the United States was grooming Japan for such a role.

The extent to which Japan can assume or has already assumed the U.S. role remains debated. General Soemitro, who was prominent in Indonesian politics before the Tanaka riots, argues that Japan cannot assume the previous U.S. role. He cites three factors: Japan's ambivalence about its defense posture, the psychological legacy from World War II affecting both Japan and Southeast Asia, and Japan's energy dependence.[67] Juwono Sudarsono, one of Indonesia's leading international relations specialists, argues that there is already a "U.S.-Japan system" that provides a basic economic, political, and social framework for the Western Pacific region and that is reinforced by an explicit security division of labor including, in recent years, collaboration for the conventional defense of Asia.[68]

One of the most important changes in Southeast Asian international relations in the past two decades is the extent to which the ASEAN countries themselves have filled the "vacuum" left by the partial withdrawal of Western powers and the far from complete advance of Japan, China, and the Soviet Union. The basic framework of political and security relationships in the region is determined by a rather stable balance between ASEAN and Vietnam. The position of the ASEAN states, as relatively conservative societies, has appeared to have been greatly strengthened in part through their external relations. Indeed, in a political sense, the ASEAN countries rather than Vietnam were on the offensive in the early 1980s.

The United States, Japan, and, to a limited degree, China are ranged in support of ASEAN. As both Indonesian statements cited above and this survey suggest, Japan seems to have little willingness or capability to develop an independent role. If the mark of a regional hegemony lies in its willingness to commit resources to establish order in the event of crisis, ASEAN in the case of the Philippines recently experienced its first serious regime crisis in fifteen years, and here the United States was the main actor from the outside. This might be true because of the special historical links between the United States and the Philippines, even if Japan had played a much larger political role, but it is doubtful that Japan would initiate and take a position of sustained leadership in the event of a political crisis involving any ASEAN country or, if it did, that it would have the broad range of economic, political, and security levers to arbitrate such a crisis.

Japan's role in ASEAN appears almost perfectly suited to that of a junior alliance partner or "supporter," to use Takashi Inoguchi's terminology. This survey has shown that Japan has filled in some of the interstices where U.S. influence or resources have declined, especially foreign investment and aid. But Japan lacks the comprehensive set of strong relationships in all spheres with the ASEAN countries that would be needed to create a viable Japanese order in the ASEAN region. Its economic value currently is weakened by the limited size of its market for imported industrial goods; its political role is constrained by a number of factors including its lack of a military role; and cultural and communications difficulties restrict a broad Japanese-ASEAN dialogue in all spheres. The potential for cooperation between Japan and the ASEAN elites thus is quite circumscribed.

Japan's foreign assistance programs provide support for governments dominated by Western-educated and -oriented elites. Japan's contacts with ASEAN nationals occur almost exclusively through the medium of Western languages and Western-derived institutions (such as foreign ministries) and reinforce the linkages that both "internationalized" Southeast Asian and Japanese elites have with Anglo-American civilization. In no sense do these contacts, in contrast to those between China and overseas Chinese or even between Middle Eastern societies and Moslems in Southeast Asia, present the prospect of an alternative order. This makes the Japanese presence accepted and welcomed by the ASEAN governments.

Japan's postwar internationalization effort has been largely in the direction of reinforcing its own relations with the United States.[69] As the U.S. presence in ASEAN itself has become less visible, Japan has become more comfortable with the notion of being a supporter in the Southeast Asian region. Two 1966 regional endeavors that did group Japan together with a number of smaller Asian-Pacific countries without the United States—ASPAC and the Ministerial Conferences for the Economic Development of Southeast Asia—had failed by the mid-1970s. The United States and Japan depend on each other to lessen what might otherwise be too imposing a presence if it were alone in the region. The Pacific economic cooperation concept represents the Asian regionalism now preferred by "internationalists" in Japan. This concept is regarded by economists as a means of better dealing with political problems that affect economic cooperation and by politicians as a means of promoting political links through increased economic cooperation, thus underscoring its overriding political—not economic—importance to both groups. For Japan, the political significance lies in Pacific cooperation as an umbrella under which the Western-oriented regional order can be supported by both the United States and Japan.

Kenneth B. Pyle

Japan, the World, and
the Twenty-first Century

The publication of a book entitled *Shōrai no Nihon* (The future of Japan) by a brilliant young journalist has electrified the Japanese reading public by its description of the changes that will transform Japan and the world in the approaching new century. The author foresees a world dominated by a new economic system, increasing interdependence and free trade, the decline of nationalism and military spending, and the emergence of a peaceful world order. The year is 1886, the author Soho Tokutomi.

Tokutomi's world view was shaped by Herbert Spencer's *Principles of Sociology*. Writing during the Pax Britannica, Spencer believed that a universal evolution of social structure was under way. The most advanced societies were leaving behind a "militant" phase and evolving toward a new "industrial" phase. Coercive, regimented, hierarchical societies were being transformed into open, democratic, commercial, and peaceful ones. Tokutomi's book drew on this analysis to interpret the changes taking place in the transition from the Tokugawa to the Meiji period and to offer his countrymen a picture of what the new century held.

A hundred years later, the Japanese are again confronting a new century, a social order transformed by a new technology, and a changing international system. Beginning in the late 1970s, interest in planning for the twenty-first century stimulated Prime Minister Masayoshi Ohira's appointment of several blue-ribbon commissions and research groups to study various aspects of the changes to be expected as Japan advanced into the new century. Their reports are collected in two volumes entitled *Kindai o koete* (Beyond the modern age), published in 1983. Aside from these officially sponsored projects, there has been a veritable tide of books and articles on Japan's place in the twenty-first century.

The task of fathoming the nation's future is more challenging than it was in Tokutomi's day because the era of Japan's late development is at an end. A fundamental transformation of the dynamics that have controlled and shaped modern Japan's history is taking place. Heretofore, the major determinant of modern Japanese development has been the timing of Japan's industrialization in relation to that of the West. Late development imposed psychological burdens, but it also offered Japanese leaders certain opportunities and advantages. First, they could see where they were going because the established industrial countries provided a historical road map. Ronald Dore, for example, observed in his comparative study of British and Japanese industrialization that because "Japan, like all follower countries, knew better where she was going," her industrial growth was more continuous and steady: "The cycles of boom and slump were not so lengthy; the troughs not so deep, their effect in tempering optimism about the prospects of long-term growth not so devastating."[1]

Second, not only could the follower countries see where they were going, but they could try to reach the destination faster, skipping over whole stages of development by borrowing from the techniques and practices of advanced societies. Trotsky defined this as the "law of combined development," which he described as a "privilege of historic backwardness."

Finally, the follower countries had the advantage of observing the mistakes and problems that the advanced countries encountered and of trying to avoid or mitigate them. Thorstein Veblen wrote in 1915 of "Japan's opportunity"—by importing modern technology and preserving feudal values intact, Japan could avoid much of the social disruption and antagonism that had attended the first industrial societies. Some of this "technology of nationalism" was also learned from Western nations.[2]

Today, the advantages and opportunities of late development are largely past. Having "caught up," Japan no longer has an "image of its future," a sense of the kind of historical development future technology is likely to promote. Nor will Japan have the problems, mistakes, and shortcomings of Western social development from which to learn.

Japan's "Information Society"

Japan finds itself in the 1980s in an unaccustomed position. As a pioneer, with no one to follow, it is seeking to formulate the future course of economic, technological, and social organization. The term most often used in Japan to sum up the bundle of ideas and images about the future is "information society" (*jōhō shakai*), which is widely regarded as the next stage of universal social evolution. "All industrial societies," writes a senior researcher at the Nomura Institute, "including Japan are expected, without exception, to move toward [an] information-centered society in the coming years."[3] In the past decade, an immense and varied literature has sprung up to describe the revolutionary consequences of this new stage of human and technological development. The coming society is intensively debated and discussed at the highest levels of government. A study commissioned by the Ministry of Finance in 1982 argues that an entirely new body of economic theory, called "softnomics," is required to analyze the transition from an emphasis on hardware and goods in industrial society to an emphasis on software, or such invisibles as information and services, in an information society.[4]

Prime Minister Yasuhiro Nakasone, addressing the Diet on February 6, 1984, shortly after his re-election, spoke of the "unknown challenges of the twenty-first century." What was striking about his vision was his stress on "the achievement of a sophisticated information society [as] an important strategic element in medium- and long-term economic development for the twenty-first century." He promised to promote policies and "establish a national consensus on what we want of the information society and to respond appropriately in a broad range of fields including frontier technology research and development."[5] This optimistic image of the Japanese future and of its revolutionary implications is one that has clearly captivated the prime minister and his advisers. In 1984, in a little-noticed address to the Japan Society in New York, following the Williamsburg summit, Nakasone envisioned Japan's future development in "the electronics and communication technology necessary to sustain an information society. . . . The achievement of the information society seems primary, since *it goes beyond changes in the production structure and . . . will mean the unfolding of a new and unprecedented stage of development* [italics added]. This may take 20 or even 30 years to realize, yet we should not let the long time span deter us."[6]

A variety of ambitious and highly visible projects receiving official encouragement and sponsorship has caught the national imagination and become symbols of the drive toward an information society. These include such new media as the Information Network System (INS), a new telecommunication network pushed by Nihon Telephone and Telegraph; Community Antenna Television (CATV); and the Character and Telephone Access Information Network (CAPTAIN) to provide vast amounts of information in the home. The fifth-generation computer has received international attention. A far more ambitious project is the plan of the Ministry of International Trade and Industry (MITI) to develop 14 "technopolises" as a means of diffusing the most advanced technologies into regional centers as the backbone of the Japanese economy in the twenty-first century.

Since Herman Kahn and other futurologists first spoke about the twenty-first century as Japan's, there has been a growing anticipation of the advent of the year 2000. There is a sense, encouraged as much by foreign as by Japanese forecasting, of the torch of world leadership passing to a new country. Daniel Bell, whose book *The Coming of Post-industrial Society* (1973) was instrumental in promoting the Japanese fascination with the concept of an information society, spoke at the 1983 Suntory Foundation Seminar of the end of "the American century." He observed that in the 1970s "Japan entered into World-History (to use Hegel's phrase)." Expounding the mystique of Japan's destiny, he continued:

At some point, a nation or a culture manifests a surge of creativity or energy which leads it to a dominant position in military power, economic or technological leadership, and artistic and cultural expression. There is an efflorescence of "genius" or uniqueness, its neighbors are overshadowed, eclipsed or even enslaved, literally or metaphorically, and its reign seems eternal. During that period of "grandeur and glory" it becomes a model for the rest of the world . . . and that leading nation establishes itself on the stage of history.[7]

Perhaps no Japanese has thought more seriously and intelligently about the present historical transition than the economist Yasusuke Murakami. In a series of recent essays, he saw the emergence of a new phase of industrial civilization following the oil crisis of 1973. This "twenty-first-century system, the system of so-called high technology" will bring with it an entirely new "paradigm": novel behavior patterns in using the new technology; new groups of specialists engaged in producing and operating the new technology; a hitherto unfamiliar set of infrastructures, including large and multipurpose cables, huge data bases, and a new educational system; and a transformed social system.[8] He observed in January 1984 that "there are more than a few people who consider the call for an 'information society' a simple dream, but broadly speaking history is moving in that direction. If the Japanese people are hesitant it is inevitable that someone else will provide the move toward an information society." The question for the coming decades, he muses, seems to be, "Will Japan be able to mature as a completely new leading nation, originating not from Europe or America?"[9]

This question of Japan's readiness for world economic leadership and for a role in the governance of the international system is on the minds of Japanese leaders. In 1984, Japan requested, and ultimately was granted, the position of second largest shareholder in the World Bank after the United States. In terms of voting power on the bank's executive board, it moved from fifth to the second spot, ahead of Britain, Germany, and France. MITI's 1984 White Paper appears to envision Japan's emergence as the center of world finance and the leading capital exporter, much as Great Britain did at the height of its power in the nineteenth century and as the United States did in the heyday of the Pax Americana immediately after World War II. Such a role is seen as resulting from inevitably recurrent Japanese trade surpluses because of such inherent structural strengths as technical innovation, productivity, and high savings that will always give Japanese manufacturers an edge over those of Japan's trading partners.

What would be the implications of Japan's achieving world economic and technological leadership and pioneering in the development of a new stage of social evolution? The relative decline of U.S. power raises serious questions about the governance of the international system. As Murakami observes, "the Pax Americana system . . . is about to be forced to undergo a reorganization because America's reliability is no longer absolute in the economic field."[10] In October 1983, George Modelski, known for his theory of long cycles in global politics, published an essay in the Japanese magazine *Voice* on "qualifications for world leadership." Modelski's hundred-year long cycles in modern history are begun and terminated by global wars that bring forth world powers that provide order for the international system. Writing for a Japanese audience, he explained that the world leaders since 1500 (Portugal, Holland, Britain, and the United States) have possessed four common characteristics: (1) a favorable geography, preferably insular; (2) a cohesive and open society; (3) a lead economy; and (4) a politico-strategic organization of global reach. Japan, he wrote, is well endowed in the first three qualifications; the fourth "is lacking at present but participation in the American system is a form of learning and investment."

Modelski wondered whether new global leaders can still emerge through warfare, given the reality of thermonuclear war, and he raised "the possibility that the single-country world leadership role might change soon." A differentiation of world leadership might take place "with different countries specializing in different functional areas." Such speculation is reminiscent of the ideas of political scientist Yonosuke Nagai, who has written that what is necessary for the advancement of human society is the "globalization of the Tokugawa system." By this, he envisions a complex system of checks and balances in which different nations fulfill different roles—much as different feudal states played different roles in the governance of the Tokugawa system.[11]

Along with the concern about Japan's readiness for leadership in the world system comes anxiety about the psychological reaction of the United States, on which Japan must rely for its security. The Comprehensive National Security Study Group, an advisory committee appointed by the late Prime Minister Ohira, hinted at this problem in its July 1980 report. The report acknowledged that U.S.-Japanese cooperation will be difficult since Japan's per capita GNP will likely overtake that of the United States; and "Japanese manufactured products will by and large be more competitive on the international market, and Japanese exports will continue to expand faster than U.S. exports. In this sense, the positions of the two economies are being reversed, and this itself will entail difficult psychological problems."[12] A highly popular science writer and senior researcher at the Nomura Research Institute, Masanori Moritani, put the matter less delicately. He wrote in 1982 that Japan's vast technological strength had come to be feared and the source of mounting frustration: "And if things continue unchanged, that fear will explode into anger. If this were not a nuclear age, it is possible that bombs might be falling on Japan even now." He concluded that restraint and caution, or "looking out when you're number one," were essential.[13]

Many leaders have sought to temper Japanese expectations and ambitions that their nation might soon exercise a decisive role in reshaping the world order, in light of the U.S. decline. In particular, it has become de rigueur among many official spokesmen to stress international cooperation and closer ties with the United States as a matter of national interest. For example, Naohiro Amaya, a former MITI counselor, wrote in May 1984 of "Japan as number two" and urged Japanese to think of their role in governing the international system as "assistant to number one" or as "vice-president" (*fuku shachō*). History shows, he argued, that world leadership requires that a nation possess the following attributes: (1) military and economic power; (2) a set of ideals with universal applicability; (3) a rational and exportable system through which it can realize its ideals; and (4) a distinct, viable, and transferable culture. Amaya holds that although Japan may be equal to the United States in economic power, in other respects "the time is far from ripe for gracing Japan with the title of 'No. 1.'" He concludes that "whether we like to admit it or not, there will be no free world and no free trading system if the United States does not preserve them for us. . . . The best Japan can aspire to is 'vice-president.' For its own sake, it must recognize this and conduct itself with the tact and discretion befitting its real position in the world community."[14] Clearly Amaya is concerned that Japanese pretensions to international leadership stirred by the recent success literature will inflame U.S. suspicions. Moreover, it is his continuing fear that runaway national pride will awaken Japanese nationalism.

The concept of an information society pioneered by Japan and representing a new historical stage in human social evolution poses profound problems for the Japanese. At the heart of the matter is their ambition for global leadership in economic and technological development and the implications of this for governance of the international system. Japan's economic power has come to be perceived as disruptive and challenging to the existing international order. French foreign trade minister Michel Jobert remarked in 1982 how quiet and peaceful the world would be without the Soviet Union and Japan.[15]

The issue of the role of this economic power in political and strategic affairs remains unanswered and the source of great debate and soul-searching reflection. Many influential Japanese profess to believe that the importance of military power in inte;national relations is declining because of the advent of nuclear weapons, increased economic interdependency, and a growing global consciousness. For the moment, at least, Amaya and other members of Japan's elite believe that Japan must continue to work closely with the United States, deferring to its overall leadership of the alliance. Hisahiko Okazaki, former director general of the Research and Planning Department of the Ministry of Foreign Affairs, observed in 1979 that "if we continue to bet on the Anglo-Saxons we should be safe for at least 20 years." [16] New conditions and new attitudes are, nevertheless, forcing the Japanese to rethink the assumptions that have guided their postwar foreign policy.

The Yoshida Doctrine and Japan's Postwar Role

Throughout the postwar decades, Japan's role in the world has been a product of the political order imposed on it by the victors and the shrewd and pragmatic policies of postwar Japanese leaders. While forging to the front rank of global economic power, Japan remained politically withdrawn, shunning initiatives and involvement in political-strategic issues. This role as a commercial democracy, aloof from international politics, has been supported by a remarkably durable popular consensus.

Japan's political passivity in the postwar era has ordinarily been understood as a product of wartime trauma, the unconditional surrender, popular pacifism, nuclear allergy, the restraints of a "peace constitution," and sometimes bureaucratic immobilism. All of these factors are without question ingredients in forming Japan's postwar international role; they have established the parameters within which political leadership has operated. Nevertheless, we would miss the essence of postwar Japanese political history if we overlooked the fact that the fundamental orientation toward economic growth and political passivity was also the product of a carefully constructed and brilliantly implemented foreign policy.

In his memoirs, *The White House Years*, Henry Kissinger concludes that Japanese decisions have been the most farsighted and intelligent of any major nation of the postwar era even while the Japanese leaders have acted with the understated, anonymous-style characteristic of their culture." [17] Kissinger was referring to the skill with which Japan has pursued its national interests by concentrating on economic development while shunning nearly all initiatives and involvements in international political-strategic issues.

The key figure in shaping the postwar conception of Japanese national purpose was Shigeru Yoshida—a man whose style was scarcely "understated" and "anonymous" in the way that characterized many Japanese leaders with whom Kissinger was familiar. A poll conducted by the magazine *Bungei shunjū* in 1984 found that an overwhelming number of Japanese regarded Yoshida as "the most important Japanese of this century." [18] Yoshida, who was prime minister for seven of the first eight and one-half years of the postwar period and who served concurrently as foreign minister during much of this time, so dominated the postwar political scene that he was frequently referred to as "One Man" Yoshida. He gathered around him a group of political disciples known as the Yoshida School, who carried on his influence in future decades. In particular, two of his protégés, Hayato Ikeda and Eisaku Sato (known as the "honor students" [*yūtōsei*] of the school), during their tenures as prime minister in the 1960s and 1970s, elaborated the implications of Yoshida's vision of Japan's fundamental purpose and orientation in the world. During the postwar decades, the Yoshida School played a shrewd and pragmatic hand, decisive when necessary, often ambiguous, but single-minded in an inconspicuous way in pursuit of Japan's national interest.

Yoshida believed that skillful diplomacy would allow Japan to win the peace. At the time that he formed his first cabinet in the spring of 1946, he observed to a colleague that "history provides examples of winning by diplomacy after losing in war." [19] That is, a defeated nation by shrewdly observing the shifting relations among world powers could take advantage of them to minimize the damage suffered as a result of defeat and could end up winning the peace. A veteran diplomat and long-time student of diplomatic history, Yoshida knew that disputes between victors over the postwar settlement with the defeated nation could be used to the latter's advantage. Although a substantial segment of Japanese opinion wanted no part in international rivalries, Yoshida saw Japan's opportunity in the U.S.-Soviet estrangement.

The critical moment for the determination of Japan's postwar orientation arrived in 1950 with the dangers and opportunities that the cold war rivalry offered Japan. The danger was that Japan would be drawn into cold war politics, expend its limited and precious resources on remilitarization, and postpone the full economic and social recovery of its people. The opportunity was to bring an early end to the Occupation, return Japan to favor with the Western democracies, establish a guarantee for its national security, and open the way to all-out economic recovery. In June 1950, on the eve of the Korean war, John Foster Dulles, special emissary of the secretary of state, came to Japan to urge Japanese rearmament. On this and subsequent occasions, Dulles sought to undo the MacArthur constitution by establishing a large Japanese military force. Yoshida, seizing the opportunity for what Yonosuke Nagai calls "blackmail by the weak," refused to accede to these demands.[20] He established a bargaining position by making light of Japan's security problems and vaguely insisting that Japan could protect itself through its own devices by being democratic and peaceful and by relying on the protection of world opinion. After all, Japan had a constitution that, inspired by U.S. ideals and the lessons of defeat, renounced arms; and the Japanese people were determined to uphold it and to adhere to a new course in world affairs.

Yoshida's "puckish" and bravado performance left Dulles (in the words of a colleague) "flabbergasted," embittered, and feeling "very much like Alice in Wonderland."[21] In succeeding meetings, Yoshida negotiated from this position. He skillfully argued that rearmament would impoverish Japan and create the kind of social unrest that the Communists wanted. (We now know that through backdoor channels he was even prevailing on Socialist party leaders to whip up anti-rearmament demonstrations and campaigns during Dulles' visits![22]) He further pointed out to Dulles the fears that other countries had of a revived Japanese military, and he enlisted MacArthur's support. MacArthur obligingly urged that Japan remain a nonmilitary nation and instead contribute to the free world through its industrial production.[23] This is, of course, what happened in the Korean war. Yoshida's firmness spared Japan military involvement in the war and allowed it instead to profit enormously from procurement orders. The result was a great stimulus to the economy, which Yoshida privately called "a gift of the gods."[24] Over the coming decades, there were to be more such gifts.

In the protracted negotiations with Dulles, Yoshida made minimal concessions; he consented to U.S. bases on Japanese soil and a very limited rearmament, sufficient to gain Dulles's agreement to a peace treaty and to a post-Occupation guarantee of Japanese security. What we may call a Yoshida Doctrine began to take shape in these negotiations. Its tenets were as follows.

1. Japan's economic rehabilitation must be the prime national goal. Political-economic cooperation with the United States was necessary for this purpose.

2. Japan should remain lightly armed and avoid involvement in international political-strategic issues. Not only would this low posture free the energies of its people for productive industrial development, it would avoid divisive internal struggles—what Yoshida called "a thirty-eighth parallel in the hearts of the Japanese people."[25]

3. To gain a long-term guarantee for its own security, Japan would provide bases for the U.S. Army, Navy, and Air Force.

It remained for Yoshida's followers to build on these foundations.

Under Yoshida's key economic adviser and finance minister, Hayato Ikeda, who became prime minister in 1960, the tenets of the Yoshida Doctrine were consolidated into a national consensus. During the late 1950s, Ikeda's predecessor, Nobusuke Kishi, had raised the divisive political issues of constitutional revision and rearmament, and his administration ended with the greatest mass demonstration in Japanese history. Ikeda returned to Yoshida's course. Working with his economic adviser, Osamu Shimomura, and the heads of the Economic Planning Agency, the Ministry of Finance, and the Ministry of International Trade and Industry, Ikeda formulated a plan for doubling the national income within a decade. Divisive political issues were put aside, and the Ikeda years (1960–64) were notable for their enthusiastic pursuit of high-growth policies. The leading historian of Japan's postwar economy writes that

Ikeda was the single most important figure in Japan's rapid growth. He should long be remembered as the man who pulled together a national consensus for economic growth and who strove for the realization of the goal. . . . From a broader perspective, however, Japan consistently adhered to Yoshida Shigeru's view that armaments should be curbed and military spending suppressed while all efforts were concentrated on the reconstruction of the economy.[26]

Under another Yoshida protégé, Eisaku Sato, who succeeded Ikeda and held the prime ministership longer (1964–72) than any other individual in Japanese history, the Yoshida Doctrine was further elaborated in terms of nuclear-strategic issues. In 1967, Sato enunciated the three nonnuclear principles, which helped to calm pacifist fears aroused by China's nuclear experiments and the escalation of war in Vietnam. The three principles held that Japan would neither produce, possess, nor permit the introduction of nuclear weapons onto its soil. Lest the principles be regarded as unconditional, Sato clarified matters in a Diet speech the following year in which he described the four pillars of Japan's nonnuclear policy: (1) reliance on the U.S. nuclear umbrella; (2) the three nonnuclear principles; (3) promotion of worldwide disarmament; and (4) development of nuclear energy for peaceful purposes. In short, the U.S. nuclear umbrella was to be the sine qua non of the nonnuclear principles. Sato was awarded the Nobel Peace Prize, but detractors like the prominent economist Shigeto Tsuru, who wanted an unconditional declaration, called it hypocrisy to proclaim nonnuclearism while taking shelter under another country's nuclear umbrella.[27]

Also in 1967, Sato added another building block to the structure of foreign policy that Yoshida had begun. To defuse domestic political turmoil and to preserve Japan's low posture in international politics, Sato formulated the policy of the Three Principles of Arms Exports (*buki yushutsu san-gensoku*), which provided that Japan would not allow the export of arms to countries in the Communist bloc, to countries covered by U.N. resolutions on arms embargoes, and countries involved or likely to be involved in armed conflicts. Subsequently, the Miki Cabinet (1974–76) extended this ban on weapons exports to all countries and defined "arms" to include not only military equipment but also the parts and fittings used in this equipment.

Constraining defense expenditures to less than 1 per cent of the gross national product became a practice in the 1960s, although it did not become official government policy until adoption of the National Defense Program Outline in 1976. The Outline contained a provision that "in maintaining the armed strength, the total amount of defense expenditure in each fiscal year shall not exceed, for the time being, an amount equivalent to 1/100th of the gross national product of the said fiscal year."

During the 1960s and 1970s, Yoshida's successors offered many formulations of both defense and foreign policy that sought to maintain Japan's low political profile and the broad domestic consensus for pursuit of the economics-first policy. One frequently cited concept was "an exclusively defensive defense" (senshu bōei), which declared that troops and weapons would have no offensive capacity. The Self-Defense Forces would not be sent abroad—even on U.N. peacekeeping missions. Weapons would be stripped of their offensive capabilities. Jets, for example, should not have bombing or midair refueling capabilities. Another concept, "comprehensive security" (sōgō anzen hoshō), was an attempt to broaden the definition of security to include such things as foreign aid and earthquake disaster relief and, therefore, to take attention away from purely military aspects of defense. "Omni-directional foreign policy" (zenhōi gaikō), which was stressed in the wake of the oil crisis, held that Japan should seek friendship with all countries in order to maintain sources of energy, raw materials, and smooth trading relations. As one Yoshida disciple who served as foreign minister in the 1970s summed it up, it was a "value-free diplomacy" that sought to avoid ideological conflict by "separating economics from politics."[28] In maintaining this broad consensus for the pursuit of economic growth, the ruling conservatives of the Liberal Democratic Party (LDP) not only avoided political conflict, they often pre-empted popular, progressive issues. A good example was Sato's 1969 initiative to establish the United Nations University in Tokyo.

The Yoshida doctrine, as it was first worked out in the Dulles-Yoshida negotiations in the early 1950s and subsequently elaborated over the next three decades by the old man's successors, was a brilliant but delicate balancing of groups and interests on the Japanese political scene. It represented a political compromise with U.S. demands for a greater Japanese military involvement. Initially, Yoshida offered military bases and a commitment to gradual rearmament; later a national defense force and other minimal concessions could be made. At the same time, Yoshida could warn the Americans of the necessity of improving living standards so as to forestall left-wing strength. Later, there seems to have been a shrewd awareness of U.S. ambivalence about Japan's remilitarization: Yoshida and his successors knew that there was apprehension in the United States, as well as in Europe and Asia, that rearmament might go too far. The danger of a nationalist revival was therefore a brake on U.S. demands.

Within Japan, the Yoshida Doctrine maintained a balance between those groups that were concerned with security even at the expense of national pride and those concerned with preservation of national autonomy and sovereignty. Keenly aware of Japan's political-economic vulnerability, Japanese leaders balanced security and economic concerns. Moreover, within the bureaucracy, the Yoshida Doctrine came to represent a balancing of bureaucratic conflicts among the Ministry of Finance, MITI, the Ministry of Foreign Affairs, and the Defense Agency. Finally, there was what appeared to be a tacit agreement with Socialist and pacifist groups that divisive issues of constitutional revision and substantial military spending would be moderated and priority given to economic growth and social welfare. In sum, the Yoshida Doctrine was a finely tuned policy for pursuing Japanese interests within the pressures and constraints at work on Japan.

Competing Views of Japan's International Role

By the late 1970s, as the conditions and constraints within which the Yoshida Doctrine had operated began to undergo substantial change, a national debate developed on Japan's future role in the world. Ostensibly it is a debate about Japan's strategic needs, but in fact it is much more than that. It is at its core a struggle to define Japan's national purpose, its fundamental values, and their relevance to international conditions in the next century.

Putting aside the finer distinctions and concentrating on the broader outlines of the options being debated, we may discern four major conceptions or schools of thought. In some sense, each is representative of a particular era of the postwar experience: (1) the progressive view emerged from the postwar reform era and flowered in the 1950s and early 1960s; (2) the merchant-nation thesis was a product of the high economic growth period of the 1960s and 1970s; (3) the changed international environment of Japan in the late 1970s led to the emergence of a realist school; and (4) the new nationalism of the 1980s, which, though still in many ways formless, is of growing influence, arose from Japan's economic achievements. Several related sets of issues serve to distinguish the different conceptions or schools of thought: (1) their view of Japan's history and traditions; (2) their assessment of Japan's strengths and weaknesses or its comparative advantage; (3) their perception of the threat to Japan and, accordingly, of the proper military force required by the nation and of the alliance with the United States; and (4) their view of the future of the international system.

It should be emphasized that these are "ideal types" or general categories of thinking, and the thinking of many well-known Japanese does not fit neatly into these categories. In fact, many Japanese vacillate between different schools. LDP leaders often seem to borrow freely of the rhetoric and ideas of all four schools, as suits their convenience. This suggests that we are dealing with modes of thought in the mainstream of thinking about Japan's future. (There are more radical approaches, but I do not attempt to deal with them here.)

The Progressive View

The finest hour of the progressives was the postwar reform era. Their idealism emerged out of the wartime disillusion, revulsion against Japanese nationalism, and the profound distrust of traditional state power. They took their stand in support of the new postwar democratic order and, above all, in support of the role that the constitution envisioned for Japan in the world. The progressives argued that Japan's unique mission in the postwar world was to demonstrate that a modern industrial nation could exist without arming itself, that Japan could show the way to a new world in which national sovereignty would be forsworn and nation-states, which were artificial creations, would disappear, allowing the naturally harmonious impulses of the world's societies to usher in a peaceful international order.

The Japanese people, having been victimized by a reactionary leadership that indoctrinated them in an artificial nationalism, had shown the demented course of the modern nation-state by their aggressions in Asia. As the first victims of the advent of atomic weapons, the Japanese people could convincingly argue that wars were ever more destructive, that a new age was accordingly at hand, and that the sovereign prerogative of war must be renounced. No other nation embraced the liberal hope for the future world order with the enthusiasm of Japan because no other nation's recent experiences seemed to bear out so compellingly the costs of the old ways. This view had a deep and profound appeal. It provided a new orientation, an idealistic mission that would expiate the sins of the past. Moreover, it provided a justification for rejecting world politics and devoting national energies entirely to rebuilding the national livelihood.

It need not be cause for surprise that some of the most uncompromising statements of this progressive-idealist vision came from Yoshida himself in the immediate postwar years—before the Dulles-Yoshida negotiations and the working out of the Yoshida Doctrine. Because he aligned Japan with the United States and led Japan to a gradual if limited rearmament, Yoshida was anathema to progressives in the 1950s. Yoshida himself bitterly attacked the most revered exponent of the progressive view, Shigeru Nambara, a distinguished political scientist and president of the University of Tokyo. In 1950 he excoriated Nambara and adherents of a position of unarmed neutrality as "literary sycophants," which caused a sensation and left the indelible impression of Yoshida as adamantly opposed to the progressive vision.[29] Nevertheless, before 1950, Yoshida had unqualifiedly and consistently expressed his support of Japanese disarmament. Moreover, he saw it as a national mission in which the Japanese people could take pride. As he said in a radio broadcast on the first anniversary of surrender, "The new constitution provides for renunciation of war, in which regard Japan leads the rest of the world. . . . Now that we have been beaten, and we haven't got a single soldier left on our hands, it is a fine opportunity of renouncing war for all time." More than three years later, in November 1949, he addressed the Diet in no less uncompromising terms: "It is my belief that the very absence of armaments is a guarantee of the security and happiness of our people, and will gain for us the confidence of the world, and will enable us as a peaceful nation to take pride before the world in our national polity." Yoshida repeatedly spoke in this period of the realism of "security without armaments" (*gumbi o motanai anzen hoshō*).[30]

As the San Francisco Treaty system and the Yoshida Doctrine were subsequently worked out, Yoshida parted company with the idealists, who set forth their own "four peace principles": no rearmament, no post-treaty U.S. military forces in Japan, a comprehensive as opposed to separate peace that excluded the Communist bloc, and permanent neutrality in the cold war. With his own new position staked out, Yoshida dismissed the idealist vision as the "babbling of a sleepwalker."[31] Nevertheless, elements of this vision were incorporated into the Yoshida Doctrine, as evidenced by the resistance to all-out armament, the abstention from power politics, and later the rejection of nuclear arms.

Although frequently scorned as "utopian pacifists" whose views are divorced from the reality of power politics, the progressives argue that military power is no longer the wave of the future and that it will not be a determinant of national greatness. Their vision of the future, in the words of Shigeto Tsuru, former Hitotsubashi University economist and subsequently editorial adviser to the *Asahi shimbun*, is of a country that will be "oriented toward respect for man." Japan should aspire to be a model of humanitarian ideals; it should strive to be known as the health-care center of the world, a country of extraordinary scenic beauty to be visited by people from all over the globe, the leader in promotion of cultural exchange, the sponsor of the United Nations University, and the most generous contributor to developing countries and to refugee relief.[32]

In an international symposium on "Japan's role in the world," held in 1979 on the occasion of the centenary celebration of the *Asahi shimbun*, Yoshikazu Sakamoto, professor of international politics at the University of Tokyo, set forth a vision of what Japan's unique role in the modern world might be, stressing the following aspects of Japan's historical experience that would constitute a unique national identity as a model society: (1) as the only nation to have suffered the effects of nuclear warfare, Japan has a mission to take the lead in opposing the spread of nuclear arms by stressing its three nonnuclear principles and working for a nuclear-free zone in Asia; (2) as the industrial nation with the fewest natural resources, Japan could serve as an example of a highly efficient society, frugal in its use of the earth's resources; (3) as a country that has suffered serious environmental crises during its industrialization, Japan could develop technology and legislation to minimize ecological destruction; and (4) as a country that has distinguished itself by its openness to foreign cultures, Japan could become a model of an open society by pursuing not only importation of culture, but an open-door policy with regard to refugees and immigration. Sakamoto concluded, "There exist in Japan the distinctive elements of a national identity which could become the core of a new and universal model of society. The role of the Japanese people in the community of mankind should be to build on this foundation a nuclear-free, pollution-free, resource-saving, and open society."[33]

Although this postwar vision retains a powerful emotional appeal for the Japanese people, it is increasingly challenged as utopian. Most progressives dismiss this charge by arguing that unarmed neutrality would offer no pretext for an invader or reason for involvement in conflict. Masashi Ishibashi, who assumed the chairmanship of the Japan Socialist Party in September 1983, makes this argument in his 1983 book *Hibusō chūritsu ron* (On unarmed neutrality), holding that if he is wrong, "the worst that could happen would be a military occupation of the Japanese archipelago." The annihilation of the race and destruction of Japanese culture that would result from involvement in a nuclear war would be averted. The implication of this viewpoint is that the progressives are prepared to risk their vision of the future, to accept the consequences if they are wrong, and to argue that the consequences would still be preferable to full-scale rearmament and involvement in power politics.

It is apparent, however, that the progressives have far less influence over Japanese opinion than they did in the 1960s. Their radical critique of Japanese society, so popular in the early postwar period, lost its strength in the aftermath of Japan's rapid economic growth and the consequent pride in Japanese social values and institutions. In a thoughtful essay on the rightward drift of opinion, Ryutaro Komiya estimates that until the mid-1960s, 80 per cent of opinion leaders were of the progressive persuasion, but that this situation has been reversed and 80 per cent are now of center or conservative leanings.[34]

Affluence has undermined the appeal of socialism, writes Kazuo Ijiri, editorial writer for the *Nihon keizai shimbun*. The overwhelming majority of Japanese identify themselves as middle class and are not persuaded by theories of conflicting class interests: "The leftist intellectuals have not been able to cope with the sweeping changes that have occurred in the masses themselves over the past 20 years or so."[35] Moreover, the traditional intellectual influences have been replaced by "middle-class intellectuals"—editorial writers, columnists in the media, bureaucrats, and businessmen, who lack the depth and background of academic intellectuals but are more in tune with middle-class values. Ijiri points to surveys showing that 90 per cent of the Japanese people now regard themselves as middle class. Progressive intellectuals have failed to provide values consonant with the real conditions of economic growth. The middle-class intellectuals, however, address themselves to the tastes and interests of this broad middle class. Above all, their writings often dwell on the Japanese character and traditions and feed the appetite for self-reflection.

What must be of growing concern to the progressives is the abandonment of their cause by the student generation. A recent study of Tokyo University freshmen shows a marked conservatism and support for the LDP, which apparently began in the late 1970s.[36] In an effort to reverse the Socialists' declining fortunes, Ishibashi, after assuming the chairmanship in 1983, proclaimed a "new realism" and announced a change in policy toward the Self-Defense Forces, which would treat them as an unconstitutional but legal entity. This convoluted attempt to break out of the pure negativism of the past threw his party into confusion and disarray. He was forced to make a tactical retreat and reassure party members that he still regarded the Self-Defense Forces as "illegitimate." Nonetheless, he continued to try to move the party in a rightward direction by improving its relations with the United States and South Korea.

Some of the idealism of the past has become tarnished, and the progressive approach is sometimes cast in cynical terms. Hideo Matsuoka, the Socialist and Communist parties' joint candidate for governor of Tokyo in 1983, argued that Japan should continue to avoid entanglement in international politics by deliberately "missing the boat" (*nori okure*);

that is, when international disputes arise, Japan should always "go to the end of the line" and wait quietly, unnoticed, while all other nations step forward to declare their positions on controversial issues. This is a "diplomacy of cowardice" (okubyō gaikō), he admitted, but it serves Japan's interests by maintaining good relations with all countries and, thus, preserves its global access to markets and raw materials.[37]

The Merchant-Nation Thesis

A second approach to Japan's role in the world is the "merchant-nation" thesis. The proponents of this school argue that a dispassionate analysis of Japan's geopolitical position, its resource endowments, and the structure of its economy leads inexorably to the conclusion that Japan's national interest is properly seen as that of a great trading nation, like that of Venice or the Netherlands in the past. This school of thought is particularly interesting since it most closely corresponds to the role that Japan has been playing in the international system since at least the mid-1960s. In an article in Chūo kōron entitled "Japan as a Maritime Nation," Masataka Kosaka, one of the country's most influential political scientists, defined the national purpose in these terms and traced its origins to Yoshida.

Japan's postwar involvement with the West . . . has been primarily economic rather than military, an emphasis chosen by Prime Minister Yoshida Shigeru at the time of Japan's negotiations with America over the 1951 San Francisco Peace Treaty. Yoshida believed that economic matters are more important than military, and, for this reason, he rejected America's suggestion that Japan rearm and spearhead American military strategy in the Far East. Japan's foreign policy has subsequently been simply a kind of "neomercantilism." . . . Yoshida's choice has proved a most adequate one for Japan. From a strictly military point of view, Japan's "neomercantilist" diplomacy has been adequate for two reasons: First, the development of nuclear weapons has greatly lessened the ethical justification as well as the effectiveness, of military power. Second, since Japan has been fully protected by the U.S. Seventh Fleet, in terms of defense her own rearmament would have been superfluous. From a political point of view, Yoshida's "neomercantilism" has harmonized with Japan's postwar democratization.[38]

Kosaka has recorded that Yoshida read this article and flatly rejected identification of his name with neo-mercantilism. "He told me there could be no such policy."[39] Yoshida was too pragmatic and non-doctrinaire to allow his views to be so simply characterized. He himself, of course, never spoke of a Yoshida Doctrine, and we can only conjecture at the ways he might have taken issue with the subsequent policies of the Yoshida School. Moreover, he was too proud and too much of a realist and nationalist to accept the implication of a politically and diplomatically passive Japan as a corollary of his policies.

In his 1981 book, Bunmei ga suibō suru toki, Kosaka elaborated on his

views. Japan should act the role of a merchant in the world community—a middleman taking advantage of commercial relations and avoiding involvement in international politics. "A trading nation (*tsūshō kokka*)
does not go to war," he wrote. "Neither does it make supreme efforts to
bring peace. It simply takes advantage of international relations created
by stronger nations. This can also be said of our economic activities. In
the most basic sense, we do not create things. We live by purchasing primary products and semifinished products and processing them. That is
to say, we live by utilizing other people's production." [40] Kosaka emphasized that this is not a popular role in the international order since it is
regarded as selfish and even immoral. It causes problems, particularly
with the United States, because "Japan has enjoyed the advantages of
being an ally and the benefits of noninvolvement." With the breakdown
of the Bretton Woods system and the oil crisis, Kosaka foresaw difficult
times as "politics and economics became more intertwined in the economic policies of nations."

Kosaka believed that Japan could adapt to the new circumstances and
survive as a trading nation if it could manage its crisis of spirit. That is,
in holding firmly to no clear principles but merely pursuing commercial
advantage, the danger was that the Japanese might lose self-respect.
This is a crisis, he wrote, that all trading nations face. "A trading nation
has wide relations with many alien civilizations, makes differing use of
various different principles of behavior, and manages to harmonize
them with each other. This, however, tends to weaken the self-
confidence and identity of the persons engaged in the operation. They
gradually come to lose sight of what they really value and even of who
they really are." To deal with this psychological burden, trading nations,
he concludes, "need the confidence that they are contributing to the
world in their own way. Only by doing so does hypocrisy (*gizen*) cease
to be hypocrisy for hypocrisy's sake. It becomes a relatively harmless
method of doing good." [41]

Naohiro Amaya was one of the most outspoken and flamboyant advocates of the merchant role. In a series of widely discussed articles
marked by their color and candor, Amaya drew analogies from Japanese
history to illustrate the role of a merchant nation, which he hoped Japan
would pursue in a consistent and thoroughgoing manner. He likened
international society to Tokugawa Japan, when society was divided into
four functional classes: samurai, peasants, artisans, and merchants. The
United States and the Soviet Union fulfill the roles of samurai, whereas
Japan bases itself on commerce and industry; Third World countries are
peasant societies. If the military role of the samurai is not exercised, as
happened in the Tokugawa period, then it might be possible to conclude
that "the world exists for Japan," but in fact international society is a

jungle and the merchant must act with great circumspection. The nation for some time has conducted itself like an international trading firm, he wrote, but it has not wholeheartedly acknowledged this role and pursued it single-mindedly.

Amaya wanted the Japanese to show the ability, shrewdness, and self-discipline of the sixteenth-century merchant princes of Hakata and Sakai, whose adroit maneuvering in the midst of a samurai-dominated society allowed them to prosper. "In the sixteenth-century world of turmoil and warfare, they accepted their difficult destiny, living unarmed or with only light arms. To tread this path, they put aside all illusions, overcame the temptation of dependency (*amae no kōzō*), and concentrated on calmly dealing with reality." By the end of the Tokugawa period, Amaya points out, merchants were so powerful that Toshiaki Honda (1744–1821) remarked, "In appearance all of Japan belongs to the samurai, but in reality it is owned by the merchants." What is required is to stay the course, to put aside the samurai's pride of principle. "For a merchant to prosper in samurai society, it is necessary to have superb information-gathering ability, planning ability, intuition, diplomatic skill, and at times ability to be a sycophant (*gomasuri nōryoku*)."

In Amaya's view, pride and principle should not stand in the way of the pursuit of profit: "From now on if Japan chooses to live as a merchant nation (*chōnin kokka*) in international society, I think it is important that it pursue wholeheartedly the way of the merchant. When necessary, it must beg for oil from the producing countries; sometimes it must grovel on bended knee before the samurai." The Tokugawa merchant was not above using his wealth to gain his way, and Amaya counsels that Japan, similarly, must be prepared to buy solutions to its political problems: "When money can help, it is important to have the gumption to put up large sums."[42]

Amaya, himself, was at the center of an international incident that attracted attention to the psychological costs of behaving in the manner he prescribed. Following the seizure of the U.S. Embassy in Teheran in November 1979, the U.S. government sought the cooperation of its allies in applying sanctions against Iran. Japan, seeking to protect its oil imports from Iran and to avoid involvement in the dispute, responded ambiguously. When it was revealed, however, that Japanese companies were continuing to make large purchases of Iranian oil, the samurai nation was angry. Secretary of State Cyrus Vance met with Foreign Minister Saburo Okita and sharply criticized Japanese insensitivity; 12 senators introduced a resolution criticizing Japan; and U.S. newspapers expressed outrage. It was time for the merchant nation to make its response.

Amaya, who was in Washington representing MITI, called a formal press conference to apologize and to assure Americans that Japanese companies would "behave themselves and never repeat such misbehavior." This indeed smacked of the merchant's "ability to be a sycophant." The submissive and abject tone of Amaya's apology was roundly criticized in Japan where it collided with the self-confidence acquired in recent years. Nobuhiko Ushiba, a veteran Foreign Ministry adviser, deplored the nation's ambivalence in the crisis and said that the failure to stand for any principles (*gensoku*) in such issues had become the "most serious disease of Japan" (*Nihon no ichiban no byōki*).[43]

What Amaya most fears is the lack of self-discipline in the merchant's role and the rebirth of an emotional nationalism that he calls "soap nationalism" (*sōpu nashonarizumu*) since it has the emotional character of a soap opera. Amaya himself feels victimized by "soap nationalism" because of the role he played in reaching a settlement of the U.S.-Japanese automobile dispute in the spring of 1981, which resulted in the decision to restrain auto export to the United States. In the same manner in which he was attacked over the Iranian crisis, he was berated for persuading the Japanese auto firms to agree to U.S. demands for self-restraint in exports.

The May 1981 issue of *Shūkan bunshun* carried an article entitled "Amaya, the Foreigner's Concubine (*rashamen*)" that described the anger of the manufacturers at Amaya's role as "Reagan's concubine (*mekake*)." In response, Amaya deplored this "soap nationalism," which failed to demonstrate the shrewdness and self-discipline required of Japan in the merchant's role. Unless Japan gave the ailing U.S. automobile industry some breathing space, Congress would pass protectionist measures that would doom the international free trade system that had so benefited Japan. Amaya stressed the fragility of the liberal economic order and reminded his readers that it depended on the future commitment of the Americans. The United States had built the free trade system and had often subordinated its immediate economic interests to the long-term political and economic advantages of strengthened economies among its allies and of a strong trading and monetary system that would link these nations. It was the better part of wisdom for Japan to encourage the United States, help to revive U.S. industry, and work for a new consensus among industrial countries to preserve the free trade system.

Through Amaya's writings runs a strain of pessimism over whether, with rising nationalism in Japan and protectionism in Europe and the United States, the mercantile diplomacy he advocates can be sustained. He concludes that if a time comes when being a merchant country cannot guarantee Japan's security, then Japan must become a samurai country.

Amaya's views have elicited sharp criticism from many quarters. Foreign affairs commentator Ken'ichi Ito called it a "kowtow foreign policy" (*dogeza gaikō*) and an "unprincipled foreign policy" (*musessō gaikō*) that would not be respected or trusted by foreign countries. Ito argued that the exclusive concern with preserving Japan's economic interests was already creating a spiritual malaise among the Japanese since it caused them to sacrifice the self-respect that comes from adherence to a clear set of moral values.[44] Similarly, the head of the Foreign Ministry's Policy Planning Division, Hiroshi Ota, wrote that the merchant-nation role had been possible for Japan in the past when U.S. political and economic power maintained a world order in which Japan was free to concentrate its efforts entirely on economic gain.[45] Both writers, however, held that the decline of U.S. power and the expansion of Japan's global interests made it impossible any longer to separate politics and economics in the way that Amaya's metaphor suggested and that Japan must join in a greater cooperative effort to ensure the security of the industrial democracies. A professor at the National Defense Academy, Masamori Sase, described Amaya's metaphor as a self-complacent and simplistic one; although bound to be appealing to residual pacifist sentiment that sought to avoid international political involvements, it would have no persuasive power abroad. A continued shunning of power politics would damage the alliance with the United States, which in the changed international environment was expecting more of Japan.[46]

Although the merchant-nation thesis has come under increasing criticism at home and abroad in the 1980s, one cannot underestimate its staying power. Prime Minister Yasuhiro Nakasone explicitly challenged the Yoshida Doctrine in the early months of his administration, but his efforts to take a more resolute stand in international political matters, though changing the tone of Japanese diplomacy, have not substantially modified its substance. Many who argue for Japan's pioneering role in establishing an information society want Japan to adhere strictly to its role as a commercial democracy. Masanori Moritani wrote in 1982 that "the characterization of Japan as a trading country no longer enjoys its former appeal, but I myself still endorse this designation." He argued that Japan should develop a technological strategy for import expansion by which it would export technology to countries everywhere and import the goods they produce with this know-how.[47] Advocacy of such "technological cooperation" has become a principal way of winning economic allies abroad, thereby overcoming trade frictions, and revitalizing the merchant-nation role. Observing the frustration of Nakasone's efforts, Yonosuke Nagai wrote in 1985 that, with the solid support of the strong economic agencies—the Ministry of Finance, the Economic Planning Agency, and MITI—and the conservative mainstream, "the Yoshida Doctrine will be permanent (*eien de aru*)."[48]

The Realist View

A third approach to Japan's role in the world is the liberal realist school of thought. It charted its position in part by opposing the progressive vision of an unarmed and neutral Japan. The realists believe that the institution of the nation-state is not about to disappear, that the strength of nationalism is unabated, and that a competition of national interests within an environment constantly approaching "international anarchy" is the only realistic way of understanding international politics. Because the realist school tends to see Japan's national interest as a cooperative defense relationship with the liberal democracies, one can trace its roots to the prewar pro–Anglo-American groups with whom Yoshida was so prominently identified and whose moderate views of foreign policy and domestic reform were overwhelmed after 1931. Although this school seeks a democratic order, it does not make the radical critique of Japanese society that the progressives have made. Nor does it have the progressives' distrust of traditional state power. In fact, typically, many of the proponents of this school have identified with liberal conservatives in the government.

A representative par excellence of this school is Yoshida's biographer, Masamichi Inoki, scholar of international communism, former president of the National Defense Academy, and now head of a research institute for peace and security. Inoki has been a steady critic of what he calls the "utopian pacifist viewpoint" for many years. With other academic scholars like Kentaro Hayashi, he has criticized the progressives for failing to make moral distinctions between communist countries and liberal democracies. Inoki opposes a massive rearmament but advocates a steady and significant increase in defense expenditure in cooperation with the Western allies. In the light of the new attitudes and conditions in Japan, the views of realists like Inoki are receiving a more respectful hearing now than probably at any time since 1945.

Inoki chaired the Comprehensive National Security Study Group, an advisory committee appointed by the late Prime Minister Ohira, which issued its report in July 1980. It represents probably the clearest statement of the realists' position to date. The report argues that "the world is not a peaceful world at present, nor is there any possibility that it will become a peaceful world in the foreseeable future." An intelligent approach to securing Japan's interests requires a joint effort with the Western allies: "Because it is not realistic (*genjitsuteki*) to place total dependence on the international order and because there is a limit to the effectiveness of self-reliant efforts, it is necessary to take an intermediate position and try to attain security by relying on cooperation among a group of nations sharing common ideals and interests." Japan must overcome the incongruity between its economic power and political weakness by accepting international responsibilities more commensurate with its economic strength. The role of "economic giant and political dwarf" must be replaced by an activist foreign policy and a substantial defense establishment that would cooperate with the Western allies in the maintenance and management of the international system. The Korean Peninsula, Southeast Asia, and the Middle East are areas where Japan must contribute politically to stability.[49]

Though appointed by the prime minister and, hence, basically friendly to sections of the Liberal Democratic Party, the group criticized the government for political expediency and lack of candor and of leadership in developing a new defense policy. The report concluded with the hope that it would serve as a catalyst for a vigorous national debate and formation of a consensus in favor of an active political and strategic role in the world.

At the heart of the realists' argument is their rejection of what we might call the notion of Japanese exceptionalism. Few aspects of Japan's foreign policy draw as sharp criticism from the realists as the contention that Japan is—in the words of former foreign minister Kiichi Miyazawa—"a special state" that, because of its exceptional historical experiences and constitutional restraints, is kept from normal participation in international politics. Realists are repelled by justifications of Japan's withdrawn international behavior that rely on Article 9 of the constitution (the no-war clause), the nuclear allergy, the three nonnuclear principles, the postwar legacy of pacifism, and other such extraordinary explanations.

Miyazawa, who authored an insider's account of the Yoshida era and who seeks to preserve the Yoshida Doctrine, argued in a 1980 interview that Japan must continue in a passive role because the constitution makes Japan "a special state" (*tokushū kokka*) and requires it to conduct "a diplomacy that precludes all value judgments" (*issai no kachi handan o shinai gaikō*). The preamble to the constitution pledges Japan to trust in "the justice and faith of the peace-loving peoples of the world" and, therefore, commits Japan to maintain friendly relations with all nations. "The only value judgments we can make are determining what is in Japan's interest. Since there are no real value judgments possible, we cannot say anything." When challenged politically, Miyazawa says, Japan has no recourse but to defer. "All we can do when we are hit on the head is to pull back. We watch the world situation and follow the trends."[50]

Masamori Sase, vocal realist, was repelled by Miyazawa's views of Japan's exceptional role in the international system. It "violates international common sense" to rely on the U.S.-Japan Mutual Security Treaty but to deny its military implications or to rely on the U.S. nuclear umbrella but not allow passage of nuclear weapons through Japanese waters. To behave like an "international eccentric" (*kokusaiteki henjin*), said Sase, is to invite scorn; to wander through international society "peddling one's special national characteristics" is to risk diplomatic isolation.[51]

Realists argue that Japan's geostrategic position makes inescapable its involvement in any superpower conflict—even if it sought to remain neutral. Hisahiko Okazaki regards the progressive view as naive: "Although leftists in Japan argue that it may be involved in a war because of the existence of the U.S.-Japan Security Treaty and of the U.S. bases in Japan, in fact it is threatened not because of its military alliance but because of its geostrategic situation. It would be unreasonable not to expect a major power to attempt to seize a geostrategically important area before its opponent utilizes it, particularly if the country at issue were inadequately armed."[52] Soviet access to the Pacific requires passage of its ships through the straits of Soya, Tsugaru, and Tsushima and makes Japan critical for control of the Western Pacific.

During his extraordinary visit to Washington in January 1983, Nakasone spoke the realist view when, as the newly elected prime minister, he sought to undo the impression of a politically passive Japan. In a series of bold public statements on strategic issues, he committed Japan to a more activist role. He decided to allow transfer of purely military technology to the United States in what amounted to a major modification of the Three Principles on Arms Exports. He further said that Japan should aim for "complete and full control" of the strategic straits controlling the sea of Japan "so that there should be no passage of Soviet submarines and other naval activities" in time of emergency. The United States had earnestly sought such a commitment, but it had been regarded as too politically sensitive for public discussion. Going still further, Nakasone said that Japan should be "a big aircraft carrier" (*ōkina koku bokan*)—his official translator interpolated this with the colorful phrase "an unsinkable aircraft carrier" (*fuchin kūbo*)—to prevent Soviet penetration of Japanese airspace. Fulfillment of this capability would require a large-scale military buildup that would far exceed the 1 per cent of GNP limitation. Finally, Nakasone repeated statements he had made in Tokyo that there should be no taboos against discussion of constitutional revision; but he added, "the Constitution is a very delicate issue and I have in mind a very long-range timetable; so to speak, but I would not dare mention it even in our Diet."[53] Although going far beyond his capacity to transform Japan's role, Nakasone gave the realists a national voice and backing unthinkable even a few years earlier.

Realists are divided over revision of Article 9. Some argue that revision is necessary to make the Self-Defense Forces constitutional, and more fundamentally, to restore full sovereignty to Japan and make it an "ordinary country" again. Others, such as Seizaburo Sato, argue that with few exceptions most countries now tolerate certain limitations on their sovereignty; it is not necessary legally to possess the right of belligerency since no country that has fought since World War II has actually declared war; therefore, it is pointless to embark on an inevitably drawn out and divisive struggle to revise the constitution.[54] What is most important is the steadily emerging consensus that Japanese rearmament is required for defense purposes and that it is not in conflict with Article 9.

Despite the enhanced strength of the realists in the 1980s, one of Japan's leading political-strategic thinkers believes that Japan's present role has extraordinary durability. In January 1981, Yonosuke Nagai wrote: "Despite the questionable nature of its origins, the new constitution has weathered 35 years, has been assimilated to Japanese traditions and culture, and, in a word, has been Japanized. In my judgment, the Japanese people will refuse ever again to become a state in the traditional sense but will choose to exist as a kind of 'moratorium state.'" Nagai believes that "the incongruity of status" between Japan's great economic power and the modest development of its political strength is appropriate to the Japanese national interest in a world dominated by nuclear weapons.

As I have emphasized, my analysis of the different schools of thought regarding Japan's future does not accurately reflect the range of differences among leading thinkers in the debate. Some writers like Masataka Kosaka could be classed as belonging to both the realist and the mercantilist schools. The position of Yonosuke Nagai, one of the most intriguing we have considered, defies easy categorization, but it deserves discussion at this point because it draws on aspects of all the schools I have thus far described. Above all, it represents a conscious attempt to adapt the Yoshida Doctrine to new conditions and to extend its life into the indefinite future. Nagai believes that despite the intense debate in the media, the Yoshida Doctrine will endure because of the strong consensus and coalition of forces that support it.[55]

Nagai, one of the best-known political scientists in Japan, sets forth a concept of what he calls the "moratorium world" and of Japan as a "moratorium state" (*moratoriamu kokka*). He describes world politics as in a state of transition from the traditional international order (the Westphalian system), in which the status of nation-states was established according to their military power, to what he calls a Kantian, peaceful world order in which the security of states will be preserved by a collective international arrangement. This transition stage is marked by a nuclear standoff or parity between the superpowers, which has created a power moratorium in the world. As a consequence, military power counts for less in determining the hierarchy of nations; international economic strength and technological know-how count for more. In other words, in this moratorium world, there is no longer a single agreed-on measure of status among nations: one state may have great military power; another may have great economic strength. There is no reason that the status of a state must be congruent on all attributes.

Therefore, the incongruity between Japan's economic power and political-military weakness is not odd, but reflects the nature of this new situation. Demands on Japan to maintain a military establishment consistent with its economic standing, writes Nagai, reflect a projection onto the world community of a drive in Western society to achieve consistency in personal status. Japanese, however, are accustomed to inconsistency of status (*chii no hikkansei*), as shown by the Tokugawa system when samurai had political power and prestige, while the merchants had economic power. In a passage reminiscent of Amaya's thesis, Nagai quotes Soko Yamaga (1622–85): "Samurai live by honor, whereas farmers, artisans, and merchants live by interest." Moreover, among the samurai, there was a complex allocation of different roles. For example, among the feudal lords, the *tozama* were given great territorial domains, but no place in the central government; the *fudai* had administrative power but little territory. The purpose of this complex system was "to prevent the centralization of power by the drive to achieve consistency of status, which is a weakness of all men." What is necessary for the advancement of human society is the "globalization of the Tokugawa system," by which Nagai appears to envision a complex system of checks and balances in which different nations fulfill different roles.

The future of Japan, for Nagai, is as a "moratorium state"; that is, in light of the current state of international politics, Japan should preserve its present constitution and "maintain the inconsistency in its status as a lightly armed, nonnuclear economic power." Strategic planning should concentrate on a limited but highly sophisticated defense posture, depending on advanced high technology such as lasers, precision-guided missiles, radar, and the like. Diplomacy should preserve the U.S.-Japan Mutual Security Treaty and seek economic cooperation with the Soviet Union so that the latter has no cause for hostilities against Japan. Should the United States increase its pressure on Japan, presumably on economic or defense issues, or should the Soviet Union build up its power unduly in the Far East, Japan always has the potential threat of a nationalist response: revision of the constitution, conversion of its industry and technology to military purposes, development of nuclear weapons, and so on. This threat gives Japan bargaining power to preserve its posture.

Nagai, who was a student of the political theorist Masao Maruyama and has progressive ties, has something in common with the progressive approach. He seeks to preserve Article 9, and he believes that Japan will "refuse to ever again become a state in the traditional sense." At one point in his essay, he writes that "Japan's 'grand experiment' could well become the military model for the industrially advanced democratic countries of the world." He believes that the world is moving toward a peaceful world order. All of these positions give him something in common with the progressives. Nevertheless, he clearly does not believe that Japan can survive as a lightly armed state without a shrewd strategy that comes to grips with power politics and the competition among nations. In this awareness, he shares the concern of the realist approach. He differs from the latter, however, in his evident lack of commitment to Western liberal values as a cause for allying with the United States and Europe. In Nagai's view, the Japanese state stands for no values; it is neutral entity. In fact, he worries, as do Kosaka and Amaya, that lacking any moral principles to guide them, but instead relying simply on national self-interest, the Japanese people may not be able to maintain their spiritual morale. Nagai is probably closest to the merchant-nation thesis in his view of the Japanese future: pure self-interest and economic nationalism are the motivations that will drive Japan.

The most significant and influential part of the debate about Japan's future role so far as immediate Japanese policy formation and assessment is concerned has been among the realists themselves. Their debate is influential and important because it goes on at the heart of Japanese government among the senior elites in the LDP, the bureaucracy, and the high financial circles. Two analysts, Professor Nagai in Japan and Professor Mike Mochizuki of Yale, have come up with a useful distinction between the "political realists" and the "military realists."[56] The former are adherents of the Yoshida Doctrine and still represent the mainstream of LDP thought; in the past they have been comfortable with the neo-mercantilist view of the Japanese nation. The military realists are largely a new phenomenon emerging in the course of this present debate; they mark a significant departure from the Yoshida Doctrine.

In tone and style, the political realists are pragmatic, cautious, often vague and ambivalent, shrewd in their narrow pursuit of Japanese self-interest, sensitive to domestic and foreign trends, and always prepared to adjust their policies to these trends. The political realists seek to keep alive the finely tuned system of checks and balances in "the domestic foreign-policy system" that Yoshida and his successors built. They are concerned with the intricate politics of balancing domestic and international concerns. Domestically they want to maintain a tranquil public opinion, neither antagonizing pacifist sentiment nor above all contributing to the rise of nationalism. The latter would mean, for them, a loss of mastery, an unleashing of latent emotions that would make the control of Japanese politics much more difficult for the elites. They also wish to limit military spending and strategic commitments because they would detract from economic growth and development of the most productive new high technologies.

Abroad, there are many concerns to be balanced. The most important is to maintain the U.S. security guarantee, which the political realists recognize will require a greater contribution as time goes on to satisfy the Americans, but this should be kept to the minimum necessary. They generally favor stringing out concessions to U.S. demands, peeling off parts of the elaborately constructed Yoshida Doctrine only as the situation demands. They regard the U.S. assessment of the Soviet threat as substantially overdrawn and believe that the Soviets are inclined to exploit instability in the Third World rather than to undertake military action against vital Western interests. Political realists worry about becoming entangled in U.S. military strategy; they would prefer to keep the Soviets at bay through trade and sale of technology. They also prefer to keep a low politico-military profile because of the vulnerability of the Japanese economy.

In contrast to this cautious pragmatism, the military realists are much more open, decisive, and clear about their policy preferences. They are forthright in their declarations that Japan is a part of the Western camp and must assume a greater share of its military burden. Moreover, their perception of a growing military threat from the Soviet Union justifies their advocacy of a substantial buildup of the Self-Defense Forces and a strengthening of the alliance with the United States. Giving priority to this military threat, they are less inclined to concern themselves with the domestic political constraints or the economic costs of a buildup. Also, they are more concerned with Soviet capabilities rather than Soviet intentions, which they regard as ephemeral. Thus, they move naturally to elaborate strategic discussions and the consideration of concrete war scenarios. Fear that the U.S. alliance will entangle Japan in U.S. military strategy is misguided, they believe, because Japan's geostrategic position makes inescapable its involvement in any superpower conflict—even if it sought to remain neutral.

The differences between political realism and military realism within the elites are epitomized in the debates between Nagai and Hisahiko Okazaki in the popular magazines. They have commented extensively on each other's views, and in 1984 they engaged in a debate on the topic

"What Is Strategic Realism?" which was published in the July 1984 *Chūō kōron*. Okazaki argued that postwar Japan has lacked any strategic doctrines, a situation that is no longer tenable given U.S.-Soviet parity and the Soviet military buildup in Northeast Asia and the Pacific. Nagai responded that the Yoshida Doctrine has been and will continue to be Japan's strategic doctrine.[57] Okazaki, who sees Nagai's views as an unworkable compromise between progressivism and the reality of Japan's defense needs, described the "moratorium state" approach as avoiding as much as possible the fulfillment of international obligations and burdens, while maintaining during a grace period a vague and unclear position and gambling on the future establishment of a new international order.[58] Dismissing the notion of the Japanese state as a neutral entity, Okazaki holds that Japan shares not only common strategic concerns with the Western democracies but also common values. Japan therefore should make a common cause with the Western community of nations.

This debate over national strategy has focused on two groups of realists and goes on at the heart of the elite leadership in Japan. Each group has strong forces behind it. The political realists, who are heirs to the Yoshida Doctrine and to the vision of Japan as a merchant state, draw their support from the most powerful elites in the Japanese political system—the mainstream of the LDP, the Ministry of Finance, MITI, the Economic Planning Agency, and leading financial circles. The military realists have the support of the anti-mainstream, right-wing LDP and, in the course of the debate, have gathered impressive new strength. In order to protect the U.S. alliance, the Ministry of Foreign Affairs has moved squarely into support of the military realist position. The Defense Agency has become more vocal and determined in pursuing its case within the party and the government. Prime Minister Nakasone has given this position a national voice, and Okazaki perceives a growing public consensus in behalf of a more forthright defense policy.

The New Nationalism

A fourth school of thought in this national debate about the future of Japan is the new nationalism. Of the four conceptions of Japan's future role, this one represents the sharpest break with the Yoshida Doctrine. It is characterized by the same recognition of the continuing role of power in the world and by the profound contempt for the progressive attitude that characterizes the realist school. It shares the realist belief that a competition of national interests within an environment constantly verging on international anarchy is the only realistic way of understanding international politics. The new nationalists likewise reject continued reliance on Japan's extraordinary and peculiar postwar political status. More resolutely than the realists, they reject important aspects of the postwar order; in sharp contrast with the realists, they do not see a shared community of interest and values with the Western democracies that would necessarily compel Japan to cooperate in an alliance framework. In this they are more akin to the economic nationalism of the merchant-nation school.

What sets the new nationalists apart is their belief that Japan should exercise an independent role in world politics. As the sociologist Ikutaro Shimizu, undoubtedly the new nationalist who has attracted the most attention, wrote in his sensational book, *Nippon yo, kokka tare* (Japan, become a state!), published in 1980, "On the one hand, Japan must encourage friendly relations with the United States, the Soviet Union, and all other countries, but at the same time we must not forget for an instant that Japan is alone. In the end we can only rely on Japan and the Japanese." [59]

The confidence that Japan is capable of an independent role is supported by an immense pride in Japan's socioeconomic and technological achievements. In the judgment of a chorus of contemporary observers, the Japanese have mastered the skills of organizing a modern industrial society with greater success than any other people. Scores of books have been written about the reasons for Japanese success; their common theme is an emphasis on the unique characteristics of the Japanese and their culture. Japan has outstripped the economic performance of other industrial countries, goes the usual explanation, because its historically formed institutions have proved more productive and competitive than those of other countries. More than one writer drew the irresistible conclusion. Wrote one widely read economist, Tsuneo Iida, who subsequently toned down his remarks: "Is it not possible that Japan might be quite different from other countries? Is it not possible that Japan might be quite superior to other countries (*yohodo sugurete iru*)?" [60]

It was inevitable that the U.S. occupation, its reforms, the war crimes trial, and the postwar self-criticism would be subject to revision. Many writers, of whom the critic Jun Eto is the most notable, are scrutinizing the procedures followed in drafting and imposing the constitution. They emphasize the censorship, the manipulation of popular opinion, and the alien and utopian nature of its provisions. The result was a constitutional system that deprived Japan of sovereign rights fundamental to a nation-state.

"The basic goal of U.S. occupation policy," wrote Eto, "was to destroy the greater Japanese empire, which had styled itself as 'unparalleled among nations' (*bankoku muhi*), and to create an ordinary Japan. Ironically, the Occupation gave birth to a Japan that is, in an entirely different sense, 'unparalleled among nations.'" Without the "right of belligerency," which was renounced in Article 9, Japan could not be a free, sovereign nation, master of its own fate.[61] Yoshida accepted this servile status and built Japan's postwar system to suit it. For Eto, "so long as we continue to set up Yoshida politics as the legitimate conservative politics, we Japanese will not escape from the shackles of the postwar period, and the road to self-recovery will be closed."[62] Since the administration of Prime Minister Ikeda, Eto believes, the government has shelved the constitutional issue, concentrated on economic development, and offered flexible interpretations of the constitution as the need arose. Eto maintains that a tacit understanding exists between the conservatives and the progressives to leave the issue unresolved.

But the time has come, he argues, to confront the issue and restore Japan's "right of belligerency" so that Japan can prepare to defend itself should the need arise. Americans, for their part, must face up to the new situation as well. They must admit that Article 9 was the result of their distrust of Japan and their fear that Japan might some day again attack the United States. "If there were among the American people the determination to wipe away completely their distrust of Japan, to tolerate a more powerful and less dependent Japan and to form an alliance with and coexist with such a Japan, then the future of Japan-U.S. relations would indeed be bright."[63]

Many writers argue that the renunciation of military power distorted national life. By relinquishing military strength, wrote Ikutaro Shimizu, Japan ceased to be a state and, instead, became simply a society whose essence is economic activity. Kichitaro Katsuda, a professor of political thought at Kyoto University, observed in his book *Heiwa kempō o utagau* (Doubts about the Peace Constitution) that the postwar liberal constitutional order, in reaction to wartime nationalism, lost sight of the concept of the state to which citizens owe their loyalty so that it can maintain order and protect the welfare of the whole community. Instead, he wrote, it is the business firms who can call on their employees for the ultimate sacrifice. When a director of Nisshō-Iwai was implicated in a scandal involving Grumman Corporation, he took his own life, leaving behind a note: "The company is eternal. Employees must die for the company."[64] An incident cited by Katsuda and other critics as illustrating the disgraceful weakness of the postwar state is the hijacking by the radical group known as the Japanese Red Army of a Japan Airlines jet in 1977. The government wholly capitulated, paying the $6 million ransom, releasing several terrorists from jail as demanded by the hijackers, and justifying its action by proclaiming that "a single human life is weightier than the earth."[65]

Shimizu is one of the most conspicuous critics of the postwar order and its values because he himself is a convert from the progressive camp. In the first decades after the war, he was one of the principal theoreticians for the progressives, exerting substantial influence over students and left-wing intellectuals. In 1960, he was a leading spokesman for the opposition to the renewal of the Mutual Security Treaty with the United States. Thereafter, his views began to change and he broke ranks with the progressives. In 1963, he urged abandonment of what he had come to regard as the simplistic and negative ways of the progressives, and he called for a new interpretation of Japanese history:

The more I learn about the efforts of many countries of Asia and Africa to modernize, the more I appreciate the understanding and skill of the Japanese leaders and people who modernized our nation during the Meiji period. The modernization process through which Japan has gone now spans a century, and that process has obviously not been just a series of unrelated episodes. It has not been just an accumulation of crimes and evil acts that can be expiated by a democratic revolution, national independence and a socialist revolution, as claimed by the advocates of the progressive view of history. The history of the Japanese, just as the histories of all great people, represents a dynamic intertwining of wisdom, energy, evil and misfortune. I believe that a new interpretation of history, accurately reflecting that dynamism, will have to be based on hypotheses that grow out of a study of the modernization process through which Japan has gone.[66]

In a recent book, *Sengo o utagau* (Doubts about the postwar period), Shimizu shows how far his views have evolved. He regards the postwar educational reforms as wholly divorced from the life of the people and concludes that the values of the 1890 Imperial Rescript on Education are still valid and appropriate.[67] He sees the premises that underlie postwar reforms as similar to the thought of the Enlightenment. The postwar reforms and their progressive adherents shared with the Enlightenment a worship of reason and of science and a contempt for history. They have, furthermore, shared the Enlightenment's faith in the fundamental goodness of human nature: if institutions were reformed, human behavior would be changed.[68] Shimizu holds, in contrast, that institutions must be rooted in the lives of the common people, and for this reason he rejects the universalist and alien nature of the postwar system.

Because of his former prominence as a leader of the progressive forces, Shimizu has been roundly excoriated for his apostasy. A close study of his earlier writing, however, reveals a notable continuity of certain themes. He has been concerned, both before and after his volte-face, with the thinking of the common man.[69] From the outset of the postwar period, he was preoccupied with the fundamental predicament and dilemma of the progressive adherents of the new order: democratic values and institutions were not the free choice of a free people, they were imposed by an occupying military authority. Like Masao Maruyama and others, he was keenly aware of the gap between the new institutions and the social values inherent in the people's everyday lives. "What are the Japanese?" he asked in 1951; "they are Asian."[70] He emphasized the need to create a concept of democracy faithful to the values and daily experience of the Japanese people. Where others of the progressive persuasion sought the destruction of Japanese institutions and values as premodern remnants, Shimizu saw a need to root democracy in the behavior of the Japanese masses.[71]

Shimizu, observing the decline in U.S. power and world commitment, now believes that Japan cannot rely on the U.S. deterrent in an emergency. As a consequence, the nationalists seek more than a modest buildup of arms. "If Japan acquired military power commensurate with its economic power," wrote Shimizu, "countries that fully appreciate the meaning of military power would not overlook this. They would defer; they would act with caution; and in time they would show respect." The time had arrived for Japan to fulfill its potential:

When Japan breaks down its postwar illusions and taboos and develops military power commensurate with its economic strength, significant political power will naturally be born. In its relations with the United States, the Soviet Union, and many countries in many degrees and meanings, Japan will gain a free hand. Even though it will be alone, if it exercises its political power wisely, Japan will gain friends that will respect it and that will readily come to its aid. With its combined economic, military, and political power, won't Japan be a proud superpower (*dōdō taru taikoku*)! Although splendidly possessing the qualities to be a superpower, Japan, whether out of inertia or lack of courage, is behaving like a physically handicapped person right in plain view of the world.[72]

Pressing on relentlessly to his most dramatic point, Shimizu observes that the nuclear powers "even though they do not use their weapons, are able to instill fears in those countries that do not have them. A country like Japan that does not possess nuclear weapons and is afraid of them will be easy game for the nuclear powers. Putting political pressure on Japan would be like twisting a baby's arm."[73] Japan, in short, must "exercise the nuclear option."

Shimizu's essay sent a shudder through Japanese society. Nonetheless, there was a certain fascination with it. Unlike the right-wing nationalists whose sound trucks in downtown Tokyo are readily ignored or Yukio Mishima's bizarre suicide, which could be dismissed as another personal aberration, Shimizu had to be taken seriously. He was a respected intellectual, a leading theoretician of postwar progressivism, and often said to be a barometer of the changing political climate in Japan. More than any other writer, he confronted directly and insistently the contradictions and incongruities that troubled Japan's postwar order, and he advocated clear and decisive resolutions that touched deep and ambivalent emotions among many Japanese.

Japan, he wrote, is a "peculiar" and "abnormal" country (*ijō na kuni*).[74] It has lived for decades under a constitutional order forced on it by occupying military forces. It has abnegated the essential characteristics of a nation-state, military power and the required loyalty of its citizens. Other nations had lost a war, but where was there another that had wholly lost its national consciousness? "The overwhelming view among intellectual circles, the media, educators, and so on is that the state, the people, and the military are more than dangerous; they are unclean."[75] These progressives, he said, do not make the same judgment of other countries. Japan has to depend on resources, food, and markets around the world, but it refuses to ensure the security of its maritime transport routes. It depends on the goodwill of other countries and idealizes the United Nations, an organization formed by the powers that defeated Japan. Japan is the third largest contributor to the United Nations, but it is still not one of the permanent members of the Security Council—all of which are nuclear powers.

Predictably, Shimizu was excoriated by progressives. But the liberal realists, as well, wrote sharp and thoughtful responses to his ideas. They were appalled not just by his more favorable view of prewar institutions and values, his sweeping rejection of the postwar order, his proposal for an all-out military buildup, and his advocacy of an independent course in foreign affairs. They saw his ideas as raising the specter of militarism and, therefore, coloring attitudes toward their own proposals for a modest rearmament. Masamichi Inoki wrote plaintively that Shimizu's volte-face threatened to confirm his worse fears: that the "utopian pacifism of postwar Japan might give way to "utopian militarism."[76] Becoming a military superpower, Shimizu's critics held, would lead to greater rather than less insecurity. Japan would be diplomatically isolated from the West, the object of suspicion among Asian countries, and because of its concentrated urban population highly vulnerable in a nuclear conflict. His critics invariably accused him of advocating ideas that would lead to a repetition of the disaster that befell Imperial Japan.

The confidence of the new nationalists that Japan is capable of an independent role in world politics is supported by the immense pride in Japan's socioeconomic and technological achievements. The most vocal of the nationalists in this regard is Yatsuhiro Nakagawa, whose prolific writings are characterized by a boldness and bombast that appeal to a mass audience. Demanding that Japan play "a positive role on the world stage," he calls Japan, in the title of a recent book "the ultra-advanced country" (*Chō-senshin koku Nippon*).[77] For some years, a bureaucrat and at one time deputy director of the Nuclear Fuel Division of the Science and Technology Agency, Nakagawa typifies the facile young writer that has gained attention in the general-interest magazines.

Nakagawa is scornful of the intellectuals who had hitherto dominated these magazines and dismisses them as "vendors of imported merchandise."[78] Unable to free themselves from Japan's traditional awe of Western countries, these intellectuals have failed to acknowledge that "Japan is the leading nation in the world in terms of the provisions that it makes for the welfare of its citizens and in terms of the abundance and affluence that its citizens enjoy in their daily lives." By his calculations, the average Japanese worker in 1978 had an aftertax income at least 1.4 times to 2.0 times that of his American counterpart. Nakagawa stresses the role of the bureaucracy in promoting the livelihood of the people because he wants to reverse the distrust of the Japanese state that has prevailed since 1945. He argues that MITI, the Ministry of Labor, the Ministry of Agriculture and Forestry, and other government agencies are devoted to Japanese workers' welfare. In fact, "in everything but name, Japan has turned itself into a textbook example of a socialist country." In describing Japan as "the worker's paradise," Nakagawa considers welfare payments, income, health care, diet, housing, and education. In these categories, he contends that Japan has outstripped Western countries and has done this without high taxes and in an extraordinarily egalitarian setting.

A National Identity for the Twenty-first Century

At the very heart of the debate over Japan's future international role is the issue of Japanese exceptionalism. Everyone involved agrees that Japan has been an exceptional nation-state since World War II, but the issue is Can and should Japan continue as an "extraordinary" nation? Or should and must it conform to new international conditions and become an "ordinary" nation? Of the four general modes of thought that we have considered, two favor continuation of the exceptional characteristics of the postwar state, and two oppose continuation. Progressivism believes it is Japan's unique "mission" to show the way to a new world. The mercantile view calculates that it is in Japan's shrewd self-interest to maintain its "incongruous" nature. But realism sees diplomatic isolation resulting from Japan's "eccentric" behavior. Finally, the new nationalism believes that Japan will be at the mercy of other countries so long as it continues as an "abnormal" country. This debate goes on today, and it will be a fundamental issue in the struggle for leadership of the LDP.

Nakasone's belief that the passive stance must be replaced by a more activist style is being challenged by Kiichi Miyazawa. In an interview with Masataka Kosaka in the July 1984 issue of *Bungei shunjū*, Miyazawa expressed satisfaction with the "postwar system," that is, with the Yoshida Doctrine. Postwar Japan had three goals, he said: to build a peaceful state (*heiwa koku*), to establish a free society, and to achieve economic prosperity and a standard of living similar to that of Western countries. With regard to the first goal, "the Japanese race has gambled its future (*unmei*) in a great experiment, the first of its kind in human history, and fortunately up to today we have succeeded." Similarly, Japan had succeeded in establishing a free society with protection for human rights and with disparities in income distribution smaller than all but two or three Scandinavian countries. "Therefore freedom has been established not only in name but in economic reality, and this country is actually the freest in the world." Finally, the nation has achieved economic prosperity, but it is important—and this was his campaign theme—to continue to pursue economic priorities in order to build up social capital for housing, schools, and to acquire the benefits of "a technological society."

One of the most noteworthy features of this debate is an emergent new sense of nationality, strikingly different from prewar nationalism. Since the end of the war, observers waiting for Japanese nationalism to come out of hiding have maintained a stakeout at the Yasukuni Shrine or at Nijūbashi, the bridges at the entrance to the Imperial Palace, assuming that these traditional symbols of nationality would be where it would appear. This is not likely. Nationalism in the 1930s had its social basis in the village, where over half the labor force was still employed in agriculture and where three-quarters of adult participants in politics had been born and raised. The bearers of nationalism were lower-middle-class groups—shopkeepers, small businessmen, grade school and elementary school teachers, clerical workers in government and business—who had risen only halfway up the educational ladder of success and who resented industrialism and the luxury, corruption, and un-Japanese cosmopolitanism of businessmen, bureaucrats, and politicians.

The social structure and politics of postwar Japan have been greatly transformed. Social and cultural divisions are lessened. Ninety per cent of the population regards itself as middle class. Japan is overwhelmingly urban, well-educated, perhaps as well informed on international conditions as any nation, and thoroughly imbued with the values and tastes of industrial society. The inchoate cultural pride that runs through the new attitudes and the debate that we have examined is more forward-looking than prewar nationalism. It builds on Japan's industrial accomplishments and finds confidence from achieving Western ends by Japanese means.

Moreover, the end of the era of late development is likely to affect the nature of Japanese nationalism. Late development entailed borrowing from the West to supplant traditional wisdom and skills and gave rise to painful cultural dislocations. A key theme in modern Japanese history has been the search for ways to reconcile the conflicting needs of cultural borrowing and national pride, to be both modern and Japanese. The burden of this historical predicament was perhaps best expressed by Natsume Soseki in his brooding speech at Wakayama in 1911. Japan, he said, was running a race with Western history; only by reaching the Western nations' advanced stage of development could it regain cultural autonomy and control of its own destiny. And yet Japan could be truly independent and self-respecting only if it were no longer "impelled from without" (*gaihatsuteki no kaika*), no longer compelled to borrow from the West, no longer forced to follow an already broken path rather than a self-determined course (*naihatsuteki no kaika*). To Soseki, Japan seemed fated to run an interminable losing race. He saw only two ways, both unsatisfactory, to try to close the gap: Japan could continue "mechanically imitating" the West (in *gaihatsu* fashion), a shortcut that destroyed integrity and self-esteem and produced a superficial civilization; or it could strive to catch up by progressing along an independent Japanese course (in *naihatsu* fashion) in the hope of reaching the West's stage of development in a fraction of the time it had taken the Western nations. But the latter alternative was unthinkable since it would require an effort so consuming and strenuous that it would lead inexorably to "nervous collapse." The "bitter truth," he concluded, was that Japan must continue in its wretched course, following abjectly in the train of Western development.[79]

The excesses of Japanese nationalism in the 1930s were partly a result of this failure to solve the dilemma of reconciling cultural borrowing with the need for national pride. The narrow Japanism of that day led to a war that ended in an imposed conception of nationality that lacked roots in the inherited tradition. In the present era, there is a widespread belief that Japan has reached the Western nations' advanced stage of development and that Japan, therefore, has regained control of its own destiny.

There is a pervasive conviction that Japan has caught up not only in a material sense but in the fulfillment of social and political values as well. Furthermore, there is confidence that these goals have been reached by a Japanese—a better—cultural route. The goals of Western liberalism have been realized without the social costs apparent in the West because they have been reached by relying on Japanese cultural values and patterns of behavior. The views of a popular economic writer, Tsuneo Iida, best illustrate this attitude:

The nature of the Japanese economy is such that, in comparison with the United States and Europe, it better observes the spirit embodied in modern economics and more effectively functions in accordance with the principles of neo-classical economic theory. In a broader perspective, one can say that the national characteristic of Japan, in comparison with the West, is to pursue more seriously such bourgeois democratic values as liberty, equality, and respect for the individual, and to realize these goals on a wider, more effective scale. *In short, the basic character of Japan consists of purified strains (junsui baiyō) of the West* [italics added].[80]

In other words, out of the chrysalis of Japanese culture has come the purest expression of modern Western values. Japan's achievement is not simply a material one of outstripping the economic growth and per capita GNP of Western societies, but of actually fulfilling the most cherished aspirations of Western civilization. Writes Iida:

Generally speaking, then, in terms of achieving the ideals of democracy, egalitarianism, and individualism and in maintaining a competitive [economic] mechanism, Japan may appear to be an ordinary nation. But this "ordinariness" is only in appearance. The fact of the matter is that what are "principles" (*tatemae*) in the Western nations have become "reality" (*honne*) in Japan.[81]

In such a view, Japan's national character is now more "Western" or modern than the prewar conception, which was fundamentally based on the formula of merging "Western science and Japanese values." Iida concludes:

As is often said, Japan relies on the West for the principles of science and technology. But in making improvements on, and in adopting [the imported science and technology], Japan often excels the West. Since this is the case with science and technology, there is nothing surprising about the fact that similar feats are being accomplished in the economic and social arenas.[82]

Above all, it is felt that Japan has a leg up on other countries in the progress toward the new high-technology–oriented society. In the words of Hiroshi Takeuchi, a prominent bank economist, "Both Japanese society and the organization of Japanese firms contain powerful built-in stimuli toward technological innovation."[83] In other words, the Japanese economy behaves in a unique and superior fashion because of distinctive cultural patterns inherent in Japanese society. For example, Naohiro Amaya stresses the formation of "collegial groups" (*nakama shūdan*) within the Japanese economy. These groups embrace a firm, its employees, other firms with which it does business, its subcontractors, and its bank. Holding these groups together is a sense of internal solidarity rooted in values of harmony that originated in the traditional village. Amaya holds that these groups are therefore a combination of Gesellschaft and Gemeinschaft elements.

Such Gemeinschaft-like interpersonal relationships are not only between a firm and its employees. They also exist between one firm and others with which it has business relationships, and between a firm and its banks. These interfirm relationships are not cold, profit-loss relationships based on calculations and contracts, but cohesive relationships that have a large margin for emotion and sense of obligation.[84]

Within the Japanese economy, Amaya contends, there is among these groups an intense competition unknown in the West. The struggles go far beyond the bounds of seeking only profit to seeking the prestige of larger market shares. Because of the collegial nature of relationships, employees are willing to sacrifice for "their company," subcontractors to absorb losses, and banks to allow "overborrowing" to facilitate expansion. Antitrust regulation to preserve competition is necessary in Western societies because they do not have the cultural forces that promote a fierce and excessive competition (katō kyōsō). This fierce competition among firms, says economist Takeuchi, is one reason for the speed of technological progress in Japan. "No one in the world today," writes Masanori Moritani, senior researcher at the Nomura Research Institute, "has made the principle of free competition work to the advantage of corporate activity and the development of new technology better than Japan."[85]

Discussion of the twenty-first century is probably more extensive in Japan than in any other country. It is remarkable for its optimism about the nature of the projected "information society" and its belief that the Japanese are best suited for the challenges of this society. One's impression is that there is less concern than in other countries about the loss of privacy, the dangers of unemployment, and the vulnerability of society to control by technocrats. Rather, there is notable self-confidence in facing this brave new world. A blue-ribbon commission of economists and bureaucrats assembled by the Ministry of Finance and known as the Study Group on the Structural Transformation of the Economy and Its Policy Implications (Keizai no Kōzō Henka to Seisaku no Kenkyūkai) concluded that, unlike the social systems of the West, Japanese society possesses characteristics well adapted to the new era. For example, Japan will be better able to deal with the dehumanizing problems of an information society because "the basic characteristic of Japanese culture is that, as shown in the Japanese word ningen, it values 'the relationship between persons' (hito to hito no aidagara)." The problem of maintaining a balance between the whole society and the individual, a relationship greatly intensified in the information society, will be better handled in the "contextualist" Japanese social pattern than in the atomistic nature of Western society.[86]

With a strong sense of having fulfilled their overriding ambition of the past century by catching up with the West, the Japanese could drift toward an assertive political nationalism or they could subside into a complacent conservatism and enjoy their hard-won affluence. Both trends are evident in Japanese society. But the elite leadership appears determined that neither trend should prevail. One of the most interesting and noteworthy developments of the past decade is the efforts of the elites to galvanize the nation and to build a consensus around a new set of national goals to replace the old fulfilled ones. These goals have a strong nationalist element, but that element is akin more to the economic nationalism that has prevailed in the postwar era than to the new nationalism of recent years. The goals envision nothing less than Japanese global leadership in economic and technological development and in a new historical stage in human social evolution. It is possible to see this development as an extension of the Yoshida Doctrine and an adjustment to new conditions. For example, Moritani has written that the "age of the American way of life, that lifestyle envied by the world since the 1950s, has ended." In place of its wasteful ways and addiction to big consumer products, Japan "should create its own 'Japanese way of life' and proselytize it throughout the world." [87]

A 1984 article by Yujiro Eguchi, a senior economist at the Nomura Research Institute, typifies much of the elite thinking. He describes the torch of world leadership passing to Japan as it once did to the United States and earlier to Britain and much earlier to the Roman Empire:

If present trends continue, Japan will doubtless become the world's leading creditor nation within a decade, assuming the position formerly held by Britain and then by the United States. Ten years from now . . . Japan will have net external assets of $500 billion, a level far in excess of America's foreign holdings at their peak. Both Britain and the United States created and ran international systems with themselves at the top when they were the leading creditors. Now it is Japan's turn to come up with an international system suited to itself. History records the Roman Empire, the British Empire, and the United States of America as major creditors. In each case the power in question created and ran an international system fitting the conditions in which it found itself. [88]

For Eguchi, the immense cost of military power means that Japan must build its international system without resorting to military power. Instead it should "concentrate on developing the software to operate an international system": a strong currency and economic reserves to invest abroad; diplomatic, cultural, and business strengths; and an information system that will permit the best country–risk analysis skills. The costly military aspects of the international system will have to be left to the United States, and this will provide a good match: "If Japan and the United States, facing each other across the Pacific Ocean, can complement each other, the former as a major creditor nation and the latter as a major debtor, the prospect for a broad-based relationship will open up." The proposal is, to say the least, breathtaking in its optimism that Japan can remain free of political-strategic concerns. What we have here is in fact the projection of the Yoshida Doctrine into the twenty-first century and the new information society: "By limiting defense strength to annual outlays of 1 per cent of GNP and putting first-rate information power to work, we can leave history a new example: a major creditor nation that is a minor military power." [89]

Clearly a kind of formless and free-floating national pride is growing. It is "formless" in comparison with prewar nationalism, which was shaped and propagated by the bureaucracy. In contrast, the disposition of contemporary Japanese leaders has usually been to try to contain this nationalism—as in the case of Amaya's rejection of "soap nationalism." Nevertheless, it is there to be exploited in building a new consensus to take the place of the catch-up psychology that has hitherto motivated the nation. The technology of an information society provides a powerful means. Many observers, as we have seen, wonder whether the Japanese people can simply rely on material self-interest to guide them or whether a new ideology is not needed. What seems clear is that the conception of Japanese national character is in an evolving and dynamic phase. The course of world events for the rest of this century will do much to shape it. And, conversely, this new sense of Japanese identity will be profoundly important for the international system.

Notes

Notes

Okimoto and Inoguchi: Introduction

1. A. F. K. Organski and Jacek Kugler, *The War Ledger* (Chicago: University of Chicago Press, 1980), pp. 144–45.

2. Robert Gilpin, *War and Change in World Politics* (Cambridge, Eng.: Cambridge University Press, 1981), pp. 156–230.

3. Herbert G. Grubel and P. J. Lloyd, *Intra-Industry Trade: The Theory and Measure of International Trade in Differentiated Products* (New York: Wiley, Halsted 1975), chap. 9. Charles Lipson, "The Transformation of Trade: The Sources and Effects of Regime Change," in Stephen D. Krasner, ed., *International Regimes* (Ithaca, N.Y.: Cornell University Press, 1983), pp. 259–62.

4. Michael J. Dahl, Daniel I. Okimoto, and Henry Rowen, *The Declining Competitiveness of the American Semiconductor Industry: Its National Security Implications* (Stanford, Calif.: Occasional Paper, Northeast Asia-United States Forum on International Policy, forthcoming).

5. Gilpin, *War and Change in World Politics*, pp. 156–85.

6. See, for example, James C. Abegglen, "Narrow Self-Interest: Japan's Ultimate Vulnerability?" in Diane Tasca, ed., *U.S.-Japanese Economic Relations: Cooperation, Competition, and Confrontation* (New York: Pergamon, 1980), pp. 21–31.

7. Hiroshi Kitamura, Ryohei Murata, and Hisahiko Okazaki, *Between Friends: Japanese Diplomats Look at Japan-U.S. Relations* (New York: Weatherhill, 1985), pp. 163–203.

8. Marvin J. Wolf, *Japanese Conspiracy: The Plot to Dominate Industry Worldwide and How to Deal with It* (New York: Empire Books, 1983), pp. 22–60.

9. E. H. Carr, *The Twenty Years' Crisis: 1919–1939* (New York: Harper and Row, 1964).

10. Gilpin, *War and Change*, p. 231; Stephen D. Krasner, "Transforming International Regimes: What the Third World Wants and Why," *International Studies Quarterly*, Vol. 25, No. 1 (Mar. 1981), pp. 119–48.

11. See Ronald Dore, "Goodwill and the Spirit of Market Capitalism" in *The British Journal of Sociology*, Vol. 34, No. 4 (1983), pp. 459–81.

12. See, for example, Charles Lipson, "The Transformation of Trade: The Sources and Effects of Regime Change," in Krasner, *International Regimes*, pp. 238–39.

Inoguchi: Foreign Policy

Some of the material in this chapter originally appeared in Takashi Inoguchi, "Japan's Images and Options: Not a Challenger, but a Supporter," *Journal of Japanese Studies*, Vol. 12, No. 1 (Winter 1986), and in Takashi Inoguchi, "Foreign Policy Background," in Herbert J. Ellison, ed., *Japan and the Pacific Quadrille* (Boulder, Col.: Westview Press, 1987). The author is grateful to the *Journal of Japanese Studies* and to Westview Press for permission to reproduce that material here.

1. For a discussion of the contending images of Japan and their relation to its place and status in the world, see Johan Galtung, "Japan and Future World Politics," *Journal of Peace Research*, Vol. 10, No. 4 (1973), pp. 355–85; and Takashi Inoguchi, "Japan's Images and Options: Not a Challenger, but a Supporter," *Journal of Japanese Studies*, Vol. 12, No. 1 (Winter 1986), pp. 95–119.

2. For a recent example of this argument, see Zbigniew Brzezinski, "Japan Must Take Steps to End Free Ride on Defense," *International Herald Tribune*, Aug. 23, 1985. Japan spends around $10 billion on defense versus $300 billion for the United States. Cumulative expenditures for 1961–80 are $1,820 billion for the United States, $239 billion for West Germany, $224 billion for France, $213 billion for Great Britain, $82 billion for Italy, and $77 billion for Japan. See Ruth L. Sivard, *World Military and Social Indicators* (Washington, D.C.: World Priorities, 1983); and Japan, Ministry of Foreign Affairs, *Sekai no ugoki*, No. 398 (1982).

3. *Nihon keizai shimbun*, May 31, 1984.

4. For a recent example of this argument, see C. Steven Solarz, "America and Japan: A Search for Balance," *Foreign Policy*, No. 49 (Winter 1982–83), pp. 74–79.

5. For Reagan's foreign policy strategy, see Takashi Inoguchi, "Daini kakumei no taigai senryaku" (The international strategy of the second revolution), *Ekonomisuto*, Apr. 16, 1985, pp. 12–22; reprinted in idem, *Kokusai kankei no seijikeizaigaku: Nihon no yakuwari to sentaku* (The political economy of international relations: Japan's roles and choices) (Tokyo: University of Tokyo Press, 1985), pp. 124–49. See also Kenneth A. Oye, "International System Structure and American Foreign Policy," in idem et al., eds., *Eagle Defiant: United States Foreign Policy in the 1980s* (Boston: Little, Brown & Co., 1983), pp. 3–32; and Mike Davis, "Reaganomics' Magical Mystery Tour," *New Left Review*, No. 149 (Jan.–Feb. 1985), pp. 45–65.

6. In 1984, Japan's ODA was $4.3 billion, and the United States' was $8.7 billion. In terms of ratios to GNP and total grants, both Japan and the United States register lower figures than other major members of the OECD Development Assistance Committee. *Asahi shimbun*, June 27, 1985, evening ed.

7. For this argument, see Ken Matsui, *Keizai kyōryoku* (Economic cooperation) (Tokyo: Yuhikaku, 1983); and Shimin no Kaigai Kyōryoku o Kangaerukai, ed., *Shimin no kaigai kyōryoku hakusho* (Citizens' white book on foreign aid) (Tokyo: Nihon Hyōronsha, 1985). See also Japan, Ministry of International Trade and Industry (MITI), *Keizai kyōryoku no genjō to mondaiten* (Economic cooperation and its problems) (Tokyo: Tsūshō Sangyō Chōsakai, 1983); Denis T. Yamamoto, *Japan and the Asian Development Bank* (New York: Praeger, 1983); Alan Rix, *Japan's Economic Aid: Policymaking and Policy* (New York: St. Martin's Press, 1980); and Sukehiro Hasegawa, *Japan's Foreign Aid: Policy Practices* (New York: Praeger, 1975).

8. Japanese aid has now come to cover all these areas and to focus on human and social development in poorer countries. See William L. Brooks and Robert M. Orr, Jr., "Japan's Foreign Economic Assistance," *Asian Survey*, Vol. 25, No. 3 (Mar. 1985), pp. 322–40. A most informative book on the subject is Asahi Shim-

bun, "Enjo" Shuzaihan, ed., *Enjo tojōkoku Nihon* (Japan as a developing aid-donor country) (Tokyo: Asahi Shimbunsha, 1985).

9. Needless to say, Japan is not the only self-seeking actor in the world: every country is.

10. See, e.g., Marvin Wolf, *Japanese Conspiracy: The Plot to Dominate Industry Worldwide and How to Deal with It* (New York: Empire Books, 1983). For the Yellow Peril image, see William Wetherall, "Paranoia Invents the Rebirth of the Yellow Peril," *Far Eastern Economic Review*, Aug. 1, 1985, pp. 41–42.

11. Immanuel Wallerstein, "Friends as Foes," *Foreign Policy*, No. 40 (Fall 1980), pp. 119–31.

12. Quoted in Steven Schlossstein, *Trade War: Greed, Power, Industrial Policy on the Opposite Side of the Pacific* (New York: Congan & Weed, 1984), pp. 201–2.

13. Winston William, "Japanese Investment: A New Worry," *New York Times*, May 6, 1984, p. F1.

14. Ibid. See also "Beikoku sangyō seisaku ni hirogaru Pentagon no kage" (The shadow of the Pentagon over U.S. industrial policy), *Nihon keizai shimbun*, May 22–24, 1984.

15. Stephen Bronte, "This Is the Decade of the Conquering Yen," *Euromoney*, Mar. 1982, pp. 71–81.

16. Zaisei Seisaku Kenkyūkai, ed., *Korekara no zaisei to kokusai hakkō* (Finance and bond issues in the future) (Tokyo: Ōkurazaimu Kyōkai, 1985), p. 112.

17. International Institute for Strategic Studies, *Military Balance, 1984–1985* (London, 1985).

18. Johan Galtung's structural theory predicts such an outcome. See his "A Structural Theory of Imperialism," *Journal of Peace Research*, Vol. 8, No. 2 (1971), pp. 81–117. See also Immanuel Wallerstein, "North Atlanticism in Decline," *SAIS Review*, No. 4 (Summer 1982), pp. 21–26.

19. MITI, *Keizai kyōryoku*.

20. See Brooks and Orr, "Economic Assistance."

21. Yamamoto, *Japan*, gives such an impression. For a contrasting view, see Stephen Krasner, "Power Structure and Regional Development Banks," *International Organization*, Vol. 35, No. 2 (Spring 1981), pp. 303–28. For the overall relationship between Japan and the Western Pacific countries, see Herbert S. Yee, "Japan's Relations with ASEAN and South Korea: From Dependence to Interdependence?" *Journal of Northeast Asian Studies*, Vol. 2, No. 2 (June 1983), pp. 29–44.

22. *Euromoney*, May 1980, pp. 64–65; Apr. 1983, pp. 24–25; Oct. 1983, pp. 166–82; Mar. 1987, pp. 14, 18. At the end of 1986, Japan's outstanding net external assets reached $1,804 billion, higher than the peak figure the United States registered in 1982, i.e., $1,495 billion. *Nihon keizai shimbun*, May 26, 1987, evening edition.

23. Japan External Trade Organization, ed., *Sekai to Nihon no kaigai chokusetsu tōshi* (The world's and Japan's direct overseas investment) (Tokyo, 1985), and *Nihon keizai shimbun*, May 29, 1987.

24. Ibid. See also Davis Bobrow, "Playing for Safety: Japan's Security Policy," *Japan Quarterly*, Vol. 31, No. 1 (Jan.–Mar. 1984), pp. 33–43; and J. W. M. Chapman, "Dependence," in idem, R. Drifte, and I. T. M. Gow, *Japan's Quest for Comprehensive Security: Defense, Diplomacy and Dependence* (London: Frances Pinter, 1983).

25. Japan, Defense Agency, *Bōei hakusho, 1985* (Defense white paper) (Tokyo, 1985).

26. See, e.g., Shinichiro Asao, "Japan's Defense Policy," *New York Times*, Feb. 29, 1984.

27. David Calleo, *The German Problem Reconsidered: Germany and the World Order, 1970 to the Present* (Cambridge, Eng.: Cambridge University Press, 1978), p. 202.

28. Takashi Inoguchi, *Gaikō taiyō no hikaku kenkyū: Chūgoku, Eikoku, Nihon* (A comparative study of diplomatic styles: China, Britain, Japan) (Tokyo: Gannandō Shoten, 1978), esp. pp. 297–308; and James Crowley, *Japan's Quest for Autonomy: National Security and Foreign Policy, 1930–1938* (Princeton: Princeton University Press, 1966).

29. See Hajime Shinohara, *Keizai taikoku no seisui* (The rise and decline of economic powers) (Tokyo: Tōyō Keizai Shimpōsha, 1981); Walt W. Rostow, *The World Economy: History and Prospect* (London: Macmillan, 1978); and Joshua S. Goldstein, "Kondratieff Waves as War Cycles," *International Studies Quarterly*, Vol. 29, No. 4 (Dec. 1985), pp. 411–44.

30. Kazushi Ohkawa and Henry Rosovsky, *Japanese Economic Growth: Trend Acceleration in the Twentieth Century* (Stanford: Stanford University Press, 1973); Takafusa Nakamura, *Senzenki Nihon keizai seichō no bunseki* (An analysis of prewar Japanese economic growth) (Tokyo: Iwanami Shoten, 1971); *Nihon keizai* (The Japanese economy) (Tokyo: University of Tokyo Press, 1978); and James W. Morley, ed., *Dilemmas of Growth in Prewar Japan* (Princeton: Princeton University Press, 1971).

31. For industrial structure, see Nakamura, *Senzenki Nihon*; Ryōshin Minami, *Nihon no keizai seichō* (Japanese economic growth) (Tokyo: Tōyō Keizai Shimpōsha, 1981); and Hugh Patrick, ed., *Japanese Industrialization and Its Social Consequences* (Berkeley: University of California Press, 1976). For political authoritarianism, see Junnosuke Masumi, *Nihon seitō shiron* (A treatise on Japanese political parties), vols. 6–8 (Tokyo: University of Tokyo Press, 1980); and Gordon M. Berger, *Parties out of Power in Japan, 1931–1941* (Princeton: Princeton University Press, 1978).

32. Alexander Gershenkron, *Economic Backwardness in Historical Perspective* (Cambridge, Mass.: Harvard University Press, 1962).

33. For Japanese technology policy, see, e.g., Masanori Yoshimi, *Nihon no sangyō gijutsu seisaku: Kokusai kyōsōryoku to gijutsu kakushin no kenkyū* (Japan's technology policy: A study of international competitiveness and technological innovation) (Tokyo: Tōyō Keizai Shimpōsha, 1985).

34. It is interesting that Britain was a rapidly declining hegemon and Germany, Japan, and the United States were all regarded as potential challengers. It may be speculated that a challenger-state that initiates a hegemonic war tends to lose and a supporter-country that allies with a hegemon tends to win. In World War II, Germany and Japan challenged and lost, whereas the United States took over hegemonic legitimacy by allying with Britain. Britain did the same when France challenged the Dutch preponderance in the seventeenth century and then established the first Pax Britannica. On this point, see Kuniko Inoguchi, "Haken no junkan to Pax Americana no ikue" (Hegemonic cycles and prospects for the Pax Americana), *Sekai*, Nov. 1985, pp. 168–83. This view differs from the hegemonic cycle model of Robert Gilpin, *War and Change in World Politics* (Cambridge, Eng.: Cambridge University Press, 1981).

35. Christopher Thorne, *Allies of a Kind: The United States, Britain, and the War Against Japan, 1941–1945* (London: Macmillan, 1978).

36. For the contrasts, see Nobuhiko Ushiba, Graham T. Allison, and Thierry

de Montbrial, *Sharing International Responsibilities Among the Trilateral Countries* (New York: Trilateral Commission, 1983).

37. For U.S. hegemony and its relative weakening in nuclear and nonnuclear areas, see Lawrence Freedman, *The Evolution of Nuclear Strategy* (London: Macmillan, 1981); and Fred L. Block, *The Origins of International Economic Disorder: A Study of United States International Monetary Policy from World War II to the Present* (Berkeley: University of California Press, 1977). See also Franz Schurman, *The Logic of World Power* (New York: Pantheon Books, 1974); Stanley Hoffman, *Primacy or World Order: American Foreign Policy Since the Cold War* (New York: McGraw-Hill, 1978); and Fred Halliday, *The Making of the Second Cold War* (London: Verso & NLB, 1983). For an emphasis on U.S. cultural hegemony despite some erosion in economic and military areas, see the paper by Russett in this volume. The most articulate scenarios on the prospects for U.S. hegemony and Japanese responses are drawn by Yasusuke Murakami, "After Hegemony Nichi-Bei keizai masatsu eno taisaku" (After hegemony: Policies for U.S.-Japanese economic conflicts), *Chūō kōron*, Nov. 1985, pp. 68–69. See also K. Inoguchi, "Haken no junkan."

38. The meaning of the U.S. umbrella over Japan in such forms as the U.S. occupation, the U.S.-Japan Mutual Security Treaty, and high economic interdependence have been topics of high interest in Japan. See, e.g., Makoto Iokibe, *Beikoku no Nihon senryō seisaku* (The U.S. occupation of Japan) (Tokyo: Chūō Kōronsha, 1985); Kazuhisa Ogawa, *Zai-Nichi Beigun* (U.S. forces in Japan) (Tokyo: Kodansha, 1984); PHP Institute, ed., *Shin Nichi-Bei kankeiron* (Japan-U.S. relations) (Kyoto, 1983); Hiroshi Kitamura et al., *Nichi-Bei o toitsumeru* (Inquiring into U.S.-Japan relations) (Tokyo: Sekai no Ugokisha, 1983); and Stephen D. Cohen, *Uneasy Partnership: Competition and Conflict in US-Japanese Trade Relations* (Baltimore: Johns Hopkins University Press, 1985).

39. OECD, *Historical Statistics, 1960–1980* (Paris, 1982).

40. I am referring to the debates on the "Japanese model." See, e.g., Tsuneo Iida, *Nihon chikarazuyosa no saihakken* (Rediscovery of Japanese strength) (Tokyo: Nihon Keizai Shimbunsha, 1979). On the debate, see the paper by Pyle in this volume; and Kozo Yamamura, "Success That Soured: Administrative Guidance and Cartels in Japan," in idem, ed., *Policy and Trade Issues of the Japanese Economy* (Seattle: University of Washington Press, 1982), pp. 77–112.

41. The most noteworthy recent example is Theodore White, "The Danger from Japan," *New York Times Magazine*, July 28, 1985, pp. 19–44.

42. Takashi Inoguchi, "Western Europe and the Western Pacific: A Comparative Assessment," in National Institute for Research Advancement, ed., *The Future of the Asia-Pacific Region* (Tokyo, 1986), pp. 107–13.

43. Shumpei Kumon, "Administrative Reform Requires New National Goals," *Economic Eye*, Vol. 3, No. 3 (1982), pp. 4–7.

44. Davis, "Reaganomics' Magical Mystery Tour." See also the references cited in note 37.

45. Ronald McKinnon, *An International Standard of Monetary Stabilization* (Cambridge, Mass.: MIT Press for the Institute for International Economics, 1984).

46. These and other problems are touched on in such works as C. Fred Bergsten, *The Dilemmas of the Dollar* (New York: New York University Press, 1975); Block, *International Economic Disorder*; and Joanne Gowa, *Closing the Gold Window: Domestic Politics and the End of Bretton Woods* (Ithaca, N.Y.: Cornell University Press, 1983).

47. See, e.g., *Nihon keizai shimbun*, May 28, 1984.

48. See ibid., May 30, 1984.

49. Kent Calder, "Opening Japan," *Foreign Policy*, No. 47 (Summer 1982), pp. 82–87; and Bobrow, "Playing for Safety." See also Raymond Vernon, *Two Hungry Giants: The United States and Japan in the Quest for Oil and Ore* (Cambridge, Mass.: Harvard University Press, 1983).

50. The most useful book on trade policies in the 1980s is William R. Cline, *Trade Policy in the 1980's* (Cambridge, Mass.: MIT Press for the Institute for International Economics, 1984). See also Robert E. Baldwin and Anne O. Krueger, eds., *The Structure and Evolution of Recent U.S. Trade Policy* (Chicago: University of Chicago Press, 1984). For Japan's trade policy, see the paper by Komiya and Itoh in this volume; and Kiyohiko Fukushima, "Japan's Real Trade Policy," *Foreign Policy*, No. 59 (Summer 1985), pp. 22–39.

51. On Japan, see Yamamura, *Policy and Trade Issues*; and Hugh Patrick and Henry Rosovsky, eds., *Asia's New Giant* (Washington, D.C.: Brookings Institution, 1976). On NICs, see OECD, *The Impact of Newly Industrializing Countries on Production and Trade in Manufactures* (Paris, 1979); Louis Turner et al., *Living with the Newly Industrializing Countries* (London: Royal Institute for International Affairs, 1980); William R. Cline, *Exports of Manufactures from Developing Countries* (Washington, D.C.: Brookings Institution, 1984); and David B. Yoffie, *Power and Protectionism: Strategies of the Newly Industrializing Countries* (New York: Columbia University Press, 1983).

52. Illuminating these processes with some exaggeration is Mancur Olsen, *The Rise and Decline of Nations: Economic Growth, Stagflation, and Social Rigidities* (New Haven: Yale University Press, 1982). See also Robert Gilpin, *War and Change in World Politics* (Cambridge, Eng.: Cambridge University Press, 1981).

53. William R. Cline, "'Reciprocity': A New Approach to World Trade Policy?" in idem, *Trade Policy*; according to another estimate, more than 50 per cent of total world trade is "controlled trade." See Japan External Trade Organization, *JETRO hakusho bōeki hen* (JETRO white paper on trade) (Tokyo, 1985). See also Robert O. Keohane, "Reciprocity as a Principle of Governance in International Relations," *International Organization*, Vol. 40, No. 1 (Winter 1986), pp. 1–27.

54. Bronte, "Conquering Yen."

55. These perspectives are presented in such works as Robert Keohane, *After Hegemony: Cooperation and Discord in the World Economy* (Princeton: Princeton University Press, 1984); and Wolfgang Hager, "Protectionism and Autonomy: How to Preserve Trade in Europe," *International Affairs*, Vol. 58, No. 3 (Summer 1982), pp. 412–28.

56. See MITI, *Tsūshō hakusho*. See also "NICs in a Twist," *Far Eastern Economic Review*, Sept. 26, 1985, pp. 99–106; Ippei Yamazawa and Takashi Nozawa, eds., *Ajia Taiheiyō shokoku no bōeki to sangyō chōsei* (Trade and industrial adjustment in Asian-Pacific countries) (Tokyo: Institute of Developing Economies, 1985); and Toshio Watanabe, *Seichō no Ajia, teitai no Ajia* (Growing Asia, stagnant Asia) (Tokyo: Tōyō Keizai Shimpōsha, 1985).

57. MITI, *Tsūshō hakusho*; and idem, *Keizai kyōryoku*.

58. *Nihon keizai shimbun*, May 31, 1984.

59. Ibid., Sept. 13, 1985, evening ed.

60. Yasusuke Murakami, "Toward a Sociopolitical Explanation of Japan's Economic Performance," in Yamamura, *Trade and Policy Issues*, pp. 3–46; and Murakami's paper in Volume I of this series. See also Yoshio Suzuki, *Money and Banking in Contemporary Japan* (New Haven: Yale University Press, 1980).

61. Yoshio Suzuki, *Nihon keizai to kin'yū* (The Japanese economy and finance) (Tokyo: Tōyō Keizai Shimpōsha, 1981); Yoshio Suzuki, *Nihon kin'yū keizai ron* (Japanese monetary economics) (Tokyo: Tōyō Keizai Shimpōsha, 1983); and the paper by Horiuchi and Hamada in Volume I of this series.

62. For the politics of government revenues and deficits, see Yukio Noguchi, *Zaisei kiki no kōzō* (The structure of the financial crisis) (Tokyo: Tōyō Keizai Shimpōsha, 1980); and Noguchi's paper in Volume I of this series.

63. On saving, see Kazuo Sato, "Japan's Savings and Internal and External Macroeconomic Balance," in Yamamura, *Trade and Policy Issues*, pp. 143–72; and Sato's paper in Volume I of this series.

64. See, e.g., Takashi Inoguchi, *Gendai Nihon seiji keizai no kōzu* (The contemporary Japanese political economy) (Tokyo: Tōyō Keizai Shimpōsha, 1983), pp. 169–97.

65. On the U.S. regulation and capital outflows for balance-of-payments reasons during the latter half of the 1960s, see Janet Kelley, *Bankers and Brokers: The Case of American Banks in Britain* (Cambridge, Mass.: Ballinger, 1977); on the U.S. deregulation since 1974 because of the transition to the floating exchange rate regime, see, e.g., M. S. Mendelsohn, *Money on the Move: The Modern International Market* (New York: McGraw-Hill, 1980). See also "A New Awakening: A Survey of Banking," *Economist*, Mar. 24, 1984, insert pp. 1–80.

66. *Nihon keizai shimbun*, May 30, 1984.

67. See Raymond Vernon, *Sovereignty at Bay: The Multinational Spread of US Enterprises* (New York: Basic Books, 1971); and Mendelsohn, *Money on the Move*.

68. See Barry Bluestone and Bennett Harrison, *The Deindustrialization of America* (New York: Basic Books, 1982). For a contrasting view, see Robert Z. Lawrence, *Can America Compete?* (Washington, D.C.: Brookings Institution, 1984).

69. See Wilkinson, "Hopes"; and Samuel Brittan, "Remedies Worse than the Disease," *Financial Times*, Sept. 16, 1985.

70. Samuel Huntington, "Renewed Hostility," in Joseph Nye, ed., *The Making of America's Soviet Policy* (New Haven: Yale University Press, 1984), pp. 265–89; Noam Chomsky, *Towards a New Cold War* (New York: Pantheon Books, 1982); Fred Halliday, *The Making of the New Second Cold War* (London: Verso & NLB, 1983); Adam Ulam, *Dangerous Relations: The Soviet Union in World Politics, 1970–1982* (New York: Oxford University Press, 1983). Hideo Ōtake, *Nihon no bōei to kokunai seiji* (Japanese defense and domestic politics) (Tokyo: San'ichi Shobō, 1983); and Raymond L. Garthoff, *Detente and Confrontation* (Washington, D.C.: Brookings Institution, 1985).

71. Quoted in Huntington, "Renewed Hostility."

72. Ibid.; and Halliday, *Post Conservative America: People, Politics and Ideology in a Time of Crisis* (New York: Random Books, 1982); and Silviu Brucan, *Post Brezhnev Era: An Insider's View* (New York: Praeger, 1984).

73. See, e.g., Jiri Valenta, "The Explosive Soviet Periphery," *Foreign Policy*, No. 51 (Summer 1983), pp. 84–100; and Zalmy Kalizad, "Soviet-Occupied Afghanistan," *Problems of Communism*, Vol. 29, No. 6 (Nov.–Dec. 1980), pp. 23–40.

74. Pierre Hassner, "The Shifting Foundation," *Foreign Policy*, No. 48 (Fall 1982), pp. 3–20; Immanuel Wallerstein, "North Atlanticism in Decline"; Nathaniel Thayer, "The Emerging East Asian Order," *SAIS Review*, Vol. 4, No. 1 (Winter–Spring 1984), pp. 1–41; and Calder, "Opening Japan."

75. See Halliday, *Second Cold War*; and Ōtake, *Nihon no bōei*.

76. See Ōtake, *Nihon no bōei*, for a detailed discussion of this trend.

77. See the symposium on Japan's defense policy, *Voice*, June 1984. See also

Mike Mochizuki, "Japan's Search for Strategy," *International Security*, Vol. 8, No. 3 (Winter 1983–84), pp. 152–79; and Ronald Morse, "Japan's Search for an Independent Foreign Policy: An American Perspective," *Journal of Northeast Asian Studies*, Vol. 3, No. 2 (Summer 1986), pp. 27–44.

78. Prime Minister Ohira's Study Group, *Sōgō anzen hoshō senryaku* (Comprehensive national security strategy) (Tokyo: Ōkurashō, 1980).

79. Japan, MITI, *Keizai anzen hoshō no kakuritsu o megutte* (Toward achieving economic security) (Tokyo: Tsūshō Sangyō Chōsakai, 1982); and Yōichi Funabashi, *Keizai anzen hoshō ron* (Economic security) (Tokyo: Tōyō Keizai Shimpōsha, 1978).

80. But despite the advent of the second cold war, Japan's basic defense posture is still based on a set of assumptions associated with the heyday of détente. It is in that respect similar to West Germany's "oasis of détente" assumption.

81. This argument is best articulated by the opposition parties, especially the Socialists and the Communists, but it is held by the government as well.

82. See Ōtake, *Nihon no bōei*, for an excellent description of domestic trends.

83. Prime Minister Ohira's Study Group, *Sōgō anzen hoshō senryaku*. For a different view, see Morse, "Japan's Search."

84. Agitation by what are called "Japan's Gaullists" is thus considered as complicating the government's task. See Tetsuya Kataoka, *Waiting for Pearl Harbor* (Stanford: Hoover Institution Press, 1980); and Yatsuhiro Nakagawa, "The WEPTO Option: Japan's New Role in East-Asia/Pacific Collective Security," *Asian Survey*, Vol. 24, No. 8 (August 1984), pp. 828–39.

85. See note 77.

86. For the perspective that focuses on domestic structures to explain foreign policy strategy, see Peter J. Katzenstein, ed., *Between Power and Plenty: Foreign Policies of Advanced Industrial Countries* (Madison: University of Wisconsin Press, 1978); idem, *Small States in World Markets: Industrial Policy in Europe* (Ithaca, N.Y.: Cornell University Press, 1985); and idem, *Corporatism and Change: Australia, Switzerland, and the Politics of Industry* (Ithaca, N.Y.: Cornell University Press, 1984). See also John Zysman, *Governments, Markets, and Growth: Financial Systems and the Politics of Industrial Change* (Ithaca, N.Y.: Cornell University Press, 1983).

87. See the 39 annual maps of world conflicts for 1945–83 in Takashi Hirose, *Clausewitz no himitsu kodo* (Clausewitz's secret code) (Tokyo: Shinchosha, 1984), pp. 24–101.

88. See J. David Singer and Melvin Small, *The Wages of War, 1816–1965* (New York: Wiley, 1972).

89. Ben-Ami Shilloni, "1945 nen natsu: Truman saidai no guko" (Summer 1945: Truman's folly), *Jiyū*, Aug. 1985, pp. 21–25; and Roger Buckley, *Occupation Diplomacy: Britain, the United States, and Japan, 1945–1952* (Cambridge, Eng.: Cambridge University Press, 1982).

90. See Iokibe, *Beikoku no Nihon senryō*; Takafusa Nakamura, ed., *Senryōki Nihon no keizai to seiji* (The economics and politics of Japan during the Occupation) (Tokyo: University of Tokyo Press, 1979); and Shinjirō Sodei, ed., *Sekaishi no naka no Nihon senryō* (The occupation of Japan in world history) (Tokyo: Nihon hyōronsha, 1985).

91. It is well known that what is called the conservative mainstream's policy line is dependent heavily on the U.S. provision of national security to Japan. See Masataka Kosaka, *Saishō Yoshida Shigeru* (Prime Minister Shigeru Yoshida) (Tokyo: Chūō Kōronsha, 1968); and Yonosuke Nagai, *Gendai to senryaku* (The contemporary age and strategy) (Tokyo: Bungei Shunjūsha, 1985). See also the paper by Muramatsu and Krauss in Volume I of this series.

92. In a recent opinion poll on the Self-Defense Forces, 63.0 per cent said that its primary role was national security; 17.2 per cent said internal security; and 13.6 per cent said disaster relief. Japan, Office of the Cabinet, Public Relations Office, ed., *Gekkan yoron chōsa*, Aug. 1985, pp. 71–120.

93. See the papers by Noguchi and by Bronfenbrenner and Yasuba in Volume I of this series.

94. See Margaret A. McKean, *Environmental Protest and Citizen Politics in Japan* (Berkeley: University of California Press, 1981).

95. Kiyofuku Chuma, *Saigunbi no seijigaku* (The politics of rearmament) (Tokyo: Chishikisha, 1985).

96. See National Institute for Research Advancement, *Seikatsu suijun no rekishiteki suii* (Historical evolution of living standards) (Tokyo, 1985), for a detailed delineation of health, education, employment, income, physical environment, security, family, community life, and social stratification and mobility during the past century.

97. For the 1950s–1960s, see, e.g., Kozo Yamamura, *Economic Policy in Postwar Japan: Growth Versus Economic Democracy* (Berkeley: University of California Press, 1967). For the 1970s–1980s, see, e.g., Nagaharu Hayabusa, "Kakegaeno nai jūgonen: Shakaishihon jūjitsu no kōki" (A crucial 15 years for social capital consolidation), *Asahi shimbun*, Sept. 1, 1985; Katsuhiko Suetsugu, "Semarareru uchinaru fukinkō zesei" (Rectification of internal disequilibrium urged), *Nihon keizai shimbun*, Sept. 29, 1985; and Davis, "Reaganomics' Magical Mystery Tour." See also Susan Chira, "In Japan, Progress Eludes Many Among the Masses," *International Herald Tribune*, Nov. 1, 1985.

98. See, e.g., Masaru Yoshitomi, *Gendai Nihon keizai ron* (Contemporary Japanese economics) (Tokyo: Tōyō Keizai Shimpōsha, 1977); Masaru Yoshitomi, *Nihon keizai* (The Japanese economy) (Tokyo: Tōyō Keizai Shimpōsha, 1981); and Takeo Komie, *Sekiyu to Nihon keizai* (Petroleum and the Japanese economy) (Tokyo: Tōyō Keizai Shimpōsha, 1982). See also Peter J. Katzenstein, ed., *Between Power and Plenty*; and Wilfred L. Kohl, ed., *After the Second Oil Crisis: Energy Policies in Europe, America, and Japan* (Lexington, Mass.: D. C. Heath, 1982).

99. Bank of Japan, *Nihon o chūshin to shita kokusai tōkei* (Japan in comparative international statistics) (Tokyo, 1985).

100. See, e.g., Yoshio Suzuki, *Nihon kin'yū keizai ron* (Japanese financial economics) (Tokyo: Tōyō Keizai Shimpōsha, 1983); Yōichi Shinkai, *Gendai makuro keizaigaku* (Contemporary macroeconomics) (Tokyo: Tōyō Keizai Shimpōsha, 1982); Seiji Shimpo, *Bunseki Nihon keizai* (The Japanese economy: An analysis) (Tokyo: Tōyō Keizai Shimpōsha, 1985); and idem, *Gendai Nihon keizai no kaimei* (Anatomy of the Japanese economy) (Tokyo: Tōyō Keizai Shimpōsha, 1979).

101. The Japanese definition of M2 + CD is cash currency in circulation + deposit money + quasi money + certificates of deposit. See Bank of Japan, *Nihon o chūshin to shita kokusai tōkei*, 1986 ed., p. 206.

102. Noguchi, *Zaisei*; Naohiro Yatsuhiro, ed., *Gyōzaisei kaikaku no kenkyū* (Studies in administrative and financial reform) (Tokyo: Tōyō Keizai Shimpōsha, 1982); Hiromitsu Ishi, *Zaisei kaikaku no ronri* (The logic of the financial reform) (Tokyo: Nihon Keizai Shimbunsha, 1982); Yukio Noguchi, "Nihon de Keinzu seisaku wa okonawareta ka" (Has Keynesian policy ever been implemented in Japan?), *Kikan gendai keizaigaku*, No. 52 (1983), pp. 163–83.

103. Zaisei Seisaku Kenkyūkai, ed., *Korekara no zaisei to kokusai hakko*, p. 46.

104. Noguchi, "Nihon de Keinzu seisaku."

105. Bank of Japan, *Nihon keizai*, p. 86.

106. See the paper by Noguchi in Volume I of this series.

107. OECD, *Historical Statistics, 1960–1980* (Paris, 1982).

108. *Yomiuri shimbun*, Aug. 2, 1985.

109. For Japanese trade policy, see the paper by Komiya and Itoh in this volume. See also Gary Saxonhouse, "The Micro- and Macroeconomics of Foreign Sales for Japan," in Cline, *Trade Policies*; idem, "Evolving Comparative Advantage and Japan's Imports of Manufactures," in Yamamura, *Policy and Trade Issues*, pp. 239–69; and the paper by Saxonhouse in this volume.

110. For the restoration of self-confidence of the conservatives in Japanese politics toward the end of the 1970s, see T. Inoguchi, *Gendai Nihon*, esp. pp. 199–245; and the paper by Muramatsu and Krauss in Volume I of this series.

111. For the poll results, see Jiji Tsūshinsha, ed., *Sengo Nihon no seitō to naikaku* (Postwar Japanese political parties and cabinets) (Tokyo, 1981), which provides monthly data compiled by the Office of the Prime Minister up to June 1981. Since Aug. 1978, the *Yomiuri shimbun* has published another series of monthly data. For a first-rate historical narrative, see Junnosuke Masumi, *Gendai seiji* (Contemporary politics) (Tokyo: University of Tokyo Press, 1983), 2 vols.; and idem, *Sengo seiji* (Postwar politics) (Tokyo: University of Tokyo Press, 1985), 2 vols. On the LDP's victory, see Takashi Inoguchi, "The Japanese Double Election of July 6, 1986," *Electoral Studies*, forthcoming.

112. For the mechanisms of these controversies, which permeate politics, see T. Inoguchi, *Gendai Nihon*, pp. 199–245.

113. Economic factors as well as policy and campaign factors do explain major portions of the increase in voter support for the LDP. See ibid.; and Takashi Inoguchi, "Keizai jōkyō to seisaku kadai" (Economic conditions and policy tasks), in Jōji Watanuki et al., *Nihonjin no senkyō kōdō* (Japanese electoral behavior) (Tokyo: University of Tokyo Press, 1985), pp. 203–36.

114. T. Inoguchi, *Gendai Nihon*, pp. 199–245.

115. Ibid.

116. Ibid.

117. On welfare, see the paper by Bronfenbrenner and Yasuba in Volume I of this series; and Stephen J. Anderson, "Nihon shakai fukushi no seisaku keisei katei" (The policy formation process of Japanese social welfare) *Jurisuto*, No. 41 (Dec. 1985), pp. 172–76.

118. T. Inoguchi, *Gendai Nihon*, pp. 199–245; on the opposition governments at the local level, see Ellis Krauss et al., eds., *Political Opposition and Local Politics in Japan* (Princeton: Princeton University Press, 1980).

119. Funabashi, *Keizai anzen*; Nobutoshi Akao, ed., *Japan's Economic Security* (New York: St. Martin's Press, 1983); Chapman et al., *Japan's Quest*; and Edward Morse, ed., *The Politics of Japan's Energy Strategy* (Berkeley, Calif.: Institute of East Asian Studies, 1981). A telling indication of Japanese preoccupation with the economic dimension of global change during this period was Prime Minister Fukuda's revelation, in a conversation with Chancellor Helmut Schmidt, of his ignorance of the SS-20s.

120. Sōgō Ansen Hoshō Kenkyū Gurūpu, *Sōgō anzen*. See also Ōtake, *Nihon no bōei*.

121. See Japan, Defense Agency, *Bōei hakusho*, 1979–85.

122. See Ōtake, *Nihon no bōei*.

123. Prime Minister Ohira's Study Group reports.

124. Rinji Gyōsei Chōsakai, *Rinchō kihon teigan* (Basic proposals of the Provisional Council [on Administrative Reform]) (Tokyo: Gyōsei Kanri Kenkyū Sentā, 1982).

125. See T. Inoguchi, *Gendai Nihon.*

126. See the paper by Noguchi in Volume 1 of this series.

127. For the Action Program, see Shijō Kaihō Mondai Kenkyūkai, ed., *Kōdō keikaku* (The Action Program) (Tokyo: Gyosei, 1985).

128. See, e.g., Keizai Seisaku Kenkyūkai, *Korekara no keizai seisaku* (Future economic policy) (Tokyo: Government Printing Bureau, 1985). See also *Asahi shimbun*, Sept. 1, 1985.

129. *Nihon keizai shimbun*, Aug. 29, 1985. Like the U.S. government, the Japanese government avoids making necessary economic reforms and blames the other side while taking advantage of the other side's policy contradictions. See also David Hale, "US and Japan Reach Historical Crossroads," *Far Eastern Economic Review*, Aug. 2, 1985; Suetsugu, "Semarareru uchinaru fukinkō zesei"; and R. Morse, "Japan's Search."

130. Japan, Ministry of Foreign Affairs, *Gaikō seisho* (Diplomatic blue book) (Tokyo, 1985), points out that the two major goals of Japanese foreign policy are to consolidate Japan's roles as a member of the industrialized countries and of the Asia-Pacific region.

131. See Hager, "Protectionism and Autonomy."

132. *Nihon keizai shimbun*, Feb. 3 and 10, 1984; and *New York Times*, Feb. 21, 1984.

133. Barry Buzan, "Economic Structure and International Security," *International Organizations*, Vol. 38, No. 4 (Autumn 1984), pp. 597–624.

134. For U.S. commercial policy, see Baldwin and Krueger, *Structure and Evolution.* See also John Zysman and Laura Tyson, eds., *American Industry in International Competition: Government Policies and Corporate Strategies* (Ithaca, N.Y.: Cornell University Press, 1983).

135. For a justification of such a U.S. policy strategy, see Keohane, *After Hegemony.*

136. Prime Minister Ohira's Policy Study Group, *Kantaiheiyō rentai no kōsō* (The idea of Pan-Pacific solidarity) (Tokyo: Government Printing Bureau, 1980).

137. See, e.g., William E. Griffith, *The Ostpolitik of the Federal Republic of Germany* (Cambridge, Mass.: MIT Press, 1978); and David Calleo, *The German Problem Reconsidered.*

138. Bruce Cummings, "The Northeast Asian Political Economy," *International Organization*, Vol. 38, No. 1 (Summer 1984), pp. 1–40.

139. Takahashi Inoguchi, "The China-Japan Relationship in Perspective" (Paper presented at the Workshop on Australia, China, Japan, Canberra, Sept. 19, 1986). See also "China's Economy: How Far? How Fast?" *Far Eastern Economic Review*, Aug. 29, 1985, pp. 50–56; and "The Readjustment in the Chinese Economy," *China Quarterly*, No. 100 (Dec. 1984), pp. 691–865.

140. See OECD, *Interfutures: Facing the Future. Mastering the Probable and Managing the Unpredictable* (Paris, 1979); and Japan, Economic Planning Agency, *Nisen nen no Nihon* (Japan in the year 2000) (Tokyo: Government Printing Bureau, 1983).

141. See Mochizuki, "Japan's Search."

142. See Nakagawa, "The WEPTO Option."

143. See R. Morse, "Japan's Search."

144. Quoted in Pierre Hassner, "Recurrent Stresses, Resilient Structures," in Robert Tucker and Linda Wrigley, eds., *The Atlantic Alliance and Its Critics* (New York: Praeger, 1983), pp. 61–94.

145. Bank of Japan, *Nihon keizai.*

146. International Bank for Reconstruction and Development, *World Development Report, 1985* (Washington, D.C., 1985). The report acknowledges the benefits for developing countries of Japan's financial contributions and development loans.

147. Hayabusa, "Kakegaeno nai jūgonen"; and Davis, "Reaganomics' Magical Mystery Tour."

148. One can no less strongly argue that the United States has been much more disquieting and disorganizing than has Japan in the 1980s.

149. Bruce Roscoe, "Against the Grain: Japan's Sudden Shift to Chinese Corn Has the U.S. Worried," *Far Eastern Economic Review*, Oct. 3, 1985, p. 60.

150. Clyde Haberman, "Japan: Uneasy on World Stage," *International Herald Tribune*, Aug. 3–4, 1985.

Kumon and Tanaka: From Prestige to Wealth

1. Comprehensive National Security Study Group, *Report on Comprehensive National Security* (Tokyo, 1980), p. 25.

2. See, e.g., Christopher K. Chase-Dunn, "International Economic Policy in a Declining Core State," in William P. Avery and David P. Rapkin, eds., *America in a Changing World Political Economy* (New York: Longman, 1982), pp. 77–96; Albert Bergesen, "1914 Again? Another Cycle of Interstate Competition and War," in P. McGowan and C. W. Kegley, Jr., eds., *Foreign Policy and the Modern World System* (Beverly Hills, Calif.: Sage, 1983), pp. 255–73; and Walter L. Goldfrank, "The Limits of Analogy: Hegemonic Decline in Great Britain and the United States," in Albert Bergesen, ed., *Crisis in the World-System* (Beverly Hills, Calif.: Sage, 1983), pp. 143–54.

3. George Modelski, "The Long Cycle of Global Politics and the Nation-State," *Comparative Studies in Society and History*, Vol. 20, No. 2 (Apr. 1978), pp. 214–35. For Modelski's most recent attempt to reformulate a "long-cycle" theory, see "The Theory of Long Cycles as a Theory of General Peace," in *The World Encyclopedia of Peace* (Oxford: Pergamon, forthcoming).

4. Robert O. Keohane, "Hegemonic Leadership and U.S. Foreign Economic Policy in the 'Long Decade' of the 1950s," and Stephen D. Krasner, "American Policy and Global Economic Stability," in Avery and Rapkin, *America*, pp. 49–76, 29–48; S. D. Krasner, "Structural Causes and Regime Consequences: Regimes as Intervening Variables," *International Organization*, Vol. 36 (1982), pp. 185–205; Robert Gilpin, *U.S. Power and the Multinational Corporation* (New York: Basic Books, 1975); and idem, *War and Change in World Politics* (Cambridge, Eng.: Cambridge University Press, 1981).

5. Our conceptualization of social games and interpretation of the modern world system based on them have evolved over the past several years. See Shumpei Kumon, *Shakai shisutemu ron* (Social systems analysis) (Tokyo: Nihon Keizai Shimbunsha, 1978); and idem, "Moderusuki chōha riron no kentō" (Examination of Modelski's long-cycle theory), in Yoshinobu Yamamoto et al., eds., *Kokusai kankei ron no shintenkai* (New developments in international relations theories) (Tokyo: University of Tokyo Press, 1984), pp. 105–33. The idea of "conventionalized prizes by conventionalized means" is from Robert Ardrey, *The Social Contract* (Huntington, N.Y.: Fontana, 1970); see also idem, *The Territorial Imperative* (Huntington, N.Y.: Fontana, 1966). For our previous attempt to contrast the nineteenth- and twentieth-century systems, see Kumon, *Tenkanki no sekai* (the world in transformation) (Tokyo: Kodansha, 1978); and Shinkichi Etō et

al., *Kokusai kankei ron* (International relations) (Tokyo: University of Tokyo Press, 1982), pp. 237–54.

6. Krasner, "Structural Causes."

7. We may be able to conceive of a social game as a situation in which many players are conducting different types of games (in the sense of game theory) with different players repeatedly over a long period. Formalization along this line has not been developed extensively. At this stage, we do not intend to formalize our theory in a mathematically rigorous fashion. We believe that the heuristic value of our theory far exceeds the pursuit of mathematical rigor.

8. Krasner, "Structural Causes," p. 186.

9. We argue later that the "knowledge game" is such a subcategory of social games, along with the power game and the wealth game.

10. Samuel E. Finer argues that "the twin process—from consolidated service to differentiated service and from differentiated territory to consolidated territory—is what constitutes *the development of the modern state*"; "State- and Nation-Building in Europe: The Role of the Military," in Charles Tilly, ed., *The Formation of National States in Western Europe* (Princeton: Princeton University Press, 1975), p. 87 (emphasis in original). For the argument that territoriality is crucial, see J. H. Herz, *International Politics in the Atomic Age* (New York: Columbia University Press, 1959), pp. 49–61. As we argue later, it was generally in the late eighteenth and the nineteenth centuries that states in Europe became *nation*-states.

11. According to Martin Wight, "The diplomatic system is the master-institution of international relations. It may be conveniently divided under two heads, resident embassies and conferences"; *Power Politics* (Harmondsworth, Eng.: Penguin Books, 1979), p. 113. We argue that the power of a state is recognized as its prestige in the diplomatic system, the concrete manifestations of which include diplomatic precedence and sites of conferences. What Masataka Kōsaka calls *koten gaikō* ("classic diplomacy") rose and fell with the prestige game in our sense; see *Koten gaikō no seijuku to hōkai* (Maturation and collapse of classic diplomacy) (Tokyo: Chūō Kōronsha, 1978). It is no accident that Hans Morgenthau, the foremost theorist of the principles of the prestige game, deplores the "decline of diplomacy" in the twentieth century: "Today diplomacy no longer performs the role, often spectacular and brilliant and always important, that it performed from the end of the Thirty Years' War to the beginning of the First World War"; *Politics Among Nations: The Struggle for Power and Peace*, 5th ed. rev. (New York: Knopf, 1978), p. 535.

12. The "military revolution" is a term used by Michael Roberts in his inaugural lecture before the Queen's University of Belfast in 1955. By this term, he emphasized the tactical innovations introduced by such figures as Maurice of Orange in the army of the Dutch Republic (e.g., the introduction of linear formations composed of small units in place of massive, deep, unwieldly squares of pikemen.) Maurice also introduced new methods of training and drill for ordinary soldiers; these subsequently became the standard for armies in Europe and throughout the world. Also emphasized by Roberts was the general increase in the size of the armies of the major powers. See "The Military Revolution, 1560–1660," in his *Essays in Swedish History* (London: Weidenfeld & Nicolson, 1967), pp. 195–225. Maurice's methods of drill are described and illustrated with fascinating pictures in Robert H. McNeill, *The Pursuit of Power: Technology, Armed Force, and Society since A.D. 1000* (Oxford: Blackwell, 1982), pp. 125–43. For some reservations to this thesis, see Geoffrey Parker, "The Military Revolution, 1560–1660—A Myth?" *Journal of Modern History*, Vol. 48 (1976), pp. 195–214. We would

also include such earlier technological changes as the adoption of artillery in warfare, the use of ships as "artillery carriers," and the invention of the broadside. See Wight, *Power Politics*, pp. 68–69; McNeill, *Pursuit of Power*, pp. 63–116; and Carlo M. Cipolla, *Guns and Sails in the Early Phase of European Expansion, 1400–1700* (London: Collins, 1965).

13. See Hermann Haken, *Synergetics—an Introduction: Nonequilibrium Phase Transition and Self-Organization in Physics, Chemistry and Biology*, 2d ed. (New York: Springer-Verlag, 1978); idem, *The Science of Structure: Synergetics* (New York: Van Nostrand Reinhold, 1984); and Ilya Prigogine and Isabelle Stenger, *Order out of Chaos: Man's New Dialogue with Nature* (Toronto: Bantam Books, 1984).

14. In addition to the prestige and wealth games, we discuss the "knowledge game" as a basic social game. These three games correspond to the three basic types of influence—threat, exchange, and persuasion—discussed by such authors as Kenneth Boulding. Our three types of social games correspond roughly with Boulding's Threat, Exchange, and Integration systems. See Kenneth Boulding, *Ecodynamics: A New Theory of Societal Evolution* (Beverly Hills, Calif.: Sage, 1978).

15. Jack S. Levy, *War in the Great Power System, 1495–1975* (Lexington: University Press of Kentucky, 1983).

16. Quincy Wright, *A Study of War* (Chicago: University of Chicago Press, 1942). Wright (p. 643) counts the Thirty Years' War as 13 distinct and overlapping wars.

17. Carl von Clausewitz, *On War*, indexed ed. (Princeton: Princeton University Press, 1984), p. 590.

18. Clausewitz (ibid.) explains the limited nature of wars in this period as follows: "The explanation why even gifted commanders and monarchs such as Gustavus Adolphus, Charles XII, and Frederick the Great, with armies of exceptional quality, should have risen so little above the common level of the times, why even they had to be content with moderate success, lies with the balance of power in Europe. With the multitude of minor states in earlier times, any one of them was prevented from rapidly expanding by such immediate and concrete factors as their proximity and contiguity, their family ties and personal acquaintances. But now that states were larger and their centers farther apart, the wide spread of interests they had developed became the factor limiting their growth. Political relations, with their affinities and antipathies, had become so sensitive a nexus that no cannon could be fired in Europe without every government feeling its interest affected. Hence a new Alexander needed more than his own sharp sword: he required a ready pen as well. Even so, his conquests rarely amounted to very much."

19. A. F. K. Organski argues: "If the theory of the balance of power has any applicability at all, it is to the politics of the first period, that preindustrial, 'dynastic' period when nations were kings and politics a sport, when there were many nations of roughly equivalent power, and when nations could and did increase their power largely through clever diplomacy, alliances, and military adventures"; *World Politics* (New York: Alfred A. Knopf, 1958), p. 307. Herz regards the eighteenth century as "the period when the balance attained perfection as an art of statecraft and a technique of diplomacy" (*International Politics*, p. 66).

20. Martin Wight, "The Balance of Power and International Order," in Alan James, ed., *The Bases of International Order* (London: Oxford University Press, 1973), p. 98.

21. Karl Polanyi, *The Great Transformation* (Boston: Beacon Press, 1944), p. 260.

22. M. G. Forsyth et al., eds., *The Theory of International Relations: Selected Texts from Gentili to Treitschke* (London: George Allen & Unwin, 1970), p. 138. A. J. P. Taylor argues that even in the nineteenth century, the "balance of power worked with calculation almost as pure as in the days before the French revolution. It seemed to be the political equivalent of the laws of economics, both self-operating. If every man followed his own interest, all would be prosperous; and if every state followed its own interest, all would be peaceful and secure"; *The Struggle for Mastery in Europe, 1848–1918* (Oxford: Oxford University Press, 1971), p. xx. This is probably analogous to the belief of many people today that the market mechanism works without government intervention.

23. Forsyth et al., *International Relations*, p. 287.

24. Finer, "State- and Nation-Building," p. 144.

25. "Automatic," "semiautomatic" and "manually operated" mechanisms are the terms that I. L. Claude, Jr., uses to distinguish types of balance-of-power theories: "The three versions of the balance of power system . . . differ fundamentally in respect to the degree of conscious motivation required for the production of equilibrium. In the automatic system, equilibrium is the valuable by-product, the unwilled dividend, of the interplay of states. In the semiautomatic system, the crucial balancer-state, and it alone, must be assumed to pursue the objective of equilibrium. In the manually operated system, the policies of most states must be rationally directed toward that objective"; *Power and International Relations* (New York: Random House, 1962), p. 50. In our argument, Claude's three versions of the balance of power represent not simply three types of balance-of-power theories but the three actual phases of the evolution of the prestige game.

26. Taylor, *Struggle for Mastery*, pp. 283–84.

27. Ibid., p. 256.

28. Hedley Bull calls this change a "return to natural law principles or to some contemporary equivalent of them"; *The Anarchical Society: A Study of Order in World Politics* (New York: Columbia University Press, 1977), p. 39. See also Wakamizu Tsutsui, *Sensō to hō* (War and law), 2d ed. (Tokyo: University of Tokyo Press, 1976).

29. Hayward R. Alker, Jr., and F. L. Sherman, "Collective Security-Seeking Practices Since 1945," in Daniel Frei, ed., *Managing International Crises* (Beverly Hills, Calif.: Sage, 1982), pp. 113–45; and R. L. Butterworth and M. E. Scranton, *Managing Interstate Conflict, 1945–74: Data with Synopses* (Pittsburgh: University Center for International Studies, 1976). For different accounts, see I. Kende, "Twenty-five Years of Local War," *Journal of Peace Research*, Vol. 8 (1971), pp. 5–22; idem, "Wars of Ten Years, 1967–1976," *Journal of Peace Research*, Vol. 15 (1978), pp. 227–41; and Ernst B. Haas, "Regime Decay: Conflict Management and International Organizations, 1945–1981," *International Organization*, Vol. 37 (1983), pp. 189–256.

30. Kozo Uno, *Principles of Political Economy: Theory of a Purely Capitalist Society* (Sussex, Eng.: Harvester Press, and Atlantic Highlands, N.J.: Humanities Press, 1980).

31. Polanyi, *Great Transformation*, p. 43.

32. Adam Smith, *An Inquiry into the Nature and Causes of the Wealth of Nations* (Tokyo: Tuttle, 1979), pp. 651, 423.

33. Smith (ibid., p. 651) argued that the state has only three duties: the defense of the country, the administration of justice, and the maintenance of certain public works. This was first an argument for the withdrawal of the state

from economic activities, but it was also a recognition that the state was capable of performing these functions.

34. For arguments for and against this proposition, see J. Gallagher and R. Robinson, "The Imperialism of Free Trade," *Economic History Review*, 2d ser., Vol. 6, No. 1 (1953). For a critical review of this debate, see Kenji Mori, *Jiyū bōeki teikokushugi* (The imperialism of free trade) (Tokyo: University of Tokyo Press, 1978).

35. The joint-stock company came into being in the seventeenth century, the East India companies of Britain and the Netherlands, the Royal African Company, and Hudson's Bay Company being examples. Although financed with private capital, they were created by public charters stipulating their activities in detail. They were, in fact, arms of the state as well as vehicles for private profit. Because of the mania of speculation in the 1720s (the South Sea Bubble), joint-stock companies were prohibited in Britain and France, with a few exceptions. See S. B. Clough and R. T. Rapp, *European Economic History* (New York: McGraw-Hill, 1975), p. 349. Only in the late nineteenth century did the corporate form prevail over other modes of ownership.

36. Ibid.

37. Yuji Yamazaki, "Kin'yū shihon no seiritsu to tenkai: Igirisu" (Establishment and development of finance capital: Britain), in Setsujirō Iriye, ed., *Kōza seiyō keizaishi, III: Teikokushugi* (Western economic history, III: Imperialism) (Tokyo: Dōbunsha, 1979), p. 88.

38. Albert Bergesen, "Long Economic Cycles and the Size of Industrial Enterprise," in Richard Rubinson, ed., *Dynamics of World Development* (Beverly Hills, Calif.: Sage, 1981), p. 183. See also idem, "Economic Crisis and Merger Movements: 1880s Britain and 1980s United States," in Edward Friedman, ed., *Ascent and Decline in the World-System* (Beverly Hills, Calif.: Sage, 1982), pp. 27–39.

39. It may be possible to argue that the formation of cartels, trusts, and Konzerns in the late nineteenth and early twentieth centuries was in fact an effort at "concert" among financial capitalists.

40. E. J. Hobsbawm, *Industry and Empire* (Harmondsworth, Eng.: Penguin Books, 1968), p. 131.

41. E. H. Carr, *Nationalism and After* (London: Macmillan, 1945), p. 17.

42. Taylor, *Struggle for Mastery*, p. 255.

43. The "crystal-ball effect" of nuclear weapons means that the consequence of a decision to start a nuclear war can be predicted by decision makers as easily and clearly as if they possessed a crystal ball. See Harvard Nuclear Study Group, *Living with Nuclear Weapons* (Cambridge, Mass.: Harvard University Press, 1983), p. 44.

44. A fascinating and first-rate computer game, "Balance of Power," by Chris Crawford (released in 1985) captures some of the essential elements of the superpower game. The game is distributed by Mindscape, Inc., Northbrook, Ill.

45. Although they have both aspects, North-South problems, we argue, are better interpreted as challenges to the working of the development game than as distribution problems in the global wealth game. If the same teams always win and the others always lose, the latter may well want to quit the game or demand changes in the rules.

46. In the previous section, we discussed the transformation of the wealth game through increasing regulation. But we do not discuss the possibility of further transformation of the wealth game comparable to the emergence of derivatives of the power game. These transformations might occur with the future

emergence of the knowledge game, which we discuss in the final section, but we do not go into this fascinating possibility in this paper.

47. See Gilpin's paper in this volume.

48. For an attempt at a 60-year cycle theory for the history of Japanese modernization since the Meiji period, see Shumpei Kumon, "Bunka no jidai to shite no 1980 nendai—6onen shūki setsu no kokoromi" (The 1980s as an era of culture—An attempt at 60-year cycle theory), in Tadao Umezao and Saburō Okita, eds., *Rentai no shisō to shin bunka* (Thought of solidarity and new culture) (Tokyo: Kodansha, 1982), pp. 13–60.

49. For the Japanese perception of the world system in the late Tokugawa period to the early Meiji period, see Masao Maruyama, "Kaikoku" (Opening the country), in *Kōza gendai rinri* (Contemporary ethics) (Tokyo: Chikuma Shobō, 1959), pp. 79–112.

50. However, as we discussed above, the nature of the wealth game gradually changed in the last two or three decades of the nineteenth century, as Japan started to modernize and industrialize itself. The Meiji government certainly learned the role of the state in economic development from such countries as Germany. Moreover, the government created the foundation of modern industries. But many government-owned industries were not profitable; the government privatized (*kangyō haraisage*) them in the 1880s and 1890s. In this sense, it may be argued that the Meiji government finally arrived at a laissez-faire economic policy after trying government intervention.

51. Takafusa Nakamura, *Nihon keizai* (Japanese economy) (Tokyo: University of Tokyo Press, 1981), p. 48.

52. Chalmers Johnson, *MITI and the Japanese Miracle: The Growth of Industrial Policy, 1925–1975* (Stanford: Stanford University Press, 1982). As Johnson's book shows, Japanese industrial policy has its origins in the prewar period. We do not take issue with this, but we argue that industrial policy as a means of the development game as we define it was utilized only after WWII. Especially important was the consciousness of prestige among the Japanese who formulated these industrial policies; they clearly considered the development of certain industries a matter of national pride. Ryutaro Komiya calls their attitude "prehistorical" in his study of industrial policy and remembers that it was difficult to conduct fruitful discussions with them because they did not share the "common language understandable in economics." Ryūtarō Komiya, Masahiro Okuno, and Kōtarō Suzumura, eds., *Nihon no sangyō seisaku* (Japan's industrial policy) (Tokyo: University of Tokyo Press, 1984), p. 6. But, we argue, that is exactly the difference between those playing the wealth game and those playing the development game.

53. This seems to contradict our statement that the United States has held the premier position in the development game. What we mean here is that Japan has been the typical (not necessarily the strongest) player of the game. The United States may have been unconscious of the existence of the development game until quite recently.

54. Hermann Hesse, *The Glass Bead Game* (Harmondsworth, Eng.: Penguin Books, 1972 [1943]).

55. Daniel Bell, *The Coming of the Post-industrial Society* (New York: Basic Books, 1973); Tadao Umezao, "Jōhō sangyō ron" (Theory of information industry), *Hōsō Asahi*, Jan. 1963; J. Naisbitt, *Megatrends: Ten New Directions Transforming Our Lives* (New York: Warner Books, 1982); and A. Toffler, *The Third Wave* (New York: W. Morrow & Co., 1980).

56. Ryūichirō Tachi, *Sofutonomikkusu: Keizai no atarashii chōryū* (Softnomics:

New trends in economics) (Tokyo: Nihon Keizai Shimbunsha, 1983); Yuichiro Nagatomi, "Japan's Informationalization and Emerging Service Economy and Its Implications for U.S.-Japan Relations" (Paper delivered at the Symposium on Japan's Emerging Service Economy and U.S.-Japan Relations, Woodrow Wilson School, Princeton University, 1984).

57. Shumpei Kumon ("Nihon kindaika no 60nen shūki setsu saikō" [The 60-year-cycle theory of Japan's modernization reconsidered], forthcoming) proposes the following objectives for Japan in the coming era: (1) to construct a highly knowledge- and information-oriented society in which the knowledge game is to be played in advance of the rest of the world; (2) to contribute much to the cooperative management of the world both in the security field and the field of economic management; and (3) to enhance industrial development and knowledge creation in order to achieve (1) and (2).

58. For various activities that Japanese firms are currently pursuing in the area of "knowledge" industry, see Hideichirō Nakamura, *Nihon sangyō no chiteki katsuryoku* (Intellectual vitality of Japanese industry) (Tokyo: Tōyō Keizai Shimpōsha, 1985).

Russett: U.S. Hegemony

I wrote this paper while a fellow at the Netherlands Institute for Advanced Study and am very grateful to the staff and other fellows for making that such a pleasant and productive environment. I am also grateful to the General Service Foundation and to the Yale Center for International and Comparative Studies for financial support, and to several colleagues—especially Robert Keohane, Stephen Krasner, Jim Lindsay, Susan Strange, William R. Thompson, and H. Bradford Westerfield—for insightful comments on an earlier draft. A version of the first sections of this paper appeared in the Spring 1985 issue of *International Organizations*.

1. E.g., Susan Strange, "Cave! Hic Dragones: A Critique of Regime Analysis," *International Organization*, Vol. 36, No. 2 (Spring 1982), pp. 299–324.

2. See Richard Rosecrance, "Introduction," in idem, ed., *America as an Ordinary Country* (Ithaca, N.Y.: Cornell University Press, 1967), p. 1; Kenneth A. Oye, "The Domain of Choice," in idem, Donald Rothchild, and Robert J. Lieber, eds., *Eagle Entangled: U.S. Foreign Policy in a Complex World* (New York: Longman, 1979), pp. 4–5; and George Liska, *Career of Empire* (Baltimore: Johns Hopkins University Press, 1978), chap. 10.

3. See Robert Gilpin, *U.S. Power and the Multinational Corporation: The Political Economy of Direct Foreign Investment* (New York: Basic Books, 1975); and idem, *War and Change in World Politics* (Cambridge, Eng.: Cambridge University Press, 1981), esp. p. 231: "By the 1980s the Pax Americana was in a state of disarray"; Stephen Krasner, "Transforming International Regimes: What the Third World Wants and Why," *International Studies Quarterly*, Vol. 25, No. 1 (Mar. 1981), pp. 119–48; Charles Kindleberger, "Systems of International Economic Organization," in David Calleo, ed., *Money and the Coming World Order* (New York: New York University Press, 1976); and also many of the contributions to the Spring 1982 special issue of *International Organization*, Vol. 36, No. 2. Robert O. Keohane's *After Hegemony: Cooperation and Discord in the World Political System* (Princeton: Princeton University Press, 1984) represents a special case. His is the most sophisticated version of hegemonic stability theory and explicitly argues against equating a decline in power base with an equivalent decline in the characteristics

of a regime. Nevertheless, he repeatedly uses phrases like "a post-hegemonic world" (p. 216) and "the legacy of American hegemony" and "hegemony will not be restored in our lifetimes" (p. 244), and the book is entitled *After Hegemony*. The only strong emphasis on the continuity of U.S. power is Susan Strange, "Still an Extraordinary Power: America's Role in a Global Monetary System," in Raymond E. Lombra and William E. Witte, eds., *Political Economy of International and Domestic Monetary Relations* (Ames: University of Iowa Press, 1982).

4. Keohane, *After Hegemony*, identifies four criteria for identifying a hegemon in the world political economy: preponderance of material resources and raw materials, capital, markets, and production of highly valued goods. A broader view of hegemony, however, requires inclusion of military, scientific, and other resources.

5. This is true, for example, with Mark E. Rupert and David P. Rapkin, "The Erosion of U.S. Leadership Capabilities," in Paul Johnson and William R. Thompson, eds., *Rhythms in International Politics and Economics* (New York: Praeger, 1985), pp. 155–80.

6. See, e.g., Kenneth Waltz, *Theory of International Politics* (Reading, Mass.: Addison-Wesley, 1979), esp. chap. 7; Waltz regards the United States as more autonomous, and hence stronger, than more internationally involved states.

7. Karl W. Deutsch, *The Analysis of International Relations*, 2d ed. (Englewood Cliffs, N.J.: Prentice-Hall, 1978).

8. Robert O. Keohane and Joseph Nye, eds., *Power and Interdependence* (Boston: Little, Brown & Co., 1977), p. 44; and Stephen Krasner, "Structural Causes and Regime Consequences: Regimes as Intervening Variables," *International Organization*, Vol. 36, No. 2 (Spring 1982), p. 199.

9. Timothy J. McKeown, "Tariffs and Hegemonic Stability Theory," *International Organization*, Vol. 37, No. 1 (Winter 1983), pp. 73–97; and Keohane, *After Hegemony*, p. 37.

10. Duncan Snidal, "Public Goods, Property Rights, and Political Organization," *International Studies Quarterly*, Vol. 23, No. 4 (Dec. 1979), pp. 532–66.

11. Stephen Krasner, "State Power and the Structure of International Trade," *World Politics*, Vol. 27, No. 3 (Apr. 1975), pp. 317–47; and John Ruggie's review of Krasner's book in *American Political Science Review*, Vol. 74, No. 1 (Mar. 1980), pp. 296–99.

12. Joe Oppenheimer, "Collective Goods and Alliances: A Reassessment," *Journal of Conflict Resolution*, Vol. 23, No. 3 (Sept. 1979), pp. 387–407.

13. George Modelski, "The Long Cycle of Global Politics and the Nation-State," *Comparative Studies in Society and History*, Vol. 20, No. 2 (Apr. 1978), pp. 214–35.

14. Karl W. Deutsch et al., *Political Community and the North Atlantic Area* (Princeton: Princeton University Press, 1957).

15. Giovanni Arrighi, "A Crisis of Hegemony," in Samir Amin et al., *Dynamics of Global Crisis* (New York: Monthly Review Press, 1982), p. 77.

16. I am aware that much of the hegemonic stability literature (for example, "founding father" Charles Kindleberger's *The World in Depression, 1929–1939* [Berkeley: University of California Press, 1973]) is concerned with specific issue-areas and goods rather than with such broader achievements or goods as peace and prosperity. Focusing on narrow issue-areas makes the thesis of a decline in U.S. hegemony more plausible—at least for those selected issue-areas. Nevertheless, the issue-areas are usually selected because they are assumed, implicitly or explicitly, to be symptomatic of a broad decline in U.S. ability to maintain the

conditions of global prosperity. Peace—harmony among the industrial capitalist powers and containment of the USSR—is one of those conditions. Thus, although some writing on hegemonic stability can escape the strictures of my critique, a general evaluation of the state of U.S. hegemony and its consequences—an evaluation that is both common and necessary—must carry the discussion beyond the selected, rather narrow, issue-areas. Gilpin, *War and Change*, and many of the contributors to the Spring 1982 special issue of *International Organization* would surely agree.

17. See Bruce Russett and Harvey Starr, *World Politics: The Menu for Choice*, 2d ed. (New York: W. H. Freeman, 1985), chap. 15; and Michael Doyle, "Kant, Liberal Legacies, and Foreign Affairs," *Philosophy and Public Affairs*, Vol. 12, No. 3 (Summer 1983), pp. 205–35.

18. The terms are, respectively, from Deutsch et al., *Political Community*; and Kenneth E. Boulding, *Stable Peace* (Austin: University of Texas Press, 1978).

19. See J. David Singer and Melvin Small, "The War-Proneness of Democratic Regimes, 1815–1965," *Jerusalem Journal of Conflict Resolution*, Vol. 1, No. 1 (1976), pp. 50–69.

20. To me, this is not the most persuasive explanation, but see Erich Weede, "Extended Deterrence by Superpower Alliance," *Journal of Conflict Resolution*, Vol. 27, No. 2 (June 1983), pp. 231–53.

21. I use the term *regime* in Krasner's sense: "principles, norms, and decision-making procedures around which actor expectations converge." See Krasner, "Structural Causes," p. 85.

22. See Arend Lijphart, *The Trauma of Decolonization: The Dutch and West New Guinea* (New Haven: Yale University Press, 1966), chap. 11; and Townsend Hoopes, *The Devil and John Foster Dulles* (Boston: Little, Brown & Co., 1973), p. 384.

23. See Zalmay Khalilzad, "Islamic Iran: Soviet Dilemma," *Problems of Communism*, Vol. 33, No. 1 (Jan.–Feb. 1984), pp. 1–20.

24. Keohane, *After Hegemony*, p. 34.

25. Melvin Small and J. David Singer, *Resort to Arms* (Beverly Hills, Calif.: Sage, 1982), p. 134.

26. For the comparative data on trade, I am indebted to Susan Strange, "Protectionism and World Politics," *International Organization*, Vol. 39, No. 2 (Spring 1985), p. 242. Helen Hughes and Jean Waelbroeck, "Foreign Trade and Structural Adjustment—Is There a New Protectionism?" in Hans-Gert Braun et al., eds., *The European Economy in the 1980s* (Aldershot, Eng.: Gower, 1983), reply that the increase in protectionism during the 1970s was small. There is some evidence that protectionism rises during periods of cyclical economic downturn, but these increases should not be mistaken for long-term trends. On the collapse of the Bretton Woods fixed exchange-rate system, see Hugh Patrick and Henry Rosovsky, "The End of Eras? Japan and the Western World in the 1970–1980s" (Paper delivered at the Japan Political Economy Research Conference, Honolulu, July 1983), p. 38: "In our view, despite excessively wide swings in real rates among currencies, the flexible exchange rate system was a way of maintaining the liberal international economic order rather than being a cause of its demise." See also Keohane, *After Hegemony*, p. 213: "Substantial erosion of the trade regime . . . has occurred, but . . . what is equally striking is the persistence of cooperation even if not always addressed to liberal ends. Trade wars have not taken place, despite economic distress. On the contrary, what we see are intensive efforts at cooperation, in response to discord in textiles, steel, electronics,

and other areas." On liberalization of the Japanese economy, see Raymond Vernon, *Two Hungry Giants: The United States and Japan in the Quest for Oil and Ores* (Cambridge, Mass.: Harvard University Press, 1983); and the paper by Komiya and Itoh in this volume.

27. Arrighi, "Crisis of Hegemony," p. 65. One could quarrel with Arrighi's use of "national interest" and qualify it by reference to the interests of the ruling classes, but on the whole I am not inclined to do so—major qualification would require some near-heroic assumptions about false consciousness.

28. Hedley Bull, *The Anarchical Society* (New York: Columbia University Press, 1977).

29. Robert O. Keohane, "The Demand for International Regimes," *International Organization*, Vol. 36, No. 2 (Spring 1984), p. 348. Keohane's discussion is reminiscent of Karl W. Deutsch, *The Nerves of Government* (New York: Free Press, 1963).

30. Robert Axelrod, *The Evolution of Cooperation* (New York: Basic Books, 1984).

31. The proposition that the burdens of empire almost inevitably outweigh its benefits is a common one. Note Mark Elvin, *The Pattern of the Chinese Past* (London: Methuen, 1973), p. 19: "The burdens of size consist mainly in the need to maintain a more extended bureaucracy with more intermediate layers, the growing difficulties of effective co-ordination as territorial area increases, and the heavier costs of maintaining troops on long front lines further removed from the main sources of trustworthy manpower and supplies."

32. Russett and Starr, *World Politics*, chap. 18.

33. Bruce Russett, *What Price Vigilance: The Burdens of National Defense* (New Haven: Yale University Press, 1970), chap. 4.

34. Karen Rasler and William R. Thompson, "Global Wars, Public Debts, and the Long Cycle," *World Politics*, Vol. 36, No. 1 (Oct. 1983), pp. 489–516, carefully recognize the particular private benefits, to the commercially extended hegemon, of providing defense and deterrence for others. This should be set against the more familiar argument that military expenditures become a private "bad" by inhibiting capital formation and growth in the hegemon. For evidence, see Rasler and Thompson, "Longitudinal Change in Defense Burdens, Capital Formation, and Economic Growth," *Journal of Conflict Resolution*, Vol. 31, No. 1 (Mar. 1987), forthcoming.

35. Arthur A. Stein, "The Hegemon's Dilemma: Great Britain, the United States, and the International Economic Order," *International Organization*, Vol. 38, No. 2 (Spring 1984), pp. 355–86. For the argument that free trade is not necessarily a collective good, see John Conybeare, "Public Goods, Prisoners' Dilemma, and the International Political Economy," *International Studies Quarterly*, Vol. 28, No. 1 (Mar. 1984), pp. 5–22.

36. Arrighi, "Crisis of Hegemony," p. 57.

37. In a brilliant paper, Duncan Snidal, "Hegemonic Stability Theory Revisited," *International Organization*, Vol. 39, No. 4 (Autumn 1985), pp. 579–617, notes that both Krasner, "State Power," and Gilpin, *War and Change*, fully recognize the degree to which the postwar regimes benefited the United States and that Gilpin particularly argues that the United States was significantly able to extract contributions as a quasi government.

38. See Keohane, *After Hegemony*.

39. See Clifford Geertz, *The Interpretation of Cultures* (New York: Basic Books, 1973).

40. Quintin Hoare and Geoffrey Nowell Smith, eds., *Selections from the Prison*

Notebooks of Antonio Gramsci (New York: International Publishers, 1971). Without tying it completely to Marxist analysis, this is akin to the concept of cultural penetration that I have employed in work with my colleagues. See Raymond Duvall et al., "A Formal Model of 'Dependencia Theory': Structure and Measurement," in Richard Merritt and Bruce Russett, eds., *From National Development to Global Community* (London: Allen & Unwin, 1981), esp. pp. 320–21. I have long been concerned with the political impact of a great power's cultural penetration; see, e.g., Bruce Russett, *Community and Contention: Britain and America in the Twentieth Century* (Cambridge, Mass.: MIT Press, 1963), chaps. 6–8.

41. Persuading someone to do something he or she would not otherwise do; see Robert A. Dahl, *Modern Political Analysis*, 4th ed. (Englewood Cliffs, N.J.: Prentice-Hall, 1984).

42. Robert W. Cox and Harold K. Jacobson, "The United States and World Order: On Structures of World Power and Structural Transformation" (Paper delivered at the Twelfth World Congress of the International Political Science Association, Rio de Janeiro, Aug. 1982), p. 7: "World hegemony is founded through a process of cultural and ideological development. This process is rooted mainly in the civil society of the founding country, though it has the support of the state in that country, and it extends to include groups from other countries." See also Norbert Elias, *The Civilizing Process*, vol. 2, *State Formation and Civilization* (Oxford: Basil Blackwell, 1982): "Just as it was not possible in the West itself, from a certain state of interdependence onwards, to rule people solely by force and physical threats, so it also became necessary, in maintaining an empire that went beyond mere plantation-land and plantation-labour, to rule people in part through themselves, through the moulding of their superegos. . . . The outsiders absorb the code of the established groups and thus undergo a process of assimilation. Their own affect-control, their own conduct, obeys the rules of the established groups. Partially they identify themselves with them, and even though the identification may show strong ambivalencies, still their own conscience, their whole superego apparatus, follows more or less the pattern of the established groups." Neither of these statements is meant to deny some reciprocal role of elites in the periphery in helping to shape the dominant world culture.

43. They form, e.g., a key element in Alker's conception of power. See Hayward R. Alker, "Power in a Schedule Sense," in idem, Karl W. Deutsch, and Antoine H. Stoetzel, eds., *Mathematical Approaches to Politics* (San Francisco: Jossey-Bass, 1973).

44. For a good but now slightly dated survey, see Marshall R. Singer, *Weak States in a World of Powers: The Dynamics of International Relationships* (New York: Free Press, 1972), chaps. 4–5. It is tempting for the cynical academic to bemoan the pervasiveness of American popular culture, from the presence of the *Today Show* by satellite in the wee hours of television programming in the Western Pacific to the Tokyo branch of Disneyland. But the influence of liberal American human rights policy must not be ignored. I was told that the Japanese government recently passed legislation for women's rights primarily out of a desire not to be embarrassed by ridicule from the U.S. delegation to the Nairobi Conference concluding the United Nations Decade for Women.

45. British influence was heavily facilitated, and consciously promoted, by the rise of English as an international language and the popularity of English literature from Shakespeare to contemporary authors. It is the United States' good fortune, for its present influence, that its language is also English. Of other countries, France has had the most success in promoting its influence through

the cultural medium of its language; one of the French motivations in trying to keep Britain out of the European Community was the hope that with Britain excluded the Germans could be made to learn French as the Community language. Japanese has not proved to be an exportable tongue. The West German government, through its Goethe Institute, has tried to promote fluency in German. But the primary German cultural product is probably music rather than literature; knowing the language is of little importance, and perhaps some artifacts (e.g., Wagnerian opera) are more attractive when one doesn't understand the words. Russian has proved not very exportable either, outside the regulated market of Eastern Europe. The classics of Russian literature (Dostoevsky, Tolstoy) are not favored by the Soviet government, Marx wrote in German, and socialist realism just is not very attractive.

46. Arthur A. Stein, "Coordination and Collaboration: Regimes in an Anarchic World," *International Organization*, Vol. 36, No. 2 (Spring 1982), p. 324.

47. Paul Kennedy, "Why Did the British Empire Last So Long?" in idem, *Strategy and Diplomacy, 1860–1945* (London: Allen & Unwin, 1984), similarly notes the role of Britain's cultural force in prolonging its influence abroad.

48. The theme of military expenditures coming at the expense of long-term economic viability is a common one, including in my own work. For some observations on the historical experience of great powers, see Paul M. Kennedy, "The First World War and the International Power System," *International Security*, Vol. 9, No. 1 (Summer 1984), pp. 7–40; and Rasler and Thompson, "Global Wars." The contemporary Soviet example also suggests how the excessive pursuit of military power produces economic stagnation.

49. Keohane, *After Hegemony*, chap. 9, gives some reasons for optimism.

50. E. H. Carr, *The Twenty Years Crisis, 1919–1939* (London: Macmillan, 1939), chap. 14, thought a "pax Americana imposed on a divided and weakened Europe would be an easier contingency to realize than a pax Anglo-Saxonica based on an equal partnership of English-speaking peoples."

51. Snidal, "Hegemonic Stability," is very good on this matter.

Hamada and Patrick: International Monetary Regime

We are indebted to Akiyoshi Horiuchi for valuable comments and to Jamie Lipson and Frances Rosenbluth for their editorial and research assistance.

1. Koichi Hamada, "The Communication Problem of Nouveau Riche," *World Economy*, Vol. 1, No. 4 (Oct. 1978), pp. 407–18.

2. See Koichi Hamada, *The Political Economy of International Monetary Interdependence* (Cambridge, Mass.: MIT Press, 1985).

3. Robert Triffin, *Gold and the Dollar Crisis* (New Haven: Yale University Press, 1960).

4. Robert A. Mundell, *Monetary Theory: Inflation, Interest and Growth in the World Economy* (Pacific Palisades, Calif.: Goodyear Publishing, 1973).

5. Hamada, *Political Economy*.

6. Ryūtarō Komiya and Miyako Suda, *Gendai kokusai kinyuron* (Contemporary international finance) (Tokyo: Nihon Keizai Shimbunsha, 1983), Vol. 2, pp. 24–25.

7. Hamada, *Political Economy*, pp. 17–21.

8. Richard N. Cooper, *The Economics of Interdependence: Economic Policy in the Atlantic Community* (New York: McGraw-Hill, 1968).

9. M. Canzoneri and J. A. Gray, "Monetary Policy Games and the Conse-

quences of Non-cooperative Behavior," *International Economic Review*, Vol. 26 (1985), pp. 547–64.

10. Max Corden, "The Logic of the International Monetary Non-system," in F. Machlup, ed., *Reflections on a Troubled World Economy* (London: Macmillan, 1983), pp. 59–74.

11. Hamada, *Political Economy*, chap. 8.

12. One might, of course, argue that it was a temporary rescuing operation during this chaotic period of major changes in rules, as we argue above.

13. See Hugh T. Patrick, "The Economic Dimensions of the U.S.-Japan Alliance," in Daniel I. Okimoto, ed., *Japan's Economy: Coping with Change in the International Environment* (Boulder, Colo.: Westview Press, 1982), pp. 149–96.

14. Dean Taylor, "Official Intervention in the Foreign Exchange Market, or Bet Against the Central Bank," *Journal of Political Economy*, Vol. 90, No. 2 (Apr. 1982), pp. 356–68. For the original argument by Friedman, see Milton Friedman, "The Case for Flexible Exchange Rates," in idem, *Essays in Positive Economics* (Chicago: University of Chicago Press, 1953), pp. 157–203.

15. Helmut Mayer and Hiroo Taguchi, *Official Interventions in the Exchange Markets: Stabilizing or Destabilizing?* BIS Economic Papers, No. 6 (Basle: Bank for International Settlements, 1983).

16. For a somewhat different view, see the paper by Shinkai in this volume. There are various issues: the degree of price elasticity of imports and exports; adjustments of underlying costs and hence changes in real exchange rates; and the time required for adjustments.

17. Sam Y. Cross, "Treasury and Federal Reserve Foreign Exchange Operations," *Federal Reserve Bank of New York Quarterly Review*, Winter 1985–86, pp. 45–48.

18. Ibid.

19. Takatoshi Ito, "The Intra Daily Exchange Rate Dynamics and Monetary Policies After G5," NBER Working Paper (Cambridge, Mass.: National Bureau of Economic Research, 1986).

20. Canzoneri and Gray, "Monetary Policy Games."

21. Rudiger Dornbusch, "Expectations and Exchange Rate Dynamics," *Journal of Political Economy*, Vol. 84 (1976), pp. 1161–76.

22. Kunio Okina, "Speculative Bubbles and Official Intervention" (Ph.D. diss., University of Chicago, 1983). What struck us during the period of overvaluation of the dollar was, however, the sustained divergence of the value of the dollar relative to other currencies, and not simply volatility. We question whether this kind of sustained divergence can be explained by "bubbles," which are presumably a short-term phenomenon.

23. Koichi Hamada and Kazumasa Iwata, "The Significance of Different Saving Ratios for the Current Account: The U.S.-Japan Case," mimeo. (Unpublished paper, 1985). This is consistent with our view that U.S. policymakers have been willing to run huge federal budget deficits and finance them in part through foreign borrowing, both direct and indirect.

24. John Williamson, *The Exchange Rate System*, rev. ed. (Washington, D.C.: Institute for International Economics, 1985).

25. Ibid., p. 34.

26. A tentative conjecture is that when the distribution of beliefs is more diverse, the effectiveness of intervention will be stronger. This is, of course, subject to further testing.

27. For a discussion of the trade regime, see the paper by Komiya and Itoh in this volume.

28. For a recent discussion of these issues, see Hugh T. Patrick and Ryuichiro Tachi, eds., *Japan and the United States Today: Exchange Rates, Macroeconomic Policies, and Financial Market Innovation* (New York: Columbia University, Center on Japanese Economy and Business, 1987).

29. Koichi Hamada and Yoshiro Nakajo, "Trade Issues and Consumer Interests: The Japanese Experience" (Paper presented at the OECD Symposium on International Trade and Consumer Interests, Paris, 1984).

30. Patrick and Tachi, *Japan and the United States*, focuses on the adjustments following the G-5 meeting to the summer of 1986, with evaluations of Japan's performance prospects and policy options in 1987–88.

31. Ryutaro Komiya, "Japan," in *Foreign Tax Policies and Economic Growth* (New York: National Bureau of Economic Research, 1966).

32. The major continental Western European countries peg their rates to each other with a small band for modest fluctuations (the snake) under the European Monetary Union. West Germany plays a major role because of the strength of its currency.

33. Mayer and Taguchi, *Official Interventions.*

34. For the internationalization of the yen, see the paper by Shinkai in this volume. For the competitive process of choosing an international currency, see F. A. Hayek, *Denationalization of Money: An Analysis of the Theory and Practice of Concurrent Currencies*, Hobart Paper Special, No. 70 (London: Institute of Economic Affairs, 1976).

35. Ronald I. McKinnon, *An International Standard for Monetary Stabilization* (Washington, D.C.: Washington Institute for International Economics, 1984).

36. Williamson, *Exchange Rate System*, esp. pp. 76–77.

37. Hamada, *Political Economy*, chap. 3.

38. Robert A. Mundell, *International Economics* (New York: Macmillan, 1968).

39. The accumulating cases of (particularly concerted) intervention provide growing research opportunities to appraise the influence of interventions on the expectations of participants in exchange rate markets. These experiences may make it possible to construct some appropriate rules of intervention to enhance stability of the exchange-rate system.

Gilpin: The Changing Trade Regime

1. Marina v. N. Whitman, *Sustaining the International Economic System: Issues for U.S. Policy*, Essays in International Finance, No. 121 (Princeton: Princeton University, Department of Economics, International Finance Section, 1977).

2. John Gerald Ruggie, "International Regimes, Transactions, and Change: Embedded Liberalism in the Postwar Economic Order," *International Organizations*, Vol. 36 (1982), pp. 379–415.

3. William R. Cline, ed., *Trade Policy in the 1980s* (Washington, D.C.: Institute for International Economics, 1983), p. 5.

4. W. M. Scammell, *The International Economy Since 1945*, 2d ed. (London: Macmillan, 1983), p. 172.

5. Ibid.

6. Ibid.

7. Council of Economic Advisers, *Economic Report of the President* (Washington, D.C.: U.S. Government Printing Office, 1985), p. 114.

8. W. M. Corden, *The Revival of Protectionism*, Occasional Papers, No. 14 (New York: Group of Thirty, 1984), p. 5.

9. Cline, *Trade Policy*, p. 9.

10. "Costs and Benefits of Protection," *OECD Observer*, No. 134 (1985).

11. John Zysman and Stephen S. Cohen, *The Mercantilist Challenge to the Liberal International Trade Order* (Study prepared for the use of U.S. Congress, Joint Economic Committee, 97th Cong. 2d Sess., 1982), pp. 42–46.

12. Cline, *Trade Policy*, p. 16.

13. Hugh Corbett, "Tokyo Round: Twilight of a Liberal Era or a New Dawn," *National Westminister Bank Quarterly Review*, Feb. 1979, pp. 19–29.

14. Whitman, *Sustaining the International Economic System*, p. 9.

15. Stephen Krasner, "The Tokyo Round—Particularistic Interests and Prospects for Stability in the Global Trading Regime," *International Studies Quarterly*, Vol. 23 (1979), pp. 491–531.

16. "Costs and Benefits of Protection," *OECD Observer*, p. 18.

17. Alan V. Deardorff and Robert M. Stern, "Methods of Measurement of Nontariff Barriers," Seminar Discussion Paper, No. 136 (University of Michigan, Department of Economics, Research Seminar in International Economics, 1984), pp. 15–16.

18. The differences between the application and the effects of Article XIX and VERs are analyzed in Brian Hindley, "Voluntary Export Restraints and the GATT's Main Escape Clause," *World Economy*, Vol. 3 (1980), pp. 313–41.

19. Robert E. Baldwin, "Trade Policies in Developed Countries," in Ronald W. Jones and Peter B. Kenea, eds., *Handbook of International Economics* (New York: North Holland, 1984), Vol. 1, pp. 610–12.

20. Carlos F. Diaz-Alejandro, "Comments," in Cline, *Trade Policy*, pp. 307–8.

21. For an examination of some of these measures, see Deardorff and Stern, "Methods of Measurement of Nontariff Barriers."

22. Corden, *The Revival of Protectionism*.

23. Cline, *Trade Policy*, p. 16.

24. Hindley, "Voluntary Export Restraints," p. 316.

25. Susan Strange and Roger Tooze, eds., *The International Politics of Surplus Capacity: Competition for Market Shares in the World Recession* (London: George Allen & Unwin, 1981).

26. Gautam Sen, *The Military Origins of Industrialization and International Trade Rivalry* (New York: St. Martin's Press, 1984), p. 191.

27. Hindley, "Voluntary Export Restraints."

28. Richard Blackhurst, Nicolas Marian, and Jan Tumlir, *Trade Liberalization, Protectionism and Interdependence*, Studies in International Trade, No. 5 (Geneva: GATT, 1977).

29. On the difficulty of measuring NTBs, see Deardorff and Stern, "Methods of Measurement of Nontariff Barriers."

30. Bruce Nussbaum, *The World After Oil: The Shifting Axis of Power and Wealth* (New York: Simon & Schuster, 1983), p. 253.

31. "Costs and Benefits of Protectionism," p. 19.

32. Ibid., p. 18.

33. Ibid.

34. Ibid.

35. Ibid.

36. Susan Strange, "Protectionism and World Politics," *International Organization*, Vol. 39 (1985), pp. 233–59.

37. Robert E. Baldwin, "Trade Policies Under the Reagan Administration," in idem, ed., *Recent Issues and Initiatives in U.S. Trade Policy*, NBER Conference Report (New York, 1984), p. 26.

38. Thorstein Veblen, *Imperial Germany and the Industrial Revolution* (New York: Viking Press, 1939).

39. Chalmers Johnson, *MITI and the Japanese Miracle: The Growth of Industrial Policy, 1925–1975* (Stanford: Stanford University Press, 1982).

40. Robert Gilpin, "Trade, Investment, and Technology Policy," in Herbert Giersch, ed., *Emerging Technologies: Consequences for Economic Growth, Structural Change, and Employment*, Symposium 1981 (Tübingen: J. C. B. Mohr for Paul Siebeck, 1982), pp. 381–409.

41. Nussbaum, *The World After Oil*.

42. Strange, "Protectionism and World Politics."

43. The author thanks Avinash Dixit for bringing these distinctions to his attention.

44. See the paper by Saxonhouse in this volume.

45. Charles Kindleberger, *Government and International Trade*, Essays on International Finance, No. 129 (Princeton: Princeton University, Department of Economics, International Finance Section, 1978), p. 5.

46. Johnson, *MITI*.

47. Frank Gibney, *Miracle by Design: The Real Reasons Behind Japan's Economic Success* (New York: Times Books, 1982), p. 5.

48. See the discussion in Baldwin, *Recent Issues*.

49. Henry K. Kierzkowski, ed., *Monopolistic Competition and International Trade* (Oxford: Clarendon Press, 1984).

50. Gene M. Grossman and J. David Richardson, *Strategic Trade Policy: A Survey of Issues and Early Analysis*, Special Papers in International Economics, No. 15 (Princeton: Princeton University, Department of Economics, International Finance Section, 1985), p. 6.

51. Avinash K. Dixit and Gene M. Grossman, "Targeted Export Promotion with Several Oligopolistic Industries," Discussion Papers in Economics, No. 71 (Princeton: Princeton University, Woodrow Wilson School, 1984), p. 1.

52. Grossman and Richardson, *Strategic Trade Policy*.

53. Gerald K. Helleiner, *Intra-firm Trade and the Developing Countries* (New York: St. Martin's Press, 1981), pp. 10–11.

54. Alan V. Deardorff, "Testing Trade Theories and Predicting Trade Flows," in Ronald W. Jones and Peter B. Kenen, eds., *Handbook of International Economics* (New York: North Holland, 1984), Vol. 1, p. 501.

55. For an examination of these matters, see Paul R. Krugman, ed., *Strategic Trade Policy and the New International Economics* (Cambridge, Mass.: MIT Press, 1986).

56. Henry Rosovsky, "Trade, Japan and the Year 2000," *New York Times*, Sept. 6, 1985.

57. Richard Cooper, "International Economics in the *International Encyclopaedia of the Social Sciences: A Review Article*," *Journal of Economic Literature*, Vol. 8 (1970), p. 437.

58. Theodore Levitt, *The Marketing Imagination* (New York: Free Press, 1983).

59. Krugman, *Strategic Trade Policy*.

60. John Williamson, *The Open Economy and the World Economy: A Textbook in International Economics* (New York: Basic Books, 1983), p. 73.

61. William R. Cline, *"Reciprocity": A New Approach to World Trade Policy?* Policy Analyses in International Economics, No. 2 (Washington, D.C.: Institute for International Economics, 1982), p. 9.

62. For the subject of how domestic policies affect trade, see Avinash K. Dixit,

"Tax Policy in Open Economies," Discussion Papers in Economics, No. 51 (Princeton: Princeton University, Woodrow Wilson School, 1983).

63. Grossman and Richardson, *Strategic Trade Policy*.

64. Cline, *Trade Policy*, p. 9.

65. Susan Strange, ed., *Paths to International Political Economy* (London: George Allen & Unwin, 1984).

66. Robert Keohane, "Reciprocity in International Relations," *International Organization*, Vol. 40 (1986), pp. 1–27.

67. Peter Robson, *The Economics of International Integration* (London: George Allen & Unwin, 1980).

68. For a list of alleged illiberal Japanese institutions and policies, see Gary Saxonhouse, "The Micro- and Macroeconomics of Foreign Sales to Japan," in Cline, *Trade Policy*, pp. 270–71.

69. Ibid., pp. 269–70.

70. The writer is indebted to Hugh Patrick for first bringing this possibility to his attention.

Komiya and Itoh: International Trade

The first draft of this paper was presented at a Japan Political Economy Research conference (JPERC), on August 5–11, 1984, at the East-West Center, Honolulu, Hawaii, and a revised one at another JPERC conference on July 23–28, 1985, in Tokyo. We are indebted to Mr. Risaburo Nezu of the Ministry of International Trade and Industry who helped us and made useful comments when we were preparing the first draft. We are also indebted to the participants of the two conferences, especially Professors Yoichi Shinkai, Hugh Patrick, and Gary Saxonhouse, and to Mr. Michiro Mizoguchi of the Ministry of Foreign Affairs for valuable comments on earlier drafts. The research underlying this paper was partly financed by grants from the Seimeikai Foundation, the Science Research Fund of the Ministry of Education, and the American Council of Learned Societies.

1. In 1953 and 1954, Japan's imports were about $2 billion, and its exports were only $1.25 billion in 1953 and $1.61 billion in 1954. Thus, Japan had a severe trade imbalance.

2. One might have a more sympathetic view of Japan's trade policy during the 1950s and 1960s if one conceives of the Japanese economy in this period as an Arthur Lewis–type dual economy with surplus labor rather than a Hecksher-Ohlin–type full-employment economy. In the former, the policy of export promotion and import restriction could increase the national income through expansion of employment in the modern manufacturing sector. Even in such an economy, however, the same result could be accomplished more easily by an exchange rate adjustment that makes the foreign exchange dearer relative to wages.

3. It is difficult to determine to what extent Japan's policy of protecting infant industries can be justified on economic grounds and how effective the policy measures undertaken for that purpose were. Economists hold varying views on this issue. For studies attempting to answer these questions, see Ryūtarō Komiya, Masahiro Okuno, and Kotarō Suzumura, eds., *Nihon no sangyō seisaku* (Japan's industrial policy) (Tokyo: University of Tokyo Press, 1984).

4. On the application of GATT Article 35 and other measures of discrimination against Japan by the major European countries and other GATT members until around 1970, see Gardner Patterson, *Discrimination in International Trade:*

The Policy Issues, 1945–1965 (Princeton: Princeton University Press, 1966), chap. 6; Kenneth W. Dam, *The GATT: Law and International Economic Organization* (Chicago: University of Chicago Press, 1970), esp. pp. 347–50; Mitsuhiko Hazumi and Kazuo Ogura, "Tai-Nichi sabetsu mondai no ippanteki haikei" (The general background of trade discrimination against Japan), in Kiyoshi Kojima and Ryūtarō Komiya, eds., *Nihon no hikanzei bōeki shōheki* (Nontariff barriers in Japan's trade) (Tokyo: Nihon Keizai Shimbunsha, 1972).

5. Some of these countries, for example, Central Africa and Chad, discriminated against Japanese products since Japan was a "cheap labor country."

6. Patterson, *Discrimination*, p. 275.

7. The facts of discrimination against Japanese exports have not been well known. There have been no official statistics or other publications on this problem, and it is very difficult to obtain factual information. There have been a few well-known cases, however. For example, France, for a long time, has restricted imports of Japanese automobiles to 3 per cent of the total number of domestically registered automobiles, and Italy allows imports of only 2,000 or so Japanese passenger cars per year. Spain still has discriminatory import embargoes on more than 140 Japanese exports.

8. The difference between the United States and European countries—especially the United Kingdom and France—in their attitudes toward Japan's participation in GATT is partly a result of their different experiences with Japanese exports in the 1930s. In 1951, the Japanese Ministry of Foreign Affairs published the following assessment of the situation in the 1930s: "Japan astonished the world by increasing her exports in 1933 in the midst of the depression . . . , and the future looked bright for the Japanese . . . . But Japan could increase exports only to those countries [or areas] that treated the Japanese goods on more or less equal and free terms, such as England . . . the Near and Middle East . . . Latin America, Thailand, and Manchuria . . . . Exports to countries that had adopted a protectionist policy, such as the Soviet Union, the United States, Australia . . . did not increase." Quoted from Masataka Kosaka, "The International Economic Policy of Japan," in R. A. Scalapino, ed., *The Foreign Policy of Modern Japan* (Berkeley: University of California Press, 1977), pp. 207–26.

9. See Kozo Yamamura, *Economic Policy in Postwar Japan: Growth Versus Economic Democracy* (Berkeley: University of California Press, 1967), chaps. 1–3, for U.S. policy toward Japan right after World War II and the way it changed.

10. According to a report Japan presented to GATT in 1968, its trading partners had requested and Japan had imposed VERs on 264 items (by the BTN four-digit classification and by the number of countries). Among them were 51 items requested by the United States.

11. Information and data on VERs are scarce. The governments and the industries concerned generally do not want to publicize their participation since they fear that VERs may spread to their exports to other countries or areas. Furthermore, it is difficult to define what is a VER and what is not. On these points, see Ryūtarō Komiya, "Yushutsu jishu kisei" (Voluntary export restraints), in Kojima and Komiya, *Nihon no hikanzei bōeki shōheki*, pp. 248–61; and Ryūtarō Komiya and Akihiro Amano, *Kokusai keizaigaku* (International economics) (Tokyo: Iwanami Shoten, 1972), pp. 256–60.

12. It is perhaps noteworthy, however, that none of these bills have so far been enacted into law or even passed by Congress. On the other hand, the U.S. government sometimes uses the fact of pending congressional consideration of protectionist bills to solicit concessions from foreign governments.

13. "The necessity of new markets for Japan as well as for developing countries" was one of the five reasons given by President Kennedy for the Trade Expansion Act of 1963, which authorized the president to enter the KR negotiations. This indicates that the United States was then still playing, or felt the need of playing, the role of Japan's patron.

14. The first to the fourth rounds of capital liberalization measures were put into effect, respectively, in July 1967, Feb. 1969, Sept. 1970, and Aug. 1971.

15. Such a bias exists more or less in all countries. Even the articles of GATT show influences of such a bias.

16. See Nihon Kanzei Kyōkai, *Bōeki nenkan* (International trade yearbook) (Tokyo, 1961), pp. 126–27.

17. For more details, see, among others, Ryūtarō Komiya, "Planning in Japan," in Morris Bornstein, ed., *Economic Planning: East and West* (Cambridge, Mass.: Ballinger, 1975); and idem, "Officers in Charge of Economic Affairs in the Japanese Government," *History of Political Economy*, Vol. 13, No. 3 (Fall 1981), pp. 600–28. See also Komiya et al., *Nihon no sangyō seisaku*.

18. In recent years, Japan requested South Korea and China to set up VERs on raw silk and certain silk textiles. However, Japan has so far refrained from restricting imports of textile products under the Multi-Fiber Agreement (MFA)— Japan is the only developed country that has not made use of the import quota system of MFA—and from requesting NICs and developing countries to set up VERs on textile products except the VERs on the silk items mentioned above. See Ippei Yamazawa, "Sen'i sangyō" (Textile industry), in Komiya et al., *Nihon no sangyō seisaku*, pp. 345–67, for further details.

19. For the details of Japan-U.S. textile negotiations, see I. M. Destler, Haruhiro Fukui, and Hideo Sato, *The Textile Wrangle: Conflict in Japanese-American Relations, 1969–1971* (Ithaca, N.Y.: Cornell University Press, 1979); and Hidezō Inaba and Toyorō Ikuta, *Nichi-Bei sen'i kōshō* (Japan-U.S. textile negotiations) (Tokyo: Kin'yū Zaisei Jijō Kenkyūkai, 1970).

20. As pointed out by J. P. Neary, "Capital Mobility, Wage Stickiness and Adjustment Assistance," in J. N. Bhagwati, ed., *Import Competition and Response* (Chicago: University of Chicago Press, 1982), pp. 39–71, the process of shifting resources from labor-intensive industries to other industries tends to cause serious structural unemployment unless wages are flexible.

21. See Komiya, "Yushutsu jishu kisei."

22. The price of electricity in Japan is now much higher even than in those other countries that depend on imported petroleum for power generation. The main reason seems the high cost of land and the large compensation payments to local residents necessary when building a new power station in Japan.

23. New ceramics, which have been spotlighted recently as one of the high-technology growth industries, also seem to be a field in which patented technologies do not play an important role and in which Japan is likely to have a strong comparative advantage.

24. Since there is a vast literature on the trade conflicts in this period, we do not go into details. For a typical American view, see Subcommittee on Trade, Committee on Ways and Means, U.S. House of Representatives, "Taskforce Report on United States–Japan Trade, with Additional Views (Jan. 1979), and "United States–Japan Trade Report" (Sept. 1980). The literature from Japan's side includes "Nichi-Bei keizai masatsu" (Japan-U.S. economic conflicts), *Kogin chōsa*, Nos. 207–8 (1981); Kazuo Ogura, *Nichi-Bei bōeki masatsu* (Japan-U.S. trade conflicts) (Tokyo: Nihon Keizai Shimbunsha, 1981); Yasutoyo Shoda and Sueo

Sekiguchi, eds., *Nichi-Bei keizai masatsu no kenkyū* (Studies on Japan-U.S. economic conflicts) (Tokyo: Nihon Keizai Kenkyū Sentā, 1983); and Masu Uekusa, et al., *Nihon sangyō no seidoteki tokuchō to bōeki masatsu* (Institutional character of Japanese industry and trade conflicts) (Tokyo: Sekai Keizai Kenkyū Kyōkai, 1983).

25. Behind this may lie the U.S. perception that the United States has given much to Japan since 1945 economically, including an open domestic market with relatively low tariff and nontariff barriers.

26. See Motoshige Itoh and Yoshiyasu Ono, "Tariffs vs. Quotas Under Duopoly of Heterogeneous Goods," *Journal of International Economics*, Vol. 17 (1984), pp. 359–73, for a theoretical analysis of this mechanism.

27. See R. C. Feenstra, "Voluntary Export Restraint in U.S. Autos, 1980–81: Quality, Employment, and Welfare Effects," in R. E. Baldwin and A. O. Krueger, eds., *The Structure and Evolution of Recent U.S. Trade Policy* (Chicago: University of Chicago Press, 1984), pp. 35–59.

28. The attitudes of the U.S. executive and Congress toward the TR differ to some extent from their attitudes toward previous tariff negotiations. The 1974 Trade Act permitted import restriction measures to mitigate balance-of-payments deficits and relaxed the conditions under which protective measures for the domestic industries can be put into effect.

29. See, e.g., A. V. Deardorff and M. Stern, "The Effects of the Tokyo Round on the Structure of Protection," in Baldwin and Krueger, *Structure and Evolution*, pp. 361–88.

30. Japan's tariffs on certain processed foods also remain high. But this is not necessarily done to protect food-processing industries. Since the domestic prices of raw materials for such industries are high because of agricultural protection, unless the tariffs on such products are kept high enough, the effective rate of protection for food processing might well be negative. Also, unless the tariff rates are high enough, the policy of agricultural protection would be partially undermined by an increase in imports of processed agricultural products.

31. Another criticism is that the Japanese distribution system is so complicated as to make it difficult for foreign manufacturers with strong preferences for traditional business relationships. Here, we simply point out that since WWII the Japanese distribution system and business relationships have been highly competitive, dynamic, and generally efficient and that quite a few foreign-owned or foreign-affiliated firms and a large number of foreign brands have been quite successful in Japan.

32. Actual administrative practices for imports may differ from the rules prescribed in the law. Many foreign complaints about the closedness of Japan's domestic market concern cumbersome importing procedures, the arbitrariness of the officers in charge, and nontransparency in decisions regarding standards for safety and consumer protection. Some of these complaints may be justified. However, unreasonable administrative practices restricting imports exist in most countries. For example, according to the *Asahi shimbun* (Apr. 18, 1985), in Jan. 1985 President Reagan approved a proclamation under the Agricultural Adjustment Act prohibiting imports of foods containing sugar for the purpose of protecting domestic sugar producers from cheap sugar imports from Canada. This is in itself a substantial nontariff barrier, but it had unexpected restrictive side effects. Traditional Japanese food imports into the United States for consumption primarily by Japanese Americans, their descendants, Japanese businessmen posted in the United States and their families, such as Japanese noodles with

soup, Japanese and Korean pickles, *kamaboko* (fishcake) and *tsukudani* (preserved food boiled down in soy sauce) were denied entry at U.S. ports because they contain or were supposed to contain sugar (as a matter of fact they contain from 0.1 per cent to 5 per cent at most). Even Japanese foods containing no sugar at all such as sesame, *mochi* (rice cakes), and *shichimi-tōgarashi* (a kind of mixed spices) could not be imported, whereas candies and *yōkan* (a sort of sweet jelly) could be. The treatment differed from port to port. Japanese exporters of these products, most of whom were small businesses, reportedly suffered large losses. Another example was the French government's sudden announcement in Oct. 1982 that customs procedures for video tape recorders could be cleared only at a customs office at an inland town on a small river called Poitiers, about 350 km southwest of Paris. Until then, VTRs could be imported through any major port or airport. Until this unusual restrictive practice was discontinued in Apr. 1983, transportation costs were increased substantially since VTRs had to be trucked to Poitiers, and the limited capacity at Poitiers caused delay and disorder.

33. Since nontariff barriers have recently been highlighted as a focal point of the U.S.-Japan trade conflict and trade negotiation, some people mistakenly think that nontariff barriers are something new. Generally speaking, nontariff barriers have become more apparent since more visible obstacles to trade have been eliminated as a result of the substantial tariff reductions in the KR and TR. Moreover, in the case of Japan, nontariff barriers have consistently been reduced since the middle of the 1960s, unlike in the United States and some other major developed countries, where new nontariff barriers such as quotas, VERs, and other trade restriction mechanisms have recently been set up.

34. See Gary Saxonhouse, "The Micro- and Macroeconomics of Foreign Sales to Japan," in W. R. Cline, ed., *Trade Policies in the 1980's* (Washington, D.C.: Institute for International Economics, 1983), pp. 259–304; and Saxonhouse's paper in this volume as well as the references cited there.

35. The situation is similar to that observed in other parliamentary democracies. For example, in the United States the executive branch is generally internationally oriented and tends to favor free trade, whereas individual industries, labor unions, and congressmen acting for particular industries and regions are inclined to protectionism, paying little attention to overall national economic welfare and the international commitments of the United States.

36. See Gerald Curzon and Victoria Curzon, "The Management of Trade Relations in the GATT," in Andrew Shonfield, ed., *International Economic Relations in Western Countries* (London: Royal Institute for International Affairs, 1976), pp. 143–283.

37. Although the Japanese government has not introduced any new quotas or strengthened quota restrictions on agricultural imports since the beginning of the 1960s, primarily because of the changing comparative advantage pattern of the Japanese economy, the implicit tariff rates of the quotas (the discrepancy between domestic and world prices for agricultural products) have generally increased in recent years.

38. Trade conflicts exist between Japan and the EC countries as well, and, one might say, even, between Japan and the ASEAN countries. But the Japan-EC conflict has been much less serious than the Japan-U.S. one and confined almost entirely to trade issues.

39. The Japanese government, on the other hand, only meekly complained about certain aspects of the U.S. economic policy: high inflation, high interest rates, large government budget deficits, and the policy of nonintervention in the foreign exchange market. Generally speaking, the U.S. government paid little

attention to such complaints of the Japanese government or of other foreign governments.

40. Fairly large current-account surpluses or deficits have not been uncommon in the international economy. Generally speaking, they do not present difficulties to other countries. For example, over the 50 years from 1860 to 1910, the United Kingdom ran current-account surpluses averaging 4 per cent of GNP, and in 1909 through 1923 and 1957 through 1975 the United States ran surpluses of 2.0 per cent and 1.1 per cent, respectively, on average. These are much larger than Japan's current surplus relative to the total volume of the world trade at the time. On the other hand, there are many examples of continued current-account deficits. For example, Canada (8.0 per cent of GNP in 1890–1910, 3.5 per cent in 1920–30), Norway (5.5 per cent in 1915–24, 11.4 per cent in 1975–78), Italy (2.2 per cent in 1921–30), and Australia (7.1 per cent in 1812–1910, 2.8 per cent in 1960–83). Steven Marris, *Dollars and the Deficits* (Washington, D.C.: Institute for International Economics, 1987).

41. Cline, *Trade Policies*, contains a number of papers dealing with this issue.

42. The Japanese government's policy toward North-South trade problems has not been much different from that of other North countries. However, Japan is the only nonwhite country without European and Christian traditions that succeeded in full-scale industrialization, and the shares of the South in Japan's trade and direct investment are much larger than those of other major industrialized countries. Hence, Japan tends to be more sympathetic to the South. Such a stance is perhaps reflected to some extent in Japan's implementation of GSP, in its attitudes to the "safeguard" issue in the TR, and to the Common Fund for price stabilization of primary products. Also, Japan is the only country among the industrialized, high-wage countries that has not yet adopted import restrictions on textiles under the MFA. Other developed countries also requested VERs on various labor-intensive products from low-wage countries, but Japan has rarely done so.

Saxonhouse: Comparative Advantage

1. The standard theories of international trade suggest that as economies' factor endowments converge, gains from international trade decline and the basis for mutually beneficial trade is removed. At the same time, it is commonly observed that most of the world's trade is among the advanced industrialized economies. For an attempted reconciliation of stylized fact and theory, see Paul R. Krugman, "Intra-industry Specialization and the Gains from Trade," *Journal of Political Economy*, Vol. 89, No. 5 (Oct. 1981), pp. 959–73.

2. This section draws heavily on Harry G. Johnson, *International Trade and Economic Growth* (Cambridge, Mass.: Harvard University Press, 1958). See also the voluminous balanced growth literature from the 1950s and 1960s, such as H. Uzawa, "On a Two-Sector Model of Economic Growth," *Review of Economic Studies*, Vol. 29 (1961), pp. 40–47; R. M. Solow and P. A. Samuelson, "Balanced Growth Under Constant Returns to Scale," *Econometrica*, Vol. 21 (1953), pp. 412–24; and P. A. Yotopoulos and L. J. Lau, "A Test for Balanced and Unbalanced Growth," *Review of Economics and Statistics*, Vol. 52 (1970), pp. 376–84.

3. In an open economy, no special assumptions about domestic demand are necessary. If, for example, it is assumed that the terms of trade facing an economy remain the same, then the analysis for the open economy follows the closed economy model.

4. See, e.g., Lawrence Krause, "Statement," submitted to the House Foreign Affairs Subcommittee on International Trade, May 9, 1985. Krause argued that Japanese policies became restrictive as the energy crisis caused a sharp deterioration in Japan's terms of trade.

5. The level of Japanese tariffs on wood products does remain an issue.

6. Julio J. Nogués, Andrez Olechowski, and L. Alan Winters, "The Extent of Non-tariff Barriers to Industrial Countries' Imports," *World Bank Economic Review*, Vol. 1 (1986), pp. 181–99.

7. Gary R. Saxonhouse, "Industrial Policy and Factor Markets: The Case of Biotechnology," *Prometheus*, Vol. 3, No. 2 (Dec. 1985), pp. 277–314. Similar results have been obtained by Hiromitsu Ishi, "Corporate Tax Burden and Tax Incentives in Japan" (Unpublished paper, May 1985). Note that in 1985 the Diet passed new legislation granting a special 7 per cent tax credit for investment in R&D-related equipment in promising high-tech fields such as biotechnology and fine ceramics.

8. U.S. Congress, *Report on the Reciprocal Trade and Investment Act of 1982* (Washington, D.C., 1982), p. 36.

9. Note, however, that in Mar. 1985 the U.S. Information Agency released the results of its annual survey of Japanese public opinion on economic issues. According to this survey, 53 per cent of its representative sample of 1,000 adults believed that Japan protects its domestic market heavily. Only 31 per cent disagreed with this evaluation. This is a marked change in perception over 1984, when 44 per cent of the sample felt that Japan engaged in heavy protectionism. See OECD, *U.S. Statement on Japanese Market Access* (1985).

10. The experience of U.S. competition with Japan's government-owned tobacco monopoly illustrates the difficulty of evaluating such anecdotes. For years, U.S. access to Japan's $12 billion cigarette market was limited. American cigarettes could be distributed only by Japan's tobacco monopoly, which was also the U.S. cigarette producers' major competitor within the Japanese market. The Japan Tobacco and Salt Public Corporation allowed only a small minority of its distributors to carry U.S. products. The distribution of foreign cigarettes has now been fully liberalized. Any retailer, whether an affiliate of the newly privatized Japan Tobacco and Salt Public Corporation or not, may now carry foreign cigarettes. Although it was confidently predicted just a few years ago that distribution restrictions were preventing billions of dollars in foreign-cigarette sales, with full liberalization and tariffs now at 20 per cent, most observers predict only a quadrupling in the 2 per cent market share held by foreign cigarettes. Some of this modest increase will be at the expense of those Japanese brands that contain a high proportion of American tobacco leaf. Cf. *Wall Street Journal*, Oct. 17, 1982, and *New York Times*, Apr. 12, 1985.

11. In particular, the General Motors plants at Fremont, Calif., and at Framingham, Mass., used U.S. steel long after simple price considerations would have dictated otherwise. The Fremont plant was shut down in the early 1980s and reopened as a joint venture between General Motors and Toyota in 1985.

12. For example, see the analysis in Jeffrey Sachs and Peter Boone, "Japanese Structural Adjustment and the Balance of Payments" (Paper presented at the Tokyo Conference on Savings: Its Determination and Macroeconomic Implications, Jan. 1988).

13. Trade barriers can affect the size of the bilateral current-account balance. Trade barriers can also affect the total volume of imports. If trade barriers limit total imports, they are also working implicitly to limit total exports. If the current-

account balance is constrained by the balance between savings and investment, then any restriction on imports is also a restriction on exports.

14. In light of the discussion in the preceding section, it might seem that the analysis here should concentrate on quantity impacts rather than on price impacts. From the perspective of welfare analysis, price impacts should be no less interesting than quantity impacts. In practice, policymakers seem increasingly interested in the trade (quantity) impact and not in the welfare impact of trade barriers.

15. This formulation rests critically on the existence of direct community utility functions. For the conditions under which this might be true, see Paul A. Samuelson, "Social Indifference Curves," *Quarterly Journal of Economics*, Vol. 70 (1956), pp. 1–22; and E. Eisenberg, "The Aggregation of Utility Functions," *Management Science*, Vol. 7, No. 4 (1961), pp. 337–50.

Applications on which the current analyses are built include Gary R. Saxonhouse, "Evolving Comparative Advantage and Japan's Imports of Manufactures," in Kozo Yamamura, ed., *Policy and Trade Issues of the Japanese Economy* (Seattle: University of Washington Press, 1982); idem, "The Micro- and Macroeconomics of Foreign Sales to Japan," in William Cline, ed., *Trade Policy for the 1980s* (Cambridge, Mass.: MIT Press for the Institute of International Economics, 1983); and idem, "Services in the Japanese Economy," in Robert P. Inman, ed., *The Services Economy: Prospects and Problems* (Cambridge, Eng.: Cambridge University Press, 1985).

16. The generalized Leontief form is discussed in W. E. Diewert, "Applications of Duality Theory," in M. E. Intriligator and D. A. Kendrick, eds., *Frontiers of Quantitative Economics*, vol. 2 (New York: Elsevier, 1974). The specific GNP function used in the analysis used here is given in Gary R. Saxonhouse, "What's Wrong with Japanese Trade Structure," *Pacific Economic Papers*, No. 136 (July 1986), pp. 1–44.

17. This follows from the application of Hotelling's lemma and is discussed in Gary Saxonhouse, "The Micro- and Macroeconomics of Foreign Sales," p. 290; and in idem, "Services."

18. The estimation of a version of equation (1) is discussed in Saxonhouse, "Evolving Comparative Advantage." The estimation of equation (2) is discussed in idem, "The Micro- and Macroeconomics of Foreign Sales." In the latter article, the problems associated with proceeding as if the number of goods is equal to the number of factors of production and the additional complications posed by intermediate and nontraded goods are discussed. Both articles discuss how a multiplicative error in a variables model can be applied to estimate the quality terms in equations (1) and (2).

19. If an alternative focus on industrial structure is appropriate, the GDP function can be used instead of the trade utility function, but otherwise the analysis proceeds as in equations (1) and (2). This approach is taken in Saxonhouse, "Services."

20. This test is related to the other tests performed on trade structure in the articles listed in note 18. With the exception of the test described in Saxonhouse, "The Micro- and Macro-economics of Foreign Sales," p. 294, n. 15, these previous tests attempted to determine which Japanese sectors might have been the specific beneficiaries of distinctive government policies and related distinctive Japanese market structures. Unlike this previous empirical work, the test performed here is a comprehensive examination of the distinctiveness of Japanese trade structure. Note that the Japanese quality terms used in this test are taken

from Saxonhouse, "The Micro- and Macroeconomics of Foreign Sales," and "Services."

21. Giving Alaska to the Japanese is a much better idea than allowing the United States to sell Alaskan oil to Japan or more generally selling Alaska as a whole to Japan. Removing the prohibition on the sale of Alaskan oil to Japan will affect only the bilateral current accounts and not the aggregate current accounts. Selling all of Alaska and not just its oil would doubtless trigger a compensating new surge of Japanese manufactured exports to the other advanced industrialized economies.

22. This simulation is conducted with 1973 data.

23. The GDP function is nothing more than an economy-wide variable profit function. The concept was first suggested by Paul H. Samuelson, "Price of Factors and Goods in General Equilibrium," *Review of Economic Studies*, Vol. 21 (1953), pp. 1–20.

24. See Krugman, "Intra-industry Specialization"; and Avinash Dixit and Joseph Stiglitz, "Monopolistic Competition and Optimum Product Diversity," *American Economic Review*, Vol. 67 (1977), pp. 297–308.

25. See, e.g., Charles Schultze, "Ford Invited Lecture," Berkeley, Calif., Jan. 31, 1983.

26. See R. E. Lipsey's review of H. C. Grubel and P. J. Lloyd's *Intra-industry Trade: The Theory and Measurement of International Trade in Differentiated Products* in *Journal of International Economics*, Vol. 6 (1976), pp. 312–14.

27. See, e.g., R. E. Baldwin, "Determinants of Commodity Structure of U.S. Trade," *American Economic Review*, Vol. 61 (1971), pp. 126–46.

28. Y. Sazanami finds that Japan, like its European Community counterparts, does participate on a regional basis in intraindustry trade. Similar to the analysis presented here, Sazanami finds that Japan's regional trading partners are not large enough to shape the character of its overall trade patterns. See "Possibilities of Expanding Intra-industry Trade," *Keio Economic Studies*, Vol. 16, No. 2 (1981), pp. 27–44.

29. J. M. Finger, "Trade Overlap and Intra-industry Trade," *Economic Inquiry*, Vol. 13 (Dec. 1975), pp. 581–90.

30. R. E. Falvey, "Commercial Policy and Intra-industry Trade," *Journal of International Economics*, Vol. 11 (1981), pp. 495–512, develops explicit theories of intraindustry trade that rely substantially on intraindustry differences in factor proportions.

31. Baldwin, "Determinants."

32. For more detail, see Saxonhouse, "The Micro- and Macroeconomics of Foreign Sales."

33. J. Jackson, *World Trade and the Law of GATT* (Indianapolis: Bobbs-Merrill, 1969), p. 273.

34. Ibid., p. 329.

35. For more detail, see Gary Saxonhouse, "Tampering with Comparative Advantage," in *Invited Testimony Before United States International Trade Commission Hearings on Foreign Targeting Practices*, June 15, 1983.

Shinkai: Internationalization of Finance

The first draft of this paper was prepared for the JPERC Volume II Conference, Aug. 6–11, 1984, and the revised version was presented at the second conference, July 23–28, 1985. In revising it, I benefited from detailed comments by

Dr. Mitsuhiro Fukao and the two discussants at the first conference: Professors Ryutaro Komiya and Ronald McKinnon. Other participants in the conferences raised a number of important points, and Professor Hugh Patrick later provided some detailed suggestions as well as a few important references. In preparing the final version, I found detailed comments at the second conference by, among others, Professors Gary Saxonhouse and Yasusuke Murakami very helpful.

1. Officially called the Working Group of the Joint Japan-U.S. Ad Hoc Group on Yen/Dollar Exchange Rate, Financial and Capital Market Issues, the group consisted of U.S. and Japanese officials from the Treasury's and Ministry of Finance's international finance bureaus, headed by the undersecretary and the deputy minister. The report to the secretary and the minister was released to the press in early June 1984. For details, see Jeffrey A. Frankel, *The Yen/Dollar Agreement: Liberalizing Japanese Capital Markets* (Washington, D.C.: Institute for International Economics, 1984).

2. Although many farm products are subject to import quotas, for example, Japanese food consumption is so internationalized that Japan imports about 50 per cent of its primary food energy, with half coming from the United States.

3. For more detailed descriptions of recent financial developments in Japan, see, e.g., Masahiro Sakamoto, "Susumu yen no kokusaika" (Internationalization of the yen in progress), *ESP*, May 1984; Yoshio Suzuki, *Kin'yū jiyūka to kin'yū seisaku* (Financial liberalization and monetary policy) (Tokyo: Tōyō Keizai Shimposha, 1985); and Masaru Yoshitomi, "Kokusai kin'yū" (International finance), *Shūkan Toyo Keizai, rinji zōkan, kin'yū to ginkō*, Apr. 13, 1984.

4. In any case, internationalization of the yen can only proceed slowly, if at all. Meanwhile, other factors that bear on the value of the yen will change in a fairly volatile way, making this factor irrelevant. As evidence that the value of an international currency can vary widely for other reasons, consider the British pound in the 1920s and the U.S. dollar in the 1970s.

5. Frankel, *Yen/Dollar Agreement*, p. 3.

6. The data in this section come from Japan, Ministry of Finance, *Kokusai Kin'yūkyoku nempō* (Annual report of the International Finance Bureau of the MOF) (Tokyo, various issues); Japan, Economic Planning Agency, *Nihon keizai no genkyō, Showa 59 nen, bunseki kekyū hen* (The present state of the Japanese economy, 1984: Supplemental analyses and studies) (Tokyo: MOF Printing Bureau, 1984); and Nomura Research Institute (written by Jun Umeda, Minoru Nakamura, and Yasuyuki Fuchida), "60 nendai no kin'yū shihon shijō no tembō" (Finance and capital markets after 1985), *Zaikai kansoku*, May 1984. See also Morgan Guaranty Trust Company, "Japan's Financial Liberalization and Yen Internationalization," *World Financial Market*, June 1984.

7. Eurodollar bonds are excluded here, as in Table 2.

8. Excluding bonds issued by governments and financial institutions.

9. See J. R. Karlik, "The Costs and Benefits of Being a Reserve-Currency Country: A Theoretical Approach Applied to the United States," in P. B. Kennen and R. Lawrence, eds., *The Open Economy* (New York: Columbia University Press, 1968). In a floating-exchange-rate period, the cost is even lower.

10. The "transparency" item in the U.S.-Japan agreement will remedy the situation somewhat.

11. Spot and forward positions are combined. Limits on spot positions, or the so-called limits on conversion in yen, were abolished in June 1984.

12. Bank transactions in government bonds in the secondary market and foreign and Japanese banks' conversion of dollars into yen have been liberalized

since July 1984. Foreign banks have been allowed to deal in government bonds since 1985.

13. See Ichiro Otani and S. Timar, "Capital Controls and Interest Rate Parity: The Japanese Experience, 1978–81," *IMF Staff Papers*, Dec. 1981.

14. See, e.g., *Business Week*, May 21, 1984.

15. See, e.g., Ronald Napier, "Japanese Capital Markets in Transition," *Program on U.S.-Japan Relations, Annual Review, 1982–83*.

16. U.S. government bond rates deflated by the CPI were 2.53 per cent (1979), 0.34 per cent (1980), 3.72 per cent (1981), and 3.76 per cent (1982). Comparable figures for Swiss government bonds were 0.15 per cent (1979), 0.87 per cent (1980), −0.93 per cent (1981), and −1.17 per cent (1982).

17. According to Napier, "Japanese Capital Markets," the U.S. real, after-tax rate fluctuated from a low of −11.8 per cent in 1974 to a high of 7.7 per cent in 1982.

18. See, e.g., Mitsuhiro Fukao, *Kawase rēto to kin'yū shijō* (Exchange rates and the financial market) (Tokyo: Tōyō Keizai Shimposha, 1983).

19. Akihiko Tanaka, Gary Saxonhouse, and Hugh Patrick pointed out to me that the United States does not want net capital exports from Japan. Ryutaro Komiya mentioned that it is some international organizations (the World Bank, for one) and some LDCs that are demanding Japanese net capital exports. I concede that there will be no explicit demand for Japanese capital exports on the part of the United States, but still I wonder if the United States doesn't really want Japan's net capital exports? At present, U.S. net capital imports are on the order of 3 per cent of GNP. If depreciation of the dollar wipes out the Japanese current-account surplus, where will the savings come from that now go to private investment? Unless the U.S. fiscal deficit is corrected, interest rates will rise and crowd out private investment. Is this acceptable? How readily can fiscal deficit be corrected?

20. E.g., Yoshitomi, "Kokusai kin'yū." See also Yoshitomi (comments by seven Japanese economists are included), "Shihon yushutsu koku to shite no Nihon no yakuwari" (The role of Japan as a capital exporter), *Nihon Keizai Kenkyū Sentā kaihō*, No. 464 (May 15, 1984).

21. The Japanese net asset position cannot be hedged; either the Japanese bear the exchange risks when assets are denominated in dollars, or Japan's debtors will bear the risk when loans are denominated in yen. For further elaboration of this point, see Fukao, *Kawase rēto*.

22. Much of the following was written after I heard the comments of the conference participants and is strongly influenced by their views.

23. Ronald McKinnon argues that in view of the possible default risks in international finance, bond issues should play a dominant role because bank loans may be incompatible with sound banking. I am inclined to agree with him.

24. See also Suzuki, *Kin'yū jiyūka*.

25. See *ibid.* for a useful discussion of past regulations and the liberalization process. Thomas F. Cargill, "A U.S. Perspective on Japanese Financial Liberalization," *Bank of Japan Monetary and Economic Studies*, No. 3 (May 1985), has a detailed chronology of events since 1975 and a long list of references.

Katzenstein: Japan, Switzerland of the Far East?

For their helpful comments on a previous draft of this paper, I would like to thank Bruce Cumings, Fred Deyo, Takashi Inoguchi, Chalmers Johnson, Michio

Muramatsu, Daniel I. Okimoto, T. J. Pempel, Richard Samuels, Manfred Schmidt, Mark Selden, Robert Smith, Keiichi Tsunekawa, Ezra Vogel, and the participants at the Japan's Political Economy in the International System conference.

1. Manfred G. Schmidt, "The Politics of Labor Market Policy: Structural and Political Determinants of Full Employment and Mass Unemployment in Mixed Economies" (Paper delivered at the World Congress of the International Political Science Association, Paris, July 20–25, 1985).

2. Felix Wehrle, "Der exportorientierte Industrialisierungsprozess in den Schwellenländern Asiens und Lateinamerikas und Japans Aufstieg zur Wirtschaftsgrossmacht—Betrachtungen aus einer schweizerischen Perspektive" (Institut für Sozialwissenschaften, University of Basel, unpublished paper, July 1983), pp. 80–81.

3. Hugh Patrick and Henry Rosovsky, eds., *Asia's New Giant: How the Japanese Economy Works* (Washington, D.C.: Brookings Institution, 1976).

4. Michael J. Piore and Charles F. Sabel, *The Second Industrial Divide: Possibilities for Prosperity* (New York: Basic Books, 1984).

5. Peter J. Katzenstein, *Corporatism and Change: Austria, Switzerland and the Politics of Industry* (Ithaca, N.Y.: Cornell University Press, 1984), pp. 162–238.

6. Silvio Borner and Felix Wehrle, *Die sechste Schweiz: Überleben auf dem Weltmarkt* (Zurich: Orell Füssli, 1984), p. 7.

7. Michèle Schmiegelow, "Cutting Across Doctrines: Positive Adjustment in Japan," *International Organization*, Vol. 2, No. 39 (Spring 1985), pp. 261–96; Bruce R. Scott and George C. Lodge, eds., *U.S. Competitiveness in the World Economy* (Boston: Harvard Business School, 1985); and Chalmers Johnson, "The Institutional Foundations of Japanese Industrial Policy," *California Management Review*, Vol. 27, No. 4 (Summer 1985), pp. 59–69.

8. Ippei Yamazawa, "Increasing Imports and Structural Adjustment of the Japanese Textile Industry," *Developing Economies*, Vol. 18, No. 4 (Dec. 1980), pp. 441–62; Brian Ike, "The Japanese Textile Industry: Structural Adjustment and Government Policy," *Asian Survey*, Vol. 20, No. 5 (May 1980), pp. 532–51; Masayuki Yoshioka, "Overseas Investment by the Japanese Textile Industry," *Developing Economies*, Vol. 17, No. 1 (Mar. 1979), pp. 3–44; I. M. Destler, Haruhiro Fukui, and Hideo Sato, *The Textile Wrangle: Conflict in Japanese—American Relations, 1969–1971* (Ithaca, N.Y.: Cornell University Press, 1979); and Richard H. Friman, "Industrial Alliances, the State, and the 'New Protectionism': Textile Protection in the United States, Japan, and West Germany. The Case of Japan" (Paper delivered at the Annual Meeting of the American Political Science Association, Washington, D.C., 1984).

9. Wehrle, "Exportorientierte Industrialisierungsprozess," pp. 74–76; and Harvard Business School, "Note on the Watch Industries in Switzerland, Japan, and the United States," 9-373-090 (Cambridge, Mass.: Harvard University, 1972).

10. T. J. Pempel, *Policy and Politics in Japan: Creative Conservatism* (Philadelphia: Temple University Press, 1982); see also Schmiegelow, "Cutting Across Doctrines."

11. Katzenstein, *Corporatism and Change*, pp. 144–54.

12. Manfred G. Schmidt, *Der schweizerische Weg zur Vollbeschäftigung: Eine Bilanz der Beschäftigung, der Arbeitslosigkeit und der Arbeitsmarktpolitik* (Frankfurt a/M.: Campus, 1985), p. 16.

13. Hanspeter Kriesi, *Entscheidungsstrukturen und Entscheidungsprozesse in der schweizer Politik.* (Frankfurt a/M.: Campus, 1980).

14. Renatus Gallati, *Der Arbeitsfriede in der Schweiz und seine wohlstandspolitische*

Bedeutung im Vergleich mit der Entwicklung in einigen andern Staaten (Bern: Lang, 1976).

15. Alexander Berenstein, "Switzerland," in *International Encyclopedia for Labour Law and Industrial Relations* (The Netherlands: Kluwer Law and Taxation Publishers, 1984), 9: 148. See also Günter Endruweitz et al., eds., *Handbuch der Arbeitsbeziehungen: Deutschland, Österreich, Schweiz* (Berlin: de Gruyter, 1985).

16. Joseph Moore, *Japanese Workers and the Struggle for Power, 1945–1947* (Madison: University of Wisconsin Press, 1983).

17. Takashi Inoguchi, "Political Surfing over Economic Waves: A Simple Model of the Japanese Political-Economic System in Comparative Perspective" (Paper delivered at the World Congress of the International Political Science Association, Moscow, 1979); idem, "Economic Conditions and Mass Support in Japan, 1960–1976," in Paul Whiteley, ed., *Models of Political Economy* (London: Sage, 1980), pp. 121–51; and idem, "Explaining and Predicting Japanese General Elections, 1960–1980," *Journal of Japanese Studies*, Vol. 7, No. 2 (Summer 1981), pp. 285–318.

18. Pempel, *Policy and Politics*.

19. John C. Campbell, "Policy Conflict and Its Resolution Within the Government System," in Ellis S. Krauss, Thomas P. Rohlen, and Patricia G. Steinhoff, eds., *Conflict in Japan* (Honolulu: University of Hawaii Press, 1984), pp. 294–334; and T. J. Pempel, "Changes in Japanese Policymaking" (Paper delivered at the American Political Science Association Convention, New Orleans, Aug.–Sept. 1985), pp. 16–17, 41.

20. OECD, *The Development of Industrial Relations Systems: Some Implications of Japanese Experience* (Paris, 1977).

21. Ichiyo Muto, "Class Struggle on the Shopfloor," *Ampo: Japan-Asia Quarterly Review*, Vol. 16, No. 3 (1984), p. 39.

22. Walter Galenson and Konosuke Odaka, "The Japanese Labor Market," in Patrick and Rosovsky, *Asia's New Giant*, pp. 587–671; and Taishiro Shirai, "Japanese Labor Unions and Politics," in idem, ed., *Contemporary Industrial Relations in Japan* (Madison: University of Wisconsin Press, 1983), pp. 331–52.

23. Haruo Shimada, "Summaries and Evaluation," in Shirai, *Contemporary Industrial Relations*, p. 366.

24. Clyde Haberman, "Labor Peace Reigns in Japan and Unions Wither," *New York Times*, June 7, 1985, p. 2.

25. Michio Muramatsu and Ellis S. Krauss, "Bureaucrats and Politicians in Policymaking: The Case of Japan," *American Political Science Review*, Vol. 78, No. 1 (Mar. 1984), pp. 126–46.

26. See the paper by Michio Muramatsu and Ellis S. Krauss in volume 1 of this series, p. 534.

27. Michio Muramatsu and Ellis S. Krauss, "The Dominant Party and Social Coalitions in Japan" (Paper delivered at the Conference on Dominant Party Systems, Cornell University, Ithaca, N.Y., Apr. 7–9, 1984), pp. 14–17.

28. Shirai, *Contemporary Industrial Relations*. See also Kozo Kikuchi, "The Japanese Enterprise Union and Its Functions," in Shigeyoshi Tokunaga and Joachim Bergmann, eds., *Industrial Relations in Transition: The Cases of Japan and the Federal Republic of Germany* (Tokyo: University of Tokyo Press, 1984), pp. 171–94.

29. Kazuo Koike, "Internal Labor Markets: Workers in Large Firms," and idem, "Workers in Small Firms and Women in Industry," in Shirai, *Contemporary Industrial Relations*, pp. 29–61, 89–115; and Ronald Dore, *British Factory—Japanese Factory: The Origins of National Diversity in Industrial Relations* (Berkeley: Univer-

sity of California Press, 1973). See also Robert E. Cole, *Japanese Blue Collar: The Changing Tradition* (Berkeley: University of California Press, 1971); Robert M. Marsh and Hiroshi Mannari, *Modernization and the Japanese Factory* (Princeton: Princeton University Press, 1976); Rodney Clark, *The Japanese Company* (New Haven: Yale University Press, 1979); Thomas P. Rohlen, *For Harmony and Strength: Japanese White-Collar Organization in Anthropological Perspective* (Berkeley: University of California Press, 1974); and Jon Woronoff, *Japan's Wasted Workers* (Tokyo: Lotus Press, 1981).

30. Taishiro Shirai, "Gegenwärtiger Stand und zukünftige Gestaltungsmöglichkeiten der Mitbestimmung in Japan," in Willy Krauss, ed., *Humanisierung der Arbeitswelt: Gestaltungsmöglichkeiten in Japan und in der Bundesrepublik Deutschland* (Tübingen: Horst Erdmann, 1979), p. 248.

31. Kazutoshi Koshiro, "Development of Collective Bargaining in Postwar Japan," in Shirai, *Contemporary Industrial Relations*, pp. 248–49; and S. J. Park, "Labour-Management Consultation as a Japanese Type of Participation: An International Comparison," in Tokunaga and Bergmann, *Industrial Relations*, pp. 153–67.

32. Taishiro Shirai, "A Theory of Enterprise Unionism," in idem, *Contemporary Industrial Relations*, pp. 140–41.

33. Ibid., p. 130.

34. Hideo Otake, "Postwar Politics: Liberalism Versus Social Democracy" *Japan Echo*, Vol. 10, No. 2 (1983), p. 47.

35. Haruo Shimada, "Japan's Postwar Industrial Growth and Labor-Management Relations," in Industrial Relations Research Association, ed., *Proceedings of the Thirty-Fifth Annual Meeting* (Madison, Wisc., 1983), p. 246.

36. George Frantz, "Government and Declining Industry: The Japanese Coal Mining Industry," (Ithaca, N.Y.: Cornell University, unpublished paper).

37. Shigeyoshi Tokunaga, "A Marxist Interpretation of Japanese Industrial Relations, with Special Reference to Large Private Enterprises," in Shirai, *Contemporary Industrial Relations*, p. 317.

38. Benjamin Martin, "Japanese Mining Labor: The Miike Strike," *Far Eastern Survey*, Vol. 30, No. 2 (Feb. 1961), pp. 26–30.

39. Frantz, "Government and Declining Industry," p. 15.

40. Ibid., p. 37.

41. Satoshi Kamata, *Japan in the Passing Lane: An Insider's Account of Life in a Japanese Auto Factory* (New York: Pantheon, 1982).

42. Muto, "Class Struggle," p. 42.

43. Knuth Dohse, Ulrich Jürgens, and Thomas Malsch, "From 'Fordism' to 'Toyotism'? The Social Organization of the Labor Process in the Japanese Automobile Industry," trans. Hugh Mosley, *Politics & Society*, Vol. 14, No. 2 (1985), pp. 115–46; Muto, "Class Struggle"; and Tokunaga, "Marxist Interpretation."

44. Dohse, Jürgens, and Malsch, "From 'Fordism' to Toyotism,'" p. 31.

45. Richard J. Schonberger, *Japanese Manufacturing Techniques* (New York: Free Press, 1982), pp. 91–92.

46. Shigeyoshi Tokunaga, "The Structures of the Japanese Labour Market," and Eisuke Daito, "Seniority Wages and Labour Management: Japanese Employers' Wage Policy," in Tokunaga and Bergmann, *Industrial Relations*, pp. 22–55, 119–30.

47. Robert E. Cole, *Work, Mobility, and Participation: A Comparative Study of American and Japanese Industry* (Berkeley: University of California Press, 1979), p. 252.

48. Otake, "Postwar Politics," p. 51.

49. Muto, "Class Struggle," p. 48.   50. Ibid.

51. Chalmers Johnson, "The Japanese Economy: A Different Kind of Capitalism" (Paper delivered at the International Conference on Technology, Enterprise, and Regional Development: Policies and Programs of Nations and States, Center for Technology and Policy, Boston University, Aug. 12–14, 1985), pp. 16–17.

52. Schmidt, *Schweizerische Weg*.

53. Angelika Ernst, *Japans unvollkommene Vollbeschäftigung: Beschäftigungsprobleme und Beschäftigungspolitik* (Hamburg: Institut für Asienkunde, 1980).

54. Koshiro, "Collective Bargaining," p. 247.

55. Manfred G. Schmidt, "The Role of the Parties in Shaping Macroeconomic Policy," in Francis G. Castles, ed., *The Impact of Parties* (Beverly Hills, Calif.: Sage, 1982), p. 135.

56. Manfred G. Schmidt, "The Welfare State and the Economy in Periods of Economic Crisis: A Comparative Study of Twenty-three OECD Nations," *European Journal of Political Research*, Vol. 11 (1983), p. 4.

57. Schmidt, "Role of the Parties," pp. 156–62.

58. Ibid., p. 147; and Manfred G. Schmidt, "The Politics of Unemployment: Rates of Unemployment and Labour Market Policy," *West European Politics*, Vol. 7, No. 3 (July 1984), pp. 11–15.

59. Schmidt, "Politics of Unemployment," pp. 27–39.

60. T. J. Pempel and Keiichi Tsunekawa, "Corporatism Without Labor? The Japanese Anomaly," in Philippe C. Schmitter and Gerhard Lehmbruch, eds., *Trends Toward Corporatist Intermediation* (Beverly Hills, Calif.: Sage, 1979), pp. 231–70.

61. Ibid., p. 245.   62. Ibid., p. 264.

63. Andrew Shonfield, *In Defense of the Mixed Economy* (Oxford: Oxford University Press, 1984), pp. 134–35.

64. Ibid., pp. 104–23.

65. Haruo Shimada, "Wage Determination and Information Sharing: An Alternative Approach to Incomes Policy?" *Journal of Industrial Relations*, Vol. 25, No. 2 (June 1983), pp. 177–200.

66. Ibid., p. 190.

67. Peter J. Katzenstein, *Small States in World Markets: Industrial Policy in Europe* (Ithaca, N.Y.: Cornell University Press, 1985), pp. 30–37.

68. Schmidt, "Role of the Parties," pp. 133, 144–45.

69. Pempel and Tsunekawa, "Corporatism Without Labor?" p. 238.

70. Shonfield, *Mixed Economy*, pp. 127–32; and Shimada, "Wage Determination."

71. Katzenstein, *Small States*.   72. Ibid.

73. Philippe Schmitter, "Interest Intermediation and Regime Governability: A Japanese Epilogue" (Unpublished paper, 1978), p. 13.

74. Ibid., pp. 16, 30.   75. Katzenstein, *Small States*.

76. Pempel and Tsunekawa, "Corporatism Without Labor?" pp. 258, 269.

77. Shimada, "Japan's Postwar Industrial Growth," p. 244.

78. Koshiro, "Collective Bargaining," p. 253.

79. Kazutoshi Koshiro, "The Quality of Working Life in Japanese Factories," in Shirai, *Contemporary Industrial Relations*, p. 77.

80. Koshiro, "Collective Bargaining," p. 249.

81. Shimada, "Wage Determination," pp. 186–91.

82. T. J. Pempel, "The Japanese Challenge: A New Capitalism" (Paper de-

livered at the Restructuring of the World Economic Hierarchy conference, Friedrich-Ebert-Stiftung, Bonn, May 28–29, 1985), p. 8.

83. J. W. M. Chapman, R. Drifte, and I. T. M. Gow, *Japan's Quest for Comprehensive Security: Defense-Diplomacy-Dependence* (N.Y.: St. Martin's Press, 1982).

84. Pempel, "Japanese Challenge," p. 10.

85. Pempel and Tsunekawa, "Corporatism Without Labor?" pp. 265–66.

86. Lawrence B. Krause and Sueo Sekiguchi, "Japan and the World Economy," in Hugh Patrick and Henry Rosovsky, *Asia's New Giant*, p. 387.

87. Shoko Tanaka, "Post-war Japanese Resource Policy: With Special Emphasis on Southeast Asia" (Cornell University, M.A. thesis, May 1982), p. 46.

88. Raymond Vernon, *Two Hungry Giants: The United States and Japan in the Quest for Oil and Ores* (Cambridge: Harvard Univ. Press, 1983), pp. 82–83.

89. Ibid., p. 94.

90. Malcolm Smith, "The Internationalization of the Japanese Economy: The Legal Framework" (Paper delivered at the Conference on Canada and International Trade, Institute of International Relations and Institute for Research on Public Policy, Vancouver, 1983).

91. Chalmers Johnson, "The 'Internationalization' of the Japanese Economy," *California Management Review*, Vol. 25, No. 3 (Spring 1983), p. 16.

92. Chalmers Johnson, "The Role of Japan in the Asian-Pacific Region and Japanese Relations with the U.S., PRC, and USSR" (Paper delivered at the Conference on the Asian-Pacific Region, sponsored by the Shanghai Institute for International Studies and the Institute of East Asian Studies, University of California, Berkeley; Shanghai, May 20–23, 1985).

93. J. D. Armstrong, "The International Committee of the Red Cross and Political Prisoners," *International Organization*, Vol. 39, No. 4 (1985), pp. 615–42.

94. Ibid., pp. 618–19.

Okimoto: Political Inclusivity

1. Michael Borrus, James Millstein, and John Zysman, *U.S.-Japanese Competition in the Semiconductor Industry* (Berkeley, Calif.: Institute of International Studies, 1982).

2. SIA (Semiconductor Industry Association), *The Effect of Government Targeting on World Semiconductor Competition* (Cupertino, Calif., 1983).

3. Stephen D. Cohen, *Uneasy Partnership: Competition and Conflict in U.S.-Japanese Trade Relations* (Cambridge, Mass.: Ballinger, 1985).

4. John Zysman, *Governments, Markets, and Growth* (Ithaca, N.Y.: Cornell University Press, 1983).

5. For Japan, Inc., see Chitoshi Yanaga, *Big Business in Japanese Politics* (New Haven: Yale University Press, 1968); James C. Abegglen, "The Economic Growth of Japan," *Scientific American*, Vol. 222 (Mar. 1970), pp. 31–37; and Eugene J. Kaplan, *Japan: The Government-Business Relationship* (Washington, D.C.: U.S. Department of Commerce, 1972). For pluralism, see Gerald L. Curtis, "Big Business and Political Influence," in Ezra F. Vogel, ed., *Modern Japanese Organization and Decisionmaking* (Berkeley: University of California Press, 1975), pp. 33–70; Michio Muramatsu and Ellis S. Krauss, "Bureaucrats and Politicians in Policymaking: The Case of Japan," *American Political Science Review*, Vol. 78 (1983), pp. 126–46; and Hideo Ōtake, *Gendai Nihon no seiji kenryoku, keizai kenryoku* (Political and economic power in contemporary Japan) (Tokyo: San'ichi Shobō, 1979). For bureaucratic statism, see Chalmers Johnson, "Japan: Who Governs? An Essay on Official Bureaucracy," *Journal of Japanese Studies*, Vol. 2 (Autumn 1975), pp. 1–28;

idem, *MITI and the Japanese Miracle: The Growth of Industrial Policy, 1925–1975* (Stanford: Stanford University Press, 1982); and T. J. Pempel, "Japanese Foreign Economic Policy: The Domestic Bases for International Behavior," in Peter J. Katzenstein, ed., *Between Power and Plenty: Foreign Economic Policies of Advanced Industrial States* (Madison: University of Wisconsin Press, 1978), pp. 139–90.

6. For elitism, see C. Wright Mills, *The Power Elite* (New York: Oxford University Press, 1959); Peter Bachrach and Morton S. Baratz, "Two Faces of Power," *American Political Science Review*, Vol. 56 (1962), pp. 947–52; and G. William Domhoff, *Who Rules America?* (Englewood Cliffs, N.J.: Prentice-Hall, 1967). For liberal pluralism, see Robert A. Dahl, *Who Governs? Democracy and Power in an American City* (New Haven: Yale University Press, 1961); Nelson W. Polsby, *Community Power and Political Theory* (New Haven: Yale University Press, 1963); and Raymond A. Bauer, Ithiel de Sola Pool, and Lewis Anthony Dexter, *American Business and Public Policy: The Politics of Foreign Trade* (New York: Atherton, 1963). For statism, see Stephen D. Krasner, *Defending the National Interest: Raw Materials Investments and U.S. Foreign Policy* (Princeton: Princeton University Press, 1978); Theda Skocpol, *States and Social Revolutions: A Comparative Analysis of France, Russia, and China* (Cambridge, Eng.: Cambridge University Press, 1979); Stephen Skowronek, *Building a New American State: The Expansion of National Administrative Capitalism* (New York: Cambridge University Press, 1982); and Eric Nordlinger, *On the Autonomy of the Democratic State* (Cambridge, Mass.: Harvard University Press, 1981).

7. For neo-corporatism, see Philippe C. Schmitter and Gerhard Lehmbruch, eds., *Trends Toward Corporatist Intermediation* (Beverly Hills, Calif.: Sage, 1979); and Suzanne D. Berger, *Organizing Interests in Western Europe: Pluralism, Corporatism, and the Transformation of Politics* (Cambridge, Eng.: Cambridge University Press, 1981). For state monopoly capitalism, see Bob Jessop, *The Capitalist State* (New York: New York University Press, 1982).

8. T. J. Pempel and Keiichi Tsunekawa, "Corporatism Without Labor? The Japanese Anomaly," in Schmitter and Lehmbruch, *Trends*, pp. 231–70.

9. Yanaga, *Big Business*.

10. Kaplan, *Japan*.

11. Akira Kubota, *Higher Civil Servants in Postwar Japan* (Princeton: Princeton University Press, 1969).

12. Graham Allison, *Essence of Decision: Explaining the Cuban Missile Crisis* (Boston: Little, Brown & Co., 1971).

13. Naohiro Amaya, *Nihon kabushiki kaisha: Nokosareta sentaku* (Japan, Inc.: The options left) (Tokyo: PHP, 1982); and I. M. Destler, Haruhiro Fukui, and Hideo Sato, *The Textile Wrangle: Conflict in Japanese-American Relations, 1969–1971* (Ithaca, N.Y.: Cornell University Press, 1979).

14. Theodore Lowi, "American Business, Public Policy Case-Studies, and Political Theory," *World Politics*, Vol. 16 (1964), pp. 677–715.

15. Dahl, *Who Governs?*; and Bauer et al., *American Business*.

16. Otake, *Gendai Nihon*; see also the paper by Kosai in Volume I of this series.

17. Ellis S. Krauss and Michio Muramatsu, "The Structure of Interest Group Influence on Public Policymaking in Japan" (Unpublished paper, 1983).

18. Krasner, *National Interest*; Skocpol, *States*; Nordlinger, *Autonomy*; and Skowronek, *New American State*.

19. SIA, *Government Targeting*; and Kozo Yamamura, ed., *Policy and Trade Issues of the Japanese Economy: American and Japanese Perspectives* (Seattle: University of Washington Press, 1982).

20. Robert N. Bellah, *Tokugawa Religion: The Values of Pre-industrial Japan* (Glencoe, Ill.: Free Press, 1957); Masao Maruyama, *Thought and Behavior in Modern Japanese Politics*, ed. Ivan Morris (New York: Oxford University Press, 1963); and Chie Nakane, *Japanese Society* (Berkeley: University of California Press, 1970).

21. Cf. Talcott Parsons, *The Structure of Social Action* (New York: McGraw-Hill, 1937); and idem, *The Social System* (Glencoe, Ill.: Free Press, 1951).

22. Bellah, *Tokugawa Religion*, pp. 11–57.

23. Alfred Stepan, *The State and Society: Peru in Comparative Perspective* (Princeton: Princeton University Press, 1978), pp. 26–45.

24. David Collier, *The New Authoritarianism in Latin America* (Princeton: Princeton University Press, 1979); and Juan J. Linz and Alfred Stepan, eds., *Breakdowns of Democratic Regimes: The European and Latin American Experience* (Baltimore: Johns Hopkins University Press, 1979).

25. Clifford Geertz, *Negara: The Theatre State in Nineteenth Century Bali* (Princeton: Princeton University Press, 1981).

26. Yasusuke Murakami, Shumpei Kumon, and Seizaburō Satō, *Bunmei to shite no ie shakai* (*Ie* society as a civilization) (Tokyo: Chūō Kōronsha, 1979).

27. Maruyama, *Thought and Behavior*; Bellah, *Tokugawa Religion*; and Barrington Moore, Jr., *Social Origins of Dictatorship and Democracy* (Boston: Beacon Press, 1966).

28. Johnson, *MITI*; and William W. Lockwood, *The Economic Development of Japan* (Princeton: Princeton University Press, 1954).

29. Murakami et al., *Ie shakai*.

30. Alexander Gerschenkron, *Economic Backwardness in Historical Perspective* (Cambridge, Mass.: Harvard University Press, 1962).

31. Linz and Stepan, *Breakdowns*.

32. Johnson, *MITI*.

33. Nakane, *Japanese Society*, p. 102.

34. Arend Lijphart, *Democracy in Plural Societies* (New Haven: Yale University Press, 1977), pp. 25–52.

35. Murakami et al., *Ie shakai*.

36. Cf. Collier, *New Authoritarianism*.

37. Murakami et al., *Ie shakai*; and John W. Hall, *Government and Local Power in Japan, 500 to 1700: A Study Based on Bizen Province* (Princeton: Princeton University Press, 1965).

38. Linz and Stepan, *Breakdowns*; Peter Duus and Daniel I. Okimoto, "Fascism and the History of Pre-war Japan: The Failure of a Concept," *Journal of Asian Studies*, Vol. 39, No. 1 (Nov. 1979), pp. 65–76.

39. Peter J. Katzenstein, "Introduction," in idem, *Between Power and Plenty*, pp. 3–22.

40. Mancur Olson, *The Rise and Decline of Nations: Economic Growth, Stagflation, and Social Rigidities* (New Haven: Yale University Press, 1982).

41. Takashi Inoguchi, *Gendai Nihon seiji keizai no kozu* (The design of politics and economics in contemporary Japan) (Tokyo: Tōyō Keizai Shimpōsha, 1983), pp. 18–22.

42. Gerald L. Curtis, *Election Campaigning, Japanese Style* (New York: Columbia University Press, 1971).

43. Joel D. Aberbach, Robert D. Putnam, and Bert A. Rockman, *Bureaucrats and Politicians in Western Democracies* (Cambridge, Mass.: Harvard University Press, 1981).

534   *Notes to Pages 318–40*

44. Barry M. Mitnick, *The Political Economy of Regulation* (New York: Columbia University Press, 1980).

45. James Q. Wilson, "The Politics of Regulation," in James W. McKie, ed., *Social Responsibility and the Business Predicament* (Washington, D.C.: Brookings Institution, 1974), pp. 135–68.

46. See, e.g., Johnson, *MITI*; Destler et al., *Textile Wrangle*; and Otake, *Gendai Nihon*.

47. Johnson, "Japan: Who Governs?"; and idem, *MITI*.

48. Bauer et al., *American Business*; and Lowi, "American Business."

49. Michio Muramatsu, *Sengo Nihon no kanryōsei* (Postwar Japan's bureaucratic system) (Tokyo: Tōyō Keizai Shimpōsha, 1981).

50. Robert A. Dahl, "Power," in *International Encyclopedia of the Social Sciences* (New York: Crowell Collier and Macmillan, 1968), 12: 405–15.

51. Mitnick, *Regulation*.

52. Wilson, "Politics of Regulation."

53. Inoguchi, *Gendai Nihon*; and Muramatsu, *Sengo Nihon*.

54. Haruhiro Fukui, "The Liberal Democratic Party Revisited: Continuity and Change in the Party's Structure and Performance," *Journal of Japanese Studies*, Vol. 10, No. 2 (Summer 1984), pp. 390–97.

55. Masumi Ishikawa, *Sengo seiji kōzō shi* (History of Japan's postwar political structure) (Tokyo: Nihon Hyōronsha, 1978).

56. Yasusuke Murakami, "The Age of New Middle Mass Politics: The Case of Japan," *Journal of Japanese Studies*, Vol. 8, No. 1 (Winter 1982), pp. 29–72.

57. Michisada Hirose, "Rieki haibun shisutemu wa henka shita ka?" (Has the system of distributing profits changed?), *Sekai*, Mar. 1983, pp. 130–50.

58. Daniel I. Okimoto, Takuo Sugano, and Franklin B. Weinstein, eds., *Competitive Edge: The Semiconductor Industries in the U.S. and Japan* (Stanford: Stanford University Press, 1984).

59. Mancur Olson, *The Logic of Collective Action* (Cambridge, Mass.: Harvard University Press, 1965).

60. Masahiko Aoki, ed., *The Economic Analysis of the Japanese Firm* (Amsterdam: North Holland, 1984).

61. Peter J. Katzenstein, *Small States in World Markets* (Ithaca, N.Y.: Cornell University Press, 1985).

62. Robert O. Keohane and Joseph S. Nye, *Power and Interdependence: World Politics in Transition* (Boston: Little, Brown & Co., 1977).

63. Kent E. Calder, "Opening Japan," *Foreign Policy*, No. 47 (Summer 1982), pp. 82–97.

64. James R. Kurth, "The Political Consequences of the Product Cycle: Industrial History and Political Outcomes," *International Organization*, Vol. 23, No. 1 (Winter 1979), pp. 1–34.

65. Hugh Patrick and Hideo Sato, "The Political Economy of United States–Japan Trade in Steel," in Yamamura, *Policy and Trade Issues*, pp. 197–238.

66. Stephen D. Krasner and Daniel I. Okimoto, "Mercantilism or Accommodation? Japan's Responses to External Pressures" (Unpublished paper, 1985).

67. On shipbuilding, see Ezra F. Vogel, *Comeback* (New York: Simon & Schuster, 1985).

68. Yamamura, *Policy and Trade Issues*.

69. Kaplan, *Japan*.

70. Aoki, *Economic Analysis*; Ken'ichi Imai and Hiroyuki Itami, "Mutual Infiltration of Organization and Market: Japan's Firm and Market in Comparison with the U.S.," Discussion Paper No. 115 (Tokyo: Hitotsubashi University, Insti-

tute of Business Research, 1983); Therese Flaherty and Hiroyuki Itami in Oki-moto et al., *Competitive Edge*, pp. 134–76; Iwao Nakatani, "The Economic Role of Financial Corporate Grouping," in Aoki, *Economic Analysis*, pp. 227–58; and Hiroshi Okumura, *Hōjin shihonshugi* (Corporate capitalism) (Tokyo: Nihon Hyō-ronsha, 1975).

71. Oliver E. Williamson, *Markets and Hierarchies: Analysis and Antitrust Implications* (New York: Free Press, 1975); and Imai and Itami, "Mutual Infiltration."

72. Okumura, *Hōjin shihonshugi*; and Ronald Dore, "Goodwill and the Spirit of Market Capitalism," *British Journal of Sociology*, Vol. 34 (1983), pp. 459–82.

73. Krasner and Okimoto, "Mercantilism."

74. Albert O. Hirschman, *Exit, Voice, and Loyalty: Responses to Decline in Firms, Organizations, and States* (Cambridge, Mass.: Harvard University Press, 1970).

75. Murakami, "New Middle Mass Politics."

Hellmann: Japanese Politics and Foreign Policy

1. See, e.g., the excellent survey article by Peter Gaurevitch, "The Second Image Reversed: The International Sources of Domestic Politics," *International Organization*, Vol. 32, No. 4 (Autumn 1978), pp. 881–911.

2. Chalmers A. Johnson, *MITI and the Japanese Miracle* (Stanford: Stanford University Press, 1982).

3. On this last point, see Yasusuke Murakami, *Shin chūkan daishi no jidai* (The age of the new middle mass) (Chūō Kōronsha, 1983), esp. pp. 201–25.

4. Giovanni Satori, *Democratic Theory* (Detroit: Wayne State University Press, 1962), p. 119.

5. Gaetano Mosca, *The Ruling Class* (New York: McGraw-Hill, 1939), pp. 462–75. On Japan, see Masao Maruyama, *Thought and Behavior in Modern Japanese Politics* (New York: Oxford University Press, 1963), esp. pp. 135–54; Seizaburō Sato, Shumpei Kumon, and Yasusuke Murakami, *Ie shakai* (Ie society) (Tokyo: Chūō Kōronsha, 1978); and Masa'aki Takane, *The Political Elite in Japan* (Berkeley: University of California Press, 1981).

6. This point is well made in Haruhiro Fukui, "Review of the Literature," in T. J. Pempel, ed., *Policymaking in Contemporary Japan* (Ithaca, N.Y.: Cornell University Press, 1977), pp. 22–59, although the discussion does not fully address the broader issue of elitism as a functional feature of Japanese politics. One notable exception is Johnson, *MITI*, in which he applies his concept of the developmental state to prewar and postwar Japanese politics and stresses that the aim of the government was to fend off pressure groups and party pressures in order to implement a coherent policy (p. 322). Curiously, Marxism, the most flawed and least relevant elitist theory, has been the one most commonly applied to Japan.

7. Joseph A. Schumpter, *Capitalism, Socialism, and Democracy* (New York: Harper Books, 1962), pp. 135–36.

8. See, e.g., Mosca, *Ruling Class*, pp. 487–88.

9. Schumpeter, *Capitalism*, p. 242.

10. On this point, see T. B. Botomore, *Elites and Society* (Baltimore: Penguin, 1964), pp. 48–68.

11. For an interesting discussion of elite consensus that synthesizes much of the relevant literature in modern social science, see Peter Bachrach, *The Theory of Democratic Elitism* (Boston: Little, Brown & Co., 1967), pp. 47–64.

12. For a good recent article on this subject, see Atsushi Odawara, "Seitō to kanryō no kankei ni tsuite" (Relations between the conservative party and the bureaucracy), *Jurisuto*, No. 35 (Summer 1984), pp. 57–63.

13. Even a casual inspection of the backgrounds of Japanese political leaders provides striking illustrations of this point, and these connections are regularly discussed in the popular political magazines. See, e.g., the elaborate report "Probe of New Family and Marriage Connections of Diet Members," *Gendai*, Oct. 1980, pp. 3–38, trans. in American Embassy, *Translations of Japanese Magazines*, Dec. 1980.

14. Gerald R. Curtis, "Japan Faces the World: Change and Continuity in Japanese Foreign Relations," in *Japan in the 1980s, I* (Atlanta: Southern Center for International Studies, 1983), p. 44.

15. Again, this is a subject that has received little scholarly treatment. In English, see Chalmers Johnson, "The Reemployment of Retired Government Bureaucrats in Japanese Big Business," *Asian Survey*, Vol. 14, No. 11 (Nov. 1974), pp. 953–65; and Tuvia Blumenthal, "The Practice of Amakudari Within the Japanese Employment System," *Asian Survey*, Vol. 25, No. 3 (Mar. 1985), pp. 310–21. In Japanese, see Michio Muramatsu, *Sengo Nihon no kanryōsei* (The bureaucracy in postwar Japan) (Tokyo: Tōyō Keizai Shimposha, 1981), esp. pp. 75–85.

16. See, e.g., Hideo Ōtake, *Gendai Nihon no seiji kenryoku, keizai kenryoku* (Political and economic power in contemporary Japan) (Tokyo: San'ichi Shobō, 1979); Jun'ichi Kyogoku, *Nihon no seiji* (Japanese politics) (Tokyo: University of Tokyo Press, 1983); and the paper by Muramatsu and Krauss in Volume I of this series.

17. The main points of the extensive literature on the relationship between public opinion and foreign policy in the United States are concisely summarized in Ernst B. Haas, *Tangle of Hopes: American Commitments and World Order* (Englewood Cliffs, N.J.: Prentice-Hall, 1969), esp. pp. 33–37, 56–59.

18. These general categories refer to *effective* public opinion, not simply to opinions held by the public. Public opinion polls deal with the latter; that is, they simply describe the opinions held on specific issues. Whether these opinions influence government decisions depends on other factors.

19. The transnational evidence for this is both startling and overwhelming, and Japan simply follows the international pattern. For example, in mid-1967, one out of three Japanese did not know that a communist government controlled China. Kyodo News Agency poll of June 1967; reported in *Asahi shimbun*, July 12, 1967.

20. For a provocative discussion of the influence of the public on policy in the United States, see Thomas R. Dye and L. Harmon Zeigler, *The Irony of Democracy* (North Scituate, Mass.: Duxbury Press, 1981), pp. 178–84.

21. For examples of this point, see Masataka Kosaka, "Saishō Yoshida Shigeru ron" (Prime Minister Shigeru Yoshida), *Chūō kōron*, Feb. 1964, pp. 80–85, 105, on Yoshida and the U.S. peace treaty; George W. Packard III, *Protest in Tokyo: The Security Treaty Crisis of 1960* (Princeton: Princeton University Press, 1966), chap. 8, on Kishi and the 1960 security treaty revisions; and D. C. Hellmann, *Japanese Domestic Politics and Foreign Policy: The Peace Agreement with the Soviet Union* (Berkeley: University of California Press, 1969), on Hatoyama and the Soviet peace agreement.

22. For elaboration, see T. J. Pempel, "Japanese Foreign Economic Policy: The Domestic Bases for International Behavior," in Peter J. Katzenstein, ed., *Between Power and Plenty: Foreign Economic Policies of Advanced Industrial States* (Madison: University of Wisconsin Press, 1978), pp. 139–90.

23. Sheldon Wolin, *Politics and Vision* (Boston: Little, Brown & Co., 1960), pp. 210–12.

24. See Fukui, "Review."

25. Johnson's stimulating *MITI* and Ezra Vogel's more popular *Japan as Number One* (Cambridge, Mass.: Harvard University Press, 1979) do address this issue directly, but both fall short in addressing the political component of the postwar elitist democracy.

26. On this point, see Giuseppe Di Palma, *The Study of Conflict in Western Society: A Critique of the End of Ideology* (Los Angeles: General Learners Press, 1973), pp. 9–10.

27. Hugh Patrick and Henry Rosovsky, *Asia's New Giant: How the Japanese Economy Works* (Washington, D.C.: Brookings Institution, 1976), p. 46.

28. This section is based largely on my "Japan and the United States in the 1980s: The Domestication of Foreign Policy" (Paper delivered at the Japan and the Pacific Quadrille: The New Phase conference, Tokyo, June 10–11, 1983).

29. One of the first and most useful discussions of this consensus is found in Gabriel Almond, *The American People and Foreign Policy* (New York: Harcourt Brace, 1950), chap. 8.

30. George F. Kennan, *Realities of American Foreign Policy* (Princeton: Princeton University Press, 1964), p. 29.

31. Marina N. Whitman, "Leadership Without Hegemony," *Foreign Policy*, No. 20 (Fall 1975), pp. 139–40.

32. On this point, see Stephen D. Krasner, *Defending the National Interest* (Princeton: Princeton University Press, 1978), pp. 83ff.

33. Leslie Gelb, "National Security and New Foreign Policy," *Parameters* (Journal of the U.S. Army War College), Nov. 8, 1978, pp. 10–11.

34. See, e.g., James C. Chase, "Is a Foreign Policy Consensus Possible?" *Foreign Affairs*, Vol. 57, No. 1 (Fall 1978); and Stanley Hoffmann, *Primacy of World Order* (New York: McGraw-Hill, 1978), esp. chaps. 3–4.

35. For an anecdotal but largely accurate account of this phenomenon, see Staff of the Asahi Shimbunsha, ed., *The Pacific Rivals* (Tokyo: Weatherhill/Asahi), pp. 293–98.

36. For a concise summary of these events, see I. M. Destler et al., *Managing an Alliance: The Politics of U.S.-Japanese Relations* (Washington, D.C.: Brookings Institution, 1976), pp. 35–45.

37. Robert O. Keohane and Joseph S. Nye, "World Politics and the International Economic System," in C. Fred Bergsten, ed., *The Future of the International Economic Order: An Agenda for Research* (Lexington, Mass.: D. C. Heath, 1973), pp. 122–25.

38. Peter J. Katzenstein, "Domestic and International Forces and Strategies of Foreign Economic Policy," in idem, *Power and Plenty*, pp. 10–11.

39. See, e.g., Morton H. Halperin, *Bureaucratic Politics and Foreign Policy* (Washington, D.C.: Brookings Institution, 1974).

40. C. Fred Bergsten, "What to Do About the U.S.-Japan Economic Conflict," *Foreign Affairs*, Vol. 60, No. 5 (Summer 1982), pp. 1059–76.

41. U.S. Department of State, Bureau of Public Affairs, *Japan and the United States: A Cooperative Relationship*, Current Policy, No. 374 (Washington, D.C., Mar. 1, 1982), p. 4.

42. Allen S. Whiting, "Japanese Public Opinion and Foreign Policy," *Asian Survey*, Vol. 22, No. 11 (Nov. 1982), pp. 1135–45.

43. See, e.g., Johnson, *MITI*; and T. J. Pempel, "Japanese Foreign Economic Policy," pp. 139–40.

44. For example, Johnson (*MITI*, p. 306) describes Japan's Greater East Asian

war as simply a failed effort to rely "on military force to achieve economic security via imperialism."

45. Ibid., p. 315.

46. On this point, see Kenneth B. Pyle, "The Future of Japanese Nationality: An Essay in Contemporary History," *Journal of Japanese Studies*, Vol. 8, No. 2 (Summer 1982), pp. 223–65.

47. See, e.g., Shumpei Kumon, "Japan Faces Its Future: Political Economics of Its Administrative Reform," *Journal of Japanese Studies*, Vol. 10, No. 1 (Winter 1984), pp. 143–66.

48. J. B. Bury, *The Idea of Progress* (New York: Macmillan, 1955), p. xxv.

49. The information cited here regarding Nakasone's political beliefs is taken mainly from Yasuhiro Nakasone, "My Life in Politics," mimeo., trans. Nathaniel Thayer (1981).

Krasner: Prospects for Stability

1. IMF figures and estimates show Japan's aggregate annual growth rate exceeding that of West Germany in every year for the period 1977–86; for the entire decade, Japan grew at an average annual rate that was 2.52 percentage points higher. Japan grew more quickly than the United States in seven out of ten years, and its average annual growth for the whole decade exceeded that of the United States by 1.52 percentage points. Japan's growth has also been more stable than that of the United States and West Germany. Figures derived from IMF, *World Economic Outlook* (1985), p. 205.

2. Figures are available in U.S., Arms Control and Disarmament Agency, *World Military Expenditures and Arms Transfers*, various issues.

3. See, e.g., the classic statement of Richard Cooper, *The Economics of Interdependence* (New York: McGraw-Hill, 1968). See also Robert O. Keohane and Joseph S. Nye, *Power and Interdependence* (Boston: Little, Brown & Co., 1977), especially the concluding chapter. None of these authors is naive about the costs associated with growing interdependence, but all emphasize the powerful independent dynamic of world market forces.

4. See Robert O. Keohane, "The Demand for International Regimes," in Stephen D. Krasner, ed., *International Regimes* (Ithaca, N.Y.: Cornell University Press, 1983), pp. 141–71.

5. David Lake, "International Economic Structures and American Foreign Economic Policy, 1887–1934," *World Politics*, Vol. 35 (July 1983), pp. 517–43.

6. See Michele Schmiegelow, "Cutting Across Doctrines: Positive Adjustment in Japan," *International Organization*, Vol. 39 (Spring 1985), pp. 261–96. See also Daniel Okimoto's discussion of the network encompassing the peak bureaucracies, big business, and the LDP in his paper in this volume.

7. For a discussion of the limited support for traditional nationalism, see Kenneth Pyle's paper in this volume. The Japanese acceptance of hierarchy is discussed in Ruth Benedict, *The Chrysanthemum and the Sword* (Cleveland: World, 1967 [1948]); and Chie Nakane, *Japanese Society* (Berkeley: University of California Press, 1970).

8. The classic presentation of the United States' liberal preoccupation is Louis Hartz, *The Liberal Tradition in America* (New York: Harcourt, Brace, 1955). Judith Goldstein elaborates the relationship between the cognitive lessons of the 1930s and contemporary U.S. policy in "The Impact of Ideas on Trade Policy: A Com-

parative Study of the Origins of U.S. Agricultural and Manufacturing Policies," mimeo. (Stanford University, 1986).

9. Robert Gilpin, *U.S. Power and the Multinational Corporation* (New York: Basic Books, 1975); and Stephen D. Krasner, "State Power and the Structure of International Trade," *World Politics*, Vol. 28 (Apr. 1976), pp. 317–47.

10. Charles Kindleberger, *The World in Depression* (Berkeley: University of California Press, 1973). Bruce Russett makes the point about the possibility of total exclusion in "The Mysterious Case of Vanishing Hegemony: Or, Is Mark Twain Really Dead?" *International Organization*, Vol. 39 (Spring 1985), p. 224.

11. George Modelski, "The Long Cycle of Global Politics and the Nation-State," *Comparative Studies in Society and History*, Vol. 20 (1978), pp. 214–35; Robert Gilpin, *War and Change in World Politics* (Cambridge, Eng.: Cambridge University Press, 1981); and A. F. K. Organski and Jacek Kugler, *The War Ledger* (Chicago: University of Chicago Press, 1981).

12. Charles Doran, "War and Power Dynamics: Economic Underpinnings," *International Studies Quarterly*, Vol. 27 (Dec. 1983), pp. 419–42; and idem, and Wes Parsons, "War and the Cycle of Relative Power," *American Political Science Review*, Vol. 74 (Dec. 1980), p. 983 for quote.

13. Gilpin, *War and Change.*

14. V. I. Lenin, *Imperialism* (New York: International Publishers, 1939; and Robert North and Nazli Choucri, *Nations in Conflict: National Growth and International Violence* (San Francisco: W. H. Freeman, 1975).

15. For a fuller discussion, see Daniel Okimoto, *Between MITI and the Market* (Stanford: Stanford University Press, forthcoming), chap. 4; as well as his paper in this volume.

16. See also I. M. Destler et al., *Managing an Alliance: The Politics of U.S.-Japanese Relations* (Washington, D.C.: Brookings Institution, 1976), pp. 101–8; and Kan Ori, "Political Factors in Postwar Japan's Foreign Policy Decisions," in Morton Kaplan and Kinhide Mushakoji, eds., *Japan, America, and the Future World Order* (New York: Free Press, 1976), p. 155.

17. Hartz, *Liberal Tradition.*

18. Stephen D. Krasner, *Defending the National Interest* (Princeton: Princeton University Press, 1978), chap. 3.

19. Murray Sayle, "Japan Victorious," *New York Review of Books*, Mar. 28, 1985, p. 34. See also Yasusuke Murakami's discussion of the *mura* form of social organization in Volume 1 of this series. Murakami is more skeptical of the contemporary saliency of group as opposed to individual sources of identification than are many other observers.

20. Consider the following two anecdotes. Murray Sayle writes: "In the village outside Tokyo in which I live, there are four gas stations, offering gasoline at four different prices. The one I patronize charges three yen a liter more than the one that happens to be closest to my house. Why don't I switch? Because the proprietor is a friend of mine, but even if he wasn't (and how could he not be, since we have done business for years?) he would still be entitled by social convention to a cash payment in compensation for the loss of my business from my new supplier; and this payment, which would have to be long and carefully negotiated between the two men, would be wholly outside my control." Sayle, "Japan Victorious," p. 36. Or consider the following statement from Warren Cromartie, an American who plays baseball for the Tokyo Yomiuri Giants. "But it's just not the hard baseball we play in the States. It's too predictable. And they

should put more emphasis on winning. They play tie games over here—I still can't get over that." Quoted in the *Peninsula Times Tribune* (Palo Alto, Calif.), June 13, 1985, p. B1. Obviously Sayle has grasped the essence of *wa* ("social harmony") more effectively than Cromartie.

21. Organski and Kugler, *War Ledger*, chap. 3.

22. Doran and Parsons, "War," p. 956.

23. Derived from figures in World Bank, *World Development Report* (1984), pp. 218–21, 223.

24. Russett, "Vanishing Hegemony?" p. 212.

25. All figures derived from information in IMF, *Direction of Trade*, various years.

26. Derived from figures in GATT, *International Trade, 1983/84*, country tables.

27. Investment figures from *Survey of Current Business*, Aug. 1983, p. 23; GNP figures from CIA, "Briefing Book for Conference on Economic Security Implications of Structural Change," Washington, D.C., June 3–4, 1985.

28. *Survey of Current Business*, Aug. 1983, p. 35.

29. Figures from U.S. Arms Control and Disarmament Agency, *World Military Expenditures and Arms Transfers, 1972–1982*.

30. Ibid.

31. David A. Lake, "Political and Cosmopolitical Economy Revisited: Japan and Theories of Trade Policy Revisited," (Paper prepared for National Bureau of Economic Research Conference on the Political Economy of Trade Policy, Dedham, Mass.: MIT Conference Center, Jan. 10–11, 1986).

32. Destler, *Managing an Alliance*, pp. 15–23; Daniel I. Okimoto, "The Economics of National Defense," in idem, ed., *Japan's Economy: Coping with Change in the International Environment* (Boulder, Colo.: Westview Press, 1982), pp. 236–39.

33. Russett, "Vanishing Hegemony?"; see also his paper in this volume.

34. See Robert Packenham, *Liberal America and the Third World* (Princeton: Princeton University Press, 1973), for a discussion of the U.S. doctrines that were applied to Japan as well as to less developed countries.

35. See Vinod Aggarwal, *Liberal Protectionism: The International Politics of Organized Textile Trade* (Berkeley: University of California Press, 1985), for a discussion of developments in the textile industry as well as an analysis of U.S. behavior emphasizing the importance of the fact that the textile industry was "nested" within the larger trade regime.

36. See Hideo Sato and Michael W. Hodin, "The U.S.-Japanese Steel Issue in 1977," and Gilbert R. Winham and Ikuo Kabashima "The Politics of U.S.-Japanese Auto Trade," in I. M. Destler and Hideo Sato, eds., *Coping with U.S.-Japanese Economic Conflicts* (Lexington, Mass.: Lexington Books, 1982).

37. John Ruggie, "Embedded Liberalism," in Krasner, *International Regimes*, pp. 195–231. Ruggie argues that the postwar trading regime has always been based on embedded liberalism. Although this may be true for Western Europe, it is much more questionable for the United States and Japan.

38. This argument is developed in Albert Hirschman's classic *National Power and the Structure of Foreign Trade* (Berkeley: University of California Press, 1945).

39. See Aggarwal, *Liberal Protectionism*.

40. Judith Goldstein's detailed analysis of restrictive measures adopted by the United States reveals that industries are much more likely to be successful in unfair trade practices cases than in escape-clause actions. See Judith Goldstein, "The Political Economy of Trade: Institutions of Protection," *American Political Science Review*, Vol. 80 (1986), pp. 161–84.

41. The phrase is from I. M. Destler et al., *The Textile Wrangle: Conflict in Japanese-American Relations, 1969–1971* (Ithaca, N.Y.: Cornell University Press, 1979).

42. See Robert Keohane, *After Hegemony* (Princeton: Princeton University Press), for a thorough discussion of regimes as instruments for facilitating agreement in non–zero sum situations.

43. Winham and Kabashima, "U.S.-Japanese Auto Trade," p. 95.

44. For instance, Kenneth Pyle reports that during the dispute over automobile quotas, a leading newspaper accused Naohiro Amaya, a councillor to MITI, of being Reagan's concubine (see Pyle's paper in this volume). During the textile dispute of the early 1970s, the national press in Japan argued that Japan should reject U.S. pressure and exercise "autonomous diplomacy." See Destler et al., *Managing an Alliance*, p. 87. Such expressions of frustration from the Japanese side are hardly surprising given the persistent emphasis of U.S. central decision makers on liberal precepts and norms. For a discussion emphasizing the importance of the overall deficit as a cause of frictions in U.S.-Japanese relations, see C. Fred Bergsten, "What to Do About U.S.-Japan Economic Conflict," *Foreign Affairs*, No. 60 (Summer 1982), pp. 1059–75.

45. The company, Ruder and Finn, publishes a regular newsletter for NTT that describes procurement activities. See also Trade Study Group, *Progress Report, 1984*, p. 55.

46. For a general discussion of the Yen-Dollar agreement, see Jeffrey A. Frankel, *The Yen/Dollar Agreement: Liberalizing Japanese Capital Markets* (Washington, D.C.: Institute for International Economics, 1984), esp. pp. 45–47.

47. Destler et al., *Managing an Alliance*, p. 148.

48. The concept of issue-specific structural theory is developed in Keohane and Nye, *Power and Interdependence*, pp. 49–52.

49. Japan's relative military weakness is a function of choice, not necessity. Japan has the basic resources needed to become a major military power. In Japan, domestic political decisions could lead to a dramatic transformation of Japan's external military position. A smaller state would not have such an option.

50. As an advocate of hegemonic stability theory, I should note that there are interpretations of contemporary events that are consistent with its assertions. For instance, one might argue, as Bruce Russett has, that U.S. hegemony has not really declined. See Russett, "Vanishing Hegemony."

Moreover, before putting hegemonic stability theory to rest, we should note that one central element of this theory, indeed the element most heavily emphasized by one of its most prominent progenitors, Charles Kindleberger, relates not to the creation or even the routine maintenance of a liberal regime but rather to outcomes under conditions of crisis. Kindleberger argues that the depression of the 1930s was a result of the failure of any major actor in the system to deal with environmentally generated pressures related to commodity prices and financial management. The current international economic system has weathered some recent crises fairly effectively. Rising and now falling oil prices and Third World debt have not led to systemic collapse, although they have severely impacted specific developing countries. Japan has been largely passive with regard to the global impact of these developments. Its capacity to assume a more effective leadership role, a role that may be thrust on it by the inevitable growth of foreign financial holdings generated by its huge global trade surplus, remains untested. The failure of Japan to exercise a leadership role in the past, as well as certain domestic considerations such as the need for consensus decision making, does not suggest that Japan would be a particularly effective partner in a crisis. For Kindleberger's arguments, see *The World in Depression*.

51. This argument is developed by Judith Goldstein in "A Reexamination of American Trade Policy: An Inquiry into the Causes of Protection" (Ph.D. diss., University of California, Los Angeles, 1983).

52. Susan Strange, "Protectionism and World Politics," *International Organization* Vol. 39 (Spring 1985), pp. 233–60. Although I find Strange's argument persuasive for recent years and adopted a similar position in explaining the outcome of the Tokyo Round of trade negotiations, it is not clear that a web-of-contracts could have developed in the first place without some confidence that liberal rules and norms would prevail—a confidence that could have been provided after World War II only by U.S. political leadership. If actors are to believe that they are in an iterative prisoners' dilemma game, that the shadow of the future is long, they need some assurance that the game will go on. See Stephen D. Krasner, "The Tokyo Round," *International Studies Quarterly*, Vol. 23 (1979), pp. 491–531. Kindleberger's analysis of the Great Depression also places great emphasis on the financial sector as a prime mover of the general collapse.

Morrison: Japan and the ASEAN Countries

1. See the paper by Inoguchi in this volume.

2. Akio Watanabe, "The United States, Japan, and the Asia/Pacific: A Japanese Perspective with Particular Reference to the Pacific Cooperation Concept" (Paper prepared for the Georgetown University Center for Strategic and International Studies, Mar. 1985, p. 10).

3. Japan, Ministry of Foreign Affairs, *Diplomatic Bluebook, 1981 Edition: Review of Recent Developments in Japan's Foreign Relations* (Tokyo: Foreign Press Center/Japan, n.d.), p. 23. Other Japanese statements make it clear that "autonomous" positions are closely linked with those of the United States and other Western democracies.

4. Nakasone, speech at the Diet session of Jan. 25, 1985; translation of Tokyo NHK television and broadcast by Foreign Broadcast Information Service, *Daily Report: Asia and Pacific* (hereafter FBIS), Vol. 4, no. 020 (Jan. 30, 1985).

5. In 1979, 78 per cent of Japan's crude oil imports, 41 per cent of its iron ore imports, 35 per cent of its steel exports, 63 per cent of its cement exports, and 38 per cent of its automobile exports passed through the Strait of Malacca.

6. Michael Leifer, *Conflict and Regional Order in South-east Asia*, Adelphi Papers No. 162 (London: International Institute for Strategic Studies, 1980), p. 18.

7. Lee quoted in Chin Kin Wah, "Singapore: Perceptions of Japan" (Unpublished paper, 1984). As early as 1973, envisioning the final collapse of the U.S. position in Vietnam, Lee advocated a joint U.S.-Japanese naval arrangement, noting that a Japanese task force "may at present be received with reservations in some countries in Southeast Asia." *Far Eastern Economic Review*, Aug. 13, 1973, referenced in Charles E. Morrison and Astri Suhrke, *Strategies of Survival: The Foreign Policy Dilemmas of Smaller Asian States* (St. Lucia: University of Queensland Press, 1978), p. 324. See also Franklin B. Weinstein, "Japan and ASEAN," in Karl D. Jackson and M. Hadi Soesastro, eds., *ASEAN Security and Economic Development*, Research Papers and Policy Studies, no. 11 (Berkeley: University of California, Institute of East Asian Studies, 1984), pp. 172–73.

8. Boonchu Rojanasathien, in a keynote address to the First Japan-Thai Symposium (Tokyo, Dec. 1979), said: "ASEAN now has no leadership by any one big

country. We know, for example, that COMECON is led by the Soviet Union, and the Western democracies are led by the United States. It is around great powers that other smaller countries rally. In this case, I would suggest that Japan has to fill the role of leader in the ASEAN region." *Japan and Thailand: New Dimensions of Dialogue,* JCIE Papers (Tokyo, 1981), pp. 6–7.

9. Ali Moertopo, "L'Indonesie et la coopération regionale et internationale," *Politique étrangère,* Vol. 38, No. 4 (1973), pp. 474–76. See also his "Peace and Security in Asia and the Pacific," in Centre for Strategic and International Studies (Jakarta), *Japan-Indonesia Relations in the Context of Regionalism in Asia* (Jakarta, 1977), pp. 10–21; and Michael Liefer, "Ali Moertopo: Regional Visionary and Regional Pragmatist," in *Sekar Semerbak: Kenangan untuk Ali Moertopo* (Reminiscences of Ali Moertopo) (Jakarta: Yayasan Proklamasi, 1985), pp. 67–76.

10. Projections made by the Council for Economic Research on the Pacific Region in the 21st Century, an advisory body to the Economic Planning Agency's Planning Bureau. See *Japan Economic Journal,* Oct. 19, 1985, p. 12.

11. See discussion in Franklin B. Weinstein, *Indonesian Foreign Policy and the Dilemma of Dependence from Sukarno to Soeharto* (Ithaca, N.Y.: Cornell University Press, 1976), pp. 262–64.

12. For elaboration on ASEAN's significance as a source of political security, see Charles E. Morrison and Astri Suhrke, "ASEAN in Regional Defense and Development," in Sundershan Chawla and D. R. Sardesai, eds., *Changing Patterns of Security and Stability in Asia* (New York: Praeger, 1980), pp. 192–214.

13. On Japan's resource-intensive development and the effect of the oil embargo, see Nobutoshi Akao, ed., *Japan's Economic Security* (New York: St. Martin's Press, 1983).

14. According to Masahide Shibusawa, the 1972–73 student demonstrations in Thailand "made Japan realize, for the first time, the enormous size and scope of its economic presence in Southeast Asia as well as the political responsibilities of carrying on such extensive activities in other countries." *Japan and the Asian Pacific Region* (London: Croom Helm, 1984), p. 75.

15. Watanabe, "United States, Japan," p. 14.

16. *Straits Times,* Feb. 26, 1977.

17. *New Straits Times,* Jan. 1, 1977.

18. Ibid., Jan. 5, 1977. For a detailed treatment of the Foreign Ministry reappraisal of Japan's ASEAN policy leading up to the Fukuda Doctrine, see Sueo Sudo, "Nanshin, Superdomino, and the Fukuda Doctrine: Stages in Japan-Southeast Relations," *Journal of Northeast Asian Studies,* Vol. 5, No. 3 (Fall 1986), pp. 40–42.

19. According to one senior Foreign Ministry official, the significance of the Fukuda Doctrine lay in the introduction of "a political dimension in Japan's foreign policy in general and her policy toward Southeast Asia in particular." Rarely had an active political interest been expressed in Japan's diplomacy before, which had concentrated primarily on the "normalization" of relations with foreign countries. Koji Watanabe, "Japan and Southeast Asia: 1980," *Asia-Pacific Community,* Spring 1980, pp. 89–90.

20. *Straits Times,* Dec. 13, 1977.

21. Tokyo JOAK Television, Aug. 22, 1977, cited in FBIS, Aug. 24, 1977.

22. *Straits Times,* June 20, 1978.

23. Renato Constantino, *The Second Invasion: Japan in the Philippines.* (Manila: The author, 1979), p. 21.

24. Akio Yamakawa, "From ASEAN to JASEAN," *Japan-Asia Quarterly Review,*

Vol. 9, No. 3 (1977), pp. 5, 7. According to an Aug. 9, 1977, commentary by *Akahata*, organ of the Japan Communist Party, "The real intention of the Japanese government is to expand Japan's influence in the ASEAN region, while increasing economic aid in place of the United States within a framework of reorganizing U.S. policy toward Asia."

25. See discussion in M. Rajendran, *ASEAN's Foreign Relations: The Shift to Collective Action* (Kuala Lumpur: Arenabuku Sdn. Bhd., 1985), pp. 109–10.

26. *Japan Times*, Nov. 3, 1985.

27. In addition to the ASEAN dialogue meetings ("six plus five" or "six plus six"), there have also been four meetings between 1980 and 1985 of the Pacific Economic Cooperation Conference (PECC), attended by academics, businessmen, and government officials in their personal capacities. Although these meetings owed their genesis to an Australian-Japanese joint communiqué at the time of Prime Minister Ohira's Jan. 1980 visit to Australia, the Japanese role has been inhibited by a number of constraints, including secure funding.

28. In Nov. 1971, the then five ASEAN governments called for the creation of a Zone of Peace, Freedom, and Neutrality [ZOPFAN] in Southeast Asia. This proposal, which remains a foreign policy aspiration of the group even though it is not actively pursued, foresees the eventual elimination of foreign military presence in the region. It is clear that in the meantime, the presence of U.S. bases in the Philippines and the Seventh Fleet continue to be valued by the ASEAN governments. Moreover, the ASEAN governments, like the Japanese government, were opposed to reducing U.S. ground forces in South Korea in the late 1970s.

29. Despite currently good Sino-Thai relations, there is considerable mistrust of China in the long term in Thailand just as there is in other Southeast Asia countries. A comprehensive survey dating from the mid-1970s found that 37 per cent of Thais thought China to be aggressive compared with 3 per cent who thought the same of Japan. China, in fact, was the most feared country, outranking Vietnam at 29 per cent and the Soviet Union at 24 per cent. A sampling of 128 members of the Thai elite, however, found that 46 per cent regarded Vietnam as aggressive, 33 per cent the Soviet Union, 13 per cent China, and only 6 per cent Japan. These results reflected Thai awareness of Japan's defense constraints and low defense spending. It could be argued that a credible Japanese commitment to the military security of Thailand would require power projection capabilities, whereas China's commitments do not, and in this sense China is the more acceptable alliance power for Thailand and other ASEAN countries. For survey results, see Khien Theeravit et al., *Japan in Thai Perspective*, Asian Studies Monograph No. 026 (Bangkok: Chulalongkorn University, Institute of Asian Studies, Jan. 1980), p. 67.

30. Comprehensive National Security Study Group, *Report on Comprehensive National Security* (trans.), July 2, 1980, referred to "traditionally contentious relations" among Vietnam, Cambodia, and Thailand and called for Japan "to perform a political role for the stabilization of these areas." It noted that ASEAN contributes to the stability of Southeast Asia (p. 29).

31. For example, "Japan's imports from ASEAN countries are increasing dramatically, with imports of manufactured products also expanding smoothly." *ASEAN and Japan: Partners for Prosperity*, p. 7. (This was a public relations booklet distributed by the Foreign Ministry on the occasion of Prime Minister Suzuki's 1981 trip to the ASEAN region.)

32. See, e.g., Donald C. Hellmann, *Japan in the Postwar East Asian International*

System (McLean, Va.: Research Analysis Corporation, 1969), pp. 23–25; and Weinstein, "Japan and ASEAN," pp. 167–68.

33. These figures exclude Brunei, which joined ASEAN in 1984. Japan's deficits with Brunei were $2.5 billion in 1982 and $2.3 billion in 1983.

34. According to The Ministry of International Trade and Industry's white papers on international trade, China's exports of crude and refined oils to Japan increased from 7.7 million kiloliters in 1977 to 10.3 million in 1981 to 10.8 million in 1983.

35. Lawrence B. Krause notes that in the 1970s the United States' structure of exports was better positioned than Japan's to benefit from the changing structure of ASEAN import demand. Japan's share of ASEAN imports declined from 24.5 per cent in 1970 to 20.6 per cent in 1979. *U.S. Economic Policy Toward the Association of Southeast Asian Nations: Meeting the Japanese Challenge* (Washington: Brookings Institution, 1982), pp. 36, 47.

36. Report of the Advisory Committee for External Economic Issues to the Government of Japan (provisional trans.), Apr. 9, 1985, p. 24.

37. Japanese tariff cuts announced on June 25, 1985, affected some 1,860 products, including 37 agricultural products of importance to ASEAN such as boned chicken, palm oil, and, seasonally, on bananas. Japan's tariff on boned chicken is 18 per cent compared with 11.3 per cent for chicken with bones. The former will be reduced to 14 per cent, the latter to 10 per cent, with parity being achieved in three years. (Thailand's tariff on chickens is 60 per cent.) Such issues, however, are largely symbolic; Thai deputy prime minister Bhichai Rattakul called the Japanese tariff concession "only a drop in the ocean." *Bangkok Post*, June 26, 1985.

38. "Forest Products Trade: A Case Study of Japan," in Korea Development Institute, *Issues and Opportunities for Pacific Economic Cooperation: Task Force Reports to the Pacific Economic Cooperation Conference IV* (Seoul: KDI Press, 1985), pp. 98–99.

39. See Teruyaki Iwasaki, "Industrial Cooperation: A Case Study of the Asahan Project" (Unpublished paper prepared for the Asian Dialogue conference, June 29–July 1, 1984).

40. Hal Hill and Brian Johns, "The Role of Direct Foreign Investment in Developing East Asian Countries" (Unpublished paper, Aug. 1984, p. 9). The United States, Western European countries, and Japan record foreign investment statistics in different ways, making comparisons difficult.

41. See Sueo Sekiguchi, ed., *ASEAN-Japan Relations: Investment* (Singapore: Institute of Southeast Asian Studies, 1983), pp. 230–37.

42. Ibid., pp. 15–16.

43. J. Panglaykim, "ASEAN and Japan: Direct Foreign Investment and Trade," in Jackson and Hadi Soesastro, *ASEAN Security*, p. 193. See also the same author's *Japanese Direct Investment in ASEAN: The Indonesian Experience* (Singapore: Maruzen Asia, 1983). Hill and Johns, "Role of Direct Foreign Investment," however, find that intrafirm trade has accounted for as much as a third of Japanese imports of manufactures from Asian developing countries and suggest that much of the investment is occurring in labor-intensive industries where Japanese domestic comparative advantage is eroding.

44. Riga Adiwoso-Suprapto, "An Exploratory Study on Indonesians' Perceptions on Japan and Japan-Indonesian Relations" (Paper delivered at the Asian Dialogue conference, June 1984). Adiwoso-Suprapto distributed questionnaires to Indonesian employees at 200 joint ventures and followed up with selected interviews. She found that employees frequently evaluated Japanese more favor-

ably in relation to other countries' nationals than did university students but that there appeared to be resentment over unequal treatment of Indonesian employees. A Thai survey of 309 employees in 53 Thai-Japanese joint ventures found that 4 per cent thought they had very good relations with Japanese experts in their companies, 33 per cent had good relations, 45 per cent normal relations, and only 6 per cent bad relations. When asked what their suggestions would be to Japanese managerial staff for improving relations, the largest share (29 per cent) urged management "to respect Thai people's capability." Banyat Surakanvit, *Thai People's Attitude Towards Japan*, Monograph No. 3 (Bangkok: Thammasat University, Japanese Studies Center, Dec. 1983), pp. 4–5.

45. Khien, et al., *Japan*, pp. 51–54, 71–73.

46. Thomas Andersson and Jan Rudengren, *External Capital Flows: The Case of Five ASEAN Countries*, Report (n.p.: Ekonomiska Forskningsinstitutet, Apr. 1984), pp. 38–39. See Hill and Johns, "Role of Direct Foreign Investment," table 1.

47. Mingsarn Santikarn has estimated that of the total number of technology agreements, those with Japan accounted for 36 per cent of Thailand's in 1980–81, 32 per cent of Malaysia's for years not specified, and 21 per cent of the Philippines' in 1978–79. Cited in Hal Hill and Brian Johns, "The Transfer of Industrial Technology to Western Pacific Developing Countries" (Paper delivered at the PECC Task Force Workshop on Foreign Investment and Technology Transfer, Oct. 9–10, 1984).

48. See, for example, Jonathan P. Stern, "Natural Gas: The Perfect Answer to Energy Diversification," in Akao, *Japan's Economic Security*, pp. 107–8.

49. Sekiguchi, *ASEAN-Japan Relations*, pp. 19–21.

50. Weinstein, "Japan and ASEAN," pp. 174–76.

51. J. Alexander Caldwell, "The Evolution of Japanese Economic Cooperation: 1950–1970," in Harold B. Malmgren, ed., *Pacific Basin Development: The American Interests* (Lexington, Mass.: Lexington Books, 1972), p. 27. Sirichai Sirikrai notes these interests remain the same. *Japan-ASEAN Relations: The Pacific Basin Cooperation*, Monograph No. 3 (Bangkok: Thammasat University, Faculty of Political Science, Research Center, 1982), p. 45.

52. Alan Rix, *Japan's Economic Aid* (New York: St. Martin's Press, 1980), p. 25.

53. Ibid., p. 222.

54. Snoh Unakul and Narongchai Akrasanee, "Structural Adjustment in Thai-Japanese Economic Relations" (Unpublished paper, Dec. 1984). The main thrust of this paper, however, is directed toward macroeconomic policy adjustments the authors believe Thailand must make in order to strengthen its balance-of-payments position.

55. Adiwoso-Suprapto, "Exploratory Study."

56. Wilifrido V. Villacorta, "Japanese Presence in the Philippines: Filipino Responses" (Unpublished paper delivered at the Asian Dialogue conference, June 1984), p. 20.

57. *Japan Times*, Sept. 27, 1985.

58. Interview on Tokyo JOAK Television, Aug. 22, 1977.

59. Cited in Villacorta, "Japanese Presence," p. 16.

60. Khien et al., *Japan*, p. 65.

61. Adiwoso-Suprapto, "Exploratory Study."

62. Japan, Ministry of Foreign Affairs, *Japan and ASEAN—Comparative Data* (Tokyo, Apr. 1983).

63. Cited in Susumu Yamakage, "Japan and ASEAN: Are They Really Becom-

ing Closer?" in Werner Pfennig and Mark M. B. Suh, eds., *Aspects of ASEAN* (Munich: Weltforum Verlag, 1984), p. 301.

64. *Japan Times*, Sept. 30, 1985.

65. There has been almost no systematic analysis of how Japanese tourism or the increase in overseas Japanese communities has affected Japan-ASEAN relations or crosscultural perceptions. Anecdotal evidence often suggests that Japanese are "clannish" and that Japanese children of overseas businessmen have little contact with the local population. Organizations in both Japan and Southeast Asia have strongly criticized "sex tours" to countries such as Thailand and the Philippines. Again, there is almost no information on how this is perceived by those societies at large. One study in 1983 of 109 Thai women who work in Japanese-style nightclubs and *karaoke* bars in Bangkok generally indicated positive answers toward questions relating to the honesty, trustworthiness, and generosity of Japanese patrons. More (29 per cent) found Japanese "polite and humble" than thought they were "arrogant" (11 per cent). About 30 per cent thought they took advantage of Thai girls to some extent, but a plurality (36 per cent) did not. More Thai hostesses (32 per cent) thought more Japanese looked down on Thai people than not (27 per cent), a finding consistent with other attitudinal surveys in the ASEAN region. Banyat Surakanvit, *Thai People's Attitude*.

66. Chin Kin Wah, "Singapore."

67. Soemitro, "Peranan Indonesia di Kawasan Asia dan Pasifik" (The role of Indonesia in the Asia-Pacific region), in *Sekar Semerbak*, p. 183.

68. Juwono Sudarsono, "Stabilitas Politik dan Ekonomi Asia Tenggara" (Political and economic stability in Southeast Asia), *Prisma*, Vol. 14, No. 1 (1985), pp. 61–64.

69. China, or Northeast Asia more generally, might provide an alternative international association. Southeast Asians, except for the overseas Chinese, are not really a part of this world, however. Japanese attention to China is jealously regarded in ASEAN. Apprehensions are usually expressed in terms of potential losses of investment funds, trade opportunities, and foreign assistance that might otherwise go to ASEAN or in terms of a longer-term security threat from a more modernized China. In a more basic sense, ASEAN fears are that Japanese aid may be going to support rather than attract an alternative civilization that would have a disruptive effect on ASEAN social organization.

Pyle: Japan and the Twenty-first Century

1. R. P. Dore, *British Factory—Japanese Factory: The Origins of National Diversity in Industrial Relations* (Berkeley: University of California Press, 1973), p. 413.

2. See my "Advantages of Followership: German Economics and Japanese Bureaucrats, 1890–1925," *Journal of Japanese Studies*, Vol. 1, No. 1 (1974), pp. 127–64; and "The Technology of Japanese Nationalism: The Local Improvement Movement, 1900–1918," *Journal of Asian Studies*, Vol. 33 (1973), pp. 51–65.

3. Hideo Miyashita, "The Information Society: What Will It Bring?" *Journal of Japanese Trade and Industry*, No. 2 (1982), p. 32.

4. Keizai no Kōzō Henka to Seisaku no Kenkyūkai, "Sofutonomikusu no teishō" (Softnomics), mimeo. (Tokyo, 1983).

5. *Japan Times*, Feb. 7, 1984.

6. *Washington Post* (weekly edition), Apr. 30, 1984.

7. *Look Japan*, Aug. 10, 1983.

8. *Japan Times*, Jan. 10, 1984.

9. Ibid.

10. Ibid.

11. Yōnosuke Nagai, "Moratoriamu kokka no bōei ron" (The defense of a moratorium country), *Chūō kōron*, Jan. 1981.

12. Sōgō Anzen Hoshō Kenkyū Gurupu, *Sōgō anzen hoshō senryaku* (A strategy for comprehensive national security) (Tokyo: Ministry of Finance, 1980), p. 22. Members of the group included Masataka Kosaka, Tsuneo Iida, Jun Eto, Masamori Sase, Seizaburo Sato, and Shoichi Watanabe.

13. Masanori Moritani, *Japanese Technology* (Tokyo: Simul Press, 1982), pp. 215, 218.

14. Naohiro Amaya, "Japan azu numba tsu" (Japan as number two), *Voice*, May 1984.

15. For a recounting of this incident, see Kumon Shumpei, "Administrative Reform Requires New National Goals," *Economic Eye*, Vol. 3, No. 3 (1982), pp. 4–7.

16. Hisahiko Okazaki, "Amerika wa tayori ni naru ka?" (Can the United States be relied on?), *Voice*, July 1979. See translation in *Japan Echo*, Vol. 6, No. 3 (1979), pp. 32–40.

17. Henry Kissinger, *The White House Years* (Boston: Little, Brown & Co., 1979), p. 324.

18. *Bungei shunjū*, Aug. 1984.

19. J. W. Dower, *Empire and Aftermath: Yoshida Shigeru and the Japanese, 1878–1954* (Cambridge, Mass.: Harvard University Press, 1979), p. 312.

20. Yōnosuke Nagai, "U.S.-Japan Relations in the Global Context" (Unpublished paper, 1983).

21. Dower, *Empire and Aftermath*, p. 383; Chihiro Hosoya, "Japan's Response to U.S. Policy on the Japanese Peace Treaty: The Dulles-Yoshida Talks of January-February 1951," *Hitotsubashi Journal of Law and Politics*, Vol. 10 (1981), p. 18.

22. Takeshi Igarashi, "Sengo Nihon 'gaikō jōsei' no keisei" (The formation of foreign affairs in postwar Japan), *Kokka gakkai zasshi*, No. 5–8 (1984), p. 486.

23. Hosoya, "Japan's Response," pp. 21–22.

24. Dower, *Empire and Aftermath*, p. 315.

25. Ibid., pp. 365, 372.

26. Takafusa Nakamura, *The Postwar Japanese Economy: Its Economy, Its Development and Structure* (Tokyo: University of Tokyo, 1981), pp. 80–81.

27. Daniel Iwao Okimoto, "Ideas, Intellectuals, and Institutions: National Security and the Question of Nuclear Armament in Japan" (Ph.D. diss., University of Michigan, 1978), p. 27; and Masamichi Inoki, "Nihon no anzen hoshō ni tsuite" (Japanese security), *Shokun*, May 1976; see translation in *Japan Echo*, Vol. 3, No. 3 (1976), pp. 51–63.

28. Kiichi Miyazawa, quoted in Soichiro Tawara, "Soren wa kowai desu ka?" (Should we fear the USSR?), *Bungei shunjū*, Mar. 1980.

29. Dower, *Empire and Aftermath*, p. 364.

30. Ibid., p. 382.

31. Ibid., p. 371.

32. Shigeto Tsuru, "Whither Japan? A Positive Program of Nation-Building in an Age of Uncertainty," *Japan Quarterly*, Vol. 27 (1980), pp. 487–98.

33. Yoshikazu Sakamoto, "Japan's Role in World Politics," *Japan Quarterly*, Vol. 27 (1980), pp. 166–73.

34. Ryūtarō Komiya, "Ureubeki migi senkai" (The worrisome turn to the right), *Gendai keizai*, Vol. 6 (Spring 1979), pp. 71–84.

35. Kazuo Ijiri, "Chishikijin to 99-hiki no mayoeru hitsujitachi" (99 lost sheep-intellectuals), *Voice*, July 1979; see translation in *Japan Echo*, Vol. 6, No. 3 (1979), pp. 85–92.

36. Takashi Inoguchi and Ikuo Kabashimo, "Genjō kōtei no hensa chi sedai" (The status quo student elite), *Chūō kōron*, Dec. 1983; see translation in *Japan Echo*, Vol. 11, No. 1 (1984), pp. 27–34.

37. Hideo Matsuoka, "'Nori-okure' gaikō no susume" ("Missing the boat" diplomacy), *Chūō kōron*, Mar. 1980.

38. Masataka Kosaka, "Japan as a Maritime Nation," *Journal of Social and Political Ideas in Japan*, Vol. 3, No. 2 (1965), pp. 49–65.

39. Masataka Kosaka, "The Quest for Credibility," *Look Japan*, Sept. 10, 1981.

40. Masataka Kōsaka, *Bunmei ga suibō suru toki* (A time of cultural decline) (Tokyo: Shinchōsha, 1981), p. 268.

41. Masataka Kōsaka, "Tsūshō kokka Nihon no unmei" (The fate of Japan as a merchant state), *Chūō kōron*, Nov. 1975.

42. Naohiro Amaya, "'Chōnin koku Nihon' tedai no kurigoto" (The complaints of a salesclerk about "Japan as a Merchant Nation"), *Bungei shunjū*, Mar. 1980; for a partial translation of this essay, see *Japan Echo*, Vol. 7, No. 2 (1980), pp. 53–62. See also idem, "Nichi-Bei jidōsha mondai to chōnin kokka" (The U.S.-Japan automobile problem and merchant states), *Bungei shunjū*, June 1980; and idem, "Sōpu nashonarizumu o haisu" (Soap nationalism), *Bungei shunjū*, July 1981.

43. Nobuhiko Ushiba, "Nihon wa gensoku o mote" (Japan should hold principles), *Ekonomisuto*, Jan. 29, 1980.

44. Ken'ichi Itō, *Amerika wa yomigaeru ka?* (Can the United States be restored?) (Tokyo: Gōdō Shuppansha, 1980), pp. 322–23.

45. Hiroshi Ōta, "1980 nendai no Nihon gaikō" (Japanese diplomacy in the 1980s), *Gaikō jihō*, Feb. 1980, pp. 5–14.

46. Masamori Sase, "'Chōnin kokka' ron o haisu" (The theory of [Japan as a] merchant state), *Bungei shunjū*, Apr. 1980.

47. Masanori Moritani, "A Technological Strategy for Import Expansion," *Economic Eye*, Vol. 3, No. 2 (June 1982), pp. 27–31.

48. Yōnosuke Nagai, *Gendai to senryaku* (Strategy in the modern world) (Tokyo: Bungei Shunjūsha, 1985), p. 67.

49. Sōgō Anzen Hoshō Kenkyū Gurupu, *Sōgō anzen*, pp. 22, 23, 49.

50. Tawara, "Soren."

51. Masamori Sase, "Nihon gaikō no tokushūsei o tsuku" (The characteristics of Japanese diplomacy), *Voice*, July 1981.

52. Hisahiko Okazaki, "Japanese Security Policy: A Time for Strategy," *International Security*, Vol. 7, No. 2 (1982), p. 191.

53. *Washington Post*, Jan. 19, 1983; see also Don Oberdorfer, "How Nakasone Lost Control of His 'Carrier,'" reprinted in *Japan Times*, Mar. 23, 1983.

54. Seizaburō Satō, "Kempō rongi e no gimon" (Some doubts on the constitutional debate), *Voice*, Apr. 1981; see translation in *Japan Echo*, Vol. 8, No. 2 (1981), pp. 94–103.

55. Nagai, "Moratoriamu kokka."

56. See Mike M. Mochizuki, "Japan's Search for Strategy," *International Security*, Vol. 8, No. 3 (1983), pp. 152–79; Nagai, *Gendai to senryaku*.

57. The 1984 edition of Okazaki's *Kokka to jōhō* (The state and intelligence) (Tokyo: Bungei Shunjūsha) contains an essay criticizing Nagai's moratorium-state thesis.

58. In an interesting exchange in their debate, Nagai insisted that just as Marx might today not be a Marxist, so it did not matter whether Yoshida was conscious of authoring a strategic doctrine:

Nagai: "I call this [grand strategy] the 'Yoshida Doctrine.' Mr. Pyle of the University of Washington also uses the same term."

Okazaki: "Yes, but Mr. Pyle clearly states in his writing that Yoshida himself declared that there was no such thing."

Nagai: "That makes no difference. . . . What Yoshida Shigeru really thought has absolutely no relation to the 'Yoshida Doctrine.'"

59. Ikutarō Shimizu, *Nippon yo, kokka tare: Kaku no sentaku* (Japan, become a state) (Tokyo: Bungei Shunjūsha, 1980), pp. 65–66.

60. Tsuneo Iida, *Nihonteki chikarazuyosa no saihakken* (The rediscovery of Japanese strengths) (Tokyo: Nihon Keizai Shimbunsha, 1979), p. 206.

61. Jun Etō, *1946 nen kempō: Sono kosoku* (The 1946 constitution: Its constraints) (Tokyo: Bungei Shunjūsha, 1980), p. 92.

62. Jun Etō, "'Yoshida seiji' o minaosu" (A reexamination of the Yoshida administration), *Seiron*, Sept. 1983.

63. Etō, *1946 nen kempō*, p. 100.

64. Kichitarō Katsuda, *Heiwa kempo o utagau* (Doubts about the Peace Constitution) (Tokyo: Kōdansha, 1981), p. 149.

65. Ibid., p. 143.

66. *Chūō kōron*, Dec. 1963; the translation is from *Journal of Social and Political Ideas in Japan*, Vol. 2, No. 2 (Aug. 1964), p. 38.

67. Ikutarō Shimizu, *Sengo o utagau* (Doubts about the postwar period) (Tokyo: Kōdansha, 1980).

68. Ibid., chap. 1.

69. See, e.g., Ikutarō Shimizu, "Shomin" (The masses), *Tembō*, Jan. 1950.

70. Ikutarō Shimizu, "Nihonjin" (The Japanese), *Chūō koron*, Jan. 1951.

71. See the essay on postwar thought by Sannosuke Matsumoto in his *Kindai Nihon no chiteki jōkyō* (Thought in contemporary Japan) (Tokyo: Chūō Kōronsha, 1974), pp. 188–243.

72. Shimizu, *Nippon yo*, p. 86.

73. Ibid., p. 91.

74. Ibid., p. 83.

75. Ibid., p. 89.

76. Masamichi Inoki, "Kūsōteki heiwa shugi kara kūsōteki gunkoku shugi e" (From the utopian Peace Constitution to utopian militarism), *Chūō kōron*, Sept. 1980; see translation in *Japan Echo*, Vol. 7, No. 4 (1980), pp. 87–98.

77. Yatsuhiro Nakagawa, *Chōsenshin koku Nippon* (Japan, an ultra-advanced country) (Tokyo: Kōdansha, 1980).

78. Yatsuhiro Nakagawa, "Nippon koso sekai-ichi no fukushi chōdaikoka da" (Japan, the welfare superpower), *Chūō kōron*, Aug. 1978; see translation in *Journal of Japanese Studies*, Vol. 5, No. 1 (1979), pp. 5–51.

79. See Kenneth B. Pyle, *The New Generation in Meiji Japan: Problems of Cultural Identity* (Stanford: Stanford University Press, 1969), pp. 190–91.

80. Iida, *Nihonteki chikarazuyosa*, p. 2.

81. Ibid., p. 32.

82. Ibid.

83. Hiroshi Takeuchi, "Nihonjin to gijutsu, ima mukashi" (The Japanese and technology, yesterday and today), *Ekonomisuto*, Apr. 10, 1981; see translation in *Japan Echo*, Vol. 10, special issue (1983).

84. Naohiro Amaya, "Dokkinhō kaisei shian ni hanron suru" (A response to the proposed revision of the Monopoly Law), *Ekonomisuto*, Nov. 19, 1974.

85. Moritani, *Japanese Technology*, p. 119. Moritani's *Kokusai hikaku: Nippon no gijutsuryoku* (The strength of Japanese technology: An international comparison) (Tokyo: Shodensha, 1980) and *Gijutsu kyōkoku: Nippon no senryaku* (A technological superpower: Japan's strategy) (Tokyo: PHP, 1981) were the basis for *Japanese Technology*.

86. Bunka Jidai no Keizai Un'ei Kenkyū Gurupu, *Hokokusho* (Report) (Tokyo, 1980), p. 72.

87. Moritani, *Japanese Technology*, p. 210.

88. Yujirō Eguchi, "Taiheiyō jidai no tōrai to Nihon no yakuwari" (The advent of the Pacific age and Japan's role), *Ekonomisuto*, Oct. 23, 1984; see translation in *Japan Echo*, Vol. 12, No. 1 (1985), pp. 9–14.

89. Ibid.

Index of Names

General Index

Action Program, 38
Administrative guidance system, 183–84, 279, 318, 339, 389. *See also* *specific ministries*
Afghanistan, 39, 56, 423
Agriculture sector, 54; EEC policy, 139; protectionism and, 181, 211, 306, 335, 407; GATT Tokyo Round and, 204; Japanese trade policy on, 206; Japanese subsidies for, 231; LDP and, 327f
Aluminum industry, 434
Amakudari, 319–21, 351
American Telephone and Telegraph Company (AT&T), 166
Anti-trust laws, 247, 339, 484
Armaments, 454ff. *See also* Nuclear armaments
Asahi shimbun, 459f
ASEAN, *see* Association of Southeast Asian Nations
Asian and Pacific Council (ASPAC), 420, 445
Asian Development Bank, 26, 420
Assets, Japanese foreign, *see* Direct foreign investment
Association of Southeast Asian Nations (ASEAN), 414–17; Japanese trade with, 415, 428–36; United States and, 417–18, 431ff, 436; China and, 419, 426, 430; Japanese national security and, 421, 425–26; Japanese culture and, 441–43. *See also* *specific countries*

Australia, 178, 232
Austria, 178, 232
Automobile industry, 2f, 148ff, 291; Japanese domestic demand and, 52; Japanese import quotas and, 191; VERs and, 203, 465; labor unions and, 291, 342; U.S. direct foreign investment and, 383, 395, 405–6

Balance-of-payments (1970–86), 112, 121, 188. *See also* Current account
Banks, 26–27; Eurodollar market and, 189; government bonds and, 251; foreign securities and, 257; segmentation of, 263, 269; Japanese subsidiaries, 408. *See also* Capital markets; *specific banks*
Bank of America, 27
Bank of Japan, 114, 119, 123, 251
Bank of Tokyo, 27, 262ff
Belgium, 178
Biotechnology, 201, 336
Bond markets, 33; Eurobonds, 25, 27; government bonds, 36, 50–51, 251; interest rates on, 125; regulations, 259, 268; Euroyen, 262; taxes and, 263. *See also* Capital markets
Bonn summit, 206
Brazil, 117, 145, 151
Bretton Woods system, 12, 108, 111–15, 133, 347
Brookings Institution, 366
Brunei, 414
Bungei shunjū, 453, 480

Israel, 55, 59
Italy, 34, 113, 154, 178, 287, 386

Jamaica, 115
Japan Airlines, 476
Japan Committee for Economic Development, 293
Japan Communist Party, 287, 317
Japan Confederation of Labor, *see* Dōmei
Japan Development Bank, 177
Japanese Red Army, 476
Japan Export-Import Bank, 315
Japan External Trade Research Organization (JETRO), 315
Japan Federation of Employers Associations (Nikkeiren), 289f, 297
Japan Foundation, 442
"Japan, Inc.," 154, 307, 373, 531
Japan National Railways, 293
Japan Productivity Center, 293
Japan Socialist Party (JSP), 286–90 *passim*, 317, 325–26, 440, 460

Kampuchea, Cambodia, 55, 418, 423
Kansai region, 196
Keidanren (Federation of Economic Organizations), 334f, 351, 433
Keirutsu organizations, 340f
Kellogg-Briand Pact, 70
Kennedy Round, GATT, 139f, 180–81
Keynesian management, 50f, 150
Kōmeitō (Clean Government Party), 317, 325f, 370
Korean War, 29, 98, 179. *See also* South Korea
Kuala Lumpur summit, 422, 441

Labor unions, 3, 284–94, 290–94; U.S. occupation and, 30, 101; protectionism and, 148, 342, 366–67; General Council of Japanese Labor Unions, 287, 290, 293, 299, 317, 326; political opposition, 287, 296, 325–26, 370; LDP and, 288, 317; Nikkeiren and, 289f; trade liberalization and, 299; NICs and, 342. *See also specific unions*
Latecomer effects, 28f
Latin America, 94
League of Nations, 70
Least developed countries (LDCs),

2, 38–39, 91, 98. *See also specific countries*
Lebanon, 55
Liberal Democratic Party (LDP), 307, 325–31, 386–87, 472; military establishment and, 43, 372; support coalition for, 52–55, 284, 316–34 *passim*; taxes and, 57; protectionism and, 210; labor unions and, 287–88; wages and, 297; family ties and, 351; foreign policy and, 376, 401, 433; agriculture and, 407–8; students and, 461
Liberalism, 161–69 *passim*, 369–71, 377, 383
Liberalization, of trade, 181–82, 192, 217–18, 251–55, 299
Life insurance, 128
Loan policy: international loans, 4, 15, 35, 255; Euromarket and, 25; consumer loans, 132; yen-denominated, 257, 266ff, 263; interest rate regulations, 259
Lockheed scandal, 53
Lomé Conventions, 141f
Luxembourg, 396

Macroeconomic policies, 25ff, 33, 35–38, 55, 108f, 112, 147 *passim*, 177, 234. *See also specific issues*
Malaysia, 414–19 *passim*, 427–42 *passim*
Management, and labor unions, 288
Manufacturing sector, 2, 112, 177; robotics and, 25; domestic demand and, 37; raw materials for, 199; Japanese comparative advantage, 200, 213; Japanese imports of, 209, 231, 241; MITI and, 338; U.S. vs. Japan, 390, 394; direct foreign investment and, 395; ASEAN markets and, 430. *See also specific industries and products*
Marketing, 200; OMA's, 141, 148, 220, 315–16
Marriages, arrangement of, 350
Marshall Plan, 99, 361
Mass media, 354
Mass production, 156, 200, 213, 283
Meiji period, 79, 177, 196, 312, 348, 477
Mercantilism, 346, 462–66